Fodor's 2010

D0459782

WITHDRAWN

WALT DISNEY WORLD

plus Universal Orlando® and SeaWorld®

Where to Stay and Eat
for All Budgets

Must-See Sights
and Local Secrets

Ratings You Can Trust

Fodor's Travel Publications   New York, Toronto, London, Sydney, Auckland
www.fodors.com

FODOR'S WALT DISNEY WORLD 2010

Editors: Joanna Cantor, Erica Duecy, Carolyn Galgano, Kelly Kealy, Alexis Kelly, Laura Kidder, Eric Wechter

Writers: Jennie Hess, Alicia Callanan Mandigo, Gary McKechnie, Rowland Stiteler

Production Editors: Evangelos Vasilakis, Kelsey Leljedal
Maps & Illustrations: David Lindroth, cartographer; Bob Blake, Rebecca Baer, *map editors*; William Wu, *information graphics*
Design: Fabrizio La Rocca, *creative director;* Guido Caroti, Siobhan O'Hare, *art directors;* Tina Malaney, Chie Ushio, Ann McBride, Jessica Walsh, *designers;* Melanie Marin, *senior picture editor*
Cover Photo (Wishes Fireworks Show, Magic Kingdom): © Disney
Production Manager: Angela McLean

SPECIAL SALES

This book is available at special discounts for bulk purchases for sales promotions or premiums. Special editions, including personalized covers, excerpts of existing books, and corporate imprints, can be created in large quantities for special needs. For more information, write to Special Markets/Premium Sales, 1745 Broadway, MD 6-2, New York, New York 10019, or e-mail specialmarkets@randomhouse.com.

AN IMPORTANT TIP & AN INVITATION

Although all prices, opening times, and other details in this book are based on information supplied to us at press time, changes occur all the time in the travel world, and Fodor's cannot accept responsibility for facts that become outdated or for inadvertent errors or omissions. So **always confirm information when it matters**, especially if you're making a detour to visit a specific place. Your experiences—positive and negative—matter to us. If we have missed or misstated something, **please write to us**. We follow up on all suggestions. Contact the Walt Disney World editor at editors@fodors.com or c/o Fodor's at 1745 Broadway, New York, NY 10019.

PRINTED IN THE UNITED STATES OF AMERICA

10 9 8 7 6 5 4 3 2 1

CONTENTS

Be a Fodor's Correspondent

Your opinion matters. It matters to us. It matters to your fellow Fodor's travelers, too. And we'd like to hear it. In fact, we need to hear it.

When you share your experiences and opinions, you become an active member of the Fodor's community. That means we'll not only use your feedback to make our books better, but we'll publish your names and comments whenever possible. Throughout our guides, look for "Word of Mouth," excerpts of your unvarnished feedback.

Here's how you can help improve Fodor's for all of us.

Tell us when we're right. We rely on local writers to give you an insider's perspective. But our writers and staff editors—who are the best in the business—depend on you. Your positive feedback is a vote to renew our recommendations for the next edition.

Tell us when we're wrong. We're proud that we update most of our guides every year. But we're not perfect. Things change. Hotels cut services. Museums change hours. Charming cafés lose charm. If our writer didn't quite capture the essence of a place, tell us how you'd do it differently. If any of our descriptions are inaccurate or inadequate, we'll incorporate your changes in the next edition and will correct factual errors at fodors.com immediately.

Tell us what to include. You probably have had fantastic travel experiences that aren't yet in Fodor's. Why not share them with a community of like-minded travelers? Maybe you chanced upon a beach or bistro or B&B that you don't want to keep to yourself. Tell us why we should include it. And share your discoveries and experiences with everyone directly at fodors.com. Your input may lead us to add a new listing or highlight a place we cover with a "Highly Recommended" star or with our highest rating, "Fodor's Choice."

Give us your opinion instantly at our feedback center at www.fodors.com/feedback. You may also e-mail editors@fodors.com with the subject line "Walt Disney World® Editor." Or send your nominations, comments, and complaints by mail to Walt Disney World® Editor, Fodor's, 1745 Broadway, New York, NY 10019.

You and travelers like you are the heart of the Fodor's community. Make our community richer by sharing your experiences. Be a Fodor's correspondent.

Happy traveling!

Tim Jarrell, Publisher

ABOUT THIS BOOK

Our Ratings

In theme-park chapters, ★, ★★, or ★★★ rates the appeal of the attraction to the audience noted. "Young children" refers to kids ages 5–7; "very young children" are those (ages 4 and under) who probably won't meet the height requirements of most thrill rides anyway. Since youngsters come with different confidence levels, exercise your own judgment with the scarier rides.

In non-theme-park chapters, black stars in the margin highlight things we deem **Highly Recommended,** places that our writers, editors, and readers praise again and again for excellence. The very best attractions, properties, and experiences get our highest rating, the orange **Fodor's Choice** symbol, throughout this book.

By default, there's another category: any place we include in this book is by definition worth your time, unless we say otherwise. And we will.

Disagree with any of our choices? Care to nominate a place or suggest that we rate one more highly? Visit our feedback center at www.fodors.com/feedback.

Budget Well

Hotel and restaurant price categories from ¢ to **$$$$** are defined in the Where to Eat and Where to Stay chapters. For attractions, we always give standard adult admission fees; reductions are usually available for children, students, and senior citizens. Want to pay with plastic? **AE, D, DC, MC, V** following restaurant and hotel listings indicate if American Express, Discover, Diners Club, MasterCard, and Visa are accepted.

Restaurants

Unless we state otherwise, restaurants are open for lunch and dinner daily. We mention dress only when there's a specific requirement and reservations only when they're essential or not accepted—it's always best to book ahead.

Hotels

Hotels have private bath, phone, TV, and air-conditioning and operate on the European Plan (aka EP, meaning without meals), unless we specify that they use the Continental Plan (CP, with a Continental breakfast), Breakfast Plan (BP, with a full breakfast), or Modified American Plan (MAP, with breakfast and dinner) or are all-inclusive (including all meals and most activities). We always list facilities but not any extra fees they might incur. Find out what's included when you book.

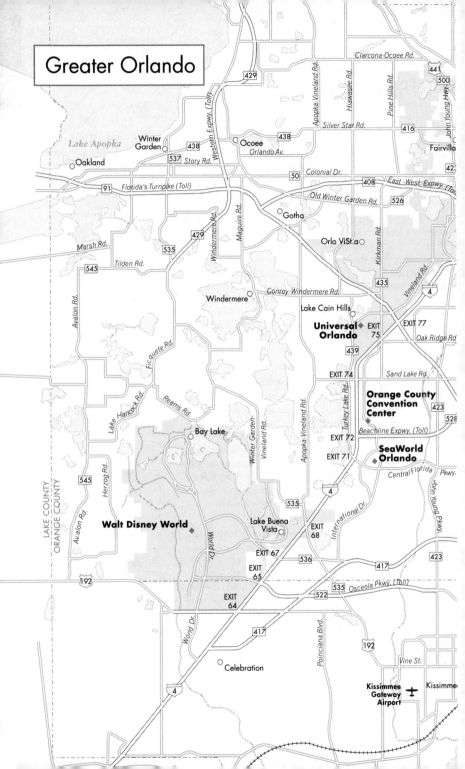

Greater Orlando

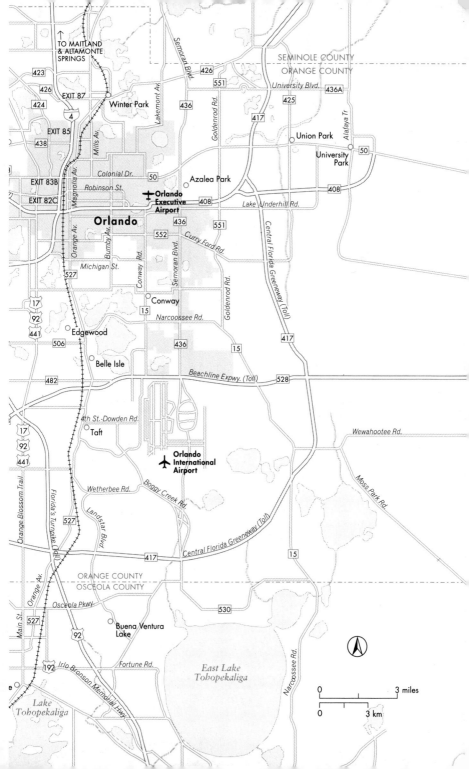

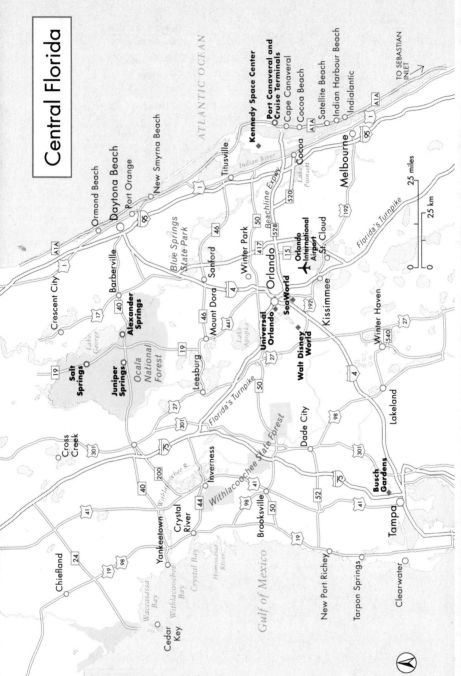

Central Florida

Before You Go

WORD OF MOUTH

"Planning is important for Disneyworld; you can read and read, but if you just wing it, you'll miss a lot. Index cards worked well for us . . . we had one card for each day and didn't feel we had to fit everything in, because we knew certain things were coming up on Day 2, Day 3, etc. We also had reminders as to what park opened early, where we had a lunch reservation, times etc. Each night the kids looked forward to reading what was on the agenda for the next day, and each card had a kid's choice afternoon, where one child picked the activities. If they argued about what to do, we would say 'we'll come back on Tuesday, when it's your afternoon to choose'."

—joesorce

Updated by
Jennie Hess

There are two types of Disney visitors. The first types just show up, trusting the theme park's reputation to guide them along. The second do some research, make dining reservations in advance, and decide which rides are must-sees ahead of time. Sure, the first types will have fun, but they'll wait in more lines, spend more money, and be more stressed out than the second types.

Chances are, that the first types—say, a family of four—arrive at the Magic Kingdom around 11, wanders along Main Street and through its stores to the other side of the iconic Cinderella Castle. At this point, one child wants to go to Space Mountain, while the other starts crying the farther the group gets from Dumbo, which now has a 90-minute line. This family might split up so each child can get in a preferred ride before lunch, or they might stick together, causing one child or the other to have a meltdown. By the time they struggle through the lines at rides and lunch counters, that late-afternoon sun is beating down.

Thanks to research and planning, the second types of visitors have learned the cardinal rule of Disney touring: arrive early. They avoid the worst lines. They avoid building unrealistic expectations that cause disappointment and tears. They enjoy their experience without stressing out about how much they need to do to justify the cost of their tickets.

The secret to enjoying Disney is to have a good plan but be willing to take detours when magical moments occur. Your children can rush to the big-deal rides early in the morning, but don't expect them to keep up that pace all day. Cushion your itinerary with extra time, and pause as much as you and your children need to. Let your mantra be "quality over quantity." It's better to tour the parks in a relaxed fashion than to flee to Pirates of the Caribbean, passing up a chance to hobnob with Princess Jasmine along the way, only to find a 30-minute wait at the ride. Jasmine definitely won't be there when you get out back.

Make each family member's top attractions part of your itinerary. Run through the plan before you enter the park; if children know that souvenirs are limited to one per person and that ice-cream snacks come after lunch, they're likely to be more patient than if they're clueless about your plans and dazzled by every trinket and treat they encounter. If you're towing an infant or toddler, be prepared to relax on a park bench while your little one snoozes in the stroller. Don't think about which ride you're missing. Just kick back and soak up the enchanting scenery.

IS MY CHILD OLD ENOUGH?

Simply stated, Disney really does have something for everyone, and we've heard parents say that even their infants were wowed by the sights and sounds. Cleverly designed playgrounds for toddlers abound, and many attractions have elements that appeal to all ages: jokes for the parents and older kids and Audio-Animatronics that move and sing for the babes. In addition, as part of the Magic Your Way Package Plus Dining plan, 1- and 2-year-olds can eat from a parent's plate at any restaurant at no charge, even when the restaurant serves buffet style.

All that said, there are many experiences very young children cannot enjoy—many of us probably remember a moment in early childhood when we went to an amusement park only to be turned away from the coolest rides because we didn't reach the height limit. Below is a list of advantages and disadvantages to bringing kids under 6 years old to the Orlando theme parks.

ADVANTAGES

Babies and tots under 3 get into the parks for free, so if you're planning a trip to Disney mainly for an older sibling, go for it.

If your children are in preschool, you can come during the off-season when the crowds are thinner and lines are shorter. It's harder for kids to miss school once they're immersed in the Renaissance and puzzling over fractions.

DISADVANTAGES

Will your 4-year-old even remember her trip to Disney after a couple of years?

You may want to go on repeat rides of the Twilight Zone Tower of Terror and Space Mountain, but any child under age 6 will probably want to ride Dumbo 100 times, splash in the fountains outside Ariel's Grotto, and collect signatures from people dressed in funny outfits.

You can still enjoy thrill attractions by taking advantage of the Baby Swap system, but you'll wind up riding with strangers instead of holding hands with your honey. The upside is that you'll meet someone new from just about anywhere in the world.

Very young children are often quite shy and easily frightened by loud noises, bright lights, and sudden movements. If your child is, he may be overwhelmed by many of the best theme-park experiences, including the 3-D shows, which don't have a minimum height.

Many children are actually seriously intimidated, and sometimes downright scared, by the characters, who are much, much larger in real life than on your TV screen.

Toddlers can get pretty impatient and cranky when they're made to adhere to adult schedules, not to mention to wait repeatedly in the hot Florida sun or to go on rides that may be too scary for them. Do you really want to spend $60-plus a day to whisk your uncomprehending tot around the parks trying to beat the crowds?

Clearly, there are some smart arguments against bringing your 5-and-under children to the theme parks. Of course, millions of parents do

Avoiding a Meltdown

■ Avoid crowded times of year (during school holidays, for example) and plan your itinerary around the days of the week and times of day when the parks are the least busy.

■ Bring a stroller, or rent one at the parks. Your child may have plenty of energy and be a great walker on a normal day, but something about pounding the pavement under the hot sun for six to nine hours can really take its toll.

■ Pack hats or visors for everyone, and insist on applying sunscreen several times daily to avoid painful sunburns that could ruin a vacation.

■ Get everybody in your family, including your children, to agree to certain basic touring plans, such as getting up early and taking afternoon naps. At the same time, leave room in your schedule to take a detour and be flexible.

■ Eat at off times to avoid crowds.

■ Give yourself more time than you think you need, and buy Park Hopper Passes so that you can always go back and see what you've missed another day.

■ Even with Fastpass, you may end up in a line or two. Pack snacks and handheld games to keep boredom at bay.

■ Save character meals for the end of your trip, when your youngsters will have become accustomed to these large, sometimes startling figures.

■ Plan for family time away from the theme parks. Spend a day at the pool or get away to the Historic Bok Sanctuary or Wekiva Springs State park.

■ Familiarize yourself with all age and height restrictions. Ideally, you should measure young children ahead of time so they won't get excited about rides they're too short to experience. However, most rides have premeasuring signs at the entrance to the queuing area, so even if you don't know how tall your child is, you won't have to wait in line before finding out.

■ Finally, be prepared for family disagreements and even tantrums. Chances are, they'll happen. Possible solutions include splitting up or leaving the parks. Missing out on a few rides while allowing everyone to cool down is better than forcing the tour to continue and testing frayed nerves.

this every year and, although they may not ride as many roller coasters as other people, they certainly have a good time. Just remember to stay flexible. If the line for Snow White's Scary Adventures is 40 minutes, skip it and let your children choose another ride or show. This strategy may result in more walking back and forth, but it's probably worth it to keep young children out of long tiresome lines.

WHEN TO GO

Timing can spell the difference between a good vacation in the theme parks and a great one. Since the Orlando area is an obvious destination for families, the area is at its most crowded during school vacations.

If you're traveling without youngsters or with just preschoolers, avoid school holidays.

SPRING Spring in Orlando is absolutely gorgeous: sunny and warm, but not killer hot and humid like it is in summer. In April and May, you may have some nippy days and others that are warm enough for the water parks. Avoid the weeks before and after Easter, which also coincide with Spring Break for a lot of schools. May, excluding Memorial Day weekend, and early June are excellent times to go.

SUMMER If water parks are a must for your family, plan your trip in summer, but be prepared for serious heat and serious crowds. Fortunately, busy periods bring longer hours and sometimes added entertainment and parades, such as the evening SpectroMagic parade in Disney's Magic Kingdom, which you can't see in quieter times. There are *slightly* fewer people in early June and late August.

FALL Summer and early fall are hurricane season, but the period from late September through November, like spring, usually brings bright beautiful days with cooler temperatures and some of the lightest crowds all year.

WINTER For most people, winter in Orlando is too chilly for swimming—and at least one of the water parks is always closed. Outside of the holidays, including Thanksgiving Day, Christmas, New Year's, Martin Luther King Jr. Day, President's Day, and Independence Day, it's the least crowded time of year.

HOW LONG TO STAY

To have a rich and full Orlando resort experience, plan on a trip of seven or eight days. This gives you time to see all of the parks at Universal and WDW and to take in at least one water park, to sample the restaurants and entertainment, and to spend a bit of time around the pool. Figure on an additional day for every other area theme park you want to visit, and then add your travel time to and from home.

> **WORD OF MOUTH**
>
> "Visit the parks in January after all the kids go back to school. This was the best trip we had at Disney. It happened to be very cold, but that was a fluke. The parks were empty—we had so much fun. We never had to rush, we had lots of picture time with sooo many characters." –MiamiBeachMomma

If you can, make time for shopping and for exploring Orlando. Central Florida has some great high-end and discount shopping and some visitor treasures like Green Meadows Farm in Kissimmee and the Charles Hosmer Morse Museum of American Art—with the world's largest collection of Tiffany glass, jewelry, and other art pieces—in Winter Park.

TAKING THE KIDS OUT OF SCHOOL

For many parents, it's worth avoiding the frustration of the crowds to take the kids out of school for a couple of days. We agree that this can make for a more enjoyable trip, but it's a good idea to consult with your child's teachers before making plans. Hopefully the teachers can advise you about the best time of year to go and help create a study plan to make certain your child's education isn't compromised.

For elementary-school kids, there are ways of making the trip educational. For example, your child could write about the different countries featured at Epcot in lieu of a missed homework assignment. One last note: although it may be fine to take an elementary-school child out of school for a few days, missing several days of middle or high school could set your child back for the rest of the semester, so consider this option very carefully.

SEASONAL CLOSURES

Disney sometimes closes rides and attractions for refurbishment or maintenance during slower seasons. Before you finalize your travel schedule, call the theme parks to find out about any planned closures so you don't show up at the Magic Kingdom to find Peter Pan's Flight grounded for the week.

OPENING HOURS

The major area theme parks, including those in Walt Disney World, are open 365 days a year. Opening times vary but generally hover around 9. Certain attractions within the parks may not open until 10 or 11 AM, however, and parks usually observe shorter hours during the off-seasons in January, February, April, May, September, and October. In general, the longest days are during prime summer months and over the year-end holidays, when the Magic Kingdom may be open as late as 11 or even midnight, and later on New Year's Eve; Epcot is open until 9 or 9:30 in the World Showcase area and at several Future World attractions, the Studios until 7 or 8:30. At other times, the Magic Kingdom closes around 7 or 8—but there are variations, so call ahead. Most of the year, the Animal Kingdom closes at 5, though during peak holiday seasons it may open at 8 and close at 7 or 8.

The parking lots open at least an hour before the parks do. If you arrive at the Magic Kingdom turnstiles before the official opening time, you can often breakfast in a restaurant on Main Street, which usually opens before the rest of the park, and be ready to dash to one of the popular attractions in other lands at Rope Drop, the Magic Kingdom's official opening time.

Hours at Typhoon Lagoon and Blizzard Beach are 9 or 10 to 5 daily (until 7—occasionally 10—in summer).

The shops at Downtown Disney stay open as late as 11 PM in summer and during holidays.

You can check exact opening and closing times by calling the parks directly or checking their Web sites.

EXTRA MAGIC HOURS

The Extra Magic Hours program gives Disney resort guests free early and late-night admission to certain parks on specified days—call ahead for information about each park's "magic hours" days to plan your early- and late-visit strategies.

CLIMATE CHART

Jan.	70F	21C	May	88F	31C	Sept.	88F	31C
	49	9		67	19		74	23
Feb.	72F	22C	June	90F	32C	Oct.	83F	28C
	54	12		74	23		67	19
Mar.	76F	24C	July	90F	32C	Nov.	76F	24C
	56	13		74	23		58	14
Apr.	81F	27C	Aug.	90F	32C	Dec.	70F	21C
	63	17		74	23		52	11

FESTIVALS AND SEASONAL EVENTS

If you've been to the parks and enjoyed the top attractions at least once, it may be time to think about a special trip around one of the many festivals and events slated throughout the year. To buy tickets for special events, call 407/824–4321 or visit ⊕*www.disneyworld.com.*

EPCOT INTERNATIONAL FOOD & WINE FESTIVAL

You won't find a food and wine festival like this six-week-long one (late September, October through mid-November) anywhere else in the world. Admission to the events like seminars on wine and beer, culinary demonstrations, pop concerts, and special exhibits is included in your theme-park ticket. International marketplaces around the World Showcase offer tastes of food, wine, and beers of the world for $2 to $5 per item. You can also make reservations for special ticketed events, ranging from a $50 Food & Wine Pairing at one of the Epcot restaurants to a $95 Master Wine Class led by a sommelier.

EPCOT INTERNATIONAL FLOWER & GARDEN FESTIVAL

Walt Disney was extremely fond of European topiaries, and he made sure that his parks had perfectly groomed green Disney characters. At this yearly festival (late March through the end of May or early June), the topiaries multiply, with colorful flowers, grasses, and mosses added to create ever more detailed characters. Gardening seminars with Disney horticulturists and celebrity gardeners, a screened butterfly garden, a fragrance garden, kids' activities, and weekend Flower Power concerts are just some of the events open to all for the cost of admission.

GAY DAYS ORLANDO

During this event (⊕*www.gaydays.com*), held the first week in June, parties and tours are organized throughout Orlando for the gay, lesbian, bisexual, and transgendered community, as well as supporters, family, and friends. The weeklong event started in 1991 when the founders encouraged the gay community to "wear red and be seen" in the Magic Kingdom on the first Saturday in June. Now thousands of red-clad folk visit during this festive week. Contact the **Gay, Lesbian & Bisexual Community Center of Central Florida (GLBCC)** (⊠*946 N. Mills Ave., Orlando* ☎*407/228–8272* ⊕*www.glbcc.org*) or visit the Gay Days official Web site for more information.

MICKEY'S NOT-SO-SCARY HALLOWEEN PARTY

Little girls dressed like fairy princesses and young boys in ninja costumes can take to the streets of the Magic Kingdom for treats (no tricks!) during the gently spooky fun of Mickey's Not-So-Scary Halloween Party, which takes place on various days throughout September and October, including the 31st. This nighttime ticketed event (about $50 for adults, $40-plus for children ages 3–9) is a great chance to meet Disney characters in their own favorite Halloween costumes and take advantage of the hottest attractions without waiting in long lines.

HOLIDAY HAPPENINGS

The Disney parks are decked out in their holiday finest beginning around Thanksgiving and continuing through the end of the year. If you've never experienced this wondrous display, it pays to book a trip during the first few weeks of December, when there's a lull between the Thanksgiving and Christmas crowds. A road trip through the kingdom to visit Disney's many adorned resort lobbies and gingerbread house displays is a must for decor devotees.

Epcot's nightly included-with-admission **Candlelight Processional** with celebrity narrators retelling the Christmas story is memorable, but you have to line up early for a seat at the America Gardens Theatre venue in Epcot. It pays to buy the Candlelight lunch or dinner package ($35–$60 for adults, $15 or more for children ages 3–9), with a meal at one of Epcot's restaurants and reserved show seating.

Mickey's Very Merry Christmas Party is a special ticketed event (about $48 for adults, $39 for children ages 3–9) happening in the Magic Kingdom over several weeks in November and December. You'll get snowed on during a stroll down Main Street, U.S.A., and you can enjoy the most popular park attractions without long waits. Complimentary cocoa and cookies, seasonal stage shows and a special holiday parade and fireworks show add to the fun.

At Disney's Hollywood Studios you can see the long-running holiday-time **Osborne Family Spectacle of Dancing Lights.** Disney's Animal Kingdom unwraps **Mickey's Jingle Jungle Parade** for the holiday festivities.

DISNEY MARATHON

At least 40,000 athletes from around the globe lace up their running shoes each January during the Walt Disney World Marathon Weekend. Goofy's Race-and-a-Half Challenge motivates runners to complete a half-marathon on Saturday and the full marathon on Sunday. The Donald Duck medal goes to half-marathoners, the Mickey medal is for full-marathoners, and the Goofy medal awaits those goofy enough to do both. The weekend also features a 5K family fun run, kids' races, and a Health and Fitness Expo at ESPN Wide World of Sports complex.

GROUP TRIPS

Groups of eight or more can take advantage of Disney's **Magical Gatherings** (☎407/934–7639 ⊕ *www.disneyworld.com/magicalgatherings*) program, through which you can access special packages that include entertainment and meals tailored to your group's interest.

Getting everyone to agree on what to do can be tricky. Preschoolers may be content on Dumbo, but thrill-seekers will want faster-paced rides. And grandparents might rather play golf than traipse around a water park. Likewise, when it comes to meals, everyone's preferences and dietary concerns may not coincide. And those doing the planning may find themselves also doing the mediating. That's where Disney's Magical Gatherings program comes in. Designed to help groups travel well together, the program, which is accessible online and over the phone, offers lots of free planning tips, plus a planner that can help you decide what to do together and when to split up.

> ### WORD OF MOUTH
>
> "Even though we knew the parks pretty well, we found [having a VIP guide] enjoyable. There's certainly a benefit to having a fast-pass for every ride... and you get pointers on things like how to max out the score on Buzz Lightyear. The guides also have interesting tidbits (i.e., what the asteroids are on Space Mountain). Our guide got us VIP parade seating, which was nice.... Schedule well ahead of time as guides book up during busy periods."   –Ryan

GUIDED TOURS

The most customizable tours are organized by Disney's **VIP Tour Services** (☎407/560–4033). These tours, for those who don't mind shelling out $1,050 or more for a day, are led by guides who will plan your day to maximize your time, enabling you to park-hop and get good seats at parades and shows with little effort. You can be as much or as little involved in the planning as you like. Note that Disney's VIP tours don't help you skip lines, as VIP tours in Universal Orlando do, but they make navigating the parks and rides easy. The guides create efficient schedules for your visit depending on your interests and lead you around the parks to the attractions you want to see. The charge is $195 per hour (or $175 an hour for Disney resort guests during non-peak times of the year), and there's a six-hour minimum for every tour. Prices go up during peak season to $215 per hour (or $195 an hour for Disney resort guests). You can book up to 90 days in advance; there's a two-hour charge if you don't cancel at least 48 hours in advance. Tour guides can lead groups of up to 10 people. Disney also offers some more affordable, topical theme-park guided tours like "Keys to the Kingdom" and the "Family Magic Tour." (*See the Guided Tours section in each theme-park chapter.*)

HOTEL AND TICKET PACKAGES

Disney's Magic Your Way value, moderate, and deluxe packages help families keep expenses in check by bundling hotel and theme-park expenses. For as low as $1,700 ($2,500 with the dining option), a family of four can plan a six-night, seven-day Magic Your Way Vacation that includes complimentary transportation from the airport and extra hours in the parks. Lower-end package rates offer value-resort accommodations; prices go up with moderate or deluxe accommodations. All Disney resort guests get free bus, boat, and monorail transportation across property. Visit ⊕*www.disneyworld.com* to explore the different package options.

MEALS AND ACTIVITIES

Specially trained vacation planners can help you book a special tour, dinner reservation, or even a photo shoot. If you have eight or more people in your group and are staying at a WDW resort, you can sign up for one of Disney's four **Grand Gatherings:**

Good Morning Character Breakfast. This is an interactive sit-down breakfast at Tony's Town Square Restaurant in the Magic Kingdom, hosted by a cast of colorful characters. You get to sing, dance, and play group games with Goofy, Pluto, and Chip 'n' Dale, and you even meet Mickey Mouse himself. ☎*$32.99 per person, $19.99 ages 3–9.*

Safari Celebration Dinner. You begin this gathering with a guided safari through the Animal Kingdom's jungles and savanna. Afterward, you head to Tusker House Restaurant for a family-style dinner and show with African singers, drummers, storytellers, and live animals. Timon of *The Lion King,* Turk of *Tarzan,* or other Disney characters make appearances. ☎*$64.99 per person, $33.99 ages 3–9.*

International Dinner and IllumiNations Dessert Reception. In Epcot's Odyssey pavilion, you dine on international cuisine in a fairy-tale setting, where children participate in a storytelling experience and enjoy a surprise character appearance. After dinner and dessert buffet, you're led outside to a private viewing area where you can watch the IllumiNations nighttime spectacular. ☎*$64.99 per person, $33.99 ages 3–9.*

Magical Fireworks Voyage. For a cruise and an after-dinner treat, meet at the Contemporary Resort for this boat ride and dessert buffet. Captain Hook and Mr. Smee playfully capture your crew and usher you onto a boat commandeered by Patch the Pirate. But don't worry about walking the plank—you'll be too busy singing seafaring songs and playing trivia games as you cruise the Seven Seas Lagoon. You get to watch the Electrical Water Pageant and the Wishes fireworks extravaganza from the boat. On the way back to shore, Patch regales you with tales of Peter Pan, who'll be waiting at the dock to sign autographs and pose for pictures. ☎*$43.99 per person, $24.99 ages 3–9.*

PEOPLE WITH DISABILITIES

The main park information centers can answer specific questions and dispense general information for guests with disabilities. Both Walt Disney World and Universal Studios publish guidebooks for guests with disabilities; allow six weeks for delivery.

DEVICES

WDW distributes maps for guests with disabilities at Guest Services (aka Guest Relations) in each park and has several free devices available for the hearing and sight impaired. **Closed captioning activators** and **assistive listening devices** are available at Guest Services in all theme parks for a $25 refundable deposit. **Handheld captioning devices** require a $100 refundable deposit, and **audio guides and tours** are available for a $25 deposit. Braille guidebooks require a $25 deposit at Guest Services. Stage shows with sign language interpreters are listed in the calendar of events. At all Disney parks, sign language interpretation at live shows is available on a rotating basis (Magic Kingdom shows on Monday and Thursday, Epcot shows on Tuesday and Friday, etc.). Guests should call for the schedule at least one-to-two weeks in advance and will be contacted by Disney with verification of seating arrangements. Call 407–824–4321 or TTY 407/827–5141.

ENJOYING THE PARKS

Attractions in all the Disney parks typically have both a visual element that makes them appealing without sound and an audio element that conveys the charm even without the visuals; many are accessible by guests using wheelchairs, and most are accessible by guests with some mobility. Guide dogs and service animals are permitted, unless a ride or special effect could spook or traumatize the animal. Large Braille maps are at centralized areas in all four Disney theme parks and at Downtown Disney Marketplace and West Side.

In some attractions, you may be required to transfer to a wheelchair if you use an ECV or scooter. In others, you must be able to leave your own wheelchair to board the ride vehicle and must have a traveling companion assist, as park staff cannot do so. Attractions with emergency evacuation routes that have narrow walkways or steps require additional mobility. Turbulence on other attractions poses a problem for some guests.

The *Guidebook for Guests with Disabilities* details many specific challenges and identifies the accessible entrances for attractions. In addition, a "guest assistance packet" of story notes, scripts, and song lyrics is available at all attractions with a story line—just ask an attractions host, who will provide a binder with the information you need.

A new standard of access was set at Walt Disney World with the opening of the Animal Kingdom, where nearly all attractions, restaurants, and shops are wheelchair accessible. Disney's Hollywood Studios comes in a close second, followed by Epcot, where some of the rides have a tailgate that drops down to provide a level entrance to the ride vehicle. Though the Magic Kingdom, now in its fourth decade, was designed before architects gave consideration to access issues, renovation plans continue. Even so, the 20 or so accessible attractions combine with the live entertainment around the park to provide a memorable experience.

GETTING AROUND

The Disney transportation system has dozens of lift- and Braille-equipped vehicles. There's ample reserved parking.

INFORMATION

Before your trip, call **Walt Disney World Information for Guests with Disabilities** (☏ *407/939–7807, 407/939–7670 TTY*) and request a copy of the *Guidebook for Guests with Disabilities* to help with planning your visit. The guidebook and Braille guides are available at Guest Services. Call **Walt Disney World Information** (☏ *407/824–4321*) two weeks in advance for a schedule of sign language–interpreted shows. Interpreters rotate daily between Disney's four major theme parks.

For accessibility information at SeaWorld and Discovery Cove, call **SeaWorld Information** (☏ *407/363–2414, 407/351–3600, 407/363–2617 TTY,*

800/837–4268 TDD). For accessibility information at the Universal parks, call **Universal Orlando Information** (☎*407/363–8000, 407/224–4414 TTY).*

WHEELCHAIR RENTALS

Probably the most comfortable course is to bring your wheelchair from home. If your chair is wider than 24½ inches and longer than 32 inches (44 inches for Electronic Convenience Vehicles or ECVs), consult attraction hosts and hostesses. Thefts of personal wheelchairs while their owners are inside attractions are rare but have been known to occur. Take the precautions you would in any public place.

Wheelchair rentals are available from area medical-supply companies that will deliver to your hotel. You can also rent by the day in major theme parks ($10 a day for wheelchairs and $8 a day for multiday use, $45 daily plus $20 refundable deposit for the limited number of ECVs, nicknamed scooters by some).

In Disney parks, since rental locations are relatively close to parking (except at the Magic Kingdom where you have to board the monorail), send someone ahead to get the wheelchair and bring it back to the car. Plan at least an extra half hour for this errand. Rented wheelchairs that disappear while you're on a ride can be replaced throughout the parks—ask any staffer for the nearest location. Attaching a small personal item like a colorful bandana to the wheelchair may prevent other guests from taking yours by mistake.

ADMISSION

Visiting Walt Disney World isn't cheap. Everyone 10 and older pays adult price. In addition, Disney changes its prices about once a year and without much notice. For that reason, you may save yourself a few bucks if you buy your WDW tickets as soon as you know for sure you'll be going.

THE TICKETING SYSTEM

Once you've decided to take the plunge, Disney fortunately makes buying tickets easy and painless. The **Magic Your Way** ticketing system is all about flexibility. You can tailor your ticket to your interests and desired length of stay. The more days you stay, the greater your savings on per-day ticket prices. A one-day ticket costs $75 for anyone age 10 and up, while a five-day ticket costs $222 or $44.40 per day.

Once you decide how many days to stay, you'll want to decide what options to add on. The **Park Hopper Pass** option lets you move from park to park within the day and adds $50 to the price of your ticket, no matter how many days your ticket covers. So it's an expensive option for a one- or two-day ticket, but it can be well worth the cost for a four-day trip, especially if you know what you want to see at each park.

The **Water Parks & More** option allows a certain number of visits to the water parks and other Disney attractions: Typhoon Lagoon, Blizzard Beach, DisneyQuest, Disney's 9-hole Oak Trail golf course, and ESPN

1

Wide World of Sports complex. You pay $50 to add this option, and you get 2 to 10 visits, depending on length of stay.

The **No Expiration** option can save you money if you know for sure you're coming back to Disney World again. For example, say you're planning a five-day trip one year, plus a weekend trip sometime the next year. You can buy a seven-day ticket, use it five days during your first trip and keep the remaining two-days' worth of theme-park fun for your next trip to Orlando. It will cost you $17 to $200 to add the No Expiration option to your two- to seven-day tickets.

Note that all Disney admission passes are nontransferable. The ID is your fingerprint. Although you slide your pass through the reader like people with single-day tickets, you also have to slip your finger into a special V-shape fingerprint reader before you'll be admitted.

BUYING TICKETS

IN ADVANCE

You can get discounted three-or-more-day tickets from the **Orlando Convention & Visitors Bureau** (⊕ *www.orlandoticketsales.com* ☎ *800/255–5786 or 407/363–5872*).

IN ORLANDO

You can buy tickets at the Ticket and Transportation Center (aka TTC) in the Magic Kingdom; at ticket booths in front of the other theme-park entrances; in all on-site resorts if you're a registered guest; at the Walt Disney World store at Orlando International Airport; and at various hotels and other sites around Orlando.

DISCOUNTS

AAA

Many of the AAA motor clubs offer discounts to Central Florida attractions, including Disney World tickets, so check with your local branch or contact the national **AAA** (☎ *866/222–7283 [866/AAA–SAVE]* ⊕ *www.aaa.com*). Also ask your local AAA office about hotel discounts and vacation packages that would include tickets, as well as special benefits within the parks including discounts on meals and nonalcoholic beverages.

MILITARY

If you are or have been a member of the U.S. or foreign military, you're eligible to purchase discounted park tickets at the Shades of Green Resort located on Walt Disney World property. The resort's ticket office is open 8 AM to 9 PM. You can also buy tickets for nonmilitary guests as long as you're traveling with them; you do not have to be a Disney resort guest to qualify for most ticket offers. If you're active-duty or retired military, National Guard, Army Reserve, a disabled veteran, foreign military stationed with U.S. armed forces, or a Department of Defense civilian with military ID, you can also stay at the on-site Shades of Green Resort (☎ *407/824–1403* ⊕ *www.shadesofgreen.org*) for a fraction of what it costs to stay at other Disney resorts.

Magic Your Way Price Chart

TICKET OPTIONS								
TICKET	**10-DAY**	**7-DAY**	**6-DAY**	**5-DAY**	**4-DAY**	**3-DAY**	**2-DAY**	**1-DAY**
BASE TICKET								
Ages 10-up	$243	$234	$231	$228	$225	$219	$156	$79
Ages 3-9	$210	$201	$198	$195	$192	$187	$133	$68
Base Ticket admits guest to one of the four major theme parks per day's use. Park choices are: Magic Kingdom, Epcot, Disney's Hollywood Studios, Disney's Animal Kingdom.								
ADD: Park Hopper	$52	$52	$52	$52	$52	$52	$52	$52
Park Hopper option entitles guest to visit more than one theme park per day's use. Park choices are any combination of Magic Kingdom, Epcot, Disney's Hollywood Studios, Disney's Animal Kingdom.								
ADD: Water Parks Fun & More	$52 10 visits	$52 7 visits	$52 6 visits	$52 5 visits	$52 4 visits	$52 3 visits	$52 2 visits	$52 1 visit
Water Parks Fun & More option entitles guest to a specified number of visits (between 2 and 10) to a choice of entertainment and recreation venues. Choices are Blizzard Beach, Typhoon Lagoon, DisneyQuest, Disney's Oak Trail golf course, and Wide World of Sports.								
ADD: No Expiration	$209	$115	$84	$73	$52	$24	$18	n/a
No expiration means that unused admissions on a ticket may be used any time in the future. Without this option, tickets expire 14 days after first use.								

MINOR PARKS AND ATTRACTIONS		
TICKET	**AGES 10-UP**	**AGES 3-9**
Typhoon Lagoon or Blizzard Beach 1-Day 1-Park	$45	$39
DisneyQuest 1-Day	$41	$35
Disney's Wide World of Sports	$11.91	$9.34
Cirque du Soleil's *La Nouba*	$67–$117	$54–$94
*All prices are subject to Florida sales tax		

FASTPASS

Imagine avoiding most of the lines at Disney. Fastpass is your ticket to this terrific scenario, and it's included in regular park admission. Pocket your theme-park ticket upon entry, then insert it into a Fastpass machine at one of several attractions at each Disney park. Out comes your Fastpass, printed with a one-hour window of time during which you can return to get into the fast line. ■ TIP➔ **Don't forget to take your park ticket back, too.** While you wait for your Fastpass appointment to mature, enjoy other attractions. (Note that you can't make another appointment until you're within the window of time for your first appointment.) Save Fastpass for the most popular attractions, and make new appointments as soon as you possibly can.

DINING AT DISNEY

CHARACTER MEALS

At special breakfasts, lunches, and dinners in many Walt Disney World restaurants, Mickey, Donald, Goofy, Chip 'n' Dale, Cinderella, and other favorite characters sign autographs and pose for snapshots. Universal's Islands of Adventure has a character breakfast, so your children can enjoy pizza or chicken fingers with Spiderman and their favorite Seuss characters. Talk with your children to find out which characters they most want to see; then call the Disney or Universal dining reservations line and speak with the representative about what's available.

Reservations are recommended because these hugging-and-feeding frenzies are wildly popular, but if you haven't reserved ahead, try showing up early and you may get lucky. It's a good idea to have your character meal near the end of your visit, when your little ones will be used to seeing these large and sometimes frightening figures; they're also a good way to spend the morning on the day you check out.

For descriptions of character meals, see Chapter 11, Where to Eat.

MEAL PLANS

If you book a package, you can add on a meal plan for more savings. The Magic Your Way Dining Plan allows you one table-service meal, one counter-service meal, and one snack per day of your trip at more than 100 theme-park and resort restaurants. You can add the plan to your package for about $42 per adult, per day, and less than $12 per child age 3–9, per day (tax and gratuities not included). When you consider that the average Disney table-service meal for a child runs about $10.99 *without* gratuity, you realize this plan is a steal. Another advantage of the plan is that you can swap two table-service meals for one of Disney's dinner shows or an evening at one of the high-end signature restaurants like California Grill.

RESERVATIONS

Make your dining reservations up to 180 days in advance of your visit through the **WDW Reservation Center** (☎*407/939–3463*) so you don't have to worry about finding a restaurant every night. Restaurants at Disney book up fast. Ask the reservationist about the cancellation policy—at a handful of restaurants, your credit card will be charged $10–$50 per person, depending on the restaurant, if you don't give 24- to 48-hours' notice. Some dinner shows and other special dining events like the Mother's Day Brunch at Epcot charge the full cost to your card if you don't cancel within 48–72 hours. Make tee time reservations to play at any of Walt Disney World's six golf courses at ⊕www.disneyworldgolf.com or by calling **WDW Golf Reservations** (☎*407/939–4653*).

WORD OF MOUTH

"The meal plan saves you money when you have kids. Irrespective of what you do, make your advance reservations (ADRs) as soon as possible; lots of places book up very, very far in advance."

–taitai

PACKING

Casual, comfortable, lightweight clothing is best. Most people walk around in shorts and T-shirts. On hot summer days, the perfect theme-park outfit begins with shorts made of a breathable, quick-drying material, topped by a T-shirt or tank top. Pockets are useful for Fastpass tickets and park maps. The entire area is extremely casual, day and night, so men need a jacket and tie in only a handful of restaurants.

We recommend bringing a change of clothes if you know you're going on a water ride that could leave you drenched. Plan ahead so you don't end up soaked and having to buy an expensive Disney outfit from a souvenir shop or leave the park early. Lightweight ponchos (available at most dollar stores) are great for water rides if you prefer not to carry a change of clothing.

In winter, be prepared for a range of temperatures: take clothing that you can layer, including a sweater and warm jacket. It can get quite cool in December, January, and February. For summer, you'll want a sun hat, and a rain poncho in case of sudden thunderstorms.

GETTING TO AND AROUND ORLANDO/DISNEY

Thousands of visitors fly into Orlando daily for a dose of vacation magic. Getting here is easy with the abundance of flights available from all destinations. Once you arrive, you'll have your pick of ground transportation options, including shuttles, taxis, limos, and rental cars. If you're booked into a Walt Disney World Resort, take advantage of the Magical Express Service that delivers you and your luggage, at no cost, from your home airport to your hotel and back again (you must book this service before departing on your trip). Disney's own fleet of buses, trams, boats, and monorail trains make it a breeze to travel throughout Mickey's world. If you're eager to explore beyond the theme parks, be sure to have a good, up-to-date map—Orlando is a sprawling metropolitan area and some areas can be tricky to traverse.

All major and most discount airlines, including American, Northwest, US Airways, Southwest, JetBlue, Spirit, Ted, and ATA fly to **Orlando International Airport** (*MCO* ☎*407/825–2001* ⊕*www.orlandoairports. net*), which serves as a secondary hub for AirTran; Southwest is the largest carrier in terms of passenger traffic The airport is divided into two terminals, A and B, and is easy to navigate thanks to excellent signs. Monorails shuttle you from gates to the core area, where you can find baggage claim. The airport is southeast of Orlando and northeast of Walt Disney World.

Flying times are 2½ hours from New York, 3½ hours from Chicago, and 5 hours from Los Angeles.

Don't forget to reconfirm your flight before you leave for the airport. Orlando's frequent summer storms can cause delays or even cancellations. You can do this on your carrier's Web site, by linking to a flight-status checker (many Web-booking services offer these), or by calling your carrier or travel agent.

AIRPORT TRANSFERS

Taxi fares start at $3–$3.50 for the first mile and add $2 for each mile thereafter. The fare from the airport to the Walt Disney World area can run $40–$60. If there are four or more people in your party, taking a taxi may cost less than paying by the head for an airport shuttle.

Mears Transportation Group whisks you away in an 11-passenger van, a town car, or a limo. Passengers who book town cars or limos are met in the baggage area by their driver. Vans run to Walt Disney World, International Drive, and along U.S. 192 in Kissimmee every 30 minutes; prices range from $20 one-way for adults ($16 for children 4–11) to $33 round-trip ($26 for children 4–11). Limo rates run $60–$70 for a town car that accommodates three or four to $180 for a stretch limo that seats eight. If you're staying at a Disney hotel (excluding the Walt Disney World Swan, Dolphin, and Downtown Disney Resort area hotels), make arrangements to use Disney's free Magical Express service, which includes shuttle transportation to and from the airport, luggage delivery, and baggage check-in at the hotel. You can't book the service once you've arrived at the airport, so be sure to reserve ahead.

Transport Contacts A-1 Taxi (☎*407/328–4555*). **Ace Metro Cab** (☎*407/855–1111*). **Checker Cab Company** (☎*407/699–9999*). **Magical Express service** (☎*866/599–0951* ⊕*www.disneyworld.com*). **Mears Transportation Group** (☎*407/423–5566* ⊕*www.mearstransportation.com*). **Star Taxi** (☎*407/857–9999*). **Yellow Cab Co.** (☎*407/422–2222*).

CAR RENTAL

You should rent a car if you're staying at an off-site hotel, want to visit sights or restaurants outside Walt Disney World, are traveling in a group (four or more people), or just like your independence. On the other hand, if you're staying at a Disney hotel and spending all or most of your trip at Disney World, you can rely on Disney's own very efficient transportation system.

RATES

Rental rates are among the lowest in the United States, but vary seasonally. They can begin as low as $30 a day and $149 a week for an economy car with air-conditioning, automatic transmission, and unlimited mileage. This does not include tax on car rentals, which is 6.5%. ■TIP➜Renting from Alamo, Avis, Budget, Dollar, or National can get you out of the airport the fastest because they have car lots on airport property, a short walk from baggage claim. The other agencies offer courtesy shuttles to their lots.

In Florida, some agencies require that you are at least 21 to rent a car. Others require that you are 25.

EMERGENCY SERVICES

If you have a cell phone, dialing *347 (*FHP) will get you the Florida Highway Patrol. Most Florida highways are also patrolled by Road Rangers, a free roadside service that helps stranded motorists with minor problems and can call for a tow truck when there are bigger problems. The **AAA Car Care Center** (☎407/824–0976) near the Magic Kingdom is a full-service operation that will provide most emergency services, including free towing even for non-AAA members on Disney property, while it's open (weekdays 7–7, Saturday 7–4). On Disney property you can flag a security guard any day until 10 PM for help with minor emergencies, such as a flat tire, dead battery, empty gas tank, or towing. Otherwise call 407/824–4777. You can also gas up on Buena Vista Drive near Disney's BoardWalk and in the Downtown Disney area across from Pleasure Island.

ROADS

The Beachline Expressway (formerly called the Beeline, aka Route 528) is the best way to get to the International Drive (also known as I-Drive) area and Walt Disney World from the OIA, though you'll pay up to $2 in tolls. SR 417, the Central Florida Greenway, is an even faster way to Disney, but tolls are heftier. Depending on the location of your hotel, follow the Beachline expressway west to International Drive, and either exit at SeaWorld for the International Drive area or stay on the Beachline to I–4 and head west for Walt Disney World and U.S. 192/Kissimmee or east for Universal Studios and downtown Orlando. Call your hotel for the best route.

I–4 is the main artery in Central Florida, linking the Gulf coast in Tampa to the Atlantic coast in Daytona Beach. Although I–4 is an east–west highway, it actually follows a north–south track through the

WORD OF MOUTH

"Disney's Magical Express takes a loooong time. The idea is great: you put special stickers on your bags, and Disney gets them from baggage claim to your hotel. In the meantime, you're in a big bus going to your hotel. However, it was 1½ hours between the time we stood in line for our bus and the time we reached our resort (ours was the last stop). And, your luggage can take up to three hours to arrive—not good if you get in at midnight and need your PJs! We would have rather hired a driver, retrieved our own bags, and gone straight to the resort."

–Attnymom

A Window on the World

1

No moss ever grows under the Mouse's trademark yellow clogs (unless it's artfully re-created moss). Since its opening in 1971, Walt Disney World has made it a point to stay fresh, current, and endlessly amusing. Disney Imagineers and producers constantly choreograph new shows and parades, revamp classic theme rides, and periodically replace an entire attraction. Yet amid all the hoopla, much remains reassuringly the same, rekindling fond memories among the generations who return.

The sheer enormity of the property—25,000 acres near Kissimmee, Florida—suggests that WDW is more than a single theme park with a fabulous castle in the center. The property's acreage translates to 40 square mi—twice the size of Manhattan. On a tract that size, 107 acres is a mere speck, yet that's the size of the Magic Kingdom. When most people imagine Walt Disney World, they think of only those 107 acres, but there's much, much more.

Epcot, the second major theme park and, at 300 acres, more than twice as big as the Magic Kingdom, is a combination of a science exploratorium and a world's fair. Disney's Hollywood Studios (formerly Disney–MGM Studios) is devoted to the world of movies and TV shows. The Animal Kingdom, the fourth major theme park, salutes creatures real, imaginary, and extinct. Add two water parks, more than two dozen hotels, a sports complex, and countless shops, restaurants, and nightlife venues, and you start to get the picture. And still there are thousands of undeveloped acres. Deer patrol grassy plains and pine forests, and white ibis inhabit swamps patched by thickets of palmettos.

Best of all, Disney has proved that it can manage its elephantine resort and make customers so happy that they return year after year. Perhaps the company's most practical innovation, the Fastpass system, lets you experience the top attractions with little or no wait. Restaurants at the parks and resorts have made great strides in an effort to cater to guests with special dietary needs and to offer family-friendly and even gourmet alternatives to the standard burger and fries. And travelers who want to vacation longer get the best ticket deals.

Disney's tradition of constant and excellent upkeep has persevered through years of ups and downs within the company. Whatever is happening in the background, all is still well on the kingdom's grounds. Walt Disney's original decree that his parks be ever changing, along with some healthy competition from Universal Studios, SeaWorld, and other area attractions, keeps the Disney Imagineers and show producers on their toes as they dream up new entertainment and install higher-tech attractions. To avoid missing anything, do plenty of research before you go, make a plan, then try to relax—and have a wonderful time.

Orlando area. ■ TIP➔Think north when I–4 signs say east and think south when the signs say west.

Two other main roads you're likely to use are International Drive and U.S. 192, sometimes called the Spacecoast Parkway or Irlo Bronson Memorial Highway. You can get onto International Drive from I–4 Exits 72, 74A, and 75A. U.S. 192 cuts across I–4 at Exits 64A and 64B.

Walt Disney World has four exits off I–4. For the Magic Kingdom, Disney's Hollywood Studios, Disney's Animal Kingdom, Fort Wilderness, and the rest of the Magic Kingdom resort area, take the one marked **Magic Kingdom–U.S. 192 (Exit 64B)**. From here, it's a 4-mi drive along Disney's main entrance road to the toll gate, and another mile to the parking area; during peak vacation periods, be prepared for serious bumper-to-bumper traffic both on I–4 nearing the U.S. 192 exit and on U.S. 192 itself. A less-congested route to the theme parks and other WDW venues is via the exit marked **Epcot/Downtown Disney (Exit 67)**, 4 mi east of Exit 64.

Exit 65 will take you directly to Disney's Animal Kingdom and ESPN Wide World of Sports as well as the Animal Kingdom resort area via the Osceola Parkway.

For access to Downtown Disney (including the Marketplace, Disney-Quest, and West Side), as well as to Typhoon Lagoon, the Crossroads Shopping Center, and the establishments on Hotel Plaza Boulevard, get off at **Route 535–Lake Buena Vista (Exit 68)**.

The exit marked **Epcot–Downtown Disney (Exit 67)** is another one to use if you're bound for those destinations or for hotels in the Epcot and Downtown Disney resort areas; you can also get to Typhoon Lagoon and the Studios from here.

RULES OF THE ROAD

All front-seat passengers are required to wear seat belts. All children under 4 years old must be in approved child-safety seats. Children older than 4 who are not strapped into a child-safety seat must wear a seat belt and, if they're shorter than 4-feet, 9-inches, should sit in a booster seat.

Florida's Alcohol/Controlled Substance DUI Law is one of the toughest in the United States. A blood alcohol level of 0.08 or higher can have serious repercussions even for the first-time offender.

In Florida you may turn right at a red light after stopping, unless otherwise posted. When in doubt, wait for the green. Be alert for one-way streets, "no left turn" intersections, and blocks closed to car traffic. Watch for middle lanes with painted arrows that point left. These are turn lanes. They are to help you make a left turn without disrupting the flow of traffic behind you. Turn your blinker on, pull into this lane, and come to a stop, if necessary, before making a left turn. Never use this lane as a passing lane. Steer clear of downtown Orlando bus lanes marked for buses only; even locals find them confusing sometimes.

Expect heavy traffic during rush hours, which are on weekdays 6–10 AM and 4–7 PM. To encourage carpooling, some freeways have special lanes for so-called high-occupancy vehicles (HOV)—cars carrying more than one passenger. The use of radar detectors is legal in Florida and its neighboring states, Alabama and Georgia. Although it's legal to talk on your cell phone while driving in Florida, it's not recommended. Dial *511 on a cell phone to hear traffic advisories for highways including I-4 and other major arteries.

TRANSPORTATION WITHIN THE PARKS

Walt Disney World has its own free transportation system of buses, trams, monorail trains, and boats that can take you wherever you want to go. If you're staying on Disney property, you can use this system exclusively. In general, allow up to an hour to travel between parks and hotels.

If you're park hopping, consider using your own car to save time. There can be 30-minute waits for park-provided bus transportation. Your parking pass is good at any of the theme parks, and parking is free if you're a resort guest.

BOAT TRAVEL

Motor launches connect WDW destinations on waterways. Specifically, they operate from the Epcot resorts—except the Caribbean Beach—to the Studios and Epcot; between Bay Lake and the Magic Kingdom; and also between Fort Wilderness, the Wilderness Lodge, and the Polynesian, Contemporary, and Grand Floridian resorts. Launches from Old Key West, Saratoga Springs, and Port Orleans all travel to Downtown Disney, as well.

BUS TRAVEL

Buses provide direct service from every on-site resort to both major and minor theme parks, and express buses go directly between the major theme parks. You can go directly from or make connections at Downtown Disney, Epcot, and the Epcot resorts, including the Yacht and Beach Clubs, BoardWalk, the Caribbean Beach Resort, the Swan, and the Dolphin, as well as to Disney's Animal Kingdom and the Animal Kingdom resorts (the Animal Kingdom Lodge, the All-Star, and Coronado Springs resorts).

Buses to the Magic Kingdom all go straight to the turnstiles, allowing you to avoid the extra step of boarding a monorail or boat at the TTC to get to the front of the Kingdom.

MONORAIL TRAVEL

The elevated monorail serves many important destinations. It has two loops: one links the Magic Kingdom, TTC, and a handful of resorts (including the Contemporary, the Grand Floridian, and the Polynesian), the other loops from the TTC directly to Epcot. Before this monorail pulls into the station, the elevated track passes through Future World—Epcot's northern half—and circles the giant silver geosphere housing the

Spaceship Earth ride to give you a preview of what you'll see.

TRAM TRAVEL

Trams operate from the parking lot to the entrance of each theme park. If you parked fairly close in, though, you may save time, especially at park closing time, by walking.

DRIVING AND PARKING

Sections of the Magic Kingdom lot are named for Disney characters; Epcot's parking lot highlights modes of exploration; those at the Studios are named Stage, Music, Film, and Dance; and the Animal Kingdom's sound like Beanie Baby

WORD OF MOUTH

"Get a room on-site. We've stayed on the monorail twice now (Grand Flo and the Poly) and loved it. We have two small kiddos, and it's completely worth it for the ease of travel and the extra magic hours. It's way too much hassle to go on and off property during the day. Plus, it's a good idea to take a break during the day for a nap/ or just rest and it's much easier."
                                    –rfolmar

names—Unicorn, Butterfly, and so on. Although in theory Goofy (row) 45 is unforgettable, by the end of the day, you'll be so goofy with eating and shopping and riding that you'll swear that you parked in Sleepy.

■TIP➔**When you board the tram, write down your parking-lot location and keep it in a pocket.** Trams make frequent trips between the parking area and the parks' turnstile areas. No valet parking is available for Walt Disney World theme parks.

For each major theme-park lot, admission is $12 for cars, $13 for RVs and campers, and free to those staying at Walt Disney World resorts. Save your receipt; if you want to visit another park the same day, you won't have to pay to park twice. If you have reservations at a Disney resort, check in early (leave baggage at the bell station if you wish) and ask for your free parking permit.

Parking is always free at Typhoon Lagoon, Blizzard Beach, Downtown Disney, and Disney's BoardWalk. You can valet park at BoardWalk for $10. Valet parking is no longer available at Downtown Disney, so it pays to arrive early in the evening—around 6 PM—and you'll get a much closer parking space; you'll also avoid long restaurant lines.

MONEY MATTERS

Be prepared to spend and spend—and spend some more. Despite relatively low airfares and car-rental rates, cash seems to evaporate out of wallets, and credit-card balances seem to increase on exposure to the hot Orlando sun. Theme-park admission is roughly $69 per day per person (for a family of two adults and two children ages 3–9)—not counting all the $2 soft drinks and $20 souvenirs. Hotels range so wildly—from $70 a night (at a few non-Disney hotels) to 10 or more times that—that you have to do some hard thinking about just how much you want to spend. Meal prices away from the theme parks are comparable to those in other midsize cities, ranging from $5 per person at a fast-food chain to $40 entrées at an upscale restaurant.

SAMPLE COSTS AT WALT DISNEY WORLD	
20 oz. bottle of water $2	Souvenir T-shirt $16–$35
20 oz. bottle of soda $2–$2.50	Roll of film (36 shots) $9.49
Cup of coffee $2–$2.25	1G digital memory card $17.95
Cheeseburger $6.10	Autograph book $6.95
French fries $2.50	Plush character toys $12–$100
Ice-cream treat $2.50–$4	

ATMS AND CREDIT CARDS

ATMs are scattered throughout the Magic Kingdom, Epcot, the Studios, Animal Kingdom, and Downtown Disney. Throughout this guide, the following abbreviations are used: **AE**, American Express; **D**, Discover; **DC**, Diners Club; **MC**, MasterCard; and **V**, Visa.

DISCOUNT COUPONS

Coupon books, such as those available from **Entertainment Travel Editions** (☎ *800/445–4137* ⊕ *www.entertainment.com*) for around $25 or $30, can be good sources for discounts on rental cars, admission to attractions, meals, and other typical purchases. Hotel and restaurant lobbies also often have racks with flyers that advertise business with coupons.

The **Orlando Magicard** (☎ *800/643–9492* ⊕ *www.orlandoinfo.com/ magicard*), offered for free by the Orlando–Orange County Convention & Visitors Bureau, provides discounts for many attractions, restaurants, and shopping-mall stores. Download it from the Web site or order it over the phone.

TIPPING

Whether they carry bags, open doors, deliver food, or clean rooms, hospitality employees work to receive a portion of your travel budget. In deciding how much to give, base your tip on what the service is and how well it's performed.

In transit, tip an airport valet and shuttle driver $1 to $2 per bag, a taxi driver 15% to 20% of the fare.

For hotel staff, recommended amounts are $1 to $2 per bag for a bellhop, $1 or $2 per night per guest for housekeeping, $5 to $20 for special concierge service, $1 to $2 for a doorman who hails a cab or parks a car, 15% of the greens fee for a caddy, 15% to 20% of the bill for a massage, and 15% of a room service bill (check first to see if gratuity is included in the room-service menu). In a restaurant, give 15% to 20% of your bill to the server and about 15% to a bartender.

PARK BASICS

BABY CARE

The Magic Kingdom's soothing, quiet **Baby Care Center** is next to the Crystal Palace, which lies between Main Street and Adventureland. The other three major Disney parks have similar baby care centers

CLOSE UP

Best Ways to Save

▪ **Consider your theme-park ticket options.** With Disney's Magic Your Way tickets, it's now worth it to buy an extra ticket on the day of your arrival or departure if you're planning to stay at least four or five days and want to cram in every bit of park time possible. It costs only $3 to upgrade from a four-day Disney adult ticket to a five-day one and $7 to upgrade from a three-day to a four-day ticket. If you're staying for just three days, however, you're probably better off spending arrival/departure days visiting Downtown Disney, Disney's Boardwalk, or Universal CityWalk, or lounging around your hotel pool.

▪ **Buy your tickets as soon as you know you're going.** Prices typically go up about once a year, so you might beat a price hike—and save a little money.

▪ **Avoid holidays and school vacation times, if possible, or go off-season.** You can see more in less time, and lodging rates are lower.

▪ **Choose accommodations with a kitchen or at least a fridge and microwave.** You can stock up on breakfast items in a nearby supermarket, and save time—and money—by eating your morning meal in your hotel room.

▪ **If you plan to eat in a full-service restaurant, do it at lunch.** Then have a light dinner. Lunchtime prices are almost always lower than dinnertime prices. Also look for "early bird" menus, which offer dinner entrées at reduced prices during late afternoon and early evening hours.

▪ **Watch your shopping carefully.** Theme-park merchandisers are excellent at displaying the goods so that you (or your children) can't resist them. You may find that some articles for sale are also available at home—for quite a bit less. One way to cope is to give every member of your family a souvenir budget—adults and children alike. Another good option is to wait until the last day of your trip to buy your souvenirs.

▪ **Refill your water bottles.** You'll be surprised at how much water you drink hiking around the parks under the hot Florida sun. Those $2 water bottles really add up, but you can save a bundle by refilling your bottles at the water fountains all over the parks.

▪ **Bring essentials with you.** Remember to pack your hat, sunscreen, camera, memory card or film, batteries, diapers, and aspirin. These items are all very expensive within the theme parks.

with nursing rooms furnished with rocking chairs. Low lighting levels make these centers comfortable for nursing, though it can get crowded in mid-afternoon in peak season. There are adorable toddler-size toilets (these may be a high point for your just-potty-trained child) as well as supplies such as formula, baby food, pacifiers, disposable diapers, and even children's pain reliever. Changing tables are in all women's rooms and most men's rooms.

BABY SWAP

Parents with small children under the height limit for major attractions have to take turns waiting in the long lines, right? Wrong. In what's unofficially known as the Baby Swap or Rider Switch, both of you queue up, and when it's your turn to board, one stays with the youngsters until the other returns; the waiting partner then rides without waiting again, and your young ones get to ride again with the other grown-up. This policy is not widely advertised at Disney, so it pays to ask attendants at individual rides if the swap is available. Universal Studios calls it a Baby Exchange and has areas set aside for it at most rides.

CAMERAS

Disposable cameras and film, batteries, and memory cards are widely available in shops throughout the theme parks and hotels. The **Camera Center,** in the Magic Kingdom Town Square Exposition Hall, is the place to buy photos that Disney photographers take of you and your family posing with characters or saying cheese at various locations around the park. A 5" × 7" photo costs $12.95 for the first print and $9.95 for each additional copy. An 8" × 10" costs $16.95. You can buy similar photos at the other Disney park Camera Centers, or you can ask for the Disney PhotoPass so you can view and order the photos online at any time.

CLINICS AND HOSPITALS

The **Centra Care** (✉ 12500 S. Apopka Vineland Rd., Lake Buena Vista ☎ 407/ 934–2273) near Downtown Disney provides free shuttle service from any of the Disney, Universal, and SeaWorld theme park's first-aid stations and from all Disney resort hotels and other area hotels. It's open weekdays 8–midnight, weekends 8–8.

For minor emergencies visit the **Main Street Physicians Clinic** (✉ 8723 International Dr., Suite 115 ☎ 407/370–4881). It's open weekdays 8–8 and weekends 9–5.

In an emergency near Celebration, head to **Florida Hospital Celebration Health** (✉ 400 Celebration Pl., Celebration ☎ 407/303–4000). If you're closer to Universal Studios, head to **Orlando Regional Medical Center/Sand Lake Hospital** (✉ 9400 Turkey Lake Rd., International Drive Area, Orlando ☎ 407/351–8500). Hospital emergency rooms are open 24 hours a day.

EMERGENCIES

In an emergency, always call **911.** Disney employees are known for their extreme helpfulness, so don't hesitate to call on anyone with a Disney name tag. All the major theme parks have first-aid centers.

LOCKERS

Lockers are available near all the theme-park entrances ($5, plus $5 deposit). If you're park hopping, you can use your locker receipt to acquire a locker at the next park you visit for no extra charge.

LOST AND FOUND

There are Lost and Found offices in the Magic Kingdom, at Epcot, in Disney's Hollywood Studios, and at Disney's Animal Kingdom. After one day, all items are sent to the Main Lost and Found office at the TCC.

Contacts **Disney's Animal Kingdom Lost and Found** (☎ 407/938–2785). **Disney's Hollywood Studios Lost and Found** (☎ 407/560–3720). **Epcot Lost and Found** (☎ 407/560–7500). **Magic Kingdom Lost and Found** (✉ City Hall ☎ 407/824–4521). **Main Lost and Found** (✉ Magic Kingdom, Ticket and Transportation Center ☎ 407/824–4245).

LOST CHILDREN

Losing a child in a crowded theme park is one of the most frightening experiences a parent can have, but the one thing to remember is that theme-park security is excellent and crime is practically nonexistent. Theme park staff members are trained to recover lost little ones and deliver them back to you safely. Disney cast members immediately accompany lost children to the Baby Care Center, where you can pick them up. But there are many ways you can avoid losing your child in the first place.

Have everyone in your family wear matching T-shirts or at least the same color, so you can easily find them and they can find you. Mobile phones are great for teens who want to split off for coaster thrills while you're entertaining younger children on kiddie rides. If you separate to use the bathroom or for any other reason, pinpoint a meeting location and time in the same area.

Hold tight to your children's hands after parades and during the massive exodus from the parks in the evening. The other times children can be easily separated are during character meet-and-greets, when parents are queuing up for Fastpass appointments, and when children are racing around play areas.

Explain to your kids ahead of time that, if they get lost, they should tell any Disney cast member right away. Cast members are easy to recognize, with their bright theme uniforms and nametags.

PACKAGE PICK-UP

Ask the shop clerk to send any large purchase you make to Package Pick-Up, so you won't have to carry it around all day. Allow three hours for the delivery. Your park guide map includes information on the designated package pickup area at the front of each theme park.

PET CARE

It's probably best to leave Rover at home, but if you just can't part with your animal, all the major Disney parks, as well as Universal and SeaWorld, have kennels. They provide a cage, water, and sometimes food. Some of the kennels, such as the one at Epcot, offer dog-walking services for an additional fee. On-site Disney resort guests can board

The Most Important Advice You'll Get

If you remember nothing else, keep in mind these essential strategies, tried and tested by generations of Disney World fans. They're the Eight Commandments for touring Walt Disney World.

■ **Make dining reservations before you leave home, especially for character dining experiences.** If you don't, you might find yourself eating a hamburger (again) or leaving Walt Disney World for dinner. The on-site restaurants book up fast.

■ **Arrive at the parks at least 30 minutes before they open.** We know, it's your vacation and you want to sleep in. So go to the Caribbean. Or the mountains. Don't go to Walt Disney World, unless you've been there a hundred times and you plan to sit by the pool and play golf more than go on rides. If you're like most families and you want to make the most of your time and money, plan to be up by at least 7:30 every day. After transit time, it'll take you 10–15 minutes to park and get to the gates. If you know you want to use the lockers or ATMs, or rent strollers, get there 45 minutes in advance.

■ **See the top attractions first thing in the morning.** And we mean first thing. As in, before 10 AM. Decide in advance which attractions you don't want to miss, find out where they are, and hotfoot it to them when the park opens. If you miss any in the morning, the other good times to see the most popular attractions are during peak meal hours, right before closing and during the parades. Otherwise, use Fastpass.

■ **Use Fastpass.** It's worth saying twice. The system is free, easy, and it's your ticket to the top attractions with little or no waiting in line.

■ **Build in rest time.** This is the greatest way to avoid becoming overly hot, tired, and grumpy. We recommend starting early and then leaving the theme parks around 3 or 4, the hottest and most crowded time of day. After a couple hours' rest at your hotel, you can have an early dinner and head back to the parks to watch one of the nighttime spectaculars or to ride a couple more of the big-deal rides (lines are shorter around closing time).

■ **Create a rough itinerary, but leave room for spontaneity.** Decide which parks to see on each day, and know your priorities, but don't try to plot your trip hour by hour. Instead, break up the day into morning, afternoon, and evening sections. If you're staying at a Disney resort, find out which parks are offering the Extra Magic Hours on which days, and plan to take advantage of the program.

■ **Eat at off-hours.** Have a quick, light breakfast at 7 or 8, lunch at 11, and dinner at 5 or 6 to avoid the mealtime rush hours. Between 11:30 and 2:30 during high season, you can wait in line up to 30 minutes for a so-called fast-food lunch in the parks.

■ **Save the high-capacity sit-down shows for the afternoon.** You usually don't have to wait in line so long for shows, and you'll be relieved at the chance to sit in an air-conditioned theater during the hottest part of the day.

their pets for $18 each per night; others pay $20 per night. The Disney day rate is $10 per pet. Book ahead and be sure to take your pet's immunization records. At SeaWorld, pets can stay for $6 a day; at Universal, the day rate is $10. Sometime in late 2009, Disney plans to open a full-service luxury pet resort operated by Best Friends Pet Care, complete with dog and cat boarding, grooming, and even bedtime stories for pet guests.

The Portofino Bay Hotel, the Hard Rock Hotel, and the Royal Pacific Resort at **Universal Orlando** (☎ *407/503–7625 or 800/232–7827*) allow your pet to stay in your room for a $25 cleaning fee, and they even offer pet room service. You must, however, provide a pet health certificate that's no more than 10 days old. You must also have a leash or cage.

STROLLER RENTALS

Renting a stroller isn't a cheap proposition, but if you weigh the rental cost against the hassle of bringing your own, it stings less. Plus, the resort's strollers are relatively lightweight and maneuverable. Single strollers are $15 a day, $13 a day for a multiday rental; double strollers are $31 a day, $27 a day for multiday rental. All strollers come with a large, visible, white card on which you can write your name. Another good trick for identifying your stroller quickly is to attach a colorful bandana or T-shirt to it.

Of course, it's never good to leave valuables in your stroller. Despite precautions, there's always the possibility that your stroller will be taken, probably by mistake because all the strollers look alike. Also, well-intentioned Disney cast members will often reorganize strollers in the stroller parking areas, so if you exit a ride to find your stroller isn't where you left it, look for it among the other strollers in the area. If you still can't find it, notify a cast member. You can pick up a new stroller free of charge if you've kept your rental receipt. If you're park hopping on the same day, turn in your old stroller when you leave the first park and show your receipt to get a new stroller at the entrance to the next park.

VISITOR INFORMATION

For general WDW information, contact Guest Information or visit Guest Services in any Disney resort. If you want to speak directly to someone at a specific Disney location, use the WDW Central Switchboard at 407/824–2222. To inquire about specific resort facilities or detailed park information, call the individual property via the switchboard. For accommodations and shows, call the Disney Reservation Center. One of the easiest ways to get Disney information is via the WDW Web site.

WALT DISNEY WORLD

WDW Information (☎ *407/824–4321, 407/827–5141 TDD* ⊕ www.disneyworld. com). **WDW Resort Reservations** (☎ *407/934–7639*). **WDW Dining reservations** (☎ *407/939–3463*).

UNIVERSAL ORLANDO

Universal Information (☎ *407/363–8000* ⊕ *www.universalorlando.com*). **Universal Resort reservations** ☎ *888/273–1311*).

SEAWORLD

SeaWorld Information (☎ 407/351–3600 or 888/800–5447 ⊕ www.seaworld. com). **Discovery Cove Information** (☎ 407/351–3600 or 877/434–7268 ⊕ www.discoverycove.com).

GREATER ORLANDO

Kissimmee/St. Cloud Convention & Visitors Bureau (☎ 407/847–5000 or 800/327–9159 ⊕ www.floridakiss.com). **Orlando/Orange County Convention & Visitors Bureau** (☎ 407/363–5872 ⊕ www.orlandoinfo.com). **Winter Park Chamber of Commerce** (☎ 407/644–8281 ⊕ www.winterpark.org or www. cityofwinterpark.org). **Visit Florida** (☎ 850/488–5607 ⊕ www.visitflorida.com).

HEAD'S UP: THE SCARY RIDES

Knowing your child's personality is half the battle when it comes to avoiding a frightening attraction. Gauge their sensitivities, and don't push them if they're unsure of a ride or attraction. Start with the milder attractions and build up to rides like the Haunted Mansion, with its dark spooky atmosphere, or Splash Mountain, with its final unnerving plunge.

Darkness, loud noises, and sudden surprises—often the main ingredients in the 3-D films—can scare children more than fast-moving coasters.

If you're unsure whether your kids will be OK on a certain ride, talk to them about it ahead of time and let them know what to expect.

Finally we suggest that you buy inexpensive earplugs (available at most pharmacies) and use them in loud theaters.

Below we've listed all of the attractions in Walt Disney World that may frighten your children and the parts that make them scary.

MAGIC KINGDOM

ADVENTURE-LAND **Pirates of the Caribbean.** The first short leg of this cruise past pirate skeletons and a cannonball battle may be a bit unsettling for young children but probably will be forgotten quickly with all the merrymaking and swashbuckling nonsense that follows.

FRONTIERLAND **Splash Mountain.** The big drop at the end is stomach-churning even for adults and those watching from the outside.

Big Thunder Mountain Railroad. Your kids *and* you will feel like you're about to go flying off the track on this high-speed and seriously bumpy roller coaster.

Haunted Mansion. The cackling ghosts and ghouls are more funny than scary to most kids, but some might find the darkness, fog, and eerie sounds, not to mention the jack-in-the-box surprises, to be pretty frightening.

FANTASYLAND **Mickey's PhilharMagic.** More intense than scary, this involves loud music and 3-D images that seem to pop out at you. Whooping and shouting audience members can also cause small children to become upset.

Snow White's Scary Adventures. The witch with her warty nose and shiny poisonous apple can spook sensitive kids under 7.

Mad Tea Party. If your child is prone to motion sickness, avoid using the ride's spinning feature.

TOONTOWN   **The Barnstormer at Goofy's Wiseacre Farm.** This is a starter coaster meant for kids, so definitely let them try this first if you're not sure if they can handle the other coasters. You can always watch it go around a few times before trying it out.

TOMORROW-   **Space Mountain.** The scariest ride in
LAND   the Magic Kingdom, this coaster whips you through space in almost total darkness. Many adults refuse to ride, but we've seen kids as young as 7 beg to ride again.

Stitch's Great Escape. Despite its cartoon host, this attraction isn't tame. Most of the show occurs in the dark with sensory surprises that can startle adults and scare kids as old as 8.

EPCOT

Honey, I Shrunk the Audience. Some of the film's 3-D and in-seat effects can startle young children; prepare them ahead of time so they'll know to expect "in your face" and "beneath the seat" surprises.

Mission Space. You're in a capsule that spins around very fast, though it feels as if you're launching straight up. It's hard enough to remember to look straight ahead—the only way to avoid serious motion sickness; in addition you're supposed to push buttons and move a joystick. We recommend keeping kids under 9 (and especially those with any health issues), as well as anyone prone to motion sickness, off this ride.

Test Track. This track ride gears up at a fairly relaxed pace and builds to a high-speed climax. Most kids don't seem bothered.

DISNEY'S HOLLYWOOD STUDIOS

Twilight Zone Tower of Terror. Your "elevator" will plunge down (and rocket skyward) 13 stories multiple times. Many people, especially "lightweights" are lifted clean out of their seats during the drops. Kids under 9 may be bothered by the scary music and story line even before the plunge.

Rock 'n' Roller Coaster Starring Aerosmith. If your child loved Space Mountain, chances are he'll love this ride, too. That said, this ride is more intense: your coaster goes a lot faster—60 MPH as opposed to 30 MPH—and you roll through high-volume hard rock music.

Muppet*Vision 3-D. OK, it's the Muppets, but like the other 3-D shows, images pop out of the screen and the soundtrack is pretty loud.

Star Tours. Riding through space in a runaway starship, you travel through an asteroid field and get shot at. We think this aging ride is fairly tame, but readers have written to us to say that their young children (think 5 years old) were pretty scared.

Sounds Dangerous Starring Drew Carey. More disturbing than scary, the loud soundtrack noises can shock some kids.

Indiana Jones Epic Stunt Spectacular. If you're going to take small children to this show, don't sit in rows close to the action—the loud gunplay by stunt performers and the fireballs produced on stage during the show can scare little ones.

CLOSE UP 1

Hidden Mickeys

Searching for Mickey? Character meals and meet-and-greets aren't the only places you can find the "big cheese." You can spot images of Mickey Mouse hidden in murals, statues, and floor tiles in queue areas and rides.

Hidden Mickeys began as an inside joke among Disney Imagineers. When finishing an attraction, they'd subtly slip a Mickey into the motif to see if co-workers and friends would notice. Today, hunting for Hidden Mickeys (and Minnies) is a great way to pass the time while standing in line. For example, as you wait to board Norway's Maelstrom ride in Epcot, you can scan the big mural for the Viking wearing mouse ears.

You can request a list of Hidden Mickeys at Guest Services in the theme parks or at Disney hotels, and the non-Disney Web site ⊕ *www. hiddenmickeys.org* has a list and photos. Before you begin your search, keep in mind that some of the images can be quite difficult to discern. (You practically need a magnifying glass to make out the profile of Minnie Mouse in the Hollywood mural at the Great Movie Ride in Disney's Hollywood Studios; she's above the roof of the gazebo.) If you're traveling with young children, you can use Hidden Mickeys as a distraction tactic, but be careful. Preschoolers might actually become frustrated trying to find him. But school-age kids might welcome the challenge of finding as many Hidden Mickeys as they can. Here are some clues.

IN THE MAGIC KINGDOM
Big Thunder Mountain Railroad. As your train nears the station, look to your right for three rusty gears on the ground.

Haunted Mansion. There's a Mouse-eared place setting on the table in the ballroom.

Snow White's Scary Adventures. In the queue-area mural, look for shorts hanging on the clothesline and at three of the stones in the chimney.

Splash Mountain. After the final drop, look for Mickey in profile lounging on his back in a cloud to the right of the Steamboat where the characters "zip-a-dee-doo-dah."

IN EPCOT
Spaceship Earth. Mickey smiles down from a constellation behind the loading area.

The American Adventure. Check out the painting of the wagon train, and look above the front leg of the foremost oxen.

AT DISNEY'S HOLLYWOOD STUDIOS
Twilight Zone Tower of Terror. In the boiler room, look for a water stain on the wall after the queue splits.

Rock 'n' Roller Coaster. A pair of Mickeys hides in the floor tile right before the doors with the marbles.

IN THE ANIMAL KINGDOM
DINOSAUR. Stare at the bark of the painted tree in the far left background of the wall mural at the entrance.

Rafiki's Planet Watch. The main Conservation Station building contains more than 25 Hidden Mickeys. Look at the animals and tree trunks in the entrance mural.

–Ellen Parlapiano

ANIMAL KINGDOM

Tree of Life—It's Tough to Be a Bug! Loud noises, scary bugs that jump out at you, spiders that descend from the ceiling—this 3-D film can scare kids as old as 9 if they're sensitive. See Mickey's PhilharMagic or Muppet*Vision 3-D to prepare for this one.

Dinosaur. Huge, lifelike dinosaurs jump out at you at several turns during this ride. There are also a couple of dips and drops. The darkness and noise alone are enough to scare many children under 8.

Primeval Whirl. A starter coaster with wilder turns and dips than the Magic Kingdom's Barnstormer, this is a good one to try out before going on to Expedition Everest.

Expedition Everest. This wild ride into the Himalayas is Disney storytelling at its fast-paced finest, and children who meet the 44-inch height requirement won't want to miss it if they like coaster-type rides and a few frights. Be warned of scary moments in the dark when the fearsome yeti appears and the ride vehicle plunges backward briefly.

Kali River Rapids. This water ride looks intimidating but it's actually pretty tame. There's one rather scary drop, but it's over quickly. The most off-putting part of the ride is the potential to get absolutely soaked. More than one child has walked away dripping wet and in tears because of it. Bring a poncho or a change of clothes and a hand towel or be prepared to buy some souvenir shorts and a T-shirt.

The Magic Kingdom

WORD OF MOUTH

"You should definitely go to Magic Kingdom. This is the quintessential Disney theme park, and there's a wide assortment of things to do. I recommend Philaharmagic: it's a 3D film featuring classic scenes from Disney movies. You must must must ride the teacups. Your children will enjoy Thunder Mountain and Splash Mountain, too."

—crazyhorse42

Updated by
Jennie Hess

Mickey Mouse. Tinkerbell. Cinderella. What would child-hood be like without the characters and magic of Disney? And when kids (and parents) say they want to go to "the" theme park, it's probably the Magic Kingdom they're think-ing of. Here you're walking amid crowds—characters like Snow White and Donald Duck strolling right alongside you—while roller coasters and rides whirl overhead and "It's a Small World" runs through your head.

The Magic Kingdom is the heart and soul of the Disney empire. Comparable (in scope) to California's Disneyland, it was the first Disney outpost in Florida when it opened in 1971, and it's the park that launched Disney's presence, with modifications, in France, Japan, and Hong Kong.

For a landmark that wields such worldwide influence, the Magic Kingdom may seem small: at 107 acres, it's smaller than Disney World's other or "Big Three" parks. But looks can be deceiving: the unofficial theme song—"It's a Small World After All"—doesn't hold true when it comes to the Magic Kingdom's attractions. Packed into seven different "lands" are nearly 50 major crowd pleasers, and that's not counting all the ancillary attractions: shops, eateries, live entertainment, Disney-character meet-and-greet spots, fireworks, parades, and, of course, the sheer pleasure of strolling through the beautifully landscaped grounds.

Many rides are geared to the young, but the Magic Kingdom is anything but a kiddie park. The degree of detail, the greater vision, the surprisingly witty spiel of the guides, and the tongue-in-cheek signs that crop up in the oddest places—for instance, in Fantasyland, the restrooms are marked "Prince" and "Princess"—all contribute to a delightful sense of discovery that's far beyond the mere thrill of a ride.

The park is laid out on a north–south axis, with Cinderella Castle at the center and the various lands surrounding it in a broad circle. Upon entering you find yourself at the foot of Main Street, U.S.A., which runs due north and ends at the Hub, a large manicured circle, properly known as Central Plaza, in front of Cinderella Castle. The castle's golden spires have been polished to perfection and street parties kick into high gear throughout 2009 in celebration of Disney's global "What Will You Celebrate?" promotion. You say it's your birthday? Then you can get in free through December 31 at the Magic Kingdom or other Walt Disney World parks or Disneyland in California.

Numbers in the margin correspond to points of interest on the Magic Kingdom map.

GETTING HERE AND AROUND

If you're staying at the Contemporary, Polynesian, or Grand Floridian, take the monorail directly to the park. If you're staying at another Disney resort, take one of the Walt Disney World shuttle buses straight to the turnstiles.

If you're driving, try to arrive extra early (45 minutes to an hour ahead of park opening), so you can park close to the Ticket and Transportation Center (TTC), where you must board the monorail or ferry to get to the park. You'll need to show your park tickets to TTC attendants, or tell them you're picking up tickets at Guest Services (aka Guest Relations). After showing your tickets to a cast member, you can choose either ferryboat or monorail transportation to the turnstiles. If the line's not prohibitive, the monorail is usually faster, and if you have children along, ask to sit up front with the driver. You might have to wait for the next train or two, but it's worth the front window view and the chance to see and talk with the driver. Trams operate from the parking lot to the TTC if you park farther away.

Once you're in the Magic Kingdom, distances are generally short, and the best way to get around is on foot. The Walt Disney World Railroad, the Main Street vehicles, and the Tomorrowland Transit Authority do help you cover some territory and can give your feet a welcome rest, but they're primarily entertainment, not transportation.

GETTING STARTED

Be prepared to open your bags for a security check before heading through the turnstile. Guest Services windows are to the right, in case you need to pick up reserved tickets or deal with any other concern. If you've taken our advice and arrived before park opening, you'll soon see Mickey and the gang ride in on the elevated Walt Disney World Railroad to welcome you to the Magic Kingdom. This little performance truly increases the excitement and anticipation. It's no wonder everyone rushes the entrance when the park finally does open.

As you pass underneath the railroad tracks, symbolically leaving behind the world of reality and entering a world of fantasy, you'll immediately notice the adorable buildings lining Town Square and Main Street, U.S.A. Cast members are available at almost every turn to help you. In fact, providing information to visitors is part of the job description of the men and women who sweep the pavement.

Before you leave Town Square, check racks beneath the Train Station or at City Hall to pick up a Guide Map, with color-coded sections to help you get around, and the Times Guide, which lists live show times, character greeting times, and special hours for attractions and restaurants that may not be open through closing.

BASIC SERVICES

BABY CARE

The Magic Kingdom's soothing, quiet **Baby Care Center** is next to the Crystal Palace, which lies between Main Street and Adventureland. Furnished with rocking chairs, it has a low lighting level that makes it

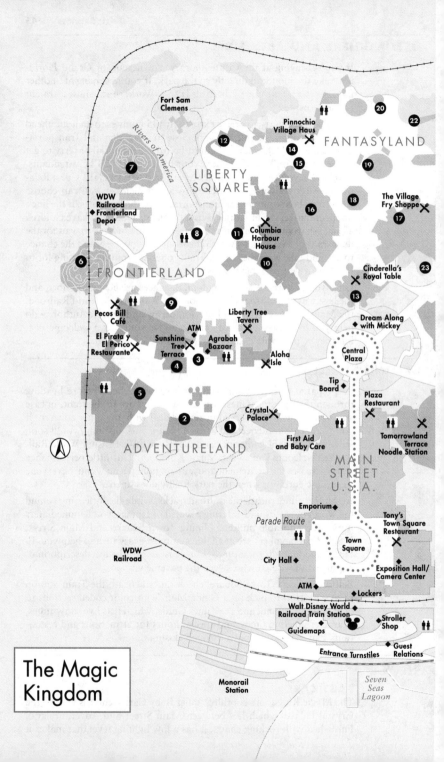

The Magic Kingdom

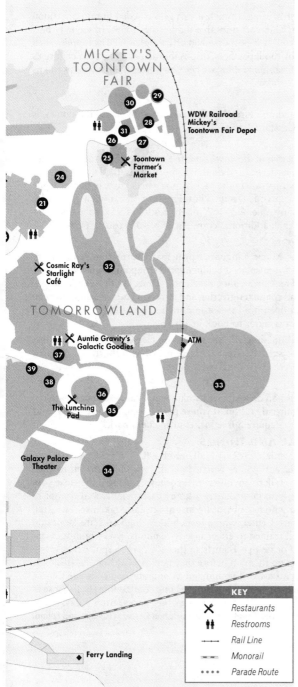

comfortable for nursing, though it can get crowded in mid-afternoon in peak season. There are adorable toddler-size toilets (these may be a high point for your just-potty-trained offspring) as well as supplies such as formula, baby food, pacifiers, disposable diapers, and even children's pain relievers. Changing tables are here, as well as in all women's rooms and most men's rooms.

FIRST AID

The Magic Kingdom's **First Aid Center,** staffed by registered nurses, is alongside the Crystal Palace.

CAMERAS

The **Camera Center,** in the Town Square Exposition Hall, opposite City Hall, sells film, batteries, and digital memory cards. If a Disney photographer took your picture in the park, this is where you can purchase the photos or pick up your **Disney PhotoPass** so you can view and order them online at any time. A 5" × 7" photo costs $12.95 for the first print and $9.95 for each additional copy. An 8" × 10" costs $16.95.

INFORMATION

City Hall is the Magic Kingdom's principal information center. Here you can search for misplaced belongings or companions, ask questions of staffers, and pick up a Guide Map and a Times Guide, with its schedule of events and character-greeting and attraction information. You can also try to find openings for last-minute lunch or dinner reservations, though it's always better to book in advance.

At the end of Main Street, on the left as you face Cinderella Castle, just before the Hub, is the **Tip Board,** a large board with constantly updated information about attractions' wait times.

LOCKERS

Lockers ($5, plus $5 deposit) are available in an arcade underneath the Main Street Railroad Station. If you're park hopping, you can use your locker receipt to acquire a free locker at the next park.

LOST PEOPLE AND THINGS

Nametags are available at City Hall or at the Baby Care Center next to the Crystal Palace, if you're worried about your children getting lost. Instruct them to talk to anyone with a Disney nametag if they lose you. If that does happen, immediately ask any cast member and try not to panic; children who are obviously lost are usually taken to City Hall or the Baby Care Center, where lost-children logbooks are kept, and everyone is well trained to effect speedy reunions. Savvy families wear matching neon or tie-dye T-shirts so that it's easy to spot stragglers in a crowd and scoop them up before they get lost. **City Hall** (☎*407/824–4521*) also has a Lost and Found and a computerized Message Center, where you can leave notes for your traveling companions, both those in the Magic Kingdom and those visiting other parks. After a day, found items are taken to the **Ticket and Transportation Center (TTC) Lost and Found.** (☎*407/824–4245*).

TOP MAGIC KINGDOM ATTRACTIONS

FOR AGES 7 AND UP

■ **Big Thunder Mountain Railroad.** This old classic coaster isn't too scary; it's just a really good, bumpy, swervy thrill.

■ **Buzz Lightyear's Space Ranger Spin.** Space ranger wannabes will love competing for the highest score on this shoot-'em-up ride.

■ *Mickey's PhilharMagic.* There are several 3-D film experiences at Disney, but this is the only one featuring the main Disney characters and movie theme songs.

■ **Space Mountain.** The Magic Kingdom's scariest ride, all you see are stars in the darkness as you zip along the tracks.

■ **Splash Mountain.** A long, tame boat ride ends in a 52½-foot drop into a very wet briar patch.

■ **Haunted Mansion.** Featuring some new razzle-dazzle special effects, this classic is always a frightful hoot.

FOR AGES 6 AND UNDER

■ **Goofy's Barnstormer.** This is Walt Disney World's starter coaster for kids who may be tall enough to go on Big Thunder Mountain and Space Mountain, but who aren't sure they can handle it. If your child loves the Barnstormer, he's probably ready for the big-kid rides.

■ **The Magic Carpets of Aladdin.** Just like Dumbo but with shorter lines, the Magic Carpets of Aladdin is a must-do for preschoolers. You can make your carpet go up and down to avoid the water as mischievous camels spit at you.

■ **The Many Adventures of Winnie the Pooh.** Hang onto your honey pot as you get whisked along on a windy-day adventure with Pooh, Tigger, Eeyore, and friends.

■ **Pirates of the Caribbean.** Don't miss this waltz through pirate country, especially if you're a fan of the movies. The scene is dark with lots of theatrical explosions, but the actual boat ride is slow and steady.

PACKAGE PICK-UP

Ask the shop clerk to send any large purchase you make to Package Pick-Up, so you won't have to carry it around all day. Allow three hours for the delivery. The Package Pick-Up area is next to City Hall.

STROLLER AND WHEELCHAIR RENTALS

The **Stroller Shop,** near the entrance on the east side of Main Street, rents both strollers and wheelchairs. Single strollers are $15 daily, $13 for multiday rental; double strollers are $31 daily, $27 for multiday rental. Wheelchairs are $10 daily, $8 for multiday rental. Electronic Convenience Vehicles (ECV) are $45 per day plus a refundable $20 security deposit. ■ **TIP→Neither wheelchairs nor ECVs are reservable, unfortunately, so arrive early to rent them. And while the park's wheelchair supply is generally plentiful, ECV availability is limited.** If any of your rentals needs replacing, ask any park cast member.

MAGIC KINGDOM TIP SHEET

■ Most families hit the Magic Kingdom early in their visit, so try to go toward the end of the week instead. Avoid weekends, since that's when locals tend to visit the park.

■ Arrive at the turnstiles at least 30 minutes before the scheduled park opening time.

■ If you're staying at a Disney resort, arrive at park opening and stay until early afternoon, then head back to the hotel for a nap or swim. You can return to the park in the mid- to late afternoon, refreshed and ready to soak up more magic.

■ Check Disney's Tip Board at the end of Main Street for good information on show times and attraction wait times—fairly reliable except for those moments when everyone follows the "See It Now!" advice and the line immediately triples.

■ Do your shopping in mid-afternoon, when attraction lines resemble a napping anaconda. During the afternoon parade, store clerks have been spotted twiddling their thumbs, so this is the time to seek sales assistance. (You can pick up purchases at Package Pick-Up next to City Hall when you're ready to leave the park.) If you shop at the end of the day, you'll be engulfed by rush-hour crowds.

■ See or ride one of the star attractions while the parade is going on, if you're willing to miss it, since lines ease considerably. But be careful not to get stuck on the wrong side of the parade route when the hoopla starts, or you may never get across.

■ At the start of the day, set up a rendezvous point and time, just in case you and your companions get separated. Good places are by the Cinderella Fountain in Fantasyland, the bottom of the staircase at the Main Street railroad station, the benches of City Hall, and the archway entrance to Adventureland.

MAIN STREET, U.S.A.

With its pastel Victorian-style buildings, antique automobiles ahoohga-oohga-ing, sparkling sidewalks, and an atmosphere of what one writer has called "almost hysterical joy," Main Street is more than a mere conduit to the other enchantments of the Magic Kingdom. It's where the spell is first cast.

Like Dorothy waking up in a Technicolor Oz or Mary Poppins jumping through the pavement painting, you emerge from beneath the Walt Disney World Railroad Station into a realization of one of the most tenacious American dreams. The perfect street in the perfect small town in a perfect moment of time is burnished to jewel-like quality, thanks to a four-fifths-scale reduction, nightly cleanings with high-pressure hoses, and constant repainting. And it's a very sunny world thanks to an outpouring of welcoming entertainment: live bands, barbershop quartets, and background music from Disney films and American musicals played over loudspeakers. Old-fashioned horse-drawn trolleys and omnibuses with their horns tooting chug along the street. Vendors in Victorian costumes sell balloons and popcorn. And Cinderella's famous castle floats whimsically in the distance where Main Street disappears.

Although attractions with a capital "A" are minimal on Main Street, there are plenty of inducements—namely, shops—to while away your time and part you from your money. The largest of these, the Emporium, is often the last stop for souvenir hunters at day's end, so avoid the crowds and buy early. You can pick up your purchases later at Package Pick-Up or have them delivered to your hotel or mailed home.

The Harmony Barber Shop is a novel stop if you want to step back in time for a haircut ($14 for children 12 and under, $17 for all others). Kids get complimentary Mickey Ears and a certificate if it's their first haircut ever. The Town Square Exposition Hall is actually a shop and exhibit center where you can see cameras of yesteryear and today. The shops in Exposition Hall are a good place to stock up on batteries, memory cards, and disposable cameras.

Main Street is also full of Disney insider fun. For instance, check out the proprietors' names above the shops: Roy O. Disney, etched above the Main Street Confectionery, is the name of Walt's brother. Dick Nunis, former chairman of Walt Disney Attractions, has an honored spot above the bakery. At the Hall of Champions, Card Walker—the "Practitioner of Psychiatry and Justice of the Peace"—is the former chairman of the company's executive committee. Longtime CEO Michael Eisner didn't get his own shop. Maybe new Disney chief Bob Iger will fare better.

WALT DISNEY WORLD RAILROAD

Duration: 21 min.

Crowds: Can be substantial late morning through late afternoon.

Strategy: Board with small children for an early start in Toontown, provided you have your own fold-up strollers to carry along on the train. If you've rented one of Disney's bulkier strollers, which cannot be loaded on the train, you may want to stick with a round-trip so you can collect your stroller outside the railroad station after you get off. Or hop aboard in mid-afternoon if you don't see a line.

Audience: All ages.

Rating: ★★

If you click through the turnstile just before 9 AM with young children in tow, wait at the entrance before crossing beneath the train station. In a few moments you'll see the day's first steam-driven train arrive laden with the park's most popular residents: Mickey Mouse, Donald Duck, Goofy, Pluto, and characters from every corner of the World. Once they disembark and you've collected the stars' autographs and photos, step right up to the elevated platform above the Magic Kingdom's entrance for a ride into living history.

Walt Disney was a railroad buff of the highest order—he constructed a one-eighth-scale train in his backyard and named it *Lilly Belle,* after his wife, Lillian. Another *Lilly Belle* rides the rails here, as do *Walter E. Disney, Roy O. Disney,* and *Roger Broggie* (named for a Disney Imagineer and fellow railroad aficionado). All the locomotives date from 1928, the same year Mickey Mouse was created. Disney scouts tracked down these vintage carriers in Mexico, where they transported sugarcane in the Yucatán, brought them back, and overhauled them. They're splendid, with striped awnings, brightly painted benches, authoritative "choo-choo" sounds, and hissing plumes of steam.

Their 1½-mi track runs along the perimeter of the Magic Kingdom, with much of the trip through the woods. Stops are in Frontierland and Mickey's Toontown Fair. The ride is a good introduction to the layout of the park and a quick trip with small children to Toontown in the morning; it's also great as relief for tired feet later in the day. The four trains run at five- to seven-minute intervals.

GROOVY SOUVENIRS

Get your collectible character pins at the **pin cart** across from the Chapeau in Town Square or at Main Street's Uptown Jewelers. Both have the park's best selections. If you spot a cast member wearing a pin you covet, ask to trade. Check www.dizpins.com (an unofficial site featuring Disney pin-trading information) for the scoop. Treats like taffy from the **Confectionery** make wonderful gifts. Serious Disney memorabilia collectors stop at the **Art of Disney**, where Mickey Mouse short cartoons from 1937 to 1940 play on a screen. One of the grooviest souvenirs is a "make-your-own-Mouse-ears-hat" option at the **Chapeau**. Pair any beanie with fuzzy pink ears, gem-studded ears, or plain black or white ears and then decorate from a selection of patches or personalize with stitching. If the sky looks dark, head to the **Emporium** for Disney's classic Mickey rain ponchos. This vast souvenir mall segues from one shop to the next and is the perfect place to buy T-shirts and the latest Disney doodads. Be on the lookout for mark downs.

ADVENTURELAND

From the scrubbed brick, manicured lawns, and meticulously pruned trees of the Central Plaza, an artfully dilapidated wooden bridge leads to the jungles of Adventureland. The landscape artists went wild here: South African cape honeysuckle droops, Brazilian bougainvillea drapes, Mexican flame vines cling, spider plants clone, and three different varieties of palm trees sway, all creating a seemingly spontaneous mess. The bright, all-American sing-along tunes that fill the air along Main Street and Central Plaza are replaced by the recorded repetitions of trumpeting elephants, pounding drums, and squawking parrots. The architecture is a mishmash of the best of Thailand, the Middle East, the Caribbean, Africa, and Polynesia, arranged in an inspired disorder that recalls comic-book fantasies of far-off places.

SWISS FAMILY TREEHOUSE

❶ **Duration:** Up to you.

Crowds: Artfully camouflaged so you may not see them—and the lines move slowly.

Strategy: Visit while waiting for your Jungle Cruise Fastpass appointment.

Audience: All ages; toddlers unsteady on their feet may have trouble with the stairs.

2

Rating: ★★

Inspired by the classic novel by Johann Wyss about the adventures of the Robinson family, who were shipwrecked on the way to America, the tree house shows what you can do with a big faux tree and a lot of imagination. The rooms are furnished with patchwork quilts and mahogany furniture. Disney detail abounds: the kitchen sink is a giant clamshell; the boys' room, strewn with clothing, has two hammocks instead of beds; and an ingenious system of rain barrels and bamboo pipes provides running water in every room. As you clamber around the narrow wooden steps and rope bridges that connect the rooms in this split-level dwelling, take a look at the Spanish moss. It's real, but the tree itself—some 90 feet in diameter, with more than 1,000 branches—was constructed by the props department. The 300,000 leaves are vinyl. It all adds up to a species of tree unofficially called *Disneyodendron eximus,* or "out-of-the-ordinary Disney tree."

▌**NEED A BREAK?** If you're looking for real refreshment and an energy boost, stop by **Aloha Isle**, where you'll find some of the tastiest and most healthful goodies. Try the fresh pineapple spears, or sip a smoothie or just some fruit juice, while you relax on one of the benches scattered in Adventureland.

JUNGLE CRUISE

② **Duration:** 10 min.
Crowds: Huge, from late morning until dinnertime; Fastpass is available.
Strategy: Go during the afternoon parade, but not after dark—you miss too much.
Audience: All ages.
Rating: ★★

On this Disney classic, you cruise through three continents and along four rivers: the Congo, the Nile, the Mekong, and the Amazon. The canopied launches are loaded, the safari-suited guides make a point of checking their pistols, and the *Irrawady Irma* or *Mongala Millie* is off for another "perilous" journey. The guide's shtick is surprisingly funny in a wry and cornball way. Along the way, you'll encounter Disney's famed Audio-Animatronics creatures of the African veld: bathing elephants, slinky pythons, an irritated rhinoceros, a tribe of hungry headhunters, and a bunch of hyperactive hippos (good thing the guide's got a pop pistol). Then there's Old Smiley, the crocodile, who's always waiting for a handout—or, as the guide quips, "a foot out." The animals are early-generation and crude by Disney standards—anyone who's seen the real thing at the Animal Kingdom or even a good zoo won't be impressed. Unless you're an old-school Disney fan, the Jungle Cruise isn't really worth a Fastpass.

THE MAGIC CARPETS OF ALADDIN

③ **Duration:** About 3 min.
Crowds: Heavy, but lines move fairly quickly.
Strategy: Visit while waiting for a Frontierland Fastpass appointment.
Audience: All ages; parents must ride with toddlers.

Rating: ★★★

Brightening the lush Adventureland landscape is this jewel-toned ride around a giant genie's bottle. You can control your own four-passenger, state-of-the-art carpet with a front-seat lever that moves it up and down and a rear-seat button that pitches it forward or backward. Part of the fun is dodging the right-on aim of a water-spewing "camel." Though short, the ride is a big hit with kids, who are also dazzled by the colorful gems implanted in the surrounding pavement.

ENCHANTED TIKI ROOM

④ **Duration:** 12 min.
Crowds: Waits seldom exceed 30 min.
Strategy: Go when you need a sit-down refresher in air-conditioning.
Audience: All ages.
Rating: ★

In its original incarnation as the Enchanted Tiki Birds, this was Disney's first Audio-Animatronics attraction. Now updated—and "under new management," as the sign out front whimsically notes—it includes the avian stars of two popular Disney animated films: Zazu from *The Lion King* and Iago from *Aladdin*. The boys take you on a tour of the original attraction while cracking lots of jokes. A holdover from the original is the ditty "In the Tiki, Tiki, Tiki, Tiki, Tiki Room," which is second only to "It's a Small World" as the Disney song you most love to hate. Speaking of which, many people really do hate this attraction, finding the talking birds obnoxious and the music way too loud and peppy.

PIRATES OF THE CARIBBEAN

⑤ **Duration:** 10 min.
Crowds: Waits seldom exceed 30 min, despite the ride's popularity.
Strategy: A good destination, especially in the heat of the afternoon.
Audience: All ages.
Rating: ★★★

This boat ride is classic Disney with a set and cast of characters created with incredible attention to detail. One of the pirate's "Avast, ye scurvy scum!" is the sort of greeting you'll want to practice on your companions. And if you've seen any of the *Pirates of the Caribbean* movies, you'll recognize many of the colorful characters and some of the scenes, as well. This is one of the few rides in the world that inspired a film (*Haunted Mansion* with Eddie Murphy was another) rather than the other way around.

The gracious arched entrance soon gives way to a dusty dungeon, redolent of dampness and of a spooky, scary past. Lanterns flicker as you board the boats and a ghostly voice intones, "Dead men tell no tales." Next, a deserted beach, strewn with shovels, a skeleton, and a disintegrating map indicating buried treasure prefaces this story of greed, lust, and destruction. Here's where the primary villain from the second "Pirates" film has been added: you'll pass right through a water-mist screen featuring the maniacal mug of Davy Jones, complete with squirming tentacle beard and barnacle-encrusted hat. Emerging from a pitch-black tunnel after a mild, tummy-tickling drop, you're caught in the middle of a furious battle. A pirate ship, cannons blazing, attacks a stone fortress. Note the pirate on board: it's gold-hungry Captain Barbossa, evil nemesis of the film's hero, Captain Jack Sparrow. Audio-Animatronics pirates hoist the Jolly Roger while brave soldiers scurry to defend the fort—to no avail. Politically correct nerves may twinge as the women of the town are rounded up and auctioned, but the wenches rule in another scene, where they chase roguish rapscallions with glee. The wild antics of the pirates—Captain Jack Sparrow pops up in several situations—result in a conflagration; the town goes up in flames, and all go to their just reward amid a catchy chorus of "A Pirate's Life For Me." Don't miss the attraction's revised ending, adjusted in the wake of the first two films—we'll tell no tales at risk of spoiling the fun.

GROOVY SOUVENIRS Among the all-time best Magic Kingdom souvenirs are the pirate hats, swords, and plastic hooks-for-hands at the **Pirate's Bazaar** near the Pirates of the Caribbean exit. Nearby, the **Agrabah Bazaar** has Jasmine-wear, including costumes and jewelry. Jasmine and other Aladdin characters are sometimes on hand to sign autographs next to the store.

FRONTIERLAND

Frontierland, in the northwest quadrant of the Magic Kingdom, evokes the American frontier. The period seems to be the latter half of the 19th century, and the West is being won by Disney cast members dressed in checked shirts, leather vests, cowboy hats, and brightly colored neckerchiefs. Banjo and fiddle music twangs from tree to tree, and snackers walk around munching turkey drumsticks so large that you could best an outlaw single-handedly with one. (Beware of hovering seagulls that migrate to the parks during cooler months—they've been known to snatch snacks from unsuspecting visitors.)

The screams that drown out the string music are not the result of a cowboy surprising an Indian. They come from two of the Magic Kingdom's more thrilling rides: Splash Mountain, an elaborate flume ride; and Big Thunder Mountain Railroad, one of the park's two roller coasters. In contrast to lush Adventureland, Frontierland is planted with mesquite, twisted Peruvian pepper trees, slash pines, and cacti.

The Walt Disney World Railroad makes a stop at Frontierland. It tunnels past a colorful scene in Splash Mountain and drops you off between Splash Mountain and Thunder Mountain.

SPLASH MOUNTAIN

Duration: 11 min.

Fodor's Choice ★

Crowds: Yes!

Strategy: If you're not in line by 9:45 AM, plan to use Fastpass or ride during meal or parade times. Parents who need to Baby Swap can take the young ones to a play area in a cave under the ride.

Audience: All except very young children, who may be terrified by the final drop. The minimum height is 40". No pregnant women or guests wearing back, neck, or leg braces.

Rating: ★★★

The second most popular thrill ride in the park after Space Mountain, Splash Mountain is a log-flume water ride, based on the animated sequences in Disney's 1946 film *Song of the South*. Here the Audio-Animatronics creations of Brer Rabbit, Brer Bear, Brer Fox, and a menagerie of other Brer beasts frolic in bright, cartoonlike settings. When you settle into the eight-person hollowed-out logs, Uncle Remus's voice growls, "Mark mah words, Brer Rabbit gonna put his foot in Brer Fox's mouth one of these days." And this just might be the day.

As the boat carries you up the mountain, Brer Rabbit's silhouette hops merrily ahead to the tune of the ride's theme song, "Time to Be Moving Along." Every time some critter makes a grab for the bunny, your log boat drops out of reach. But Brer Fox has been studying his book *How to Catch a Rabbit,* and our lop-eared friend looks as if he's destined for the pot. Things don't look so good for the flumers, either. You get one heart-stopping pause at the top of the mountain—just long enough to grab the safety bar—and then the boat plummets down into a gigantic, very wet briar patch. In case you want to know what you're getting into, the drop is 52½ feet—that's about five stories—at a 45-degree angle, enough to reach speeds of 40 MPH and make you feel weightless. Try to smile through your clenched teeth: as you begin to drop, a flashbulb pops. You can purchase a photographic memento of the experience before exiting the ride. Brer Rabbit escapes—and so do you, wet and exhilarated—to the tune of "Zip-a-Dee-Doo-Dah," the bouncy, best-known melody from the film. If you want to get really wet—and you will get splashed from almost every seat—ask the attendant to seat you in the front row.

BIG THUNDER MOUNTAIN RAILROAD

7 **Duration:** 4 min.

Fodor'sChoice **Crowds:** Large.

★ **Strategy:** Use Fastpass unless the wait is less than 15 min. The ride is most exciting at night, when you can't anticipate the curves and the track's rattling sounds as if something's about to give.

Audience: All except young children; the minimum height is 40". No pregnant women or guests wearing back, neck, or leg braces.

Rating: ★★★

Set in gold-rush days, the theme of this thrilling roller coaster is a runaway train. It's a bumpy ride with several good drops and moments when you feel like you're going to fly right off the tracks, but there are no inversions and at least you can see where you're going (unlike in Space Mountain). Overall it's more fun than scary, and you'll see kids as young as 7 lining up to ride. The design is fabulous, too. The train rushes and rattles past 20 Audio-Animatronics figures—including donkeys, chickens, a goat, and a grizzled old miner surprised in his bathtub—as well as $300,000 worth of genuine antique mining equipment, tumbleweeds, a derelict mining town, hot springs, and a flash flood.

The ride was 15 years in the planning and took two years and close to $17 million to build. This 1979 price tag, give or take a few million, equaled the entire cost of erecting California's Disneyland in 1955. The 197-foot mountain landscape is based on the wind-swept scenery of Arizona's Monument Valley, and thanks to 650 tons of steel, 4,675 tons of concrete, and 16,000 gallons of paint, it replicates the area's gorges, tunnels, caverns, and dry river beds.

TOM SAWYER ISLAND
8 Duration: Up to you.
Crowds: Seldom overwhelming, and, here, the more the merrier.
Strategy: Try it as a refreshing afternoon getaway.
Audience: Most appealing to kids ages 5 to 13.
Rating: ★★

An artfully ungrammatical sign tells you what to expect: "IF'N YOU LIKE DARK CAVES, MYSTERY MINES, BOTTOMLESS PITS, SHAKY BRIDGES 'N' BIG ROCKS, YOU HAVE CAME TO THE BEST PLACE I KNOW." Aunt Polly would have walloped Tom for his orthography, but she couldn't have argued with the sentiment. Actually two islets connected by a swing bridge, Tom Sawyer Island is a playground of hills, trees, rocks, and shrubs.

The main island, where your raft docks, is where most of the attractions are found. The Mystery Mine is like a secret passageway to exploration. Children love Injun Joe's Cave, where there are lots of columns and crevices from which to jump out and startle siblings and where the wind wails for a spooky effect. In a clearing atop the hill, there's a rustic playground. As you explore the shoreline on the dirt paths, watch out for the barrel bridge—the whole contraption bounces at every step.

On the other island is Fort Langhorn, a log fortress from which you can fire air guns with great booms and cracks at the passing *Liberty Belle* riverboat. It's guarded by a snoring Audio-Animatronics sentry, working off his last bender. Both islands are sprinkled with lookouts for great views to Thunder Mountain and Frontierland, as well as Liberty Square's Haunted Mansion

COUNTRY BEAR JAMBOREE
9 Duration: 17 min.
Crowds: Large, considering the relatively small theater.
Strategy: Visit before 11 AM, during the afternoon parade, or after most small children have left for the day. Stand to the far left in the anteroom, where you wait to end up in the front rows; to the far right if you want to sit in the last row, where small children can perch on top of the seats to see better.
Audience: All ages; even timid youngsters love the bears.
Rating: ★★★

Wisecracking, cornpone, lovelorn Audio-Animatronics bears joke, sing, and play country music and 1950s rock-and-roll in this stage show. The emcee, the massive but debonair Henry, leads the stellar cast of

Grizzly Hall, which includes the robust Trixie, who laments love lost while perching on a swing suspended from the ceiling; Bubbles, Bunny, and Beulah, harmonizing on "All the Guys That Turn Me On Turn Me Down"; and Big Al, the off-key cult figure who has inspired postcards, stuffed animals, and his own shop next door. Don't miss the bears' seasonal show in late November and December, when they deck the halls for a special concert.

GROOVY SOUVENIRS Cowboy hats and Davy Crockett coonskin caps at **Big Al's**, across from the County Bear Jamboree, are fun to try on even if you don't take one home. And families with a passion for pin trading can choose from among a selection of 400 Disney pins, including limited-edition pieces, at the **Frontier Trading Post. The Prairie Outpost & Supply** carries gourmet goodies.

LIBERTY SQUARE

The rough-and-tumble Western frontier gently folds into colonial America as Liberty Square picks up where Frontierland leaves off. The weathered siding gives way to solid brick and neat clapboard. The mesquite and cactus are replaced by stately oaks and masses of azalea. The theme is colonial history, which Northerners will be happy to learn is portrayed here as solid Yankee. The buildings, topped with weather vanes and exuding prosperity, are pure New England.

A replica of the Liberty Bell, crack and all, seems an appropriate prop to separate Liberty Square from Frontierland. There's even a Liberty Tree, a more than 150-year-old live oak found elsewhere on Walt Disney World property and moved to the Magic Kingdom. Just as the Sons of Liberty hung lanterns on trees as a signal of solidarity after the Boston Tea Party, the Liberty Tree's branches are decorated with 13 lanterns representing the 13 original colonies. Around the square are tree-shaded tables for an alfresco lunch and plenty of carts and fast-food eateries to supply the goods.

NEED A BREAK? **Sleepy Hollow** offers quick pick-me-ups in the form of funnel cakes, soft-serve ice cream, espresso drinks, root beer floats, and caramel corn.

HALL OF PRESIDENTS: A CELEBRATION OF LIBERTY'S LEADERS

⑩ Duration: 25 min.
Crowds: Expected to be heavy with addition of Barack Obama and an enhanced show.
Strategy: Go first thing in the morningor during the parade.
Audience: Older children and adults.
Rating: The updated show had not yet opened for review at press time.

This multimedia tribute to America and its presidents caused quite a sensation when it opened in 1971; it was here that the first refinements of the Audio-Animatronics system of computerized robots could be seen. Today it's still worth a visit, especially after a major rehab of

CLOSE UP

Behind the Scenes

As you stroll down Main Street, U.S.A., Disney cast members are dashing through tunnels in a bustling underground city, the nerve center of the Magic Kingdom. The 9-acre corridor system beneath the park leads to behind-the-scenes areas where employees create their Disney magic. It also ensures that you'll never see a frontiersman ambling through Tomorrowland. There's the Costuming Department with miles of racks, and Cosmetology, where Cinderella can touch up her hair and makeup. At the heart of this domain is Engineering Central, from which many of the Magic Kingdom attractions are still run.

The only way to see what goes on in Disney's tunnels is by taking one of two backstage tours: the **Keys to the Kingdom** lasts more than four hours

and costs $65, including lunch but not park admission; and **Backstage Magic** lasts seven hours and costs $219, including peeks at Epcot and Disney's Hollywood Studios, as well as lunch (park admission not included or required). These tours are restricted to people age 16 and older. Security measures prevent access to most of the concrete tunnels, so it's unlikely you'll bump into Mickey without his head on. (And don't expect to take photos. Disney guards its underground treasures carefully!) If you visit in December, you can take the three-and-half hour daily **Yuletide Fantasy** tour ($69)—an insider's look at how Disney's elves transform its parks and resorts. Reserve a spot several months in advance. For details, call ☎407/939–8687.

2

the show and the addition of a latest-generation Audio-Animatronics version of President Barack Obama.

Instead of its previous focus on the U.S. Constitution and civil rights, the new show (as described by a Disney Imagineer) "tells the moving story of the bond between the presidents and 'We, the People.'" Producers reshot the accompanying film in high-definition video and added more than 130 new images culled from the National Archives, Library of Congress, and other collections to tell the story. A digital soundtrack, LED lighting, new musical score, and new narration by Morgan Freeman further enhance the experience. The film covers 220 years of U.S. history and emphasizes presidents who've reached out to people in times of strife. Both George Washington and Abraham Lincoln get more of the spotlight during the new film, the latter by delivering his famous Gettysburg Address.

For most visitors, the best part of the show is a roll call of all 43 U.S. presidents. (Fun fact: Obama is officially the 44th president because Grover Cleveland is counted twice due to his having served nonconsecutive terms.) Each chief executive responds with a nod, and those who are seated rise (except for wheelchair-bound Franklin Delano Roosevelt, of course). The detail is lifelike, right down to the brace on Roosevelt's leg. The robots can't resist nodding, fidgeting, and even whispering to each other while waiting for their names to come up. The audience might fidget too as they wait for Obama's turn, which includes his presidential Oath of Office (recorded in the White House by Imagineers) and a speech about The American Dream. Anyone interested in presidential artifacts will enjoy their wait in the redecorated lobby area, where First Ladies' dresses, presidential portraits, and even George Washington's dental instruments are on display.

LIBERTY SQUARE RIVERBOAT

⑪ Duration: 15 min.

Crowds: Moderate, but capacity is high, so waits are seldom trying.

Strategy: Check Times Guide—the riverboat is open seasonally. Go when you need a break from the crowds.

Audience: All ages.

Rating: ★

An old-fashioned steamboat, the *Liberty Belle* is authentic, from its calliope whistle and the gingerbread trim on its three decks to the boilers that produce the steam that drives the big rear paddle wheel. In fact, the boat misses authenticity on only one count: there's no mustachioed captain to guide it during the ride around the Rivers of America. That task is performed by an underwater rail. The 1½-mi cruise is slow and not exactly thrilling, except, perhaps, to the kids getting "shot at" by their counterparts at Fort Langhorn on Tom Sawyer Island. But it's a relaxing break for all concerned, and children like exploring the boat.

HAUNTED MANSION

⑫ Duration: 8 min.

Crowds: Substantial, but high capacity and fast loading usually keep lines moving.

Strategy: Go early in the day or when crowds have gathered to wait for a parade. Nighttime adds an extra fright factor, and you may be able to line right up during the evening parade in peak season.

Audience: All but very young children who are easily frightened.

Rating: ★★★

The special effects here are a howl crossed with a scream. Disney Imagineers recently kicked the effects up a few notches, so you're in store for extra thrills and chills. You're greeted at the creaking iron gates of this Hudson River Valley Gothic mansion by a lugubrious attendant, who has one of the few jobs at Disney for which smiling is frowned upon, and ushered into a spooky picture gallery. A disembodied voice echoes from the walls: "Welcome, foolish mortals, to the Haunted Mansion. I am your ghost host." A new audio system with 30-plus surround-sound speakers ups the ghost-host fright factor. A scream shivers down, the room begins to "stretch," and you're off into one of Disney's classic attractions. ■ TIP➔**Don't rush out of this room when other visitors depart; linger for some ghoulish bonus whispers.**

Consisting mainly of a slow-moving ride in a black, cocoonlike "doom buggy," the Haunted Mansion is only really scary for younger children, and that's mostly because of the darkness. Everyone else will just laugh (or ooh and ah) at the special effects. Watch the artfully strung liquid cobwebs pass you by; the suit of armor that comes alive; the shifting walls in the portrait gallery that make you wonder if they are moving up or if you are moving down; the ghostly ballroom dancers; and, of course, Madame Leota's talking disembodied head in the crystal ball, which floats realistically in the wake of technical enhancements. Other additions: ghostly footprints moving along a staircase and a new "bride in the attic" scene, where you should keep an eye on the portraits as your doom buggy eases past. Just when you think the Imagineers have exhausted their bag of ectoplasmic tricks, along comes another one; you suddenly discover that your doom buggy has gained an extra passenger. As you approach the exit, your ghoulish guide intones, "Now I will raise the safety bar, and the ghost will follow you home." Thanks for the souvenir, pal. And speaking of souvenirs, if you can't resist bringing home more than a friendly ghost, you can get Disney's Clue Haunted Mansion board game at the park's Emporium gift shop or at Once Upon a Toy in Downtown Disney.

FANTASYLAND

Walt Disney called this "a timeless land of enchantment." Fantasyland does conjure up pixie dust. Perhaps that's because the fanciful gingerbread houses, gleaming gold turrets, and, of course, rides based on Disney-animated movies are what the Magic Kingdom is all about.

With the exception of the slightly spooky Snow White's Scary Adventures, the attractions here are whimsical rather than heart-stopping. Like the animated classics on which they're based, these rides, which could ostensibly be classified as rides for children, are packed with enough delightful detail to engage the adults who accompany them. Unfortunately, Fantasyland is always the most heavily trafficked area in the park, and its rides are almost always crowded.

You can enter Fantasyland on foot from Liberty Square, Tomorrowland, or Mickey's Toontown Fair, but the classic introduction is through Cinderella Castle. To get in an appropriately magical mood—and to provide yourself with a cooling break—turn left immediately after you exit the castle's archway. Here you'll find a charming and often overlooked touch: Cinderella Fountain, a lovely brass casting of the castle's namesake, who's dressed in her peasant togs and surrounded by her beloved mice and bird friends.

Photographers will want to take advantage of one of the least-traveled byways in the Magic Kingdom. From the southern end of Liberty Square, turn left at the Sleepy Hollow snack shop. Just past the outdoor tables is a shortcut to Fantasyland that provides one of the best, unobstructed ground-level views of Cinderella Castle in the park. It's a great spot for a family photo.

CINDERELLA CASTLE

 This quintessential Disney icon, with its royal blue turrets, gold spires, and glistening white towers, was inspired by the castle built by the mad Bavarian king Ludwig II at Neuschwanstein, as well as by drawings prepared for Disney's animated film of the French fairy tale. Although often confused with Disneyland's Sleeping Beauty Castle, at 180-plus feet this castle is more than 100 feet taller; and with its elongated towers and lacy fretwork, it's immeasurably more graceful. Don't miss the elaborate mosaic murals on the walls of the archway as you rush toward Fantasyland from the Hub. The five panels, measuring some 15 feet high and 10 feet wide, were designed by Disney artist Dorothea Redmond and created from a million bits of multicolor Italian glass, silver, and 14-karat gold by mosaicist Hanns-Joachim Scharff. The mosaics tell the story of the little cinder girl as she goes from pumpkin to prince to happily ever after.

The fantasy castle has feet, if not of clay, then of solid steel beams, fiberglass, and 500 gallons of paint. Instead of dungeons, there are service tunnels for the Magic Kingdom's less-than-magical quotidian operations, such as Makeup and Costuming. These are the same tunnels that honeycomb the ground under much of the park. And upstairs doesn't hold, as rumor has it, a casket containing the cryogenically preserved body of Walt Disney. Instead, there's a suite where some lucky families enjoyed a "dream come true" overnight stay when Disney held its "Year of a Million Dreams" celebration. Within the castle's archway is the recently opened **Bibbidi Bobbidi Boutique,** a kiddie salon where the "royal treatment" transforms little girls age 3 and older into "Disney Divas," "Pop Princesses," or "Fairy-Tale Princesses." Hair and makeup are by a "Fairy Godmother-in-training." Boys aren't left out of the picture; they can grab a chair for their own "Cool Dude" transformation involving colorful hair gels and other accoutrements. The boutique replaces the former **King's Gallery,** where Disney once sold delicate crystal symbols of fairy-tale magic, including Cinderella's glass slipper in many colors and sizes. No worries; you can still find these treasures at **Uptown Jewelers** on Main Street.

If you have reservations to dine at **Cinderella's Royal Table,** you enter the castle by way of an ascending spiral staircase where costumed waiters attend to your meal. Cinderella, her Fairy Godmother, and other princesses join you at what is one of the most popular character-greeting experiences offered at Walt Disney World. ■TIP➔**Call 90 days ahead, or as soon as you can, to reserve the character breakfast or lunch.**

IT'S A SMALL WORLD

⑭ Duration: 11 min.
Crowds: Steady, but lines move fast.
Strategy: Go back later if there's a long wait, since crowds ebb and flow here. Tots may beg for a repeat ride; it's worth another go-round to see all that you missed on the first trip through.
Audience: All ages.

Rating: ★★

Visiting Walt Disney World and not stopping for this tribute to terminal cuteness—why, the idea is practically un-American. The attraction is essentially a boat ride through several candy-color lands, each representing a continent and each crammed with musical moppets, all madly singing. Disney raided the remains of the 1964–65 New York World's Fair for sets, and then appropriated the theme song of international brotherhood and friendship for its own. Some claim that it's the revenge of the "audio-animatrons," as 450 simplistic dolls differentiated mostly by their national dress—Dutch babies in clogs, Spanish flamenco dancers, German oompah bands, Russians playing balalaikas, sari-wrapped Indians waving temple bells, Tower of London guards in scarlet beefeater uniforms, Swiss yodelers and goatherds, Japanese kite fliers, Middle East snake charmers, and young French cancan dancers, to name just a few—parade past, smiling away and wagging their heads in time to the song. But somehow, by the time you reach the end of the ride, you're grinning and wagging, too, with the one-verse theme song indelibly impressed in your brain. Now all together: "It's a world of laughter, a world of tears. It's a world of hope and a world of fears. . . ."

PETER PAN'S FLIGHT

15 **Duration:** 2½ min.
Crowds: Always heavy, except in the evening and early morning.
Strategy: Get a Fastpass, and enjoy other attractions while you wait.
Audience: All ages, but best for the preschool set.
Rating: ★★

This wonderful indoor ride was inspired by Sir James M. Barrie's 1904 novel about the boy who wouldn't grow up, which Disney animated in 1953. Aboard two-person magic sailing ships with brightly striped sails, you soar into the skies above London en route to Neverland. Along the way you can see Wendy, Michael, and John get sprinkled with pixie dust while Nana barks below, wave to Princess Tiger Lily, meet the evil Captain Hook, and cheer for the tick-tocking, clock-swallowing crocodile who breakfasted on Hook's hand and is more than ready for lunch. Despite the absence of high-tech special effects, children love this ride. Adults enjoy the dreamy views of London by moonlight, a galaxy of twinkling yellow lights punctuated by Big Ben, London Bridge, and the Thames River. The only negative is the ride's brevity. Avoid the regular line or upon exiting you may find yourself annoyed at having waited for an hour for a 2½-minute ride.

MICKEY'S PHILHARMAGIC

16 **Duration:** 12 min.
Fodor'sChoice   **Crowds:** Heavy.
★   **Strategy:** You could grab a Fastpass, but they're probably better spent on Pooh and Peter Pan. It's a big theater, so you shouldn't have to wait long. Go during the parade for the shortest lines.
Audience: All ages; some effects may startle small children.
Rating: ★★★

Mickey Mouse may be the headliner here, but it's Donald Duck's misadventures—reminiscent of Mickey's as the sorcerer's apprentice in *Fantasia*—that set the comic pace in this gorgeous, 3-D animated film. As you settle into your theater seat, the on-screen action takes you behind the curtains at a grand concert hall where Donald and Mickey are preparing for a musical performance. But when Donald misuses Mickey's magical sorcerer's hat, he suddenly finds himself on a whirlwind journey that includes a magic carpet ride and an electrifying dip under the sea. And you go along for the ride. On the way you meet favorite Disney characters including Ariel, Simba, Aladdin, and Jasmine, and Peter Pan and Tinker Bell. The film startles with its special-effects technology—you'll smell a fresh-baked apple pie, feel the rush of air as champagne corks pop, and get lost in the action on one of the largest screens ever created for a 3-D film: a 150-foot-wide canvas. The film is beautifully scored and marks the first time that classic Disney characters appear in a computer-generated animation attraction.

SNOW WHITE'S SCARY ADVENTURES

(17) Duration: 3 min.
Crowds: Steady from late morning until evening.
Strategy: Go very early, during the afternoon parade, or after dark. Skip if the wait is more than 15 min.
Audience: All ages; may be frightening for young children.
Rating: ★

What was previously an unremittingly scary indoor spook-house ride where the dwarves might as well have been named Anxious and Fearful is now a kinder, gentler experience with six-passenger cars and a mini-version of the movie. There's still the evil queen, the wart on her nose, and her cackle, but joining the cast are the Prince and Snow White herself. Although the trip is packed with plenty of scary moments, an honest-to-goodness kiss followed by a happily-ever-after ending might even get you "heigh-ho"-ing on your way out.

CINDERELLA'S GOLDEN CARROUSEL

(18) Duration: 2 min.
Crowds: Lines during busy periods but they move fairly quickly.
Strategy: Go while waiting for your Peter Pan's Flight Fastpass reservation, during the afternoon parade, or after dark.
Audience: A great ride for families and for romantics, young and old.
Rating: ★★

It's the whirling, musical heart of Fantasyland. This ride encapsulates the Disney experience in 90 prancing horses and then hands it to you on a 60-foot moving platter. Seventy-two of the dashing wooden steeds date from the original carousel built in 1917 by the Philadelphia Toboggan Company; additional mounts were made of fiberglass. All are meticulously painted—it takes about 48 hours per horse—and each one is completely different. One wears a collar of bright yellow roses; another, a quiver of Native American arrows. The horses gallop ceaselessly beneath a wooden canopy, gaily striped on the outside and decorated on the inside with 18 panels depicting scenes from Disney's 1950 film *Cinderella*. As the platter starts to spin, the mirrors sparkle, the fairy lights glitter, and the band organ plays favorite tunes from Disney movies. If you wished upon a star, it couldn't get more magical.

DUMBO THE FLYING ELEPHANT

 Duration: 2 min.

Crowds: Perpetual, except in very early morning, and there's little shade—in summer, the wait is truly brutal.

Strategy: Come as soon as the park opens or head for the similar Magic Carpets of Aladdin instead.

Audience: Toddlers and young children.

Rating: ★★

Hands down, this is one of Fantasyland's most popular rides. Although the movie has one baby elephant with gigantic ears who accidentally downs a bucket of water spiked with champagne and learns he can fly, the ride has 16 jolly Dumbos flying around a central column, each pachyderm packing a couple of kids and a parent. A joystick controls each of Dumbo's vertical motions, so you can make him ascend or descend at will. Alas, the ears do not flap. Keep an eye out for Timothy Mouse atop the ride's colorful balloon.

ARIEL'S GROTTO

Duration: Up to you.

Strategy: Check your Times Guide for appearance times, and arrive at least 20 min ahead.

Audience: Young children, especially little girls.

Rating: ★★

A "beneath the sea" motif distinguishes this starfish-scattered meet-and-greet locale. Ariel the Little Mermaid appears here in person, her carrot-red tresses cascading onto her glittery green tail. Just across the ropes from the queue area are a group of wonderfully interactive fountains that are perfect for little kids who love to splash.

THE MANY ADVENTURES OF WINNIE THE POOH

Duration: About 3 min.

Crowds: Large.

Strategy: Use the Fastpass setup; if the youngsters favor immediate gratification, go early in the day, late in the afternoon, or after dark.

Audience: All ages.

Rating: ★★★

The famous honey lover and his exploits in the Hundred Acre Wood are the theme for this ride. You can read posted passages from A.A. Milne's stories as you wait in line. Once you board your honey pot, Pooh and his friends wish you a "happy windsday." Pooh flies through the air, held aloft by his balloon, in his perennial search for "hunny," and you bounce along with Tigger, ride with the Heffalumps and Woozles, and experience a cloudburst. When the rain ends at last, everyone gathers again to say "Hurray!" This ride replaced Mr. Toad's Wild Ride; look for the painting of Mr. Toad handing the deed to Owl.

POOH'S PLAYFUL SPOT

Duration: Up to you.

Crowds: Heaviest in midday.

Strategy: When the kiddies get tired of the stroller or standing in lines, this is the place to let them burn off some energy.

Audience: Children ages 2 to 5 and parents.
Rating: ★★★

Let your toddler have some free time at this playground based on tales from the Hundred Acre Wood. Tots and preschoolers crawl through faux hollow logs and honey pots, clamber around in Pooh's tree house complete with gnarled roots, zoom down a slide, and splash in fountains. Tired parents relax on log-style benches and keep an eye on the wee ones without fear of losing them. Pooh and friends meet and greet fans in an area right next to the park, so children can decide if they're ready for a close encounter. Though shade is limited, Pooh's spot is nevertheless an enchanted place.

FAIRYTALE GARDEN: STORY TIME WITH BELLE

(23) Duration: 25 min, several times daily (check your Times Guide).
Crowds: Heaviest in midday.
Strategy: Arrive early for a good seat on one of the benches.
Audience: All ages.
Rating: ★

Disney's beloved bookworm makes an appearance at the Fairytale Garden several times daily and brings *Beauty and the Beast* to life, using her audience as cast members. Storytelling was never so much fun.

MAD TEA PARTY

(24) Duration: 2 min.
Crowds: Steady from late morning on, with slow-moving lines.
Strategy: Skip this ride if the wait is longer than 30 min and if spinning could ruin your day.
Audience: Preschool and grade-school kids.
Rating: ★

This carnival staple is for the vertigo addict looking for a fix. The Disney version is based on its own 1951 film *Alice in Wonderland*, in which the Mad Hatter hosts a tea party for his un-birthday. You hop into oversize, pastel-color teacups and whirl around a giant platter. Add your own spin to the teacup's orbit with the help of the steering wheel in the center. If the centrifugal force hasn't shaken you up too much, check out the soused mouse that pops out of the teapot centerpiece and compare his condition with your own.

MICKEY'S TOONTOWN FAIR

This concentrated tribute to the big-eared mighty one was built in 1988 to celebrate the Mouse's Big Six-O. Owing to its continual popularity with the small-fry set, it's now an official Magic Kingdom land, a 3-acre niche set off to the side of Fantasyland. As in a scene from a cartoon, everything is child size. The pastel houses are positively Lilliputian, with miniature driveways, toy-size picket fences, and signs scribbled with finger paint. Toontown Fair provides great one-stop shopping (better known as meet-and-greets) for your favorite Disney characters—hug them, get autographs, and take photos. The best way to arrive is on the Walt Disney World Railroad, the old-fashioned choo-choo that also stops at Main Street and Frontierland. Note that Mickey's Toontown Fair is completely accessible.

THE BARNSTORMER AT GOOFY'S WISEACRE FARM

25 Duration: 1 min.
Crowds: Heaviest in mid-morning.
Strategy: Visit in the evening, when many tykes have gone home.
Audience: Younger kids, especially preschoolers and grade-schoolers, but no one under 35 inches.
Rating: ★★★

Traditional red barns and farm buildings form the backdrop at Goofy's Wiseacre Farm. But the real attraction is the Barnstormer, a roller coaster whose ride vehicles are 1920s crop-dusting biplanes—designed for children but large enough for adults as well. Hold on to your Mouse ears. This attraction promises tummy-tickling thrills to young first-time coaster riders. If you're uncertain whether your children are up to Big Thunder Mountain Railroad, this is the test to take.

TOON PARK

26 Duration: Up to you.
Crowds: Moderate and seldom a problem.
Strategy: Go anytime.
Audience: Young children mainly, but everyone enjoys watching them.
Rating: ★★

This spongy green, maize, and autumn-orange play area formerly featured foam farm critters suitable for kiddie climbing. Now the fenced-in area is shaded by an awning and includes a giant tree trunk for scrambling in, around, and under; a tiny yellow and blue playhouse; and a gazebo-style structure leading to a tunnel and slide. Festive multicolor lights add a carnival mood by night.

DONALD'S BOAT

27 Duration: Up to you.
Crowds: Can get heavy in late morning and early afternoon.
Strategy: Go whenever the kids need some play time.
Audience: Young children and their families.
Rating: ★★

A cross between a tugboat and a leaky ocean liner, the *Miss Daisy* is actually a water-play area, with lily pads that spray without warning. Although it's intended for kids, grown-ups also take the opportunity to cool off on a humid Central Florida afternoon.

NEED A BREAK?

The **Toontown Farmer's Market** sells simple, healthful snacks and fresh fruit, plus juices, lemonade slush drinks and soda. If you're lucky, you can find a place on the park bench next to the cart and give your feet a rest.

MICKEY'S COUNTRY HOUSE

28 Duration: Up to you.
Crowds: Moderate.
Strategy: Go first thing in the morning or during the afternoon parade.

MAGIC KINGDOM

NAME	Min. Height	Type of Entertainment	Duration	Suits	Crowds	Strategy
Main Street U.S.A.						
Walt Disney World Railroad	n/a	train	21 min.	All	Heavy	Board with small children for an early start in Railroad Toontown or hop on midafternoon.
Adventureland						
Enchanted Tiki Room	n/a	show	12 min.	All	30 min.	Go when you need a refresher in an air-conditioned room.
Jungle Cruise	n/a	boat	10 min.	All	Yes!	Go during the afternoon parade, but not after dark—you miss too much.
The Magic Carpets of Aladdin	n/a	kid thrill ride	3 min.	All	Fast lines	Visit while waiting for Frontierland Fastpass.
Pirates of the Caribbean	n/a	boat	10 min.	All	30 min.	A good destination, especially in the heat of the afternoon.
Swiss Family Treehouse	n/a	walk-through	Up to you.	All	Slow lines	Visit while waiting for Jungle Cruise Fastpass.
Frontierland						
★ Big Thunder Mountain Railroad	40"	thrill ride	4 min.	5 and up	Heavy	Fastpass. Most exciting at night when you can't anticipate the curves.
Country Bear Jamboree	n/a	show	17 min.	All	Heavy	Visit before 11 am. Stand to the far left lining up for the front rows.
★ Splash Mountain	40"	thrill ride	11 min.	5 and up	Yes!	Fastpass. Get in line by 9:45 am or ride during meal or parade time. Bring a change of clothes.
Tom Sawyer Island	n/a	play area	Up to you.	5 to 13	ok	Afternoon refresher. It's hard to keep track of toddlers here.
Liberty Square						
Hall of Presidents	n/a	show	30 min.	9 and up	Light	Go in the afternoon for an air-conditioned break.
Haunted Mansion	n/a	ride	8 min.	All	Fast lines	Nighttime adds extra fear factor.
Liberty Square Riverboat	n/a	boat	17 min.	All	ok	Good for a break from the crowds.
Fantasyland						
Ariel's Grotto	n/a	meet & greet, play area	Up to you.	Little kids	Yes!	Arrive 20 min. or more before autograph time.
Cinderella's Golden Carrousel	n/a	carousel	2 min.	All	Fast lines	Go while waiting for Peter Pan's Flight Fastpass, during afternoon parade, or after dark.
Dumbo the Flying Elephant	n/a	kid thrill ride	2 min.	Little kids	Slow lines	Go at Rope Drop. No shade in afternoon.

2

					Midday	
Fairytale Garden	n/a	show	25 min.	All		Arrive early for a bench.
it's a small world	n/a	boat ride	11 min.	All	Fast lines	Tots may beg for a repeat ride; it's worth it.
Mad Tea Party	n/a	thrill ride	2 min.	3 to adult	Slow lines	Go in the early morning. Skip if wait is 30 min.
The Many Adventures of Winnie the Pooh	n/a	thrill ride	3½ min.	All	Heavy	Use Fastpass. Go early, late in the afternoon, or after dark.
★ Mickey's PhilharMagic	n/a	3-D film	12 min.	All	Heavy	Use Fastpass or arrive early or during a parade.
Peter Pan's Flight	n/a	ride	2½ min.	All	Slow lines	Try evening or early morning. Use Fastpass first.
Snow White's Scary Adventures	n/a	kid thrill ride	3 min.	All	Steady	Go very early, during the afternoon parade, or after dark. May scare toddlers and pre-schoolers.
Mickey's Toontown Fair						
The Barnstormer at Goofy's Wise-acre Farm	35"	kid thrill ride	1 min.	3 and up	Steady	Go during evening if your child can wait.
Tomorrowland						
Astro-Orbiter	n/a	thrill ride	2 min.	All	Slow lines	Skip unless there's a short line.
Buzz Lightyear's Space Ranger Spin	n/a	interactive thrill ride	5 min.	3 and up	Fast lines	Go in the early morning and use Fastpass. Kids will want more than one ride.
Monster's Inc. Laugh Floor	n/a	interactive film	15 min.	All	Heavy	Go when you're waiting for your Buzz Lightyear or Space Mountain Fastpass.
★ Space Mountain	44"	thrill ride	2½ min.	7 and up	Yes!	Use Fastpass, or go at the beginning or the end of day or during a parade.
Stitch's Great Escape	40"	sim. exp.	20 min.	4 and up	Heavy	Use Fastpass. Visit early after Space Mountain, Splash Mountain, Big ThunderMountain, or during a parade.
Tomorrowland Indy Speedway	54" to drive	racetrack	5 min.	Big kids	Steady	Go in the evening or during a parade; skip on a first-time visit. No height requirement to ride shotgun.
Tomorrowland Transit Authority	n/a	tram on track	10 min.	All	ok	Go with young kids if you need a break.
Walt Disney's Carousel of Progress	n/a	show	20 min.	All	ok	Skip on a first-time visit unless you're heavily into nostalgia.

★ = Fodor's Choice

Audience: All ages, although teens may be put off by the terminal cuteness of it all.

Rating: ★★

Begin here to find your way to the mouse. As you walk through this slightly goofy piece of architecture right in the heart of Toontown Fairgrounds, notice the radio in the living room, "tooned" to scores from Mickey's favorite football team, Duckburg University. Down the hall, Mickey's kitchen shows the ill effects of Donald and Goofy's attempt to win the Toontown Home Remodeling Contest—with buckets of paint spilled and stacked in the sink and paint splattered on the floor and walls. The Judge's Tent just behind Mickey's house is where the mouse king holds court as he doles out hugs and autographs and mugs for photos with adoring fans.

JUDGE'S TENT

㉙ Duration: Plan to wait it out if an audience with Mickey is a priority.

Strategy: If you can't get there early, try a lunchtime visit.

Audience: Young children and families.

Rating: ★★★

If you want to spend a few moments with the big cheese himself, load your camera, dig out a pen, and get in line here. You can catch Mickey in his personal dressing room for the ideal photo opportunity and autograph session.

TOONTOWN HALL OF FAME

㉚ Duration: Up to you.

Crowds: Can get heavy in late morning and early afternoon.

Strategy: Go first thing in the morning or after the toddlers have gone home.

Audience: Young children.

Rating: ★★★

Stop here to collect an autograph and a hug from Disney princesses like Cinderella and Snow White. Pluto and Goofy have moved on to other meet-and-greet areas in the park to make room for the popular

> ### WORD OF MOUTH
>
> "If it is imperative that your little princesses get the autographs of the big princesses, go straight to their line at the Toontown Hall of Fame the minute Toontown opens (usually 45 minutes after the park opens). We went one day 25 minutes after Toontown opened and there was a 2-hour wait."
>
> –missypie

new Fairies from Pixie Hollow. Check out the blue ribbon–winning entries from the Toontown Fair. **County Bounty** sells stuffed animals and all kinds of Toontown souvenirs, including autograph books.

MINNIE'S COUNTRY HOUSE

㉛ Duration: Up to you.

Crowds: Moderate.

Strategy: Go first thing in the morning or during the afternoon parade.

Audience: All ages, although teens may find it too much to take.

Rating: ★★

Unlike Mickey's house, where ropes keep you from going into the rooms, this baby-blue-and-pink house is a please-touch kind of place.

In this scenario, Minnie is editor of *Minnie's Cartoon Country Living* magazine, the Martha Stewart of the mouse set. While touring her office, crafts room, and kitchen, you can check the latest messages on her answering machine, bake a "quick-rising" cake at the touch of a button, and, opening the refrigerator door, get a wonderful blast of arctic air while checking out her favorite ice cream flavor: cheese-chip.

TOMORROWLAND

The "future that never was" spins boldly into view as you enter Tomorrowland, where Disney Imagineers paint the landscape with whirling spaceships, flashy neon lights, and gleaming robots. This is the future as envisioned by sci-fi writers and moviemakers in the 1920s and '30s, when space flight, laser beams, and home computers were fiction, not fact. Retro Jetsonesque styling lends the area lasting chic.

TOMORROWLAND INDY SPEEDWAY

③② **Duration:** 5 min.

Crowds: Steady and heavy from late morning to evening.

Strategy: Go in the evening or during a parade; skip on a first-time visit unless you've been through all the major attractions.

Audience: Older children. Children riding with an adult must be at least 32" tall; those who wish to ride alone must reach 54".

Rating: ★

This is one of those rides that incite instant addiction in children and immediate hatred in their parents. The reasons for the former are easy to figure out: the brightly colored Mark VII model cars that swerve around the four 2,260-foot tracks with much vroom-vroom-vrooming. Kids will feel like they're Mario Andretti as they race around. Like real sports cars, the gasoline-powered vehicles are equipped with rack-and-pinion steering and disc brakes; unlike the real thing, these run on a track. However, the track is so twisty that it's hard to keep the car on a straight course—something the race-car fanatics warming the bleachers love to watch. You may spend a lot of time waiting, first to get your turn on the track, then to return your vehicle after your lap. All this for a ride in which the main thrill is achieving a top speed of 7 MPH.

SPACE MOUNTAIN

③③ **Duration:** 2½ min.

Fodor's Choice **Crowds:** Large and steady, with long lines from morning to night despite ★ high capacity.

Strategy: Get a Fastpass ticket, or go at the beginning of the day, the end, or during a parade.

Audience: All except young children. No pregnant women or guests wearing back, neck, or leg braces. The minimum height is 44".

Rating: ★★★

The needlelike spires and gleaming white concrete cone of this 180-foot-high attraction are almost as much of a Magic Kingdom landmark as Cinderella Castle. Inside is what is arguably the world's most imaginative roller coaster. Although there are no loop-the-loops, gravitational whizbangs, or high-speed curves, the thrills are amply provided by

Disney's masterful brainwashing as you take a trip into the depths of outer space—in the dark.

■ TIP→The wait to ride Space Mountain can be an hour or more if you don't have a Fastpass, so do your best to get one in the morning. As you walk to the loading area, you'll pass whirling planets and hear the screams and shrieks of the riders and the rattling of the cars, pumping you up for your own ride. Once you wedge yourself into the seat and blast off, the ride lasts only 2 minutes and 38 seconds, with a top speed of 28 MPH, but the devious twists and invisible drops in the dark make it seem twice as long. Stow personal belongings securely or have a non-rider hold onto them.

WALT DISNEY'S CAROUSEL OF PROGRESS

③④ **Duration:** 20 min.
Crowds: Moderate.
Strategy: Skip on a first-time visit unless you're heavily into nostalgia. May be closed in low season.
Audience: All ages.
Rating: ★

Originally seen at New York's 1964–65 World's Fair, this revolving theater traces the impact of technological progress on the daily lives of Americans from the turn of the 20th century into the near future. Representing each decade, an Audio-Animatronics family sings the praises of modern-day gadgets that technology has wrought. Fans of the holiday film *A Christmas Story* will recognize the voice of its narrator, Jean Shepard, who injects his folksy, all-American humor as father figure through the decades.

TOMORROWLAND TRANSIT AUTHORITY

③⑤ **Duration:** 10 min.
Crowds: Not one of the park's most popular attractions, so lines are seldom long, and they move quickly.
Strategy: Go if you want to preview Space Mountain, if you have very young children, or if you simply want a nice, relaxing ride that provides a great bird's-eye tour of Tomorrowland.
Audience: All ages.
Rating: ★

A reincarnation of what Disney old-timers may remember as the WED-way PeopleMover, the TTA takes a nice, leisurely ride around the perimeter of Tomorrowland, circling the Astro-Orbiter and eventually gliding through the middle of Space Mountain. Some fainthearted TTA passengers have no doubt chucked the notion of riding the roller coaster after being exposed firsthand to the screams emanating from within the mountain—although these make the ride sound worse than it really is. Disney's version of future mass transit is smooth and noiseless, thanks to an electromagnetic linear induction motor that has no moving parts, uses little power, and emits no pollutants.

ASTROORBITER

③⑥ **Duration:** 2 min.
Crowds: Often large, and the line moves slowly.

2

Strategy: Visit while waiting out your Space Mountain Fastpass appointment or skip on your first visit if time is limited, unless there's a short line.

Audience: All ages.

Rating: ★★

This gleaming superstructure of revolving planets has come to symbolize Tomorrowland as much as Dumbo represents Fantasyland. Passenger vehicles, on arms projecting from a central column, sail past whirling planets; you control your car's altitude but not the velocity. The line is directly across from the entrance to the TTA.

STITCH'S GREAT ESCAPE

37 **Duration:** 15 min.

Crowds: Large.

Strategy: Use Fastpass if you've already been on Splash Mountain, Space Mountain, and Big Thunder Mountain, or see it during a parade.

Audience: All but young children, who may be frightened by shoulder restraints, periods of darkness, and loud, startling noises. Minimum height is 40".

Rating: ★★

Once again, Disney seizes upon a hit film to create a crowd-pleasing attraction. This time the film is *Lilo & Stitch,* and the attraction is built around a back-story to the film, about the mischievous alien, Stitch, before he meets Lilo in Hawaii. You're invited, as a new security recruit for the Galactic Federation, to enter the high-security teleportation chamber, where the ill-mannered Stitch is being processed for prison. In the form of a 3½-foot-tall Audio-Animatronics figure, Stitch escapes his captors and wreaks havoc on the room during close encounters with the audience in near-darkness. Sensory effects and tactile surprises are part of the package. Beware the chili-dog "belch" and a spray that prompts more than a few gasps of surprise (Hint: Stitch is the first Audio-Animatronics figure to spit).

> ### WORD OF MOUTH
>
> "I have been on [Stitch's Great Escape] three times. It is one of the more disappointing attractions in WDW. There are several parts when it is very dark and lights are flashing and there are hard to identify noises (Stitch running around). All three times, there was more than one terrified toddler screaming. Also, the design of the seating makes it difficult to hold your child and comfort them if they panic."   –scarboroughmom

BUZZ LIGHTYEAR'S SPACE RANGER SPIN

38 **Duration:** 5 min.

Crowds: Substantial, but lines move fast.

Strategy. Go first thing in the morning, get your Fastpass appointment time, then return when scheduled. If you're with children, time the wait and ride twice if it's only 15 or 20 min. Youngsters like a practice run to learn how to hit the targets.

Audience: Kids 3 to 100.

Rating: ★★★

Based on the wildly popular *Toy Story,* this ride gives you a toy's perspective as it pits you and Buzz against the evil Emperor Zurg. You're seated in a fast-moving two-passenger Star Cruiser vehicle with an infrared laser gun in front of each rider and a centrally located lever for spinning your ship to get a good vantage point. You shoot at targets throughout the ride to help Disney's macho space toy, Buzz, defeat the emperor and save the universe—you have to hit the targets marked with a "Z" to score, and the rider with the most points wins. As Buzz

likes to say, "To infinity and beyond!" The larger-than-life-size toys in the waiting area are great distractions while you wait.

MONSTERS, INC. LAUGH FLOOR

(39) **Duration:** 15 min.
Crowds: Heavy.
Strategy: Go when you're waiting for your Buzz Lightyear or Space Mountain Fastpass appointment.
Audience: All ages.
Rating: ★★

The joke's on everyone at this interactive attraction starring Mike Wazowski, the one-eyed hero from Disney-Pixar's hit film *Monsters, Inc.* The old Timekeeper theater has been fitted with 400 seats so you can interact with an animated Mike and his sidekicks in the real-time, unscripted way that the character Crush from *Finding Nemo* performs at Epcot in Turtle Talk with Crush at "The Seas with Nemo & Friends." Here the premise is that Mike realizes laughter can be harnessed as a power source, and Mike's new comedy club is expected to generate power for the future. The more the audience yuks it up, jokes, and matches wits with Mike's comedian-wannabes, the greater the power produced. A new technological twist: you can text-message jokes from cell phones to the show's producer; they might even be used in the show.

ENTERTAINMENT, PARADES, AND FIREWORKS

The headliners are, of course, the Disney characters, especially if you're traveling with children. In what Disney calls "character greetings," these lovable creatures and fairy-tale celebrities sign autographs and pose for snapshots throughout the park—line up in Town Square when the gates open, or snag Mickey's autograph at the Judge's Tent in Mickey's Toontown Fair. Ariel's Grotto in Fantasyland is also a great place for autographs, and Goofy is often making waves at Splash Mountain. During Disney's "What Will You Celebrate?" promotion, the park adds a lively note three times daily with the "Move It, Shake It, Celebrate It!" musical street party of Disney characters, stilt walkers, and other performers. Characters including the Mad Hatter and Lumiere pop out of gift-wrapped float packages, and Mickey Mouse and other Disney favorites mix it up with some dance moves. The daily Times Guide lists most show hours and character meet-and-greet times and windows, so keep it handy.

DREAM ALONG WITH MICKEY
Duration: 20 min.
Crowds: Heavy, as with all new and limited-time shows.
Strategy: Arrive 30–40 min early to grab one of the scattered benches, though your view of the stage may disappear as the audience gathers for standing room. If you have children, plan to stand or sit on the pavement near the stage for an unobstructed view.
Audience: All ages. Older kids may want to skip it in favor of rides.
Rating: ★★

The Cinderella Castle forecourt provides the perfect location for several daily performances of this Disney character spectacle starring Donald Duck, Mickey Mouse, Minnie Mouse, Goofy, and others. As the show begins, Donald is a "dreams-come-true" skeptic, but he has joined his optimistic pals anyway at a party where Disney princes and princesses dance in a romantic, dreamy number. There's adventure, too, when Peter Pan, pirates, and wenches take the stage. When pesky Disney villains crash the party, Donald decides to challenge evil and fight for the dreams of all his character friends and family. Pick up a Times Guide at City Hall or in most park shops for performance times and a schedule of character meet-and-greets. Based on Disney's record for creating new live productions, don't be surprised if something replaces Dream Along with Mickey by 2010.

CELEBRATE A DREAM COME TRUE PARADE
Duration: About 25 min.
Crowds: Heavy.
Strategy: Arrive 20–30 min in advance of the 3 PM start time. If you're watching in Town Square, you'll wait until almost 3:30 PM for the parade's first float to get to that point.
Audience: All ages. Older kids may want to skip it in favor of rides, which will have shorter lines until the parade ends.
Rating: ★★

The Magic Kingdom often tweaks or revamps its afternoon parade, but you don't have to worry about missing your favorite characters in this park mainstay, which begins in Frontierland, proceeds around the castle hub, and continues down Main Street to Town Square. Floats feature Mickey, Goofy, and most of the Disney storybook gang. The "Celebrate" theme rings out, though classic Disney tunes are woven into the score to accompany the story told by each float, including "You Can Fly" with Peter Pan and "Chim Chim Cher-ee" with Mary Poppins. Mickey Mouse and main squeeze Minnie lead off on a festive float that spells "party time" with decorations of oversize fireworks and noisemakers. Dozens of performers in bright costumes wave flags and streamers and kick up their heels along the route; the parade stops at three locations for high-energy dance numbers. Six other floats are crowd pleasers, with Disney stars like Pinocchio, Snow White, Cinderella, Belle, Beast, Ariel, Prince Ali, Mary Poppins, Alice (of Wonderland), and others. The villains float scares up laughs with Cruella de

Vil, Maleficent, The Wicked Queen, and Jafar. The warm and fuzzy finale features Pluto, Goofy, and Chip 'n' Dale.

SPECTROMAGIC PARADE

Fodor'sChoice **Duration:** 20 min.
★ **Crowds:** Heavy.
Strategy: Take your place on the curb at least 40 min before the parade begins.
Audience: All ages.
Rating: ★★★

The magic truly comes out at night when the parade rolls down Main Street, U.S.A., in a splendidly choreographed surge of electro-luminescent, fiber-optic, and prismatic lighting effects that bring to life peacocks, sea horses, fountains, fantasy gardens, and floats full of colorful Disney characters. Plenty of old-fashioned twinkle lights are thrown in for good measure, and familiar tunes are broadcast over 204 speakers with 72,000 watts of power. Mickey, as always, is the star. But Practical Pig, from one of Disney's prewar Silly Symphony cartoons, steals the show. With the flick of a paintbrush, he transforms more than 100 feet of multicolor floats into a gleaming white-light dreamscape.

WISHES

Duration: 12 min.
Crowds: Heavy.
Strategy: Find a place near the front of the park so you can make a quick exit at the end of the show.
Audience: All ages.
Rating: ★★★

When the lights dim on Main Street and orchestral music fills the air, you know this fireworks extravaganza is about to begin. In Wishes, Jiminy Cricket returns to convince you that your wishes really can come true, and he is supported by Disney characters from such classic films as *Pinocchio, Fantasia, Cinderella,* and *The Little Mermaid.* Songs from the movies play over loudspeakers as more than 680 individual fireworks paint the night sky. Oh, and don't worry that Tinker Bell may have been sealed in her jar for the night—she comes back to fly above the crowd in grand pixie-dust style.

DISABILITIES AND ACCESSIBILITY

Overall, the Magic Kingdom gets decent marks from visitors with disabilities. All restaurants and shops have level entrances or are accessible by ramps. Before your trip, call and request a copy of the *Guidebook for Guests with Disabilities.* This guide, assistive listening systems, reflective captioning equipment, hand-held captioning devices, Braille and audio guides, and sign-language interpretation schedules are available in the park at Guest Services. The park's guide for guests with disabilities tells you where you can use the various devices, which attractions have sign-language interpretation on specific days, and wheelchair access details. Devices require deposits, but no fees. Call **Walt Disney World Information** (☎*407/824–4321*) then wait until the end of the menu to touch 0 to reach someone who can help. Dial 407/939–7807 or 407/939–7670 TTY for accessible accommodations and guidebook information.

To board the **Walt Disney World Railroad** at the Main Street Station, you must transfer from your wheelchair, which can be folded to ride with you or left in the station. Alternatively, board at Frontierland or Mickey's Toontown Fair. The **Main Street Vehicles** can be boarded by those with limited mobility as long as they can fold their wheelchair and climb into a car. There are curb cuts or ramps on each corner. At the hub by the Tip Board across from Casey's Corner, there's a large Braille map of the park.

In Adventureland, the **Magic Carpets of Aladdin** has ramp access for guests in wheelchairs and a customized control pendant for manipulating the "carpet's" height and pitch movement. The **Swiss Family Treehouse,** with its 100 steps and lack of narration, gets low ratings among those with mobility and visual impairments. At the **Jungle Cruise,** several boats have lifts that allow access for visitors in wheelchairs; people with hearing impairments can pick up Assistive Listening receivers at Guest Services for use on the boats. Boarding **Pirates of the Caribbean** requires transferring from a nonfolding to a folding wheelchair, available at the entrance; the very small flume drop may make the attraction inappropriate for those with limited upper-body strength or those wearing neck or back braces. Because of gunshot and fire effects, service animals should stay behind.

Frontierland is the only area of the park, aside from Main Street, that has sidewalk curbs; there are ramps by the Mile Long Bar and east of Frontierland Trading Post. To ride **Big Thunder Mountain Railroad** and **Splash Mountain,** you must be able to step into the ride vehicle and walk short distances, in case of an emergency evacuation; those with limited upper-body strength should assess the situation on-site, and those wearing back, neck, or leg braces shouldn't ride. Service animals aren't allowed on these rides. **Tom Sawyer Island,** with its stairs, bridges, inclines, and narrow caves, isn't negotiable by those using a wheelchair. The *Country Bear Jamboree* is completely wheelchair accessible; if you lip-read, ask to sit up front. The **Frontierland Shootin' Arcade** has two guns set at wheelchair level.

The **Hall of Presidents** and *Liberty Belle* Riverboat, in Liberty Square, are wheelchair accessible. At the **Haunted Mansion,** those in wheelchairs must transfer to the "doom buggies" and take one step; however, if you can walk as much as 200 feet, you'll enjoy the preshow as well as the sensations and eerie sounds of the rest of the ride.

Mickey's PhilharMagic has special viewing areas for guests in wheelchairs. **it's a small world** can be boarded without leaving your wheelchair, but only if it's standard size; if you use a scooter or an oversize chair, you must transfer to one of the attraction's standard chairs, available at the ride entrance. To board **Peter Pan's Flight, Dumbo the Flying Elephant, Cinderella's Golden Carrousel,** the **Mad Tea Party,** and

BLITZ TOURS

BEST OF THE PARK

Arrive at the parking lot 30 to 45 minutes before opening, and once in the park, dash left, or hop the **Walt Disney World Railroad,** to Frontierland and claim an early Fastpass time for **Splash Mountain.** Head over for **Big Thunder Mountain Railroad,** then ride **Pirates of the Caribbean.** By now, your Fastpass ticket should be valid to ride Splash Mountain. Next go to Liberty Square and experience the **Haunted Mansion** if the wait's not long; otherwise, see the **Hall of Presidents** with its new Audio-Animatronics President Obama, the **Country Bear Jamboree** show, or ride **it's a small world** and return to the mansion later. When you're finished, sprint to Tomorrowland and pick up a Fastpass for **Space Mountain** or **Stitch's Great Escape.** Try to time this so that you can have some lunch and then see **Dream-Along with Mickey**. If you have longer to wait, head to the *Monsters, Inc.* **Laugh Floor** or the **Carousel of Progress**. By now it'll be time for Space Mountain or Stitch. Afterward, pick up a Fastpass for **Buzz Light-year's Space Ranger Spin.** Then ride the **Tomorrowland Transit Authority** or squeeze in any missed attractions.

If you haven't seen the 3 PM parade, look for a viewing spot at 2:30 or earlier. Once you settle on a curb, send a member of your group to pick up Fastpass tickets for the **Many Adventures of Winnie the Pooh.** If the crowds aren't too thick, the second floor of the train station makes a nice parade viewing spot. After the parade, hop the train to Mickey's Toontown Fair for some fun photos. From here, stroll into Fantasyland for your Fastpass appointment with Pooh. Afterward, get Fastpass appointment for **Mickey's PhilharMagic** or **Peter Pan's Flight.** While you wait, take a spin on **Cinderella's Golden Carrousel** and check out the **Cinderella Castle** mosaics, or pop over to Liberty Square or Frontierland to catch what you missed earlier.

You may have time to get dinner and return to your hotel for a short breather before the **SpectroMagic** parade and **Wishes** fireworks show. Or you could chill out, have dinner in the park and get a viewing spot early. If you watch the fireworks from Town Square, you can readily grab a monorail seat back to the parking lot as soon as it ends. Or you can ride Splash Mountain or Space Mountain again; lines will be short now, and you can see the fireworks from anywhere in the park.

ON RAINY DAYS

Unlike those at Disney's Hollywood Studios and Epcot's Future World, however, many of the Magic Kingdom's attractions are outdoors. If you don't mind getting damp, pick up a poncho with Mickey insignia ($8 adults, $7 children) in almost any Disney shop and soldier on.

WITH SMALL CHILDREN

At Rope Drop, go directly to Fantasyland and get a Fastpass return-time ticket at the **Many Adventures of Winnie the Pooh.**

Then ride **Dumbo the Flying Elephant.** Next, check showtimes for **Mickey's PhilharMagic** 3-D extravaganza and see it before moving on to a new land. While you wait for the show and your appointment with Pooh, take a whirl on **Cinderella's**

Golden Carrousel and, moving clockwise, other attractions without prohibitive waits. You can also head for a character greeting (check your Times Guide). By now it should be time to use your Fastpass ticket at the Many Adventures of Winnie the Pooh, and the wee ones may want to romp in Pooh's Playful Spot. While they do, send an adult from your group to get everyone a Fastpass for **Peter Pan's Flight.** Next head to **it's a small world.** If you have time before Peter Pan, visit **Ariel's Grotto** to pose for snapshots with the Little Mermaid, catch Storytime with Belle at the **Fairytale Garden,** or see a performance of **Dream-Along with Mickey.**

Small children often are happiest with a quick lunch at one of the counter-service restaurants. For a full-service lunch, proceed to **Cinderella's Royal Table** at Cinderella Castle or **Liberty Tree Tavern** in Liberty Square (reserve seating in advance). **The Crystal Palace** buffet is a great option complete with character visits. Depending on your lunch location, either take the train or walk to Mickey's Toontown Fair. Lunch can digest while the children get their autographs and photos with Mickey Mouse and other Disney celebrities. Then on to the **Barnstormer** to test their coaster mettle. Taking the **Walt Disney World Railroad** is the most relaxing way to return to Frontierland, where you can pick up your Fastpass for **Splash Mountain.** Then claim a piece of pavement across the street from the **Country Bear Jamboree** for the 3 PM parade so you can make a quick exit to line up for **Big Thunder Mountain Railroad**—if your kids can handle the thrills and are tall enough. For

the shortest lines, go *during* the parade. By now, it should be time for your Fastpass reservation for Splash Mountain. After the ride, check out either the *Country Bear Jamboree* or the **Haunted Mansion.**

Late afternoon is a nice time to hitch a raft to **Tom Sawyer Island.** When you return, head straight for Adventureland. Proceed across the Adventureland plaza to the **Jungle Cruise.** Pick up another Fastpass here if the line is long. Then do **Pirates of the Caribbean** and the **Magic Carpets of Aladdin.** If you still have time and energy left, scramble around the **Swiss Family Treehouse** and then head back for your Fastpass to the Jungle Cruise.

Stroll across the Main Street hub to Tomorrowland and pick up a Fastpass ticket for **Buzz Lightyear's Space Ranger Spin.** While you wait, see **Monsters, Inc. Laugh Floor** or **Stitch's Great Escape.** Then climb aboard **Tomorrowland Transit Authority** and, if the line's not prohibitive, **Astro-Orbiter.** By now it's time to join Buzz on his intergalactic mission and, if there's time afterward, to take a spin at the nearby **Mad Tea Party.**

If you have the stamina, hike toward the front of the park after dinner and grab a rocker on the porch of **Tony's Town Square Restaurant** or stake out a curb an hour before the evening **SpectroMagic** parade and **Wishes** fireworks show.

Snow White's Scary Adventures, guests using wheelchairs must transfer to the ride vehicles. The Dumbo and Peter Pan rides aren't suitable for service animals. For **the Many Adventures of Winnie the Pooh,** people who use wheelchairs wait in the main queue and are then able to roll right onto an individual honey pot to ride, with one member of their party accompanying them. There are amplifiers for guests with hearing impairments.

Mickey's Toontown Fair is accessible, though guests who ride the Barnstormer must transfer from a wheelchair to the ride vehicle.

In Tomorrowland, **Stitch's Great Escape** requires guests in motorized scooters to transfer to an on-site standard wheelchair for the show's duration. *Monsters, Inc.* **Laugh Floor** and the **Carousel of Progress** are barrier-free for those using wheelchairs. To board **Buzz Lightyear's Space Ranger Spin** you must transfer to a standard wheelchair; for **Astro-Orbiter** and the **Tomorrowland Transit Authority,** you must be able to walk several steps and transfer to the ride vehicle. To drive **Tomorrowland Indy Speedway** cars, you must have adequate vision and be able to steer, press the gas pedal, and transfer into the low car seat. The cautions for **Big Thunder Mountain Railroad** and **Splash Mountain** also apply to **Space Mountain.**

EATING IN THE MAGIC KINGDOM

Dining options are mainly counter service—and every land has its share of fast-food restaurants serving burgers, hot dogs, grilled-chicken sandwiches, and salads. The walkways are peppered with carts dispensing popcorn, ice-cream bars, lemonade, bottled water, and soda. The Magic Kingdom's widest variety of counter-service menu options—including Kosher burgers, hot dogs, rotisserie chicken, vegetarian wraps, soups, and desserts—are available at Cosmic Ray's Starlight Cafe in Tomorrowland.

FULL-SERVICE RESTAURANTS

Reservations are usually essential for the three most popular table-service restaurants in the Magic Kingdom. You can make them through the Disney reservations line up to 180 days in advance; it's a risk to wait until the day you want to eat.

The fare at **Cinderella's Royal Table** includes Caesar salads, braised lamb shank, pan-seared salmon, cheese tortellini, and roast chicken. But the real attraction is that you get to eat inside Cinderella Castle in an old mead hall, where Cinderella herself is on hand—with other princesses during the breakfast and lunch character meals—in her shiny blue gown. For dinner, Cinderella appears with her Fairy Godmother. A photo package is now included in all Royal Table dining experiences. *Fantasyland.*

Decorated in lovely Williamsburg colors, with Early American–style antiques and lots of brightly polished brass, **Liberty Tree Tavern** is a pleasant place even when jammed. The menu is all-American, with oversize sandwiches, stews, and chops—a good bet for an à la carte lunch. Dinnertime is a "revolutionary" feast of smoked pork, turkey, carved beef, and all the trimmings. *Liberty Sq.*

Tony's Town Square Restaurant is named after the Italian restaurant in *Lady and the Tramp,* where Disney's most famous canine couple share their first kiss over a plate of spaghetti. In fact, the video plays on a TV in the restaurant's waiting area. Lunch and "Da Dinner" menus offer pastas, of course, along with Italian twists on beef, pork, seafood, and chicken. Breakfast is offered as one of Disney's reservations-only Magical Gatherings experiences for groups of eight or more. *Main St.*

Contacts Disney Reservation Center (☎ *407/939–3463*).

SELF-SERVICE RESTAURANT
In the **Crystal Palace,** the "buffets with character" are pleasant. Winnie the Pooh and his pals from the Hundred Acre Wood visit tables in this glass-roof conservatory, and the offerings at breakfast, lunch, and dinner are varied, generous, and surprisingly good. Healthy doses of American regional cuisine include offerings inspired by the season, and there's a sizable choice of pastas, soups, freshly baked breads, and salads that varies from day to day. The place is huge but charming with its numerous nooks and crannies, comfortable banquettes, cozy cast-iron tables, and abundant sunlight. It's also one of the few places in the Magic Kingdom that serve breakfast. *At the Hub end of Main St. facing Cinderella Castle.*

GUIDED TOURS

A number of **guided tours** (☎ *407/939–8687*) are available. Arrive 15 minutes ahead of time to check in for all of them. Some companies— such as Visa, the official credit card company of Walt Disney World, and AAA—offer discounts for some of the tours; make sure to ask ahead about special discounts.

The 4½-hour **Keys to the Kingdom Tour** is a good way to get a feel for the layout of the Magic Kingdom and what goes on behind the scenes. The walking tour, which costs $65, includes lunch but not admission to the park itself. No one younger than 16 is allowed. Tours leave from City Hall daily at 8:30, 9, and 9:30 AM. Included are visits to some of the "backstage" zones: the parade staging area, the wardrobe area, and other parts of the tunnels that web the ground underneath the Magic Kingdom.

The **Family Magic Tour** is a two-hour "surprise" scavenger hunt in which your tour guide encourages you to find things that have disappeared. Disney officials don't want to reveal the tour's components—after all, it's the Family "Magic" Tour—but they can say that a special character-greeting session awaits you at the end of the adventure. Tours leave City Hall at 10 AM daily ($30 for adults and children 3 and up).

Railroad enthusiasts will love the **Magic Behind Our Steam Trains,** which gives you an inside look at the daily operation of the WDW railroad. This tour became so popular that it was lengthened from two to three hours and is offered on four days. Tours begin at the front entrance turnstile at 7:30 AM Monday through Saturday. Those over 10 years old may participate. The cost is $45 per person, plus park admission.

Backstage Magic takes you on a tour of the Magic Kingdom, Epcot, Disney's Hollywood Studios, and the resort's behind-the-scenes Central Shop area, where repair work is done. The cost for the seven-hour tour, which is for those 16 and older, is $219 per person. Tours depart at 9 AM on weekdays. The fee includes lunch but does not include park admission, which isn't required for the tour itself.

Mickey's Magical Milestones chronicles the development and influence of the Big Cheese himself and includes details about how the Disney icon affected pop culture and the Disney theme parks. A VIP meeting with Mickey Mouse and special seating at *Mickey's PhilharMagic* are included in the two-hour tour, which departs at 9 AM on Monday, Wednesday, and Friday. The cost is $25 per person for guests ages 3 and older, and park admission is required.

Epcot

3

WORD OF MOUTH

"Epcot is one of my favorite parks, and it is both educational and fun. Mission: Space may be a little too intense for your children, but I recommend Soarin' and Fast Track. The World Showcase has some amazing food from the different countries."

—crazyhorse42

Updated by
Jennie Hess

Epcot, which stands for an "Experimental Prototype Community of Tomorrow," was the original inspiration for Walt Disney World. Disney envisioned a future in which nations coexisted in peace and harmony, reaping the miraculous harvest of technological achievement. As early as 1966, Disney said that Epcot would "take its cue from the new ideas and new technologies that are now emerging from the creative centers of American industry." He wrote that Epcot, never completed, always improving, "will never cease to be a living blueprint of the future . . . a showcase to the world for the ingenuity of American free enterprise."

But the permanent settlement that he envisioned wasn't to be and, instead, has taken an altered shape in Disney's Celebration, an urban planner's dream of a town near fast-growing Kissimmee. Epcot, which opened in 1982, 16 years after Disney's death, is a showcase, ostensibly, for the concepts that would be incorporated into the real-life Epcots of the future. It's composed of two parts: Future World, where most pavilions are colorful collaborations between Walt Disney Imagineering and major U.S. corporations and are designed to demonstrate technological advances through innovative shows and attractions; and the World Showcase, where exhibition areas complete with shops, restaurants, attractions, and live entertainment are microcosms of 11 countries from four continents.

Epcot today is both more and less than Walt Disney's original dream. Less because the World Showcase presents views of its countries that are, as an Epcot guide once put it, "as Americans perceive them"— highly idealized. But this is a minor quibble in the face of the major achievement: Epcot is that rare paradox—an educational theme park— and a very successful one, too.

Although several attractions, such as Soarin', Test Track, and Mission: SPACE, provide high-octane kicks, the thrills are mostly for the mind. Epcot is best for school-age children and adults. But that doesn't mean the little ones can't have a great time here. Much of the park's entertainment and at least half of its attractions provide fun diversions for preschool children overstimulated by the Magic Kingdom's pixie dust. If you're traveling with younger children, don't miss the Kidcot Fun Stops for hands-on crafts at every World Showcase pavilion and at Future World's Test Track, the Land and the Seas with Nemo & Friends.

GETTING THERE AND AROUND

The monorail and WDW buses drop you off at the main entrance in front of Future World. But if you're staying at one of the Epcot resorts (i.e., the BoardWalk, Yacht Club, Beach Club, Dolphin, or Swan), you can use the International Gateway entrance, which lets you into the World Showcase between France

> **COVERING THE DISTANCE**
>
> Even if your preschooler is a good walker, we highly recommend bringing or renting a stroller so you can cover Epcot's long distances without losing steam.

and the United Kingdom, via water launches or a walkway. However, since Future World generally opens two hours earlier than the World Showcase, you'll have to walk briskly through the park to the Future World pavilions to get a head start on the crowd.

Trams operate from the parking lot to the entrance of each theme park. If you parked fairly close, though, you may save time, especially at park closing time, by walking.

Epcot is a big place; a local joke suggests that the acronym actually stands for "Every Person Comes Out Tired." But still, the most efficient way to get around is to walk. Just to vary things, you can cruise across the lagoon in one of the air-conditioned, 65-foot water taxis that depart every 12 minutes from two World Showcase Plaza docks at the border of Future World. The boat closer to Mexico zips to a dock by the Germany pavilion; the one closer to Canada heads to Morocco. You may have to stand in line for your turn to board, however.

GETTING STARTED

Once you go through security and the turnstiles at either the main Future World entrance or the back World Showcase entrance, make a beeline for Mission: SPACE and Test Track (for the fast-paced thrills) or for the Seas with Nemo & Friends and Soarin' (for two terrific family-fun experiences), where the longest lines form first.

BASIC SERVICES

BABY CARE

Epcot has a **Baby Care Center** as peaceful as the one in the Magic Kingdom; it's in the Odyssey Center in Future World. Furnished with rocking chairs, it has a low lighting level that makes it comfortable for nursing, and cast members have supplies such as formula, baby food, pacifiers, and disposable diapers for sale. Changing tables are available here, as well as in all women's rooms and some men's rooms. You can also buy disposable diapers and wipes near both park entrances at the stroller rental stations.

CAMERAS AND FILM

Disposable cameras and memory cards are widely available. At Disney's other three theme parks you can get your digital memory card downloaded onto a CD for $11.99 plus tax, but Epcot no longer provides

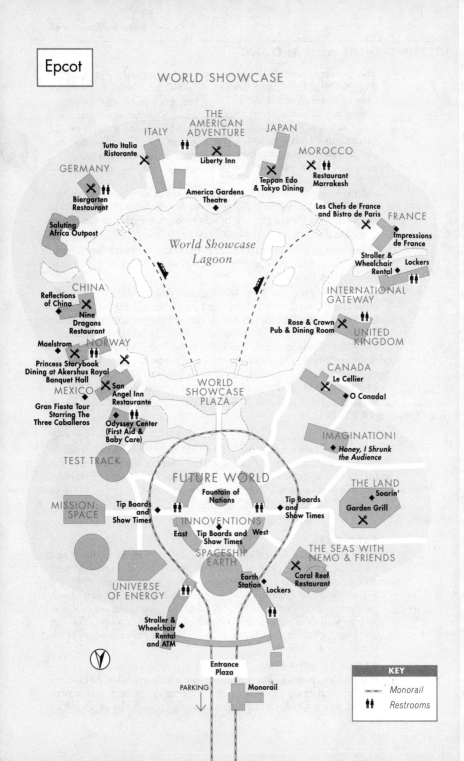

TOP 6 EPCOT ATTRACTIONS

■ **The American Adventure.** Many adults and older children love this patriotic look at American history.

■ **IllumiNations.** This amazing musical laser-and-fireworks show is Disney nighttime entertainment at its best.

■ **Mission: SPACE.** Blast off on a simulated ride to Mars, if you can handle the turbulence.

■ **The Seas with Nemo & Friends.** Ride in your own mobile clamshell and marvel as Nemo and his cartoon friends are placed inside a gigantic aquarium filled with real sea life. "Turtle Talk with Crush" is a great follow-up act.

■ **Soarin'.** Feel the sweet-scented breeze as you fly over California's beautiful landscapes.

■ **Test Track.** Your car revs up to 60 MPH on a hairpin turn in this wild ride on a General Motors proving ground.

the service. All other camera and photo services are available at the **Kodak Camera Center,** in the Entrance Plaza, and at **Cameras and Film,** at the Imagination! pavilion. For photos snapped by Disney photographers, get the **Disney PhotoPass,** which allows you to keep track of digital photos of your group shot in the parks. Later you can view and purchase them online.

FIRST AID
The park's **First Aid Center,** staffed by registered nurses, is in the Odyssey Center on the path between Test Track in Future World and Mexico in the World Showcase.

INFORMATION
Guest Services (aka **Guest Relations**), on the east side of Spaceship Earth, is the place to pick up schedules of live entertainment, park brochures, maps, and the like. Map racks are also at the park's International Gateway entrance between the U.K. and France pavilions, and most shops keep a stack handy. Guest Services cast members will assist with dining reservations, ticket upgrades, and services for guests with disabilities.

LOCKERS
Lockers ($5, $5 deposit) are to the west of Spaceship Earth and in the Bus Information Center by the bus parking lot.

LOST PEOPLE AND THINGS
If you're worried about your children getting lost, get nametags for them at either Guest Services or the Baby Care Center. Instruct them to speak to someone with a Disney nametag if you become separated. Immediately report your loss to any cast member and try not to panic; the staff here is experienced at reuniting families, and there are lost-children logbooks at Guest Services and the Baby Care Center. Guest Services also has a computerized **Message Center,** where you can leave notes for your traveling companions in any of the parks.

For the **Lost and Found** (☏*407/560–7500*), go to the west edge of the Entrance Plaza. After one day, all articles are sent to the **Main Lost and**

Found office (✉ *Magic Kingdom, Ticket and Transportation Center [TTC]* ☎ 407/824–4245).

PACKAGE PICK-UP

Ask shop clerks to forward any large purchases you make to Package Pick-Up at the Gift Stop in the Main Entrance Plaza and at the World Traveler at International Gateway, so that you won't have to carry them around all day. Allow three hours.

STROLLER AND WHEELCHAIR RENTALS

For stroller and wheelchair rentals, look for the special stands on the east side of the Entrance Plaza and at World Showcase's International Gateway. Single strollers are $15 daily, $13 for multiday rental; double strollers are $31 daily, $27 for multiday rental. Wheelchairs are $10 daily, $8 for multiday rental. Electronic Convenience Vehicles (ECV) are $45 per day plus a refundable $20 security deposit. Neither wheelchairs nor ECVs are reservable, so arrive early to rent them. And while the park's wheelchair supply is generally plentiful, ECV availability is limited. If any of your rentals needs replacing, ask any park cast member.

KIDCOT FUN STOPS
Children ages 3 to 10 will love these activity and craft areas sprinkled throughout Future World and the World Showcase. They can get their Epcot passports ($9.95 plus tax at any of the shops) stamped, make puppets, draw pictures, and even create a Moroccan fez.

FUTURE WORLD

Future World is made up of two concentric circles of pavilions. The inner core is composed of the Spaceship Earth geosphere and, just beyond it, a plaza anchored by the wow-generating computer-animated Fountain of Nations, which is as mesmerizing as many a more elaborate ride or show. Bracketing it are the crescent-shaped Innoventions East and West.

Six pavilions compose the outer ring. On the east side they are, in order, the Universe of Energy, Mission: SPACE, and Test Track. The east pavilions present a single, self-contained ride and an occasional postride showcase; a visit rarely takes more than 30 minutes, but it depends on how long you spend in the postride area. On the west side there are the Seas with Nemo & Friends, the Land, and Imagination! These blockbuster exhibits contain both rides and interactive displays; you could spend at least 1½ hours at each of these pavilions, but there aren't enough hours in the day, so prioritize.

SPACESHIP EARTH

Duration: 15 min.
Crowds: Longest during the morning and shortest just before closing.
Strategy: Ride while you're waiting for your Mission: SPACE or Test Track appointments.
Audience: All ages.
Rating: ★★★

Balanced like a giant golf ball waiting for some celestial being to tee off, the multifaceted silver geosphere of Spaceship Earth is to Epcot

TIP SHEET

■ Don't try to do it all. Epcot is so vast and varied that you really need two days to explore everything. If you only have one day, visit just the attractions and pavilions that most interest you.

■ The best days to go are early in the week, since most people tend to go to Disney's Animal Kingdom and the Magic Kingdom first.

■ Arrive at the turnstiles 15 to 30 minutes before opening, so you can avoid some of the lines. Make Mission: SPACE, Test Track, and Soarin' your first stops, and be sure to use your Fastpass option whenever possible.

■ Plan to have at least one relaxed meal. With children, you may want to make reservations (try to make them 90 days in advance) for Princess Storybook Breakfast, Lunch, or Dinner at Norway's Akershus, or for dinner at the Land's Garden Grill, a revolving restaurant that features character appearances by Chip 'n' Dale. Or opt for an early seafood lunch at the Coral Reef in the Seas with Nemo & Friends. A late lunch or an early dinner at one of the World

Showcase restaurants is another great option.

■ Upon entering, check one of Epcot's Tip Boards past Spaceship Earth and just outside either Innoventions building, and modify your strategy if there's a short line at a top attraction.

■ Walk fast, see the exhibits when the park is at its emptiest, and slow down and enjoy the shops and the live entertainment when the crowds thicken.

■ If your family loves festivals, go for either the Epcot International Flower & Garden Festival (late March through late May or early June) or the Epcot International Food & Wine Festival (late September through mid-November); you'll get extra bang for the admission buck.

■ Set up a rendezvous point and time at the start of the day, just in case you and your companions get separated. Some good places in Future World include in front of Gateway Gifts near Spaceship Earth and in front of the Fountain of Nations; in World Showcase, in front of your country of choice.

what Cinderella Castle is to the Magic Kingdom. As much a landmark as an icon, it can be seen on a clear day from an airplane flying down either coast of Florida.

Inside the ball, the Spaceship Earth ride transports you past a series of tableaux that explore human progress and the continuing search for better forms of communication. In 2008 Disney Imagineers upgraded the ride to present new and enhanced scenes with more vibrant sets and lighting effects. Most of the Audio-Animatronics figures received hair and costume makeovers, and their movements were tweaked so they appear noticeably more lifelike. The script, by science-fiction writer Ray Bradbury, in the past was narrated by Walter Cronkite and, more recently, Jeremy Irons. For the updated experience, Oscar-winner Dame Judi Dench narrates the journey that begins in the darkest tunnels of time, proceeds through history, and ends poised on the edge of the future. For the first time on a Disney ride, the narration also is offered in French, Japanese, German, Spanish, and Portuguese. Ten-time Emmy winner Bruce Broughton composed the new musical score.

Audio-Animatronics figures present Cro-Magnon man daubing mystic paintings on cave walls, Egyptian scribes scratching hieroglyphics on papyrus, Roman centurions building roads, Islamic scholars mapping the heavens, and 11th- and 12th-century Benedictine monks hand-copying ancient manuscripts. As you move into the Renaissance, Michelangelo paints the Sistine Chapel, Gutenberg invents the printing press, and in rapid succession, the telegraph, radio, television, and computer come into being. New scenes depict a family viewing the

> **DID YOU KNOW?**
>
> Everyone likes to gawk at the giant "golf ball," but there are some truly jaw-dropping facts about it: it weighs 1 million pounds and measures 164 feet in diameter and 180 feet in height ("Aha!" you say. "It's not really a sphere!"). It also encompasses more than 2 million cubic feet of space, and it's balanced on six pylons sunk 100 feet into the ground. The anodized-aluminum sheath is composed of 954 triangular panels, not all of equal size or shape. And, last, because it's not a geodesic dome, which is only a half sphere, the name "geosphere" was coined.

moon landing on TV, a massive two-story computer room circa 1960s, and a '70s garage where the personal computer was born. As your ride vehicle swings backward and descends slowly, there's new interactive fun for riders. Touch screens quiz guests about how they envision their own future, then play back an animated, "Jetsonesque" scenario based on the answers. Siemans, which presents the higher-tech attraction, created a fun-packed post show with high-demand interactive games that involve simulated driving, piecing together a digital human body, and managing a growing city's power grid. As you exit the ride and enter the post show, watch the giant digital map screen to see your photo taken during the ride and posted in your hometown location.

INNOVENTIONS

Duration: Up to you.
Crowds: Largest around the popular computer displays.
Strategy: Go before 10 AM or after 2 PM.
Audience: All ages, but primarily for the grade-school set. A few games are designed with preschoolers in mind.
Rating: ★★★

Innoventions is a two-building, 100,000-square-foot, walk-through attraction that you can visit at your own pace. Hands-on interactive exhibits entertain kids and adults as they investigate the innovations now improving the world around us. Innoventions East is filled with activities meant to inspire and entertain. At Waste Management's "Don't Waste It!" exhibit, you become an environmental steward working to dispose a year's worth of trash while creating energy to power a city. At the Test the Limits Lab, you can be product testers for Underwriters Laboratories trying to break TV screens, slam doors, crush helmets, and put other home products through their paces. StormStruck, presented by FLASH, serves up severe weather in a 3-D theater with tips on how to protect your home and family from future storms. And for the first time, Innoventions features a ride by Raytheon for the engineer in all of us. Using math and science challenges, you can create a thrill ride, then you and one other person can board a robotic simulator and try it out.

At Innoventions West, you can test drive the Segway Human Transporter at Segway Central. The transporter is so popular that it's used by some Disney personnel to wheel across the park and has been incorporated into Epcot and Fort Wilderness guided tours. Liberty Mutual's "Where's the Fire?" interactive experience is a terrific way to review fire safety and prevention. Families can enjoy the game house, where they team up with other guests to find and extinguish as many fire hazards as possible. At the Velcro Companies Slapstick Studios, you can join a high-energy game show to solve "sticky" problems using Velcro-branded products. At ThinkPlace, IBM puts you in a game where you can create an avatar of yourself who's able to jump, run, and dance through a video game starring (you guessed it) you! You can even watch your cash reserves grow as T. Rowe Price shows you how to save and invest for your future dreams at the Great Piggy Bank Adventure.

If you can't resist an interactive escapade, sign up here for the Kim Possible World Showcase Adventure. You'll receive your own "Kimmunicator"—a hand-held wireless controller connecting you with several Kim Possible characters who provide clues to stop comical villains from taking over the world with their mad inventions. At your own pace, you can scour the World Showcase for clues and solve challenges encountered during the experience. Whew! Once your heroic deed is done, you may need to grab a frozen treat and kick back on a park bench to recover.

If you're a collector of the myriad Disney pins that are sold in nearly all the theme-park shops, the Pin Station at Innoventions Plaza has quite a collection.

NEED A BREAK? Enter the indoor refrigerator that is **Club Cool**, where Coca-Cola's bold red-and-white colors guide you to a room full of soda machines and logo merchandise. You can sample (for free) the cola king's products from around the world: Vegitabeta from Japan, Smart Watermelon from China, Kinley Lemon from Israel. It's entertaining to watch the faces of those who discover a not-so-yummy flavor.

MISSION: SPACE

Duration: 4 min.

Crowds: Heavy, since this is Disney's most technologically advanced attraction and one of only a handful of thrill rides at Epcot.

Strategy: Arrive before 10 AM or use Fastpass. Don't ride on a full stomach.

Audience: Adults and children over 8. Pregnant women and anyone with heart, back, neck, balance, blood pressure, or motion sickness problems shouldn't ride. Minimum height: 44".

Rating: ★★★

It took five years for Disney Imagineers, with the help of 25 experts from NASA, to design Mission: SPACE, the first ride ever to take people "straight up" in a simulated rocket launch. The story transports you and co-riders to the year 2036 and the International Space Training Center, where you are astronauts-in-training about to embark on your first launch. Before you board the four-person rocket capsule, you're assigned to a position: commander, navigator, pilot, or engineer. And at this point you're warned several times about the intensity of the ride and the risks for people with health concerns.

For those who can handle the intense spinning, the sensation of lift-off is truly amazing. You'll feel the capsule tilt skyward and, on a screen that simulates a windshield, you'll see the clouds and even a

> ## MISSION: SPACE CAUTION
>
> Parents should exercise caution when deciding whether to let their children ride Mission: Space. Even if your child meets the height requirement, she may not be old enough to enjoy the ride. In the capsule, you're instructed to keep your head back against the seat and to look straight ahead for the duration of the ride. (Closing your eyes or not looking straight ahead can bring on motion sickness.) Your role as a "crew member" also means you're supposed to hold onto a joystick and push buttons at certain times. All these instructions can confuse kids and get in the way of their enjoyment of the ride.

flock of birds pass over you. Then you launch—a turbulent and heart-pounding experience that flattens you against your seat. Once you break into outer space, you'll even feel weightless. After landing, you exit your capsule into the Training Lab, where you can rejoin your little ones playing space-related games. ■ TIP→ **Note that many people come off this ride feeling nauseated and disoriented from the high-speed spinning of the vehicle, which is the technology that makes you feel as if you're rocketing into space. Keep in mind that these effects are cumulative. You may feel OK after your first ride but totally ill after your second or third ride in a row.**

TEST TRACK
Duration: 5 min.
Crowds: Heavy.
Strategy: Go first thing in the morning and get a Fastpass ticket, or you will wait—a long time. Note that the ride can't function on wet tracks, so don't head here right after a downpour.
Audience: All but young children: the line-area message will be lost on them, and the speeds and other effects may prove frightening. No pregnant women or guests wearing back, neck, or leg braces. Minimum height: 40".
Rating: ★★★

This small-scale-with-big-thrills version of a General Motors vehicle proving ground takes you behind the scenes of automobile testing. The line area showcases many of these tests in informative, action-packed exhibits, which make the wait fun, but if you enter with a Fastpass, you'll miss these features. On the ride, sporty convertible Test Track vehicles take you and five other passengers through seven performance tests. In the Brake Test your ride vehicle makes two passes through a circular setup of traffic cones, and you learn how antilock brakes can make a wildly out-of-control skid manageable. In the Environmental Chamber, vehicles are exposed to extreme heat, bone-chilling cold, and a mist that simulates exposure to corrosive substances. After leaving these test chambers, vehicles accelerate quickly up a switchback "mountain road" in the Ride Handling Test. There's also a too-close-for-comfort view of a Barrier Test. The best part, the High-Speed Test, is last: your vehicle goes outside the Test Track building to negotiate a steeply banked loop at a speed of nearly 60 MPH. Outside the pavilion, kids can get a soaking in the Cool Wash, an interactive water area that lets them pretend they're in a car wash.

UNIVERSE OF ENERGY

The first of the pavilions on the left, or east, side of Future World, the Universe of Energy occupies a large, lopsided pyramid sheathed in thousands of mirrors—solar collectors that power the attraction inside. Though it's a technologically complex show with a ride, film, and large Audio-Animatronics dinosaurs, the attraction could use some updating. One of the special effects includes enough cold, damp fog to make you think you've been transported to the inside of a defrosting refrigerator. ("We don't want to go through that fog again," one child announced after emerging from a particularly damp vision of the Mesozoic era.)

ELLEN'S ENERGY ADVENTURE
Duration: 30 min.
Crowds: Steady but never horrible; 600 people enter every 15 min.
Strategy: To be at the front of the ride and have your experience of the primeval landscape unspoiled by rows of modern heads, sit in the seats to the far left and front of the theater; to get these seats position yourself similarly in the preshow area.
Audience: All ages.
Rating: ★★

In the Universe of Energy show, comedian Ellen DeGeneres portrays a woman who dreams she's a contestant on *Jeopardy!* only to discover that all the categories involve a subject she knows nothing about—energy. Her challengers on the show, hosted by Alex Trebek himself, are Ellen's know-it-all former college roommate (played to the irritating hilt by Jamie Lee Curtis) and Albert Einstein. Enter Bill Nye, the Science Guy, Ellen's nice-guy neighbor and all-around science whiz, who guides Ellen (and you) on a crash course in Energy 101.

First comes the history of the universe—in one minute—on three 70-mm screens, 157 feet wide by 32 feet tall. Next the theater separates into six 96-passenger vehicles that lurch into the forest primeval. Huge trees loom out of the mists of time, ominous blue moonbeams waver in the fog, sulfurous lava burbles up, and the air smells distinctly of Swamp Thing. Through this unfriendly landscape, apatosauruses wander trailing mouthfuls of weeds, a tyrannosaurus fights it out with a triceratops, pterodactyls swoop through the air, and a truly nasty sea snake emerges from the swamp to attack the left side of the tram. A terrified Ellen is even cornered by a menacing elasmosaurus.

The ride concludes with another film in which Ellen learns about the world's present-day energy needs, resources, and concerns. It's shown on three screens, each 30 feet tall, 74 feet wide, and curved to create a 200-degree range of vision. Does Ellen win in her *Jeopardy!* dream? You'll have to travel back in time for the answer.

THE SEAS WITH NEMO AND FRIENDS

This pavilion, known for years as the Living Seas, has always been a draw with its 5.7-million-gallon aquarium filled with 65 species of sea life, including sharks. To capitalize on the huge popularity of the Disney-Pixar hit film, *Finding Nemo*, Disney Imagineers reworked the attraction using clever technology that makes it look like Nemo and pals are on an adventure in the aquarium along with the real fish. While inside, don't miss the terrific Turtle Talk with Crush interactive, real-time film attraction.

THE SEAS WITH NEMO AND FRIENDS EXPERIENCE
Duration: As long as you like. Turtle Talk with Crush lasts 20 min.
Crowds: Heavy to moderate.
Strategy: If you have small children or Nemo fans, go early in the morning; the wait for both the new ride and the cannily interactive Turtle Talk with Crush will get longer.
Audience: All ages, but especially kids under 9.
Rating: ★★★

Hop into a "clamobile" and take a ride under the sea to look for Nemo, who has wandered off from Mr. Ray's class field trip. This ride adds fresh zip to an aging, but relevant, attraction—an astonishing animation projection effect makes it appear as if Nemo and his pals are swimming among the marine life of the actual Seas aquarium. As your ride progresses, Dory, Nemo's spacey sidekick, helps Bruce, Squirt, and other pals find him. After the ride, head for the Sea Base area to line up for Turtle Talk with Crush, starring, of course, Crush the ancient sea turtle from the *Finding Nemo* film. In this real-time animated show, Crush "chats" and "jokes" so convincingly with kids in the small theater, that some walk up and touch the screen where Crush "swims," eyes wide as sand dollars. There's often a wait for this cartoon chat, but it's a hit with preschoolers and young schoolchildren, as well as their parents. Take a few minutes to walk around the tank at the pavilion's core and check out Bruce's Shark World for some fun photo ops and shark facts with graphics, plus displays about the endangered Florida manatee and dolphins.

THE LAND

Shaped like an intergalactic greenhouse, the enormous, skylighted Land pavilion dedicates 6 acres and a host of attractions to everyone's favorite topic: food. You can easily spend two hours exploring here, more if you take one of the guided greenhouse tours available throughout the day.

NEED A BREAK?

Talk about a self-contained ecosystem: The Land pavilion grows its own produce, including tomatoes and cucumbers, some of which shows up on the menu at the **Sunshine Seasons** healthful food court. Much of the fare is cooked on a 48-inch Mongolian grill. You order at a counter, then carry your meal or snack to a table. The eatery's Asian shop offers chicken noodle bowls and spicy stir-fries. A sandwich shop delivers oak-grilled veggie or ham sandwiches on fresh breads, and a yummy turkey on focaccia with chipotle mayonnaise. The salad shop also wows with roasted beets, goat cheese, and seared tuna—among other options—over mixed greens. Wood-fired grills and rotisseries sizzle with chicken, pork, and salmon, and the bakery is a sure bet for fresh pastries. To avoid the crowds, plan to eat at nonpeak times—after 2 for lunch and before 5 or after 7 for dinner.

SOARIN'

Fodor's Choice ★

Crowds: Heavy.
Strategy: Go early and grab a Fastpass, or go just before park closing.
Audience: Adults and children 40" or taller. This is a mild flight with a thrilling view; even very shy children will love it.
Rating: ★★★

WORD OF MOUTH

"We love Soarin' and always ask the cast member to sit in the front row. That way you don't see dangling feet in your line of view."
—mma

If you've ever wondered what it's like to fly, or at least hang glide, this attraction is your chance to enjoy the sensation without actually taking the plunge. It's based on the popular attraction Soarin' Over California at Disney's California Adventure in Anaheim. It uses motion-based technology to literally lift you in your seat 40 feet into the air within a giant projection-screen dome. As you soar above the Golden Gate Bridge, Napa Valley, Yosemite, and other California wonders, you feel the wind and smell pine forests and orange blossoms. Navy buffs get a kick out of swooping over a massive aircraft carrier. Duffers can't help but duck when that golf ball heads their way. The accompanying score created by Jerry Goldsmith (*Mulan, Star Trek*) builds on the thrill, and the crispness and definition of the film, projected at twice the rate of a typical motion picture, adds realism.

LIVING WITH THE LAND

Duration: 14 min.
Crowds: Moderate all day.
Strategy: The line moves fairly quickly, so go anytime. Use Fastpass in the case of peak season crowds.
Audience: Teens and adults.
Rating: ★★★

A boat ride into a faux rain forest is just the beginning of this entertaining tour that focuses on strides in agriculture and aquaculture. You climb aboard a canopied boat that cruises, accompanied by recorded narration, through three biomes—rain forest, desert, and prairie ecological communities—and into an experimental greenhouse that demonstrates how food sources may be grown in the future, not only on the planet but also in outer space. Shrimp, sunshine bass, tilapia, eels, catfish, and alligators are raised in controlled aquacells, and tomatoes, peppers, and squash thrive in the Desert Farm area via drip irrigation that delivers just the right amount of water and nutrients to their roots. Gardeners are usually interested in the section on integrated pest management, which relies on "good" insects like ladybugs to control more harmful predators. Everyone enjoys seeing Mickey Mouse–shaped fruits and vegetables (there may be pumpkins, cucumbers, or watermelons) nurtured with the help of molds created by the Land's science team; scientists also are growing a "tomato tree"—the first of its kind in the United States—that yields thousands of tomatoes from a single vine. Many of the growing areas are actual experiments-in-progress, in which Disney and the U.S. Department of Agriculture have joined forces to produce, say, a sweeter pineapple or a faster-growing pepper. The plants (including the tomato tree's golf-ball-size tomatoes) and fish that grow in the greenhouse are regularly harvested for use in the Land's restaurants.

> ### WORD OF MOUTH
>
> "Epcot has an area in the front that will appeal to a four year old. There is a Nemo ride and my 4 year old really enjoyed the ride through the Disney green houses. And then in each country, there is a kid station where you add little country tags to a mask that they give you. The kids really get into collecting these tags. Plus there are some attractions that are fun in the countries such as the boat ride through Mexico." –kelliebellie

CIRCLE OF LIFE
Duration: 20 min.
Crowds: Moderate to large, all day.
Strategy: Hit this first in the Land.
Audience: Enlightening for children and adults; a nap opportunity for toddlers.
Rating: ★★

Featuring three stars of *The Lion King*—Simba the lion, Timon the meerkat, and Pumbaa the waddling warthog—this film delivers a powerful message about protecting the world's environment for all living things. Part animation, part *National Geographic*–like film using spectacular 70 mm live-action footage, Circle of Life tells a fable about a "Hakuna Matata Lakeside Village" that Timon and Pumbaa are developing by clearing the African savanna. Simba cautions about mistreating the land by telling a story of a creature who occasionally forgets that everything is connected in the great Circle of Life. "That creature," he says, "is man." The lilting accompaniment is Tim Rice and Elton John's popular song, and the narration is provided by James Earl Jones.

IMAGINATION!

The theme here is the imagination and the fun that can be had when you let it loose. The leaping fountains outside make the point, as does the big attraction here, the 3-D film *Honey, I Shrunk the Audience*.

The Journey into Imagination with Figment ride can be capped by a stroll through Image Works, a sort of interactive fun house devoted to music and art.

HONEY, I SHRUNK THE AUDIENCE

Duration: 14 min.

Crowds: Large theater capacity should mean a relatively short wait, but the film's popularity can make for big crowds.

Strategy: Go first thing in the morning or just before closing, or utilize Fastpass.

Audience: All but easily frightened children. For most, the humor quotient outweighs the few scary moments.

Rating: ★★★

Don't miss this 3-D adventure about the futuristic "shrinking" technologies demonstrated in the hit films that starred Rick Moranis. Moranis reprises his role as Dr. Wayne Szalinski, who's about to receive the Inventor of the Year Award from the Imagination Institute. While Dr. Szalinski is demonstrating his latest shrinking machine, though, things go wrong. Be prepared to laugh and scream your head off, courtesy of the special in-theater effects and 3-D film technology that are used ingeniously, from start to finish, to dramatize a hoot of a story.

JOURNEY INTO IMAGINATION WITH FIGMENT

Duration: 8 min.

Crowds: Lines move fairly quickly here.

Strategy: Ride while waiting for your Honey, I Shrunk the Audience Fastpass appointment.

Audience: Children and adults. Prepare preschoolers for the brief period of darkness and the slightly disorienting scanner at the end.

Rating: ★★

Figment, a fun-loving dragon, is teamed with Dr. Nigel Channing, the presenter of Dr. Szalinski's award in *Honey, I Shrunk the Audience*. The pair take you on a sensory adventure designed to engage your imagination through sound, illusion, gravity, dimension, and color. After the ride, you can check out Image Works, where several interactive displays allow you to further stretch your imagination.

WORLD SHOWCASE

Nowhere but at Epcot can you explore a little corner of almost a dozen countries in one day. As you stroll the 1⅓ mi around the 40-acre World Showcase Lagoon, you circumnavigate the globe according to Disney by experiencing the native food, entertainment, culture, and arts and crafts at pavilions representing 11 countries in Europe, Asia, North Africa, and the Americas. Pavilion employees are from the countries they represent—Disney hires them to live and work for up to a year as part of its international college program.

Instead of rides, you have breathtaking films at the Canada, China, and France pavilions; several art exhibitions; and the chance to chat in the native language of the friendly foreign staff members. Each pavilion also has a designated Kidcot Fun Stop, open daily from 11 AM or noon until around 8 or 9 PM, where youngsters can try their hands at crafts projects—they might make a Moroccan fez or a Norwegian troll, for instance. Live entertainment is an integral part of the pavilions' presentations, and some of your finest moments here will be watching incredibly talented Dragon Legend Chinese Acrobats, singing along with a terrific band of Fab Four impersonators in the U.K. pavilion and the rockin' Off Kilter band in Canada, or laughing along with some improv fun in the Italy courtyard. Dining is another favorite pastime at Epcot, and the World Showcase offers tempting tastes of the authentic cuisines of the countries that have pavilions. In recent years Disney has worked to increase dining initiatives across its theme-park and resort properties, and Epcot recently debuted several new and enhanced restaurant experiences (*see details in Italy, Japan, China and Mexico sections*).

WHEN TO GO

The best times to visit are April through early June, during the Epcot International Flower & Garden Festival, and October through mid-November, during the Epcot International Food and Wine Festival. Keep in mind, however, that crowds do get heavier during these festivals, even though they're scheduled outside the peak season.

EN ROUTE A World Showcase Passport ($9.95) is a wonderful way to keep a kid interested in this more adult area of Epcot. The passports, available at vendor carts, come with stickers and a badge, and children can have them stamped at each pavilion. The World Showcase is also a great place to look for unusual gifts—you might pick up silver jewelry in Mexico, a teapot in China, or a kimonoed doll in Japan.

CANADA

"Oh, it's just our Canadian outdoors," said a typically modest native guide upon being asked about the model for the striking rocky chasm and tumbling waterfall that represent just one of the high points of Canada. The beautiful formal gardens do have an antecedent: Butchart Gardens, in Victoria, British Columbia. And so does the Hôtel du Canada, a French Gothic mansion with spires, turrets, and a mansard roof; anyone who's ever stayed at Québec's Château Frontenac or Ottawa's Château Laurier will recognize the imposing style favored by architects of Canadian railroad hotels. Like the size of the Rocky Mountains, the scale of the structures seems immense; unlike the real thing, it's managed with a trick called forced perspective, which exaggerates the smallness of the distant parts to make the entire thing look gigantic. Another bit of design legerdemain: the World Showcase Rockies are made of chicken wire and painted concrete mounted on a movable platform similar to a parade float. Ah, wilderness!

Canada also contains shops selling maple syrup, lumberjack shirts, and other trapper paraphernalia. Its restaurant, Le Cellier Steakhouse, is a great place to stop for a relaxing lunch or dinner and may be easier to get into than the higher-demand Chefs de France and the new Teppan Edo in the Japan pavilion.

O CANADA!

Duration: 17 min.
Crowds: Can be thick in late afternoon.
Strategy: Go when World Showcase opens or in the evening.
Audience: All ages, but no strollers permitted, and toddlers and small children can't see unless they're held aloft.
Rating: ★★★

That's just what you'll say after seeing this CircleVision film's stunning opening shot—footage of the Royal Canadian Mounted Police surrounding you as they circle the screen. From there, you whoosh over waterfalls, venture through Montréal and Toronto, sneak up on bears and bison, mush behind a husky-pulled dogsled, and land pluck in the middle of a hockey game. This is a standing-only theater.

UNITED KINGDOM

Never has it been so easy to cross the English Channel. The United Kingdom rambles between the elegant mansions lining a London square to the bustling, half-timber shops of a village high street to thatched-roof cottages from the countryside. (The thatch is made of plastic broom bristles in deference to local fire regulations.) And of course there's a pair of the familiar red phone booths that were once found all over the United Kingdom but are now on their way to being relics. The pavilion has no single major attraction. Instead, you can wander through shops selling tea and tea accessories, Welsh handicrafts, Royal Doulton figurines, and English lavender fragrance by Taylor of London. Theme chess sets with characters from *Alice in Wonderland* and *Robin Hood* catch the eye at the Crown & Crest. Outside, the strolling World Showcase Players coax audience members into participating in their definitely lowbrow versions of Shakespeare. There's also a lovely garden and park with benches in the back that's easy to miss—relax and kick back to the tunes of the British Invasion, a band known for its on-target Beatles performances. Kids love to run through the hedge maze as the parents travel back in time to "Yesterday." Check the Times Guide and arrive 30 minutes early for a bench or 15 minutes early for a curb.

NEED A BREAK? Revive yourself with a pint of the best—although you'll be hard-put to decide between the offerings—at the **Rose & Crown**, a pub that also offers traditional afternoon tea on the outdoor terrace. The adjacent dining room serves more substantial fare for lunch and dinner (reservations often required). The terrace outside is one of the best spots for watching IllumiNations; arrive at least an hour or so in advance to get a seat. If you're in a hurry, grab fish-and-chips to go from Yorkshire County Fish Shop.

FRANCE

You don't need the scaled-down model of the Eiffel Tower to tell you that you've arrived in France, specifically Paris. There's the poignant accordion music wafting out of concealed speakers, the trim sycamores pruned in the French style to develop signature knots at the end of each branch, and the delicious aromas surrounding the Boulangerie Pâtisserie bake shop. This is the Paris of dreams, a Paris of the years just before World War I, when solid mansard-roof mansions were crowned with iron filigree, when the least brick was drenched in romanticism. Here's a replica of the conservatory-like Les Halles—the iron-and-glass barrel-roof market that no longer exists in the City of Light; there's an arching footbridge; and all around, of course, there are shops. You can inspect Parisian impressionist artwork at Galerie des Halles; sample Guerlain perfume and cosmetics at La Signature; and acquire a bottle of Bouzy Rouge at Les Vins de France. If you plan to dine at Les Chefs de France, make a reservation for a late lunch or dinner; the second-floor Bistro de Paris (dinner only) is a gourmet treat.

NEED A BREAK? The frequent lines at **Boulangerie Pâtisserie**, a small Parisian-style sidewalk café, are worth the wait. Have a creamy café au lait and an éclair, Napoleon, or some other French pastry while enjoying the fountains and floral displays.

IMPRESSIONS DE FRANCE
Duration: 18 min.
Crowds: Steady from World Showcase opening through late afternoon.
Strategy: Visit anytime during your stroll around the World Showcase.
Audience: Adults and children age 7 and up.
Rating: ★★★

The intimate Palais du Cinema, inspired by the royal theater at Fontainebleau, screens this homage to the glories of the country. Shown on five screens spanning 200 degrees, in an air-conditioned, sit-down theater, the film takes you to vineyards at harvest time, Paris on Bastille Day, the Alps, Versailles, Normandy's Mont-St-Michel, and the stunning châteaux of the Loire Valley. The musical accompaniment also hits high notes and sweeps you away with familiar segments from Offenbach, Debussy, and Saint-Saëns, all woven together by longtime Disney musician Buddy Baker.

MOROCCO

No magic carpet is required as you enter Morocco—just walk through the pointed arches of the Bab Boujouloud gate and you'll find yourself exploring the mysterious North African country of Morocco. The arches are ornamented with beautiful wood carvings and encrusted with intricate mosaics made of 9 tons of handmade, hand-cut tiles; 19 native artisans were sent to Epcot to install them and to create the dusty stucco walls that seem to have withstood centuries of sandstorms. Look closely and you'll see that every tile has a small crack or some other imperfection, and no tile depicts a living creature—in deference to the Islamic belief that only Allah creates perfection and life.

Koutoubia Minaret, a replica of the prayer tower in Marrakesh, acts as Morocco's landmark. Winding alleyways—each corner bursting with carpets, brasses, leatherwork, and other North African craftsman-

PHOTO TIP

You'll get a great shot of Space-ship Earth across the lagoon by framing it in the torii gate.

ship—lead to a beautifully tiled fountain and lush gardens. The full-service Restaurant Marrakesh is a highlight here if you enjoy eating couscous and roast lamb while distracted by a lithesome belly dancer. And one of the hottest fast-food spots on the Epcot dining scene is Tangierine Café, with tasty Mediterranean specialties like chicken kebabs, lentil and couscous salads, and freshly baked Moroccan bread. Both eateries are open for lunch and dinner.

JAPAN

A brilliant vermilion torii gate, based on Hiroshima Bay's much-photographed Itsukushima Shrine, frames the World Showcase Lagoon and stands as the striking emblem of Disney's serene version of Japan. During the Epcot International Flower & Garden Festival, the view is more spectacular, as the gate also showcases a display of award-winning bonsai.

Disney horticulturists deserve a hand for creating an authentic land-scape: 90% of the plants they used are native to Japan. Rocks, pebbled streams, pools, and carefully pruned trees and shrubs complete the meticulous picture. At sunset, or during a rainy dusk, the twisted branches of the corkscrew willows frame a perfect Japanese view of the five-story winged pagoda that is the heart of the pavilion. Based on the 8th-century Horyuji Temple in Nara, the brilliant blue pagoda has five levels, symbolizing the five elements of Buddhist belief—earth, water, fire, wind, and sky.

The peace is occasionally interrupted by authentic performances on drums and gongs. Other entertainment is provided by demonstrations of traditional Japanese crafts, such as kite-making or Miyuki, a type of candy art. Mitsukoshi Department Store, an immense three-centuries-old retail firm known as Japan's Sears Roebuck, is a favorite among Epcot shoppers and carries everything from T-shirts to kimonos and row upon row of Japanese dolls. For lunch and dinner, diners are entertained by the culinary feats of chefs at Teppan Edo (which carries on the chop-toss-applaud antics of the original Teppanyaki Dining Room). Disney recently replaced Japan's Tempura Kiku and Matsu No Ma Lounge with Tokyo Dining, which focuses on presentation of traditional ingredients and cuisine from Japan, including sushi, at slightly lower prices than those at Teppan Edo.

AMERICAN ADVENTURE

In a Disney version of Philadelphia's Liberty Hall, the Imagineers prove that their kind of fantasy can beat reality hands down. The 110,000 bricks, made by hand from soft pink Georgia clay, sheathe the familiar structure, which acts as a beacon for those across Epcot's lagoon. The pavilion includes an all-American fast-food restaurant, a shop, lovely rose gardens, and an outdoor theater.

◗ NEED A BREAK? What else would you order at the counter-service **Liberty Inn** but burgers, apple pie, and other all-American fare? If the weather's cool enough, you can relax at an outdoor table and watch the world go by. On a warm summer evening, this is the place to get an ice-cream sundae before Illumi-Nations starts. On a chilly winter day, the hot cocoa is a hit.

THE AMERICAN ADVENTURE
Duration: 30 min.
Crowds: Large, but the theater is huge, so you can almost always get into the next show.
Strategy: Check the entertainment schedule and arrive 10 min before the Voices of Liberty and the Spirit of America Fife & Drum Corps are slated to perform. See the drum corps outside, then grab a bench or a spot on the floor inside to enjoy the Voices' a cappella tunes before the show.
Audience: All ages.
Rating: ★★★

The pavilion's key attraction is this 100-yard dash through history, and you'll be primed for the lesson after reaching the main entry hall and hearing the stirring a cappella Voices of Liberty. Inside the theater, the main event begins to the accompaniment of "The Golden Dream," performed by the Philadelphia Orchestra. This show combines evocative sets, the world's largest rear-projection screen (72 feet wide), enormous movable stages, and 35 Audio-Animatronics players that are impressive but could use some upgrading. Ben Franklin still climbs up the stairs, but his movements are more tentative when compared with newer-generation figures. Beginning with the arrival of the Pilgrims at Plymouth Rock and their grueling first winter, Ben Franklin and a wry, pipe-smoking Mark Twain narrate the episodes, both praiseworthy and shameful, that have shaped the American spirit. Disney detail is so painstaking that you never feel rushed, and, in fact, each speech and scene seems polished like a little jewel. You feel the cold at Valley Forge and the triumph when Charles Lindbergh crosses the Atlantic; you're moved by Nez Percé chief Joseph's forced abdication of Native American ancestral lands and by women's rights campaigner Susan B. Anthony's speech; you laugh with Will Rogers's aphorisms and learn about the pain of the Great Depression through an affecting radio broadcast by Franklin Delano Roosevelt.

AMERICA GARDENS THEATRE
Crowds: Large during festival and holiday performances and celebrity concerts.
Strategy: Check the entertainment schedule and arrive one hour or so ahead of time for holiday and celebrity performances.
Audience: Varies with performance.

On the edge of the lagoon, directly opposite Disney's magnificent bit of colonial fakery, is this open-air, partially tree-shaded venue for concerts and shows. Some are of the "Yankee Doodle Dandy" variety. Others are hot tickets themed to such Epcot events as the Flower Power concerts with '60s pop legends during the March or April-through-early-June Epcot International Flower & Garden Festival and Eat to the Beat! concerts during the October-through-mid-November Epcot International Food & Wine Festival. This is also the setting for the annual yuletide Candlelight Processional—a not-to-be-missed event if you're at WDW during the holidays. The Candlelight Dinner Package (available through Disney's dining reservations hotline) includes dinner in a select World Showcase restaurant and preferred seating for the moving performance.

ITALY

In WDW's Italy, the star is the architecture: reproductions of Venice's Piazza San Marco and Doge's Palace, accurate right down to the gold leaf on the ringlets of the angel perched 100 feet atop the Campanile; the seawall stained with age, with barbershop-stripe poles to which two gondolas are tethered; and the Romanesque columns, Byzantine mosaics, Gothic arches, and stone walls that have all been carefully antiqued. Mediterranean plants such as grapevines, kumquat, and olive trees add verisimilitude. Shops sell Venetian beads and glasswork, leather purses and belts, olive oils, pastas, and Perugina cookies and chocolate kisses. At Tutto Italia Ristorante, cuisine is from several regions of Italy— Italian wines, handmade mozzarella, and freshly made breads are featured. Limited outdoor dining beneath umbrellas is lovely.

GERMANY

Germany, a make-believe village that distills the best folk architecture from all over that country, is so jovial that you practically expect the Seven Dwarfs to come "heigh-ho"-ing out to meet you. Instead, you'll hear the hourly chimes from the specially designed glockenspiel on the clock tower, musical toots and tweets from multitudinous cuckoo clocks, folk tunes from the spinning dolls and plush lambs sold at Der Teddybär, and the satisfied grunts of hungry visitors chowing down on hearty German cooking. The Biergarten's wonderful buffet serves several sausage varieties, as well as sauerkraut, spaetzle, and roasted potatoes, rotisserie chicken, and German breads, all accompanied by yodelers, dancers, and other lederhosen-clad musicians who perform a year-round Oktoberfest show. There are also shops aplenty, including Die Weihnachts Ecke (the Christmas Corner), which sells nutcrackers and other Christmas ornaments; Volkskunst, with a folk-crafts collection

BLITZ TOUR

BEST OF THE PARK

Plan to arrive in the parking lot 30 minutes before the official park opening. Decide ahead of time whether you want to begin with the high-octane thrills of **Mission: SPACE** or with the remarkable but not stomach-churning high of **Soarin'**. As soon as you pass through the turnstile race over to either **Mission: SPACE** or **Soarin'** and wait in line to ride or get a Fastpass appointment. Afterward, choose either the East or West Future World track to continue.

East Track: After Mission: SPACE, either ride or pick up a Fastpass to return later for **Test Track**. Then backtrack to **Spaceship Earth**. Upon leaving Spaceship Earth, head to Soarin'.

West Track: After **Soarin'** at the Land pavilion, take the **Living with the Land** boat ride, then proceed to the **Seas with Nemo & Friends**; if the wait is long, plan to return when the masses have migrated to the World Showcase. At the **Imagination!** pavilion, get another Fastpass ticket for *Honey, I Shrunk the Audience*. Visit **Journey into Imagination with Figment,** and if you have time left, meander through Image Works before returning to Honey, I Shrunk the Audience.

Head counterclockwise into the World Showcase, toward **Canada,** while everyone else is hoofing it toward Mexico. If it's lunchtime, you may be able to get a table right away at **Le Cellier Steakhouse,** one of Epcot's lesser-known dining gems. Then try to catch a performance of the World Showcase Players or British Invasion in the United Kingdom before crossing the bridge into **France**, where you can snap up an éclair or Napoleon at **Boulangerie Pâtisserie.** Shop in Morocco and Japan; then see the **American Adventure Show,** timing it to a Voices of Liberty performance. If there are lines at **Norway** by the time you get there, grab a Fastpass for the Maelstrom ride, then head for **Innoventions, Ellen's Energy Adventure** at the Universe of Energy, or one of the greatest hits like **Soarin'** or the **Seas with Nemo & Friends** that you may have missed earlier due to long lines.

Now's the time to head back to Norway and Maelstrom, followed by an early dinner at France, Italy, Mexico, or another inviting spot. See any attractions or shows that you missed, remembering that parts of Future World sometimes close ahead of the rest of the park. Stick around for **IllumiNations,** and stake out a spot early by the lagoon wall at Italy, on the International Gateway Bridge between France and the United Kingdom, or at an outdoor U.K. table. Make sure the wind is to your back so fireworks and special effects smoke don't waft your way and obscure the scene. Take your time on the way out—the park seems especially magical after dark.

ON RAINY DAYS

Although attractions at Future World are largely indoors, Epcot's expansiveness and the largely outdoor attractions of the World Showcase make the park a poor choice on rainy days. Still, if you can't go another day, bring a poncho and muddle through.

that includes cuckoo clocks ranging from hummingbird scale to the size of an eagle; and Glas und Porzellan, one of only eight outlets in the world to carry a complete collection of M.I. Hummel figurines.

NEED A BREAK? Bratwurst and cold beer from the **Sommerfest cart**, at the entrance of the Biergarten restaurant, make a perfect quick and hearty lunch, while the soft pretzels and strudel are ever-popular snacks. There's not much seating, so you may have to eat on the run.

The **Saluting Africa–Outpost**, between Germany and China, isn't one of the 11 World Showcase pavilions, but kids love to test their drumming skills on bongos and other drums that invite players to improvise their own African folklore performances. Village Traders sells African handicrafts and—you guessed it—souvenirs relating to *The Lion King*. Buy an ice cream or frozen yogurt at the Refreshment Outpost and enjoy the break at a table by the lagoon. A cool mist is set up to offer respite on hot days.

CHINA

A shimmering red-and-gold, three-tier replica of Beijing's Temple of Heaven towers over a serene Chinese garden, an art gallery displaying treasures from the People's Republic, a spacious emporium devoted to Chinese goods, and two restaurants. The gardens, planted with a native Chinese tallow tree, water lilies, bamboo, and a 100-year-old weeping mulberry tree, are one of the most peaceful spots in the World Showcase. Piped-in traditional Chinese music flows gently over the peaceful hush of the gardens, which come alive with applause and cheers when the remarkable Dragon Legend Acrobats tumble into a roped-off area for their breathtaking act. China's popular Nine Dragons Restaurant reopened recently with a redesigned dining room, new costumes for servers, and new menu items including shrimp summer rolls, Chinese chicken salad, and salt-and-pepper shrimp with spinach noodles.

NEED A BREAK? The **Lotus Blossom Café** is beautifully decorated and offers some authentic Chinese tastes, no reservation required. Pot stickers, soups, and egg rolls are popular; new among finger foods is the Rou Jia Mo, a Chinese-style beef sandwich. Entrées include Beijing-style barbecue chicken and garden vegetables and tofu stir-fry. The new **Joy of Tea** outdoor cart serves hot and cold tea, plus trendy green tea frozen drinks and plum wine.

REFLECTIONS OF CHINA
Duration: 19 min.
Crowds: Steady from World Showcase opening through late afternoon, but the theater's high capacity means you can usually get into the next show.

Strategy: Go anytime.

Audience: All ages, but no strollers permitted, and small children have to be held aloft to see.

Rating: ★★★

Think of the Temple of Heaven as an especially fitting theater for a movie in which sensational panoramas of the land and people are dramatically portrayed on a 360-degree CircleVision screen. Highlights include striking footage of Hong Kong, Shanghai, and Macao. This may be the best of the World Showcase films—the only drawback is that the theater has no chairs; lean rails are provided.

NORWAY

Among the rough-hewn timbers and sharply pitched roofs here—softened and brightened by bloom-stuffed window boxes and figured shutters—are lots of smiling young Norwegians, all eager to speak English and show off their country. The pavilion complex contains a 14th-century, fortresslike castle that mimics Oslo's Akershus, cobbled streets, rocky waterfalls, and a stave church modeled after one built in 1250, with wood dragons glaring from the eaves. The church houses an exhibit called "To the Ends of the Earth," which uses vintage artifacts to tell the story of two early-20th-century polar expeditions. It all puts you in the mood for the pavilion's shops, which sell spears, shields, and other Viking necessities. At the restaurant, Akershus, breakfast is served. Visit the Norwegian *koldtbord* (buffet) for smoked salmon, fruit, and pastries, followed by a family-style hot breakfast of eggs, meats, and other treats served at the table. For lunch and dinner, you'll find cold dishes like chilled shrimp, salads, and cheeses on the traditional *koldtbord* ; hot entrées served at the table may include glazed salmon, lamb stew, or a traditional ground beef and pork patty called kjottkake. The restaurant is the only one in the park where you can have breakfast, lunch, or dinner with Disney princesses, including Aurora, Belle, and Snow White. You can reserve up to 90 days in advance, and we recommend booking as early as possible. However, you can always check at Guest Services for seats left by cancellations.

NEED A BREAK? You can order smoked salmon and other open-face sandwiches, plus Norwegian Ringnes beer at **Kringla Bakeri Og Kafe**. The pastries here are worth the stop. Go early or late for speediest service and room to sit in the outdoor seating area.

MAELSTROM

Duration: 10 min.

Crowds: Steady, with slow-moving lines from late morning through early evening.

Strategy: Grab a Fastpass appointment so you can return after lunch or dinner.

Audience: All ages.

Rating: ★★

In Norway's dandy boat ride, you pile into a 16-passenger, dragon-headed longboat for a voyage through time that, despite its scary name

and encounters with evil trolls, is actually more interesting than frightful. The journey begins in a 10th-century village, where a boat, much
like the ones used by Eric the Red, is being readied for a Viking voyage.
You glide steeply up through a mythical forest populated by trolls, who
cause the boat to plunge backward down a mild waterfall, then cruise
amid the grandeur of the Geiranger fjord. Then you experience a storm
in the North Sea and, as the presence of oil rigs signals the 20th century,
end up in a peaceful coastal village. Disembarking, you proceed into a
theater for a quick and delightful film about Norway's scenic wonders,
culture, and people.

AGE OF THE VIKING SHIP
Duration: As long as you want.
Crowds: Not that bad.
Strategy: Go anytime.
Audience: Toddlers and elementary-school-age children.
Rating: ★★

Children adore this replica of a Viking ship, an interactive playground
filled with ropes and climbing adventures from bow to stern.

MEXICO

Housed in a spectacular Maya pyramid surrounded by dense tropical
plantings and brilliant blossoms, Mexico welcomes you onto a "moonlit" plaza that contains the Gran Fiesta Tour boat ride, an exhibit of
pre-Columbian art, a very popular restaurant, and, of course, shopping
kiosks where you can unload many, many pesos.

Modeled on the market in the town of Taxco, Plaza de los Amigos is
well named: there are lots of friendly people—the women dressed in
ruffled off-the-shoulder peasant blouses and bright skirts, the men in
white shirts and dashing sashes—all eager to sell you trinkets from a
cluster of canopied carts. The perimeter is rimmed with stores with tile
roofs, wrought-iron balconies, and flower-filled window boxes. What
to buy? Brightly colored paper blossoms, sombreros, baskets, pottery,
leather goods, and colorful papier-mâché piñatas, which Epcot imports
by the truckload.

One of the pavilion's key attractions is the San Angel Inn Restaurante,
featuring traditional Mexican cuisine, wine and beer, and overlooking
the faux "moonlit" waterway traversed by Gran Fiesta Tour boats. At
this writing, a new tequila bar is slated to open in fall 2010 next to the
San Angel Inn, and the more casual, outdoor Cantina de San Angel is
expected to expand along the World Showcase Lagoon with more seating for diners eager to sample a new menu of Mexican treats.

GRAN FIESTA TOUR STARRING THE THREE CABALLEROS
Duration: 9 min.
Crowds: Moderate, slow-moving lines expected from late morning
through late afternoon.
Strategy: Because the ride has been updated and rethemed, it's probably
worth a visit, especially if you have small children, who usually enjoy
the novelty of a boat ride.

Audience: All ages.
Rating: ★★

Donald Duck goes to Mexico in this fresher, lighter version of the original El Rio del Tiempo ride, which was basically a floating travelogue. In this attraction—which shines with the polish of enhanced facades, sound system, and boat-ride props—Donald teams with old pals Jose Carioca (the parrot) and Panchito (the Mexican charro rooster) from the 1944 Disney film *The Three Caballeros*. The *Gran Fiesta Tour* film sweeps you along for an animated jaunt as the caballeros are reunited for a grand performance in Mexico City. Donald manages to disappear for his own tour of the country, leaving Jose and Panchito to search for their missing comrade.

ENTERTAINMENT AND FIREWORKS

Some of the most enjoyable entertainment takes place outside the pavilions and along the promenade. Live shows with actors, dancers, singers, mime routines, and demonstrations of folk arts and crafts are presented at varying times of day; get times in your Epcot Times Guide. Or look for signs posted at the pavilions. The **World Showcase Players** of Italy and the United Kingdom, plus U.K.'s **British Invasion**, Morocco's **Mo' Rockin'**, Mexico's **Mariachi Cobre,** and China's incredible **Dragon Legend Acrobats** keep audiences coming back.

A group that calls itself the **JAMMitors** plays up a storm several days during the week (check the Times Guide) at various Future World locations, using the tools of the janitorial trade—garbage cans, wastebaskets, brooms, mops, and dustpans. If you hear drumming from the vicinity of Japan, scurry on over to watch the **Matsuriza** Taiko drummers in action. And the American Adventure's **Spirit of America Fife & Drum Corps** will take you back a few hundred years with a patriotic nod to the birth of a nation.

ILLUMINATIONS: REFLECTIONS OF EARTH

Fodor'sChoice **Duration:** 13 min.
★ **Crowds:** Heavy.
Strategy: For best views (and if you have young children), find your place 45 min in advance.
Audience: All ages.
Rating: ★★★

The marvelous nighttime spectacular takes place over the World Showcase Lagoon every night before closing. Be sure to stick around for the lasers, lights, fireworks, fountains, and music that fill the air over the water. Although there's generally good viewing from all around the lagoon, some of the best spots are in front of the Italy pavilion, on the bridge between France and the United Kingdom, on the promenade in front of Canada, at the World Showcase Plaza, and on the bridge between China and Germany, which will give you a clear shot, unobstructed by trees. After the show, concealed loudspeakers play the theme music manipulated into salsa, polka, waltz, and even—believe it or not—Asian rhythms.

DISABILITIES AND ACCESSIBILITY

Accessibility standards in this park are high. Many attractions and most restaurants and shops are fully wheelchair accessible. The *Guidebook for Guests with Disabilities* lays out services and facilities available and includes information about companion restrooms. Call **WDW Information** (☎*407/824–4321 or 407/939–7807, 407/827–5141 TTY*) a few weeks in advance if you want to arrange sign-language interpretation on a day not scheduled. The guidebook, assistive listening systems, video captioning equipment, handheld captioning devices, Braille and audio guides, and sign-language interpretation schedules are available in the park at Guest Services Be sure to ask for the special guide map for guests with disabilities. It's filled with accessibility details and shows which attractions have reflective captioning and compatibility with all the devices available. Devices require a deposit, but no fee. Closed-captioning is available on TV monitors at attractions that have pre-shows. Large Braille maps of the park are near the Guest Services lobby in Future World and International Gateway, and also to the left of the walkway from Future World to the World Showcase Plaza.

At Future World, to go on the **Spaceship Earth Ride,** you must be able to walk four steps and transfer to a vehicle; in the unusual case that emergency evacuation may be necessary, it's by way of stairs. Service animals shouldn't be taken on this ride. Although much of the enchantment is in the visual details, the narration is interesting as well. **Innoventions** is completely wheelchair accessible—some exhibits inside this always-evolving attraction may require transferring from a wheelchair. **Universe of Energy** is accessible to guests using standard wheelchairs and those who can transfer to them. Because this is one of the attractions that has sound tracks amplified by rental personal translator units, it's slightly more interesting to those with hearing impairments than to those with visual impairments.

At **Test Track,** one TV monitor in the preshow area is closed-captioned for people with hearing impairments. Visitors in wheelchairs are provided a special area where they can practice transferring into the ride vehicle before actually boarding the high-speed ride. **Mission: SPACE** also requires a transfer from wheelchair to seat. In the **Seas with Nemo & Friends,** guests in standard wheelchairs can wheel onto an accessible "clamshell" vehicle; those in electronic scooters must be able to transfer to a standard wheelchair or the ride vehicle; guests using wheelchairs also have access to the aquarium area and shows like Turtle Talk with Crush.

In the **Land, Circle of Life** and the greenhouse tour are completely wheelchair accessible. "Reflective captioning," in which captions are displayed at the bottom of glass panes mounted on stands, is available at the Circle of Life. If you can read lips, you'll enjoy the greenhouse tour. As for the **Living with the Land** boat ride, those using an oversize wheelchair or a scooter must transfer to a Disney chair. And in the new **Soarin'** riders must transfer from their wheelchairs to the ride system. Guests who wish to board the **Journey into Imagination with Figment** ride can remain in their wheelchairs. The theater that screens *Honey, I*

Shrunk the Audience is completely accessible, although you must transfer to a theater seat to experience some of the special effects. The preshow area has one TV monitor that is closed-captioned. The hands-on activities of **Image Works** have always been wheelchair accessible and should continue to be.

WORD OF MOUTH

"We love both the Coral Reef and either of the French restaurants. Save room for desert and grab one from the French pastry shop. If you go to the Coral Reef, request a seat by the tank."
–LindaLa

At World Showcase, most people stroll about, but there are also Friendship boats, which require those using oversize wheelchairs or scooters to transfer to Disney chairs; **American Adventure, France, China,** and **Canada** are all wheelchair accessible; personal translator units amplify the sound tracks here. **Germany, Italy, Japan, Morocco,** and the **United Kingdom** all have live entertainment, most with strong aural as well as visual elements; the plaza areas where the shows are presented are wheelchair accessible. In **Norway** you must be able to step down into and up out of a boat to ride the Maelstrom, and an emergency evacuation requires the use of stairs; service animals are not allowed. In **Mexico** the Gran Fiesta Tour boat ride is accessible to guests using wheelchairs, but those using a scooter or oversize chair must transfer to a Disney model.

During **IllumiNations,** certain areas along the lagoon's edge at Showcase Plaza, Canada, and Germany are reserved for guests using wheelchairs. Arrive at least 45 minutes before show time to stake out a spot.

EATING IN EPCOT

In World Showcase every pavilion sponsors at least one and often two or even three eateries. Where there's a choice, it's usually between a full-service restaurant with commensurately higher prices; a more affordable, ethnic fast-food spot; and carts and shops selling snacks ranging from French pastries to Japanese ices—whatever's appropriate to the pavilion. France has two full-service restaurants; Chefs de France is open for lunch and dinner; Bistro de Paris opens for dinner only. Lunch and dinner reservations usually are essential at the full-service restaurants; you can make them up to 180 days in advance by calling ☎407/939–3463 or going in person to Guest Services at the park (only on the day of the meal) or to the restaurants themselves when they open for lunch, usually at noon. Some of these rival Orlando's best dining options.

In Future World a large fast-food emporium, **Electric Umbrella,** dominates the Innoventions East Plaza area. The fare here is chicken sandwiches, burgers, and salads. At the Land's **Garden Grill,** you can eat solid American family-style dinner fare as the restaurant revolves, giving you an ever-changing view of each biome on the boat ride. Besides the Princess dining in Norway, this is the only Epcot restaurant that includes mealtime Disney character meet-and-greets—here, Chip 'n'

Dale are your hosts. **Sunshine Seasons** in the Land is a food court with healthful Asian-inspired cuisine, including sushi, as well as souped-up salads and inspired sandwiches. The Seas with Nemo & Friends' **Coral Reef** serves excellent seafood in addition to chicken, steak, and special kids' entrées; one of its walls is made entirely of glass and looks directly into the attraction's 5.7-million-gallon aquarium full of interesting critters. Recent changes and enhancements to restaurants in Italy, China, and Japan pavilions have kicked up meal options several notches; all are worth considering for a solid dining experience. *See Chapter 11, Where to Eat, for full descriptions of Epcot restaurants.*

GUIDED TOURS

Reserve with **WDW Tours** (☎407/ 939–8687) up to six weeks in advance for a behind-the-scenes tour, led by a knowledgeable Disney cast member. Don't forget to ask about tour discounts; some companies, such as Visa, offer them. Several tours give close-up views of the phenomenal detail involved in the planning and maintenance of Epcot. Tours are open only to those 16 years of age and over (proof of age is required) unless otherwise noted.

The UnDISCOVERed Future World ($55, plus park admission) leaves at 9 AM Monday, Wednesday, and Friday from the Guest Services lobby just inside Epcot's main entrance. The four-hour behind-the-scenes walking tour covers all Future World pavilions, some VIP lounges, and includes peeks at backstage areas such as the barge marina where Disney stores its IllumiNations show equipment. Take the three-hour **Gardens of the World Tour** ($59, plus park admission) to see the World Showcase's realistic replicas of exotic plantings up close and to get tips for adding landscape magic to your own garden. The tour runs on Tuesday and Thursday at 9 AM, plus Saturday during the Epcot International Flower & Garden Festival from mid-March to late May or early June.

Ever since the Segway Human Transporters (featured at Innoventions) became a novelty, a number of Disney employees have used them for speedy transportation around the park's World Showcase. Curious guests can now take their own two-hour Segway guided tour, called the **Around the World at Epcot Tour,** daily at 7:45, 8:30, 9, or 9:30 AM. Billed as "the world's first self-balancing, electric-powered personal transportation device," the Segway takes only a brief training session to master. Once you've learned the moves and strapped on your helmet, you can cruise with the group from one World Showcase country to the next. The tour begins at Guest Services ($95, park admission required).

EPCOT

NAME	Min. Height	Type of Entertainment	Duration	Suits	Crowds	Strategy
Future World						
Ellen's Energy Adventure (Universe of Energy)	n/a	ride	30 min.	All	ok	Best seats are to the far left and front of the theater.
★ *Honey, I Shrunk the Audience* (Imagination!)	n/a	show	18 min.	All	Yes!	Go in the early morning or just before closing. Take off the 3-D glasses if little kids get scared.
Innoventions	n/a	walk through	Up to you.	3 and up	at displays	Go before 10 am or after 2 pm.
Journey into Imagination with Figment (Imagination!)	n/a	ride	8 min.	5 and up	Fast lines	Ride while waiting for Honey, I Shrunk the Audience Fastpass. Toddlers may be scared by darkness and scanner at the end of the ride.
Living with the Land (The Land)	n/a	boat	4 min.	Teens	ok	The line moves quickly, so go anytime.
Mission: SPACE	44"	thrill ride	4 min.	8 and up	Heavy	Get there before 10 am or use Fastpass. Don't ride on a full stomach.
★ Soarin' (The Land)	40"	sim. ride	5 min.	5 and up	Heavy	Go early, use Fastpass, or just before park closing.
Spaceship Earth	n/a	ride	15 min.	All	Morning	Ride while waiting for Mission: SPACE or just before closing.
Test Track	40"	thrill ride	5 min.	5 and up	Heavy	Go in morning with Fastpass. The ride can't function on wet tracks, so don't go after a downpour.

The Circle of Life (The Land)	n/a	film	20 min.	All	Steady	Go early or for your toddler's afternoon nap.
The Seas with Nemo & Friends	n/a	ride, film, interactive exhibits	Up to you	All	Heavy	Get Nemo fans here early in the morning.
World Showcase						
Age of the Viking Ship	n/a	play area	Up to you	3 and up	ok	Go anytime.
America Gardens Theatre	n/a	show	Varies	Varies	Varies	Arrive 30 min. to 1 hr. ahead of time for holiday and celebrity performances.
Gran Fiesta Tour Starring the Three Caballeros	n/a	boat	9 min.	All	Moderate	Good if you have small children.
Impressions de France	n/a	film	18 min.	7 and up	Steady	Come after dinner.
Maelstrom	n/a	thrill ride	10 min.	All	Steady	Use Fastpass for after lunch or dinner.
O Canada!	n/a	film	17 min.	All	late afternoon	Go when World Showcase opens or in the evening. No strollers permitted.
Reflections of China	n/a	film	19 min.	All	Yes!	Go anytime. No strollers permitted.
The American Adventure Show	n/a	show	30 min.	All	Fast lines	Arrive 10 min. before the Voices of Liberty or the Spirit of America Fife & Drum Corps are slated to perform.

★ = Fodor$Choice

3

If you want to get into the swim—and you have documentation of your scuba open-water adult certification—try the Seas with Nemo & Friends' **Epcot Divequest** ($175, park admission not required or included). Discounts may be available. Guests of divers who want to watch must pay admission. The tours last three hours and, under the supervision of one of the Seas with Nemo & Friends' master divers, you can spend 40 minutes underwater in the mammoth aquarium. The tours take place daily at either 4:30 or 5:30. Guests 10 and up must have scuba certification and children under 17 must be accompanied by a parent or legal guardian. **Dolphins in Depth** ($175, neither park admission nor diving certification required) is an experience that encourages interaction with your favorite water friends. Tour officials meet you at the entrance at 9:45, where you'll be escorted to the Seas with Nemo & Friends pavilion. Tours run weekdays and last about three hours; you'll still need to pay park admission if you want to remain after the tour. Participants must be 13 or older; anyone under 18 must be accompanied by a participating parent or legal guardian.

The **Epcot Seas Aqua Tour** ($140, no park admission required or included) is designed for nondivers who want to get in with the fish. You wear a flotation device and diving gear, but you remain at the surface. Anyone age 8 and older can join the tour (those ages 8–11 must have a parent or legal guardian participating); tours are limited to 12 guests. The tour meets daily at 12:30 and runs about 2½ hours, with 30 minutes spent in the water. **Behind the Seeds at Epcot** is a one-hour tour of the Land pavilion's greenhouses. It costs $16 for ages 10 and up, $12 for ages 3–9. Park admission is required.

A seasonal tour that holiday fans will enjoy is **Yuletide Fantasy,** a 3½-hour visit through the theme parks and several resorts to see how Disney's elves weave decorations and holiday traditions throughout the 40-square-mi property. One day it's a tropical paradise, the next it's a winter wonderland. The $69 tour departs daily during December at 9 AM from Epcot and is for those 16 and older.

Disney's Hollywood Studios

WORD OF MOUTH

"It's not a marathon, remember to relax and enjoy your surroundings. While I think newbies going to DW should definitely have done research and have a plan in place, too often I think visitors get caught up in seeing x number things and it almost becomes an exercise in crossing things off their list. No one hands out awards for most things seen."
—klam_chowder

"A short list of must-dos to us would include: the stunt driving show, MuppetVision, Tower of Terror, Fantasmic (night show)."
—DancingBearMD

Updated by
Jennie Hess

The park's old-time Hollywood ambience begins with a rosy-hue view of the moviemaking business presented in a dreamy stage set from the 1930s and '40s, amid sleek Art Moderne buildings in pastel colors, funky diners, kitschy decorations, and sculptured gardens populated by roving actors playing, well, roving actors, as well as casting directors, gossip columnists, and other colorful characters.

When Michael Eisner opened the then named Disney–MGM Studios in May 1989, he welcomed attendees to "the Hollywood that never was and always will be." Attending the lavish, Hollywood-style opening were celebrities that included Bette Midler, Warren Beatty, and other Tinseltown icons. Disney explains the recent name change as a way to "better reflect not only the Golden Age of Tinseltown, but all that today's Hollywood has to offer in movies, music, theater, and television."

Unlike the first movie theme park—Universal Studios in Southern California—Disney–MGM Studios combined Disney detail with MGM's motion-picture legacy and Walt Disney's own animated film classics. The park was designed to be a trip back in time to Hollywood's heyday, when Hedda Hopper, not tabloids, spread celebrity gossip and when the girl off the bus from Ohio could be the next Judy Garland. The result blends a theme park with movie and television production capabilities, breathtaking rides with insightful tours, and nostalgia with high-tech wonders. In a savvy effort to grab a big piece of the pop-culture pie, Disney opened its own *American Idol* attraction in late 2008. Performers with the most votes compete in an end-of-day finale that guarantees the winner a place in the TV show's regional audition process.

Thanks to a rich library of film scores, the park is permeated with music, all familiar, all uplifting, all evoking the magic of the movies, and all constantly streaming from the camouflaged loudspeakers at a volume just right for humming along. The park icon, a 122-foot-high Sorcerer Mickey Hat that serves as a gift shop and Disney pin-trading station, towers over Hollywood Boulevard. Unfortunately, the whimsical landmark blocks the view of the park's Chinese Theater, a more nostalgic introduction to old-time Hollywood. Watching over all from the park's back lot is the Earful Tower, a 13-story water tower adorned with giant mouse ears.

The park is divided into sightseeing clusters. Hollywood Boulevard is the main artery to the heart of the park, where you find the glistening red-and-gold replica of Graumann's Chinese Theater. Encircling it in a roughly counterclockwise fashion are Sunset Boulevard, the Animation Courtyard, Pixar Place, Commissary Lane, the Streets of America area, and Echo Lake.

The entire park is small enough—about 154 acres, and with fewer than 20 major attractions, as opposed to the more than 40 in the Magic Kingdom—that you should be able to cover it in a day and even repeat a favorite ride.

Numbers in the margin correspond to points of interest on the Disney's Hollywood Studios map.

GETTING THERE AND AROUND

If you're staying at one of the Epcot resorts (the BoardWalk, Yacht Club, Beach Club, Swan, or Dolphin), getting here on a motor launch that leaves from one of several boat docks is part of the fun. Disney resort buses will deposit you at the park's front entrance. If you're staying off property, it costs $12 to park in the lot, but you can use that same parking ticket to visit another Disney park later in the day if you have the stamina. Once the turnstiles open at 9 AM, make a beeline for the Hollywood Junction information window at the corner of Hollywood and Sunset if you need to make same-day dining reservations. Distances are short inside the Studios, and walking is the only way to get around unless you use a wheelchair or motor-powered chair.

4

BASIC SERVICES

BABY CARE

At the small **Baby Care Center,** you'll find facilities for nursing and changing infants and/or toddlers. Formula, baby food, pacifiers, and disposable diapers are for sale next door at Movieland and also at Oscar's Super Service. There are also diaper-changing areas in all women's rooms and some men's rooms.

FIRST AID

First Aid is in the Entrance Plaza adjoining Guest Services (aka Guest Relations).

CAMERAS AND FILM

Walk through the aperture-shaped door of **Darkroom** (or **Cover Story,** the shop next door—the two are connected) on Hollywood Boulevard, where you can buy memory cards, film, and disposable cameras. You can even have a cast member download your memory card onto a CD for $11.99 plus tax. If a Disney photographer takes your picture in front of the Chinese Theater, for example, or with Mickey Mouse on Sunset Boulevard, be sure to pick up a **Disney PhotoPass,** which will allow you to see the pictures online before or after you return home. You can purchase prints ($16.95 for an 8" × 10" photo; other sizes available), at the park or from home if you like.

INFORMATION

Guest Services is just inside the turnstiles on the left side of the Entrance Plaza.

At the corner where Hollywood Boulevard intersects with Sunset Boulevard is the **Studios Tip Board,** a large board with constantly updated information about attractions' wait times—reliable except for those

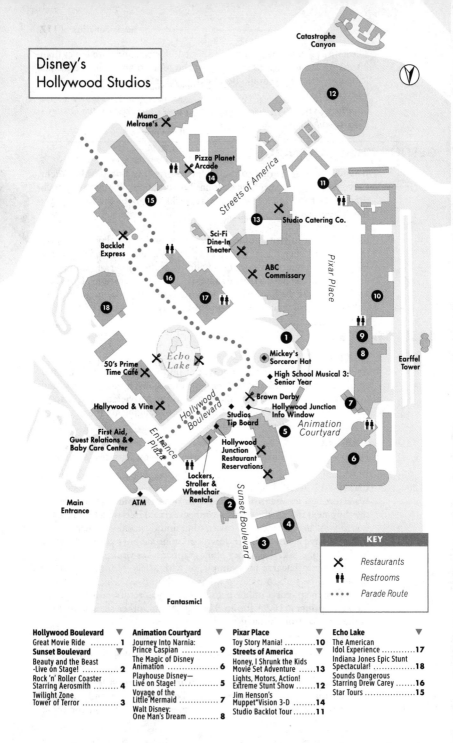

Disney's Hollywood Studios

Catastrophe Canyon

12

Mama Melrose's ✕

Pizza Planet Arcade ✕
14

11

Streets of America

15

13 **Studio Catering Co.** ✕

Backlot Express ✕

Sci-Fi Dine-In Theater

16

ABC Commissary ✕

Pixar Place

18

17

10

Echo Lake

1

9

8

Mickey's Sorcerer Hat

Earffel Tower

50's Prime Time Café ✕

◆ **High School Musical 3: Senior Year**

✕ **Brown Derby**

7

Hollywood & Vine ✕

Hollywood Boulevard

◆ **Studios Tip Board**

Hollywood Junction Info Window

5

Animation Courtyard

First Aid, Guest Relations & Baby Care Center ◆

Entrance Plaza

Hollywood Junction Restaurant Reservations

6

Lockers, Stroller & Wheelchair Rentals

Main Entrance

ATM

2

Sunset Boulevard

4

3

Fantasmic!

KEY

✕	*Restaurants*
🚻	*Restrooms*
• • • •	*Parade Route*

TIP SHEET

■ It's best to go to Disney's Hollywood Studios—like Epcot—early in the week, while most other people are rushing through Disney's Animal Kingdom and the Magic Kingdom.

■ Plan to arrive in the parking lot 30 minutes ahead of opening, so you can get to the entrance 15 minutes ahead.

■ Check the tip board periodically for attractions with short wait times that you can visit between Fastpass appointments.

■ Be at the Fantasmic! amphitheater at least 60 minutes before show time; if you booked the Fantasmic! dinner package, you can show up a bit later.

■ If you plan to have a fast-food lunch, try to eat early or late. The Studios' counter-service places get especially packed between 11 and 2:30.

■ Set up a rendezvous point and time at the start of the day, just in case you and your companions get separated. Two excellent spots are by the giant Sorcerer Mickey Hat and at an outdoor table in front of the Starring Rolls Café near the intersection of Hollywood and Sunset.

moments when everyone follows the "See It Now!" advice, and the line immediately triples. Just behind the Tip Board is the Hollywood Junction information window, where you can make dining reservations or get answers to just about any Studios-related question.

LOCKERS

You can rent lockers at Oscar's Super Service, to the right of the entrance plaza after you pass through the turnstiles, or at Crossroads of the World. The cost is $5, with a $5 refundable deposit for the key. Bring your key to the Crossroads location for your refund.

LOST PEOPLE AND THINGS

If you're worried about your children getting lost, get name tags for them at Guest Services, and instruct them to go to a Disney staffer, anyone wearing a name tag, if they can't find you. If the worst happens, ask any cast member before you panic; logbooks of lost children's names are kept at Guest Services.

Guest Services also has a computerized Message Center, where notes can be left for traveling companions at this and other parks. Report any lost or found articles at Guest Services in the Entrance Plaza or call **Disney's Hollywood Studios Lost and Found** (☎*407/560–3720*). Articles lost for more than one day should be sought at the **Main Lost and Found** (✉*Magic Kingdom, Ticket and Transportation Center [TTC]* ☎*407/824–4245*).

PACKAGE PICK-UP

Ask the shop clerk to forward any large purchase you make to Package Pick-Up next to Oscar's Super Service in the Entrance Plaza, so you won't have to carry them around all day. Allow three hours for it to get there.

TOP HOLLYWOOD STUDIOS ATTRACTIONS

FOR AGES 8 AND UP

The American Idol Experience. Rock-star wannabes get their shot at theme-park fame and maybe even a "Dream Ticket" to the American Idol TV show auditions. Show audiences get to vote on the top singers.

Fantasmic! The ultimate battle between good and evil is staged on the moat and island of an outdoor amphitheater. Get ready for a cracking loud, fiery battle that involves water in a most unusual way. Many children under 8 love this show, but toddlers and babies, as well as some sensitive children, are frightened of the loud noises. Performances are twice a week, so check the park's schedule ahead of your visit.

The Magic of Disney Animation. Take a behind-the-scenes look at the making of a Disney animated film; children love the hands-on activities.

Rock 'n' Roller Coaster Starring Aerosmith. Many people think this high-speed, hard-core roller coaster is the best ride at Walt Disney World.

Twilight Zone Tower of Terror. Scare up some nerve and defy gravity inside this haunted hotel. You'd be better off taking the stairs—if there were any to take. As they say, the 13th story is killer.

FOR AGES 7 AND UNDER

Block Party Bash. Get ready for a high-energy, immersive parade where you can play along with the toys from Toy Story, shout it out with Mike and Sully of Monsters, Inc., and dance with Flick and Atta from A Bug's Life. Some floats double as dance stages and trampolines, and the scene hops with acrobats, stilt walkers, and dancers.

Honey I Shrunk the Kids Movie Set Adventure. Preschoolers and gradeschoolers love to romp among the giant blades of grass and bugs at this adorable, creative playground. They can hide inside Lego pieces and slide down a strip of film coming out of a film canister.

Muppet*Vision 3-D. Children shriek with laughter and most adults crack up, too, during this 3-D movie in which Kermit, Miss Piggy, and other lovable Muppets vie for your attention.

Playhouse Disney—Live on Stage! The preschool crowd can't get enough of popular Disney Channel characters from "Mickey Mouse Clubhouse," "Little Einsteins," and "Handy Manny" who show up for the newest version of this hoppin', boppin' kidfest. Streamers, bubbles, and other effects are the icing on this rich party fare.

Voyage of the Little Mermaid. This classic animated film is a kiddie favorite, and seeing Ariel live and in person as she sings "Part of Your World" from her grotto is a kick for fans. Evil Ursula can be a fright, however, for kids who are easily upset.

Beauty and the Beast—Live on Stage! The beloved fairy tale of Belle and her Beast plays out perfectly on the stage with charming performances by Mrs. Potts, Chip, Lumiere, and Cogsworth. Dancing chefs, and a sherbet parfait that transforms into a luminous showgirl, delight the little ones.

STROLLER AND WHEELCHAIR RENTALS

Oscar's Super Service, to the right in the Entrance Plaza, is the place for stroller, wheelchair, and ECV rentals. Single strollers are $15 daily, $13 for multiday rental; double strollers are $31 daily, $27 for multiday rental. Wheelchairs are $10 daily, $8 for multiday rental. Electronic Convenience Vehicles (ECV) are $45 per day plus a refundable $20 security deposit. Neither wheelchairs nor ECVs are reservable, so arrive early to rent them. And while the park's wheelchair supply is generally plentiful, ECV availability is limited. If any of your rentals needs replacing, ask any park cast member.

HOLLYWOOD BOULEVARD

4

With its palm trees, pastel buildings, and flashy neon, Hollywood Boulevard paints a rosy picture of 1930s Tinseltown. There's a sense of having walked right onto a movie set in the olden days, what with the art deco storefronts, strolling brass bands, and roving starlets and nefarious agents—actually costumed actors known as the Citizens of Hollywood. These are frequently joined by characters from Disney movies new and old—from *Mickey Mouse* to *Toy Story* friends—who pose for photos and sign autographs.

NEED A BREAK?

For a sweet burst of energy, snag a freshly baked chocolate chip cookie or a pastry and an espresso at **Starring Rolls Cafe,** at the corner of Hollywood and Sunset near the Brown Derby. Sandwiches are also on the menu here, and outdoor tables offer great people-watching.

GREAT MOVIE RIDE

❶ **Duration:** 22 min.
Crowds: Medium. If it's peak season and the inside lines start spilling out the door, expect at least a 25-min wait.
Strategy: Go while waiting out a Fastpass appointment for another attraction.
Audience: All but young children, for whom it may be too intense.
Rating: ★★★

At the end of Hollywood Boulevard, just behind the Sorcerer Mickey Hat, are the fire-engine-red pagodas of a replica of Graumann's Chinese Theater, where you enter this attraction. The line takes you through the lobby past such noteworthy artifacts as Dorothy's ruby slippers from *The Wizard of Oz,* a carousel horse from *Mary Poppins,* and the piano played by Sam in *Casablanca.* You then shuffle into the preshow area, an enormous screening room with continuously running clips from *Mary Poppins, Raiders of the Lost Ark, Singin' in the Rain, Fantasia, Footlight Parade,* and, of course, *Casablanca.* Once the great red doors swing open, it's your turn to ride.

Disney cast members dressed in 1920s newsboy costumes usher you onto open trams waiting against the backdrop of the Hollywood Hills, and you're off on a tour of cinematic climaxes—with a little help from Audio-Animatronics, scrim, smoke, and Disney magic. First comes the world of musical entertainment with, among others, Gene Kelly clutching that immortal lamppost as he begins "Singin' in the Rain" and Mary Poppins with her umbrella and her sooty admirers reprising "Chim-Chim-Cher-ee." Soon the lights dim, and your vehicle travels into a gangland shoot-out with James Cagney snarling in *Public Enemy.* Gangsters or Western gunslingers (it depends on which tram you board) hijack your tram and whisk you off to a showdown. Soon, you'll be waving at John Wayne on horseback as you escape the line of fire.

Nothing like a little time warp to bring justice. With pipes streaming fog and alarms whooping, the tram meets some of the slimier characters from *Alien*—look up for truly scary stuff—and then eases into the cobwebby, snake-ridden set of *Indiana Jones and the Temple of Doom,* where your hijacker attempts to steal an idol and gets his or her just desserts.

Each time you think you've witnessed the best scene, the tram moves into another set: Tarzan yodels and swings on a vine overhead; then Bogey bids Bergman goodbye with a "Here's looking at you, kid" in front of the plane to Lisbon. The finale has hundreds of robotic Munchkins cheerily enjoining you to "Follow the Yellow Brick Road," despite the cackling imprecations by the Wicked Witch of the West. Remember to check out Dorothy's tornado-tossed house—those on the right side of the tram can just spot the ruby slippers. The tram follows the Yellow Brick Road, and then there it is: a view of the Emerald City before you're brought back to reality.

SUNSET BOULEVARD

This avenue pays tribute to famous Hollywood monuments, with facades derived from the Cathay Circle, the Beverly Wilshire Theatre, and other City of Angels landmarks. As you turn onto Sunset Boulevard from Hollywood Boulevard, you'll notice the Hollywood Junction information window, where reservations can be made for restaurants throughout the park.

NEED A BREAK?

Grab lunch or a quick snack at one of the food stands along Sunset Boulevard. You can get a burger (meat or veggie) or chicken strips at **Rosie's All-American Cafe,** a slice of pizza from **Catalina Eddie's,** a fruit salad from the **Anaheim Produce Company,** or a turkey leg or chili dog at **Toluca Legs Turkey Company.** Grab a sweet treat at **Hollywood Scoops Ice Cream,** where you can get two scoops in a cone or cup; for the diet conscious, there's fat-free, sugar-free vanilla.

BEAUTY AND THE BEAST—LIVE ON STAGE!

❷ **Duration:** 30 min.
Crowds: Almost always.
Strategy: Line up at least 30 min prior to showtime for good seats, especially with children. Performance times vary from day to day, so check ahead.

CLOSE UP

15 Romantic Things to Do at the Parks

Not everything at Disney World involves children. Let the kids have fun at one of Disney's resort kids' clubs or get a babysitter (available for a fee through Kid's Nite Out) and enjoy some private time, just the two of you.

1. Dress up and make dinner a very special occasion at the truly grand Victoria & Albert's restaurant in the Grand Floridian. Remember to make a reservation three months in advance.

2. Share expertly crafted sushi before dinner and perfectly paired wines at the California Grill on the top floor of Disney's Contemporary Resort. Watch the sun set over the Seven Seas Lagoon, or see the Magic Kingdom fireworks from your seat or the restaurant's outdoor viewing spot.

3. Rent a boat for a cruise on the Seven Seas Lagoon or the waterways leading to it. Bring champagne and glasses.

4. Take a nighttime whirl on Cinderella's Golden Carrousel in Fantasyland. Sparkling lights make it magical.

5. Have your picture taken and grab a kiss in the heart-shaped gazebo in the back of Minnie's Country House.

6. Plan a day of couples pampering at the Grand Floridian Spa.

7. Buy a faux diamond ring at the Emporium on Main Street in the Magic Kingdom. Propose to your sweetheart at your favorite spot in the World.

8. Hold hands and share the wonder of the surreal Cirque du Soleil show La Nouba at Downtown Disney West Side.

9. Sit by the fountain in front of Epcot's France pavilion and share a pastry and café au lait.

10. Have a drink at the cozy Crew's Cup Lounge in the Yacht Club hotel.

11. Stroll the BoardWalk. Play croquet. Watch IllumiNations from the bridge to the Yacht and Beach Club. Then boogie at the Atlantic Dance Hall.

12. Tie the knot all over again at the Wedding Pavilion or during an intimate ceremony on one of Disney's beaches. Invite Mickey and Minnie to the reception.

13. Rent a hot-air balloon for a magical tour of Walt Disney World.

14. Take a golf lesson with one of Disney's pros, then enjoy time together on one of the resort's lushly land-scaped courses.

15. Enjoy a British lager outside at Epcot's Rose & Crown Pub—a perfect IllumiNations viewing spot. Book ahead and ask for a table with a view.

4

Audience: All ages.
Rating: ★★★

This wildly popular stage show takes place at the Theater of the Stars, a re-creation of the famed Hollywood Bowl. The long-running production is a lively, colorful, and well-done condensation of the animated film. As you arrive or depart, it's fun to check out handprints and footprints set in concrete of the television celebrities who've visited Disney's Hollywood Studios.

TWILIGHT ZONE TOWER OF TERROR

3 **Duration:** 10 min.
Crowds: Yes!
Strategy: Get a Fastpass reserved-time ticket. Otherwise, go early or wait until evening, when the crowds thin out.
Audience: Older children and adults. No pregnant women or guests with heart, back, or neck problems. Minimum height: 40".
Rating: ★★★

Ominously overlooking Sunset Boulevard is a 13-story structure that was once the Hollywood Tower Hotel, now deserted. You take an eerie stroll through an overrun, mist-enshrouded garden and then into the dimly lighted lobby. In the dust-covered library a bolt of lightning suddenly zaps a television set to life. Rod Serling appears, recounting the story of the hotel's demise and inviting you to enter the Twilight Zone. Then, it's onward to the boiler room, where you climb aboard the hotel's giant elevator ride. As you head upward past seemingly empty hallways, ghostly former residents appear in front of you. The Fifth Dimension awaits, where you travel forward past recognizable scenes from the popular TV series. Suddenly—faster than you can say "Where's Rod Serling?"—the creaking vehicle plunges downward in a terrifying, 130-foot free-fall drop and then, before you can catch your breath, shoots quickly up, down, up, and down all over again. No use trying to guess how many stomach-churning ups and downs you'll experience—Disney's ride engineers have upped the ride's fright factor by programming random drop variations into the attraction. It's a different thrill every time. As you recover from your final plunge, Serling warns, "The next time you check into a deserted hotel on the dark side of Hollywood, make sure you know what vacancy you'll be filling, or you'll be a permanent member of . . . the Twilight Zone!"

ROCK 'N' ROLLER COASTER STARRING AEROSMITH

4 **Duration:** Preride 2 min; Ride 1 min, 22 seconds.
Crowds: Huge.
Strategy: Ride early in the day, then pick up a Fastpass to go again later, especially if you're visiting with older children or teens.
Audience: Older children, teens, and adults. No guests with heart, back, or neck problems or motion sickness. Minimum height: 48".
Rating: ★★★

Although this is an indoor roller coaster like Space Mountain in the Magic Kingdom, the similarity ends there. With its high-speed launch (0 to 60 in 2.8 seconds), multiple inversions, and loud rock music, it generates delighted screams from coaster junkies, though it's smooth enough and short enough that even the coaster-phobic have been known to enjoy it. The vehicles look like limos, and the track resembles the neck of an electric guitar that's been twisted; a hard-driving rock sound track by Aerosmith blasts from speakers mounted in each vehicle to accentuate the flips and turns. There's rock-and-roll memorabilia in the line area, and Aerosmith stars in the preshow film.

ANIMATION COURTYARD

As you exit Sunset Boulevard, veer right through the high-arched gateway to the Animation Courtyard. Straight ahead are Playhouse Disney—Live on Stage!, the Magic of Disney Animation, and Voyage of the Little Mermaid.

PLAYHOUSE DISNEY—LIVE ON STAGE!

❺ Duration: 22 min.

Crowds: Not a problem, but lines tend to be heavy in mid-afternoon.

Strategy: Go first thing in the morning, when your child is most alert.

Audience: Toddlers, preschoolers.

Rating: ★★★

Playhouse Disney—Live on Stage! is one of the best Walt Disney World shows for children. A cast of Disney Channel characters joins the show's perky, primary-color-clad host on a larger-than-life "storybook stage." Mickey Mouse, Donald Duck, Daisy, and Goofy puppets team up on the "Mickey Mouse Clubhouse" set to prep for a surprise birthday bash for Minnie. As party plans simmer, Handy Manny and his box of tools take the stage for a fix-it project involving a bubble machine—during one viewing, a preschooler tried to storm the stage twice to join Manny and his claw hammer. Next, puppets Leo, Annie, Quincy, and June of the "Little Einsteins" arrive with an animated Rocket and music by Korsakov for a great rocket race with nemesis "Big Jet." Finally, Winnie the Pooh and Tigger become "supersleuths" to rescue Roo's kite trapped high in a tree. Throughout the 22-minute show, preschoolers and even toddlers sing and dance along as the characters cha-cha-cha their way through lively stories laced with lessons ("when you have a problem, think, think, think!"). Floating bubbles, flying confetti, animated effects, and other treats are icing on Minnie's birthday cake.

THE MAGIC OF DISNEY ANIMATION

❻ Duration: About 30 min.

Crowds: Steady all day.

Strategy: Go in the morning or late afternoon, when you can get in with less waiting. If you want to test your talents at the Animation Academy, go straight to that line after the *Drawn to Animation* show and visit the interactive touch-screen zone later.

Audience: All but toddlers, who may be unwilling to sit still for the Animation Academy.

Rating: ★★★

This journey through the Disney animation process is one of the park's most engaging attractions. More than any other backstage peek, this tour truly takes you inside the magic as you follow the many steps of 2-D animation, an art expected to be totally replaced in years to come by computer-generated films such as the Disney/Pixar blockbusters *Toy Story* and *Finding Nemo*. The animation studio was a satellite of Walt Disney's original California studio from 1988 through 2003. It was here that *Brother Bear, Lilo & Stitch,* and *Mulan* were produced, as were several Disney short films and portions of other popular Disney features.

You begin the tour in a small theater with a performance of *Drawn to Animation,* in which a real actor plays the role of an animator interacting with Mushu, the wise-cracking animated character from *Mulan.* Mushu prances between two screens above the stage. In their very funny exchange, the two explain how an animated character evolves from original concept. The animators who actually created the spunky dragon appear on screen to help tell the story. Depending on when you visit, new characters from upcoming Disney films may be introduced near the end of this show.

> **WHO'S THAT GUY?**
>
> Keep an eye out for the wacky "Citizens of Hollywood" characters—detectives, starlets, movie directors, and public works employees—who pop up on Hollywood or Sunset boulevards for impromptu entertainment that usually involves some guest participation.

Next, you enter a creative zone where kiosks of computer touch screens invite you to add color to your favorite characters and even find out which Disney character is most like you (answer a brief quiz and you can't help but smile when you find your animated character double). In the Sound Stage area, your interactive computer lets you choose from four film scenes, then cues you to voice the characters—it's a hoot when you play it back! Watch for popular Disney toon stars to appear in this area for autographs and photos.

The final stop is the Animation Academy, a delightful crash course in how to draw an animated character. Children and adults can sit side-by-side at one of 38 backlighted drafting tables as an artist gives easy-to-follow instructions on drawing a Disney character. Your sketch of Donald Duck (or the character du jour) is your souvenir. As you exit, check out the collection of drawings and cels, the clear celluloid sheets on which the characters were drawn for *Snow White, Fantasia,* and other Disney classics. Here, too, are the actual Academy Awards that Disney has won for its animated films.

VOYAGE OF THE LITTLE MERMAID

❼ **Duration:** 17 min.
Crowds: Perpetual.
Strategy: If you decide not to ride the Rock 'n' Roller Coaster or Tower of Terror, go first thing in the morning, putting the Fastpass to good use. Otherwise, wait until the stroller brigade's exodus after 5.
Audience: All ages, though small children may be frightened by the dark theater and the evil, larger-than-life Ursula.
Rating: ★★★

A boxy building on Mickey Avenue invites you to join Ariel, Sebastian, and the underwater gang in this stage show, which condenses the movie into a marathon presentation of the greatest hits. In an admirable effort at verisimilitude, a fine mist sprays the stage; if you're sitting in the front rows, expect to get spritzed.

WALT DISNEY: ONE MAN'S DREAM

❽ **Duration:** 20 min or longer, depending on your interest in artifacts.
Crowds: Heavy.

Strategy: Get your Fastpass appointment to see one of the high-demand attractions like Rock 'n' Roller Coaster, then see this attraction while waiting.

Audience: Ages 10 and up.

Rating: ★★

Next door to the Mermaid show, One Man's Dream is a photo, film, and audio tour through Walt's life. You get to peek at his Project X room, where many of his successes were born, and hear him tell much of his own story on tapes never before made public. If you qualify as a baby boomer, it's a real nostalgia trip to see Walt resurrected on film as his "Wonderful World of Color" intro splashes across the screen. And if you're into artifacts, there's plenty of Walt memorabilia to view as you absorb the history of this entertainment legend.

4

JOURNEY INTO NARNIA: PRINCE CASPIAN

9 Duration: 15 min.

Crowds: Small and steady.

Strategy: "Narnia" fans should check this out while waiting for a Fastpass appointment elsewhere.

Audience: Ages 5 and up.

Rating: ★

Just after the 2008 motion picture release of *The Chronicles of Narnia: Prince Caspian,* Disney launched this "behind-the-scenes" tour of props, costumes, concept art, and storyboards similar to an earlier presentation promoting *The Lion, The Witch and The Wardrobe.* As you enter, you step inside a faux stone castle interior—standing room only. Four screens encircling the room play scenes from the film, while a special effect makes it appear that the Ice Witch is emerging from a huge ice block in the "castle" wall. When the video ends, guests walk past displays of artifacts and costumes worn in the film by characters including Prince Caspian, Lucy, Peter, and Edmund. If you're not a fan of the film, you may want to skip this one.

PIXAR PLACE

Once known as Mickey Avenue, Pixar Place has a fresh new look tied into one of the parks biggest attractions, Toy Story Mania! Where television and film production soundstages once stood, warm brick facades welcome guests to the land of Woody and Buzz. On your left, open-air kiosks invite shoppers to browse for themed toys and souvenirs. The brick Camera Department building is the place to mix and mingle with character stars from the blockbuster movie, *Toy Story.* Check character schedules on your Times Guide before lining up for autographs and photos.

10 TOY STORY MANIA!

Duration: 7 min.

Crowds: Heavy

Strategy: If Fastpass is offered, take one and return later. The ride's interactive fun is addictive, so you may want to visit first thing in the morning and return later for another spin with your Fastpass.

Audience: All ages.
Rating: ★★★

Great toys like Mr. Potato Head, Woody, and Buzz Lightyear from Disney's hit film *Toy Story* never lose their relevance. So it makes perfect sense that the hottest new theme park ride in Disney's collection of classics would take place inside the toy box of Andy, the boy whose toys come to life when he's gone. When you enter this new attraction, you'll queue past an oversize Mr. Potato Head and grab a pair of 3-D glasses before boarding your jazzed-up ride vehicle. Soon, you're whirling onto the midway where you can use your car's spring-action shooters to launch darts at balloons, toss rings at aliens, and splatter eggs at barnyard targets. Just as in the Magic Kingdom's Buzz Lightyear's Space Ranger Spin, you'll rack up points for targets hit and see your tally at ride's end. Frequent riders can hone a rat-a-tat shooting system to increase scores each ride; if you get caught up in intense competition with your riding partner, your shooting arm may ache by the time you've hit your last target. Don't let Rex's fear of failure slow you down—shoot for the stars and you'll deserve a salute from the Green Army Men.

STREETS OF AMERICA

It's well worth touring the New York, San Francisco, and Chicago sets here on foot—as long as crews aren't filming—so that you can check out the windows of shops and apartments, the taxicabs, and other details.

STUDIO BACKLOT TOUR

⑪ **Duration:** 35 min.
Crowds: Steady through the afternoon, but lines seem to move quickly.
Strategy: As you enter the tram, remember that people sitting on the left get wet. Go early; it closes at dusk.
Audience: All but very young children, who might be scared in Catastrophe Canyon.
Rating: ★★

The first stop on this tour, which you enter at the far end of Pixar Place where it meets Streets of America, is an outdoor special-effects water tank, where audience members are recruited for an unforgettable (and very wet) video moment. (In winter, when guests aren't fond of walking through the park with damp clothing, this audience-participation scene may be canceled.) Then it's time to line up for the tram ride. As you walk through the line, you're also touring a huge prop warehouse, which stores everything you could possibly imagine, from chairs to traffic lights to British phone booths.

Board the tram for a tour of the back lot's different departments: set design, costumes, props, lighting, and a standout movie set—Catastrophe Canyon. The tram's announcer swears that the film that's supposedly shooting in there is taking a break. But the next thing you know, the tram is bouncing up and down in a simulated earthquake, an oil tanker explodes in a mass of smoke and flame, and a water tower crashes to the ground, touching off a flash flood, which douses the tanker and threatens to drown the tram. As the tram pulls out, you see the backstage workings of the catastrophe: the canyon is actually a mammoth steel slide wrapped in copper-color concrete, and the 70,000 gallons of floodwater—enough to fill 10 Olympic-size swimming pools—are recycled 100 times a day, or every 3½ minutes. You'll also ride past the Streets of America back lot, where you can glimpse New York Street, with its brownstones, marble, brick, and stained glass that are actually expertly painted facades of fiberglass and Styrofoam. Grips can slide the Empire State and Chrysler buildings out of the way anytime. You'll have to walk the Streets set after exiting the tram to see the San Francisco and Chicago side streets. Word on Pixar Place is that Catastrophe Canyon may be torn down by 2011 in preparation for a new thrill attraction, so see it now!

LIGHTS, MOTORS, ACTION! EXTREME STUNT SHOW

12 **Duration:** 33 min.

Crowds: Heavy due to attraction's newness.

Strategy: You should be able to get into the theater even if you arrive close to show time; some days there are as few as two shows a day.

Audience: All, though babies and young children may be frightened by loud noises.

Rating: ★★

In today's light-speed society, it makes sense that action films gross some of the highest figures at box offices around the world. And with the success of the high-octane vehicle stunt show at Disneyland Paris, it's only natural that Disney show designers would model this new stunt extravaganza after its action-packed counterpart. Here, Disney designers made it their mission to reveal the secrets behind Hollywood's greatest stunts, including heart-pounding car chases and explosions. The scene is a 177,000-square-foot Mediterranean village "movie set" inside a 5,000-seat, open-air theater. The premise? Filmmakers are producing a spy thriller on the set, and the director is organizing different out-of-sequence stunts. Heroes and villains perform high-speed spinouts, two-wheel driving, jumps, and high falls using various vehicles, including watercraft. Besides experiencing the thrill of seeing choreographed stunts live, you'll learn how filmmakers combine shots of various stunts to create a completed scene, which plays on the stadium's mammoth video wall. Keep in mind that this show is pretty long, and you're sitting on a hard bench with no back the whole time. If you have small children or if you think you might want to leave during the show, sit toward the back.

HONEY, I SHRUNK THE KIDS MOVIE SET ADVENTURE

13 **Duration:** Up to you.

Crowds: Steady.

Strategy: Come after you've done several shows or attractions and your children need to cut loose.

Audience: Preschoolers and young school-age children.

Rating: ★★★

Let your youngsters run free in this playground based on the movie, where there are scenes of Lilliputian kids in a larger-than-life world. They can slide down a gigantic blade of grass, crawl through caves, climb a mushroom mountain, inhale the scent of a humongous plant (which will then spit water back in their faces), and dodge sprinklers set in resilient flooring made of ground-up tires. All the requisite playground equipment is present: net climbs, ball crawls, caves, and slides. Because the area is enclosed, there's often a line to get in—but attraction hosts don't fudge on capacity limits, which maintains a comfort zone for those inside. ■ TIP➜ Keep a close eye on your toddler. It's easy to lose track of children in the caves and slides of this wacky playground.

MUPPET*VISION 3-D

⑭ **Duration:** 25 min total.
Crowds: Moderate, but the theater is high capacity, so if you get there 10 min early you can get in.
Strategy: Arrive 10 min early. And don't worry—there are no bad seats.
Audience: All ages.
Rating: ★★★

You don't have to be a Miss Piggyphile to get a kick out of this combination 3-D movie and musical revue, although all the Muppet characters make appearances, including Miss Piggy in roles that include the Statue of Liberty. In the waiting area, Muppet movie posters advertise the world's most glamorous porker in Star Chores and To Have and Have More, and Kermit the Frog in an Arnold Schwarzenegger parody, Kürmit the Amphibian, who's "so mean, he's green." When the theater was constructed, special effects were built into the walls; the 3-D effects are coordinated with other sensory stimulation so you're never sure what's coming off the screen and what's being shot out of vents in the ceiling and walls.

ECHO LAKE

Segue from Streets of America to Echo Lake, an idealized southern California. In the center is the cool, blue lake of the same name, an oasis fringed with trees and benches and ringed with landmarks: pink-and-aqua restaurants trimmed in chrome, presenting sassy waitresses and black-and-white television sets at the tables; the shipshape Min and Bill's Dockside Diner, which offers snacks; and Gertie, a dinosaur that dispenses ice cream, Disney souvenirs, and the occasional puff of smoke in true magic-dragon fashion. Look for Gertie's giant footprints in the sidewalk. (Gertie, by the way, was the first animated animal to show emotion—an inspiration to the pre-Mickey Walt.) The hot ticket here is the American Idol Experience, where park guests can act out their own *American Idol* ambitions. You'll also find two of the park's longest-running attractions, the Indiana Jones Epic Stunt Spectacular! and Star Tours.

EN
ROUTE Adventurous types should check out the genuine Indiana Jones bull-whips and fedoras sold at the **Indiana Jones Adventure Outpost,** next to the stunt amphitheater, and the Yoda backpacks, interactive Droids, and "Darth Tater" Mr. Potato Head kits at **Tatooine Traders,** outside of Star Tours.

STAR TOURS

15 **Duration:** 5 min.

Crowds: Lines swell periodically when the Indiana Jones Epic Stunt Spectacular! lets out.

Strategy: To make sure you'll walk right on, go shortly before closing or first thing in the morning. Otherwise cruise on with the help of a Fastpass timed ticket. When you line up to enter the simulation chamber, keep to the far left to sit up front and closer to the screen for the most realistic sensations (the ride is rougher in back but the sensations of motion less exhilarating).

Audience: *Star Wars* fans, adults and children 40" or taller. No pregnant women, children under 3, or guests with heart, back, neck, or motion sickness problems; children under 7 must be accompanied by an adult.

Rating: ★★

Although the flight-simulator technology used for this ride was long ago surpassed on other thrill rides, this adventure (inspired by the *Star Wars* films) is still a pretty good trip. "May the force be with you," says the attendant on duty, "'cause I won't be!" Piloted by *Star Wars* characters R2D2 and C-3PO, the 40-passenger *StarSpeeder* that you board is supposed to take off on a routine flight to the moon of Endor. But with R2D2 at the helm, things quickly go awry: you shoot into deep space, dodge giant ice crystals and comet debris, innocently bumble into an intergalactic battle, and attempt to avoid laser-blasting fighters as you whiz through the canyons of some planetary city before coming to a heart-pounding halt.

NEED A
BREAK? If you have a sweet tooth, you should be sure to save room for some soft-serve Ice Cream of Extinction at **Gertie's,** the ice-cream bar and snack shop inside the big green dinosaur on the shore of Echo Lake. Nearby, **Min & Bill's Dockside Diner** is the spot for a stuffed pretzel or specialty shake. You can even buy a beer here. Step right up to the counter.

INDIANA JONES EPIC STUNT SPECTACULAR!

18 **Duration:** 30 min.

Crowds: Large, but the theater's high capacity means that everyone who wants to get in usually does, so don't waste a Fastpass here.

Strategy: Go at night if there's a late performance scheduled, when the idols' eyes glow red. If you sit up front, you can feel the heat when Marian's truck catches fire.

Audience: All but young children.

Rating: ★★★

The rousing theme music from the Indiana Jones movies heralds action delivered by veteran stunt coordinator Glenn Randall, whose credits include *Raiders of the Lost Ark, Indiana Jones and the Temple of*

Doom, E.T., and *Jewel of the Nile.* Presented in a 2,200-seat amphitheater, the show starts with a series of near-death encounters in an ancient Maya temple. Clad in his signature fedora, Indy slides down a rope from the ceiling, dodges spears that shoot up from the floor, avoids getting chopped by booby-trapped idols, and snags a forbidden gemstone, setting off a gigantic boulder that threatens to render him two-dimensional.

Though it's hard to top that opener, Randall and his pals do just that with the help of 10 audience participants. "Okay, I need some rowdy people," the casting director calls. While the lucky few demonstrate their rowdiness, behind them the set crew casually wheels off the entire temple. Two people roll the boulder like a giant beach ball and replace it with a Cairo street, circa 1940. Then the nasty Ninja-Nazi stuntmen come out, and you start to think that this is one of those times when it's better to be in the audience. Eventually Indy comes sauntering down the "street" with his redoubtable girlfriend, Marian Ravenwood, portrayed by a Karen Allen look-alike. She's kidnapped and tossed into a truck while Indy fights his way free with bullwhip and gun, and bad guys tumble from every corner and cornice. Motorcycles buzz around; the street becomes a shambles; and, as a stunning climax, the truck carrying Marian flips and bursts into flame. The actors do a great job of explaining the stunts. You see how they're set up, watch the stars practice them in slow motion, and learn how cameras are camouflaged behind imitation rocks for trick shots. Only one stunt remains a secret: how do Indy and Marian escape the explosion? That's what keeps 'em coming back.

THE AMERICAN IDOL EXPERIENCE

(17) **Duration:** 25-min preliminary show; 45-min finale show.
Crowds: Heavy; theater seats 1,000 guests each performance.
Strategy: Arrive at least 30 min before showtime.
Audience: School-age children and up.
Rating: ★★★

So you want to be a rock star? How about an American Idol? If you're 14 or older and can sing on key, make sure you head to auditions as soon as you enter the park in the morning. You may be chosen by a Disney casting director to belt out a tune on The American Idol Experience stage. Three guests are chosen to sing their hearts out for each scheduled show. At the end of the day, the top singers are invited back for a grand finale show, and the winning performer earns The American Idol Experience "Dream Ticket"—a sort of Fastpass to the front of the line at a future regional audition for the *American Idol* television show.

Not an *Idol* fan? No problem. This show, performed on a high-tech Hollywood-style stage complete with neon flash and high-energy show hosts, is a blast for all who enjoy live entertainment. Idol wannabes can choose their tunes from many music genres, so performers and songs vary with every show. You might hear the sweet lyrics of "Colors of the Wind" from Disney's *Pocahontas* just before the edgy Aretha Franklin hit "Respect." The best part? You and every other audience member cast a vote for the show's top singer, who then has a chance to appear in the daily finale show.

As you line up outside the theater's entrance, a quick-witted warm-up host revs up the audience; he reappears on stage with a fun, fast-paced monologue that explains how to react to singers and judges and how to vote for your favorite. Enter the show host, who introduces three judges with show-biz experience who deliver kudos or critiques to each performer. (Don't be afraid to boo one judge who enjoys his role as caustic critic.) Near the end of the show, your armrest keypad lights up for 10 seconds so you can place your vote; while votes are tallied, you're treated to a big-screen music video starring 2007 *American Idol* champion Jordin Sparks. Other American Idol stars, including host Ryan Seacrest and recent champ David Cook, make video appearances.

Dying to see who wins the Dream Ticket but can't get into the theater for the evening finale? Take heart. A stadium-size LED screen outside the theater offers a live simulcast and draws crowds for the dramatic Idol conclusion.

4

SOUNDS DANGEROUS STARRING DREW CAREY

16 **Duration:** Continuous 12-min shows; operates seasonally.
Crowds: Steady.
Strategy: Arrive 10–15 min before showtime.
Audience: School-age children and up.
Rating: ★★

A demonstration of the use of movie sound effects, this show uses many of the gadgets created by sound master Jimmy MacDonald, who became the voice of Mickey Mouse during the 1940s and invented some 20,000 sound effects during his 45 years at Walt Disney Studios. Most qualify as gizmos—a metal sheet that, when rattled, sounds like thunder; a box of sand for footsteps on gravel; and other noises made from nails, straw, mud, leather, and other ordinary components. The premise of the show is that you will help Drew Carey, who portrays an undercover cop, find out who smuggled the diamonds from the snow globe. To do so, you don headphones to follow Carey's progress and to hear the many sounds that go into the production of a movie or television show.
■TIP➔**Most of the show takes place in utter and complete darkness and it's *very* loud—preschoolers will be frightened.** Carey's bumbling detective provides plenty of laughs for adults and older kids.

EN
ROUTE

If you like to sift through antiques and novelty wares, make a stop at **Sid Cahuenga's One-of-a-Kind,** where you can find authentic Hollywood collectibles, curios, and autographed items that once belonged to celebrities. You'll find the latest trendy clothing and other merchandise—think *Pirates of the Caribbean* and *High-School Musical*—at **Legends of Hollywood** near the corner of Sunset and Hollywood.

DAILY PERFORMANCES

BLOCK PARTY BASH
Duration: 25 min.
Crowds: Heavy.
Strategy: Stake out your curb spot an hour early and hang on to it.

Audience: All ages.
Rating: ★★★

Energetic pop tunes, innovative floats, and a platoon of popular Disney characters give the Studios' parade hip new style as it wends its way mid-day up Hollywood Boulevard. The Green Army Men of *Toy Story* crash onto the scene to lead the moving spectacle packed with Disney characters like Woody and Buzz Lightyear from *Toy Story* and Flik and Atta from *A Bug's Life*. Dancers, stilt-walkers, and acrobats draw guests into the fun that's enhanced by special effects and floats that double as dance stages and trampoline-style performer launch pads. Watch for a surprise finale with Mr. and Mrs. Incredible.

HIGH SCHOOL MUSICAL 3: SENIOR YEAR
Duration: 20 min.
Crowds: Heavy.
Strategy: The show runs several times daily. Stake out a spot near Mickey's Sorcerer's Hat icon 30–45 min early; ask Disney cast members for tips on best viewing.
Audience: All ages.
Rating: ★★

Five or six times each day, pop culture hits Hollywood Boulevard with sing-along, dance-along 'tweener tunes when a lively team of theme-park performers brings Disney Channel's *High School Musical* to the Studios' streets. Much like the park's previous High School Musical 2 version, the live show spreads "Wildcat Fever" through the crowd, and kids get to sing and dance in the street along with "East High" performers to the tunes of "A Night to Remember" and "The Boys Are Back."

FANTASMIC!
Duration: 25 min, performance times vary.
Crowds: Heavy.
Strategy: Arrive at least an hour early and sit toward the rear, near the entrance/exit. Consider the Fantasmic! dinner package, which includes seating for the show.
Audience: Adults and kids over 6.
Rating: ★★★

The Studios' after-dark show wows audiences of thousands with its 25 minutes of special effects and Disney characters. The omnipresent Mickey, in his Sorcerer's Apprentice costume, plays the embodiment of Good in the struggle against forces of Evil, personified by Disney villains and villainesses such as Cruella DeVil, Scar, and Maleficent. In some of the show's best moments, animated clips of images of these famous bad guys alternate with clips of Disney nice guys (and dolls), projected onto screens made of water—high-tech fountains surging high in the air. Disney being Disney, it's Good that emerges triumphant, amid a veritable tidal wave of water effects and flames, explosions, and fireworks worthy of a Hollywood shoot-'em-up. Show up early at the 6,500-seat Hollywood Hills Amphitheatre opposite the Twilight Zone Tower of Terror. *Fantasmic!* is (usually) only performed just two days a week, so check the schedule days ahead before planning your Studios visit.

CLOSE UP

Fantasmic! Dinner Package

If getting to the Fantasmic! amphitheater 60 minutes ahead of show time doesn't sound like your cup of tea, you can shave some time off and still get a good seat by booking a Fantasmic! dinner package. Here's how it works: You get a prix-fixe meal at the buffet-style Hollywood & Vine or the table-service Hollywood Brown Derby or Mama Melrose's, plus a special pass to the show's amphitheater that gives preferred entry and lets you sidestep the main line. The price of the package depends on the restaurant you choose. At Hollywood & Vine, the buffet is $30.99 for adults and $15.99 for kids ages 3 to 9, including nonalcoholic beverage and dessert. At the Brown Derby, the adult dinners are $46.99 and children's meals $11.99, including beverage, and dessert. At Mama Melrose's, adults pay $32.99 and children's meals are $11.99. Prices don't include park admission, tax, or gratuity.

Reserve dinner for at least two or three hours before the show, though you can also dine much earlier if you prefer. After dinner, you can spend more time in the park if it's early, or go straight to the amphitheater and choose your seat. Don't arrive at the last minute, though, or your seating choices will be limited. Without the dinner package, you need to arrive 60 to 90 minutes early. That extra time saved can make a big difference if you're traveling with tired and antsy children. Book the package by calling 407/939–3463 or stop by the Hollywood Junction information window as you enter Disney's Hollywood Studios in the morning to see if reservations are available. They often are. One caveat: Fantasmic! is an outdoor show and if it rains, the show can be canceled, even at the last minute. You still get your dinner, but you're not reimbursed for losing out on your preferred seating.

It's best to book your Fantasmic! dinner package a couple of months in advance, but you might be able to get a last-minute reservation.

DISABILITIES AND ACCESSIBILITY

Check in at Guest Services to pick up a copy of the Studios guide map for guests with disabilities. Studio attractions are wheelchair accessible, with certain restrictions on the Star Tours thrill ride, Rock 'n' Roller Coaster, and Twilight Zone Tower of Terror. Guests with hearing impairments can obtain closed-captioning devices for use in most of the attractions. You can reserve time with a sign-language interpreter by calling **WDW Guest Information** (☎ *407/824–4321, 407/827–5141 TTY*) at least two weeks in advance. There's a large Braille map of the park located where Hollywood intersects with Sunset, near the Tip Board.

To board the **Great Movie Ride,** on Hollywood Boulevard, you must transfer to a Disney wheelchair if you use an oversize model or a scooter; the gunshot, explosion, and fire effects mean that service animals cannot be taken on the rides.

To board Sunset Boulevard's **Twilight Zone Tower of Terror,** you must be able to walk unassisted to a seat on the ride and have full upper-body

BLITZ TOUR

BEST OF THE PARK

Arrive well before the park opens. When it does, run right up Hollywood Boulevard, hang a right at Sunset Boulevard, and dash to the 13-story **Twilight Zone Tower of Terror.** You can make a Fastpass appointment here, then go next door to ride **Rock 'n' Roller Coaster Starring Aerosmith.** *American Idol* fans should check the Time Guide to determine which performance of the **American Idol Experience** you'll want to attend. If talent shows and stomach-churning thrills aren't top priority, shoot straight for **Toy Story Mania!** on Pixar Place, where lines may be long. If Fastpass is offered, grab yours and return later. After your Twilight Zone plunge, you may want to get a Fastpass for a second go-round on your favorite of these two thrill rides. With kids and 'tweens, catch a performance of **High School Musical 3: Senior Year.** Then make the **Great Movie Ride** at the Chinese Theater your next stop. If you're still waiting to return for your Fastpass appointment at the Tower of Terror or Rock 'n' Roller Coaster, catch the **Magic of Disney Animation** or, if you have small children, **Playhouse Disney— Live on Stage!** Once you've used your Fastpass, head over to the **Indiana Jones Epic Stunt Spectacular!** If the line is long get a Fastpass.

For lunch, grab a sandwich on the run at the **ABC Commissary,** or do table-service at the **Sci-Fi Dine-In Theater Restaurant,** where you can sit in a 1950s-era convertible with built-in tables and watch B-movie trailers on a large drive-in movie screen. Then take in the **Lights, Motors, Action! Extreme Stunt Show** or return to Indiana Jones if you're holding a Fastpass appointment. Afterward, dash over to **Star Tours,** where you should take a Fastpass timed ticket unless the line is very short. While you wait for your appointment, catch **Muppet*Vision 3-D** or the **Block Party Bash** parade. If there's still time before your Star Tours return, check out *Sounds Dangerous* **Starring Drew Carey** or the **Studio Backlot Tour.** Those who "just say no" to thrill rides can catch **Voyage of the Little Mermaid** or soak up some Disney history at **Walt Disney: One Man's Dream.** Don't miss the interactive **Toy Story Mania!** ride. Then, keep your Star Tours appointment, and let the kids scramble around on the **Honey, I Shrunk the Kids Movie Set Adventure,** or explore Sunset Boulevard, where the shops sell much of the same merchandise as those on Hollywood Boulevard but are less crowded. Try to catch a late performance of **Beauty and the Beast—Live on Stage!** Finally, line up for a grand finale to cap the night with fireworks, lasers, fountains, and the cast of popular Disney characters—*Fantasmic!* (performed two evenings a week). Remember to turn at the gate for one last look at the Earful Tower, its perky appendages outlined in gold lights.

ON RAINY DAYS

Plan your day around the indoor attractions and make Fastpass appointments back to back. Enjoy a relaxing lunch at the Brown Derby or a zany time in the 50's Prime Time Café, where a great cast of servers and a peanut-butter-and-jelly milk shake will help you forget all about the weather.

strength. The ride's free falls make it unsuitable for service animals. **Beauty and the Beast—Live on Stage!** at the Theater of the Stars is completely accessible to guests using wheelchairs. To ride the **Rock 'n' Roller Coaster Starring Aerosmith,** guests who use wheelchairs must transfer to a ride vehicle—an area in which to practice the transfer is available. At Animation Courtyard, **Voyage of the Little Mermaid, Playhouse Disney—Live on Stage!,** and the **Magic of Disney Animation** are wheelchair accessible; all have preshow areas with TV monitors that are closed-captioned.

You can roll a wheelchair throughout **Journey Into Narnia: Prince Caspian** and the **Walt Disney: One Man's Dream** attraction, which features captioning in the theater. At **Toy Story Mania!** scooter occupants must transfer to a standard wheelchair. The **StudioBacklot Tour** is wheelchair accessible, too. Guests with hearing impairments who lip-read should request a seat near the tour guide. The earthquake, fire, and water effects of the Catastrophe Canyon scene make the attraction inappropriate for service animals. The **Lights, Motors, Action!—Extreme Stunt Show** accommodates wheelchairs and is compatible with assistive listening devices acquired at Guest Services.

On New York Street, the **Honey, I Shrunk the Kids Movie Set Adventure** is barrier-free for most guests using wheelchairs, although the uneven surface may make maneuvering difficult. **Muppet*Vision 3-D** is also completely wheelchair accessible and features reflective captioning; contact a host to use the system. Those with hearing impairments may request a personal audio link that will amplify the sound here. A TV monitor in the pre-show area is closed-captioned.

At Echo Lake, the **Indiana Jones Epic Stunt Spectacular!** is completely wheelchair accessible. Explosions and gunfire may make it inappropriate for service animals. **Star Tours,** a turbulent ride, is accessible by guests who can transfer to a ride seat; those lacking upper-body strength should request an extra shoulder restraint. Service animals should not ride. **Sounds Dangerous Starring Drew Carey** is completely wheelchair accessible. However, the entertainment value is derived from the different sound effects, so you may decide to skip this one if you have a hearing impairment.

All restaurants and shops are fully wheelchair accessible, but there are no Braille menus or sign-language interpreters. Most live entertainment locations are completely wheelchair accessible. Certain sections of parade routes are always reserved for guests with disabilities. The noise and explosions in **Fantasmic!** may frighten service animals.

EATING IN DISNEY'S HOLLYWOOD STUDIOS

FULL-SERVICE RESTAURANTS

The magic continues inside the park's full-service restaurants. Where else but at Disney World can you watch '50s sitcoms nonstop while you devour veal-and-shiitake-mushroom meat loaf? Waits can be long. To make priority seating reservations, call the **Disney Reservation Center** (☎407/939–3463) up to 90 days in advance, or stop in person at the

DISNEY'S HOLLYWOOD STUDIOS

NAME	Min. Height	Type of Entertainment	Duration	Suits	Crowds	Strategy
Hollywood Blvd.						
Great Movie Ride	n/a	tour	22 min.	5 and up	Medium	Go while waiting for Fastpass on another ride. Lines out the door mean 25-min. wait.
Sunset Blvd.						
Beauty and the Beast—Live on Stage!	n/a	show	30 min.	All	Yes!	Go 30 min. before showtime for good seats. Performance days vary, so check ahead.
★ Rock 'n' Roller Coaster Starring Aerosmith	48"	thrill ride	3 min.	7 and up	Huge	Ride early, then use Fastpass for another go later.
★ Twilight Zone Tower of Terror	40"	thrill ride	10 min.	7 and up	Yes!	Use Fastpass. Go early or late evening.
Animation Courtyard						
Playhouse Disney— Live on Stage!	n/a	show	22 min.	toddlers & pre-schoolers	Afternoon	Go first thing in the morning, when your child is most alert.
★ The Magic of Disney Animation	n/a	tour	15-30 min.	All	Steady	Go in the morning or late afternoon. Toddlers may get bored.
Voyage of the Little Mermaid	n/a	show	17 min.	All	Yes!	Go first thing in the morning. Otherwise, wait until after 5.
Walt Disney: One Man's Dream	n/a	film	20 min. or longer	10 and up	Steady	See this attraction while waiting for a Fastpass appointment.
Journey Into Narnia: Prince Caspian	n/a	tour	15 min.	5 and up	Steady	Go anytime while waiting for Fastpass appointment.
Pixar Place						

Toy Story Mania	n/a	thrill ride	varies	All	Heavy	Go early, use Fastpass.
Streets of America						
Honey, I Shrunk the Kids Movie Set Adventure	n/a	play area	Up to you	All	Steady	Come after you've done several shows and your kids need to cut loose.
Muppet*Vision 3-D	n/a	3-D film	25 min.	All	Moderate	Arrive 10 min. early. And don't worry—there are no bad seats.
Lights, Motors, Action! Extreme Stunt Show	n/a	show	33 min.	All	Heavy	You should be able to get into the theater even if you arrive close to showtime. For the best seats, line up for the show while others are lining up for the parade.
Studio Backlot Tour	n/a	tour	30 min.	All	Fast lines	People sitting on the left get wet. Go early; it closes at dusk.
Echo Lake						
The American Idol Experience	n/a	live show	25 min. /45 min.	5 and up	Yes!	Arrive at least 30 min. before showtime
Indiana Jones Epic Stunt Spectacular!	n/a	stunt show	30 min.	All	Fast lines	Go at night, when the idol's eyes glow red. Sit up front to feel the heat of a truck on fire.
Sounds Dangerous Starring Drew Carey	n/a	show	12 min.	6 and up	steady	Arrive 15 min. before show. You sit in total darkness.
Star Tours	40"	sim. ride	5 min.	3 and up	Fast lines	Go before closing, early morning, or get a Fastpass. Keep to the left in line for best seats.
Daily Performances						
Block Party Bash	n/a	parade	25 min.	All	Heavy	Stake out your curb spot an hr. early and hang on to it.
★ Fantasmic!	n/a	show	25 min.	6 and up	Heavy	Arrive at least 1 hr. early and sit toward the rear, near the entrance/exit, or buy the Fantasmic! dinner package for preferred admission.
High School Musical 3: Senior Year	n/a	show	20 min.	All	Heavy	*Stake out a spot 30–45 min early.*

★ = **Fodor's**Choice

restaurant or first thing in the morning at the Hollywood Junction information window, just to the right of the Studios Tip Board, at the intersection of Hollywood and Sunset boulevards.

With its staff in black tie and its airy, palm-fronded room positively exuding Hollywood glamour, the spacious **Hollywood Brown Derby** is one of the nicest—and most expensive—places to eat in the park. The Cobb salad was invented at the restaurant's Hollywood namesake. The wine list is excellent, and you can count on creative chef specials. The butter comes in molds shaped like Mickey Mouse heads. If you request the Fantasmic! dinner package and make a reservation for no later than two hours before the start of the show, you receive a pass to skip the line.

Spend a leisurely lunch at the **50's Prime Time Café**, where video screens constantly show sitcoms, place mats pose television trivia quizzes, and waitresses play "Mom" with convincing enthusiasm, insisting that you clean your plate. The menu is what your own mom might have made were she a character on one of those video screens—meat loaf, broiled chicken, pot roast, hot roast beef sandwiches—all to be washed down with root-beer floats and ice-cream sodas.

To replace the energy you've no doubt depleted by miles of theme-park walking, you can load up on carbs at **Mama Melrose's Ristorante Italiano.** The menu has pastas, seafood, pizza baked in brick ovens, and several vegetarian entrées, including eggplant Parmesan. Ask for the Fantasmic! dinner package if you want faster access to the show.

If you don't mind zombies leering at you while you consume chef salads, smoked turkey, and grilled chicken sandwiches, seared marinated tofu, and Milky-Way-Out Milk Shakes, then head to **Sci-Fi Dine-In Theater Restaurant,** a re-creation of a drive-in. All the tables are set in candy-color '50s convertibles and face a large screen, on which a 45-minute reel of the best and worst of science-fiction trailers plays in a continuous loop.

SELF-SERVICE RESTAURANTS

The **ABC Commissary** serves a full breakfast menu before 10:30 AM and has a refreshingly different fast-food menu that includes Cuban sandwiches, Asian salad, and fish-and-chips. At the **Backlot Express**, in Echo Lake, you don't need a reservation to enjoy the burgers, hot dogs, grilled veggie sandwiches, and chef salads.

A buffet of rotisserie meats and poultry, salads, seafood, and fresh pastas makes up the dinner fare at **Hollywood & Vine.** This casual eatery, with a Hollywood theme, is a real charmer—totally '50s and vaguely deco—and Playhouse Disney characters are on hand for breakfast and lunch. In Echo Lake, **Min & Bill's Dockside Diner** is the spot for a stuffed pretzel or specialty shake. The **Studio Catering Company,** near the Studio Backlot Tour exit, has specialty sandwiches, salads, and desserts. **Pizza Planet Arcade** is for kids who need some amusement with their pizza—video games and other diversions allow parents to relax with a cup of coffee or cocoa while their children stay entertained.

Disney's Animal Kingdom

WORD OF MOUTH

"I think kids will really enjoy Disney's Animal Kingdom. In addition to wonderful attractions like the Safari, the shows (Nemo, Lion King, etc.) are exceptional and both parents and kids will enjoy them."

—WDW_Radio_Show

"My parents took my niece to Animal Kingdom not long after coming back from a safari in Tanzania. My mom was struck by how similar the Disney safari was to the Tanzanian safari—the land rovers, the bumpy roads, the radio reporting game sightings, etc. Of course, it was Disney-fied, but she was impressed by how much thought they put into it."

—lifelist

Updated by
Jennie Hess

Humankind's enduring love for animals is the inspiration for WDW's fourth theme park, Disney's Animal Kingdom. Opened in 1998, the park explores the stories of all animals—real, imaginary, and extinct.

At 500 acres and five times the size of the Magic Kingdom, Animal Kingdom is the largest in area of all Disney theme parks worldwide. The space gives Disney Imagineers plenty of scope for their creativity, and it allows for growth, an example of which is Expedition Everest. Opened in 2006 it's the park's biggest thrill attraction—a runaway train ride on a rugged mountain complete with icy ledges, dark caves, and a yeti legend.

As you enter the park through the Oasis, exotic background music plays, and you're surrounded by a green grotto, gentle waterfalls, and gardens alive with exotic birds, reptiles, and mammals. The Oasis opens early, so you can do a lot of critter-watching before its inhabitants settle down to snooze through the heat of the day.

Just before the park opens (or an hour before it opens on Extra Magic Hours mornings when resort guests are admitted early), Minnie Mouse, Pluto, and Goofy arrive at the iconic Tree of Life in a safari vehicle to welcome the first guests into the heart of the park. (Keep an eye out for Mickey waving from a distance.)

In the park, animals thrive in careful re-creations of natural landscapes in exotic lands ranging from Thailand and India to southern Africa. You'll also find rides, some of Disney's finest musical shows, eateries, and, of course, Disney characters—where else does the Lion King truly belong? Cast members come from all over the world—Kenya and South Africa as often as Kentucky and South Carolina. That's part of the charm of the place. All this is augmented by an earnest educational undercurrent that's meant to foster a renewed appreciation for the animal kingdom.

The park is laid out very much like its oldest sibling, the Magic Kingdom. The hub of this wheel is the spectacular Tree of Life in the middle of Discovery Island. Radiating from Discovery Island's hub are several spokes—the other "lands," each with a distinct personality. South of Discovery Island is Camp Minnie-Mickey, a character-greeting and show area.

Numbers in the margin correspond to points of interest on the Disney's Animal Kingdom map.

GETTING THERE AND AROUND

To get to the Animal Kingdom your options are to take a Disney bus, if you're staying on-site, or to drive ($12 parking fee, good at other Disney parks throughout the day). Although this is technically Disney's largest theme park, most of the land is reserved for the animals. The pedestrian areas are actually quite compact with relatively narrow passageways. The only way to get around is on foot.

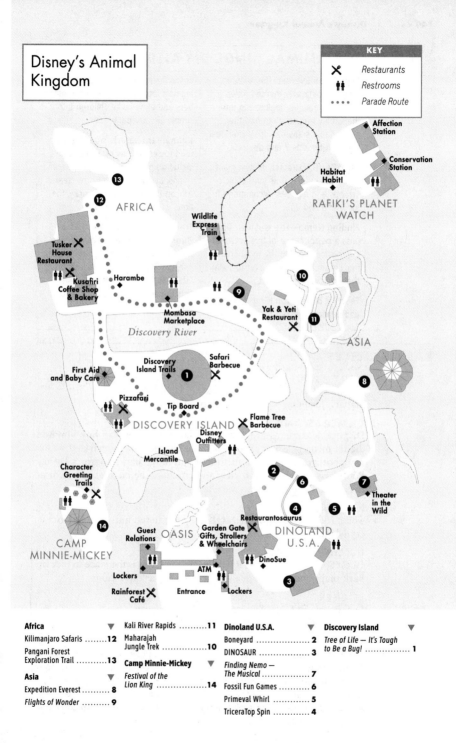

Disney's Animal Kingdom

Affection Station

Conservation Station

Habitat Habit!

RAFIKI'S PLANET WATCH

AFRICA

Wildlife Express Train

13

12

Tusker House Restaurant ✕

Kusafiri Coffee Shop & Bakery ✕

Harambe

Mombasa Marketplace

Discovery River

10

9

Yak & Yeti Restaurant ✕

11

ASIA

8

Discovery Island Trails

Safari Barbecue ✕

1

Tip Board

First Aid and Baby Care

Pizzafari ✕

DISCOVERY ISLAND

Flame Tree ✕ Barbecue

Disney Outfitters

Island Mercantile

Character Greeting Trails

2

6

7

Theater in the Wild

4

5

Restaurantosaurus ✕

14

CAMP MINNIE-MICKEY

OASIS

Guest Relations

Garden Gate Gifts, Strollers & Wheelchairs ✕

DINOLAND U.S.A.

DinoSue

3

Lockers

Rainforest ✕ Café

ATM

Entrance

Lockers

TOP ANIMAL KINGDOM ATTRACTIONS

Expedition Everest. The Animal Kingdom's cleverly themed roller coaster is a spine-tingling trip into the snowy Himalayas to find the abominable snowman. It's a ride best reserved for kids 7 and up.

DINOSAUR. Extremely lifelike giant dinosaurs jump out as your vehicle swoops and dips. We recommend it for kids 8 and up.

Finding Nemo—The Musical. Don't miss a performance of this outstanding musical starring the most charming, colorful characters ever to swim their way into your heart.

Festival of the Lion King. Singers and dancers dressed in fantastic costumes representing many wild animals interact with audience members and even invite children into a simple circular parade.

Kilimanjaro Safaris. You're guaranteed to see dozens of wild animals, including giraffes, zebras, hippos, and rhinos, living in authentic, re-created African habitats. If you're lucky, the lions will be stirring, too.

Tree of Life—It's Tough to Be a Bug! This adorable 3-D movie starring Flik from the Disney film *A Bug's Life*, is full of surprises, including "shocking" special effects. Some kids under 7 are scared of the loud noises.

BASIC SERVICES

BABY CARE
The **Baby Care Center** is in Discovery Island. You can buy disposable diapers, formula, baby food, and pacifiers.

CAMERAS AND FILM
Disposable cameras are widely available, and you can buy film and digital memory cards at several shops throughout the park. If a Disney photographer takes a picture of you in the park, ask for a **Disney PhotoPass**—later, you can view and purchase the pictures online or at the park's Photo Center in the Oasis.

FIRST AID
The park's First Aid Center, staffed by registered nurses, is in Discovery Island.

INFORMATION
Guest Services (aka Guest Relations) in the Oasis is the place to pick up park maps and entertainment schedules and ask questions.

LOCKERS
Lockers are in Guest Services ($5, $2 key deposit).

LOST PEOPLE AND THINGS
If you're worried about your children getting lost, get name tags for them at Discovery Island. Instruct them to speak to someone with a Disney name tag if you become separated. If you do become separated from your child, immediately report your loss to any cast member. Lost-children logbooks are at the Baby Care Center on Discovery Island and at Guest Services at the park's main Oasis entrance. **Animal Kingdom Lost**

and Found is at Guest Services, also. (☎*407/938–2785*). To retrieve lost articles after leaving the park, call Lost and Found on the same day, or call **Main Lost and Found** (✉*Magic Kingdom Ticket and Transportation Center [TTC]* ☎*407/824–4245*) if more than a day has passed since you've lost the article.

PACKAGE PICK-UP
You can have shop clerks forward any large purchases to Package Pick-Up near the Main Entrance Plaza in the Oasis, so that you won't have to carry them around all day. Allow three hours for the journey.

STROLLER AND WHEELCHAIR RENTALS
Garden Gate Gifts, in the Oasis, rents strollers, wheelchairs, and ECVs. Single strollers are $15 daily, $13 for multiday rental; double strollers are $31 daily, $27 for multiday rental. Wheelchairs are $10 daily, $8 for multiday rental. Electronic Convenience Vehicles (ECV) are $45 per day plus a refundable $20 security deposit. Neither wheelchairs nor ECVs are reservable, so arrive early to rent them. And while the park's wheelchair supply is generally plentiful, ECV availability is limited. If any of your rentals needs replacing, ask any park cast member.

THE OASIS

This lush entrance garden makes you feel as if you've been plunked down in the middle of a rain forest. Cool mist, the aroma of flowers, and playful animals and colorful birds all enliven a miniature landscape of streams and grottoes, waterfalls, and glades fringed with banana leaves and jacaranda. On the finest Orlando mornings, when the mists shroud the landscape, it's the scene-setter for the rest of your day. It's also where you can take care of essentials before entering the park. Here you'll find stroller and wheelchair rentals, Guest Services, and an ATM.

EN ROUTE Before you pass through the turnstiles on your way into the Animal Kingdom, stop at the **Outpost Shop** for a must-have safari hat with Mouse ears. Once in Discovery Island, look for a Minnie Mouse headband with a safari-style bow at **Creature Comforts.**

DISCOVERY ISLAND

Primarily the site of the Tree of Life, this land is encircled by Discovery River, which isn't an actual attraction but can be viewed from a bridge in Harambe. The island's whimsical architecture, with wood carvings handmade in Bali, adds plenty of charm and a touch of fantasy to this park hub. The verdant **Discovery Island Trails** that lead to the Tree of Life provide habitats for kangaroos, lemurs, Galapagos tortoises, and other creatures you won't want to miss while here. It's hard to tear the kids from the glass panel in a cavelike observation area where you can see river otters frolic underwater and above. You'll find some great shops and some good counter-service eateries here, and the island is also the site of the daily Mickey's Jammin' Jungle Parade. Visitor services that aren't in the Oasis are here, on the border with Harambe, including the Baby Care Center and the First Aid Center.

TIP SHEET

■ Try to visit the Animal Kingdom during the week. The pedestrian areas of the park are relatively compact and the park can feel horribly packed on weekends when it's especially crowded.

■ Arrive a half hour before park opening to get a jump on the crowds and to see the wild animals at their friskiest.

■ Check the park's Tip Board for the latest information on lines just after crossing the bridge into Discovery Island.

■ Set up a rendezvous point and time at the start of the day, just in case you and your companions get separated. Some good places include the outdoor seating area of Tusker House restaurant in Africa, in front of DinoLand U.S.A.'s Boneyard, and at the entrance of the Festival of the Lion King show.

TREE OF LIFE—IT'S TOUGH TO BE A BUG!

❶ **Duration:** 20 min.

Crowds: Moderate to heavy.

Strategy: Get a Fastpass reservation after you've been on Kilimanjaro Safaris. If the line is 40 min or less, however, save your Fastpass for another ride, such as DINOSAUR, and get into the regular line that meanders along the Discovery Island Trails. As you stroll the winding trail around the Tree of Life, it's fun to spot animals like ring-tailed lemurs, Galapagos tortoises, and red kangaroos in their habitats and to see how many of the creature carvings you can find on the trunk, branches, and roots of the mammoth icon.

Audience: All ages, but the show is very loud and some effects will frighten children under 8. There's often at least one screaming toddler during the show.

Rating: ★★★

A monument to all earth's creatures, the park's centerpiece is an imposing 14 stories high and 50 feet wide at its base. Its 100,000-plus leaves are several shades of green fabric, each carefully placed for a realistic effect. Carved into its thick trunk, gnarled roots, and soaring branches—some of which are supported by joints that allow them to sway in a strong wind—are nearly 350 intricate animal forms that include a baboon, a whale, a horse, the mighty lion, and even an ankylosaurus. Outside, paths tunnel underneath the roots as the fauna-encrusted trunk towers overhead. It's a rich and truly fascinating sight—the more you look the more you see. The path leads you inside the tree trunk to the star attraction of Discovery Island, where you get a bug's-eye view of life. The whimsical 3-D film adventure *It's Tough to Be a Bug!* is modeled vaguely on the animated film *A Bug's Life* from Disney-Pixar, the creators of *Toy Story.* Special film and theater effects spray you with "poison," zap you with a swatter, and even poke you with a stinger. It's all in good fun—and the surprise ending is too playful to give away.

DINOLAND U.S.A.

Just as it sounds, this is the place to come in contact with re-created prehistoric creatures, including the fear-inspiring carnotaurus and the gentle iguanodon. The landscaping includes live plants that have evolved over the last 65 million years. In collaboration with Chicago's Field Museum, Disney has added a complete, full-scale skeleton cast of Dino-Sue—also known as "Sue"—the 65-million-year-old Tyrannosaurus rex discovered near the Black Hills of South Dakota. After admiring "Sue," you can go on the thrilling Dinosaur ride, amble along the Cretaceous Trail, play in the Boneyard, or take in the Finding Nemo–The Musical show at the Theater in the Wild. Kids will want to hitch a dino-ride on the TriceraTop Spin and on the Primeval Whirl family coaster, which has spinning "time machines." There's no need to dig for souvenirs at Chester and Hester's Dinosaur Treasures gift shop—all you need is your wallet.

NEED A BREAK? Famished, but no time for lunch? Make tracks for **Trilo-Bite** and dig into a hearty turkey leg. Wash it down with a frozen lemonade, and you'll be ready to take on a T. rex.

BONEYARD

❷ Duration: Up to you and your children.
Crowds: Can be heavy mid-morning to early afternoon.
Strategy: Let the kids burn off energy here while waiting for your Fastpass appointment for DINOSAUR, or head over late in the day when kids need a break to run free.
Audience: Toddlers, school-age children, and their families.
Rating: ★★★

Youngsters can slide, dig, bounce, slither, and stomp around this archaeological dig site–cum–playground, the finest play area in any of the four Disney parks. In addition to a huge sand pit where children can dig for mammoth bones, there are twisting short and long slides, climbing nets, caves, and a jeep to climb on. Stomp on the dino-footprints to make 'em roar.

DINOSAUR

❸ Duration: Not quite 4 min.
Crowds: Can get heavy mid-morning.
Strategy: Go first thing in the morning or at the end of the day, or use the Fastpass.
Audience: All ages except very young children, pregnant women, or guests with back, neck, or heart problems. The realistic carnivores frighten a lot of children under 8. Minimum height: 40".
Rating: ★★★

This wild adventure through time puts you face-to-face with huge dinosaurs that move and breathe with uncanny realism. When a carload of guests rouses a cantankerous carnotaurus from his Cretaceous slumber, it's showtime. You travel back 65 million years on a fast-paced, twisting adventure and try to save the last living iguanodon as a massive asteroid hurtles toward Earth. Exciting Audio-Animatronics and special effects bring to life dinosaurs like the raptor, pterodactyl, styracosaurus, alioramus, and compsognather. Be prepared for a short but steep drop toward the end of the ride.

TRICERATOP SPIN

 Duration: About 2 min.

Crowds: Heavy.

Strategy: Ride early or line up while waiting for your Fastpass appointment for DINOSAUR.

Audience: Toddlers, school-age children and their families.

Rating: ★★

TriceraTop Spin is designed for playful little dinophiles who ought to get a kick out of whirling around this ride's giant spinning toy top and dodging incoming comets in their dino-mobiles. "Pop!" goes the top and out comes a grinning dinosaur as four passengers in each vehicle fly in a circle and maneuver up and down.

PRIMEVAL WHIRL

Duration: About 2½ min.

Crowds: Heavy.

Strategy: Kids may want to ride twice, so take your first spin early, then get a Fastpass to return later if the wait is longer than 20 min. Minimum height: 48".

Rating: ★★★

In a free-spinning, four-passenger vehicle, you head on a brief journey back in time on this outdoor open-air coaster, twisting, turning, and even venturing into the jaws of a dinosaur "skeleton." As you ride, crazy cartoon dinosaurs in shades of turquoise, orange, yellow, and purple pop up along the track bearing signs that warn "The End Is Near." More signs warn of "Meteors!" and suggest that you "Head for the Hills!"—coaster hills, that is. Halfway through the ride, your car seems to spin out of control and you take the next drop backward. The more weight there is in the vehicle, the more you spin.

FOSSIL FUN GAMES

Duration: Up to you.

Cost: Varies.

Strategy: Bring a pocketful of change and a stash of ones.

Audience: Older children and adults.

Rating: ★

A carnival-style midway in the middle of DinoLand U.S.A., this fun fair draws crowds with games like Whack a Packycephalosaur and the mallet-strength challenge, Dino-Whamma. The prehistoric fun comes at a price, however, and stone currency is not accepted. Prizes are mostly of the plush-character variety—you might win your sweetheart a stuffed Nala.

FINDING NEMO–THE MUSICAL

Duration: 30 min.

Crowds: Expected to be heavy, as with all new attractions.

Strategy: Arrive 40 min before showtime.

Audience: All ages, especially fans of the film.

Rating: ★★★

This is a fish tale of magnificent scale; a show so creative and fun that many audience members have likened it to a first-rate Broadway show. In fact, Disney Imagineers collaborated with several Broadway talents to produce this richly staged musical brimming with special effects and elaborate, larger-than-life puppets acted by gifted performers, dancers, and acrobats. It's all choreographed to bring you

> **TIMING TIP**
>
> Because of the proximity of the two attractions, Finding Nemo–The Musical is a good place to take younger kids while older siblings wait in line and ride Expedition Everest. If there's not a long wait for Everest, however, the entire family should see Nemo together.

into Nemo's big blue world. The sweet story remains the same as in the movie—Nemo and his father Marlin go on separate journeys that ultimately teach them how to understand each other. Zany Dory, with her hilarious memory lapses, cool Crush the sea turtle dude, tap dancing sharks, and other characters give memorable supporting-role turns. Original songs by Tony Award–winning *Avenue Q* co-composer-creator Robert Lopez and a cappella musical *Along the Way* co-creator Kristen Anderson-Lopez add new depth and energy to the story. Michael Curry, who co-designed the character puppets of Broadway's *The Lion King,* created the musical's eye-popping puppetry; Peter Brosius, artistic director of the Children's Theatre Company of Minneapolis and winner of a regional theater Tony Award, directed the show. Expect multigenerational humor and Broadway- and pop-inspired tunes.

ASIA

Meant to resemble a rural village somewhere in Asia, this land is full of remarkable rain-forest scenery and ruins. Groupings of trees grow from a crumbling tiger shrine and two massive towers, one representing Thailand, the other Nepal. The towers are the habitat for two families of gibbons, whose hooting fills the air at all hours of the day. While you're here, take a wild ride on Expedition Everest, stroll the Maharajah Jungle Trek, see the Flights of Wonder bird show, and raft the Kali River Rapids.

EXPEDITION EVEREST

8 Duration: 2½ min.

Crowds: Huge for this park's wildest thrill ride yet.

Strategy: Rush here as soon as the park opens and enter the line if the wait isn't too long—the detail of this re-created Himalayan village is worth soaking up as you walk through; otherwise, grab a Fastpass.

Audience: Since the coaster is supposed to be less intense than, say, Space Mountain, brave children who meet the 44"-minimum height requirement can ride.

Rating: ★★★

Disney really turned up the thrill factor in the Animal Kingdom with Expedition Everest, a roller coaster coiling through a 200-foot-high faux Himalayan mountain. The story goes that a fierce yeti guards the route to Mt. Everest. Of course, you're willing to risk running

CLOSE UP

Books on Disney

Neal Gabler's *Walt Disney: The Triumph of the American Imagination* (2006) gives the full story that led to Walt's "synergistic empire," and has earned rave reviews. One of the most perceptive books on Walt Disney and his works is *The Disney Version* (third edition, 1997), by Richard Schickel. For a good read about Disney and other animators, look for *Of Mice and Magic* (1990), by Leonard Maltin. A comprehensive history of the great Disney animation tradition is provided in *Disney Animation: The Illusion of Life*, by Frank Thomas and Ollie Johnston (1995).

Walt Disney: An American Original (1994), by Bob Thomas, is full of anecdotes about the development of WDW. Rollins College professor Richard Fogelsong questions the "economic marriage" between Disney and Orlando in his book *Married to the Mouse* (2003).

across the big guy in your quest to reach the summit. So, you board an "aging," seemingly innocuous, 34-passenger, steam-engine train into the mountains. You roll past bamboo forests, thundering waterfalls, and sparkling glacier fields as you climb higher through snowcapped peaks. All of a sudden your trip turns perilous: the train becomes a runaway, barreling forward then backward around icy ledges and through dark snowy caverns. Nearly a mile of twists and turns cut through the dark mountain, and at one point your train plunges a harrowing 80 feet. Will you find the yeti? Do you even want to? Well, what's a Disney ride without a mammoth, lifelike, Audio-Animatronics monster?

For adults who yearn to travel to far-off places like Nepal, the line area is an architectural marvel that enriches the yeti story. The buildings, inside and out, are created in the same style as Himalayan mountain dwellings and teem with cultural references that include prayer flags, totems, and other artifacts from Tibet, Nepal, and the entire region. Photographs of Himalayan people are displayed in the line gallery.

FLIGHTS OF WONDER

⑨ Duration: 30 min.
Crowds: Not a problem.
Strategy: Arrive 15 min before showtime and find a shaded seat beneath one of the awnings—the sun can be brutal in summer.
Audience: All.
Rating: ★★

This outdoor show area near the border with Africa is the place for spectacular demonstrations of skill by falcons, hawks, and other rare and fascinating birds, which swoop down over the audience.

MAHARAJAH JUNGLE TREK

⑩ Duration: As long as you like.
Crowds: Not bad because people are constantly moving.
Strategy: Go anytime.
Audience: All ages.
Rating: ★★★

Get an up-close view of some unusual and interesting animals along this trail: a Komodo dragon perched on a rock; Malayan tapirs near the wooden footbridge; families of giant fruit bats that hang to munch fruit from wires and fly very close to the open and glass-protected viewing areas; and Bengal tigers in front of a maharajah's palace. The tigers have their own view (with no accessibility, of course) of a group of Asian deer and a herd of black buck, an antelope species. At the end of the trek, you walk through an aviary with a lotus pool. Disney interpreters, many from Asian countries, are on hand to answer any and all questions.

KALI RIVER RAPIDS

⑪ **Duration:** About 7 min.
Crowds: Long lines all day.
Strategy: Use your Fastpass, or go during the parade.
Audience: All but very young children and adults with heart, back, or neck problems or motion sickness. Minimum height: 38".
Rating: ★★★

Asia's thrilling adventure ride is to the Animal Kingdom what Splash Mountain is to the Magic Kingdom. Aboard a round raft that seats 12, you run the Chakranadi River. After passing through a huge bamboo tunnel filled with jasmine-scented mist, your raft climbs 40 feet upriver, lurches and spins through a series of sharp twists and turns, and then approaches an immense waterfall, which curtains a giant carved tiger face. Past rain forests and temple ruins, you find yourself face-to-face with the denuded slope of a logged-out woodland burning out of control. There are many more thrills, but why spill the beans? **You will get wet, and there's an 80% chance you will get so soaked you'll have to wring out your clothing in the nearest restroom afterward.** If you don't mind the extra baggage, plan ahead with a change of clothing and a plastic bag or, at the very least, bring a poncho.

AFRICA

This largest of the lands is an area of forests and grasslands, predominantly an enclave for wildlife from the continent. The focus is on live animals at the key attractions. Harambe, on the northern bank of Discovery River, is Africa's starting point. Inspired by several East African coastal villages, this Disney town has so much detail that it's mind-boggling to try to soak it all up. Signs on the apparently peeling stucco walls of the buildings are faded, as if bleached by the sun, and everything has a hot, dusty look. For souvenirs with both Disney and African themes, browse through the Mombasa Marketplace and Ziwani Traders. Safari apparel, decorative articles for the home, and jewelry make souvenir shopping more fun.

NEED A BREAK? The tantalizing aroma of fresh-baked cinnamon buns leads to the **Kusafiri Coffee Shop & Bakery,** where, after just one look, you may give in to the urge. These buns are worth the banknotes, and they pair well with a cappuccino or espresso. Kids may opt for a giant cookie and milk.

KILIMANJARO SAFARIS

12 **Duration:** 20 min.

Crowds: Heavy in the morning.

Strategy: Arrive in the park first thing in the morning—it's worth the trouble—and come straight here using the Fastpass if necessary. If you arrive at the park late morning, save this for the end of the day, when it isn't so hot. You'll probably see about the same number of animals as in early morning.

Audience: All ages—parents can hold small tykes and explain the poacher fantasy.

Rating: ★★★

A giant Imagineered baobab tree is the starting point for this adventure into the up-country. Although re-creating an African safari in the United States may not be a new idea, this safari goes a step beyond merely allowing you to observe rhinos, hippos, antelope, wildebeests, giraffes, zebras, elephants, lions, and the like. There are illustrated game-spotting guides above the seats in the open-air safari vehicles, and as you lurch and bump over some 100 acres of savanna, forest, rivers, and rocky hills, you'll see most of these animals—sometimes so close you feel like you could reach out and touch them. It's easy to suspend disbelief here because the landscape is so effectively modeled and replenished by Disney horticulturists. This being a theme park, dangers lurk in the form of ivory poachers, and it suddenly becomes your mission to save a group of elephants from would-be poachers. Even without the scripted peril, there's enough elephant excitement on the savanna to impress everyone. In the past several years, four baby elephants have been born—the first, a male calf named Tufani, born May 22, 2003, is the fourth surviving elephant calf in North America resulting from artificial insemination. The second, a female named Kianga, arrived July 6, 2004, as part of the park's breeding program coordinated by the American Zoo and Aquarium Association; on December 19, 2005, the 233-pound female calf Nadirah was born at the park. The park's fourth baby elephant, a male calf named Tsavo, arrived June 28, 2008. The growing youngsters hang out with the rest of the herd. Other babies born at the park and thriving in their habitats are a white rhinoceros and baby giraffe.

PANGANI FOREST EXPLORATION TRAIL

13 **Duration:** Up to you.

Crowds: Heavy in the morning, but there's room for all, it seems.

Strategy: Go while waiting for your safari Fastpass; try to avoid going at the hottest time of day, when the gorillas like to nap.

Audience: All ages.

Rating: ★★★

Calling this a nature walk doesn't really do it justice. A path winds through dense foliage, alongside streams, and past waterfalls. En route there are viewing points where you can stop and watch a beautiful rare okapi (part of the giraffe family) munching the vegetation, a family and a separate bachelor group of lowland gorillas, hippos (which you usually can see underwater), comical meerkats (a kind of mongoose), graceful gerenuk (an African antelope), exotic birds, an antelope species called the yellow-backed duiker, and a bizarre colony of hairless mole rats. Native African interpreters are on hand at many viewing points to answer questions.

RAFIKI'S PLANET WATCH

Take the Wildlife Express steam train to this unique center of eco-awareness. Rafiki's, named for the wise baboon from *The Lion King*, is divided into three sections. At the Conservation Station, you can meet animal experts and gather round for a critter encounter, enjoy interactive exhibits, learn about worldwide efforts to protect endangered species and their habitats, and find out ways to connect with conservation efforts in your own community. At the Habitat Habit! section, cotton-top tamarins (small white-headed monkeys) play while you learn how to live with all earth's animals. And you don't have to be a kid to enjoy the Affection Section, where young children and adults who are giving their inner child free rein get face-to-face with goats and some rare domesticated critters from around the world. ■TIP→ **Crowds can get heavy mid-morning. Go in late afternoon if you've hit all key attractions.**

CAMP MINNIE-MICKEY

This Adirondack-style land is the setting for live performances at the Lion King Theater, as well as meet-and-greet trails where Disney characters gather for picture-taking and autographs.

FESTIVAL OF THE LION KING

⑮ **Duration:** 28 min.

Crowds: Not a problem.

Strategy: Arrive 40 min before showtime. If you have a child who might want to go on stage, sit in one of the front rows to increase his or her chance of getting chosen.

Audience: All ages.

Rating: ★★★

If you think you've seen enough *Lion King* to last a lifetime, you're wrong unless you've seen this show. In the air-conditioned theater-in-the-round, Disney presents a delightful tribal celebration of song, dance, and acrobatics that uses huge moving stages and floats. The show's singers are first-rate; lithe dancers wearing exotic animal-theme costumes portray creatures in the wild. Timon, Pumba, and other Lion King stars have key roles.

BLITZ TOUR

BEST OF THE PARK

Whatever you do, arrive early. Get to the parking lot a half hour before the official park opening. Make a beeline for **Expedition Everest** and ride right away (if the wait is 20 minutes or less) or grab a Fastpass. After your yeti encounter, head straight over to Africa and ride **Kilimanjaro Safaris** or get a Fastpass. If you're waiting for a Fastpass appointment, explore the **Pangani Forest Exploration Trail.** If you need a snack, get one of the huge, hot, cinnamon rolls at **Kusafiri Coffee Shop & Bakery.** Next, head over to the **Tree of Life—It's Tough to Be a Bug!** Don't bother with the Fastpass here unless the line wait is longer than 40 minutes. The line meanders along paths that encircle the Tree of Life and allows great views of the tree's animal carvings and animal habitats along the way.

Now zip over to **DINOSAUR** in Dino-Land U.S.A. to pick up a timed Fastpass ticket. Then try to grab a ride on **TriceraTop Spin** or **Primeval Whirl** before heading to **Restaurantosaurus** for a bite to eat. Kids love the food; parents, the music. Afterward, let the children explore the **Boneyard** while you digest. By now it should be time to return to DINOSAUR. Try to time your ride either before or just after the next performance of **Finding Nemo—The Musical** at the Theater in the Wild. Don't forget to check the entertainment schedule so you know when to find your spot for **Mickey's Jammin' Jungle Parade.** If the line's not too long and you're in the mood to get wet, take the plunge on **Kali River Rapids,** then dry out during a stroll along the **Maharajah Jungle Trek** or during the next **Flights of Wonder** show. Then, do a half circle around Discovery Island and head on into Camp Minnie-Mickey, where you and the kids can have your pictures taken with—who else?—Mickey, Minnie, and several of their character friends. Then catch **Festival of the Lion King.** Later, shop in Discovery Island. If time allows, and especially if the kids are along, take the train to **Rafiki's Planet Watch.**

If the wait's not too long, have dinner at the **Rainforest Café**; the surroundings alone are worth the visit.

ON RAINY DAYS

The animals love a cool, light rain, so don't avoid this park in wet weather unless you're feeling wimpy. You're going to get wet on Kali River Rapids anyway!

PARADE

MICKEY'S JAMMIN' JUNGLE PARADE

Duration: 12 min.
Crowds: Heavy.
Strategy: Choose your spot along the parade route early, as this is one of Disney's most creative parades, and you should try not to miss it.
Audience: All ages.
Rating: ★★★

The parade takes off at about 4 PM daily (times may vary, so check Times Guide) on a route beginning at the Kilimanjaro Safaris entrance and continuing around Discovery Island with a "characters on safari" theme. Rafiki in his adventure Rover, Goofy in a safari jeep, and Mickey in his "Bon Voyage" caravan join other popular characters each day for the festive daytime fanfare. Adding to the pomp are a batch of oversize puppets—snakes, giraffes, frogs, tigers, monkeys, and others—created by famed designer Michael Curry, known for the puppet costumes of *The Lion King* on Broadway. Throw in some fanciful "party-animal" stilt walkers and animal rickshaws carrying VIPs or lucky park guests, and you've got another reason to strategize your day carefully.

DISABILITIES AND ACCESSIBILITY

All restaurants, shops, and attractions are completely wheelchair accessible, including the theater-in-the-round at Camp Minnie-Mickey, the Finding Nemo—The Musical at the Theater in the Wild, and at the Tree of Life theater showing It's Tough to Be a Bug!, which are also accessible to electric scooters. However, to fully experience all the bug movie's special effects, guests who use wheelchairs should transfer to one of the theater seats. Check the *Guidebook for Guests with Disabilities* or the park's own guide map for information about closed-captioning boxes for the monitor-equipped attractions such as the Tree of Life and how to get a sign-language interpretation schedule. Scripts and story lines for all attractions are available, and sign-language interpreters can be booked with at least a one-week notice. Braille guides are available at Guest Services; a large Braille map of the park is by the Guest Services lobby and near the Tip Board at the entrance to Discovery Island. Call **WDW Information** (☏ *407/824–4321, 407/827–5141 TTY*) for more details.

In DinoLand U.S.A., you must transfer from your wheelchair to board the **DINOSAUR** thrill ride. Note that you will be jostled quite a bit on this twisting, turning, bumpy ride. **Primeval Whirl** requires a transfer, but **TriceraTop Spin** is wheelchair accessible. To board **Kali River Rapids** in Asia, you'll need to transfer from your wheelchair to one of the ride rafts. If you're like most of the passengers who get soaked on this water ride, you'll be soggy for hours unless you have a change of clothing handy. You must transfer from your wheelchair to board **Expedition Everest.** In Africa, you can roll your wheelchair on board the Wildlife Express train to **Rafiki's Planet Watch,** where you'll need it to traverse the path from the train stop to the station. The **Kilimanjaro Safaris** attraction is also wheelchair accessible, but those in scooters must transfer to a standard wheelchair. Service animals are allowed in most areas of the park; however, some areas are off-limits, including the Affection Section petting-zoo area of Rafiki's Planet Watch, the aviaries of **Pangani Forest Exploration Trail** and **Maharajah Jungle Trek,** and the Expedition Everest, Primeval Whirl, DINOSAUR, and Kali River Rapids rides.

ANIMAL KINGDOM

NAME	Min. Height	Type of Entertainment	Duration	Suits	Crowds	Strategy
Discovery Island						
★ Tree of Life—It's Tough to Be a Bug!	n/a	3-D film	20 min.	All but toddlers	Heavy	Do this after Kilimanjaro Safaris. Good photo op. Fastpass available. Small children may be frightened.
DinoLand U.S.A.						
Boneyard	n/a	play area	Up to you	Under 9	Heavy	Play here while waiting for DINOSAUR Fastpass, or come late in the day.
Cretaceous Trail	n/a	walk through	Up to you	All	ok	Stroll along here as you head toward Chester and Hester's for souvenirs or while you wait for the next *Finding Nemo* show.
Dinosaur	40"	thrill ride	4 min.	5 and up	Mid-morning	Go first thing in the morning or at the end of the day, or use Fastpass.
Fossil Fun Games	n/a	arcade	Up to you	6 and up	ok	Bring a pocketful of change
Finding Nemo—The Musical	n/a	show	30 min.	All	Heavy	Arrive 40 min. before showtime. Take little kids here while big kids wait for Expedition Everest.
Primeval Whirl	48"	thrill ride	2 1/2 min.	All	Heavy	Kids may want to ride twice. Take your first spin early, then Fastpass if the wait is more than 20 min.
TriceraTop Spin	n/a	thrill ride	2 min.	Best for small kids	Heavy	Ride early while everyone else heads for the safari, or queue up while waiting for your Fastpass appointment for DINOSAUR.
Asia						
★ Expedition Everest	44"	thrill ride	2 1/2 min.	7 and up	Yes!	Use Fastpass. This is the park's biggest thrill ride.
Flights of Wonder	n/a	show	30 min.	All	ok	Arrive 15 min before showtime and find a shaded seat beneath one of the awnings—the sun can be brutal.

5

				4 and up		
Kali River Rapids	38"	thrill ride	7 min.	All	Yes!	Use your Fastpass or go during the parade. You'll get wet.
Maharajah Jungle Trek	n/a	animal habitat walk	Up to you	All	ok	Go anytime.
Africa						
★ Kilimanjaro Safaris	n/a	tour	18 min	All	Morning	Do this first thing in the morning. If you arrive at the park late morning, save this for the end of the day, when it's not so hot.
Pangani Forest Exploration Trail	n/a	animal habitat walk	Up to you	All	ok	Go while waiting for your safari Fastpass; try to avoid going at the hottest time of day, when the gorillas like to nap.
Rafiki's Planet Watch	n/a	walk through	Up to you	All	Midmorning	Go in the late afternoon after you've hit all key attractions.
Wildlife Express Train	n/a	train ride	5 min.	All	Steady	Head straight to Affection Section with little kids to come face-to-face with domesticated critters.
Camp Minnie-Mickey						
★ Festival of the Lion King	n/a	show	28 min.	All	ok	Arrive 40 min before showtime. Sit in one of the front rows to increase your kid's chance of being chosen.
Entertainment						
★ Mickey's Jammin' Jungle Parade	n/a	parade	12 min.	All	Heavy	Choose your spot along the parade route early, as this is one of Disney's most creative parades, and you should try not to miss it.

★ = **Fodor's**Choice

EATING IN THE ANIMAL KINGDOM

Restaurants inside Disney's Animal Kingdom serve mostly fast food, but now there are two full-service restaurants. For reservations, call the **Disney Reservation Center** (☎ *407/939–3463*) at least one day ahead.

FULL-SERVICE RESTAURANTS

The **Rainforest Café**, part of the international chain of the same name, is appropriately situated right outside the Animal Kingdom entrance. It's truly a jungle in there, and the occasional orchestrated "thunderstorms" and robotic elephant, monkey, and other creatures make the experience a real treat for kids. A meal here really isn't about the food (though much of it is quite good), but about the moving animals, strange jungle sounds, and other made-for-kids distractions.

The **Yak & Yeti Restaurant** is a new eatery in the Asia area that serves lunch and dinner "Pan Asian" style. The large dining room overflows with artifacts and intricate carvings; plates are covered with miso salmon, honey chicken, and tempura shrimp. Chilled sake, beers from India, and other exotic drinks are on the bar menu.

SELF-SERVICE RESTAURANTS

At Discovery Island's **Flame Tree Barbecue** you can dig into ribs, brisket, and pulled pork with several sauce choices. There are also fresh tossed salads. The tables, set beneath intricately carved wood pavilions, make great spots for a picnic.

On the other side of Discovery Island from Flame Tree Barbecue, **Pizzafari** serves individual pizzas, salads, and sandwiches. There's plenty of self-service seating in spacious rooms. First thing in the morning, you can even grab a quick breakfast pizza or egg and hash brown platter here en route to your safari ride.

Restaurantosaurus, in DinoLand U.S.A., is open for counter-service lunches and dinners featuring burgers, fries, chicken nuggets, and salads. The wacky decor and "prehistoric" tunes make refueling more fun.

Tusker House Restaurant, in Harambe, is a buffet restaurant in a colorful indoor-outdoor marketplace setting where flavorful dishes, including spit-roasted meats, are seasoned with an African touch. Donald's Safari Breakfast greets morning guests with a buffet spread hosted by Donald Duck and his Disney character pals.

If you don't have time for its full-service counterpart, the **Yak & Yeti Local Food Cafes** in Asia offers a quick stop for counter-service fried rice, egg rolls, and sweet-and-sour pork dishes.

GUIDED TOURS

Call 407/939–8687 to arrange for an Animal Kingdom tour.

Backstage Safari takes an in-depth look at animal conservation every Monday, Wednesday, Thursday, and Friday 8:30–11:30 and also 1:30–4:30, stopping at the animal hospital and other behind-the-scenes areas. It's a great way to learn about animal behaviors and how handlers care for the critters in captivity, but don't expect to see many animals on this tour. Book ahead; you can make reservations up to a year in advance. Those in your party must all be at least 16 years old to participate and the cost is $70 plus park admission.

Wild by Design offers participants 14 and older insights into the creation of Disney's Animal Kingdom every Monday, Wednesday, Thursday, and Friday, from 8:30 to 11:30. The tour touches on the park's art, architecture, history, and agriculture, and reveals how stories of exotic lands are told at the park. You get a glimpse of behind-the-scenes buildings to see custodians taking care of the animals. The tour price is $60; park admission is required as well.

5

The Water Parks

WORD OF MOUTH

"I prefer Typhoon Lagoon over Blizzard Beach even though it's older. Blizzard is different, with ski lifts and the snow look, but I felt the lazy river ride at Typhoon was better, and they have a spot to snorkel and the lines weren't as long."

— Brooke

"Go to Blizzard Beach, the Disney water park. Arrive EARLY. You'll be cool all day there! The kids love it. [The water parks] also have a lazy river that goes round and round."

— AttyWSW

Updated by
Jennie Hess

There's something about a water park that brings out the kid in all of us, and there's no denying that the Disney water parks are two of the best in the world. What sets them apart? It's really the same thing that differentiates all Disney parks—the detailed themes.

Whether you're cast away on a balmy island at Typhoon Lagoon or washed up on a ski resort-turned-seaside playground at Blizzard Beach, you can be sure that the landscaping and clever architecture will add to the traditional fun of flume and raft rides, wave pools, and splash areas for the youngest children. Another plus: the vegetation has matured enough to allow lots of shade for those who need a break from the sun. The Disney water parks give you that lost-in-paradise feeling on top of all those high-speed wedgie-inducing waterslides. Blizzard Beach and Typhoon Lagoon are so popular with visitors and locals that crowds often reach overflow capacity in summer. And your children may like them so much that they simply must go again during your stay. That's why we recommend that you plan your water-park visit on a day early in your visit. If you're going to Disney World five days or more between April and October, we suggest adding the Water Park Fun & More option to your ticket. Of course, check the weather in advance to make sure the temperatures are to your liking for running around in a swimsuit.

GETTING THERE AND AROUND

You can either take WDW bus transportation or drive to the water parks. There's no charge to park your car at either Typhoon Lagoon or Blizzard Beach. Once inside, your options are to walk, swim, or slide. Arrive 30 minutes ahead of park opening and get ready to race to the tallest slides.

TYPHOON LAGOON

According to Disney legend, Typhoon Lagoon was created when the quaint, thatched-roof, lushly landscaped Placid Palms Resort was struck by a cataclysmic storm. It left a different world in its wake: surfboards sundered trees, once-upright palms imitated the Leaning Tower of Pisa, and part of the original lagoon was cut off, trapping thousands of tropical fish—and a few sharks. Nothing, however, topped the fate of *Miss Tilly*, a shrimp boat from "Safen Sound, Florida," which was hurled high in the air and became impaled on Mt. Mayday, a magi-

WHICH PARK'S FOR ME?

Most people agree that kids under 7 and older adults prefer Typhoon Lagoon, while bigger kids and teens like Blizzard Beach better because it has more slides and big-deal rides.

TIP SHEET

■ There's really only one problem with the water parks—they're crowd pleasers. In summer and on weekends, the parks often reach capacity by mid-morning.

■ If you must visit in summer, go during late afternoon when park hours run later or when the weather clears up after a thundershower. Typically, rainstorms drive away the crowds.

■ If you plan to make a whole day of it, avoid weekends—the water parks are big among locals as well as visitors.

■ Arrive 30 minutes before opening time so you can park, buy tickets, rent towels, and snag inner tubes before the hordes descend. Set up camp and hit the slides and whitewater rides first.

■ Women and girls should wear one-piece swimsuits unless they want to find their tops somewhere around their ears at the bottom of the waterslide.

■ One word—sunscreen. OK, so you know why it's important. But it's easy to lose track of time and forget to reapply, which can be a big mistake even on partly cloudy Florida days. Set your waterproof watch alarm or plan a sunscreen dousing during lunch, snack, or early dinner gatherings. Remember, that boiled-lobster look is neither attractive nor healthy.

■ An inexpensive pair of water shoes will do wonders to save the feet—especially children's tender footsies—from hot sand and walkways, and from grimy restroom floors.

■ Review the park layout with children, and help orient them to the spot where you've chosen to camp out for the day.

■ If you're visiting during a cooler time of year, go in the afternoon, when the water will have warmed up a bit.

cal volcano that periodically tries to dislodge *Miss Tilly* with huge geysers of water.

Ordinary folks, the legend continues, would have been crushed by such devastation. But the resourceful residents of Placid Palms were made of hardier stuff—and from the wreckage they created 56-acre Typhoon Lagoon, the self-proclaimed "world's ultimate water park."

Typhoon Lagoon offers a full day's worth of activities. You can bob along in 5-foot waves in a surf lagoon the size of two football fields, speed down waterslides, bump through rapids, go snorkeling, and, for a mellow break, float in inner tubes along the 2,100-foot Castaway Creek, rubberneck from specially constructed grandstands as human cannonballs are ejected from the storm slides, or merely hunker down in one of the many hammocks or lounge chairs and read a book. A children's area replicates adult rides on a smaller scale. It's Disney's version of a day at the beach—complete with friendly Disney lifeguards.

The layout is so simple that it's hard to get lost. The wave and swimming lagoon is at the center of the park; the waves break on the beaches closest to the entrance and are born in Mt. Mayday at the other end of the park. Castaway Creek encircles the lagoon. Anything requiring a gravitational plunge—storm slides, speed slides, and raft trips down rapids—starts around the summit of Mt. Mayday. Shark Reef and Ketchakiddie Creek flank the head of the lagoon, to Mt. Mayday's right and left, respectively, as you enter the park.

There are plenty of lounge chairs and a number of hammocks but definitely not enough beach umbrellas. If you crave shade, commandeer a spot in the grassy picnic area around Getaway Glen on the left side of the park just past the Leaning Palms concession. If you like moving about, people-watching, and having sand in your face, go front and center at the surf pool. For your own patch of sand and some peace and quiet, head for the coves and inlets on the left side of the lagoon.

Numbers in the margin correspond to points of interest on the Typhoon Lagoon map.

GETTING STARTED

DISABILITIES AND ACCESSIBILITY

The park gets high ratings in the accessibility department. All paths that connect the different areas of Typhoon Lagoon are wheelchair accessible. Those who use a wheelchair and who can transfer to a raft or inner tube can also float in **Typhoon Lagoon** and on **Castaway Creek.** Wheelchairs are available in the entrance turnstile area—a limited number are built to go into the water—and are free with ID.

DRESSING ROOMS AND LOCKERS

There are men's and women's thatched-roof dressing rooms and two sizes of full-day lockers ($5 and $7, plus $5 deposit for either) to the right of the entrance on your way into the park; a second, less-crowded set is near Typhoon Tilly's. The towels you can rent (for $2) at the stand to the right of the main entrance are a little skimpy; bring your own beach towel or buy one at Singapore Sal's if you like. The Typhoon Lagoon Imagineers thoughtfully placed restrooms in every available nook and cranny. Most have showers and are much less crowded with clothes-changers than the main dressing rooms.

FIRST AID

The small First-Aid Stand, run by a registered nurse, is on your left as you enter the park, not far from the Leaning Palms food stand.

INFORMATION

The staff at the **Guest Services** (aka Guest Relations) window outside the entrance turnstiles, to your left, can answer many questions; a chalkboard inside gives water temperature and surfing information. During off-season, which encompasses October through April, the park closes for several weeks for routine maintenance and refurbishment. Call **WDW Information** (☎ *407/824–4321*) or check disneyworld.com for days of operation.

Typhoon Lagoon

LOST PEOPLE AND THINGS

Ask about your misplaced people and things at the Guest Services window near the entrance turnstiles, to your left as you enter the park. Lost children are taken to an area by the Tip Board near the front of the park.

PICNICKING

Picnicking is permitted, but you won't be allowed to bring in a cooler too large for one person to carry. Tables are set up at Getaway Glen and Castaway Cove, near Shark Reef. Bring a box lunch from your hotel or pick up provisions from the Goodings supermarket at the Crossroads shopping center (off SR 535), and you'll eat well without having to line up with the masses. Although you can find alcoholic beverages at Typhoon Lagoon, don't bring along your own or you'll be walking them back to the car. Glass containers are also prohibited.

> **FOR YOUNG ONES ONLY**
>
> Most kids under 6 would be just as happy splashing around in a hotel pool as at a water park, but rest assured that there are designated kiddie areas at the water parks so toddlers can play without the danger of being bowled over by bigger kids.

SUPPLIES

The **rental-rafts concession,** the building with the boat sticking through the roof to the left of the entrance, past the Leaning Palms food concession, offers free inner tubes. You need to pick them up only for the lagoon; they're provided for Castaway Creek and all the white-water rides. You can borrow snorkels and masks at **Shark Reef,** but you may not bring your own equipment into Typhoon Lagoon. Free life vests are available at **High and Dry Towels.** You must leave an ID such as a credit card, driver's license, or car keys as collateral.

Singapore Sal's, to the right of the main entrance (on the way into the park), is the place to buy sunscreen, hats, sunglasses, and other beach paraphernalia.

TYPHOON LAGOON ATTRACTIONS

❶ Typhoon Lagoon Surf Pool. This is the heart of the park, a swimming area that spreads out over 2½ acres and contains almost 3 million gallons of clear, chlorinated water. It's scalloped by lots of little coves, bays, and inlets, all edged with white-sand beaches—spread over a base of white concrete, as body surfers soon discover when they try to slide into shore. Ouch! The main attraction is the waves. Twelve huge water-collection chambers hidden in Mt. Mayday dump their load with a resounding "whoosh" into trapdoors to create waves large enough for Typhoon Lagoon to host amateur and professional surfing championships. A piercing double hoot from *Miss Tilly* signals the start and finish of wave action: every 2 hours, for 1½ hours, 5-foot waves issue forth every 90 seconds; the next half hour is devoted to moderate bobbing waves. Even during the big-wave periods, however, the waters in Blustery Bay and Whitecap Cove are protected enough for timid swimmers. Surfers who don't want to risk a fickle ocean can surf here on certain days before the park opens (call ahead for the schedule). Instruction and surfboard are included in the $150 cost, and the surfing experience lasts for 2½ hours. Reserve your waves by calling ☎407/939–7529.

❷ **Castaway Creek.** This circular, 15-foot-wide, 3-foot-deep waterway is everyone's water fantasy come true. Snag an inner tube and float along the creek that winds around the entire park, a wet version of the Magic Kingdom's Walt Disney World Railroad. You pass through a rain forest that showers you with mist and spray, you slide through caves and grottoes, you float by overhanging trees and flowering bushes, and you get dumped on at the Water Works, whose "broken" pipes the Typhoon Lagooners never got around to fixing. The current flows a gentle 2½ feet per second; it takes about 30 minutes to make a full circuit. Along the way there are exits where you can hop out and dry off or do something else—and then pick up another inner tube and jump right back in.

❸ **Shark Reef.** If you felt like leaping onto the stage at the Studios' Voyage of the Little Mermaid or jumping into the tank at Epcot's the Seas with Nemo & Friends, make tracks for this 360,000-gallon snorkeling tank. The coral reef is artificial, but the 4,000 tropical fish—including black-and-white-striped sergeant majors, sargassum trigger fish, yellowtail damselfish, and amiable leopard and bonnet-head sharks—are quite real. To prevent algae growth, Shark Reef is kept at a brisk 72°F, which is about 15 degrees cooler than the rest of Typhoon Lagoon. A sunken tanker divides the reef; its portholes give landlubbers access to the underwater scene and let them go nose-to-nose with snorkelers. Go first thing in the morning or at the end of the day if you want to linger. During the warmest weather, adults and children ages 5 and over can take a personal supplied-air snorkeling lesson at about $20 per half hour. If your kids want to learn how to explore the depths of the ocean Disney style, sign them up at Guest Services when you purchase your tickets.

❹ **Crush 'N' Gusher.** If flume rides, storm slides, and tube races aren't wild enough for your inner thrill-seeker, get ready to defy gravity on Disney's first water coaster. Designed to propel you uphill and down along a series of flumes, caverns, and spillways, this ride should satisfy the most enthusiastic daredevil. Keeping with park lore, Crush 'N' Gusher flows through what appears to be a rusted-out tropical fruit factory, weaving in and out of the wreckage and debris that once transported fruit through the plant's wash facilities. Three fruit spillways are aptly named Banana Blaster, Coconut Crusher, and Pineapple Plunger. ☞*Audience: Children under 48" are not allowed on this ride. No pregnant women or guests with heart, back; or neck problems or other physical limitations.*

6

When you need to regain your energy, head to **Leaning Palms**, to your left as you enter the park, for standard beach fare—burgers, dogs, pizzas, chef salads, beer, and, of course, ice cream and frozen yogurt. For adults, **Let's Go Slurpin'** is a beach shack on the edge of Typhoon Lagoon that dispenses frozen margaritas as well as wine and beer. **Typhoon Tilly's**, on the right just south of Shark Reef, also serves burgers, dogs, and salads, and pours mostly sugary, nonalcoholic grog—though you can grab a Davy Jones lager if you must.

❺ Humunga Kowabunga. There's little time to scream, but you'll hear just such vociferous reactions as the survivors emerge from the catch pool opposite Shark Reef. The basic question is: want to get scared out of your wits in three seconds flat—and like it enough to go back for more? The two side-by-side Humunga Kowabunga speed slides rightly deserve their acclaim among thrill lovers, as they drop more than 50 feet in a distance barely four times that amount. For nonmathematicians, that's very steep. Oh yes, and then you go through a cave. In the dark. The average speed is 30 MPH; however, you can really fly if you lie flat on your back, cross your ankles, wrap your arms around your chest, and arch your back. Just remember to smile for the rubberneckers on the grandstand at the bottom. ☞ *Audience: Children under 48" are not allowed on this ride. No pregnant women or guests with heart, back, or neck problems or other physical limitations.*

❻ Storm Slides. Each of these three body slides is about 300 feet long and snakes in and out of rock formations, through caves and tunnels, and under waterfalls, but each has a slightly different view and offers a twist. The one in the middle has the longest tunnel; the others' secrets you'll have to discover for yourself. Maximum speed is about 20 MPH, and the trip takes about 30 seconds.

❼ Mt. Mayday. What goes down can also go up—and up and up and up and up. "It's like climbing Mt. Everest," wailed one teenager about a climb that seems a lot steeper than this 85-foot peak would warrant. However, it's Mt. Everest with hibiscus flowers, a rope bridge, stepping-stones set in plunging waters, and—remember that typhoon?—a broken canoe scattered over the rocks near the top. The view encompasses the entire park.

Lovers of white-water rafting should head to Mayday Falls, Keelhaul Falls, and Gangplank Falls at Mt. Mayday. These white-water raft rides in oversize inner tubes plunge down the mount's left side. Like the Storm Slides, they have caves, waterfalls, and intricate rockwork, but with some extra elements.

❽ Mayday Falls. The 460-foot slide over Mayday Falls in blue inner tubes is the longest and bumpiest of the three falls; it's a straight slide over the falls into a catchment, which gives you just enough time to catch your breath before the next plunge.

❾ Keelhaul Falls. This spiraling, 400-foot ride in yellow inner tubes through raging rapids seems way faster than the purported 10 MPH.

⑩ Gang Plank Falls. If you climb up Mt. Mayday for this ride, you'll go down in four-person, 6½-foot-long inflated rafts that descend crazily through 300 feet of rapids. This is a great ride for adventurous families to enjoy together—the rafts can hold five if some of the passengers are kids.

⑪ Ketchakiddie Creek. Typhoon Lagoon's children's area has slides, mini-rapids, squirting whales and seals, bouncing barrels, waterfalls, sprinklers, and all the other ingredients of a splash fiesta. The bubbling sand ponds, where youngsters can sit in what seems like an enormous whirlpool bath, are special favorites. ☞ *All adults must be accompanied by a child or children under 48" and vice versa.*

⑫ Bay Slides. These scaled-down versions of the Storm Slides are geared to younger kids, who must be under 60 inches to ride.

BLIZZARD BEACH

With its oxymoronic name, Blizzard Beach promises the seemingly impossible—a seaside playground with an alpine theme. As with its older cousin, Typhoon Lagoon, the Disney Imagineers have created an entire legend to explain the park's origin: after a freak winter storm dropped snow over the western side of Walt Disney World, entrepreneurs decided to create Florida's first downhill ski resort. Saunalike temperatures soon returned. But just as the resort's operators were ready to close up shop, they spotted a playful alligator sliding down the "liquid ice" slopes. The realization that the melting snow had created the tallest, fastest, and most exhilarating water-filled ski and toboggan runs in the world gave birth to the ski resort–water park.

Disney Imagineers have gone all out here to create the paradox of a ski resort in the midst of a tropical lagoon. Lots of verbal puns and sight gags play with the snow-in-Florida motif. The park's centerpiece is Mt. Gushmore, with its 120-foot-high Summit Plummet, as well as other toboggan and water-sled runs with names such as Teamboat Springs; Toboggan Racer; Slush Gusher; and Runoff Rapids. Between Mt. Gushmore's base and its summit, swim-skiers can also ride a chairlift converted from ski-resort to beach-resort use—with umbrellas and snow skis on their undersides. Devoted waterslide enthusiasts generally prefer Blizzard Beach to the other water parks.

Numbers in the margin correspond to points of interest on the Blizzard Beach map.

GETTING STARTED

DISABILITIES AND ACCESSIBILITY

Most paths are flat and level. If you use a wheelchair, you'll also be able to float in **Cross Country Creek,** provided you can transfer to a large inner tube. Other guests with limited mobility might also be able to use the inner tubes at some of the park's tamer slides. A limited number of wheelchairs—some suitable to wheel into the water—are available near the park entrance and are free if you leave an ID.

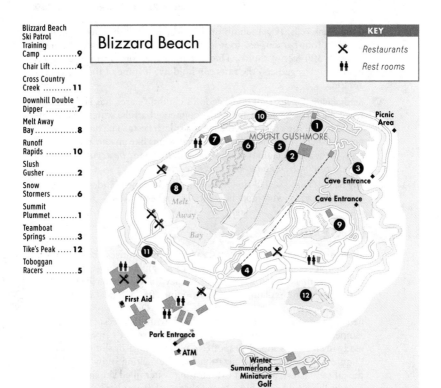

DRESSING ROOMS AND LOCKERS

Dressing rooms are in the Village area, just inside the main entrance. There are showers and restrooms here as well. Lockers are strategically located near the entrance, next to Snowless Joe's Rentals and near Tike's Peak, the children's area (more convenient if you have little swim-skiers in tow). At Snowless Joe's it costs $5 to rent a small locker, $7 for a large one; plus a $5 deposit required. Only small lockers are available at Tike's Peak. Restrooms are conveniently located throughout the park; there are facilities in the Village area near the entrance, in Lottawatta Lodge, at the Ski Patrol Training Camp, and just past the Melt Away Bay beach area. Towels are available for rent at Snowless Joe's ($2), but they're tiny. If you care, buy a proper beach towel in the Beach Haus or bring your own.

FIRST AID

The First-Aid Stand, overseen by a registered nurse, is in the Village, between Lottawatta Lodge and the Beach Haus.

INFORMATION

Disney staffers at the Guest Services window, to the left of the ticket booth as you enter the park, can answer most of your questions. Each year, the park closes for several weeks during the fall or winter months for routine maintenance and refurbishment. For the park's days of operation, call **Blizzard Beach** (☎407/824–4321) or check the disneyworld.com Web site.

LOST PEOPLE AND PEOPLE

Start your visit by naming a specific meeting place and time. Instruct your youngsters to let any lifeguard know if they get lost. If they do get lost, don't panic: head for the Tip Board near the front of the park where lost children are recovered.

PICNICKING

You're not allowed to bring glass containers or your own alcoholic beverages into the park. Picnicking is welcome, however, and several areas are pleasant lunch spots, most notably the terrace outside Lottawatta Lodge and its environs. Coolers must be small enough for one person to handle; otherwise, you won't be able to take them into the park.

SUPPLIES

Personal flotation devices, better known as life jackets, are available free to children and adults at **Snowless Joe's** (leave your ID with an attendant until you return them). You can't rent inner tubes here: they're provided at the rides.

Sunglasses, sunscreen, bathing suits, waterproof disposable cameras, and other sundries are available at the **Beach Haus,** along with Blizzard Beach logo merchandise. Check out the ski equipment hanging from the ceiling. The **Sled Cart,** a kiosk-style shop, sells souvenirs, suntan lotion, and water toys.

6

BLIZZARD BEACH ATTRACTIONS

❶ **Summit Plummet.** This is Mt. Gushmore's big gun, which Disney bills as "the world's tallest, fastest free-fall speed slide." From Summit Plummet's "ski jump" tower, it's a wild 55-MPH plunge straight down to a splash landing at the base of the mountain. It looks almost like a straight vertical drop. If you're watching from the beach below, you can't hear the yells of the participants, but rest assured—they're screaming their heads off. ☞*Minimum height: 48".*

❷ **Slush Gusher.** This speed slide, which drops through a snow-banked mountain gully, is shorter and less severe than Summit Plummet but a real thriller nonetheless. ☞*Minimum height: 48".*

❸ **Teamboat Springs.** Six-passenger rafts zip along in one of the world's longest family white-water raft ride. Since its original construction, it has doubled its speed of departure onto its twisting, 1,200-foot channel of rushing waterfalls. This is great for families—a good place for kids too big for Tike's Peak to test more grown-up waters.

❹ **Chair Lift.** If you're waterlogged, take a ride from the beachfront base of Mt. Gushmore up over its face and on to the summit—and back down again. Children must be at least 48 inches tall to ride alone, or 32 inches tall to ride accompanied by an adult.

⑤ Toboggan Racers. On this ride you grab a mat and swoosh down an eight-lane waterslide over Mt. Gushmore's "snowy" slopes.

⑥ Snow Stormers. No water park would be complete without a fancy water-slide, and Blizzard Beach has one—actually three flumes that descend from the top of Mt. Gushmore along a switchback course of ski-type slalom gates.

⑦ Downhill Double Dipper. These side-by-side racing slides are where future Olympic hopefuls 48 inches and taller can compete against one another.

NEED A BREAK?

Lottawatta Lodge—a North American ski lodge with a Caribbean accent—is the park's main emporium of fast food. Lines are long at peak feeding times.

The **Warming Hut**, which is open seasonally, offers smoked turkey legs, salads, hot dogs, and ice cream. Hot dogs, snow cones, and ice cream are on the menu at **Avalunch**. **Frostbite Freddie's** and **Polar Pub** on the main beach both sell frozen drinks and spirits.

⑧ Melt Away Bay. The park's main pool is a 1-acre oasis that's constantly fed by "melting snow" waterfalls. The man-made waves are positively oceanlike. If you're not a strong swimmer, stay away from the far end of the pool, where the waves originate. You can get temporarily stuck in a pocket even if your head is still above water.

⑨ Blizzard Beach Ski Patrol Training Camp. The preteens in your crowd may want to spend most of their time on the T-bar drop, bungee-cord slides, and culvert slides here. In addition, there's a chance to take on Mogul Mania, a wide-open area where you can jump from one slippery mogul to the next. The moguls really look more like baby icebergs bobbing in a swimming pool.

⑩ Runoff Rapids. You have to steel your nerves to climb into an inner tube for these three twisting, turning flumes—even one that's in the dark. But once you're in, it's way more fun than scary.

⑪ Cross Country Creek. Just grab an inner tube, hop on, and circle the entire park on this creek during a leisurely 45-minute float. Along the way, you'll get doused with frigid water in an ice cave—wonderful on a steamy Florida day.

⑫ Tike's Peak. Disney is never one to leave the little ones out of the fun, and this junior-size version of Blizzard Beach, set slightly apart from the rest of the park, has scaled-down elements of Mt. Gushmore. Adults must be accompanied by children under 48 inches tall.

Disney Cruises

WORD OF MOUTH

"The kids' programs are the absolute best! They do science projects (they make them fun, really), plays, games, etc. At night in the kids' area they have a huge screen where they show the latest Disney movies and they bring out little cots for the kids to sit on, and warm freshly baked cookies and milk! They think of everything. We had to drag our kids out of there. Try to get them to leave to see the shows though. They are really fantastic productions."

—nina

Updated by
Jennie Hess

With Disney's reach extending all the way to the high seas on two cruise ships, the *Disney Magic* and the *Disney Wonder,* there's an alternative vacation for "sail" beyond the Orlando kingdom. The Disney Cruise Line (DCL) ships, each with 875 staterooms and a capacity of 2,700, offer several excursions from Port Canaveral, Florida, to eastern and western Caribbean destinations, with stops at a nice mix of ports and at Disney's own private island, Castaway Cay.

Periodically, the ships offer alternative sailings to the Mexican Riviera, Mediterranean ports, and southern Caribbean islands. In 2010, the Disney Magic launches its first sailing to Northern European capitals with stops at Oslo, Copenhagen, and St. Petersburg, among others.

Aboard the *Magic,* Mickey's silhouette is on the funnels and Goofy clings to the stern. Styled like a classic liner, the ship sails on a seven-night eastern Caribbean cruise, stopping at St. Maarten or St. Croix, St. Thomas (with excursions to St. John), and Castaway Cay. On alternate weeks, the *Magic* follows a western Caribbean itinerary to ports of call in Key West, Grand Cayman, and Cozumel, with the grand finish at Castaway Cay. In 2010, the Magic crosses the pond in late April to begin a series of Northern European and Mediterranean cruises that continue through September; the ship then returns to resume its Caribbean sailings. The art nouveau–inspired *Wonder* also mixes up its 2010 schedule a bit, adding new twists to its popular-with-first-time-cruisers three- or four-night Bahamian cruises. A new five-night sailing adds Key West to the Nassau and Castaway Cay stops; another five-night cruise makes two stops at the idyllic Castaway Cay on the way to and from Nassau. Plus, you can combine this ocean getaway with a stay at Walt Disney World Resort for a seamless land-and-sea vacation. You check in just once: your room key at your Disney resort hotel becomes both your boarding pass at Disney's terminal at Port Canaveral and the key to your stateroom. A top draw of Disney's cruises is the private island Castaway Cay where there are separate beaches for adults, families, and teens, as well as good snorkeling and a family-friendly stingray adventure. Parents can enjoy some private time on the island while well-tended kids forget they're even around. Then everyone can share family time on the beach or in the water.

CRUISE PACKAGES

Packages include room, meals, and activities but not transportation to and from the ship (unless you book air travel at the same time) or shore excursions. Prices can vary greatly depending on the destination, the time of year you sail, and even depending which week you book. You might get a better rate by booking early, but occasionally you'll get a bargain by booking at the last minute on a ship that hasn't filled. The larger your stateroom and the better the location, the higher the price will be.

To book any Disney cruise, call **Disney Cruise Line** (☎800/370–0097 ⊕*www.disneycruise.com*). If you want to dig for a discount on your Disney cruise, locate a travel agent who specializes in cruises at www.travelsense.org.

SPECIAL-OCCASION PACKAGES

Special-occasion cruises have become hot tickets as cruising gains popularity generally, and DCL will help you celebrate. One popular add-on package is the Romantic Escape at Sea ($359 per couple) with champagne breakfast in bed, passes to the ship spa's Tropical Rain Forest sauna, steam room, and other amenities, priority seating at the adults-only restaurant, Palo, a romantic gift amenity and "romance turn-down service." A Disney Fairy Tale Weddings specialist will help couples plan weddings or vow renewals on the ship. If you want to surprise someone with a birthday bouquet or special gift, you can arrange it ahead of time with your Disney Cruise planner.

7

STATEROOMS

Cabins are ranked by category and range from standard inside staterooms (Categories 11 and 12, 184 square feet; sleeps 3 in Category 12, and 3 to 4 in Category 11) and deluxe inside staterooms (214 square feet; sleeps 3 to 4) to deluxe ocean-view rooms (Categories 8 and 9, 214 square feet; sleeps 3 to 4) to suites that sleep seven and provide sweeping views from a spacious balcony (Categories 1 and 2, from 945 to 1,029 square feet). In between the high and low ends are deluxe one-bedroom suites with verandas (Category 3, 614 square feet; sleeps 4 to 5); deluxe family stateroom with veranda (Category 4, 304 square feet; sleeps 5); and deluxe ocean-view staterooms with verandas (Categories 5 to 7, 268 square feet; Category 7 sleeps 3 and Categories 6 to 7 sleeps 3 to 4). The most luxurious and expensive staterooms are Category 1 Royal Suites, with private verandas and all the amenities you could dream of, including a media library and dining salon.

Quite a few of the staterooms feature a clever pull-down bunk-bed setup that saves space until bedtime and draws cheers from children.

On each ship, 73% of rooms have ocean views and 44% have private verandas. All are elegantly appointed with natural wood furniture. In addition, all except Category 11 and 12 rooms have split bathrooms, one with shower and sink, the other with toilet and sink, which allow couples and families to get ready in half the time.

Disney does a commendable job of keeping all rooms and much of the rest of the ship smoke-free while setting aside some deck, bar, and private veranda areas for smokers. Accessible staterooms for people with disabilities have ramps, handrails, fold-down shower seats, and handheld showerheads; special communications kits are available with phone alerts, amplifiers, and text typewriters.

SHORE EXCURSIONS

At various ports of call, Disney offers between one and two dozen organized shore excursions, from snorkeling and diving to sightseeing and shopping. For example, at Grand Cayman you can visit a butterfly farm or sign up for a trip to Stingray City, not really a city, but a long sandbar where hundreds of rays live. During a stop at Cozumel, you can explore the magnificent Mayan ruins of Tulum and strike a bargain for handcrafted Mexican hats, toys, and knickknacks. At St. Maarten you can sign up for a mountain-biking adventure, and on St. John, you can join a sail-and-snorkel expedition. All activities are rated from "leisurely" to "strenuously active." For full descriptions of the many shore excursions, go to ⊕*www.disneycruise.com.*

ADULT ACTIVITIES

When people think Disney cruise, they often think it's a family-only affair. Not necessarily so. Sure, families get the best of all worlds on each of these elegant ships, there's no reason why adults (especially those who want to be kids again) have to miss out on the fun. On both ships, several areas are just for grown-ups, including one of the three pools. Poolside games, wine tastings, dessert-making, and even navigational demonstrations by the ship's bridge officers are among the diversions just for adults. The ship's spa is a don't-miss for those who need some pampering; the best time slots fill quickly, though, so book either when you buy your package or as soon as you board.

For a romantic dinner, book an evening at the intimate, adults-only **Palo** (both ships), with its sweeping ocean views. Expect a fantastic wine list and dishes like grilled salmon with creamy risotto; warm shrimp salad with crispy pancetta, white beans, and grilled asparagus; and grilled filet mignon with a Port wine reduction and Gorgonzola cheese sauce. Reserve early, as it's a hot ticket. The champagne brunch on four-night-or-longer cruises is another great Palo dining event, with menu goodies like eggs Florentine; sweet pizza with mango, raspberries, and crème fraiche; and carpaccio of grilled eggplant with shaved prosciutto and truffle-oil dressing. Both dinner and brunch cost $15 per person on top of your cruise package.

Beat Street, a nightclub on the *Magic,* has the Rockin' Bar D dance club and Sessions, a piano bar. **Route 66,** the *Wonder*'s nightclub, has the WaveBands dance club and the Cadillac Lounge piano bar. If you're looking for something more low-key, check out **Diversions,** a sports pub on both ships. Or take in a first-run film at the ships' plush Buena Vista Theatre, where full-length features really pop with new digital 3-D technology. At the Cove Café, you can enjoy a gourmet coffee, watch TV, check e-mail, and socialize.

CHILDREN'S ACTIVITIES

On both the *Magic* and the *Wonder,* there's nearly an entire deck reserved for kids. When you drop them off, pick up a pager to stay in touch with the activities counselors. Babysitting is available for children under 3 at **Flounder's Reef Nursery** for $6 per hour (two-hour minimum) and $5 an hour for each additional sibling. To make traveling with babies easier on guests, Disney now offers a groundbreaking online service, Babies Travel Lite, which lets parents order all their baby's travel products, including diapers and formula, and have them shipped to their stateroom before the cruise begins.

The well-run **Oceaneer Club** is part of the cruise package, providing non-stop activities for kids ages 3 to 7, and giving parents the opportunity to enjoy some R&R. Little ones have a ball in the colorful playroom designed to look like Captain Hook's pirate ship. Kids can scramble around on a slide and rope bridge, play with a trunk full of costumes, watch a Disney movie, and get creative with crafts and interactive fun that's part of the new Toy Story Boot Camp. Counselors tailor activities to kids ages 3 to 4 and 5 to 7 separately.

Kids 8 to 12 can head for the high-tech, outer-space-theme **Oceaneer Lab.** There are fun science experiments, sports challenges, and karaoke jams. A new program inspired by the High School Musical craze features a ship-wide scavenger hunt and "Wild Cat Spirit" talent show. With their parent's permission and a Lab Pass sticker on their Key to the World card, children can check themselves in and out of the Lab as they please.

Teens up to age 17 can chill out at their own getaway called the Stack on the *Disney Magic* and Aloft on the *Disney Wonder.* Here teens can tune in to music, watch plasma-screen TVs, play board- and video games, or just hang out and meet new friends. Organized activities for teens include trivia games and evening dance parties. The new T.O.R.C.H (Teen Only Resource and Communication Hub) is a new social Web site with message-, photo-, and video-posting designed for teens cruising aboard a Disney ship.

DINING AND ENTERTAINMENT

RESTAURANTS

Disney offers early and late dinner seating times. Request the best seating time for your family when you book your cruise. Cruise dining coordinators will do their best to seat you at the requested time, but if you're placed on a wait list and scheduled for another seating, you can appeal to restaurant managers for a change once you're on board. Families with small children usually prefer earlier seatings. If you miss your seating, you can always find pizza or a simple buffet served elsewhere on the ship.

The dining coordinators will arrange for you to alternate restaurants each night so you have the chance to sample all three. At **Animator's Palate** (both ships), the color scheme goes from black-and-white to Technicolor as the meal progresses. Dining is slightly more formal at **Lumiere's**, on the *Magic*, where beef tenderloin, lamb shank, and other entrées are served French-style in a grand dining room reminiscent of those aboard classic transatlantic ocean liners. At **Triton's**, on the *Wonder*, seafood, roast duck, pasta, and other selections are served in an elegant, art deco, under-the-sea-theme dining room. At the Caribbean-theme **Parrot Cay** restaurant, the mood is both casual and festive. Character breakfasts and high tea with Wendy of *Peter Pan* fame are options aboard the *Magic* (but not the *Wonder*).

AFTER DARK

All Disney Cruise itineraries include the **Pirates IN the Caribbean** party, during which swashbuckling servers dish up an "argh" or two, a cup of grog, and (on all seven-night cruises) a pirate bandanna for every guest at dinner. After dinner, you head off to a deck party where Captain Hook, Mr. Smee, and others appear for some high-spirited action, dancing, and a grand finale of fireworks.

Lavish shows and variety acts entertain families every night of every cruise. The hottest new show to debut aboard the Disney Wonder is Toy Story–The Musical, a larger-than-life stage version of the film classic. The Golden Mickeys is a high-tech salute to the animation of Walt Disney in the form of a Hollywood-style award ceremony. Twice Charmed is a Broadway-style production adding a twist to the Cinderella story. And Disney Dreams is a sweet bedtime story starring Peter Pan, Aladdin, Ariel, and other popular Disney characters with updated enhancements that provide animation, pyrotechnic and laser features, snow effects, and mechanisms that let characters "fly" more convincingly. Each ship also has a **cinema** screening classic Disney films, and every guest will have the opportunity to experience a show or film featuring the new Disney Digital 3-D enhancements.

Assistive listening systems for guests with disabilities are available in the ships' main theaters, and sign language interpretation is offered for live performances on specified cruise dates.

CASTAWAY CAY

Disney has its own private island, and you're invited. White-sand beaches, towering palms, and swaying hammocks beckon at Castaway Cay, the final stop of every Disney cruise. You're free to roam the island, relax on the beach, or join an excursion such as snorkeling or parasailing. Castaway Ray's Stingray Adventure, a calmer take on Grand Cayman's Stingray City, is a program that lets adults and kids age 5 and up touch, feed, and even snorkel with stingrays in an island lagoon. Tours and programs book up quickly so make your reservations when you buy your package.

If you're not traveling with children or if you've dropped them off at Scuttle's Cove to take part in the kids' programs, hop a tram to Serenity Bay. This is a beach just for adults, where you can melt under the influence of a cabana-sheltered Swedish massage (reserve in advance) or sip a rum punch from Castaway Air Bar. A barbecue lunch buffet is served on both the family and adult ends of the island. Sand-accessible wheelchairs are available for guests who need them.

7

Universal Orlando

WORD OF MOUTH

"One of the wonderful things about Universal is you can walk anywhere. The walk between the two parks is no big deal and City Walk is right in between them."

—schmerl

Updated
by Gary
McKechnie

For nearly 20 years Universal and Disney have been going head to head. When one park adds a resort hotel, the other follows. When a hot new attraction is unveiled at Disney, you can bet on the arrival of hot new attraction at Universal. With the addition of Blue Man Group, Hollywood Rip Ride Rocket—a new, interactive rollercoaster—and a Harry Potter–theme land set to open at Islands of Adventure, the competition is sure to continue into the next decade.

Universal is not just a theme park. In substance as well as style, it's a complete resort destination. Borrowing a concept from Walt Disney World Resort, which encompasses theme parks and hotels, Universal Orlando Resort refers to the conglomeration of Universal Studios Florida (the original theme park), Islands of Adventure (the second theme park), CityWalk (the dining-shopping-nightclub complex), and three fabulous on-property hotels.

Located halfway between Walt Disney World and downtown Orlando, and just off heavily trafficked International Drive, Universal is surprisingly secluded. You drive into one of two massive parking complexes (at 3.4 million square feet they're the largest on earth) and take moving walkways to the theme parks. Or, if you're staying at a Universal hotel, you can take a motor launch or stroll to the entrance. When you arrive you'll notice a few things . . .

While Disney creates a fantasy world for people—especially young children—who love fairy tales, Universal Orlando is geared to older kids, adults, and anyone who enjoys high-energy thrills and pop culture. Movie and TV fans will love this place. But along with pop culture comes plenty of commercialism: cash-depleting distractions like rock-climbing walls, souvenir kiosks, and other such traces of tackiness. To be fair, Disney is adding such distractions, and Universal does show an impressive commitment to creativity, presentation, and cutting-edge technology through newer attractions. In recent years they have jettisoned several old attractions to spotlight current favorites like Shrek, Jimmy Neutron, the Mummy, and the Simpsons Ride, and then premiered the dazzling Blue Man Group. Two major events are planned for 2009: The new Hollywood Rip Ride Rockit roller coaster at Universal Studios and the Wizarding World of Harry Potter at Islands of Adventure. What would really put things over the top is if Universal took some tips from the competition on employee hospitality and the value of presentation. And when you want to forsake land-based action rides, you can head over to Wet 'n Wild (owned by Universal, but not a part of Universal Orlando Resort) for an afternoon of aquatic adrenaline and a place to cool off.

TICKET	ADULTS	AGES 3–9
1 day, 1 park	$79	$69
1 day, 2 parks	$90	$80
2 days, 2 parks *second day expires within six days of first stamp; for unlimited expiration, add $10*	$119.99	$109.99
5-park FlexTicket	$234.95	$214.95

ADMISSION

For the most significant savings of time and money, buy your tickets online (⊕*www.universalorlando.com*) *or* on the phone ahead of time. You'll avoid the incredibly long and slow lines (even in low season) at the ticket booths at the park entrances and won't be subjected to the full-priced "at the gate" fees and the confusing smorgasbord of prices. Plus, there are no shipping costs because you can print your tickets directly from your computer. One such online-only bargain is the Early-Bird Exclusives Ticket. For about $95 you receive unlimited admission to both theme parks and CityWalk for seven consecutive days—quite a savings. Here are your other ticket options (tax not included).

You may also want to consider FlexTickets, which let you add visits to SeaWorld, Wet 'n Wild, and Busch Gardens Tampa Bay, and Aquatica onto visits to Universal. These FlexTickets are good for unlimited admission for 14 consecutive days.

People with a disability that limits enjoyment of the park are eligible for a 15% discount off the ticket price. Also, American Automobile Association members get 10% off, sometimes more, at AAA offices. There are discount coupons for most theme parks in tourist flyers distributed around Orlando and if you buy tickets at the **Orlando/Orange County Convention & Visitors Bureau Orlando/Orange County Convention & Visitors Bureau**(⊠*8723 International Dr.* ☎*407/363–5871*), you can save about $5 per adult ticket ($3 on children's prices).

BABY CARE

There are diaper-changing tables in men's and women's restrooms. Nursing facilities and complimentary diapers are at the Health Services/First Aid centers (two per park). Many shops stock basic baby care items—wipes, etc.—but they are kept out of sight at the cash registers, so you have to ask for them. Also, check the park maps: a baby bottle symbol lets you know which ones carry the items.

CHILD SWAP

All rides have Child Swap areas, so that one parent or adult party member can watch a baby or toddler while the other enjoys the ride or show. The adults then do the swap, and the former caretaker rides without having to wait in line all over again.

GETTING THERE AND AROUND

Driving east on I–4 (from WDW and the Tampa area), get off at Universal Boulevard (Exit 75A). Then take a left onto Universal Boulevard and follow the signs.

Driving west on I–4 (from the Daytona and Jacksonville areas), take Universal Boulevard (Exit 74B). Turn right onto Hollywood Way and follow the signs.

Both Universal Studios and Islands of Adventure (sometimes called simply IOA) are large parks that require a lot of walking. At IOA, sights are organized in a big circle, so if you plan carefully—that is, arrive early—you only have to walk around the doughnut once. Avoid backtracking if you're with small children or senior citizens. At the Studios, you may have to cross the park a couple of times, especially if it's crowded and your Universal Express appointments are at inconvenient times.

HAND STAMPS
If you want to leave the park and come back the same day, have your hand stamped when you leave, and show your hand and ticket when you return.

HOURS
Universal Studios and Islands of Adventure are both open 365 days a year, from 9 to 7, with hours as late as 10 in summer and holiday periods.

INFORMATION
Call **Universal Orlando** (☎ *407/363–8000 or 888/331–9108* ⊕ *www.universalorlando.com*) for tickets, hotel reservations, and information.

PARKING
Universal's parking garage complex, which serves both theme parks and CityWalk, is the world's largest. Definitely write down your parking space, because everything looks the same inside and after a few go-rounds on the Hulk you might have a hard time remembering whether you parked at King Kong 104 or Jaws 328. Because your vehicle is covered, it's not so sweltering at the end of the day even when it's hot. The cost is $12 for cars and motorcycles, $15 for campers. Valet parking, which puts you just a short walk (and about 15 minutes closer) to the entrance of Universal Studios, is available for $10 if you're there less than two hours, $20 if more. Parking in the garage is $3 after 6 PM, free after 10 PM.

STAYING ON SITE
When you stay at one of Universal's resort hotels—the Portofino Bay, Hard Rock Hotel, or Royal Pacific—you receive early admission to the parks, unlimited access to the express lines at rides, and priority seating at some restaurants. And in minutes you can walk to CityWalk and the parks. All three resorts are luxurious, fantasy-theme palaces, with room rates to match (though bargains can be had in the off-season). *For detailed property descriptions, see Chapter 12, Where to Stay.*

UNIVERSAL EXPRESS
The Universal Express Pass works much like Disney's Fastpass. You make appointments to get into the express line at certain popular attractions by inserting your theme-park ticket into a machine and getting a Universal Express Pass. The free pass is printed with the times between which you should show up for the ride, which means you'll likely wait no longer than 15 minutes for even the most popular attractions. Smart.

You can't get another pass, or appointment, until your current one is used or the time expires.

With a Universal Express-PLUS-Pass, you get front-of-the-line access to rides and attractions without having to make or wait for an appointment. Prices vary depending on the season and number of days, but a one-day/one-park pass costs $20 and up; a two-day/two-park pass runs $25 and up. If you're a Universal hotel guest, you actually get this perk for free, or rather, as part of your room rate. You use your hotel key card to access the express lines.

ISLANDS OF ADVENTURE

The creators of Islands of Adventure (IOA) brought theme-park attractions to a new level. From Marvel Super Hero Island and Toon Lagoon to Seuss Landing, Jurassic Park, and the Lost Continent, almost everything is impressive, and the shows, attractions, and at times the rides can even out-Disney Disney.

The park's five theme islands, connected by walkways, are arranged around a large central lagoon. The waterside is a good place to relax, either as a way to escape crowds or to recuperate from an adrenaline-surging coaster.

After passing the turnstiles, you arrive at the Port of Entry plaza. This international bazaar brings together bits and pieces of architecture, landscaping, music, and wares from many lands: you may see Dutch windmills, Indonesian pedicabs, African masks, and Egyptian figurines. But don't stop here. Head directly for the massive archway inscribed with the notice THE ADVENTURE BEGINS. You won't be disappointed.

Numbers in the margin correspond to points of interest on the Islands of Adventure map.

8

BASIC SERVICES

CAMERAS **DeFotos** is a camera shop in the Port of Entry on your right after the turnstiles. They sell disposable cameras both with and without flash for about $20, as well as digital memory cards and sticks, and very basic digital cameras for about $60.

HEALTH SERVICES There are two Health Services/First Aid centers at Islands of Adventure: one at the front entrance inside Guest Services, and the main center near Sindbad's Village in the Lost Continent.

INFORMATION **Guest Services** (☎407/224–6350) is just before the turnstiles on your right before you enter the park. Step through the turnstiles and you can find a rack of brochures and maps in French, Spanish, Portuguese, Japanese, and German, as well as English. If you have questions prior to visiting, call **Universal's main line** (☎407/363–8000).

Studio Information Boards are at the Port of Entry in front of the Lagoon (where the circular walk around the park splits). The boards are posted with up-to-the-minute ride and show operating information—including the length of lines at the major attractions.

LOCKERS There are $8-a-day lockers across from Guest Services at the entrance, with $10 family-size models available; you have unlimited access to

UNIVERSAL ORLANDO TIP SHEET

Universal Orlando is big, but it's not nearly the size of Walt Disney World, so navigating it is much easier.

■ Get there early—at 8 AM if the parks open at 9. Seriously. Seeing the park with about 100 other people is far better than seeing it with thousands. Plus, it's cooler in the morning.

■ Try to visit on a weekday, as locals crowd the parks on weekends.

■ If you aren't a resort guest, arrive in the parking lot at least 45 minutes early.

■ Write down your parking location.

■ Don't forget anything in your car. The parking garage is at least a half-mile from both park entrances and a return round-trip will eat up valuable time.

■ If you're running late, skip the gargantuan parking garage and follow the signs to valet parking. For $18—almost twice the price of regular parking—you'll be in a lot just a few steps from the entrance to CityWalk and have a head start in reaching the parks.

■ If you're a Florida resident, you'll qualify for substantial discounts on admission to these parks. Buying online can save you even more.

■ If you're visiting during busy times, seriously consider buying the Universal Express PLUS Pass for an extra $15 and up (depending on the season and day of the week). It's well worth it to avoid waiting in line.

■ Theme park food can be pricey. Consider the Universal Meal Deal ($20.99 for adults, $10.99 for kids), which pays for meals (one entrée platter and one dessert) at four specific restaurants per park throughout the day. Meal Deals for both parks are $24.99 for adults and $12.99 for kids. A souvenir cup for an additional $8.99 offers unlimited beverages. No sharing.

■ If you're in a hurry to reach the park and don't feel you can stop for a bite, don't worry—there are a Starbucks, a Cinnabon, and other quick-bite eateries at CityWalk. But we still recommend building in 10 minutes for a quick breakfast.

■ If you're overwhelmed by what to see and do, check with Guest Services, where Universal reps will create an itinerary for you, free of charge, based on your interests and available time.

■ One of the best perks of riding solo, if you don't mind breaking up your group, is the advantage of going into the fast-moving Single Rider line. Use it early and often anywhere it's offered.

■ If you're toting a baby around with you, check out the Child Swap areas. Although you won't be able to ride with your spouse, one parent can enter the attraction, take a spin, and then return to take care of the baby while the other parent rides without having to wait in line again.

■ Eat at off times, like 11 AM and 3 PM, to avoid the midday rush for food.

IN UNIVERSAL STUDIOS

■ When entering Universal Studios, many people start a clockwise loop of the park. Instead, head to the right to avoid crowds, especially early in the day.

■ Set up a rendezvous point and time early in the day, just in case you and your companions get separated. Good places include in front of the Lucy Tribute near the entrance, by the stage area across from Mel's Drive-In, and by the seating area of Beetlejuice's Graveyard Revue.

■ Expect kids to get wet at Fievel's Playland and absolutely drenched at Curious George Goes to Town—bring a bathing suit or change of clothing, and stash spare clothes in a nearby locker.

IN ISLANDS OF ADVENTURE

■ Tour the park counter-clockwise, zipping through Seuss Landing to get to Dueling Dragons, if you want to avoid the morning crowds. When you get to the Hulk coaster, you can use an Express Pass.

■ In case someone gets lost, set up a rendezvous point and time at the start of the day. Don't pick an obvious and crowded location (such as the Hulk entrance), but a small restaurant or bridge between two islands.

■ If you plan to ride Dueling Dragons or the Incredible Hulk Coaster, wear shoes that are strapped firmly onto your feet—no flip-flops or heel-less sandals. If you wear glasses, consider pocketing them or wearing a sports strap to keep them firmly against your head when you're flung upside down. Neither coaster is so rough that you're certain to lose your glasses, but better safe than sorry.

■ You should also leave loose change in one of the lockers.

Be ready to get totally drenched on Dudley Do-Right's Ripsaw Falls. Putting your bag under your feet should protect it in large part, but we still recommend a waterproof backpack. There are restrooms near the exit of the ride where you can go to change into your extra set of clothes. Avoid jeans!

WORD OF MOUTH

"We just got back from Universal with our teenage son. My biggest tip is this: Leave the backpack or pocketbook locked up at your hotel. Many of the rides (Men In Black, The Mummy) will not let you carry on anything that can't fit into your pockets. You have to use one of the provided lockers."   –Weadles

8

TOP ISLANDS OF ADVENTURE ATTRACTIONS

FOR AGES 8 AND UP

The Amazing Adventures of Spider-Man. Easily the best ride in town. Get ready to fight the bad guys and put your life in danger. You'll understand what all the brightest engineers and technology wizards are doing with their time after this one.

Dudley Do-Right's Ripsaw Falls. Prepare to be completely soaked on this log flume ride, which has an even scarier dive than Splash Mountain.

Dueling Dragons. Two floorless coasters go through multiple inversions and approach each other at a combined speed of nearly 120 MPH. At times they come so close together you feel as though you're going to hit the passengers on the other track.

Eighth Voyage of Sindbad. Jumping, diving, punching—is it another Tom Cruise action film? No, it's a cool, live stunt show with a love story to boot.

Incredible Hulk. Florida's best and scariest coaster shoots you skyward and sends you on no less than seven inversions. It's hard to walk straight after this one.

FOR AGES 7 AND UNDER

The Cat in the Hat. Take a seat on a moving couch and see what it's like to have the Cat in the Hat come to babysit for a while. Ever wanted to enter a Dr. Seuss book? That's what this ride is like.

Popeye and Bluto's Bilge-Rat Barges. This tumultuous raft ride is perfect for kids under 7 who want to go on a big-deal ride but are too young for the Hulk and Dudley Do-Right's Rip Saw Falls. It's not too scary—just wild and wet.

both types throughout the day. Scattered strategically throughout the park—notably at Dueling Dragons, the Incredible Hulk Coaster, and Jurassic Park River Adventure—are so-called Smart Lockers that are free for the first 45 to 60 minutes, but are $2 per hour afterward and max out at $14 per day. Stash backpacks and cameras here while you're being drenched or going through the spin cycle.

LOST PEOPLE AND THINGS If you've misplaced something, return to the last attraction where you had it. If it's not there, head to Guest Services in the Port of Entry. If you lose your children or others, head directly to Guest Services.

STROLLER AND WHEELCHAIR RENTALS You can rent strollers ($13 per day for singles, $21 for doubles) manual wheelchairs ($12 per day), and electric scooters ($45 per day) at the Port of Entry to your left after the turnstiles. Photo ID or a $50 deposit on a credit card is required for either. If the wheelchair breaks down, disappears, or otherwise needs replacing, speak to any shop attendant. Since it's a long way between the parking garages and the park entrance, you may want to rent a push wheelchair at the garages and upgrade to an ECV (electric convenience vehicle) when you reach the park entrance. Quantities are limited, so it's recommended that you reserve in advance.

Islands of Adventure

Harry Potter
(open 2010)

Smart Lockers ◆ 12

JURASSIC PARK

TOON LAGOON

THE LOST CONTINENT

MARVEL SUPER HERO ISLAND

SEUSS LANDING

PORT OF ENTRY

Smart Lockers

Lockers

First Aid

KEY

✗	Restaurants
🚻	Restrooms

MARVEL SUPER HERO ISLAND

This island may return you to the halcyon days of yesteryear, when perhaps you were able to name every hero and villain in a Marvel comic book. The facades along Stanley Boulevard (named for Marvel's famed editor and co-creator Stan Lee) put you smack in the middle of these adventures, with cartoony colors and flourishes. Although the spiky, horrific tower of **Doctor Doom's Fearfall** makes it a focal point for the park, the **Amazing Adventures of Spider-Man** is the one attraction to see. At various times Doctor Doom, Spider-Man, and the Incredible Hulk are available for photos, and sidewalk artists are on hand to paint your face like your favorite hero (or villain). Also dominating the scenery is the Hulk's own vivid-green coaster. Along with a hard-driving rock sound track, the screams emanating from Doctor Doom's and from the Hulk Coaster set the mood for this sometimes pleasant, sometimes apocalyptic world.

INCREDIBLE HULK COASTER

❶ Duration: 2¼ min.
Crowds: All the time.
Strategy: You can use Universal Express Pass here; otherwise, make a beeline either to this coaster or to Dueling Dragons as soon as you arrive in the park.
Audience: Coaster lovers. No pregnant women or guests with heart, back, or neck problems. Minimum height: 54".
Rating: ★★★

If you follow a clockwise tour of IOA, this is the first ride that will catch your attention and probably the first you'll want to ride. The first third of the coaster is directly above the sidewalk and lagoon. You can watch as cars are spit out from a 150-foot catapult that propels them from 0 to 40 MPH in less than two seconds. If that piques your interest, then enter the line where the walls are illustrated with artwork explaining how the superheroes and villains got their powers. After you get on the coaster, prepare yourself for flesh-pressing g-forces that match those of an F-16 fighter. Instantly you are whipped into an upside-down, zero-g position 110 feet above the ground. That's when you go into the roller-coaster's traditional first dive—straight down toward the lagoon below at some 60 MPH. Racing along the track, you then spin through seven rollovers in all and plunge into two deep, foggy subterranean enclosures. And just when you think it's over, it's not. It just keeps rolling along way after you've exhausted your supply of screams and shrieks. Powerful.

Note that the fog effects are most vivid first thing in the morning; darkness enhances the launch effect, since you can't see the light at the end of the tunnel. Front and rear seats give you almost entirely different experiences. The ride is fastest in the rear and has fine views, but is roughest on the sides; the front row, with its fabulous view of that green track racing into your face, is truly awesome—but you have to wait even longer for it.

STORM FORCE ACCELATRON

2 **Duration:** 2 min.

Crowds: Not a problem.

Strategy: Go whenever—except after you've eaten.

Audience: Older children and adults. No pregnant women or guests with heart, back, or neck problems.

Rating: ★★

This whirling ride is supposed to demonstrate the power of nature. Cartoon character Storm (of the X-Men) harnesses the power of weather to battle her archenemy Magneto (What?! *A story line?*) by having people like you board Power Orbs. These containers convert human energy into electrical forces through the power of "cyclospin." Strip away the veneer, however, and what you've got is a mirror image of Disney World's twirling teacups. Definitely not a good idea if you get motion sickness.

DOCTOR DOOM'S FEARFALL

3 **Duration:** 1 min.

Crowds: Can get crowded, but the line moves fairly fast.

Strategy: You can use Universal Express Pass here; otherwise, go later in the day, when crowds are thinner, but not on a full stomach.

Audience: Older children and adults. No pregnant women or guests with heart, back, or neck problems or motion sickness. Minimum height: 52".

Rating: ★

Although the 200-foot-tall towers look really, really scary, the ride is really just pretty scary. After being strapped into a chair, a silent countdown begins as you wait nervously while the disembodied voice of Dr. Doom tells you the contraption is designed to extract your fear, with which he'll rule the world. After a few anxious seconds, in a flash your chair is snapped with great speed to the peak of the tower, held there so you can realize just how high up you really are, and then dropped to earth. The process is then repeated, but just once. The ride is so short that it actually feels sort of anticlimactic. Check the time and estimate your desire to see a panoramic view of Universal's parks and possibly the Orlando skyline (depending on which side of the ride you're on). Leave loose items in the bins provided; no one else can reach them while you're on your trip.

AMAZING ADVENTURES OF SPIDER-MAN

4 **Duration:** 4½ min.

Crowds: Usually inescapable unless you use Universal Express Pass.

Strategy: You can use Universal Express Pass here; otherwise, go early in the day or at dusk. If you don't know much about Spider-Man's villains, check out the wanted posters on the walls.

Audience: All but timid young children; youngsters accustomed to action TV shows should be fine. No pregnant women or guests with heart, back, or neck problems. Minimum height: 40"; children under 48" must be accompanied by an adult.

Rating: ★★★

Even if you've never heard of Peter Parker or J. Jonah Jameson, the 4½ minutes spent in this building can make an hour standing in line worthwhile. Unlike any other ride at any theme park, this one combines moving vehicles, 3-D film, simulator technology, and special effects. Unless you use the Universal Express Pass, expect a winding and torturous walk in line through the Daily Bugle's offices. You learn that members of the Sinister Syndicate (Doctor Octopus [aka Doc Oc], Electro, Hobgoblin, Hydro Man, and deadly Scream) have used their Doomsday Anti-Gravity Gun to steal the Statue of Liberty. None of this matters, really, since once you board your car and don your 3-D glasses, you're instantly swept up into a weird cartoon battle. When Spider-Man lands on your car, you feel the bump; when Electro runs overhead, you hear his footsteps following you. You feel the sizzle of electricity, a frigid spray of water from Hydro Man, and the heat from a flaming pumpkin tossed by the Hobgoblin. No matter how many times you visit this attraction, you cringe when Doc Oc breaks through a brick wall, raises your car to the top of a skyscraper, and then releases you for a 400-foot free fall to the pavement below. The bizarre angles and perspective at which scenes are shown are so disorienting, you really do feel as if you're swinging from a web. Do not miss this one.

TOON LAGOON

As you leave Marvel's world, there's no water to separate it from Toon Lagoon, just a change of pavement color and texture, midway games along the walkway, and primary colors turning to purple and fuchsia. Toon Lagoon's main street, Comic Strip Lane, makes use of cartoon characters that are instantly recognizable to anyone—anyone born before 1942, that is. Pert little Betty Boop, gangling Olive Oyl, muscle-bound Popeye, Krazy Kat, Mark Trail, Flash Gordon, Pogo, and Alley Oop are all here, as are the relatively more contemporary Dudley Do-Right, Rocky, Bullwinkle, Beetle Bailey, Cathy, and Hagar the Horrible. The colorful backdrop and chirpy music are as cheerful as Jurassic Park next door is portentous. There are squirting fountains for kids, hidden alcoves, and elevated cartoon balloon captions to pose under for photos.

EN ROUTE Get your Betty Boop collectibles at the Betty Boop Store. Poncho collectors can get one at Gasoline Alley, along with clever blank books, and cartoon-character hats and wigs that recall Daisy Mae and others.

DUDLEY DO-RIGHT'S RIPSAW FALLS

⑤ Duration: 5½ min.
Crowds: Varies by season, but very heavy in summer.
Strategy: You can use Universal Express Pass here; otherwise, go in late afternoon, when you're hot as can be, or at day's end, when you're ready to head back to your car. There's no seat where you can stay dry.
Audience: All but the youngest children. No pregnant women or guests with heart, back, or neck problems. Minimum height: 44"; children under 48" must be accompanied by an adult.
Rating: ★★★

Inspired by set-ups and a locale used on the popular 1960s animated pun-fest Rocky and Bullwinkle, this twisting, up-and-down flume ride through the Canadian Rockies is definitely wet and wild. You're supposed to help Dudley rescue Nell, his belle, from the evil and conniving Snidely Whiplash. By the time your mission is accomplished, you've dropped through the rooftop of a ramshackle dynamite shack and made an explosive dive 15 feet below water level into a 400,000-gallon lagoon, and you're not just damp—you're soaked to the skin. Actually, the final drop looks much scarier than it really is; the fact that the ride vehicles have no restraining devices at all is a clue to how low the danger quotient actually is here. You never know quite what's ahead—and you're definitely not expecting the big thrill when the time comes. If the weather is cold and you absolutely must stay dry, pick up a poncho at Gasoline Alley, opposite the entrance.

NEED A BREAK? On Toon Lagoon, you'll find Blondie's Deli: Home of the Dagwood. The jumbo sandwich that creates the restaurant's marquee is a hoot, and you can buy the real thing, by the inch, inside.

POPEYE AND BLUTO'S BILGE-RAT BARGES

6 **Duration:** 5 min.
Crowds: Heavy all day.
Strategy: You can use Universal Express Pass here; otherwise, go first thing in the morning or about an hour before closing.
Audience: All but young children. No pregnant women or guests with heart, back, or neck problems or motion sickness. Minimum height: 42"; children 42"–48" must be accompanied by an adult.
Rating: ★★★

At times this river-raft ride is quiet, but often it's a bumping, churning, twisting white-water tumult that will drench you and your fellow travelers. As with every ride at IOA, there's a story line here, but the real attraction is boarding the wide circular raft with 11 other passengers and then getting soaked, splashed, sprayed, or deluged. The degree of wetness varies, since the direction your raft spins may or may not place you beneath torrents of water flooding from a shoreline water tower or streaming from water guns from an adjacent play area.

ME SHIP, THE OLIVE

7 **Duration:** As long as you wish.
Crowds: Fairly heavy all day.
Strategy: If you're with young children, go in the morning or around dinnertime.
Audience: Young children.
Rating: ★★

From bow to stern, dozens of participatory activities keep families busy as they climb around this jungle-gym boat moored on the edge of Toon Lagoon. Toddlers enjoy crawling in Swee' Pea's Playpen, and older children and their parents take aim at unsuspecting riders locked into the Bilge-Rat Barges. Primarily, this is designed for kids, with whistles, bells, and organs to trigger, as well as narrow tunnels to climb through and ladders to climb up. Check out the view of the park from the top of the ship.

JURASSIC PARK

Walking through the arched gates of Jurassic Park brings a distinct change in mood. The music is stirring and slightly ominous, the vegetation tropical and junglelike. All this, plus the high-tension wires and warning signs, does a great job of re-creating the Jurassic Park of Steven Spielberg's blockbuster movie—and its insipid sequels. The half-fun, half-frightening Jurassic Park River Adventure is the island's standout attraction, bringing to life key segments of the movie's climax.

EN ROUTE The Dinostore, on the pathway between Jurassic Park and the Lost Continent, has a Tyrannosaurus rex that looks as if he's hatching from an egg, and (yes, mom) educational dino toys, too.

PTERANODON FLYERS

❽ Duration: 2 min.

Crowds: Perpetual. Since the ride loads slowly, waits can take as much as an hour.

Strategy: Skip this on your first few visits.

Audience: All ages. Children 36" to 56" tall must be accompanied by an adult.

Rating: ★

These gondolas are eye-catching and can't help but tempt you to stand in line for a lift. The problem is that the wide, wing-spanned chairs provide a very slow, very low-capacity ride that will eat up a lot of your park time. Do it only if you want a prehistoric-bird's-eye view of the Jurassic Park compound.

NEED A BREAK? The Thunder Falls Terrace, near the grand finale of the Jurassic Park River Adventure, is open for lunch and dinner during peak seasons. One terrace side, entirely glass, gives an optimal view of the plunge, and you can also sit outdoors next to the river's thundering waterfall. Nearby, Burger Digs and Pizza Predattoria are year-round dining options.

CAMP JURASSIC

❾ Duration: As long as you want.

Crowds: Sometimes more, sometimes less.

Strategy: Go anytime.

Audience: One and all.

Rating: ★★

Remember when you were a kid content with just a swing set and monkey bars? Well, those toys of the past have been replaced by fantastic play areas like this, which are interwoven with the island's theme. Though the camp is primarily for kids, some adults join in, racing along footpaths through the forests, slithering down slides, clambering over swinging bridges and across boiling streams, scrambling up net climbs and rock formations, and exploring mysterious caves full of faux lava. Keep an eye open for the dinosaur footprints; when you jump on them, a dinosaur roars somewhere (different footprints are associated with different roars). Watch out for the watery cross fire nearby—or join in the shooting yourself.

JURASSIC PARK RIVER ADVENTURE

⑩ **Duration:** 6 min.

Crowds: Heavy except early in the morning.

Strategy: You can use Universal Express Pass here; otherwise, go early or late.

Audience: All but young children, who may be frightened. No pregnant women or guests with heart, back, or neck problems. Minimum height: 42".

Rating : ★★★

You're about to take a peaceful cruise on a mysterious river past friendly, vegetarian dinosaurs. Of course, something has to go amiss or it wouldn't be much fun at all. A wrong turn is what it takes, and when you enter one of the research departments and see that it's overrun by spitting dinosaurs and razor-clawed raptors, things get plenty scary. This is all a buildup to the big finish: guarding the exit is a towering, roaring T. rex with teeth the size of hams. By some strange quirk of fate, a convenient escape arrives via a tremendously steep and watery 85-foot plunge that will start you screaming. Smile! This is when the souvenir photos are shot. Thanks to high-capacity rafts, the line for this water ride moves fairly quickly.

JURASSIC PARK DISCOVERY CENTER

⑪ **Duration:** As long as you like.

Crowds: People mingle throughout, so that crowded feeling is almost extinct.

Strategy: Go anytime.

Audience: Older children and adults.

Rating: ★★

If there's a scintilla of information your kids don't know about dinosaurs, they can learn it here. There are demonstration areas where a realistic raptor is being hatched and where you can see what you'd look like (or sound like) if you were a dino. In the Beasaurus area ("Be-a-Saurus"), you can look at the world from a dinosaur's point of view. There are numerous hands-on exhibits and a Jeopardy!-style quiz game where you can test your knowledge of dinosaur trivia. The casual restaurant upstairs is a nice place to take an air-conditioned break, and tables on the balcony overlook the lagoon.

LOST CONTINENT

Ancient myths from around the world inspired this land. Just past a wooden bridge and huge mythical birds guarding the entrances, the trees are hung with weathered metal lanterns. From a distance comes the sound of booming thunder mixing with shimmering New Agey chimes and vaguely Celtic melodies. Farther along, things start to look like a sanitized version of a Renaissance Fair. Seers and fortune-tellers in a tent decorated with silken draperies and vintage Oriental carpets are on hand at Mystics of the Seven Veils. The gifted women read palms, tarot cards, and credit cards. In a courtyard outside the Sindbad show, a Talking Fountain offers flip responses to guest questions, such as "Is there a God?" Answer: "Yes. He's from Trenton and his name is Julio." Answers are followed by the fountain spraying unsuspecting guests.

EN ROUTE

Dragon's Keep carries Celtic jewelry along with stuffed dragons, toy swords in various sizes and materials, and perfectly dreadful fake rats, mice, and body parts. Treasures of Poseidon is stocked with shells and baubles made from them, while a heavy drop hammer pounds out signs and symbols on classy medallions at the interesting Coin Mint.

FLYING UNICORN

⑫ Duration: Less than a minute.

Crowds: Moderate, but since the ride is so brief, lines move quickly. You can use Universal Express Pass here if the lines are heavy.

Audience: Kids under 7, with adults riding along for moral support. Minimum height: 36".

Rating: ★★★

If you made the mistake of putting your kid on Dueling Dragons, the antidote may be this child-size roller coaster. Following a walk through a wizard's workshop, the low-key thrill ride places kids on the back of a unicorn for a very, very brief ride through a mythical forest. This is the park's equivalent of Universal Studios' Woody Woodpecker coaster. Kids lacking thrill-ride experience should enjoy this immensely.

NEED A BREAK?

If you're ready to toast your conquest of mortal fear, head straight across the plaza to the Enchanted Oak Tavern, ingeniously sprawled inside the huge base of a gnarled old oak tree. Chow down on barbecue chicken and ribs or corn on the cob, although the cool, cozy surroundings surpass the food's quality. In the adjacent Alchemy Bar, order a pint of beer including the park's own Dragon Scale Ale.

DUELING DRAGONS

⑬ Duration: 2¼ min.

Crowds: Perpetual.

Strategy: You can use Universal Express Pass here; otherwise, ride after dark, when most visitors are going home, or go early. For the most exciting ride, go for the rear car of the Fire Dragon or the front car of the Ice Dragon; note that lines for the front car of both coasters are much longer.

Audience: Older children with roller-coaster experience and adults with cast-iron stomachs. No pregnant women or guests with heart, back, or neck problems. Minimum height: 54".

Rating: ★★★

Since the cars of this high-test and extremely popular roller coaster are suspended from the track, your feet will be flying off into the wild blue yonder as you whip through corkscrews and loops and are flung upside-down and around. The twin coasters are on separate tracks so the thrill is in the near misses, which makes front-row seats a prized commodity (there's a separate, much longer line if you just have to ride in the lead car). Coaster weights are checked by a computer, which programs the cars to have near misses as close as 12 inches apart. Top speed on the ride ranges 55–60 MPH, with the Fire Dragon (red) offering more inversions and the Ice Dragon (blue) providing more cornering. Either way, take advantage of the small lockers (free for 45 minutes) in which you can stash your stuff: wallets, glasses, change, and, perhaps, an air-sickness bag.

EIGHTH VOYAGE OF SINDBAD

🔟 **Duration:** 25 min.
Crowds: Not a problem, due to size of the open-air auditorium.
Strategy: Stake out seats about 15 min prior to show time. Don't sit too close up front—you won't see the whole picture as well.
Audience: Older children and adults.
Rating: ★★★

The story line of this stunt show is simple and satisfying: Sindbad and his sidekick Kabob arrive in search of treasure, get distracted by the beautiful Princess Amoura, and are threatened by the evil sorceress Miseria. That's enough to get the good guy started off on 25 nonstop minutes of punching, climbing, kicking, diving, leaping, and Douglas Fairbanks–ing his way through the performance amid water explosions, flames, and pyrotechnics that end with a daring flaming high dive. Kids love the action, and women love Sindbad. The 1,700-seat theater can be a nice place to sit a spell, replenish your energy, and watch a swashbuckler in action.

POSEIDON'S FURY

🔟 **Duration:** 20 min.
Crowds: Usually heavy.
Strategy: You can use Universal Express Pass here; otherwise, go at the end of the day. Stay to the left against the wall as you enter and position yourself opposite the podium in the center of the room. In each succeeding section of the presentation, get into the very first row, particularly if you aren't tall.
Audience: Older children and adults.
Rating: ★★

Following a long walk through cool ruins guarded by the Colossus of Rhodes, a young archaeologist arrives to take you on a trek to find Poseidon's trident. Although each chamber you enter on your walk looks interesting, the fact that very little happens in most of them can wear down the entertainment quotient. To reach the final chamber, you walk through a tunnel of water that suggests being sucked into a whirlpool—hard to describe, hard to forget. Then when the wall disappears, you're watching a 180-degree movie screen on which actors playing Poseidon and his archenemy appear. Soon, they're shouting and pointing at each other and triggering a memorable fire- and water-works extravaganza where roughly 350,000 gallons of water, 200 flame effects, massive crashing waves, thick columns of water, and scorching fireballs begin erupting all around you. Although the first 15 minutes don't offer much, the finale is loud, powerful, and hyperactive. Is it worth the time investment? That's up to you.

SEUSS LANDING

This 10-acre island is the perfect tribute to Theodor Seuss Geisel, putting into three dimensions what had for a long time been seen only on the printed page. While adults recall why Dr. Seuss was their favorite author, kids are introduced to the Cat, Things One and Two, Horton, the Lorax, and the Grinch.

Visually, this is the most exciting parcel of real estate in America. From the topiary sculptures to the jumbo red-and-white-stripe hat near the entrance, the design is as whimsical as his books. Fencing is bent into curvy shapes, lampposts are lurching, and Seussian characters placed atop buildings seem to defy gravity. Everything, even the pavement, glows in lavenders, pinks, peaches, and oranges. Flowers in the planters echo the sherbet hues of the pavement.

From the main avenue, you can follow the webbed footprints to Sneetch Beach, where the Sneetches are frolicking in the lagoon alongside a strand littered with their beach things; the Seussonic boom box even has its own sound track, complete with commercials. Look carefully in the sand and you can see where the Sneetches jumped the fence to get to the beach, fell flat on their faces, and finally started dragging their radio rather than carrying it. Nearby is the Zax Bypass—two Zaxes facing off because neither one will budge. And keep an eye peeled for the characters—the grouchy Grinch, Thing One and Thing Two, and even the Cat himself.

EN ROUTE

Stores such as **Cats, Hats & Cats, Hats & Things,** and **Mulberry Mulberry Store** stock wonderful Seussian souvenirs, from funny hats to Cat-top pencils and red-and-white-stripe coffee mugs. And when you're inspired to acquire a bit of two-dimensional Dr. Seuss, you can stop into **Dr. Seuss' All the Books You Can Read.** For a last-minute spree, the **Islands of Adventure Trading Company,** in the Port of Entry, stocks just about every kind of souvenir you saw elsewhere in the park.

IF I RAN THE ZOO

16 **Duration:** Up to you and your young ones.
Crowds: Probably heaviest early in the day.
Strategy: If you can talk your kids into waiting, come at the end of your visit.
Audience: Young children.
Rating: ★★★

In this Seussian maze, kids can ditch the adults and have fun at their level. Here they encounter the trademarked fantasy creatures as they climb, jump, push buttons, and animate strange and wonderful animals. Park designers have learned that kids' basic needs include eating, sleeping, and getting splashed, so they've thoughtfully added interactive fountains.

NEED A BREAK?

Would you eat ice cream on a boat? Would you drink juice with a goat? Taste vanilla on a cone? Sip some grape juice all alone? Then there are places you must stop. Stop at the **Hop on Pop Ice Cream Shop?** What do you say after Moose Juice Goose Juice? Say, thank you, thank you, Dr. Seuss.

Grab a quick bite inside the **Circus McGurkus** fast-food eatery. Check out the walrus balancing on a whisker and the names on the booths: Tum-tummied Swumm, Rolf from the Ocean of Olf, the Remarkable Foon. Occasionally, a circus master–calliope player conducts a sing-along with the diners below. If you prefer dining with large groups of people, keep looking: the cavernous dining room seldom looks even partially full.

THE HIGH IN THE SKY SEUSS TROLLEY TRAIN RIDE

 Duration: 3 min.
Crowds: Heavy
Strategy: Kids love trains, so get in line.
Audience: All ages, but mostly for toddlers and young children. Children 34"–48" must be accompanied by an adult.
Rating: ★★

Offering an aerial view of the Seuss Landing, trains on separate tracks embark on a slow and pleasing tour of the area, with a Seuss-like narrative detailing sights along the route. Although it can be a lengthy wait to get on board, this is a nice and relaxing miniature train journey and it can be especially enjoyable for kids when the trolley rolls right through the Circus McGurkus Café Stoo-pendous, and along the shores of the lagoon where you can see the Sneetches as they enjoy the beaches.

CARO-SEUSS-EL

Duration: 2 min.
Crowds: Lines move pretty well, so don't be intimidated.
Strategy: You can use Universal Express Pass here; otherwise, make this a special end to your day.
Audience: All ages. Children under 48" must be accompanied by an adult.
Rating: ★★★

The centerpiece of Seuss Landing could have come straight from the pages of a Seuss book. Ordinary horse-centered merry-go-rounds may seem passé now that Universal has created this menagerie: the cowfish from *McElligot's Pool,* the elephant birds from *Horton Hatches the Egg,* and the Birthday Katroo from *Happy Birthday to You!*—an ark of imaginary animals. The 54 mounts are interactive: the animals' eyes blink and their tails wag when you get on. It's a cliché, but there's a good chance you'll feel like a kid again when you hop aboard one of these fantastic creatures.

ONE FISH, TWO FISH, RED FISH, BLUE FISH

Duration: 2-plus min.
Crowds: Thick all day.
Strategy: You can use Universal Express Pass here; otherwise, go very early or at the end of your visit when the tykes have left, so you can be a kid at heart. Otherwise, skip on your first visit.
Audience: Young children. Children under 48" must be accompanied by an adult.
Rating: ★★

Dr. Seuss put elephants in trees and green eggs and ham on trains, so it doesn't seem far-fetched that fish can circle "squirting posts" to a Jamaican beat. After a rather lengthy wait for what seems like a very short experience, you climb into your fish and, as it spins around a center pole, you (or your child) control its up-and-down motion. The key is to follow the lyrics of the special song—if you go down when the song tells you to go up, you may be drenched courtesy of the aforementioned "squirting post." Mighty silly, mighty fun.

THE CAT IN THE HAT

Duration: 4½ min.
Crowds: Heavy.
Strategy: You can use Universal Express Pass here; otherwise, go early or near the end of the day, when the children go home.
Audience: All ages. Children under 48" must be accompanied by an adult.
Rating: ★★★

If you ever harbored a secret belief that a cat could actually come to your house to wreak havoc while your mom was out, then you get to live the experience here. After boarding a couch that soon spins, whirls, and rocks through the house, you roll past 18 scenes, 30 characters, and 130 effects that put you in the presence of the mischievous cat. He balances on a ball; hoists china on his umbrella; introduces Thing One and his wild sibling, Thing Two; and flies kites in the house while the voice of reason, the fish in the teapot, sounds the warning about the impending return of the family matriarch. As the tension builds so does the fun.

ENTERTAINMENT

Throughout the day there are character greetings and shows in each of the Islands. In Toon Lagoon, you may run into the **Toon Trolley,** which carries an assortment of Universal-related characters who disembark to sign autographs and pose for pictures. Adjacent to Ripsaw Falls, the Pandemonium Amphitheatre is usually dark, but does stage seasonal and/or special performances such as the skateboard and bicycle stunts of Extreme Adventures.

During the holidays, the **Grinchmas** celebration brings live shows and movie characters to Seuss Landing, and at Marvel Super Hero Island the **X-Men** make a guest appearance. During summer and holiday periods, when the park is open late, there's a big fireworks show that can be seen anywhere along the lagoon bordering the islands—the lagoon-side terrace of the Jurassic Park Discovery Center has a fairly unimpeded view.

DISABILITIES AND ACCESSIBILITY

As at Universal Studios, Islands of Adventure has made an all-out effort not only to make the premises physically accessible for those with disabilities but also to lift barriers created through the attitudes of others. All employees attend workshops to remind them that people with

BLITZ TOUR

BEST OF THE PARK

To see everything in Islands of Adventure, a full day is necessary, especially since the large number of thrill rides guarantees that long lines will greet you just about everywhere. To see the most without waiting, stay at a Universal resort hotel or arrive in the parking lot 45 minutes before the park's official opening. Also, take advantage of Universal Express Pass ticketing.

This plan involves a lot of walking and retracing. It sounds crazy but it just…might…work. Unless you have preschoolers and need to see Seuss Landing first, take a left after the Port of Entry and head for the best and most popular attractions, starting with the **Incredible Hulk Coaster** and then the **Amazing Adventures of Spider-Man**. Then double back, skipping Toon Lagoon in favor of the **Jurassic Park River Adventure**. In the Lost Continent next door, do **Dueling Dragons**. If it's showtime, next catch the **Eighth Voyage of Sindbad.** On the way back to Toon Lagoon, let the kids see either the **Jurassic Park Discovery Center** or **Camp Jurassic**, or both.

At Toon Lagoon, see **Dudley Do-Right's Ripsaw Falls** before or after the drenching at **Popeye & Bluto's Bilge-Rat Barges**. By now, if you're in luck, the young Dr. Seuss fans and their families will have left the park, so it's time to hit Seuss Landing. Go to **Cat in the Hat** first, then on to **One Fish, Two Fish, Red Fish, Blue Fish**. Make a stop at the **Green Eggs and Ham Café** to see how those green eggs are made, even if you're not ready to chow down. **Caro-Seuss-el** lets you be a kid again. Before you exit, walk through **If I Ran the Zoo**. The unusual animals here are definitely worth a look. If the line is short and you can walk right on, consider boarding **The High in the Sky Seuss Trolley Train Ride**—otherwise wait until you're back in the neighborhood.

The remaining attractions are worthwhile if you've happened to arrive on a slow day and finish ahead of time: **Doctor Doom's Fearfall** and **Storm Force Accelatron** in Marvel Super Hero Island, the **Pteranodon Flyers** at Jurassic Park, and the **Flying Unicorn** and **Poseidon's Fury** in the Lost Continent.

ON RAINY DAYS

Except during Christmas week, expect rainy days to be less crowded—even though the park is in full operation. (Coasters do run in the rain—although not in thunderstorms.) However, since most attractions are out in the open, you'll get very wet.

8

disabilities are people first. And you can occasionally spot staffers using wheelchairs. Most attractions and all restaurants are wheelchair accessible. Ask for the comprehensive *Rider's Guide* at Guest Services. Also, additional information for travelers with disabilities is available online (⊕*www.universalorlando.com*; from the home page, click "Hours & Info" and then on Guest Services).

ATTRACTIONS All attractions are completely accessible to guests who use wheelchairs with the exception of the **Incredible Hulk Coaster, Doctor Doom's Fearfall,** and **Dueling Dragons,** for which you must transfer from your chair to ride. Ask an attendant for assistance or directions to wheelchair access.

SERVICES Many employees have had basic sign-language training; even some of the animated characters sign, albeit sometimes in an adapted manner. There's an outgoing TTY series hearing-impaired system on the counter in Guest Services.

> WORD OF MOUTH
>
> "If you want exotic (not the food), fun, and interesting, go to Mythos. Food is good, surroundings really unusual; I think everyone will love it!"
>
> —Sylvia3

EATING AT ISLANDS OF ADVENTURE

Sit-down restaurants and fast-food eateries are scattered throughout Islands of Adventure. For the most part, trans-fat foods are out and a line of healthy side dishes and snacks is in. Mythos and Confisco Grille accept "priority seating," which is not a reservation but an arrival time that's issued—you receive the first available seat after that particular time. To make arrangements up to 30 days in advance, just call **Guest Services** (☎407/224–6350). You can also visit Guest Services or the restaurant in person when you arrive.

FULL-SERVICE RESTAURANTS

The park's fancy mealtime option is the sophisticated and gorgeous **Mythos Restaurant** (☎407/224–4534), in the Lost Continent. The ambitious menu favors continental cuisine and changes seasonally, although the warm and gooey warm chocolate-banana cake is a constant.

Confisco's Grill (☎407/224–9255) is near the lagoon at the intersection of Port of Entry and Seuss Landing. Meals include steaks, salads, sandwiches, soups, and pastas—and there's even a neat little pub.

The **Thunder Falls Terrace** (☎407/224–4461), in Jurassic Park, serves rotisserie chicken and ribs, although the restaurant may close when crowds are light.

SELF-SERVICE RESTAURANTS

On Toon Lagoon **Blondie's Deli: Home of the Dagwood** serves the jumbo sandwich that creates the restaurant's marquee by the inch. At Seuss Landing's **Green Eggs and Ham Cafe** traditional breakfast fare is also available. In Jurassic Park, you can have Caesar salad on a pizza crust, along with more traditional versions of the Italian specialty, at **Pizza Predatoria.** Check out the rapacious raptors on the sign.

UNIVERSAL STUDIOS FLORIDA

Disney does an extraordinary job when it comes to showmanship, which may be why Universal Studios has taken advantage of its distinctly non-Disney heritage to add attitude to its presentations. Universal Studios performers aren't above tossing in sometimes risqué jokes and asides to get a cheap laugh.

Although this theme park has something for everyone, its primary appeal is to those who like loud, fast, high-energy attractions. If you

TOP UNIVERSAL STUDIOS ATTRACTIONS

FOR AGES 7 AND UP

Revenge of the Mummy. A pretty good indoor coaster that takes you past scary mummies and billowing balls of fire (really).

Universal Horror Make-Up Show. This sometimes gross, often raunchy, but always entertaining demonstration merges the best of stand-up comedy with creepy effects.

The Simpsons Ride. A full-immersion ride that takes you on a wild journey through the Simpsons' hometown of Springfield. It's the closest you may ever come to appearing in a Simpsons episode.

FOR AGES 6 AND UNDER

Animal Actors on Location! A perfect family show starring a menagerie of animals whose unusually high IQs are surpassed only by their cuteness and cuddle-ability.

A Day in the Park with Barney. Small children love the big purple dinosaur and the chance to sing along.

want to calm down, there are quiet, shaded parks and a children's area where the adults can enjoy a respite while the kids are ripping through assorted playlands at 100 MPH. There are some visitors, however, who miss the sort of connection that Disney forges with the public through its carefully developed history of singable songs and cuddly characters.

The park has 444 acres of stage sets, shops, reproductions of New York and San Francisco, and anonymous soundstages housing themed attractions, as well as genuine moviemaking paraphernalia. On the map, it's all neatly divided into six neighborhoods, which wrap themselves around a huge lagoon. The neighborhoods are **Production Central,** which spreads over the entire left side of the Plaza of the Stars; **New York,** with excellent street performances at 70 Delancey; the bicoastal **San Francisco/Amity; World Expo; Woody Woodpecker's KidZone;** and **Hollywood.**

Although the park looks easy to navigate on the map, a blitz tour through it can be difficult, since it involves a couple of long detours and some backtracking. If you need help, theme-park hosts are trained to provide more information than you thought you needed. Also keep in mind that some rides—and many restaurants—delay their openings until late morning, which may throw a kink in your perfectly laid plans. In fact, if you arrive when the gates open, it's kind of eerie walking around in a nearly deserted theme park where it's just you and the staff. To make sure you maximize your time and hit all the best rides, follow this chapter's Blitz Tour.

Numbers in the margin correspond to points of interest on the Universal Studios map.

BASIC SERVICES

CAMERAS Just inside the Universal Studios main entrance, at the **On Location** shop in the Front Lot, you can find nearly everything you need to make your vacation picture-perfect. The store sells disposable cameras both with and without flash for about $20, digital memory cards and sticks, and very basic digital cameras for about $60.

HEALTH SERVICES   Universal Studios' First Aid centers are between New York and San Francisco (directly across from *Beetlejuice's Graveyard Revue*) and at the entrance between the bank and the Studio Audience Center.

INFORMATION   Visit **Guest Services** (☎407/224–6350) in the Front Lot to the right after you pass through the turnstiles, for brochures and maps in French, Spanish, Portuguese, Japanese, and German, as well as English. The brochures also lay out the day's entertainment, tapings, and rare film shoots. If you have questions prior to visiting, call **Universal's main line** (☎407/363–8000) or Guest Services.

Studio Information Boards in front of Studio Stars and Mel's Drive-In restaurants provide up-to-the-minute ride and show operating information—including the length of lines at the major attractions.

LOCKERS   Locker rental charges are $8 for small lockers and $10 for family-size ones per day and both offer unlimited access. The high-price lockers are clustered around the courtyard after you've cleared the turnstiles. Keep in mind it can be a long walk back to the gate when you're on the other side of the park. If you time it right, you may not need a locker here because Universal also has Smart Lockers at major thrill rides. These are free for up to 90 minutes.

LOST PEOPLE AND THINGS   If you lose something, return to the last attraction or shop where you recall seeing it. If it's not there, head to Guest Services. If you lose a person, there's only one place to look: head directly to Guest Services near the main entrance.

STROLLERS AND WHEELCHAIRS   Strollers (singles $13, doubles $21), manual wheelchairs ($12 per day), and electric scooters ($45 per day) can be rented just inside the main entrance and in San Francisco/Amity. Photo ID or a $50 deposit on a credit card is required for either. If the wheelchair breaks down, disappears, or otherwise needs replacing, speak to any shop attendant. It's a long, long way from the parking garage to the entrance. Consider renting a push wheelchair from the central concourse between the parking garages. You can upgrade to an ECV (electric convenience vehicle, or scooter) when you reach the park entrance. Quantities are limited, so it's recommended that you reserve in advance.

PRODUCTION CENTRAL

Composed of six huge warehouses with once-active soundstages, this area has plenty of attractions that appeal to preteens. Follow Nickelodeon Way left from the Plaza of the Stars.

EN ROUTE   Every ride and attraction has its affiliated theme shop, and it's important to remember that few attraction-specific souvenirs are sold outside of their own shop. So if you're struck by a movie- and ride-related pair of boxer shorts, seize the moment—and the shorts. Choice souvenirs include Universal Studios' trademark movie clipboard, available at the **Universal Studios Store,** on the Plaza of the Stars, and movie star memorabilia is available at **Silver Screen Collectibles,** across from Terminator 2 3-D.

JIMMY NEUTRON'S NICKTOON BLAST

 Duration: 8 min.
Crowds: Heaviest early in the day because it's near the entrance.
Strategy: If you can talk your kids into waiting, come at the end of the day.
Audience: All ages.
Rating: ★★★

Jimmy has arrived with a virtual-reality ride. The boy genius is joined by a large collection of Nickelodeon characters, including SpongeBob SquarePants and the Rugrats, as he demonstrates his latest invention (the powerful Mark IV rocket). Things go awry when evil egg-shaped aliens make off with the rocket and threaten to dominate the world. Computer graphics and high-tech, high-speed gizmos wow your senses as your rocket car dives, bounces, and skips its way through Nick-based cartoon settings. If your kids are regular Jimmy viewers or can sing SpongeBob's theme song, you have to do this ride. Be prepared: the show empties to a large gift shop selling Blues Clues, Dora the Explorer, Rugrats, Jimmy Neutron, and SpongeBob souvenirs.

SHREK 4-D

❷ **Duration:** 12 min.
Crowds: Will likely remain heavy as long as the movie remains popular.
Strategy: Use a Universal Express Pass if possible.
Audience: All ages.
Rating: ★★

Mike Myers, Eddie Murphy, Cameron Diaz, and John Lithgow reprise their vocal roles as the swamp-dwelling ogre, Shrek; his faithful chatterbox companion, Donkey; Shrek's bride, Princess Fiona; and the vengeful Lord Farquaad in this animated 3-D saga. Grab your "OgreVision" glasses and prepare for a tumultuous ride as Shrek tries to rescue Fiona from Lord Farquaad's ghost. If she won't be his wife in life, he figures she ought to be in death. When the show begins, the showdown puts you at the center of a 3-D movie adventure that includes a battle between fire-breathing dragons and a pretty scary plunge down a deadly 1,000-foot waterfall. Specially built theater seats and a few surprising sensory effects—mainly blasts of air and sprinkles of water—make the "4-D" part. Even with the show's capacity for 300, you'll probably have to wait in line an hour just to reach the pre-show, which stars the Gingerbread Man and the Magic Mirror and is slightly entertaining, but at 13 to 15 minutes, lasts longer than the film itself.

NEED A BREAK? **Classic Monsters Cafe** resembles a mad scientist's laboratory. The self-serve restaurant is open seasonally and offers wood-fired oven pizzas, pastas, chopped chef salads, four-cheese ravioli, and rotisserie chicken. Frankenstein's monster and other scary characters from vintage Universal films make the rounds of the tables as you eat. Be sure to check out the monster-meets-celebrity pictures at the entrance.

8

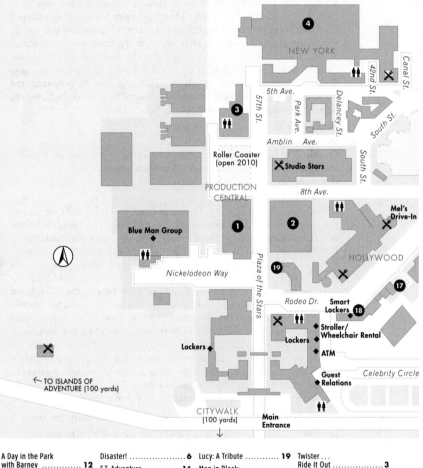

Universal Studios

NEW YORK

4

Canal St.

42nd St.

5th Ave.

Park Ave.

Delancey St.

South St.

3

57th St.

Amblin Ave.

Roller Coaster
(open 2010)

✕ Studio Stars

South St.

8th Ave.

PRODUCTION
CENTRAL

1

2

Mel's
Drive-In

Blue Man Group

HOLLYWOOD

Nickelodeon Way

19

17

Plaza of the Stars

Rodeo Dr.

Smart
Lockers

18

Lockers

Stroller/
Wheelchair Rental

Lockers

ATM

← TO ISLANDS OF
ADVENTURE (100 yards)

Guest
Relations

Celebrity Circle

CITYWALK
(100 yards)
↓

Main
Entrance

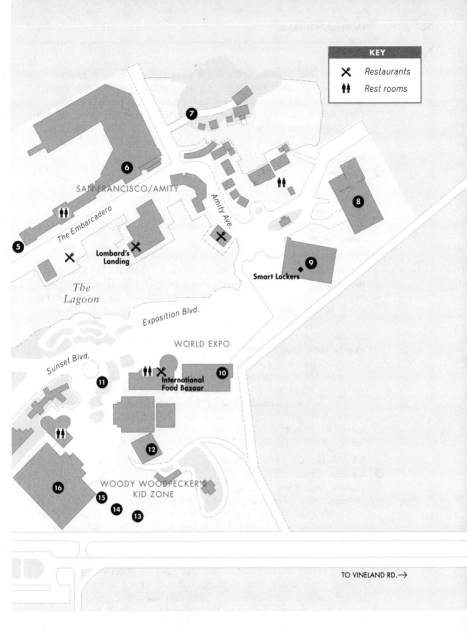

KEY

✗ Restaurants
🚻 Rest rooms

7

6

SAN FRANCISCO/AMITY

Amity Ave.

8

The Embarcadero

5

✗ Lombard's
Landing

✗

The
Lagoon

Smart Lockers

9

Exposition Blvd.

WORLD EXPO

Sunset Blvd.

11

🚻 ✗ International
Food Bazaar

10

12

16

15

WOODY WOODPECKER'S
KID ZONE

14 13

TO VINELAND RD. →

NEW YORK

This Universal take on the Big Apple recalls the original—right down to the cracked concrete and slightly stained cobblestones. Many of the sets you see are used in music videos and commercials. The **Blues Brothers Bluesmobile** regularly cruises the neighborhood, and musicians hop out to give scheduled performances at 70 Delancey. The show is surprisingly popular, with crowds congregating in the street for the live show.

TWISTER . . . RIDE IT OUT

❸ Duration: 3 min.

Crowds: Expect very long lines.

Strategy: You can use Universal Express Pass here; otherwise, go first thing in the morning or at closing.

Audience: All but young children, who may be frightened.

Rating: ★★

This attraction accomplishes in two minutes what it took the highly contrived movie two long hours to do—and overall it's far more exciting. After enduring a slow line and a fairly boring lecture from the movie's stars about the destructive force of tornadoes, you're eventually ushered into a standing-room theater where a quiet country scene slowly transforms into a mighty scary make-believe windstorm. An ominous, five-story-high funnel cloud weaves in from the background to take center stage as 110 decibels of wind noise, crackling electrical lines, and shattered windows add to the confusion. A truck, signs, car, and cow are given frequent-flyer points as they sail across the stage; and even though you know you're in a building and more victims are waiting patiently outside, when the roof starts to fly away your first instinct is to head for the root cellar. Don't. Watch the whole thing and marvel at the special-effects masters who put this together—and tear it apart every few minutes.

REVENGE OF THE MUMMY

❹ Duration: 3 min.

Crowds: Expect very long lines.

Strategy: Use Universal Express Pass or go first thing in the morning. If you don't mind riding alone, make tracks for the strategic single-rider line—strongly recommended. **Audience:** All but young children, who may be frightened. Minimum height: 48".

Rating: ★★★

Action, adventure, and horror—the staples of the *Mummy* movies—are in abundance in this spine-tingling thrill ride. First you enter the tomb of a pharaoh and walk through catacombs and past Egyptian artifacts before boarding a coaster car. Then you're taken into a haunted labyrinth, where you're given an opportunity to sell your soul for safety and riches. Opting against it, you're sent hurtling through underground passageways and Egyptian burial chambers on a $40 million ride that combines roller-coaster technology, pyrotechnics, and some super-scary skeletal warriors. Highlights include running past a phalanx of towering mummy guards, escaping a beetle-infested burial chamber, zipping backwards through fog, and racing full-tilt into the mummified mouth of Imhotep. Coaster junkies take note: you'll feel the 1.5 g-force as you fly uphill, and almost the entire ride takes place in the dark.

SAN FRANCISCO/AMITY

This area combines two sets. One part is the wharves and warehouses of San Francisco's Embarcadero and Fisherman's Wharf districts, with cable-car tracks and the distinctive redbrick Ghirardelli chocolate factory; the other is the New England fishing village terrorized in *Jaws*.

EN ROUTE

Shaiken's Souvenirs on the Embarcadero sells supercool Blues Brothers sunglasses and hats, among other movie apparel and accessories.

BEETLEJUICE'S GRAVEYARD REVUE

5 **Duration:** 25 min.
Crowds: Steady, but high capacity of amphitheater means no waiting.
Strategy: You can use Universal Express Pass here; otherwise, go when ride lines are at capacity or after dark on hot days.
Audience: Older children and adults.
Rating: ★★

Whew! This is *some* show. In an amphitheater, a Transylvanian castle is the backdrop for Beetlejuice, who takes the stage and warms up the audience with his snappy lines, rude remarks, and sarcastic attitude. Then for some reason, which is hard or useless to remember, he introduces the stars of the show: Frankenstein's monster and his bride, the Werewolf, and Dracula. Thus begins a stage show never before seen on this planet. At some point, the monsters doff their traditional costumes in favor of glitzy and hip threads and sing the greatest hits of such diverse artists as Bruce Springsteen, the Village People, and Van Halen—albeit with "monster" changes, that is, "Jesse's Girl" becomes "Frankie's Girl." Upping the weirdness factor, the Ghoul Girl cheerleaders, Hip and Hop, are here to add sex appeal to the production. We are not kidding. Despite a sense of pity (or, perhaps, grudging admiration) for the performers (which once included 'N Sync's Joey Fatone and comedian Wayne Brady), this may be the only place you could see Frankenstein's monster pretending to play an electric guitar and shout "Are you ready to rock, Orlando?" Don't be fooled by imitators.

NEED A BREAK?

If you plan to have a full-service dinner in the evening, a quick burger may be all you need to make it through the day. **Richter's Burger Co.** lets you drop in and create your own burger or grilled chicken sandwich. Pretty quick, pretty convenient, and there are seats inside and out.

DISASTER!

6 **Duration:** 20 min.
Crowds: Heavy.
Strategy: You can use Universal Express Pass here; otherwise, go early or late.
Audience: All but young children. No pregnant women or guests with heart, back, or neck problems or motion sickness. Minimum height: Without adult, 40".
Rating: ★★

8

Dusting off a tired, old attraction based on a forgotten '70s film, Universal retooled the first half of Earthquake to change the attraction's storyline and add a much-needed makeover of comedy and energy. With all their actors in rehab, the assistant of disaster movie producer Frank Kincaid is in a hurry to cast park guests in roles for his latest blockbuster. Even the casting is fun, with the harried assistant seeking actors such as "A Martha Stewart–type without the prison time . . ." When the casting is complete, you enter the next room where, through an old magician's trick known as "Pepper's ghost," Kincaid (Christopher Walken) actually appears to take the stage and interact with the production assistant as he frantically tries to coordinate the elements for his next project, Mutha Earth. The show leads to the soundstage where the previously selected actors run through seemingly senseless actions before everyone boards trams to experience a two-minute, 8.3–Richter scale tremor that includes trembling earth, collapsing ceilings, blackouts, explosions, fire, and a massive underground flood coming from every angle. It's all very exciting, and is capped off on the return trip when you watch the hilarious "finished" film on the tram's monitors. The guest-starring clips shot before your journey now make sense as you see them interspersed into a "Mutha Earth" trailer starring Dwayne "The Rock" Johnson as a heroic park ranger. Disaster's sure to be a new guest favorite.

JAWS
❼ Duration: 7 min.
Crowds: Lines stay fairly long most of the day, but nothing like those at *Shrek* 4-D.
Strategy: You can use Universal Express Pass here; otherwise, go early or after dark for an even more terrifying experience—you can't see the attack as well, but can certainly hear and feel it.
Audience: All but young children, who will be frightened. No pregnant women or guests with heart, back, or neck problems or motion sickness.
Rating: ★★★

Perhaps because this is another attraction based on an old movie, Jaws, too, is looking a little tired. A lot tired. Still, that doesn't stop most guests from lining up for a ride around the 7-acre lagoon. There's a fairly fast-moving line, but if it slows down you can always watch WJWS, a fake TV station airing joke commercials for products like used recreational vehicles and candied blowfish. You can guess what happens when you board your boat for a placid cruise around the bay. That's right. A 32-foot killer shark zeroes in at 20 MPH, looking for a bite of your boat. Even though you know the shark is out there, things can still get pretty frightening with surprise attacks, explosions, and the teeth-grinding sounds on the side of your boat. And don't think you're safe just because you've reached the boathouse. The special effects on this ride really shine, especially the heat and fire from electrical explosions that could singe the eyebrows off Andy Rooney. Try it after dark for an extra thrill, and then cancel the following day's trip to the beach.

FEAR FACTOR LIVE

8 **Duration:** 25 min.

Crowds: Expect large crowds as with all new attractions, though the 2,000-seat amphitheater means you should be able to get in close to showtime.

Strategy: For a premium seat, arrive 30 min in advance or use Universal Express.

Audience: All ages, though small children may not be entertained.

Rating: ★★★

If you can't get enough of watching people grasping for temporary and misguided fame by eating worms, being sealed up in a roach-filled box, or wetting their pants as they're suspended from a helicopter, well, you can witness, and even participate in, stunts like this live at this show, which marks the first time a TV reality show has become a theme-park attraction. If you dare to compete, sign up at the audience-participation desk near the front of the attraction. Of course, since there are physical stunts involved, there are plenty of restrictions: you must be 18 or older, 5' to 6'2" tall, 110 to 220 pounds, and in good health. Apply as early as possible, as slots for the six daily shows fill quickly. If you're in the audience, you can still get in on the action by blasting contestants with water and air.

WORLD EXPO

The far corner of the park contains one of Universal Studios' most popular attractions **Men in Black: Alien Attack,** as well as the **Simpsons Ride,** which opened in 2008 within the real estate formerly occupied by Back to the Future.

NEED A BREAK? **The International Food Bazaar,** International Food Bazaar near the Simpsons, is an efficient, multiethnic food court serving Italian (pizza, lasagna), American (fried chicken, meat loaf), Greek (gyros), and Chinese (orange chicken, stir-fried beef) dishes at affordable prices—usually $7 to $9.

MEN IN BLACK: ALIEN ATTACK

9 **Duration:** 4½ min.

Crowds: Up to an hour in busy season.

Strategy: You can use Universal Express Pass here; otherwise, go first thing in the morning. Hint: solo riders can take a faster line so if you don't mind splitting up for a few minutes, you'll save a lot of time.

Audience: Older children and adults. The spinning nature of the cars may cause dizziness, so use caution: no guests with heart, back, or neck problems or motion sickness.

Rating: ★★★

This star attraction is billed as the world's first "ride-through video game." The pre-show provides the story line: to earn membership into MIB, you and your colleagues have to round up aliens who escaped when their shuttle crashed on Earth. A laser gun is mounted on your futuristic car, but unfortunately, since the gun's red laser dot is just a pinpoint, sometimes it can be hard to see what you've hit (which is why your score is tallied and displayed on an onboard computer). Basically,

Backstage at Universal

Odds are that while you're midway through a 100-foot spiral and g-forces are pushing your forehead through your feet, you won't be thinking about the technological soup of rotors, generators, and gears it took to get you there. But every time you board a ride at Universal Studios or Islands of Adventure, what you experience is just the tip of a high-tech iceberg. Lasers, 3-D imaging, holograms, pulleys, motors, hydraulics, and supercharged power supplies are working like mad to ensure that, for a few minutes at least, you really think Poseidon is sparking lightning bolts or Spider-Man has joined you on a trip through New York.

Think of what your day would be like minus all this mechanical acumen. The Incredible Hulk Coaster, for instance, would be just a lump of metal and plastic. But add four massive motors spinning fast enough to generate power to 220 smaller motors, and you're whipping up enough force to throw this 32,000-pound vehicle (a mass equal to eight Mercedes-Benz cars) up a 150-foot track at a 30-degree incline, to rocket you from 0 to 40 MPH *in less than two seconds.* If you want to experience a similar sensation, climb into an F-16 fighter jet and take it for a spin.

At the **Amazing Adventures of Spider-Man,** 3-D effects, sensory drops, and virtual reality will fool you into believing you're actually being subjected to an assault of flaming pumpkins, careening garbage trucks, electric bolts, antigravity guns, swirling fog, frigid water, and an incredibly intense 400-foot, white-knuckle, scream-like-a-baby sensory drop.

The volume of air that rushes through **Twister . . . Ride It Out** could fill more than four full-size airborne blimps in *one minute.* Its 110-decibel sound system uses 54 speakers cranking out 42,000 watts; enough wattage to power five average homes.

In **E.T. Adventure,** there are 4,400 illuminated stars in the sky, 3,340 miniature city buildings, 250 cars on the street, and 140 streetlights in the city. The ride utilizes 284 mi of electrical wiring, 250 mi of fiber optics, 68 show control computers, and 2,500 separate commands from those computers.

Jaws' 7-acre lagoon contains 5 million gallons of water, 2,000 mi of wire, and 10,000 cubic yards of concrete reinforced with 7,500 tons of steel. The 32-foot steel and Fiberglass shark weighs 3 tons and swims at 20 feet per second.

Each time you step inside a Universal attraction, there are more high-tech happenings going on behind the scenes . . . or right before your eyes.

you're on a trip through dark New York streets, firing blindly at aliens to rack up points. And they can fire back at you, sending your car spinning out of control. Be prepared to stomach the ending, when your car ends up swallowed by a 30-foot-high bug. Depending on your score, the ride wraps up with one of 35 endings, ranging from a hero's welcome to a loser's farewell. And you can compare scores with your friends. All in all, it's pretty exciting, if a bit confusing.

THE SIMPSONS RIDE

⑩ **Duration:** 6 min.
Crowds: Expect an hour-long wait.
Strategy: You can use Universal Express Pass here.
Audience: Older children and adults. No pregnant women or guests with heart, back, or neck problems or motion sickness. Minimum height: 40"; adults must accompany kids between 40" and 48".
Rating: ★★★

You know things will be a little different when you enter this attraction by walking through Krusty the Clown's gaping mouth—right away you wonder where you'll exit. On video monitors in the carnival-style queue area you'll be greeted by recognizable citizens of Springfield, including police chief Clancy Wiggum, who reminds you that if you must get sick, do it in your hat. That sets the tone for the attraction, where cartoon colors and video clips prepare you for the preshow that explains that the ever-entrepreneurial Krusty has expanded his empire to include a theme park, but it's also revealed that his disgruntled former sidekick, Sideshow Bob, has plans to sabotage it. Since little Maggie is too young to ride, she's left with Grandpa. If you can keep your eyes open as the virtual reality ride throws you around like you're in a super-size paint shaker, you'll see that after a fairly tame start, your coaster is flying all over Springfield, plunging toward the businesses and buildings you know, and narrowly escaping disaster as Sideshow Bob tears up the tracks. In the end, you end up safe thanks to the split-second timing of an unexpected hero. Weigh your love of the Simpsons against the will of your stomach. If you have even a scintilla of motion sickness, this one will throw you for a colorful, cartoonish loop.

WOODY WOODPECKER'S KIDZONE

Universal Studios caters to preschoolers with this compilation of rides, attractions, shows, and places for kids to get sprayed, splashed, and soaked. It's a great place for children to burn off their energy and give parents a break after nearly circling the park.

ANIMAL ACTORS ON LOCATION!

⑪ **Duration:** 20 min.
Crowds: Can get crowded in peak times.
Strategy: Go early for a good seat.
Audience: All ages.
Rating: ★★★

Animal shows are usually fun, and this one is better than most. An arkful of animals are the stars here, and the tricks (or *behaviors*) they perform are loosely based on shows from the cable network: *Emergency Vets, Planet's Funniest Animals,* and *The Jeff Corwin Experience.* A raccoon opens the show, and Lassie makes a brief appearance, followed by an audience-participation segment in the clever, funny, and cute Dog Decathlon. Next, Gizmo the parrot from *Ace Ventura: Pet Detective* arrives to fly in front of a wind machine and blue screen, the televised image showing him soaring across a desert, a forest, and then in outer space. In the grand finale Bailey the orangutan does some impressions (how an ape does Ricky Martin is a mystery), then there's an overpoweringly adorable chimpanzee and, finally, a brief peek at a boa constrictor. If your family loves animals, then this is an entertaining show that shouldn't be missed.

A DAY IN THE PARK WITH BARNEY

⑫ **Duration:** 20 min.
Crowds: Room for all.
Strategy: Arrive 10–15 min early on crowded days for a good seat—up close and in the center.
Audience: Young children.
Rating: ★★

If you can't get enough of the big purple dinosaur, here he is again. After a long preshow starring a goofy, kid-friendly emcee, parents tote their preschoolers into a pleasant theater-in-the-round filled with brilliantly colored trees, clouds, and stars. Within minutes, the kids will go crazy as their beloved TV playmate (and Baby Bop) dance and sing though clap-along, sing-along monster classics including "Mr. Knickerbocker," "If You're Happy and You Know It," and (of course) "I Love You." Following the very pleasing and thoughtful show and a chance to meet Barney up close, you'll exit to a fairly elaborate play area featuring hands-on activities—a water harp, wood-pipe xylophone, and musical rocks—that propel the already excited kids to even greater heights.

CURIOUS GEORGE GOES TO TOWN

⑬ **Duration:** As long as you like.
Crowds: Heavy in mid-morning.
Strategy: Go in late afternoon or early evening.
Audience: Toddlers through preteens and their parents.
Rating: ★★★

The celebrated simian visits the Man with the Yellow Hat in a no-line, no-waiting, small-scale water park. The main town square has brightly colored building facades, and the plaza is an interactive aqua play area that adults avoid but kids are drawn to like fish to water. Yes, there's water, water everywhere, especially atop the clock tower, which periodically dumps a mighty huge 500 gallons down a roof and straight onto a screaming passel of preschoolers. Kids love the levers, valves, pumps, and hoses that gush at the rate of 200 gallons per minute, letting them get sprayed, spritzed, splashed, and splattered. At the head of the square, footprints lead to a dry play area, with a rope climb and a ball cage where youngsters can frolic among thousands of foam balls. Parents can get into the act, sit it out on nearby benches, or take a few minutes to buy souvenir towels to dry off their waterlogged kids.

FIEVEL'S PLAYLAND

⑭ **Duration:** Up to your preschooler.
Crowds: Not significant, although waits do develop for the waterslide.
Strategy: On hot days, go after supper.
Audience: Toddlers, preschoolers, and their parents.
Rating: ★★

Another Spielberg movie spin-off, this one from the animated film *An American Tail*, this playground's larger-than-life props and sets are designed to make everyone feel mouse-size. Boots, cans, and other ordinary objects disguise tunnel slides, water play areas, ball crawls, and a gigantic net-climb equipped with tubes, ladders, and rope bridges. A harmonica slide plays music when you slide along the openings, and a 200-foot waterslide gives kids (and a parent if so desired) a chance to swoop down in Fievel's signature sardine can. It should keep the kids entertained for hours. The downside? You might have to build one of these for your backyard when you get home.

WOODY WOODPECKER'S NUTHOUSE COASTER

⑮ **Duration:** 1½ min.
Crowds: Heavy in mid-morning and early afternoon, when the under-2 set is out in force.
Strategy: Go at park closing, when most little ones have gone home.
Audience: Young children and their parents.
Rating: ★★★

Unlike the maniacal coasters that put you through zero-g rolls and inversions, this low-speed, mild-thrill version (top speed 22 MPH) makes it a safe bet for younger kids and action-phobic adults. (It's the same off-the-shelf design used on Islands of Adventure's Flying Unicorn and Goofy's Barnstormer at the Magic Kingdom.) The coaster races (a relative term) through a structure that looks like a gadget-filled factory; the coaster's cars look like shipping crates—some labeled "mixed nuts," others "salted nuts," and some tagged "certifiably nuts." Woody's Nuthouse has several ups and downs to reward you for the wait, and children generally love the low-level introduction to thrill rides.

E.T. ADVENTURE

⑯ **Duration:** 5 min.
Crowds: Sometimes not bad, but can be heavy during busy seasons.
Strategy: You can use Universal Express Pass here; otherwise, go early.
Audience: All ages. No guests with heart, back, or neck problems or motion sickness.
Rating: ★★★

Like other attractions here, this well-meaning ride is looking (and even smelling) a little bit tired. If it's your first time to Universal, however, you may still get a kick out of Steven Spielberg's update on *E.T.* Once you've learned that it's your mission to help E.T. return to his planet, you board bicycles mounted on a movable platform and fly 3 million light years from Earth (in reality just a few hundred yards), past a squadron of policemen and FBI agents to reach E.T.'s home. Here the music follows the mood, and the strange sounds in E.T.'s world are as colorful as the characters, which climb on vines, play xylophones, and

8

swing on branches in an alien Burning Man festival. Listen very, very closely at the end when E.T. offers you a personalized good-bye.

HOLLYWOOD

Angling off to the right of Plaza of the Stars, Rodeo Drive forms the backbone of Hollywood.

EN ROUTE

Stop by the **Brown Derby Hat Brown Derby Hat Shop** for the perfect topper, from red-and-white *Cat In The Hat* stovepipes to felt fedoras to bush hats from *Jurassic Park*.

UNIVERSAL HORROR MAKE-UP SHOW

⑰ **Duration:** 25 min.
Crowds: Not daunting.
Strategy: You can use Universal Express Pass here; otherwise, go in the afternoon or evening.
Audience: All but young children, who may be frightened; older children eat up the blood-and-guts stories.
Rating: ★★★

One of the funniest and most entertaining shows of any theme park, this attraction begins in an intriguing preshow area where masks, props, and rubber skeletons from horror films like *Van Helsing and Frankenstein* make a great backdrop for a family photo. Beyond this, the real fun kicks off in the theater when a host brings out a special-effects expert to describe what goes into (and what oozes out of) some of the creepiest movie effects. Corn syrup and food coloring make for a dandy blood substitute, for example. Despite the potentially frightening topic, teens, adults, and seniors get a kick out of the whole show because the subject is handled with an extraordinary amount of dead-on humor and totally engaging audience participation. As movie secrets are betrayed, actors add in one-liners with comedy-club timing. Throw in some knives, guns, loose limbs, and a surprise ending, and you've got yourself a recipe for edge-of-your-seat fun. It's absolutely flat-out good.

NEED A BREAK?

Schwab's Pharmacy is a re-creation of the legendary drugstore where—studio publicists claim—Lana Turner was discovered. What you'll discover is a quick stop where you can order ice cream as well as hand-carved turkey and ham sandwiches.

TERMINATOR 2 3-D

⑱ **Duration:** 21 min, with preshow.
Crowds: Always.
Strategy: You can use Universal Express Pass here; otherwise, go first thing in the morning.
Audience: All but very young children, who may be frightened.
Rating: ★★★

California's governor said he'd be back, and he is, along with the popular film's other main characters, including a buff Linda Hamilton and an older Edward Furlong, aka young John Connor. Directed by James *Titanic* Cameron, who also directed the first two *Terminator* movies, the 12-minute show is—frame for frame—one of the most expensive live-action films ever produced. The attraction begins when you enter the headquarters of the futuristic consortium, Cyberdyne, and a "community relations and media control" hostess greets your group and introduces their latest line of law-enforcing robots. Things go awry (of course), and the Schwarzenegger film, combined with icy fog, live actors, gunfights, and a chilling grand finale, keeps the pace moving at 100 MPH—although the 3-D effects seem few and far between. Kids may be scared silly and require some parental counseling, but if you can handle a few surprises, don't miss this one.

LUCY: A TRIBUTE

⑲ Duration: About 15 min.
Crowds: Seldom a problem.
Strategy: Save this for a peek on your way out or for a hot afternoon.
Audience: Adults.
Rating: ★

If you smile when you recall Lucy stomping grapes, practicing ballet, gobbling chocolates, or wailing when Ricky won't let her be in the show, then you need to stop here. This mini-museum (and major gift shop) pays tribute to Lucille Ball through scripts, props, costumes, awards, and clips from the comedian's estate. A challenging trivia quiz game has you trying to get Lucy, Ricky, Fred, and Ethel across country to Hollywood. It's a nice place to take a break and spend time with one of the funniest women of television.

ENTERTAINMENT

If you're in Orlando at the right time of year, don't miss Universal's evening seasonal parties—most notably **Mardi Gras** (early February through early April), **Rock the Universe** (Christian music, September), the wildly popular **Halloween Horror Nights** (October), and **Macy's Holiday Parade** (December and January). There are also CityWalk celebrations, including **Tony Hawk's Skate Bash, Orlando Beer Festival,** and **Reggae Fest.**

DISABILITIES AND ACCESSIBILITY

In addition to being physically accommodating, Universal has a professional staff that is quite helpful. At each park's Guest Services desk, you can pick up a *Studio Guide for Guests with Disabilities* (aka *Rider's Guide*), which contains information for guests who require specific needs on rides and offers details on interpreters, Braille scripts, menus, and assisted devices. Walking areas for service animals are available at the Nickelodeon Courtyard and at Men in Black: Alien Attack.

During orientation, all employees learn how to accommodate guests with disabilities, and you can occasionally spot staffers using wheelchairs. Additionally, power-assist buttons make it easier to get past heavy, hard-to-open doors; lap tables are provided for guests in shops; and already accessible bathroom facilities have such niceties as insulated under-sink pipes and companion restrooms.

Many of the cobblestone streets have paved paths, and photo spots are arranged for wheelchair accessibility. Various attractions have been retrofitted so that most can be boarded directly in a standard wheelchair; those using oversize vehicles or scooters must transfer to a standard model available at the ride's entrance—or into the ride vehicle itself. All outdoor shows have special viewing areas for people in wheelchairs, and all restaurants are wheelchair accessible.

ATTRACTIONS **Animal Actors on Location!,** the **Universal Horror Make-Up Show, Beetlejuice's Graveyard Revue, Twister . . . Ride It Out,** and **Terminator 2 3-D** are all completely wheelchair-accessible, theater-style attractions. Good scripts and songs mean that even those with visual impairments can enjoy parts of all of these shows.

No motorized wheelchairs or electric convenience vehicles (ECVs) are permitted on any ride vehicle, at either park. To ride **E.T. Adventure** you must transfer to the ride vehicle or use a standard-size wheelchair. Service animals are not permitted. There is some sudden tilting and accelerating, but even those with most types of heart, back, or neck problems can ride in E.T.'s orbs (the spaceships) instead of the flying bicycles. Those who use wheelchairs must transfer to the ride vehicles to experience **Woody Woodpecker's Nuthouse Coaster,** but most of **Curious George Goes to Town** is barrier-free.

If you use a standard-size wheelchair or can transfer to one or to the ride vehicle directly, you can board **Disaster!, Jaws,** and **Men in Black** directly. Service animals should not ride, and neither should you if you find turbulence a problem. Note that guests with visual impairments as well as those using wheelchairs should cross San Francisco/Amity with care. The cobblestones are rough on wheelchair and stroller wheels.

One vehicle in **Jimmy Neutron's Nicktoon Blast** is equipped with an access door that allows for standard-size wheelchairs, and two vehicles in the back of the attraction have closed caption screens. **Shrek 4-D** has eight handicap-equipped seats. Assisted listening devices are available at Guest Services.

Lucy: A Tribute is wheelchair accessible, but the TV-show excerpts shown on overhead screens are not closed-captioned. The line for the **Simpsons Ride** is accessible to people who use wheelchairs, but riders with either wheelchairs or ECVs must transfer to the ride's seating.

SERVICES Many Universal Studios employees have had basic sign-language training; even some of the animated characters speak sign, but since many have only four fingers, it's an adapted version. Like Walt Disney World, Universal supplements the visuals with a special guidebook containing story lines and scripts for the main attractions. The *Studio Guide for Guests with Disabilities* pinpoints special entrances available for those with disabilities; these routes often bypass the main line. You can get this and various booklets at Guest Services, just inside the main entrance and to the right. There's an outgoing TTY series hearing-impaired system on the counter in Guest Services.

UNIVERSAL STUDIOS BLITZ TOUR

BEST OF THE PARK

If you want to attempt to see everything in one day, arrive early so that you can take care of business and see the top attractions before the park gets very crowded. Another way to increase your attraction quota is to ignore the faux Hollywood streets and the gift shops. During peak seasons, you can avoid long waits at major attractions with the highly recommended Universal Express and Express PLUS Passes. These admit you to the attractions with little or no wait in line.

If you're one of the first people in the park and have plenty of early energy, circle the park twice to catch the A-list rides first, then pick up the B-list later. If you're dying to see **Shrek 4-D,** you'll need to hit it first (it's straight ahead on the right), and then backtrack and turn left to follow up with **Terminator 2** 3-D. Next, make tracks down the street to the **Simpsons Ride** while the lines are still at a minimum. As you continue counterclockwise, **Men in Black: Alien Attack** is next, followed by **Jaws,** then **Disaster!,** then the must-see **Revenge of the Mummy** attraction and, finally, back near the entrance to see **Twister – Ride It Out.** Anywhere along the line, if you time it right so you don't have to wait, consider dropping in to see the live action show, **Fear Factor Live.**

You've just circled the park, and chances are the crowds have arrived. Based on your preferences, you can backtrack to pick up other entertaining attractions like **Jimmy Neutron's Nicktoon Blast, Animal Actors** on *Location!,* and the **Universal Horror Make-Up Show.** The remaining rides and attractions are up to you. If the lines are short, all that remains are the ride and show collection at **Woody Woodpecker's KidZone** and **Lucy: A Tribute.** It's been a full day. Go get some rest.

ON RAINY DAYS

Unless it's the week after Christmas, rainy days mean that the crowd will be noticeably thinner. Universal is one of the area's best bets in rainy weather—the park is fully operational, and there are many places to take shelter from downpours. Only a few street shows are canceled during bad weather.

8

EATING AT UNIVERSAL STUDIOS

Most restaurants are on Plaza of the Stars and Hollywood Boulevard. Several accept "priority seating," which is not a reservation but an arrival time. You'll receive the first available seat after that particular time.

You can make arrangements up to 30 days in advance by calling or dropping by **Guest Services** (☎ *407/224–6350*) when you arrive or by heading over to the restaurant in person. In a sign of the times, transfat foods are out and healthful food is in.

FULL-SERVICE
RESTAURANTS

San Francisco/Amity's **Lombard's Landing** (☎ *407/224–6400*) is designed to resemble a warehouse from 19th-century San Francisco. The specialty is seafood (of course), including clams, shrimp, mussels, and catch of the day, but you can also get hamburgers, pastas, steak, and chicken.

UNIVERSAL ORLANDO

NAME	Min. Height	Type of Entertainment	Duration	Suits	Crowds	Strategy
UNIVERSAL STUDIOS						
A Day in the Park with Barney	n/a	show	20 min.	Under 7	ok	Arrive 10–15 min. early on crowded days for a good seat—up close and in the center.
★ *Animal Actors on Location!*	n/a	show	20 min.	All	Peak times	Stadium seating, but come early for a good seat.
Beetlejuice's Graveyard Revue	n/a	show	25 min.	5 and up	Heavy, but fast lines	Use Universal Express Pass here or go after dark on hot days.
Curious George Goes to Town	n/a	play area	Up to you.	Under 7	Midmorning	Go in late afternoon or early evening. Bring a towel.
Disaster!	40"	thrill ride	20 min.	7 and up	Heavy	Come early, before closing or use Universal Express Pass. This is loud.
E.T. Adventure	n/a	ride	5 min.	All	ok	Go early morning or use Universal Express Pass.
Fear Factor Live	n/a	show	25 min.	All	Fast lines	Stadium seating, but arrive 30 min. early for good seats. Or use Universal Express Pass. Toddlers may be bored.
Jaws	n/a	thrill ride	7 min.	10 and up	Heavy	Come after dark for a more terrifying ride.
Jimmy Neutron's Nicktoon Blast	40"	sim. ride	8 min.	All	Morning	Come at the end of the day. Under 40", can experience the ride from a stationery location. Use Universal Express or single rider line.
Lucy: A Tribute	n/a	walk through	15 min.	Adults	ok	Save this for a hot afternoon.
Men in Black: Alien Attack	42"	thrill ride	4½ min.	10 and up	Peak season	Solo riders can take a faster line so split up. Spinning ride.
Revenge of the Mummy	48"	thrill ride	3 min.	7 and up	Yes!	Use Universal Express Pass or go first thing in the morning.
Shrek 4-D	n/a	4-D film	13 min.	All	Yes!	Very popular. Use Universal Express Pass.
The Simpsons Ride	40"	thrill ride	6 min.	10 and up	Heavy	Use Universal Express Pass. It's also a simulator ride.
Terminator 2 3-D	n/a	3-D film	21 min.	7 and up	Yes!	Go first thing in the morning or use Universal Express Pass.
Twister…Ride It Out	n/a	sim. ride/show	3 min.	10 and up	Yes!	Go first thing in morning or at closing. This "ride" involves standing and watching the action unfold.
★ *Universal Horror Make-Up Show*	n/a	show	25 min.	All	Not daunting	Go in the afternoon or evening. Young children may be frightened; older children eat up the blood-and-guts stories.
Woody Woodpecker's Nuthouse Coaster	36"	thrill ride	1½ min.	Toddlers	Midmorning	Go at park closing, when most little ones have gone home.

UNIVERSAL ISLANDS OF ADVENTURE

★ The Amazing Adventures of Spider-Man	40"	sim. ride	4½ min.	5 and up	Yes!	Use Universal Express Pass or go early or late in day. See bad guys in the wanted posters.
Camp Jurassic	n/a	play area	Up to you	All	ok	Go anytime.
Caro-Seuss-el	n/a	carousel	2 min.	All	Fast lines	Use Universal Express Pass or end your day here.
The Cat in the Hat	n/a	thrill ride	4½ min.	All	Heavy	Use Universal Express Pass here or go early or at the end of the day.
Doctor Doom's Fearfall	52"	thrill ride	1 min.	10 and up	Fast lines	Use Universal Express Pass or go later in the day, on an empty stomach.
★ Dudley Do-Right's Ripsaw Falls	44"	thrill ride	5½ min.	All	Summer	Ride the flume in late afternoon to cool down, or at day's end. There's no seat where you can stay dry.
★ Dueling Dragons	54"	thrill ride	2¼ min.	10 and up	Yes!	Ride after dark or early morning. Go for the rear car of Fire Dragon.
★ Eighth Voyage of Sinbad	n/a	show	25 min.	All	Fast lines	Stadium seating, but arrive atleast 20 minutes early. Don't sit too close up front.
Flying Unicorn	36"	thrill ride	1 min.	Under 7	Fast lines	Use Universal Express Pass if crowded. This thrill ride is mild.
High in the Sky Seuss Trolley Train Tour	34" *	ride	3 min.	All	Heavy	Relatively new. You may have to wait. 34" to 48" can ride but must do so with an adult.
★ Incredible Hulk Coaster	54"	thrill ride	2¾ min.	10 and up	Yes!	Come here first. Effects are best in the morning. The front row is best.
Jurassic Park Discovery Center	n/a	walk through	Up to you	10 and up	ok	Go anytime.
Jurassic Park River Adventure	42"	thrill ride	6 min.	All	Yes!	Universal Express Pass. Toddlers may be scared.
One Fish, Two Fish, Red Fish, Blue Fish	n/a	ride	2+ min.	Under 7	Yes!	Use Universal Express Pass or come early or late in day.
Popeye & Bluto's Bilge-Rat Barges	42"	thrill ride	5 min.	All	Yes!	Come early in the morning or before closing. You will get wet.
Poseidon's Fury	n/a	show	20 min.	6 and up	Heavy	Come at the end of the day. Stay to the left for best spot. Get in first row each time.
Pteranodon Flyers	36"**	ride	2 min.	All	Perpetual	Skip this on your first visit. 36" to 48" can ride but must do so with an adult.
Storm Force Accelatron	n/a	thrill ride	2 min.	10 and up	ok	Go whenever—except after you've eaten.

★ = Fodor'sChoice

8

Hidden in Production Central, **Finnegan's Bar & Grill** (☎ 407/363–8757) is an Ellis Island–era New York dining room serving shepherd's pie, Irish stew, fish-and-chips, and steaks. Main courses start at $10; and Guinness, Harp, and Bass are on tap. Live Irish folk music completes the theme.

At the corner of Hollywood Boulevard and 8th Avenue—which turns into Sunset Boulevard along the bottom shore of the lagoon—is **Mel's Drive-In** (☎ 407/363–8766) (no reservations), a flashy '50s eatery with a menu and decorative muscle cars straight out of *American Graffiti*. For burgers and fries, this is one of the best choices in the park, and it comes complete with a roving doo-wop group. You're on vacation— go ahead and have that extra-thick shake. Mel's is also a great place to meet, in case you decide to go your separate ways in the park.

SELF-SERVICE RESTAURANTS   The **International Food Bazaar,** a food court near the Simpsons Ride, has pizza, lasagna, fried chicken, meat loaf, gyros, stir-fried beef, and other multicultural dishes at affordable prices—usually $7 to $9. The Italian Caesar and Greek salads are especially welcome on a muggy day.

Production Central's **Classic Monsters Cafe** resembles a mad scientist's laboratory. The self-serve restaurant is open seasonally and offers wood-fired oven pizzas, pastas, chopped chef salads, four-cheese ravioli, and rotisserie chicken. Frankenstein's monster and other scary characters from vintage Universal films make the rounds of the tables as you eat. Be sure to check out the monster-meets-celebrity pictures at the entrance.

GUIDED TOURS

Universal has several variations on **VIP Tours** (☎ 407/363–8295), which offer what's called "front-of-the-line access" or, in plain English, the right to jump the line. Originally created for visiting celebrities, this is the ultimate capitalist fantasy and worthwhile if you're in a hurry, if you're with a large group, if the day is crowded, and if you have the money to burn. The five-hour one-day/one park VIP tour costs $120 per person and for one-day/two parks $150 **and each can accommodate as many as a dozen people.** The tours do not include park admission—that is a separate fee. Exclusive one-day/one park eight-hour tours (which are reserved for your group only) start at $1,600, not including sales tax, while a one-day/two park tour tallies in at $2,000. For $3,000, sign up for a two-day tour of both parks, which includes backstage access and discussions on the park's history, decorating, and landscaping. The tours also offer extras and upgrades such as priority restaurant seating, bilingual guides, gift bags, complimentary refreshments at check-in, free wheelchairs and strollers if needed, and valet parking. Best of all, the guides can answer practically any question you throw at them—they're masters of Universal trivia. Keep in mind, the shorter tours are nonexclusive, which means you'll be touring with other park guests. Eight-hour VIP tours are exclusive and geared to the desires and interests of your group, **and the group can be up to 15 people.**

UNIVERSAL CITYWALK

CityWalk is Universal's answer to Downtown Disney. They've gathered theme retail stores and kiosks, restaurants, and nightclubs in one spot— here they're right at the entrance to both Universal Studios Florida and Islands of Adventure. CityWalk attracts a mix of conventioneers, vacationers, and what seems to be Orlando's entire youth market. You may be too anxious to stop on your way into the parks and too tired to linger on your way out, but at some point on your vacation you may drop by for a drink at **Jimmy Buffett's Margaritaville,** a meal at **Emeril's,** a concert at **Hard Rock Live,** take in the **Blue Man Group,** or pick up a souvenir from one of several gift stores. Visiting the stores and restaurants is free, as is parking after 6 PM. The only price you'll have to pay is a cover charge for the nightclubs, or you can invest in the more sensible $9.95 Party Pass for admission to all the clubs all night long. Pay $13 and you can add a movie to your evening out. *See Chapter 13, Nightlife, for descriptions of CityWalk's bars and clubs.*

WET 'N WILD

The world's first water park (as confirmed by *Aquatics International*), Wet 'n Wild opened in 1977 and quickly became known as the place for thrilling waterslides. Although it's now far from alone, Wet 'n Wild is still the nation's most popular water park, thanks to its quality, service, innovations, and ability to create more heart-stopping waterslides, rides, and tubing adventures than its competitors. There's a complete water playground for kids, numerous high-energy slides for adults, a lazy river ride, and some quiet sandy beaches on which you can stretch out and get a tan.

After skimming down a super-speedy waterslide, it may be time for a break. You can bring a cooler or stop for lunch at one of several food courts and find a picnic spot at various pavilions near the lakeside beach, pools, and attractions. Pools are heated in cooler weather, and Wet 'n Wild is one of the few water parks in the country to be open year-round.

If you're not a strong swimmer, don't worry. Ride entrances are marked with warnings to let you know which ones are safe for you, there are plenty of low-key attractions available, and during peak season as many as 400 lifeguards are on duty daily.

ADMISSION

Admission without tax is $44.95 for adults (10 and above) and $38.95 for children ages 3 to 9. The price drops by $10 roughly three to four hours before the park closes. Since closing times vary, call in advance to find out when the discount begins. For information about the Orlando FlexTicket, a combination ticket for all of the Universal Studios parks, see the Admission section at the front of this chapter. Parking is $10 for cars, $11 for RVs.

WET 'N WILD TIP SHEET

■ Unless you have to travel in summer, try to avoid the peak months of June, July, and August.

■ Arrive 30 minutes before the park opens in the morning, or come on a cloudy day.

■ On the surface, there doesn't seem to be much reason to go to this park when it's gray and drizzly, but as a Wet 'n Wild spokeswoman observes, "This is a water park. If you aren't coming here to get wet, why are you here?" OK. If you do come on a day that rains, it will likely be a quick summer afternoon shower that will close attractions and clear pools only until 30 minutes or so after the thunder and lightning pass. If it looks like a soggy, thorough, all-day rain, skip it.

■ Wear a bathing suit (and a one-piece suit is better than a bikini). You can't wear cutoffs or anything that has rivets, metal buttons, or zippers.

■ If your bare feet aren't used to it, the rough and hot surface of the sidewalks and sandpaperlike pool bottoms can do a number on your soles. Bring a pair of wading slippers when you're walking around, but be ready to carry them as you're plunging down a slide.

■ Keep money, keys, and other valuables in a locker. They could get lost on the super slides. If you wear prescription sunglasses, you can bring them on the rides; just take them off and clutch them tightly before you take the plunge.

■ Keep in mind that lines here are Disney-esque. Once you think you're almost there, you discover there's another level or two to go. Get ready to be patient.

■ Bring a towel, but leave it behind when you ride.

■ Wear high SPF sunblock, and remember that you can get a sunburn even on a cloudy day.

■ Eat a high-protein meal to keep your energy going. A day here involves nearly nonstop walking, swimming, and climbing.

BASIC SERVICES

FACILITIES AND SUPPLIES   Don't think the expenses stop with parking and admission. If you came without a towel, you can rent one for $2 with a $2 deposit. Mighty small lockers, $8 with a $2 deposit, are near the entrance and at handy locations throughout the park. Tubes for the Wave Pool cost $4 with a $2 deposit. To save you $2, a combination package of all three is available.

There are dressing rooms (with lockers), showers, and restrooms to the left just after the main entrance. Additional restrooms are near the Bubble Up, First Aid, and the Surge.

Life jackets are provided by the staff. If you're looking for sunscreen, sunglasses, bathing suits, camera film, and other necessities, stop in the Breakers Beach Shop near the park entrance.

FIRST AID   The First Aid Stand is between Surf Grill and Pizza & Subs.

HOURS   Wet 'n Wild is open 365 days a year, weather permitting, usually from 10 AM to 6 PM, with summer hours extending from until 9:30 AM until 9 PM. Call for exact hours during holiday periods.

INFORMATION The Guest Services desk is to the left as you enter the park. For general information, call **Wet 'n Wild** or visit online (☎ *407/351–3200 recorded information, 407/351–1800 park operations* ⊕ *www.wetnwildorlando. com*).

LOST PEOPLE AND THINGS If you plan to split up, be sure everyone knows where and when you plan to meet. Lifeguards look out for kids who might be lost. If they spot one, they'll take the child to Guest Services, which will page the parent or guardian. The Lost and Found is at Guest Services, to the left just after you walk through the entrance to Wet 'n Wild.

PICNICKING You are welcome to picnic and to bring coolers with food into the park. However, glass containers and alcoholic beverages are not permitted. There are many picnic areas scattered around Wet 'n Wild, in both covered and open areas.

WHEELCHAIRS Many of the paths are flat and easily accessible in a wheelchair; however, no rides accommodate people using wheelchairs. Wheelchairs are available for $5 with a $25 refundable deposit.

WET 'N WILD ATTRACTIONS

Black Hole: The Next Generation. One of the park's most popular attractions was enhanced with new effects. A dynamic display of lights and energy surround you as you're hurtled through the mysterious cosmos in a two-person "hydra-capsule." You'll scream your head off as you zip through space and encounter the gravitational effects of Worm Holes and Black Holes before splashing back to earth. *Minimum height: 36 ", 48 " without an adult.*

The Blast. This two-passenger ride sends you and a friend bumping down twists and turns through explosive pipe bursts and drenching waterspouts leading up to a final waterfall plunge. *Minimum height: 36 ", 48 " without an adult.*

Bomb Bay. Lines move quickly here, but not because the capacity is great. It's because a lot of kids chicken out once they reach the top. If you challenge yourself to the ultimate free fall, here's what happens: you step inside a large enclosed cylinder mounted above a nearly vertical drop. The attendant looks through the glass door to make sure your arms and legs are crossed (thereby preventing wedgies), and then punches a button to release the trapdoor. Like a bomb dropping out of a plane, you free-fall for 76 feet and then skim down the long, steep slide. The force of the water on your feet, legs, and back can be substantial, rivaling the emotional toll it took to do it in the first place. *Minimum height: 48 " without an adult.*

Brain Wash. A great name goes along with one of the water park's newest thrill rides. Climbing into an inner tube designed for two or four passengers, there are lights, video, and surreal sounds that wash around you as you and your tube as you commit to a 53-foot vertical drop—but that's only half of it. Once you've survived the drop, you'll find yourself at the rim of a 65-foot domed funnel where you begin swishing and swirling back and forth around the massive bowl before finally

8

dropping through into the waters below. *Minimum height: 48" without an adult.*

Bubba Tub. Because up to four people can take this ride together, this is one of the park's most popular attractions. After scaling the platform, your group boards a huge waiting inner tube. From the top of the six-story slide it flows over the edge and starts an up-and-down, triple-dip, roller-coaster ride that splashes down into a watery pool. *Minimum height: 36", 48" without an adult.*

Bubble Up. After catching sight of this enormous (about 12 feet tall), wet beach ball, many kids race right over to try to climb to the top and then slide back down. Surrounding the ball is a wading pool, a respite between attempts to scale the watery mountain. *Height: 42"–64" only.*

Der Stuka. Adjacent to Bomb Bay is a steep slide that offers a similar thrill to that of Bomb Bay, but without the trap-door drop. *Der Stuka,* "steep hill" in German, is hard to beat for sheer exhilaration. After climbing the winding six-story platform, you sit down on a horizontal slide, nudge yourself forward a few inches, and then gravity takes over. You're hurtling down a slippery, 250-foot-long speed slide that will tax your back and test the security of your bathing suit. This one's a real scream. *Minimum height: 48".*

Disco H20. Here's something even the folks at Studio 54 never dreamed of: a four-person raft that floats into a swirling aquatic nightclub. Once inside the 70-foot-tall building, your raft goes into a spin cycle as you're bombarded with sparkling lights, disco balls, and the sounds of the '70s greatest hits. You must be 36 inches in height or you'll upset the bouncer. *Minimum height: 36", 48" without an adult.*

The Flyer. This four-person toboggan carries you into switchback curves and down suddenly steep drops. The turns are similar to those on a real toboggan run. *Minimum height: 36", 48" without an adult.*

Kids' Park. Designed for children under 48 inches, Kids' Park is like a day at the beach. There's a kid-size sand castle to play in, and a 5-foot-tall bucket that dumps 250 gallons of water every few minutes onto a seashell-decorated awning, where it splashes off to spray all and sundry. In the center is a pool surrounded by miniaturized versions of the more popular grown-up attractions and rides. Children overjoyed when they play with a garden hose will go absolutely nuts when they see that they can slide, splash, squirt, and swim on rides here. Tables and chairs go fast, with many families here for nearly their whole visit.

Knee Ski/Wakeboard. A molasses-slow line marks the entrance to this seasonal attraction, which requires an additional fee. A moving cable with ski ropes attached encircles a large lake. After donning protective headgear and a life vest, you kneel on a knee board or try to balance yourself on a wakeboard, grab a ski rope, and are given the opportunity to circumnavigate the lake. The ½-mi ride includes five turns: roughly 75% of the riders wipe out after turn number one, and 90% are gone by turn two. Only the agile and athletic few make it the distance. Hint: if you wipe out before turn one, you get to go back and try again. *Minimum height: 56".*

Lazy River. Had enough? Then settle into an inner tube for a peaceful trip down a gently moving stream. Bask in the sun as you drift by colorful flowers and tropical greenery. It's a nice break when your body just can't handle any more 45-degree drops.

Mach 5. After grabbing a soft foam board, you scale a few steps and arrive at one of three waterslides. Conventional wisdom says that Lane B is the best, but it's possible all three are the same. Riding on your belly, you zip through some great twists, feel the sensation of hitting the high banks, and then splash down in a flood of water. It's mucho fun. *No height requirement, but participants must be able to control the board.*

The Storm. At the top of the tower, two tubes carry a torrent of water. Climb in the tube, shove off in the midst of a tidal wave, and the slow, curving arc takes you around and around until you reach a 30-foot diameter bowl. Now you spin around again like soap suds whirling around a sink drain. After angular momentum has had its fun, you drop through a hole in the bottom of the bowl into a small pool. After you get your bearings and find the surface, you may be tempted to climb up and do it again. *Minimum height: 48".*

Surf Lagoon. This 17,000-square-foot lagoon is as close to a beach as you'll get in the park, which explains why it's generally packed. Also known as the Wave Pool, it's just past the turnstiles. Every so often, the lagoon is buffeted by 4-foot-high waves, which elicit screams of delight from kids. Likewise, adults are thrilled to find that the money they spent on the kid's floats, surfboards, and inner tubes was worth it.

The Surge. The title overstates the thrill of this ride, although it borders on exhilarating. Up to four passengers can fit in this giant raft: once you've gone over the lip of the first drop, there's no turning back. The raft zips down five stories while twisting and turning through a series of steeply banked curves and beneath waterfalls. If you or your kids are too nervous for rides like Bomb Bay or the Black Hole, then this is probably a safe bet. *Minimum height: 36", 48" without an adult.*

The Wild One. Open seasonally (usually April through September), this is a large, two-person inner tube that's towed around the lake. The ease of staying afloat is countered by the challenge of hanging on when you cross the boat's wake. Like the knee skis, this requires an additional fee. *Minimum height: 51".*

8

SeaWorld, Discovery Cove, and Aquatica

WORD OF MOUTH

"Our tip for SeaWorld is if you wish to feed the animals spend a little time listening to the experts. To feed the stingrays you have to hold the fish pointing up between your fingers (so your hand is flat and the fish is sticking up at 90 degrees to your hand). You then allow the stingrays to glide over your hand and take the fish. So many kids and adults were having a hard time getting the stingrays to take the fish because they weren't using the right technique."

—highflyer

Updated
by Gary
McKechnie

Ten minutes from Universal and Walt Disney World, Sea-World and Discovery Cove are designed for animal lovers and anyone who prefers more natural pleasures. Both parks offer a relatively low-key, ocean-themed experience. Sea-World's new water park, Aquatica, which opened in early 2008, will suit those who are looking for more action, with water slides, lagoons, and beaches.

Sister parks SeaWorld and Discovery Cove differ in price and activities. At SeaWorld you'll watch a series of high-energy circus shows involving dolphins, whales, sea lions, a huge walrus, and even cats and dogs. Plus you can ride three thrilling roller coasters, one of which (Kraken) is considered one of the scariest rides in Florida. The second is the watery Journey to Atlantis flume ride, and the third, new in 2009, is Manta, a coaster designed to make you feel like you're sailing along with a giant manta ray. Discovery Cove is more of a laid-back oasis. You change into your bathing suit and spend the day snorkeling among tropical fish, relaxing on the beach, and, for a short period, interacting with dolphins. You can also get up close to tropical birds in the aviary. For the luxury of visiting a faux tropical island, you'll pay roughly four times as much as a ticket to SeaWorld, but your ticket actually includes a pass to either SeaWorld or Busch Gardens in Tampa (which must be used within seven days).

SEAWORLD ORLANDO

There's a whole lot more to SeaWorld than Shamu, the "stage name" used for its mammoth killer-whale mascots. Sure, you can be splashed by the whales, stroke a stingray, see manatees face-to-snout, learn to love an eel, and be spat at by a walrus. But as the world's largest marine adventure park, SeaWorld celebrates all the mammals, birds, fish, and reptiles that live in and near the ocean.

Although SeaWorld can't rival Disney World when it comes to park design and attention to detail, it does offer a somewhat gentler and less-hurried touring experience governed mostly by show schedules. Every attraction is designed to showcase the beauty of the marine world and demonstrate ways that humans can protect its waters and wildlife. And because there are more exhibits and shows than rides—believe it or not, there are only four actual rides in the entire park—you can go at your own pace without that hurry-up-and-wait feeling. First-timers may be slightly confused by the lack of distinct "lands" here—SeaWorld's performance venues, attractions, and activities surround a 17-acre lake, and the artful landscaping, curving paths, and concealing greenery sometimes lead to wrong turns. But armed with a map that lists show times, it's easy to plan a chronological approach that flows

TOP SEAWORLD ATTRACTIONS

Kraken. SeaWorld's main thrill ride takes you on a high-speed chase with a dragon. But who's chasing who? Just don't disturb the dragon eggs on your way out.

Pets Ahoy. Anyone who has ever loved a pet, or wanted one, has to see the talented cats, dogs, birds, and pig in this show.

Journey to Atlantis. This somewhat dated Splash Mountain–esque ride still provides thrills on its last, steep, wet drop.

Believe. The park's flagship attraction and mascot are irresistible. In a show four years in the making, you'll see several Shamus performing graceful aquabatics that are guaranteed to thrill.

Clyde and Seamore Take Pirate Island. Head for Sea Lion & Otter Stadium to watch this slapstick comedy routine starring an adorable team of water mammals and their trainers.

easily from one show and attraction to the next and allows enough time for rest stops and meal breaks.

Numbers in the margin correspond to points of interest on the Sea-World map.

ADMISSION

At this writing, regular one-day tickets to SeaWorld cost $74.95 for adults, and $64.95 for children ages 3 to 9, not including tax. For permission to bypass the admission line at the park, purchase and print out your tickets online at ⊕*www.seaworld.com.*

DISCOUNTS Standard discounts are available for senior citizens, AAA members, military personnel, and guests with disabilities. Guests with visual or hearing impairments are eligible for 50% off the ticket price. Florida residents have the added advantage of buying a Fun Card, which offers unlimited admission between January 1 and December 31 at the same rate as a one-day admission.

As SeaWorld, Discovery Cove, Aquatica, and Busch Gardens Tampa Bay (about an hour from Orlando on I–4) fall under the same corporate umbrella (Busch Entertainment Corporation), there are incentives for purchasing combination tickets to these parks as well as the Universal Orlando attractions Islands of Adventure, Universal Studios, and Wet 'n Wild. Visit www.seaworld.com for the pricing options.

BABY CARE

Diaper-changing tables are in or near most women's restrooms and in the men's restroom at the front entrance, near Shamu's Emporium. You can buy diapers at machines in all changing areas and at Shamu's Emporium. A special area for nursing is alongside the women's restroom at Friends of the Wild gift shop, equidistant from SeaWorld Theater, Penguin Encounter, and Sea Lion & Otter Stadium.

Gerber baby food is sold by request at most restaurants (for yourself you may want to order a more substantial entrée), as well as at the Children's Store. For more infant items you'll have to leave the park for

SeaWorld Orlando

KEY WEST

→ Discovery Cove

First Aid

Dolphin Cove ◆

Sharks Underwater Grill

Paddle boats

The Waterfront

Anheuser-Busch Hospitality Center

First Aid

Mango Joe's Café

Atlantis Bayside Stadium

Seafire Inn

Makahiki Luau

Lockers ◆

Show Schedules ◆

Guest Relations, Information

Main Entrance

Lagoon

KEY

✗ Restaurants

†† Rest rooms

A'lure, the
Call of the Ocean **15**
Blue Horizons **6**
Clydesdale Hamlet **16**
Dolphin Nursery **1**
Journey to Atlantis **8**
Key West at SeaWorld **5**

Kraken **9**
Manatees: The
Last Generation? **7**
Manta **2**
Pacific Point
Preserve **13**
Penguin
Encounter **10**

Pets Ahoy **11**
Sea Lion &
Otter Stadium **12**
Shamu Stadium–
Believe **18**
Shamu's Happy
Harbor **17**
Shark Encounter **14**

Sky Tower **19**
Stingray Lagoon **4**
Turtle Point **3**
Wild Arctic **20**

a short drive to a nearby supermarket or drugstore. Ask for directions to local supermarkets and drugstores on nearby International Drive or Central Florida Parkway.

CAMERAS AND FILM
Memory cards for digital cameras, as well as disposable cameras both with and without flash, are available at many gift shops.

GETTING THERE AND AROUND
SeaWorld is just off the intersection of I–4 and the Beachline Expressway, 10 minutes south of downtown Orlando and 15 minutes from Orlando International Airport. Of all the Central Florida theme parks, it's the easiest to find. If you're heading west on I–4 (toward Disney), take Exit 72 onto the Beachline Expressway (aka Highway 528) and take the first exit onto International Drive and follow signs a short distance to the parking lot. Heading east, take Exit 71.

HEALTH SERVICES/FIRST AID
First Aid Centers, staffed by registered nurses, are behind Stingray Lagoon and near Shamu's Happy Harbor. In case of an emergency ask any SeaWorld employee to contact Security.

HOURS
SeaWorld opens daily at 9 AM, but closing hours vary between 6 and 7 PM, and, during the holidays, as late as 11 PM. To be safe, call in advance for park hours.

INFORMATION
The **Main Information Center** is just inside the park, near the entrance. This should be one of your first stops since it's where you can pick up a wonderful map of the park, which contains a wealth of information on showtimes, restaurants, attractions, and inside tips on wheelchair accessibility, strollers, Braille menus, smoking areas, and more. Here you can also buy tickets for the luau, Discovery Cove, and guided tours, as well as make dinner reservations. The hosts are here to help you plan your day and point you toward the attractions and shows that will pique your interest. For general information, contact **SeaWorld Orlando** (☎ *407/351–3600 or 800/327–2420* ⊕ *www.seaworld.com*).

LOCKERS
Coin-operated lockers are available inside the main entrance and to the right as you enter, next to Shamu's Emporium. There are also lockers throughout the park and, conveniently, by the wild coaster, Kraken. The cost ranges between 50¢ and $1.50, depending on size.

LOST PEOPLE AND THINGS
All employees who see lost-looking children take them to the Information Center, where you can also go to report lost children. A parkwide paging system also helps reunite parents with kids. The Information Center also operates as the park's Lost and Found.

PACKAGE PICK-UP
Purchases made anywhere in the park can be sent to Package Pick-Up, in Shamu's Emporium near the park entrance, on request. Allow two hours for your purchases to make it there.

TIP SHEET

■ Avoid a weekend visit or one during school holidays if you can, since those are the busiest times.

■ Wear comfortable sneakers—no heels or slip-on sandals—since you may get your feet wet on the water rides.

■ Pack dry clothes for yourself and your children if you intend to get wet by sitting close to the front at the Shamu show or riding Journey to Atlantis.

■ If you prefer to take your own food, remove all plastic straws and lids before you arrive—they can harm fish and birds.

■ Budget ahead for food for the animals—feeding time is a major part of SeaWorld charm. A small carton of fish costs $5.

■ Arrive at least 30 minutes early for the Shamu show, which generally fills to capacity on even the slowest days. Prepare to get wet in the "splash zone" down front.

PARKING
Parking costs $10 per car, $12 for an RV or camper. Preferred parking, which costs $15, allows you to park in the six rows closest to the front gate.

PET CARE CENTER
For $6, the pet care center near the main entrance accommodates dogs, cats, hamsters, and whatever other creatures you may be traveling with. Dogs must be walked every two to three hours throughout the day. For meals, you're expected to bring food for your pet, but SeaWorld will provide water.

QUICK QUEUE
In the style of Disney's Fastpass and Universal's Express Pass, SeaWorld has introduced this front-of-line option. A Quick Queue pass, which costs $15–$25 per person depending on the season, will get you to the front of the line at major attractions and shows. Keep in mind that there are only a handful of "major attractions" and the space is seldom a problem at major shows that seat hundreds, if not thousands.

STROLLER AND WHEELCHAIR RENTALS
Strollers ($10 for a single and $18 for a double), standard wheelchairs ($10), and electric wheelchairs ($38) can be rented at the Information Center.

SEAWORLD ATTRACTIONS

DOLPHIN NURSERY
 Crowds: Not a problem.
Strategy: Go during a Shamu show so the kids can be up front.
Audience: All ages.
Rating: ★★

In a large pool, dolphin moms and babies (with birth dates posted on signs) play and leap and splash. You can't get close enough to pet or feed them, so you'll have to be content peering from several feet away and asking the host questions during a regular Q and A session. Here's a popular answer: No, you can't take one home. Hint: if you just *have* to touch a dolphin, head over to Dolphin Cove in the Key West section.

MANTA

2 Crowds: May be large.

Strategy: To beat the crowds, go first thing or late in the day, or purchase a Quick Queue pass for front-of-line access.

Audience: Kids will love the aquarium entrance; older children and adults will love the thrill of the ride itself. Note that kids must be at least 54" tall (4½') to ride.

Rating: ★★★

Inspired by the sleek form of its namesake aquatic creature, Manta takes you on a lightning-fast twirl through water and sky. Artwork and mosaics in the cavernous queue area pay tribute to rays; large windows reveal thousands of fish, sea dragons and horses, and many species of rays swimming contentedly within the nearly 200,000-gallon aquarium. When you actually board the ride, you'll be suspended horizontally beneath a 12-foot ray-shaped roller coaster car, then whisked off on a ½-mi race of loops and spins around and above the aquarium that reaches as high as 140 feet. At times you'll be so close to the water that the coaster's wings will actually skim the surface, though you're not likely to get drenched the way you would on a real water ride.

TURTLE POINT

3 Crowds: Sporadically crowded, but generally enough space for all to get a good view.

Strategy: Go anytime.

Audience: All ages.

Rating: ★★

There's nothing flashy or extravagant about this re-creation of a small beach and lagoon, but it's fascinating because you get to watch gigantic sea turtles (loggerheads, green, and hawksbill) basking in the sun or drifting in the water. Many of these giant cuties were rescued from predators or fishing nets and their injuries make it impossible for these lumbering beauties to return to the wild. They found a good home here. A kiosk is filled with sea turtle info, and an educator is usually on hand to answer questions. The kiosk is well worth a brief look.

STINGRAY LAGOON

4 Crowds: Can make it hard to get to the animals during busy seasons.

Strategy: Walk by if it's crowded, but return before dusk, when the smelt concession stand closes.

Audience: All ages.

Rating: ★★★

In a broad shallow pool, dozens and dozens of stingrays are close enough to touch, as evidenced by the many outstretched hands surrounding the rim. Smelts, silversides, shrimp, and squid are available for $5 a tray (two for $9 and four for $15) at nearby concession stands. Why do you want them? Because the fishy treats are a delicacy for the rays, and when they flap up for lunch you can feed them and stroke their velvety skin. Even though they still have their stingers they won't hurt you; they just want food. This is one of the most rewarding experiences for everyone, and the animals are obligingly hungry all day. Look for the nursery pool with its baby rays.

KEY WEST AT SEAWORLD

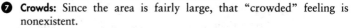 **Crowds:** Can get thick but not overwhelming.
Strategy: While on your way to or from a show, carve out some time to see the dolphins. If things are too crowded, go shopping until the crowds disperse.
Audience: All ages.
Rating: ★★★

This laid-back 5-acre area is modeled after Key West, Florida's southernmost outpost, where the sunsets are spectacular and the mood is festive. There are no distinct "lands" within SeaWorld, but Key West at SeaWorld comes close, containing individual tropical-style shows and attractions within its loosely defined borders. Along with an obvious Jimmy Buffett-y "island paradise" feel, a huge pool holds a few dozen Atlantic bottlenose dolphins that you can feed and pet. Fish trays cost $5.

BLUE HORIZONS

Duration: 20 min.
Crowds: Heavy due to the attraction's newness.
Strategy: Arrive 20 min early.
Audience: All ages.
Rating: ★★

The story of Blue Horizons is a fairy tale of sorts, starting with a young girl's fantasy of life in the sea, which is enough to lead off a high-energy and crowd-pleasing show that features high dives, dolphins, and astounding feats of aquabatics. There's rarely a pause as the performers present this Cirque du Soleil–style show by incorporating dolphins—first one, then two, and eventually as many as nine—that conduct a series of perfectly coordinated leaps, arcs, and splashes throughout the show. At some point, performers are skiing atop the back of two dolphins as another, dressed in a resplendent costume of feathers, performs an aerial ballet. Next, a series of high dives are presented as divers repeatedly leap from two high towers as two acrobats portraying the villains perform impressive and repeated synchronized jumps on bungee cords. The tale concludes with little Marina getting a chance to surf on the back of a dolphin and even fly. Overall, this is a great family show that blends together everything SeaWorld does best above and below the water.

MANATEES: THE LAST GENERATION?

Crowds: Since the area is fairly large, that "crowded" feeling is nonexistent.
Strategy: Go during a Shamu show and not right after a dolphin show.
Audience: All ages.
Rating: ★★★

If you don't have time to explore Florida's springs in search of manatees in the wild, then don't miss the chance to see this. The lumbering, whiskered manatees, which look like a cross between walruses and air bags, were brought here after near-fatal brushes with motorboats, and are returned to their homes when they're healthy. Tramping down a clear tunnel beneath the naturalistic, 3½-acre lagoon, you enter Manatee Theater, where a film describes the lives of these gentle giants and the ways in which humans threaten the species' survival. In Manatee Habitat, a 300,000-gallon tank with a 126-foot seamless acrylic viewing panel, you can look in on the lettuce-chomping mammals as well as native fish, including tarpon, gar, and snook. Keep an eye out for mama manatees and their nursing calves.

EN ROUTE
It's hard to pass up a plush Shamu—not least because the dolls are available all over the park. But if you're looking for a slightly less conventional souvenir, consider a soft manatee. You can buy either one at **Manatee Gifts.** Proceeds from the toys go to benefit a manatee preservation organization.

JOURNEY TO ATLANTIS
8 **Duration:** 6 min.
Crowds: Large.
Strategy: Make a beeline here first thing in the morning or go about an hour before closing; going at night is definitely awesome, and the wait, if there is one, will be cooler.
Audience: Older children and adults; definitely not for the faint of heart or for anyone with a fear of dark, enclosed spaces. Minimum height: 42".
Rating: ★★★

This was SeaWorld's first entry in Florida's escalating "coaster wars" and, in a way, it's a testament to coaster breakthroughs that it now seems a little outdated—the new arrivals have surpassed it. To be fair, this is really a hybrid coaster, combining elements of a high-speed water ride and a roller coaster with lavish special effects. There are frequent twists, turns, and short, shallow dives but few hair-raising plunges except for the first, which sends you nearly 60 feet into the main harbor (plan on getting soaked to the skin), and the final drop, a 60-foot nosedive into S-shaped, bobsledlike curves. Like most other attractions, this has a story line that doesn't really matter, but here it is: the lost continent of Atlantis has risen in the harbor of a quaint Greek fishing village, and you board a rickety Greek fishing boat to explore it. Once you're inside, an ominous current tugs at your boat, and an old fisherman offers a golden sea horse (actually Hermes—the messenger of the gods—in disguise!) to protect you from the evil Sirens. That's it. The wild, watery battle between Hermes and Allura (queen of the Sirens) is all a ploy to crank up effects using liquid crystal display technology, lasers, and holographic illusions.

KRAKEN
9 **Duration:** 6 min.
Crowds: Expect lines.
Strategy: Get to the park when it opens and head straight to Kraken; otherwise, hit it close to closing or during the Blue Horizons show.
Audience: Older children and adults. Minimum height: 54".
Rating: ★★★

Many people head straight for Kraken when the park opens, and as soon as you see its loops and dips, you'll know why. At 149 feet, Kraken is the second-tallest coaster in Florida (right after SheiKra at Busch Gardens). Named after an angry monster, this wickedly fast coaster will plunge you underground three times, lift you higher, drop you longer, and spiral you faster than any coaster in Florida. Aside from the coveted front seats, the capacity for this attraction is fairly high so the line moves pretty quickly. Once you're on board, you're poised for a thrill that'll take you to the highest heights and into the crook of high-speed whiplash turns and drops. Kraken packs a serious punch and part of its appeal is its floorless seats (your legs dangle loosely), seven inversions, and moments of weightlessness. No bags are allowed past the turnstiles; and it'll cost 50¢ to leave them in a locker. It's worth the investment—this is one cool coaster.

PENGUIN ENCOUNTER

Duration: Stay as long as you like.

Crowds: Sometimes gridlocked despite the moving walkway nudging visitors past the glassed-in habitat.

Strategy: Go while the dolphin and sea lion shows are on, and before you've gotten soaked at Journey to Atlantis, or you'll feel as icy as the penguins' environment.

Audience: All ages.

Rating: ★★

If you saw *March of the Penguins,* you'll have to visit the stars of this low-key walk-through attraction. In a large white building between the Dolphin Stadium and the Sea Lion & Otter Stadium, 17 species of penguin scoot around a refrigerated re-creation of Antarctica. They're as cute as can be, waddling across icy promontories and plopping into frigid waters to display their aquatic skills. You watch an average day in their world through the thick see-through walls. A moving walkway rolls you past at a slow pace, but you can also step off to an area where you can stand and marvel at these tuxedo-clad creatures as they dive into 45°F (7°C) water and are showered with three tons of snow a day. Nearby, a similar viewing area for puffins and murres is nearly as entertaining. Afterward, spend a little time in the plaza outside where there are caricature artists, artists working in pastels, gift shops, and soothing music to enjoy.

PETS AHOY

Duration: 15–20 min.

Crowds: Can be substantial on busy days.

Strategy: Gauge the crowds and get there early if necessary.

Audience: All ages.

Rating: ★★★

A dozen dogs, 18 cats, and an assortment of ducks, doves, parrots, and a pig (nearly all rescued from the local animal shelter) are the stars of this lively, hilarious show. The animals perform a series of complex stunts on a stage that looks like a seaside village. No matter how many times you see it, Pets Ahoy will never fail to amaze you. These cute-as-a-button actors perform feats that are each more incredible than the last, eventually culminating in a hilarious finale. Look around and you'll notice the show is just as appealing to foreign guests; you don't have to speak English to enjoy what is essentially a live version of a silent movie. Surely this is one of the best family friendly shows in Florida. Stick around and you'll have a chance to shake paws with the stars.

SEA LION & OTTER STADIUM

 Duration: 40 min, including the 15-min preshow.
Crowds: No problem.
Strategy: Sit toward the center for the best view, and don't miss the beginning.
Audience: All ages.
Rating: ★★★

Along with shows starring Shamu and the dolphins, the show here is one of the park's top crowd-pleasers. A multilevel pirate ship forms the set for Clyde and Seamore Take Pirate Island, a drama in which Sea-World's celebrated otters, walruses, and California sea lions prevail over piratical treachery. During the performance, they prove that they can outperform the human actors in a hilarious swashbuckling adventure that revolves around lost loot, pirate plunder, and misadventure on the high seas. Get ready for plenty of audience interaction, cheap laughs, and good-natured gags designed to please the kids as the animal actors waddle, dive, slide, dance, and scoot, adding their thespian talents to this melodrama. Be sure to arrive at least 15 minutes early to catch the preshow—the mime is always a crowd favorite.

PACIFIC POINT PRESERVE

Crowds: Not a problem.
Strategy: Go anytime.
Audience: All ages.
Rating: ★★★

A nonstop chorus of "aarrrps" and "yawps" coming from behind Clyde and Seamore's stadium will lead you to the 2½-acre home for California sea lions and harbor and fur seals. A naturalistic expanse of beaches, waves, and huge outcroppings of upturned rock designed to duplicate the rocky northern Pacific coast have a calming effect. You can stroll around the edge of the surf zone, a favorite hangout for fun-loving pinnipeds, and peep at their underwater activities through the Plexiglas wall at one side of the tank. Buy some smelts and watch the sea lions sing for their supper from close up.

SHARK ENCOUNTER

Duration: Plan to spend 20 min.
Crowds: Most significant when adjacent sea lion show gets out.
Strategy: Go during the sea lion show.
Audience: All ages.
Rating: ★★★

Within this large, innocuous white structure are some thoroughly creepy critters: eels, barracuda, sharks, and poisonous fish. You walk through large transparent tubes as the fish and eels swim all around you. There's a chance you'll come across a few creatures that you've probably never seen or even imagined before, like the weedy sea dragon and his cousin, the leafy sea dragon, which are cute little creatures that look like branches of a tree. For truth in advertising, there are a half dozen species of shark alone in some 300,000 gallons of water. You can time your visit to coincide with a meal at the extraordinarily well-designed **Sharks Underwater Grill,** where you can order fresh fish and Floribbean cuisine while watching your entrées' cousins.

A'LURE, THE CALL OF THE OCEAN

15 **Duration:** 20 min.

Crowds: Heavy, but the auditorium seats more than 1,000 so you won't feel packed in.

Strategy: Arrive at least 15 min before curtain for a wide choice of seats.

Audience: All ages.

Rating: ★★

SeaWorld never holds back when it comes to stage shows, and its latest presentation, A'Lure, is no exception. A'Lure, which replaced Odyssea, consists of a series of dazzling feats of acrobatics and pageantry framed by the story of a fisherman who falls overboard and into a new world beneath the waves. The colorful, costumed inhabitants of this underwater kingdom astound the fisherman with their amazing talents on the trampoline, and then rocket themselves through hoops, and leap onto towering poles and stick to them like chameleons. The storyline, of course, is just a backdrop for the performance of the acrobats, who march into the audience with festive Chinese dragons, find wonderful new uses for hula hoops, and perform impressive feats with hanging strips of silk. This is a thrilling, surreal, and somewhat touching presentation that is certain to please kids and adults. You'll want to see it twice—there's so much taking place you're likely to miss some wonderful moments.

CLYDESDALE HAMLET

16 **Duration:** You'll probably stay between 10 and 15 min.

Crowds: Very light.

Strategy: Go anytime.

Audience: All ages.

Rating: ★

At its core, this is a walk around the stable where the hulking Budweiser Clydesdales are kept, and a look at the clean corral where they get a chance to romp and play. A statue of a mighty stallion—which kids are encouraged to climb upon—makes a good theme-park photo opportunity.

SHAMU'S HAPPY HARBOR

17 **Crowds:** Often a challenge.

Strategy: Don't go first thing in morning or you'll never drag your child away; but if you go mid-afternoon or near dusk, expect plenty of hubbub. Bring a towel to dry them off.

Audience: Toddlers through grade-schoolers.

Rating: ★★★

If you want to take a break while your kids exhaust the last ounce of energy their little bodies contain, bring them here. This sprawling, towering, 3-acre outdoor play area has places to crawl, climb, explore, bounce, and get wet. There's also a four-story net climb and adjacent arcade with midway games. Youngsters go wild for the tent with an air-mattress floor, pipes to crawl through, and "ball rooms," one for toddlers and one for grade-schoolers, with thousands of plastic balls to wade through. With big sailing ships to explore and water to play in and around, Happy Harbor is sure to be a favorite of any high-energy kid.

SHAMU STADIUM (BELIEVE)

18 **Duration:** 30 min.
Crowds: Sometimes a problem.
Strategy: Go 30 min early for early-afternoon show. Close-up encounters through the Plexiglas walls are not to be missed, so trot on down.
Audience: All ages.
Rating: ★★★

This is the place. Within this stadium is Shamu, SeaWorld's orca mascot, starring in *Believe,* which (because we're talking about whales here) took more than four years to perfect. In the show, Shamu et al. perform awe-inspiringly choreographed moves against the backdrop of an elaborate three-story set, and an 80-foot panoramic LED screen within the shape of a tail fluke helps illuminate the action. It's quite amazing, really. As whales weighing as much as *10,000 pounds* demonstrate their grace and agility, they are actually performing a kind of breathtaking "killer whale ballet" to the corresponding beat of an original musical score. The show is also proof that trainers, who are propelled through the water on the whales' backs or bellies, balance on their noses, and are launched into spectacular high dives, have one of the best jobs on earth. In peak seasons when the park is open late, the special evening show is the always enjoyable and oddly patriotic. Shamu Rocks is performed, like all whale shows should be, to the accompaniment of a live guitarist. The anthem-heavy music and visual effects will speak most loudly to you and your teens, but at heart it's a sweet animal show appropriate for all, assuming it doesn't clash with any bedtimes. When the whales want to soak you, they'll throw thousands of gallons of water into the stands with their tail flukes or a well-placed belly flop. Even in the upper reaches of the splash zones, you'll still get drenched—fun at the time, but less so a few hours later if you didn't bring a change of clothes.

9

NEED A BREAK? A boardwalk leads from Shamu Stadium across the lagoon to the **Waterfront**, a Mediterranean-style faux waterfront village lined with shops, eateries, kiosks, and street performers. Even more laid-back than the rest of the park, this is a perfect spot to relax if you can remember that's the purpose of your vacation. Although there are scheduled performances, chances are you'll just wander through the area en route to another attraction and catch some strolling musicians. The restaurants have entertainment, too, like at **Seafire Inn** where guests can enjoy a live family-friendly musical stage. Shops include **Oyster's Secret**, where guests can choose an oyster and find a pearl inside; and **Allura's Treasure Trove**, a toy shop featuring candy and toys. Summer and holiday fireworks displays go up from the Waterfront.

SKY TOWER

⑲ Crowds: Fairly light.
Strategy: Look for a line and go if there's none.
Audience: All ages.
Rating: ★★

The focal point of the park is this 400-foot-tall tower, the main mast for a revolving double-decker platform. During the six-minute rotating round-trip up and down, you'll get the inside scoop on the park's history, its attractions, and surrounding sights. There's a separate $3 admission for this tower ride. Adjacent to the tower is Oyster's Secret, a small area where you can sit and watch pearl divers snag oysters.

WILD ARCTIC

⑳ Crowds: Expect a wait during peak seasons.
Strategy: Go early, late, or during a Shamu show. You can skip the simulated helicopter ride if you just want to see the mammals.
Audience: All ages. Minimum height for motion option: 42".
Rating: ★★★

Inside this pseudo–ice station, you embark on one of SeaWorld's three rides, a flight-simulator helicopter ride leading to rooms with interactive, educational displays. If your stomach can handle the rolls and pitches of a virtual helicopter, it makes for scary, enjoyable, queasy fun. Afterward, there are above- and below-water viewing stations where you can watch beluga whales blowing bubble rings, polar bears paddling around with their toys, and groaning walruses trying to hoist themselves onto a thick shelf of ice.

DISABILITIES AND ACCESSIBILITY

ATTRACTIONS With wide sidewalks and gentle inclines to the seats at shows, SeaWorld may be Florida's most accessible theme park. The **Dolphin Stadium, Sea Lion & Otter Stadium, SeaWorld Theater,** and **Shamu Stadium** all provide reserved seating areas that are accessible and have entry via sloping ramps. The stadium shows usually fill to capacity, so for your choice of seats plan to arrive 30 minutes before each show, 45 minutes in peak seasons.

At Shamu Stadium, the reserved seating area is inside the splash zone, so if you don't want to get soaking wet, get a host or hostess to recommend another place to sit.

Penguin Encounter, Shark Encounter, Tropical Reef, and **Journey to Atlantis** are all wheelchair accessible. To ride the moving-sidewalk viewing areas in Penguin Encounter, Shark Encounter, and Journey to Atlantis, you must transfer to a standard wheelchair, available in the boarding area, if you do not already use one. Tropical Reef and Penguin Encounter have minimal entertainment value for guests with visual impairments, but being hearing-impaired does not detract from the enjoyment. To ride **Kraken** you must transfer to the ride vehicles.

Shamu's Happy Harbor has some activities that are accessible to children using wheelchairs, including many of the games in the midway. Most of the other attractions are geared toward those who can climb, crawl, or slide.

RESTAURANTS AND SHOPS
Restaurants are accessible, but drinking straws are not provided here out of concern for the safety of the animals. Shops are level, but many are so packed with merchandise that maneuvering in a wheelchair can be a challenge.

SERVICES
There are outgoing TTY hearing-impaired systems in the lobby of Guest Services and across from the Dolphin Stadium. Sign-language interpreters for guided tours are available with advance notice.

EATING AT SEAWORLD

Burgers, barbecue, and other standard theme-park offerings are available at restaurants and concessions throughout the park. For reservations at full-service restaurants, call 407/351–3600 or 800/327–2424.

DINNER SHOW
The enjoyable **Makahiki Luau,** held in the Seafire Inn at the Waterfront, combines a Polynesian-Tahitian-Hawaiian feast with interactive entertainment. The evening begins with a welcome drink, a quick hula lesson, and the arrival of the Grand Kahuna, who arrives on a motorized pontoon boat rather than an outrigger canoe. What follows is a family-friendly stage show that includes sing-alongs, a drumming contest, and torch twirling. Reservations are required and may be made in advance or on the same day at the information counter near the park entrance. The cost is $48.94 for adults and $31.90 (tax included) for children ages 8 to 12, which includes unlimited nonalcoholic drinks and one cocktail for adults. If you have luau reservations and arrive about an hour before the show, you can spend a little time inside the park before the luau begins. Just let the attendants at the parking lot and front gate know and they'll admit you for free.

FULL-SERVICE RESTAURANTS
Sharks Underwater Grill, near Shark Encounter, is the park's most upscale restaurant, and the setting and service are extraordinary for a theme park. You walk through an underwater grotto into a cavernous restaurant that looks like it could be the secret headquarters of a James Bond villain. Five bay windows separate the dining room from a 660,000-gallon aquarium with sand tiger, sandbar, nurse, black nose, and Atlantic black tip sharks. Three tiers of booths and tables fill the room and each of the 240 seats is perfect for watching the deep blue waters. The menu is Floribbean, with Caribbean-spice seafood pasta, blackened sea scallops, jumbo lump crab cakes, pan-seared snapper, coconut-crust chicken spears, filet mignon with jerk seasoning, and pork medallions with black-bean sauce. Two extra menus—one for teens and one for kids under age 9—are also offered. There's a bar in a quiet alcove near the entrance. Reserve in advance for priority seating, or visit the host stand at the restaurant.

Dine with Shamu. This buffet, which is served in a pavilion next to Shamu Stadium, is one of the park's most popular dining options. The buffet includes salads, pastas, seafood, beef, chicken, and desserts, plus a meeting with a marine animal trainer who will share information about the nearby whales. The buffet costs $42 per adult and $22 per child age 3 to 9, and includes complimentary soft drinks, though beer now costs extra. There are three seatings daily, at 11:30, 3:30, and 6:30; about 200 guests can be accommodated per seating. Reservations are recommended (☎ 800/327–2424).

Beneath the Sky Tower, the **SandBar** is a pub designed to look like an ancient fortress. Overlooking the harbor, it's a nice spot to enjoy sushi platters, shrimp cocktails, fresh fruit and cheese plates, as well as martinis and live music.

At **Mango Joe's Cafe,** a cafeteria near Shamu Stadium, you can find fresh fajitas, hefty salads, and a delicious key lime pie. Many of the umbrella-shaded tables are right on the lake. **Smoky Creek Grill** serves up barbecue chicken and ribs near the Penguin Encounter. To accommodate health-conscious guests, **Mama's Kitchen** switched from home foods to a healthy menu that features sandwiches, salads, and pastas. The **Waterfront Sandwich Grill** carves its sandwich fillings to order and also grills big, juicy hamburgers. Close to the Dolphin Cove in Key West, **Captain Pete's Island Eats** has quick bites including chicken fingers, hot dogs, and fresh funnel cakes, plus smoothies and cold drinks.

In an old shipbuilder's hall on the Waterfront, **Voyagers Wood Fired Pizzas** has hand-tossed pizzas, salads, pastas, and decadent desserts. Also at the Waterfront, the **Spice Mill** serves Cajun jambalaya, Caribbean jerk chicken sandwiches, chicken tenders, and a range of salads. At the **Seafire Inn,** chefs prepare stir-fry dishes on a 4-foot Mongolian wok for everyone to see. Hamburgers, sandwiches, and coconut-fried shrimp are also on the menu.

GUIDED TOURS

Unlike other theme parks, SeaWorld has created a variety of programs that—for a price—will get animal lovers up close and personal with their favorite creatures. Some tours also provide special access to show. Register for all tours and programs by calling the **Guided Tour Center** (☎ 800/432–1178, 800/406–2244, or 407/363–2398 ⊕ www.seaworld. com). When at the park, you can also go to the tour desk to the left of Guest Services (aka Guest Relations) at the park entrance to see what's available that day.

There are two hour-long **Spotlight** tours to choose from. **Penguin Spotlight** takes you from pole-to-pole in a behind-the-scenes look at the Penguin Encounter. If you think these waddling birds are cute from a distance, just wait until you see them up close—you might even get to pet them. You'll be accompanied by one of SeaWorld's animal care experts, so you and the kids can ask all the questions you'd like. The tour requires you to climb stairs and walk on some icy or wet surfaces. At **Dolphin Spotlight,** you walk backstage at the Whale and Dolphin stadium to see how the trainers take care of and train the dolphins that appear in Blue Horizons. You'll also visit Dolphin Cove, where you can touch and feed a dolphin. Prices for each spotlight tour vary seasonally but are around $50 for adults and $40 for children. Tours depart every 30 minutes until 3 PM.

For an in-depth SeaWorld experience (as well as a chance to cut in line), the seven-hour **VIP Tour** includes a comprehensive tour of all park attractions, a poolside buffet lunch hosted by SeaWorld trainers, and reserved seating at shows. An educator is assigned to your group to answer questions, and the group is limited to 18 people. The cost is $125 per adult and $100 for children on top of park admission. The tour also includes fish to feed the dolphins, stingrays, and sea lions; instant admission to Kraken, Journey to Atlantis, and Wild Arctic; and reserved seating at two select shows, including *Believe*. You can make reservations in person at the guided-tour center or by phone. The Elite VIP Tour, which is only for private groups, includes all the elements of the VIP Tour plus lunch at Sharks Underwater Grill. Your group will pay $1,800 for up to a dozen people plus $200 for each additional guest.

There's much more than you'd expect happening behind the scenes at SeaWorld, which is why you might enjoy the 90-minute **Behind-The-Scenes Tour.** An animal expert give you the backstage tour of the park's rescue and rehabilitation program, telling you how the park is called upon to rescue injured birds, turtles, manatees, and dolphins and bring them back to SeaWorld for some TLC. At the end of the tour, you'll meet a shark (watch your fingers), pet a penguin, and visit a hidden polar bear den.

Your kids should be tickled to know that SeaWorld's education department also offers more than 200 **summer camp programs** (☏*407/363–2380 or 866/479–2267* ⊕*www.swbgadventurecamps.com*), including sleepovers and educational adventures for kids. They're not the only ones having fun—there are also Adventure Camp opportunities for the whole family.

DISCOVERY COVE

Moving away from the traditional theme-park format, SeaWorld took a chance when it opened Discovery Cove, a 32-acre limited-admission park that's a re-creation of a Caribbean island, complete with coral reefs, sandy beaches, and a signature experience, a dolphin encounter, for which you must be 6 or older (there is a park admission option that does not include the swim).

Here's how it works: after you enter a huge thatch-roof tiki building, you register and are given a reserved time to swim with the dolphins, the highlight of your Discovery Cove day; the pre-appointed time also makes planning your day simple, as you can fill in with anytime-swims and meals or snacks before and after your dolphin time. With your admission, everything is included—food, lockers, snorkel and mask, wet suit or swim vest, fins (the use of fins is discouraged, as they annoy the fish), and towels. Each guest is also issued a park-approved packet of sunblock: apply it early and often, especially to your face and shoulders. And if you've got a peckish and picky brood, it's a pleasure to go to the all-you-can eat cafeteria or simply walk up to snack stop and snatch some bottled water, chips, a hot pretzel, and other goodies. **Since most of the rest of Orlando is not all-inclusive, it's probably best to grab snacks on behalf of your younger kids so they don't get used to the idea of theme-park snack stations being "free."**

Once inside, you're confronted with rocky lagoons surrounded by lush landscaping, intricate coral reefs, and underwater ruins. It's at this point that the daily cap on crowds and the park's design bring you to a welcome realization: There are times, as you wend your way through rises and dips of the seemingly isolated paths or troop through the sandy white beaches that you and your family will feel you have the park to yourselves. Navigating the grounds is simple; posted signs point you toward swimming areas, cabanas, or the free-flight aviary, aflutter with exotic birds, which can be reached by way of a walkway or by swimming beneath a waterfall. Perhaps the most underhyped aspect of Discovery Cove are the snorkeling pools. While there's on-site instruction, it's a real thrill to float lazily and silently as an explosion of tropical fish swim swarm around you, staying out of your way. It's also fun to snorkel past the cascading waterfalls and a shipwreck; just be mindful of the coral, which is unkind to bare feet.

Although the rate may seem steep, you're getting a lot for your money, if you have time to take advantage of it: Discovery Coveadmission includes 14 consecutive days of unlimited admission to either SeaWorld *or* Busch Gardens Tampa. When you consider that a dolphin swim in the Florida Keys runs approximately $175, Discovery Cove may start to look like a bargain.

ADMISSION
If you're committed to visiting Discovery Cove, make reservations well in advance—attendance is limited to about 1,000 people a day. Tickets (including dolphin swim) cost $289 year-round, $100 less without the dolphin swim. Either ticket includes unlimited access to all beach and snorkeling areas and the free-flight aviary; all meals and snacks; use of a mask, snorkel, swim vest, towel, locker, and other amenities; parking; and a pass for 14 consecutive days of unlimited, come-and-go-as-you-please admission to SeaWorld Orlando or Busch Gardens in Tampa. For reservations and additional information, call **Discovery Cove** (☎ *877/434–7268* ⊕ *www.discoverycove.com*).

DISABILITIES AND ACCESSIBILITY
Wheelchairs with wide, balloonlike tires that roll over the sand are available. Call to request one in advance so that they have one waiting for you at the reception.

HOURS
Discovery Cove is open daily from 9 to 5:30, with extended hours in summer and on some holidays. Allow a full day to see all attractions.

EXPLORER'S AVIARY
Rating: ★★★
The entrance to this 12,000-square-foot birdhouse is a kick. To get here you can walk in from the beach or, better yet, swim into it from the river that snakes through the park by going under a waterfall. You arrive in a small-bird sanctuary populated with more than 250 exotic

TIP SHEET

■ Make reservations three to four months in advance for peak seasons. Admission slots for June start selling out in March.

■ The masks Discovery Cove provides don't accommodate glasses, so wear contacts if you can. Otherwise, try to get one of the limited number of prescription masks. No deposit is required, but you will be responsible if they're lost or damaged.

■ Don't bother to pack your own wet suit or fins. Wet suits or vests are available here; the wet suit is the way to go for anyone in your party who thinks the water is cold regardless of its temperature.

■ You can leave your keys, money, and other personal belongings in your locker all day. The plastic passes you're given upon entering the park are all you need to pick up your meals and (nonalcoholic) drinks.

■ If it becomes an all-day thunder and lightning rainstorm on your reserved day, attempts will be made to reschedule your visit when you're in town. If that's not possible, you'll have to settle for a refund.

birds including darting hummingbirds, tiny finches, and honeycreepers. In the large-bird sanctuary, you get up close to perched and wandering toucans, red-legged seriema, and other colorful and exotic birds who stand as tall as four feet. Look for attendants who have carts filled with complimentary fruit and birdfeed that you can use to attract the birds. It's a beautiful experience—especially when a bird hops onto your shoulder to say hello. Get the camera ready.

BEACHES
Rating: ★★

Lined with swaying palms, tropical foliage, and quaint thatched huts, this is where you claim your own private spot in the sand, with shady umbrellas, hammocks, lounges, or beach chairs. Since the park's biggest-selling feature is limited guest capacity, the most seductive aspect is staking out your private stretch of sand and leaving the real world behind. For the most privacy, head to the far west end of Discovery Cove. A few cabanas and tents are available on a first-come, first-served basis, and towels and beach chairs are plentiful.

DOLPHIN LAGOON
Duration: 45–60 min.
Audience: Anyone age 6 and older.
Rating: ★★★

Before you get too excited about Discovery Cove's top attraction, remember that your "swim" with the dolphins is supervised and restricted to what's safe for both you and the dolphins; the real deal may not line up with your fantasy of frolicking with these playful creatures. But despite the limitations, the attraction offers you the truly unique chance to touch, feed, play with, and even kiss a bottlenose dolphin, one of the most social and communicative marine animals.

Before you can get into the lagoon, you have to sit through a some-what tedious 15-minute orientation with the rest of your group. The orientation consists of a film plus a few words from a dolphin trainer. Afterward, after your group is split up—there will be several of you per dolphin—you proceed to the lagoon where you enter the surprisingly chilly water for roughly 25 minutes of "interaction" with one of 25 dolphins. You spend most of the time in knee-deep water, and a flota-tion vest is required. Discovery Cove trainers teach you about dolphin behavior, and you discover the hand signals used to communicate with them. Your dolphin may roll over so you can touch his or her belly, and, at your signal, leap into the air. Near the end of the session you have a chance to swim out to deeper water, catch hold of the dolphin's fin and have him or her pull you back to shore. At some point, you pose for pictures, which you'll be coaxed into buying immediately after leaving the water.

TROPICAL REEF
Rating: ★★★

Snorkelers follow butterfly fish, angelfish, parrotfish, and a few dozen other species through this authentic-looking coral reef. The brighter the day, the more brilliant the colors. Stingrays sail slowly and gracefully past as you float above. Some of the fish may come within touching distance, but when you reach out to them they scatter in nanoseconds. Also inside the coral reef is an artificial shipwreck where panels of Plexiglas in the hull reveal a pool filled with barracudas and sharks—you'll get the heebie-jeebies when you see them face to face. The same sensation may carry over to the lagoon, where dozens of southern and cow-nosed rays skim around the shallows. Don't be afraid to wade in and play—they've had their barbs removed. Often, several rays get together and make loops around the pool, so if you stay in one spot they'll continue to glide past you.

RAINFOREST RIVER
Rating: ★

The Rainforest River meanders its way throughout most of Discovery Cove. River swimmers float lazily through different environments—a sunny beach; a dense, tropical rain forest; an Amazon-like river; a tropical fishing village; an underwater cave; and the aviary. The only drawback here is that the bottom of the river is like the bottom of a pool and the redundancy of the scenery along the way can make it a little tedious.

GUIDED TOURS

Discovery Cove's **Trainer for a Day** program allows up to 24 guests a day to work side by side and behind the scenes with animal experts and interact with dolphins, birds, rays, and tropical fish. Whether they have an in-water training experience with a dolphin, pamper a pygmy falcon, feed tropical fish, or play with an anteater, participants have the hands-on opportunity to train and care for these unique animals. You'll receive a reserved dolphin swim, an enhanced dolphin interaction, and a chance to feed and take care of exotic birds in the aviary. Plus, you have behind-the-scenes access to small-mammal playtime and training, animal food preparation and record review, and behavioral training instruction. You'll walk away with a lot of memories as well as a souvenir shirt and waterproof camera. Be sure about this one. It starts at $488 (plus 6.5% sales tax) in peak season but it does include the regular admission price plus tickets valid for 14 consecutive days of unlimited admission to SeaWorld Orlando or Busch Gardens Tampa Bay. For an additional $70, you can upgrade to 14 days' admission to SeaWorld and Bush Gardens and Aquatica.

AQUATICA

Sixty acres of waterpark just across I-Drive from SeaWorld, Aquatica is the new kid in town angling to lure water babies away from Disney's Typhoon Lagoon and Blizzard Beach. Aquatica's outfitted with the slides and thrills you'd expect from an Orlando water park, but with plenty of whimsical SeaWorld touches as well.

A tranquil South Seas look belies the active nature of the park; like its competition, key here is a series of super-fast water slides, coupled in this case with some serene crystal blue streams and white-sand beaches. Hidden grottos and waterfalls and brightly colored, quirky buildings topped with pitched roofs feed a laid-back feel. As at SeaWorld, wildlife plays a major role here, with black and white Commerson's dolphins (smaller dolphins that look a little like Shamu) and colorful fish figuring literally in a couple rides and prominently in Maori-style totem poles and fountains.

In addition to two serviceable restaurants—Waterstone Grill (sandwiches, wraps, kiddie meals) and Banana Beach Cookout (all-you-can eat burgers and the like), as well as grab-and-go spot Mango Market, the park has sporadic refreshment stations available as well as gift shops, lockers, and facilities for towel rentals and stroller and wheelchair rentals.

Admission is $44.95 for adults and $38.95 for children 3–9, excluding tax. Visit ⊕*www.aquaticabyseaworld.com* for more details.

DOLPHIN PLUNGE
Zipping 250 feet down a narrow tube is only half the fun of the park's signature ride. The other half is finding that the tube plunges through a lagoon filled with Commerson's dolphins. The bottom part of the tube is see-through, which means, theoretically, you can see the dolphins as you zip by, but this can be a challenge, as the slide moves you awfully fast and there's water splashing your eyes at the base as you empty into a waiting pool. There are only two slides going on this ride, so expect to wait about an hour at peak times for the chance to plunge.

TAUMATA RACER
In the aquatic equivalent of a bobsled run, you climb into one of eight lanes and start your descent down 300 feet of slides, which includes a 360-degree turn at the top. The thrill as you crest the top of the slide is palpable (be sure to hold tightly to your blue mat) and the eight

SEAWORLD ORLANDO AND DISCOVERY COVE

NAME	Min Height	Type of Entertainment	Duration	Suits	Crowds	Strategy
A'Lure, the Call of the Ocean	n/a	show	20 min.	All	Heavy	Plenty of seats, but arrive 15 min. early fr a wide selection.
Aviary	n/a	aviary	Up to you	All	ok	Be sure your camera has memory.
Beaches	n/a	pool	Up to you	All	ok	Go to Discovery Cove for privacy.
Blue Horizon	n/a	show	30 min.	All	Heavy	Arrive 20 min early.
Clydesdale Hamlet	n/a	zoo	Up to you	All	ok	Go anytime.
Coral Reef	n/a	pool	Up to you	All	ok	See barracudas and sharks here.
Dolphin Lagoon	n/a	pool	60 min.	6 and up	ok	Beware: you'll be cajoled to buy photos.
Dolphin Nursery	n/a	touch pool	Up to you	All	ok	Go during Shamu show so the kids can be up front.
Explorer's Journey to Atlantis	42"	thrill ride	6 min.	7 and up	Large	Make a beeline here first thing or go about an hr. before closing; this is best at night.
★ Key West at SeaWorld	n/a	touch pool	Up to you	All	ok	If too crowded, wander until crowds disperse. Feed the dolphins.
★ Kraken	54"	thrill ride	6 min.	8 and up	Yes!	Get to the park when it opens and head straight to Kraken; otherwise, hit it near closing time.
Manatees: The Last Generation?	n/a	touch pool	Up to you	All	ok	Go during a Shamu show and not right after a dolphin show.
Manta	54"	thrill ride	6 min.	8 and up	Large	Go first thing or late in the day, or purchase a Quick Queue pass for front of ride access.
Odyssea	n/a	show	30 min.	All	Fast lines	Arrive 15 min. before curtain for a choice of seats. Entertaining pre-show.

Pacific Point Preserve	n/a	sea lions	Up to you	All	ok	Go anytime.
Penguin Encounter	n/a	touch pool	Up to you	All	Yes!	Go during dolphin and sea lion shows, and before you've gotten soaked at Journey to Atlantis, or you'll freeze.
Pets Ahoy	n/a	show	15–20 min.	All	Sometimes	Gauge the crowds and get there early if necessary.
Rainforest River	n/a	pool	Up to you	All	ok	Go anytime.
Ray Lagoon	n/a	pool	Up to you	All	ok	Swim with barbless stingray.
★ Sea Lion & Otter Stadium	n/a	show	40 min.	All	ok	Sit toward the center for the best view, and don't miss the beginning.
★ SeaWorld Theater— Pets Ahoy	n/a	show	20–25 min.	All	Busy	Gauge the crowds and get there early if necessary.
★ Shamu Stadium	n/a	show	30 min.	All	Busy	Go 45 min. early for early-afternoon show. Don't miss Close-up Encounters.
Shamu's Happy Harbor	n/a	play area	Up to you	Toddlers	Busy	Don't go first thing in morning or you'll never drag your child away; go midafternoon or toward dusk. Bring a towel to dry them off.
Shark Encounter	n/a	aquarium	20 min.	All	Sometimes	Go during the sea lion show.
Sky Tower	n/a	great view	6 min.	All	ok	Look for a line and go if there's none.
Stingray Lagoon	n/a	aquarium	Up to you	All	Moderate	Walk by if it's crowded, return before dusk.
Tropical Reef	n/a	aquarium	Up to you	All	ok	Go at the end of the day—because it's near the entrance, most people stop here on their way in.
Tropical River	n/a	aquarium	Up to you	All	ok	Go anytime.
Turtle Point	n/a	zoo	Up to you	All	ok	Go anytime.
Wild Arctic	42"	sim. ride	Up to you	All	Peak season	Go during a Shamu show. You can skip the ride if you just want to see the mammals.

★ = Fodor'sChoice

9

lanes mean that the line for this slide should move more quickly than Dolphin Plunge's.

ROA'S RAPIDS

A flowing but low-key current is the highlight of this attraction that takes you along gentle rapids and occasional waterfalls. Roa's is a lot of bang for the buck: there's no line (though the waters can get crowded with visitors at times) and after strapping on your life jacket you'll wade into the rapids via a wide entrance lane (and you can exit the same way). You can easily hold on to one of your kids as you bob around, and you're free to circle the rapids as many times as you wish.

LOGGERHEAD LANE

More low-key than the gentle rapids is this easy-flowing stream, which you'll navigate atop individual rubber tubes. A highpoint is that the lane eventually leads to a 10,000-gallon grotto filled with thousands of colorful fish and also offers a view of the Commerson's dolphins. This is indeed a lazy river: there's next to no pull, so you might have to paddle a bit, especially if you want to choose the turn with the fish grotto.

BIG SURF SHORES AND CUTBACK COVE

Twin side-by-side lagoons yield wave experiences that are either tame or squeal-worthy; since the pools are independent, one can generate crashing waves with 5-foot swells while the other provides gently rolling surf that laps the shore. A plus for parents is that it's easy to move from one pool to the other, and the park's white-sand beach faces the pools, providing a good base of operations if you're spending a lot of time in this area.

WALKABOUT WATERS

A colorful 60-foot fortress anchors 15,000 square feet of family slides, pools, water cannons, and two rather large buckets that periodically dump water on frolickers below. This is a well-executed playspace; your kids can treat it as a playground and avoid getting too soaked. Plus, the slides attached to the play structure flow slowly enough for beginners (note that kids are not permitted to ride on grown-up's laps on this one). Another area geared toward young children, **Kata's Kookaburra Cove** has more open splashable space as well as fountains and slides.

Adrenaline junkies will also want to sample the five-story **Whanau Way** slide and six-story **Hooroo Run; Walhalla Wave,** sharing the same tower and splash pool as Hooroo, is more family-oriented, with round rafts accommodating four riders at a time. And if literally feeling flushed is your thing, there's **Tassie's Twister,** yielding a massive basin where the water spins you and your raft around and around and around until you drop into the pool below.

Side Trips

WORD OF MOUTH

"My family is spending next week in Orlando, 12 of us including 9 yr. old and 14 yr. old. Any suggestions besides Disney? Maybe a dinner theater?"
—gingschultz

"Kids love Gatorland. How about Kennedy Space Center? I honestly couldn't recommend any of the dinner theaters."
—321go

Revised by Jennie Hess

Starting to feel irritable? Claustrophobic? It's called theme-park syndrome, and it often strikes four days or so into a vacation. You start to feel like you can't wait to get away from the crowds, hot pavement, and Candyland surroundings of the parks. If this sounds familiar and you need a break from theme-park mania, or if you'd simply like to see more of Central Florida than what you can view from the top of a roller-coaster track, then this chapter is for you.

For a breath of fresh air and a look at what the accommodating climate of Central Florida has to offer, you can escape to the Ocala National Forest or Wekiwa Springs State Park. If you need a museum fix and maybe some shopping in a quintessential Florida village, head for Winter Park and the Charles Hosmer Morse Museum with its stunning collection of Tiffany glass. Got kids to educate and entertain? Take them to WonderWorks or the Orlando Science Center. Do they like rockets and astronauts? Don't miss a day trip to the incomparable Kennedy Space Center. You'll soon discover abundant Central Florida sights that are equally enjoyable and often less crowded and less expensive than those at the theme parks. But take care—the sights listed below are fairly spread out from the northern suburbs to Florida's east coast and to communities south of Disney World. Note their locations on a map before heading out to visit them.

Numbers in the margin correspond to points of interest on the Away from the Theme Parks map.

KISSIMMEE

10 mi southeast of WDW; take I–4 Exit 64A.

Although Kissimmee is primarily known as the gateway to Walt Disney World, its non-WDW attractions just might tickle your fancy.

❶ Long before Walt Disney World, there was **Gatorland**. This campy attraction near the Orlando–Kissimmee border on U.S. 441 has endured since 1949 without much change, despite competition from the major parks. In November 2006, however, a fire destroyed the park's main entrance and gift shop, though its monstrous aqua gator-jaw icon remained standing. And the park's thousands of alligators and crocodiles swimming and basking in the Florida sun remained unscathed. The park reopened a month later with makeshift facilities and has since rebuilt its popular gift shop and admission complex. Its bounce-back spirit intact, Gatorland opened the Gator Gulley Splash Park in spring 2007, complete with giant "egrets" spilling water from their beaks, dueling water guns mounted atop giant "gators," and other theme splash areas. There's also a small petting zoo and an aviary. A free train ride provides

TOP ATTRACTIONS

Charles Hosmer Morse Museum. Known as the "Tiffany museum," the galleries here hold the largest and most comprehensive collection of art by Louis Comfort Tiffany, from stained-glass windows and lamps to blown-glass vases and gem-studded jewelry.

Gatorland. Thousands of alligators and crocodiles swim around and bask in the sun at this reptile-oriented park. Don't miss the Gator Wrestlin' Show.

Historic Bok Sanctuary. The beautifully landscaped gardens and marble-and-seashell tower provide the backdrop for relaxing walks, picnics, and music recitals. The landscape was designed by Frederick Law Olmsted Jr., son of the planner of New York's Central Park.

Kennedy Space Center. If you've ever been fascinated by space travel or wanted to be an astronaut, don't miss the chance to see shuttles up close.

Wekiwa Springs State Park. Celebrate the out-of-doors with a day fishing, boating, canoeing, or swimming in the Wekiva River. This park spans nearly 7,000 acres of virgin Florida land.

WonderWorks. The building clues you in to what you'll find here—it's upside down and sinking into the ground. Kids go nuts for the simulators that let you survive an earthquake and pilot a jet.

an overview of the park, taking you through an alligator breeding marsh and a natural swamp setting where you can spot gators, birds, and turtles. A three-story observation tower overlooks the breeding marsh, swamped with gator grunts, especially come sundown during mating season.

For a glimpse of 37 giant rare and deadly crocodiles, check out the exhibit called **Jungle Crocs of the World.** To see eager gators leaping out of the water to catch their food, see the **Gator Jumparoo Show.** The most thrilling is the first one in the morning, when the gators are hungriest. There's also a **Gator Wrestlin' Show,** and although there's no doubt who's going to win the match, it's still fun to see the handlers take on those tough guys with the beady eyes. In the educational **Up Close Animal Encounters Show,** 30 to 40 rattlesnakes fill a pit around the show's host. This is a real Florida experience, and you leave knowing the difference between a gator and a croc. ⊠*14501 S. Orange Blossom Trail, between Orlando and Kissimmee* ☎*407/855–5496 or 800/393–5297* ⊕*www.gatorland.com* ⊠*$22.99 adults, $14.99 children 3–12; discount coupons online* ⊗*Daily 9–5.*

★ ☺ ❷ Friendly farmhands keep things moving on the two-hour guided tour of **Green Meadows Farm**—a 40-acre property with almost 300 animals. There's little chance to get bored and no waiting in line, because tours are always starting. Everyone can milk the fat mama cow, and chickens and geese are turned loose in their yard to run and squawk while city slickers try to catch them. Children take a quick pony ride, and everyone gets jostled about on the old-fashioned hayride. Youngsters come away saying, "I milked a cow, caught a chicken, petted a pig, and fed a

10

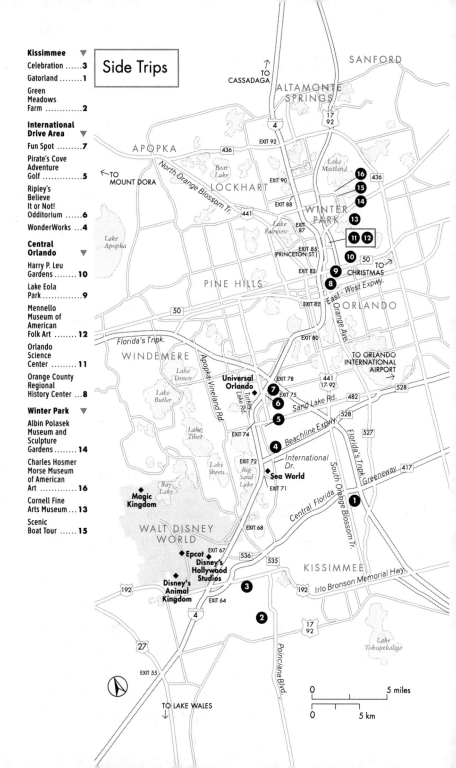

Side Trips

goat." Take U.S. 192 for 3 mi east of I–4 to South Poinciana Boulevard; turn right and drive 5 mi. ✉*1368 S. Poinciana Blvd.* ☎*407/846–0770* ⊕*www.greenmeadowsfarm.com* ✆*$21, children 2 and under free; discount coupons online* ⊙*Daily 9:30–5:30; last tour at 4* PM.

CELEBRATION

❸ *6 mi south of Epcot; take I–4 to Exit 64A and follow "Celebration" signs.*

This Disney-created community, in which every blade of grass in every lawn is just right, looks like something out of *The Stepford Wives*. But Celebration, which draws on vernacular architecture from all over the United States and was based on ideas from some of America's top architects and planners, offers a great retreat from the theme parks and from the garish reality of the U.S. 192 tourist strip 1 mi to the east. The shell of it appears to be nearly as faux as Main Street, U.S.A., but as the town evolves, you see signs that real life is being lived here—and a good life it is. Celebration is a real town, complete with its own hospital and school system. Houses and apartments, which are built to conform to a strict set of design guidelines, spread out from the compact and charming downtown area, which wraps around the edge of a lake. The town is so perfect it could be a movie set, and it's a delightful place to spend a morning or afternoon. Sidewalks are built for strolling, restaurants have outdoor seating with lake views, and inviting shops beckon. After a walk around the lake, take your youngsters over to the huge interactive fountain and have fun getting sopping wet. The town stays busy with events ranging from pie festivals to art shows, and the Sunday Farmers' Market at the Town Center is worth a visit. Starting the last Saturday in November and continuing through New Year's Eve, honest-to-goodness snow sprinkles softly down over Main Street every night on the hour from 6 to 9, to the absolute delight of children of all ages. Search ⊕*www.celebrationfl.com* for event listings or call 407/566–1200.

INTERNATIONAL DRIVE AREA

7 mi northeast of WDW; take I–4 Exit 74 or 75 unless otherwise noted.

A short drive northeast of WDW are a number of attractions that children adore; unfortunately, some may put wear and tear on parents.

Just up the street, the Ripley's Believe It or Not! building seems to be sinking into the ground, but true to Orlando tradition, the newer attraction, **WonderWorks**, one-ups the competition: it's sinking into the ground at a precarious angle and upside down. If the strange sight of a topsy-turvy facade complete with upended palm trees and simulated FedEx box doesn't catch your attention, the swirling "dust" and piped-out creaking sounds will. Inside, the upside-down theme continues only as far as the lobby. After that, it's a playground of 100 interactive experiences—some incorporating virtual reality, others educational (similar to those at a science museum), and still others just pure entertainment. Here are just some of the things you can do: experience an earthquake or a hurricane, pilot a fighter jet or land a space shuttle using simulator controls, make giant bubbles in the Bubble Lab, play laser tag in the largest laser-tag arena and arcade in the world, design and ride your own roller coaster, lie on a bed of real nails, and play basketball with a 7-foot opponent. ⊠*9067 International Dr.* ☎*407/352–8655* ⊕*www.wonderworksonline.com* 🖾*$19.95 adults, $14.95 children 4–12; higher-price combo packages include laser tag and Outta Control Magic Comedy Dinner Showparking costs $2–$6; see online coupons* ⊗*Daily 9 AM–midnight.*

🌀 **❺** You can play the crème de la crème of miniature golf at the two **Pirate's Cove Adventure Golf** locations. Each site has two 18-hole courses that wind around artificial mountains, through caves, and into lush foliage. The beginner's course is called Captain Kidd's Adventure; a more difficult game can be played on Blackbeard's Challenge. The courses are opposite Mercado Mediterranean Village and in the Crossroads of Lake Buena Vista shopping plaza. Arrive by 11 PM if you want to play a round before closing. ⊠*8501 International Dr.* ☎*407/352–7378* ⊕*www. piratescove.net* ⊠*12545 SR 535 Lake Buena Vista, Crossroads Center, I–4 Exit 68* ☎*407/827–1242* 🖾*I-Drive location, $9.95 adults, $8.95 children 4–12; both courses $13.95 adults, $12.50 children; Crossroads location, $9.95 adults, $8.95 children 4–12; both courses $13.95 adults, $12.50 children* ⊗*Daily 9 AM–11:30 PM.*

❻ **Ripley's Believe It or Not! Odditorium** challenges the imagination. A 10-foot-square section of the Berlin Wall. A pain and torture chamber. A Rolls-Royce constructed entirely of matchsticks. A 26' × 20' portrait of van Gogh made from 3,000 postcards. These and almost 200 other oddities (shrunken heads included) speak for themselves in this museum-cum-attraction in the heart of tourist territory on International Drive. The building itself is designed to appear as if it's sliding into one of Florida's notorious sinkholes. Give yourself an hour or two to soak up the weirdness here, but remember, this is a looking, not touching, experience, which may drive antsy youngsters—and their parents—crazy. The museum is ¼ mi south of Sand Lake Road. ⊠*8201 International Dr.* ☎*407/363–4418 automated, 407/351–5803 live attendant, or 800/998–4418 Ext. 3* ⊕*www.ripleysorlando.com* 🖾*$18.95 adults, $11.95 children 4–12* ⊗*Daily 9:30 AM–midnight; last admission at 11 PM.*

🌀 **❼** **Fun Spot.** Four go-kart tracks offer a variety of driving experiences for children and adults. Though drivers must be at least 10 years old and meet height requirements, parents can drive smaller children in two-seater cars on several of the tracks, including the Conquest Track. Six family and thrill rides range from the dizzying Paratrooper to an old-fashioned Revolver Ferris Wheel. Seven kiddie rides include twirling toddler Teacups. Inside the arcade, traditional Whack a Mole and Spider Stompin' challenges get as much attention as the interactive high-tech video games. From Exit 75A, turn left onto International Drive then left on Grand National to Del Verde Way. (Older teens looking for "extreme" go-kart and ride thrills may want to head to sister park

Fun Spot USA in Kissimmee—check Web site for details). ⊠*5551 Del Verde Way, I–4 to Exit 75A* ☎*407/363–3867* ⊕*www.fun-spot.com* ✉*$14.95–$34.95 depending on go-kart and ride package(discount coupon online); arcade tokens 25¢ each or $25 for 120* ☉*Daily 10* AM–*midnight.*

CENTRAL ORLANDO

Fifteen miles northeast of WDW, take I–4 Exit 82C or 83B eastbound, or Exit 85 for Loch Haven Park sights. Downtown Orlando is a dynamic area with high-rises, sports venues, interesting museums, restaurants, and nightspots. Numerous parks and lakes provide pleasant relief from the tall office buildings. A few steps away from downtown's tourist centers are delightful residential neighborhoods with brick-paved streets and live oaks dripping with Spanish moss.

🐚 ❽ The **Orange County Regional History Center** takes you on a journey back in time to discover how Florida's Paleo-Indians hunted and fished the land; what the Sunshine State was like when Spaniards first arrived in the New World; and how life in Florida was different when citrus was king. Visit a cabin from the late 1800s, complete with Spanish moss–stuffed mattresses, mosquito netting over the beds, and a room where game was preserved prerefrigeration. Seminole Indian displays include interactive screens, and tin-can tourist camps of the early 1900s preview Florida's destiny as a future vacation mecca. ⊠*65 E. Central Blvd.* ☎*407/836–8500 or 800/965–2030* ⊕*www.thehistorycenter.org* ✉*$12 adults, $9 students and senior citizens, $7 children 5–12; discount coupon online* ☉*Mon.–Sat. 10–5, Sun. noon–5.*

🐚 ❾ In the heart of downtown is **Lake Eola Park,** with its signature fountain in the center. The 42-acre park represents an inner-city victory over decay. Established in 1892, the now family-friendly park experienced a series of ups and downs that left it very run-down by the late 1970s. With the support of determined citizens, the park gradually underwent a renovation that restored the fountain and added a wide walkway around the lake. Now families with young children use the well-lighted playground in the evening and downtown residents toss bread to the ducks, swans, and birds and walk their dogs late at night in relative safety. The lakeside **Walt Disney Amphitheater** is a dramatic site for the annual Shakespeare Festival (April and May) as well as for weekend concerts and other events.

Don't resist the park's biggest draw, a ride in a swan-shaped pedal boat. Two adults or one adult and two children can fit comfortably into the boats. Children under 16 must be accompanied by an adult.

Bring a blanket and pack a picnic, or visit one of several good restaurants by the park and in the nearby Thornton Park neighborhood; there's a nice mix of indoor-outdoor dining. The view at dusk, as the fountain lights up in all its colors and the sun sets behind Orlando's ever-growing skyline, is spectacular. ⊠*Robinson St. and Rosalind Ave., Downtown Orlando* ☎*407/246–2827 park, 407/232–0111 Swan Boats* ✉*Swan Boat rental $12 per ½ hr; Gondola rental $15 per*

10

½ hr ⊙*Park daily 6* AM*–midnight; Swan Boats weekdays noon–dusk, weekends 10–dusk.*

⑩ The **Harry P. Leu Gardens,** a few miles outside of downtown on the former lakefront estate of a citrus entrepreneur, are a quiet respite from the artificial world of the theme parks. On the grounds' 50 acres is a collection of historical blooms, many varieties of which were established before 1900. You can see ancient oaks, a 50-foot floral clock, and one of the largest camellia collections in eastern North America (in bloom November–March). **Mary Jane's Rose Garden,** named after Leu's wife, is filled with more than 1,000 bushes; it's the largest formal rose garden south of Atlanta. The simple 19th-century **Leu House Museum,** once the Leu family home, preserves the furnishings and appointments of a well-to-do, turn-of-the-20th-century Florida family. ⊠*1920 N. Forest Ave., North-Central Orlando* ☎*407/246–2620* ⊕*www.leugardens. org* ✉*$7 adults, $2 children kindergarten–12th grade; toddlers and preschoolers free; also free to all Mon. 9–noon* ⊙*Garden daily 9–5; guided house tours Aug.–June, daily on hr and ½ hr 10–3:30.*

★ ☾ ⑪ With all the high-tech glitz and imagined worlds of the theme parks, is it worth visiting the reality-based **Orlando Science Center**? That depends. If you're into hands-on educational exhibits about the human body, mechanics, electricity, math, nature, the solar system, and optics, you'll really like the science center. It's in a gorgeous building with, besides the exhibits, a wonderful atrium that's home to live gators and turtles. There's a great DinoDigs room for the dinosaur-crazed, and Kids Town for children 7 and under is a wonderland of hands-on fun. The Dr. Phillips CineDome, a movie theater with a giant eight-story screen, offers large-format IWERKS films (Ub Iwerks was an associate of Walt Disney's in the early days), as well as planetarium programs. The science center is home to Florida's largest publicly accessible refractor telescope as well as smaller telescopes, and some weekend days you can safely check out sunspots and solar flares on the sun's surface. Night viewing to see the four moons of Jupiter, the rings of Saturn, and deep sky objects including galaxies, nebulas, and double stars occurs only during quarterly events called "Cocktails and the Cosmos." Guests don't have to pay extra to visit the observatory those evenings unless they wish to buy drinks or dinner. (Call ahead or check the Web site for observatory events.) ⊠*777 E. Princeton St.* ☎*407/514–2000 or 888/672–4386* ⊕*www.osc.org* ✉*$17 adults, $16 students and senior citizens with ID, $12 children 3–11; parking $5; tickets include all permanent and special exhibits, films, live science presentations, and planetarium shows (4* PM*, 1st and 3rd Fri.)* ⊙*Sun.–Tues. 10–5, Thurs.–Sat. 10–5.*

⑫ The **Mennello Museum of American Folk Art** is one of the few museums in the United States, and the only one in Florida, devoted to folk art. Its intimate galleries, some with lovely lakefront views, contain the nation's most extensive permanent collection of Earl Cunningham paintings as well as works by many other self-taught artists. There's a wonderful video about Cunningham and his serendipitous discovery in Saint Augustine; temporary exhibitions have included the works of Wyeth, Cassatt, Michael Eastman, and others. At the museum shop you can purchase folk art books, toys, and unusual gifts. ⊠*900 E. Princeton St.*

☎407/246–4278 ⊕*www.mennellomuseum.com* ✉*$4 adults, $1 students, children under 12 free, $3 senior citizens 60 and older* ☉*Tues.–Sat. 10:30–4:30, Sun. noon–4:30.*

WINTER PARK

20 mi northeast of WDW; take I–4 Exit 87 and head east 3 mi on Fairbanks Ave.

This peaceful, upscale community may be just north of the hustle and bustle of Orlando, but it feels miles away.

★ You can spend a pleasant day here shopping, eating, visiting museums, and taking in the scenery along **Park Avenue,** in the center of town. This inviting brick street has chic boutiques, sidewalk cafés, restaurants, and hidden alleyways that lead to peaceful nooks and crannies with even more restaurants and shops. Park Avenue is definitely a shopper's heaven.

When you want a rest, look for a bench in the shady **Central Park,** which has lovely green lawns, a rose garden, a fountain, and a gazebo. On the southwest corner, the **Winter Park Farmer's Market** lures locals and visitors each Saturday morning. If you don't want to browse in the shops across the street, a walk through the park beneath the moss-covered trees is a delightful alternative. Also consider a cruise on the area's canal-linked lakes to see wildlife and the old estates.

 Fodor's Choice ★ The world's most comprehensive collection of the work of Louis Comfort Tiffany, including immense stained-glass windows, lamps, watercolors, and desk sets, is at the **Charles Hosmer Morse Museum of American Art.** The museum's constant draws include exhibits on the Tiffany Long Island mansion, Laurelton Hall, and the 1,082-square-foot Tiffany Chapel, originally built for the 1893 world's fair in Chicago. It took craftsmen 2½ years to painstakingly reassemble the chapel here. Also displayed at the museum are collections of paintings by 19th- and 20th-century American artists, and jewelry and pottery, including a fine display of Rookwood vases. ✉*445 N. Park Ave.* ☎*407/645–5311* ⊕*www.morsemuseum.org* ✉*$3 adults, $1 students, children under 12 free; Nov.–Apr., Fri. free 4–8* ☉*Tues.–Sat. 9:30–4, Sun. 1–4; Nov.–Apr., Fri. until 8.*

⑬ On the Rollins College campus, the **Cornell Fine Arts Museum** houses the oldest collection of art in Florida, its first paintings acquired in 1896. The collection includes more than 6,000 works, from Italian Renaissance paintings to 19th- and 20th-century American and European paintings, decorative arts, and sculpture. Artists represented include William Merritt Chase, Childe Hassam, and Pietro Liberi. In addition, outstanding special exhibitions are scheduled throughout the year. Outside the museum, a small but charming garden overlooks Lake Virginia. ✉*Rollins College, 1000 Holt Ave, Winter Park* ☎*407/646–2526* ⊕*www.rollins.edu/cfam* ✉*$5 adults, free for children and students with ID* ☉*Tues.–Fri. 10–4, weekends noon–5.*

★ **⑮** From the dock at the end of Morse Avenue you can depart for the **Scenic Boat Tour,** a Winter Park tradition that's been in continuous operation for

10

A Pocket of Old Florida Charm

If you take a seat on a bench near the rose garden in Central Park and listen as the Amtrak passenger train rolls by the west end of the park, it's not hard to imagine how Winter Park looked and sounded in the late 19th century.

The town's name reflects its early role as a warm-weather haven for northerners. From the late 1880s until the early 1930s, each winter hundreds of vacationers from northern states like New York and Pennsylvania would travel to Florida by rail to escape the harsh weather. For many, Winter Park was the final destination. Here visitors would relax amid the orange groves and stroll along Park Avenue, which attracts window-shoppers and tea drinkers to this day. The lovely, 8-square-mi village retains its charm with brick-paved streets, historic buildings, and well-maintained lakes and parkland. Even the town's bucolic 9-hole golf course is on the National Register of Historic Places.

For the quintessential Winter Park experience, spend a few hours taking in the sights on Park Avenue. Serious shoppers can spend hours dipping into the small boutiques and upscale chain stores that line the avenue. But save at least an hour or two for the **Charles Hosmer Morse Museum of American Art,** which has the largest collection of artwork by Louis Comfort Tiffany. This is where you'll find such treasures as the Tiffany Chapel and dozens of Tiffany's beautiful stained-glass windows, lamps, and pieces of jewelry. Many of the works were rescued from Tiffany's Long Island estate, Laurelton Hall, after a 1957 fire destroyed much of the property. The museum also contains collections of American decorative art from the mid-19th to the early 20th centuries and American paintings from the same period.

Another fine museum is on the Rollins College campus. The **Cornell Fine Arts Museum** has a collection of 6,000 art objects, including 19th- and 20th-century American and European paintings and sculptures. North of the college on Osceola Avenue is the **Albin Polasek Museum and Sculpture Gardens,** where you can get a guided tour of the former home of the prolific Czech-American sculptor Albin Polasek (1879–1965). On-property examples of Polasek's works include statues in several mediums.

Perhaps one of the loveliest ways to visit the village is on the **Scenic Boat Tour** (⊕ *www.scenicboattours. com*), in operation since 1938. The 18-passenger pontoon boat cruises 12 mi of Winter Park waterways, including three lakes and oak- and cypress-shaded canals built in the 1800s as a transportation system for the logging industry. A well-schooled skipper shares stories about the moguls who built their mansions along the shore. You can spot countless ducks and wading birds, including egrets, blue herons, and the enigmatic "snakebird," or anhinga—often seen drying its wings while perched on shore or diving beneath the lake surface for dinner. You may even glimpse an alligator or see an osprey or bald eagle soar overhead.

more than 60 years. The relaxing, narrated one-hour pontoon boat tour, which leaves hourly, cruises by 12 mi of Winter Park's opulent lakeside estates and travels through narrow canals and across three lakes. ✉*312 E. Morse Blvd.* ☎*407/644–4056* ⊕*www.scenicboattours.com* 🖃*$10 adults, $5 children 2–11* ☉*Daily 10–4.*

Stroll along on a guided tour through lush gardens showcasing the graceful sculptures created by internationally known sculptor Albin Polasek (1879–1965) at the **Albin Polasek Museum and Sculpture Gardens.** The late artist's home, studio, galleries, and private chapel are centered on 3 acres of exquisitely tended lawns, colorful flower beds, and tropical foliage. Paths and walkways lead past classical life-size, figurative sculptures and whimsical mythological pieces. Inside the museum are works by Hawthorne, Chase, Mucha, and Saint-Gaudens. ✉*633 Osceola Ave. 32789* ☎*407/647–6294* ⊕*www.polasek.org* 🖃*$5 adults, $3 students ages 13 and up with student ID, children under 12 free* ☉*Sept.–June, Tues.–Sat. 10–4, Sun. 1–4; July and Aug., only gardens open weekdays 10–4 (free).*

WEKIWA SPRINGS STATE PARK

13 mi northwest of Orlando, 28 mi north of WDW.

Where the tannin-stained Wekiva River meets the crystal-clear Wekiwa headspring, there's a curious and visible exchange—like strong tea infusing water. Wekiva is a Creek Indian word meaning "flowing water"; wekiwa means "spring of water."

Wekiwa Springs State Park sprawls around this area on 6,400 acres. The parkland is well suited to camping, hiking, and picnicking; the spring to swimming; and the river to canoeing and fishing. Canoe trips can range from a simple hour-long paddle around the lagoon to observe a colony of water turtles to a full-day excursion through the less-congested parts of the river that haven't changed much since the area was inhabited by the Timacuan Indians. Take I–4 Exit 94 (Longwood) and turn left on Route 434. Go 1¼ mi to Wekiwa Springs Road; turn right and go 4½ mi to the entrance, on the right. ✉*1800 Wekiva Circle, Apopka 32712* ☎*407/884–2008* ⊕*www.myflorida.com* 🖃*$3–$5 per vehicle* ☉*Daily 8–dusk.*

EN ROUTE As you drive northwest on U.S. 441, you head into aptly named **Lake County,** an area renowned for its pristine water and excellent fishing. Watch the flat countryside, thick with scrub pines, take on a gentle roll through citrus groves and pastures surrounded by live oaks.

KENNEDY SPACE CENTER VISITOR COMPLEX

17 mi north of Cocoa.

The must-see **Kennedy Space Center Visitor Complex,** just southeast of Titusville, is one of Central Florida's most popular sights. Following the lead of the theme parks, they've switched to a one-price-covers-all admission. To get the most out of your visit to the space center, take the bus tour (included with admission), which makes stops at several

10

facilities. Buses depart every 15 minutes, and you can get on and off any bus whenever you like. As you approach the Kennedy Space Center grounds, tune your car radio to AM1320 for attraction information.

The newest Space Center addition is Eye on the Universe: The Hubble Space Telescope Exhibit, scheduled to remain at KSC through early fall 2010. This multimedia presentation surrounds guests with fascinating Hubble images of deep space nebulas, ancient stars, and galaxies. If you want to feel as if you're headed into space, the Shuttle Launch Experience lets you hear the rumble and feel the g-forces of a rocket during launch. Once you're strapped into the space shuttle motion simulator, special light and sound effects dramatize prelaunch moments; then, you'll feel the force of liftoff and the exhilaration of rocket booster separation, main engine cutoff and external tank separation. The sensation of weightlessness follows as the simulator mimics space entry and the payload bay doors open to frame the ultimate view of Earth.

The first stop on the bus tour is the Launch Complex 39 Observation Gantry, which has an unparalleled view of the twin space-shuttle launchpads. At the Apollo/Saturn V Center, don't miss the presentation at the Firing Room Theatre, where the launch of America's first lunar mission, 1968's *Apollo VIII*, is re-created with a ground-shaking, window-rattling lift-off. At the Lunar Surface Theatre, recordings from *Apollo XI* offer an eerie and awe-inspiring reminder that when Armstrong and Aldrin landed, they had less than 30 seconds of fuel to spare. In the hall it's impossible to miss the 363-foot-long *Saturn V* rocket. A spare built for a moon mission that never took place, this 6.2-million-pound spacecraft has enough power to throw a fully loaded DC-3 all the way to the sun and back!

Don't miss the outdoor Rocket Garden, renovated to showcase more dramatically, through special lighting effects, the historic Atlas, Redstone, and Titan rockets of the early space program. You can travel back in time by climbing inside the Apollo, Gemini, and Mercury capsules to get a sense of the early astronauts' cramped spaces.

The most moving exhibit is the Astronaut Memorial, a tribute to those who have died while in pursuit of space exploration. A 42½-foot-high by 50-foot-wide "Space Mirror" tracks the movement of the sun throughout the day, using reflected sunlight to brilliantly illuminate the names of the 24 fallen U.S. astronauts that are carved into the monument's 70,400-pound polished granite surface.

During the Astronaut Encounter, in a pavilion near the center's entrance, an astronaut who's actually flown in space hosts a daily Q&A session to tell visitors about life in zero gravity, providing insights to an experience only a few hundred people have ever shared. If you'd like to have a closer encounter with an astronaut, you can purchase a special ticket option to Lunch with an Astronaut (adults $60.99, children 3–11 $43.99, includes general complex admission and lunch). For a more in-depth experience, take the NASA Up Close tour (adults $59, children 3–11 $43, includes admission), which brings you to sights seldom accessible to the public, such as the NASA Press Site Launch Countdown Clock, the Vehicle Assembly Building, the shuttle landing strip, and the 6-million-pound crawler that transports the shuttle to its launchpad. Or see how far the space program has come with the Cape Canaveral: Then and Now tour ($59 adults, $43 children), which visits America's first launch sites from the 1960s and the 21st century's active unmanned rocket program.

The only back-to-back twin **IMAX theater complex** in the world is in the complex, too. The dream of space flight comes to life on a movie screen five stories tall with dramatic footage shot by NASA astronauts during missions. Realistic 3-D special effects will make you feel like you're in space with them. Films alternate throughout the year. Call for specific shows and times. ⊠ *Rte. 405, Kennedy Space Center* ☎ *321/449–4444 or 866/737–5235* ⊕ *www.kennedyspacecenter.com* ✉ *General admission ticket is valid for 2 days of admission used within a 7-day time period and includes bus tour, IMAX movies, and Astronaut Hall of Fame; adults $38, $28 children 3–11; packages available for guided tours and activities* ⊙ *Space Center daily 9–6, last regular tour at 2:45* PM; *closed certain launch dates; IMAX I and II theaters daily 10–5:40.*

The original *Mercury 7* team and the later *Gemini, Apollo, Skylab,* and shuttle astronauts contributed to make the **United States Astronaut Hall of Fame** the world's premium archive of astronauts' personal stories. Recently, the archive has expanded to include a new Space Shuttle wing that allows guests to relive the missions of several astronauts and to examine personal artifacts from these space heroes. Authentic Hall of Fame astronaut memorabilia and equipment tell a vivid story of human space exploration. You'll watch videotapes of historic moments in the space program and see one-of-a-kind items like Wally Schirra's relatively archaic *Sigma 7* Mercury space capsule, Gus Grissom's spacesuit (colored silver only because NASA thought silver looked more "spacey"), and a flag that made it to the moon.

The exhibit First on the Moon focuses on crew selection for *Apollo 11* and the Soviet Union's role in the space race. Definitely don't miss the Astronaut Adventure, a hands-on discovery center with interactive exhibits that help you learn about space travel. One of the more challenging activities is a space-shuttle simulator that lets you try your hand at landing the craft—and afterward replays a side view of your rolling and pitching descent.

If that gets your motor going, consider enrolling in ATX (Astronaut Training Experience). Held at the Hall of Fame, this is a two-day program that includes one full day of intense training where you can dangle from a springy harness for a simulated moonwalk, spin in ways you never thought possible in a multi-axis trainer, and either work Mission Control or helm a space shuttle (in a full-scale mock-up) during a simulated landing. Veteran astronauts helped design the program, and you'll hear firsthand from them as you progress through your training. Your first day includes a VIP tour of the Kennedy Space Center plus overnight accommodations at the Hampton Inn Cocoa Beach. Space is limited (no pun intended), so call in advance. Also included in the program ($625, first two family participants—one adult, one child (8 or older)—and $275 for each additional adult or child; maximum four people) is your astronaut gear and lunch. A new half-day program called ATX Core is offered to individual guests 16 and older for $145. ⊠ *Rte. 405, Kennedy Space Center* ☎ *321/449–4444 or 866/737–5235, 321/449–4400 ATX* ⊕ *www.kennedyspacecenter.com* ☒ *Hall of Fame only, $17 adults, $13 children 3–11* ⊙ *Daily 9–7.*

EN ROUTE ★ The 57,000-acre **Canaveral National Seashore** is on a barrier island that's home to more than 1,000 species of plants and 300 species of birds and other animals. The unspoiled area of hilly sand dunes, grassy marshes, and seashell-sprinkled beaches is a large part of NASA's buffer zone. Surf and lagoon fishing are available, and a hiking trail leads to the top of a Native American shell midden at Turtle Mound. A visitor center is on Route A1A. Weekends are busy, and parts of the park are closed before launches, sometimes as much as two weeks in advance, so call ahead at 321/267–1110.

Fodor'sChoice ★ If you prefer wading birds over waiting in line, don't miss the 140,000-acre **Merritt Island National Wildlife Refuge,** which adjoins the Canaveral National Seashore. It's an immense area dotted by brackish estuaries and marshes and patches of land consisting of coastal dunes, scrub oaks, pine forests and flatwoods, and palm and oak hammocks. You can borrow field guides and binoculars at the visitor center to track down various types of falcons, osprey, eagles, turkeys, doves, cuckoos, loons, geese, skimmers, terns, warblers, wrens, thrushes, sparrows, owls, and woodpeckers. ⊠ *Rte. 402, across Titusville causeway* ☎ *321/861–0667* ⊕ *www.fws.gov/merrittisland* ☒ *Free* ⊙ *Daily dawn–dusk; visitor center weekdays 8–4:30, Sat. 9–5, Sun. (Nov.–Mar.) 9–5.*

MOUNT DORA

★ *35 mi northwest of Orlando and 50 mi north of WDW; take U.S. 441 (Orange Blossom Trail in Orlando) north or take I–4 to Exit 92, then Rte. 436 west to U.S. 441, and follow signs.*

The unspoiled Lake Harris chain of lakes surrounds remote Mount Dora, an artsy valley community with a slow and easy pace, a rich history, New England–style charm, and excellent antiquing. Although the town's population is only about 10,000, there's plenty of excitement here, especially in fall and winter. The first weekend in February is the annual Mount Dora Art Festival, which opens Central Florida's spring art-fair season. Attracting more than 250,000 people over a three-day period, it's one of the region's major outdoor events. During the year there's a sailing regatta (April), a bicycle festival (October), a crafts fair (October), and many other happenings. Mount Dora draws large crowds during monthly (third weekend, except December) antiques fairs and thrice-yearly antiques "extravaganzas" (third weekends of January, February, and November) at popular Renninger's Twin Markets, an antiques center plus farmers' and flea markets.

Take a walk down Donnelly Street. The yellow Queen Anne–style mansion is **Donnelly House** (⊠ *515 Donnelly St.*), an 1893 architectural gem. Notice the details on the leaded-glass windows. Built in the 1920s, what was once known as the Dora Hotel is now **The Renaissance** (⊠*413 Donnelly St.*), a shopping arcade with restaurants and an Icelandic pub.

If you walk along 5th Avenue you'll pass a number of charming restaurants and gift and antiques shops. At **Uncle Al's Time Capsule** (⊠*140 E. 4th Ave.* ☎*352/383–1958*), you can sift through some terrific Hollywood memorabilia and collectibles.

☼ **Gilbert Park** has a public dock and boat-launching ramp, a recently renovated playground, nature trail, and a two large picnic pavilions with grills. ⊠*Tremain St. and Liberty Ave.* ☉*Daily Sunrise to sunset.*

A stroll around the lakefront grounds of the **Lakeside Inn** (⊠*100 N. Alexander St.* ☎*352/383–4104*), a country inn built in 1883, makes you feel as if you've stepped out of the pages of *The Great Gatsby*; there's even a croquet court.

A historic train depot serves as the offices of the **Mount Dora Chamber of Commerce.** Stop in and pick up a self-guided tour map that tells you everything you need to know—from historic landmarks to restaurants. Don't forget to ask about the trolley tour, during which a guide gives you the skinny on local historical spots and throws in a ghost story. ⊠*341 Alexander St., at 3rd Ave.* ☎*352/383–2165* ⊕*www.mountdora. com* ☉ *Weekdays 9–5, Sat. 10–4, Sun. 10–2; after hrs, maps on display at kiosk.*

☼ The **Inland Lakes Railway** offers scenic train excursions via the Mount Dora Champion, pulled by Herbie, a 1942 locomotive-driven coach that takes you on a 75-minute ride. Lunch and dinner trains are available from Eustis station. ⊠*Alexander St. and 3rd Ave.* ☎*352/589–4300* ⊕*www.inlandlakesrailway.com* ⊠*$12 adults, $8 children 2–12* ☉ *Wed.–Sat., times vary.*

OCALA NATIONAL FOREST

60 mi northwest of WDW; take I–4 east to Exit 92, and head west on Rte. 436 to U.S. 441, which you take north to Rte. 19 north.

☼ Between the Oklawaha and the St. Johns rivers lies the 366,000-acre **Ocala National Forest.** Clear streams wind through tall stands of pine or hardwoods. This spot is known for its canoeing, hiking, swimming, and camping, and for its invigorating springs. Here you can walk beneath tall pine trees and canoe down meandering streams and across placid lakes. Stop in at the **Ocala National Forest Visitor Center** (⊠*45621 Rte. 19, Altoona* ☎*352/669–7495*) for general park information. The center is open daily 9–4:30.

Fodor$Choice ★

10

HISTORIC BOK SANCTUARY

57 mi southwest of Orlando; 42 mi southwest of WDW.

If after several days at the theme parks you find that you're in need of a back-to-nature fix, head south along U.S. 27 to the small town of **Lake Wales.** Along the way you see what's left of Central Florida's citrus groves (many of them remain). But the main reason to take this drive is to get to the **Historic Bok Sanctuary,** known for years as Bok Tower Gardens, an appealing sanctuary of plants, flowers, trees, and wildlife. Shady paths meander through pine forests in this peaceful world of silvery moats, mockingbirds and swans, blooming thickets, and hidden sundials. You'll be able to boast that you stood on the highest measured point on Florida's peninsula, a colossal 298 feet above sea level. The majestic, 200-foot Bok Tower is constructed of coquina—from seashells—and pink, white, and gray marble, and it was refreshed for the sanctuary's 75th anniversary celebration in February 2004. The tower houses a carillon with 57 bronze bells that ring out each day at 1 and 3 PM during 30-minute live recitals, which may include early American folk songs, Appalachian tunes, Irish ballads, or Latin hymns. The bells are also featured in recordings every half hour after 10 AM, and sometimes even moonlight recitals.

The landscape was designed in 1928 by Frederick Law Olmsted Jr., son of the planner of New York's Central Park. The grounds include the 20-room, Mediterranean-style **Pinewood Estate,** built in 1930. Take I–4 to Exit 55, and head south on U.S. 27 for about 23 mi. Proceed past Eagle Ridge Mall, then turn left after two traffic lights onto Mountain Lake Cut Off Road and follow signs. ⊠*1151 Tower Blvd., Lake Wales* ☎*863/676–1408* ⊕*www.boktower.org* ⊠*$10 adults, $3 children 5–12, 50% off admission Sat. 8–9; Pinewood Estate general tour $6 adults, $5 children 5–12; holiday tour prices higher* ⊙*Daily 8–6; check Web site or call for Pinewood Estate tour schedule, which varies seasonally; holiday tours late Nov.–early Jan.*

Where to Eat

WORD OF MOUTH

"A couple of nice dinner options are Flying Fish (great food!) and Bluezoo in the Dolphin hotel. Whatever dining options you decide upon, try to reserve as far in advance as they book up months ahead. You can always cancel if you change your mind."

—mouseRD

"If you are willing to leave the park for dinner, try Citricos at The Grand Floridian. We also liked Artist Point at the Wilderness Lodge, and The Kona Cafe at the Polynesian. If you want to pile lots of food on your plate, try 'Ohana at the Polynesian. Not my style, but it is often crowded."

—Ryan

Revised by
Rowland
Stiteler

There used to be a running joke among dining critics in Florida that if one looked closely at the Orlando City Seal, it contained a Latin inscription that translated to read "bus drivers eat free." That was certainly the culinary mantra of central Florida. Quantity had priority over quality, and most cuisine seemed to have a grease content sufficient to make it flammable. Those days are gone forever.

Now with international culinary superstars like Emeril Lagassee, Wolfgang Puck, Todd English, and Norman Van Aken—not to mention local luminary Louis Perrotte of Le Coq au Vin—firmly established in eateries around the city, Orlando is making its way into the big leagues of fine dining in this country. And hovering just below that top level of cuisine as an art form in Orlando there's another level that can best be described as not fancy—but extremely good—cooking. Stop into one of the restaurants along Sand Lake Road (Exit 74 from I–4) and you can feast on worthy offerings ranging from a good paella to an expertly cooked chateaubriand to compelling Lebanese shish kebab to a tasty central American empanada.

In part because the almost 50 million visitors who come to Orlando every year hail from all over the world, so does the cuisine. And you can largely thank the increasingly high quality that travelers demand for the steady upward surge the quality of Orlando cuisine has seen in the past dozen years.

Food in the parks ranges from fast to fabulous. Hamburgers, chicken fingers, and fries dominate at most of the counter-service places, but fresh sandwiches, salads, and fruit are always available, too. Of course, the full-service restaurants offer the best selection, from the Hollywood Brown Derby's signature Cobb salad to steak at Le Cellier. Priority-seating reservations are generally essential for restaurant meals, especially at dinner. Without reservations, you may find yourself having a burger (again) for dinner, or having to leave Walt Disney World, which some people prefer to do anyway.

DRESS

Because tourism is king around Orlando, casual dress is the rule. Men need jackets only in the priciest establishments.

MEALTIMES

When you're touring the theme parks, you can save a lot of time by eating in the off-hours. Lines at the counter-service places can get very long between noon and 2 PM, and waiting in line for food can get more frustrating than waiting in line for a ride. Try eating lunch at 11 AM and dinner at 5 PM, or lunch at 2:30 PM and dinner at 9 PM.

TOP 5 DISNEY RESTAURANTS

Boma. African-inspired dishes like spiced, roasted chicken and curried coconut seafood stew are a hit with parents and kids at this casual buffet in the Animal Kingdom Lodge.

California Grill. This restaurant hits the top of the favorites list for most people for its innovative American cuisine and incredible views of the Magic Kingdom. Reserve months in advance for a window seat during the fireworks.

Jiko. Superb southern-African cuisine paired with an exceptional wine list and incredibly knowledgeable servers, Jiko is perfect for a romantic dinner for two.

Mama Melrose's. You can't go wrong with solid Italian pastas and *secondi* like osso buco. This casual *ristorante* in Disney's Hollywood Studios is great for families, and you get free drink refills if you sign up for the Fantasmic! dinner package.

Victoria & Albert's. Want to go all out? Treat yourself to a seven-course prix-fixe meal at the restaurant many consider to be Central Florida's best. The Victorian dining room and costumed servers transport you to another time and place, while every mouthful of the haute cuisine is a sensuous delight.

RESERVATIONS

All WDW restaurants and most restaurants elsewhere in greater Orlando take "priority seating" reservations. A priority-seating reservation is like a Fastpass to a meal. You don't get your table right away, but you should get the next one that becomes available. Say you make your reservation for 7 PM. Once you arrive, the hostess will give you a round plastic buzzer that looks sort of like a hockey puck. Then you can walk around, get a drink at the bar, or just wait nearby until the buzzer vibrates and flashes red. That means your table is ready and you can go back to the hostess stand to be seated. You will most likely be seated within 15 minutes of your arrival.

For restaurant reservations within Walt Disney World, call 407/939–3463 or 407/560–7277. And, although you can't make reservations online at ⊕*www.disneyworld.com,* you can certainly get plenty of information, like the hours, price range, and specialties of all Disney eateries. For Universal Orlando reservations, call 407/224–9255.

In reviews, reservations are mentioned only when they're essential or not accepted. Unless otherwise noted, the restaurants listed are open daily for lunch and dinner.

PRICES

WHAT IT COSTS				
¢	$	$$	$$$	$$$$
AT DINNER under $8	$8–$14	$15–$21	$22–$30	over $30

Prices are per person for a median main course, at dinner, excluding tip and tax.

BEST BETS FOR ORLANDO DINING

If it can be fried and put under a heat lamp you can probably find it in Orlando, but the dining scene both within the parks and the city itself has long transcended fast food. Quality restaurants operate within the parks, Downtown Disney, and several central Orlando neighborhoods. Here are our top recommendations, organized by price, cuisine, and experience. The restaurants we consider the very best are indicated in the listings with the Fodor's Choice logo.

Fodor'sChoice ★

Artist Point, p. 295
Bice, p. 305
Bistro de Paris, p. 285
Boma, p. 295
Bonefish Grill, p. 316
Bravo! Cucina Italiana, p. 316
Emeril's, p. 303
Jiko, p. 296
Le Coq au Vin, p. 324
Les Chefs de France, p. 286
Mama Melrose's Ristorante Italiano, p. 290
Seasons 52, p. 320
Victoria & Albert's, p. 298

By Price

¢

Baja Burrito Kitchen, p. 322
Flame Tree Barbecue, p. 290
Johnny's Fillin' Station, p. 324
Moe's, p. 318
Picabu Buffeteria, p. 297

$

50s Prime Time Café, p. 289
ESPN Club, p. 294
Little Saigon, p. 325
Mythos, p. 302

$$

Antonio's, p. 315
Bonefish Grill, p. 316
Bravo! Cucina Italiana, p. 316
Café d'Antonio, p. 308
Cantina Laredo, p. 317
Mama Melrose's Ristorante Italiano, p. 290

$$$

Artist Point, p. 295
Biergarten, p. 285
Boma, p. 295
Cuba Libre, p. 311
Emeril's, p. 303
Jiko, p. 296
Le Cellier, p. 286
Le Coq au Vin, p. 324
Les Chefs de France, p. 286
Seasons 52, p. 320

$$$$

A Land Remembered, p. 310
Bice, p. 305
Bistro de Paris, p. 285
Cinderella's Royal Table, p. 283
Norman's, p. 313
Texas de Brazil, p. 314
The Venetian Room, p. 307
Victoria & Albert's, p. 298

By Cuisine

AFRICAN

Boma, p. 295
Jiko, p. 296

AMERICAN

A Land Remembered, p. 310
Chef Mickey's, p. 295
Cinderella's Royal Table, p. 283
Confisco Grille, p. 302
ESPN Club, p. 294
Johnny's Fillin' Station, p. 324
NBA City, p. 304
Rainforest Café, p. 290, 293
Seasons 52, p. 320

CARIBBEAN

Bahama Breeze, p. 310
Bongo's, p. 291
Tommy Bahama's Tropical Café, p. 314

CHINESE

Ming Court, p. 312
Nine Dragons, p. 287
P.F. Chang's, p. 328

CONTINENTAL

Chef Justin's Park Plaza Gardens, p. 327
The Venetian Room, p. 307
Victoria & Albert's, p. 298

ECLECTIC

The Boheme Restaurant, p. 323
Café Tu Tu Tango, p. 311
Citricos, p. 296
Mythos, p. 302
Villa de Flora Marketplace and Restaurant, p. 308

FAST FOOD

Anthony's Pizzeria and Restaurant, p. 322
Cosmic Ray's Starlight Cafe, p. 283
Moe's, p. 318

FRENCH

Bistro de Paris, p. 285
La Coquina, p. 299
Le Coq au Vin, p. 324
Les Chefs de France, p. 286

IRISH

Finnegan's Bar & Grill, p. 301
Raglan Road Irish Pub, p. 293

ITALIAN

Antonio's, p. 315
Bice, p. 305
Bravo! Cucina Italiano, p. 316
Enzo's on the Lake, p. 329
Fiorella's Cucina Toscana, p. 312
Mama Melrose's Ristorante Italiano, p. 290

JAPANESE

Amura, p. 322
Kimonos Sushi Bar, p. 296
Ran-Getsu, p. 313
Seito Celebration, p. 309
Seito Sushi, p. 329
Tokyo Dining and Teppan Edo, p. 288

LATIN

Columbia Restaurant, p. 309
The Latin Quarter, p. 304
Numero Uno, p. 325
Samba Room, p. 319

MEXICAN

Baja Burrito Kitchen, p. 322
Cantina Laredo, p. 317
Moe's, p. 318
San Angel Inn, p. 287

PIZZA

Alfonso's Pizza & More, p. 322

Anthony's Pizzeria and Restaurant, p. 322
NYPD Pizza, p. 325
Wolfgang Puck, p. 293

SEAFOOD

Bonefish Grill, p. 316
Cityfish, p. 323
Flying Fish, p. 294
Fulton's Crab House, p. 292
Landry's Seafood House, p. 300
Oceanaire Seafood Room, p. 313
Sunset Sam's Fish Camp, p. 307

STEAK

Linda's La Cantina, p. 325
Morton's of Chicago, p. 319
Old Hickory Steak House, p. 306
The Palm, p. 305
Shula's Steak House, p. 297
Texas de Brazil, p. 314
Vito's Chop House, p. 315
Yachtsman Steak House, p. 299

By Experience

BUFFET

Biergarten, p. 285
Garden Grill, p. 285
Hollywood & Vine, p. 289
Picabu Buffeteria, p. 297

Villa de Flora Marketplace and Restaurant, p. 308

CHARACTER MEAL

Chef Mickey's, p. 295
Cinderella's Royal Table, p. 283
Royal Akershus Banquet Hall, p. 287

BEST VIEWS

California Grill, p. 295
Enzo's on the Lake, p. 329
LakeView Restaurant, p. 300
Old Hickory Steak House, p. 306

FUN PERFORMANCES

'Ohana, p. 297
Marrakesh, p. 286
Taverna Opa, p. 314

LATE-NIGHT DINING

B-Line Diner, p. 310
ESPN Club, p. 294
Raglan Road Irish Pub, p. 293

SPECIAL OCCASION

Le Coq Au Vin, p. 324
Norman's, p. 313
Victoria & Albert's, p. 298

SUNDAY BRUNCH

The Boheme Restaurant, p. 323
House of Blues, p. 292
La Coquina, p. 299

TOP 4 OFF-SITE RESTAURANTS

Bonefish Grill. Standout seafood like grilled sea bass, tilefish, and rainbow trout is served in a casually elegant dining room.

Bravo! Cucina Italiana. Stellar Italian cooking with a menu that changes frequently, plus a pleasant outdoor dining area worthy of spending an afternoon with a meal and a few drinks.

Le Coq au Vin. Souped-up French country fare, like bronzed grouper with roasted pecans and the namesake chicken with red wine sauce,

makes this fine little eatery in south-central Orlando worth seeking out.

Seasons 52. What's on the menu this month won't be on it next month at this new-concept restaurant where the ingredients in the dishes are served at the time of year when they are most ripe and flavorful. The dishes are not only flavorful, they are healthy as well. Meats and fish tend to be grilled not baked. And the decadent desserts are served in shot-glass sizes.

WINE AND ALCOHOL

The Magic Kingdom's no-liquor policy, a Walt Disney tradition that seems almost quaint in this day and age, does not extend to the rest of Walt Disney World, and in fact, most restaurants and watering holes, particularly those in the on-site hotels, mix elaborate fantasy drinks based on fruit juices or flavored with liqueurs.

WALT DISNEY WORLD AREA

CHARACTER MEALS

At these breakfasts, brunches, and dinners staged in hotel and theme-park restaurants all over Walt Disney World, kids can snuggle up to all the best-loved Disney characters. Sometimes the food is served buffet style; sometimes it's served to you banquet style. The cast of characters, times, and prices increase frequently (although locations of performances remain fairly constant), so be sure to call ahead.

Reservations are always available and often required; some meals can fill up more than 60 days in advance. However, you can frequently book by phone on the same day you plan to dine, depending on the specific location you choose. It never hurts to double-check the character lineup before you leave for the meal. If you have your heart set on a specific meal, make your reservations when you book your trip—up to six months in advance. Smoking is not permitted.

BREAKFAST

Main Street, U.S.A.'s **Crystal Palace Buffet** (☎ *407/939–3463* 🖃 *$19 adults, $11 children ages 3–9*) has breakfast with Winnie the Pooh, Eeyore, Tigger, Piglet, and friends daily from 8 to 10:30 AM. Disney–Hollywood Studios's **Hollywood & Vine** (☎ *407/939–3463* 🖃 *$23 adults,*

$13 children ages 3–9) hosts *Playhouse Disney* stars Jo Jo and Goliath from "Jo Jo's Circus" and June and Leo from "The Little Einsteins."

At Disney's Beach Club, characters including Goofy, Chip 'n' Dale, and Pluto are on hand at the **Cape May Café** (☎*407/939–3463* ✉*$19 adults, $11 children ages 3–9)* from 7:30 to 11 AM daily. At the Contemporary Resort, Chef Mickey, Goofy, and Chip 'n' Dale are on hand at **Chef Mickey's** (☎*407/939–3463* ✉*$22.99 adults, $12.99 children ages 3–9)* which has a no-holds-barred buffet from 7 to 11:15 AM daily. The Polynesian Resort's characters including Lilo and Stitch, Pluto, and Mickey are on hand at **'Ohana** (☎*407/939–3463* ✉*$19 adults, $11 children ages 3–9)*, which serves breakfast with Mickey and his friends daily from 7:30 to 11 AM.

At the Swan, the weekend Good Morning Character Breakfast with Goofy and Pluto convenes at the **Garden Grove Café** (☎*407/934–3000* ✉*$18 adults, $9.50 children ages 3–9)* from 8 to 11 AM. This location is typically not crowded, and makes a good place to take your kids if you can't get a character breakfast seating elsewhere.

At the Wyndham Palace Resort & Spa you can drop in Sunday from 8 to 10:30 AM for a character meal at the **Watercress Restaurant** (☎*407/827–2727* ✉*$25 adults, $13 children ages 3–9)*.

At the **Covington Mill Restaurant** at the Walt Disney World Hilton, a rotating cast of Disney characters appear Sunday from 8:30 to 11 AM (☎*407/827–4000* ✉*$18.50 adults, $8.50 children ages 3–9)*.

At the **Regal Sun Resort** (formerly the Grosvenor) on Disney Hotel Row, Pluto and Goofy appear from 8:30 to 10:30 AM on Tuesday, Thursday, and Saturday in what is one of the WDW area's least expensive character breakfasts (☎*407/828–4444* ✉*$13 adults, $6 children ages 3–9)*.

BY
RESERVATION
ONLY

The Princess Storybook Breakfasts with Snow White, Sleeping Beauty, and at least three other princesses are held at Epcot Center in the Norway exhibit at **Royal Akershus Banquet Hall** (☎*407/939–3463* ✉*$24 adults, $13 children ages 3–9)* in the Norway Pavilion from 8:30 to 10:30 AM daily. Donald Duck and his friends are at Donald's Breakfastosaurus 8:10 to 10 AM daily at the **Restaurantosaurus** (☎*407/939–3463* ✉*$18.99 adults, $10.99 children ages 3–9)*, in Disney's Animal Kingdom. Mary Poppins and the Alice in Wonderland characters including the Mad Hatter preside at **1900 Park Fare Restaurant** (☎*407/824–2383* ✉*$249 adults, $13 children ages 3–9)* in the Grand Floridian from 7:30 to 11:30 AM daily. Cinderella herself hosts Magic Kingdom breakfasts from 8 to 10 AM daily at **Cinderella's Royal Table** (☎*407/939–3463* ✉*$35 adults, $24 children ages 3–9)*. This breakfast is extremely popular, so book six months in advance to be assured seating. (Prices jump to $37 for adults and $25 for children during holiday periods that include Thanksgiving, Christmas, and Easter.)

Fodor'sChoice
★

LUNCH

At Cinderella Castle, **Cinderella's Royal Table** (☎*407/939–3463* ✉*$38 adults, $25 children ages 3–9)* is a popular lunchtime option. Your picture is taken as you arrive, then presented to you—in a Cinderella frame,

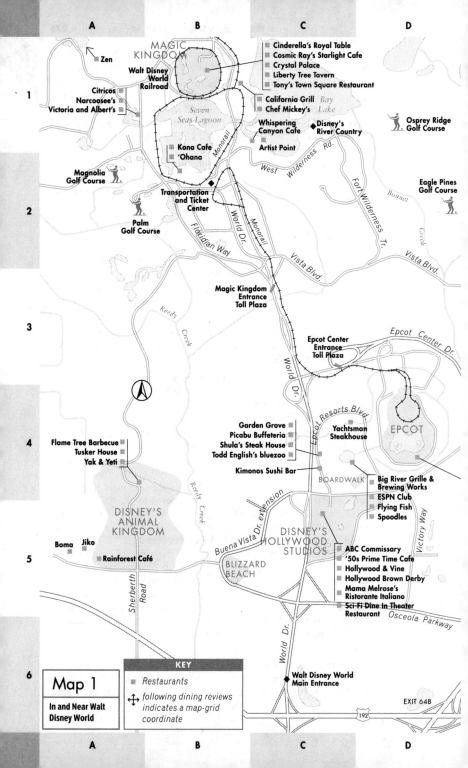

MAGIC KINGDOM

Zen

Walt Disney World Railroad

Citricos
Narcoosee's
Victoria and Albert's

Cinderella's Royal Table
Cosmic Ray's Starlight Cafe
Crystal Palace
Liberty Tree Tavern
Tony's Town Square Restaurant

California Grill
Chef Mickey's

Bay Lake

Whispering Canyon Cafe

Disney's River Country

Osprey Ridge Golf Course

Seven Seas Lagoon

Artist Point

Kona Cafe
'Ohana

Magnolia Golf Course

West Wilderness Rd.

Eagle Pines Golf Course

Bonnet

Transportation and Ticket Center

Palm Golf Course

Monorail

World Dr.

Monorail

Vista Blvd.

Fort Wilderness Tr.

Vista Blvd.

Floridian Way

Magic Kingdom Entrance Toll Plaza

Reedy Creek

Epcot Center Dr.

Epcot Center Entrance Toll Plaza

World Dr.

Epcot Resorts Blvd.

EPCOT

Garden Grove
Picabu Buffeteria
Shula's Steak House
Todd English's bluezoo

Yachtsman Steakhouse

Flame Tree Barbecue
Tusker House
Yak & Yeti

Kimonos Sushi Bar

BOARDWALK

Big River Grille & Brewing Works
ESPN Club
Flying Fish
Spoodles

DISNEY'S ANIMAL KINGDOM

Reedy Creek

Buena Vista Dr. extension

DISNEY'S HOLLYWOOD STUDIOS

Victory Way

Boma Jiko

Rainforest Café

BLIZZARD BEACH

ABC Commissary
'50s Prime Time Cafe
Hollywood & Vine
Hollywood Brown Derby
Mama Melrose's Ristorante Italiano
Sci-Fi Dine In Theater Restaurant

Sherberth Road

World Dr.

Osceola Parkway

Map 1

In and Near Walt Disney World

KEY

■ Restaurants

following dining reviews indicates a map-grid coordinate

Walt Disney World Main Entrance

EXIT 64B

192

A   B   C   D

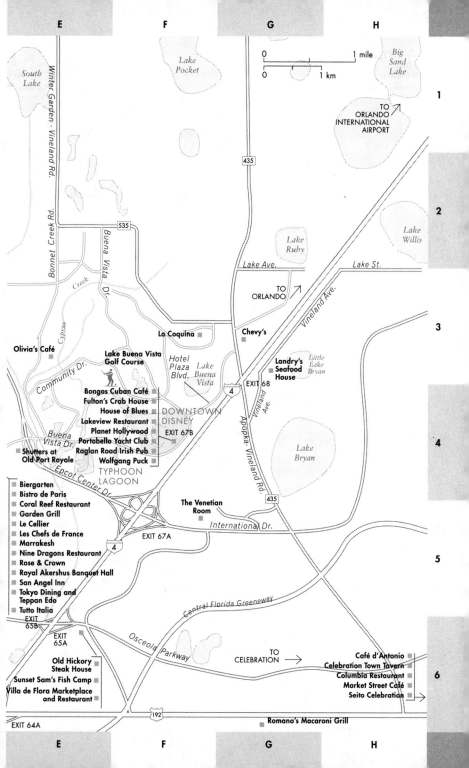

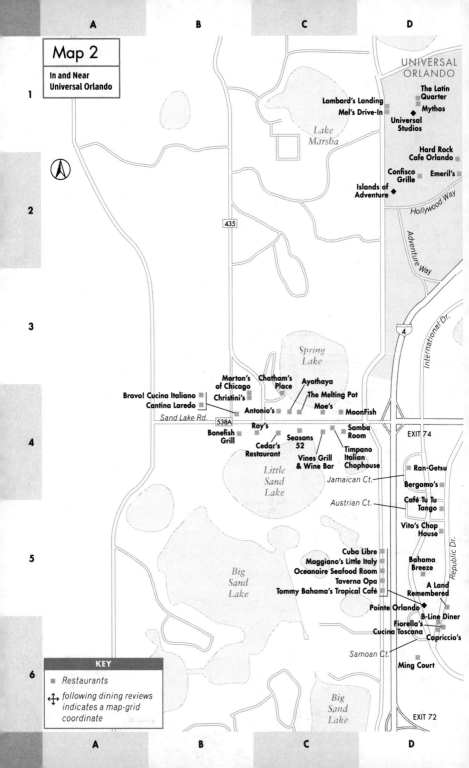

Map 2

In and Near Universal Orlando

1

UNIVERSAL ORLANDO

Lake Marsha

Lombard's Landing
Mel's Drive-In
The Latin Quarter
Mythos
Universal Studios

Hard Rock Cafe Orlando

Confisco Grille
Emeril's

2

Islands of Adventure

Hollywood Way

Adventure Way

3

Spring Lake

International Dr.

Morton's of Chicago
Chatham's Place
Ayothaya
The Melting Pot
Bravo! Cucina Italiano
Christini's
Cantina Laredo
Antonio's
Moe's
MoonFish

Sand Lake Rd.

538A

4

Bonefish Grill
Roy's
Seasons 52
Samba Room
Cedar's Restaurant
Vines Grill & Wine Bar
Timpano Italian Chophouse

EXIT 74

Little Sand Lake

Ran-Getsu
Bergamo's
Jamaican Ct.
Café Tu Tu Tango
Austrian Ct.
Vito's Chop House

5

Big Sand Lake

Cuba Libre
Maggiano's Little Italy
Oceanaire Seafood Room
Taverna Opa
Tommy Bahama's Tropical Café
Bahama Breeze
A Land Remembered
Pointe Orlando
B-Line Diner
Fiorella's
Cucina Toscana
Capriccio's

Republic Dr.

Samoan Ct.

Ming Court

6

Big Sand Lake

EXIT 72

KEY

■ Restaurants

✦ following dining reviews indicates a map-grid coordinate

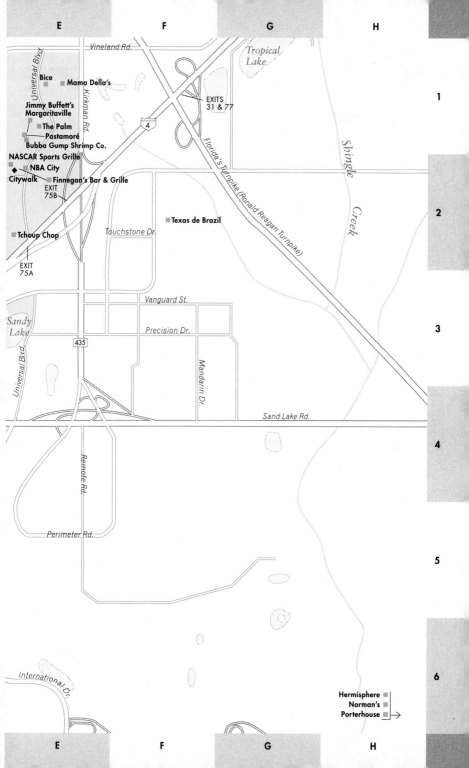

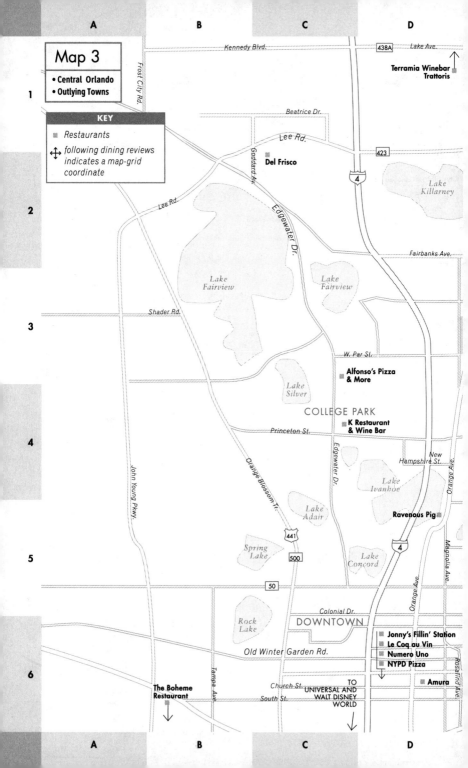

Map 3

- Central Orlando
- Outlying Towns

KEY

- ■ Restaurants
- ✛ following dining reviews indicates a map-grid coordinate

A **B** **C** **D**

Kennedy Blvd.

438A   Lake Ave.

■ Terramia Winebar Trattoris

1

Frost City Rd.

Beatrice Dr.

Lee Rd.

423

■ **Del Frisco**

Goddard Av.

Lee Rd.

Edgewater Dr.

I-4

Lake Killarney

2

Fairbanks Ave.

Lake Fairview

Lake Fairview

Shader Rd.

3

W. Par St.

Lake Silver

■ **Alfonso's Pizza & More**

COLLEGE PARK

■ **K Restaurant & Wine Bar**

Princeton St.

4

John Young Pkwy.

Orange Blossom Tr.

New Hampshire St.

Lake Ivanhoe

Edgewater Dr.

Orange Ave.

441

Lake Adair

■ **Ravenous Pig** ■

500

Spring Lake

Lake Concord

4

Orange Ave.

Magnolia Ave.

5

50

Rock Lake

Colonial Dr.

DOWNTOWN

■ **Jonny's Fillin' Station**
■ **Le Coq au Vin**
■ **Numero Uno**
■ **NYPD Pizza**

Tampa Ave.

Old Winter Garden Rd.

Rosalind Ave.

6

■ **The Boheme Restaurant**
↓

Church St.
South St.

TO UNIVERSAL AND WALT DISNEY WORLD
↓

■ **Amura**

A **B** **C** **D**

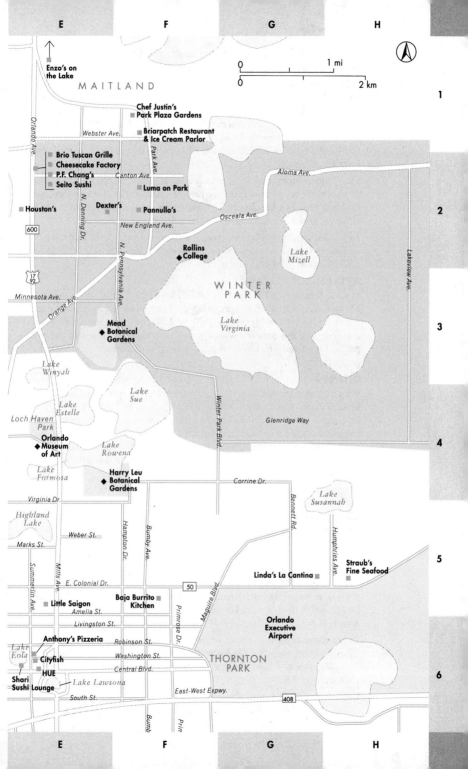

of course. (Prices jump to $40 for adults and $26 for children during holiday periods that include Thanksgiving, Christmas, and Easter.)

Winnie the Pooh, Tigger, and Eeyore come to the **Crystal Palace Buffet** (☎407/939–3463 ✉*$21 adults, $12 children ages 3–9*) on Main Street, U.S.A., from 11:10 AM to 2:30 PM. This is a popular location for character meals, and reservations are essential here. Mickey, Pluto, and Chip 'n' Dale are on hand from noon to 3:50 PM at the **Garden Grill** (☎407/939–3463 ✉*$22 adults, $12 children ages 3–9*) in the Land pavilion at Epcot.

The Princess Storybook Lunches with Snow White, Sleeping Beauty, and at least three other princesses are held at Epcot at the Norway Pavilion in **Royal Akershus Banquet Hall** (☎407/939–3463 ✉*$31 adults, $19 children ages 3–9*) from 11:40 AM to 2:50 PM.

Jo Jo, Goliath, June, and Leo from *Playhouse Disney* make a comeback at Disney's Hollywood Studios' **Hollywood & Vine** (☎407/939–3463 ✉*$25 adults, $14 children ages 3–9*).

AFTERNOON SNACKS

For the Wonderland **Tea Party** (☎407/939–3463 ✉*$30 including tax*) at the Grand Floridian Resort, Alice and other characters preside over afternoon tea weekdays from 1:30 to 2:30 PM. With the cast's help, children can bake their own cupcakes and then eat them at the tea party. Open only to children ages 3 to 10; all participants must be potty-trained.

DINNER

All character dinners require reservations. At Cinderella Castle, the **Dreams Come True Dinner** (☎407/939–3463 ✉*$41 adults, $26 children ages 3–9*) includes an appearance by the Fairy Godmother. Your evening concludes with the presentation of a framed photo of you and your child at the dinner. (Prices jump to $44.99 for adults and $27.99 for children during holiday periods that include Thanksgiving, Christmas, and Easter.)

Minnie Mouse, Goofy, Pluto, and friends (which in this case does not include Mickey) get patriotic during their evening appearance at the Liberty Square **Liberty Tree Tavern** (☎407/939–3463 ✉*$29 adults, $14 children ages 3–9*). A "revolutionary" feast of smoked pork, turkey, carved beef, and all the trimmings is served nightly from 4 to 8:40 PM. Farmer Mickey, along with Chip 'n' Dale and Pluto appear at the Land Pavilion at Epcot's **Garden Grill** (☎407/939–3463 ✉*$29 adults, $14 children ages 3–9*) from 4 to 8 PM daily. Winnie the Pooh and friends appear at a nightly buffet from 4 to 8:45 PM at the **Crystal Palace Buffet** (☎407/939–3463 ✉*$29 adults, $14 children ages 3–9*) on Main Street, U.S.A.

Every night at 8 PM (7 PM in winter), near Fort Wilderness's Meadow Trading Post, there's a **Character Campfire** (☎407/824–2727) with a free sing-along. Chip 'n' Dale are frequent attendees, among other characters.

Cinderella's Gala Feast is held at the Grand Floridian's **1900 Park Fare** (☎407/939–3463 ✉*$33 adults, $15 children ages 3–9*), for a buffet served from 4:30 to 8:20 PM daily. The Contemporary Resort hosts a popular dinner starring Mickey at **Chef Mickey's** (☎407/939–3463 ✉*$30 adults, $15 children ages 3–9*), from 5 to 9:15 PM daily. At the Walt Disney World Swan, you can dine with *Lion King* characters Monday and Friday from 5:30 to 10 PM at **Garden Grove** (☎407/934–1609). Known as the Garden Grove Café during the day, Gulliver's Grill hosts Goofy and Pluto the other five nights of the week. Dinner is $32 adults, $13 children ages 3 to 9.

The Princess Storybook Dinner with Snow White, Sleeping Beauty, and at least three other princesses are held at Epcot Center at the Norway Pavilion in **Restaurant Akershus** (☎407/939–3463 ✉*$36 adults, $20 children ages 3–9*) from 4:20 to 8:40 PM.

> **HAPPILY EVER AFTER**
>
> Some 1,500 couples tie the knot at Walt Disney World every year. At the **Fairy Tale Wedding Pavilion** (☎*407/828–3400*) near the Grand Floridian Resort and many other locations across Disney property, the bride can ride in a Cinderella coach, have rings borne to the altar in a glass slipper, and invite Mickey and Minnie to attend the reception. Check out the interactive Web site, ⊕**www.disneyweddings. com,** for photos, testimonials, and wedding ideas.

MAGIC KINGDOM

Dining options in the Magic Kingdom are mainly counter service, and every land has its share of fast-food places selling burgers, hot dogs, grilled-chicken sandwiches, and salads. The walkways are peppered with carts dispensing popcorn, ice-cream bars, lemonade, bottled water, and soda.

For a meal in one of the full-service restaurants in the Kingdom, you must make priority-seating reservations. You can make them at the restaurants on the day you want to eat or through the **Disney Reservations Center** (☎407/939–3463).

$$$$
AMERICAN

✕**Cinderella's Royal Table.** Cinderella and other Disney princesses appear at breakfast time at this eatery in the castle's old mead hall; you should book reservations up to 180 days in advance to be sure to see them. Breakfast and lunch are preplated meals. Breakfast, which includes scrambled eggs, sausages, bacon, Danishes, potatoes, and beverages is $35 for adults, $24 for children. Lunch, which includes entrées like herb-crusted pork tenderloin with mustard cheese grits and pan-seared salmon with saffron crab risotto, is $38 for adults, $24 for children. The prix-fixe dinner is $43 for adults, $27 for children. When you arrive at the Cinderella Castle, a photographer snaps a shot of your group in the lobby. A package of photographs will be delivered to your table during your meal. ✉*Cinderella Castle* ☎407/939–3463 ⚑*Reservations essential* ▭*AE, MC, V* ✛*1:B1.*

¢–$
AMERICAN

✕**Cosmic Ray's Starlight Cafe.** Burgers, rotisserie chicken, barbecued ribs, grilled chicken sandwiches, hot dogs, and chicken strips, all served with potato croquettes (ranging in price $7–$14) are available at the counter of this fast-food outlet in Tomorrowland. Kid's meals are as low as $4.60, including a good version of the ubiquitous peanut butter and jelly sandwich. The triple chocolate cake is the best of the desserts. Robotic Las Vegas–style lounge singer Sonny E. Clipse (who is billed as a lounge lizard and is literally one—in that the singer is a robotic lizard)—croons for the crowds. ⊠*Tomorrowland* ☎*407/503–3463* ▤*AE, MC, V* ✛*1:B1.*

$$–$$$
AMERICAN

✕**Crystal Palace.** Named for the big glass atrium surrounding the restaurant, the Crystal Palace is a great escape in summer, when the air-conditioning is turned to near meat-locker level. The buffet-style meal includes items like ancho-rubbed Atlantic salmon, rotisserie chicken, roasted adobo pork soups, pastas, fresh-baked breads, and ice-cream sundaes, all part of a one-price package (dinner price is $29 for adults). There's also a kids-only buffet with what many youngsters consider the basic food groups: macaroni and cheese, pizza, and chocolate chip cookies for $14 per child. The Crystal Palace is huge but charming with numerous nooks and crannies, comfortable banquettes, cozy cast-iron tables, and abundant sunlight. It's also one of the few places in the Magic Kingdom that serves breakfast. Winnie the Pooh, Tigger, Piglet, and Eeyore visit at breakfast, lunch, and dinner. ⊠*At Hub end of Main St. facing Cinderella Castle* ☎*407/939–3463* ▤*AE, MC, V* ✛*1:B1.*

$–$$$
AMERICAN

✕**Liberty Tree Tavern.** This "tavern" is dry, but it's a prime spot on the parade route, so you can catch a good meal while you wait. Order colonial-period comfort food like smoked pork ribs, hearty pot roast cooked with a cabernet wine and mushroom sauce, or turkey and dressing with mashed potatoes. Lunch prices are à la carte, with the least expensive sandwich for adults—a cheeseburger—going for $12. Dinner is a prix-fixe meal that costs $29 for adults, $13 for children. The restaurant is decorated in lovely Williamsburg colors, with Early American–style antiques and lots of brightly polished brass. ⊠*Liberty Sq.* ☎*407/824–6461* ▤*AE, MC, V* ✛*1:B1.*

$$–$$$
ITALIAN

✕**Tony's Town Square Restaurant.** Inspired by the animated classic *Lady and the Tramp,* Tony's offers everything from spaghetti with meatballs, to a New York strip steak, to a catch of the day served with orzo pasta. There's no wine list, but you can get the smoothie of the day or a collector's mug of lemonade. The most tempting desserts are the tiramisu or the pistachio crème brûlée. If you can't get a table right away, you can watch *Lady and the Tramp* in the waiting area. ⊠*Main St., U.S.A., Liberty Sq.* ☎*407/939–3463* ▤*AE, MC, V* ✛*1:B1.*

EPCOT

Epcot's World Showcase offers some of the finest dining in Orlando. Every pavilion has at least one and often two or even three eateries. Where there's a choice, it's between a relatively expensive full-service restaurant and a more affordable, ethnic fast-food spot, plus carts and shops selling snacks ranging from French pastries to Japanese ices—whatever's appropriate to the pavilion.

Lunch and dinner priority-seating reservations are essential at the full-service restaurants; you can make them up to 60 days in advance by calling 407/939–3463 or going in person to Guest Services (aka Guest

Relations) at the park (only on the day of the meal) or to the restaurants themselves when they open for lunch, usually at noon. No matter how you book, show up a bit early to be sure of getting your table.

$$$
GERMAN

✕**Biergarten.** Oktoberfest runs 365 days a year here. The cheerful, some-times raucous, crowds are what you would expect in a place with an oompah band. The menu and level of frivolity are the same at lunch and dinner. For a single price ($20 for adults, $11 for kids ages 3–9 at lunch; $29 for adults and $14 for children at dinner), mountains of sauerbraten, bratwurst, chicken or pork schnitzel, German sausage, spaetzle, apple strudel, Bavarian cheesecake, and Black Forest cake await you at the all-you-can-eat buffet. And if you aren't feeling too Teutonic, there's also rotisserie chicken and roast pork. Patrons pound pitchers of all kinds of beer and wine on the long communal tables—even when the yodelers, singers, and dancers aren't egging them on. ✉*Germany* ▤*AE, MC, V* ✛*1:D4.*

$$$$
Fodor's Choice
★
FRENCH

✕**Bistro de Paris.** The great secret in the France pavilion—and, indeed, in all of Epcot—is the Bistro de Paris, upstairs from Les Chefs de France. The sophisticated menu changes regularly and reflects the cutting edge of French cooking; representative dishes include pan-seared lobster, roasted rack of venison with black-pepper sauce, and seared scallops with truffle-potato puree. An excellent appetizer is the Escargot and Mushroom Cassolette with parsley butter, frog leg fritters, and water-cress veloute. If eating cooked snails isn't your thing, go for the Country Style Meat Plate, which includes homemade pâté, beef croquette, duck rillette, and smoked duck magret. Save room for the Grand Marnier flambéed crepes. Come late, ask for a window seat, and plan to linger to watch the nightly Epcot light show, which usually starts around 9 PM. Moderately priced French wines are available by the bottle and the glass. If you like French cuisine but don't know much about it, the six-course, prix-fixe meal, $75 per person without wine, or $120 with wine parings, is a good way to go. ✉*France* ▤*AE, MC, V* ✛*1:D4.*

$$$–$$$$
SEAFOOD

✕**Coral Reef Restaurant.** One of this restaurant's walls is made entirely of glass and looks directly into the 6-million-gallon Living Seas aquarium, where you can get tantalizingly close to sharks, stingrays, groupers, tarpons, sea turtles, and even the occasional scuba diver. And with a three-tiered seating area, everyone has a good view. Edible attractions include seared Sterling salmon with ratatouille, grilled mahimahi with couscous, and pan-seared ahi Tuna. If you prefer red meat, go for the 12-ounce New York strip with potatoes au gratin. Finish up with the butterscotch crème brûlée. ✉*The Living Seas* ▤*AE, MC, V* ✛*1:D4.*

$$$
AMERICAN

✕**Garden Grill.** Solid family-style lunch or dinner fare is served here as the restaurant revolves, giving you an ever-changing view of each biome on the Living with the Land boat ride. The restaurant offers an all-you-can-eat buffet ($29 at dinner, $14 for children 3–9). Typical choices include rotisserie pork, fried catfish, chicken strips, flank steak with cabernet mushroom sauce and macaroni and cheese. The big, fluffy buttermilk biscuits are a specialty here. Besides the Princess breakfast in Norway, this is the only Epcot restaurant that has Disney character meet-and-greets during meals. Wine is served by the glass at lunch and dinner. ✉*The Land* ▤*AE, MC, V* ✛*1:D4.*

$$$–$$$$
CANADIAN

✕ **Le Cellier.** With the best Canadian wine cellar in the state, this charming eatery with stone arches and dark-wood paneling has a good selection of Canadian beer as well. Aged beef is king, although many steaks appear only on the dinner menu. The chefs have chosen a representative menu for a fixed price dinner for $37 for adults (and an $8 menu for kids). The prix-fixe menu for adults has choices ranging from pan-seared salmon to porcini mushroom ravioli. But you can also go à la carte. If you're a carnivore, go for the herb-crusted prime rib. Even though the menu changes periodically (gone are the buffalo steaks, alas), they always have the pan-seared Canadian salmon and free-range chicken with a mustard marinade. For a light meal, try the Prince Edward Island mussels, or a bowl of the hearty beef and barley soup. Desserts pay tribute to the land up north with a crème brûlée made with maple sugar, and a Canadian Club chocolate cake. ⊠ *Canada* ▤ *AE, MC, V* ✛ *1:D4.*

> **WORD OF MOUTH**
>
> "Our favorite is Le Cellier, in Canada—excellent food that is quite pricey. As far as the resorts go, Kona Cafe in the Polynesian is a good one, but always sooo crowded. Boma offers superb food (buffet style)…a truly great dining experience." –Randa

$$$–$$$$
Fodor'sChoice
★
FRENCH

✕ **Les Chefs de France.** What some consider the best restaurant at Disney was created by three of France's most famous chefs: Paul Bocuse, Gaston Lenôtre, and Roger Vergé. Classic escargots, a good starter, are prepared in a casserole with garlic butter; you might follow up with duck à l'orange or grilled beef tenderloin with a black pepper sauce. Make sure you finish with crepes *au chocolat.* The best guilty pleasure: a sinful version of macaroni and cheese made with cream and Gruyère cheese, is a bargain at $18. The nearby Boulangerie Pâtisserie, run by the same team, offers tarts, croissants, eclairs, napoleons, and more, to go. And if you want an oxymoron—inexpensive haute cuisine, try the three course, prix-fixe meal available until 7 PM for $34 per person. ⊠ *France* ▤ *AE, MC, V* ✛ *1:D4.*

$$–$$$
MOROCCAN

✕ **Marrakesh.** Chef Abrache Lahcen of Morocco presents the best cooking of his homeland in this ornate eatery, which looks like something from the set of *Casablanca.* Your appetizer might be *harira,* a soup with tomatoes, lentils, and lamb that is traditionally served during Ramadan. From there, move on to the chicken, lamb, or vegetable couscous, Morocco's national dish. A good way to try a bit of everything is the Marrakesh Royal Feast ($43 per person), which includes chicken *bastilla* (chicken in phyllo pastry) and beef *brewat* (minced beef in a layered pastry dusted with cinnamon and powdered sugar), plus vegetable couscous and assorted Moroccan pastries. A slightly less expensive option is "A Night in Casablanca," a sampler plate of roast lamb Meshoui, chicken kebab, and seafood bastilla with vegetable couscous. The best choice for dessert is a sweet bastilla in which the pastry is stuffed with vanilla cream and toasted almonds. Traditional belly dancers perform periodically throughout the day in a show that is completely G-rated. ⊠ *Morocco* ▤ *AE, MC, V* ✛ *1:D4.*

$$–$$$
CHINESE

✕**Nine Dragons Restaurant.** Though the restaurant is a showcase for all regions of Chinese cooking, including Szechuan and Hunan, the majority of the menu is Cantonese, including the excellent sweet-and-sour pork and the Kung Pao chicken with peanuts and dried chili peppers. Other good choices are the Cantonese roast duckling. For a really memorable experience, try the three-course Five-Spiced Fish, light, sautéed whitefish fillets with a classic Chinese five-spice sauce, served with an appetizer or soup, like the shrimp summer rolls or the chicken consommé with dumplings, and a dessert (the coconut rice pudding is a good choice). The strawberry red-bean ice cream is a great finale to your meal. One of the best ways to enjoy a good cross-section of the cuisine is to order the Nine Dragons family style meal, including one soup, one entrée, and one dessert for $19 per person at lunch and $24 at dinner. The distinctive building has a curved, yellow-tile roof with ornate carvings inspired by the Forbidden City. ⊠*China* ▤*AE, MC, V* ✛*1:D4.*

$$–$$$
BRITISH

✕**Rose & Crown.** If you're an Anglophile and you love a beer so thick you could stand a spoon up in your mug, this is the place to soak up both the suds and the British street culture. "Wenches" serve up traditional English fare—fish-and-chips, shepherd's pie (available only at lunch), and the ever-popular bangers and mash (sausage over mashed potatoes). Potato and leek soup or smoked Scottish salmon on a potato cake make good appetizers. Vegetarians will even find a tasty vegetable curry with Italian bread. For dessert try the chocolate Scotch cake or the warm apple crumble with ice cream. If you're not driving soon after the meal, try the Imperial Ale sampler, which includes five 6-ounce glasses for $9.35. The terrace has a splendid view of IllumiNations. ⊠*United Kingdom* ▤*AE, MC, V* ✛*1:D4.*

$$$$
SCANDINAVIAN

✕**Royal Akershus Banquet Hall.** In recent years, this Norwegian restaurant has become the site of character buffets at all three meals, with an array of Disney princesses, including Ariel, Belle, Jasmine, Snow White, Princess Aurora from Sleeping Beauty, Mulan, Mary Poppins, and even an occasional cameo appearance by Cinderella. The Norwegian buffet at this restaurant is as extensive as you'll find on this side of the Atlantic. Appetizers usually include herring, prepared several ways, and cold seafood, including *gravlax* (cured salmon served with mustard sauce) or *fiskepudding* (a seafood mousse with herb dressing). For your main course, you might try some hot sausages, venison stew, or grilled Atlantic salmon. The à la carte desserts include raspberry tarts, bread pudding, and chocolate mousse with strawberry sauce. Breakfast prices average $28 for adults and $18 for kids 3–9; lunch is $31 for adults and $19 for kids, and dinners run $36 for adults and $20 for kids. Call 407/939–3463 for reservations. ⊠*Norway* ▤*AE, MC, V* ✛*1:D4.*

$$–$$$
MEXICAN

✕**San Angel Inn.** In the dark, grottolike main dining room, a deep purple, dimly lighted mural of a night scene in Central Mexico seems to envelop the diners. San Angel is a popular respite for the weary, especially when the humidity outside makes Central Florida feel like equatorial Africa. At dinner, guitar and marimba music fills the air. Start with the *sopa Azteca,* (a traditional tortilla soup with avocado, cheese, and pasilla pepper) and then try the authentic *filete motuleno* (grilled beef tenderloin over black beans and melted cheese, ranchero sauce, and poblano pepper strips) or the *pollo a las rojas* (grilled chicken with red peppers, onion strips, and cream sauce). For dessert, try the flan, served with a piña colada sauce or the rice pudding with rice and cinnamon. ⊠*Mexico* 🖃*AE, MC, V* ✛*1:D4.*

$$–$$$ ✕ **Tokyo Dining and Teppan Edo.** Formerly three restaurants in a complex
JAPANESE called Mitsukoshi (which is also the name of a giant Tokyo department store) have now evolved into two restaurants, **Teppan Edo**, a teppanyaki steak house were chefs do performance cooking at 20 grills, and **Tokyo Dining.** Menu standouts at Teppan Edo include the New York strip, the filet mignon, and the Tori chicken breast. Teppan Edo also has a small sushi selection, ranging from $5 to $8 per serving, and a kids' menu that avoids the typical mac and cheese, and instead offers Teppan-style chicken or shrimp with rice and veggies. Tokyo Dining is the part of the twin-restaurant operation that is more serene and specializes in sushi, serving a wider variety than its neighbor, with the addition of tempura dishes like shrimp, scallops, or veggies. You can also opt for a sushi-tempura combo, such as the Ginza gozen plate. Both restaurants have something great to watch: Teppan Edo has the performing chefs; Tokyo Dining has a great view of the Japan pavilion. ⊠*Japan* 🖃*AE, MC, V* ✛*1:D4.*

$$$–$$$$ ✕ **Tutto Italia.** After a generation as the culinary pillar of the Italy sec-
ITALIAN tion at Epcot, L'Originale Alfredo di Roma Ristorante disappeared in summer 2007 and was replaced by Tutto Italia, located in the same building, with the same formality—servers wear white shirts and black ties. Even though the typical diner is wearing shorts, a T-shirt, and flip-flops, they're still welcome at the starch-tablecloth-covered tables, where they can enjoy a four-course Italian meal, as pricey as it is tasty. For instance, the "family table," a four-course dinner with two entrées, costs $60 for adults (which is anyone 10 years or older) and $18.50 for children 9 and under; à la carte dinner entrées run from $24 to $36. Offerings include a decent tortelloni stuffed with veal and served with white truffle cream, and spaghetti and meat balls with a slant—these are made with veal and pomodoro sauce. Desserts include mocha tiramisu and the cannoli stuffed with chocolate, sweet ricotta, and candied orange. Expect a wait at peak lunch and dinner times; outdoor seating is also available. ⊠ *Italy* 🖀*407/939–3463* ♨*Reservations essential* 🖃*AE, MC, V* ✛*1:D4.*

DISNEY'S HOLLYWOOD STUDIOS

The Studios tends to offer more casual American cuisine than the other parks. In other words, it's cheeseburger city. However, there are some good, imaginative offerings, too. Where else but here can you watch '50s sitcoms nonstop while you devour veal-and-shiitake-mushroom meat loaf? Waits can be long. To make priority-seating reservations, call 407/939–3463 up to 180 days in advance, or stop in person at the restaurant or first thing in the morning at Hollywood Junction Restaurant Reservations. There are four ways to book dinner packages that include the Fantasmic! after-dark show: by phone, in person at a Disney hotel, at the park's Guest Services, and at Hollywood Junction.

$-$$

AMERICAN

✕ **50s Prime Time Café.** Who says you can't go home again? If you grew up in middle America in the 1950s, just step inside. While *I Love Lucy* and *The Donna Reed Show* play on a television screen, you can feast on meat loaf, pot roast, or fried chicken, all served on a Formica tabletop. At $15, the meat loaf is one of the best inexpensive dinners in any local theme park. Follow it up with angel food cake with whipped cream and fresh berries or an ice-cream soda—available in chocolate, strawberry, vanilla, even peanut butter and jelly. The place offers some fancier dishes, such as olive-oil poached salmon, which are good but out of character with the diner theme. If you're not feeling totally wholesome, go for Dad's Electric Lemonade (rum, vodka, blue curacao, sweet-and-sour mix, and Sprite), which is worth every bit of the $9.50 price tag. Just like Mother, the menu admonishes, "Don't put your elbows on the table!" ⊠*Echo Lake* ☎*407/939–3463* ▤*AE, MC, V* ✛*1:C5.*

¢–$

FAST FOOD

✕ **ABC Commissary.** This place has a refreshingly different fast-food menu than the rest, including fast-but-tasty treats, such as the tortilla wrap filled with tabbouleh, hummus, and marinated tomatoes. Indoor seating offers great respite from the heat in summer. The menu here is by no means exotic or even creative, but it offers the virtue of having some healthy eating choices in a fast-service environment. Chicken curry with rice makes a good alternative to a cheeseburger, and there's a no-sugar-added strawberry parfait. The place is not usually crowded. ⊠*Echo Lake* ▤*AE, MC, V* ✛*1:C5.*

$$–$$$

AMERICAN

✕ **Hollywood & Vine.** This restaurant is designed for those who like lots of food and lots of choices. You can have everything from frittatas to fried rice at the same meal. Even though the buffet ($25 for adults, $13 for children ages 3–9) is all-you-can-eat at a relatively low price, it does offer some upscale entrées like oven-roasted prime rib, sage-rubbed rotisserie turkey, or grilled sirloin in a red wine demi-glace, plus a fresh fish of the day. There are plenty of kids' favorites, such as mac and cheese, hot dogs, and fried chicken. Minnie, Goofy, Pluto, and Chip 'n' Dale put in appearances at breakfast and lunch character meals. There's a Hollywood theme to the place; characters and servers are just hoping to be discovered by some passing Hollywood agent. Priority seating reservations are a must. ⊠*Echo Lake* ☎*407/939–3463* ⌂*Reservations essential* ▤*AE, MC, V* ✛*1:C5.*

$$–$$$

AMERICAN

✕ **Hollywood Brown Derby.** At this reproduction of the famous 1940s Hollywood restaurant, the walls are lined with movie-star caricatures, just like in Tinseltown, and the staff wears black bow ties. The house specialty is the Cobb salad, which by legend was invented by Brown Derby founder Robert Cobb; the salad consists of lettuce enlivened by loads of tomato, bacon, turkey, blue cheese, chopped egg, and avocado, all tossed table-side. Other menu choices include grilled salmon on creamy polenta and Gorgonzola with sun-dried tomatoes and baby arugula; and pan-roasted duck breast and venison sausage with celery root puree. For dessert, try the Brown Derby grapefruit cake with layers of cream cheese icing. If you request the Fantasmic! dinner package, make a reservation for no later than two hours before the start of the show. ⊠*Hollywood Blvd.* ☎*407/939–3463* ▤*AE, MC, V* ✛*1:C5.*

$$–$$$ ✕**Mama Melrose's Ristorante Italiano.** To replace the energy you've no
Fodor'sChoice   doubt depleted by miles of theme-park walking, you can load up on
★   carbs at this casual Italian restaurant that looks like an old warehouse.
ITALIAN   Good main courses include Italian sausage served atop rigatoni pasta
with tomato basil sauce, and grilled salmon with sun-dried tomato
pesto, or the oven-roasted chicken Parmesan over spaghetti. Wood-fired
flatbreads are available as an entrée choice here (a great bargain at $12)
with toppings ranging from pepperoni to grilled chicken with sun-dried
tomato pesto. The sangria, available by the carafe, flows generously.
One of the best desserts is the warm chocolate truffle cake. Ask for the
Fantasmic! dinner package if you want priority seating for the show.
✉*Street of America* ☎*407/939–3463* ▭*AE, MC, V* ✛*1:C5.*

$$–$$$ ✕**Sci-Fi Dine-In Theater Restaurant.** If you don't mind zombies leering at
AMERICAN   you while you consume chef salads, barbecue pork sandwiches, char-
broiled sirloin, and Milky-Way-Out Milk Shakes, then head to this
enclosed faux drive-in, where you can sit in a fake candy-color '50s
convertible and watch trailers from classics like *Attack of the Fifty-
Foot Woman* and *Teenagers from Outer Space.* The menu includes
choices like slow-roasted barbecue ribs, a beef and blue cheese salad,
sautéed shrimp with bow-tie pasta, and a huge Reuben sandwich with
fries or melon slices. The hot fudge sundaes are delicious. ✉*Echo Lake*
☎*407/939–3463* ▭*AE, MC, V.* ✛*1:C5*

DISNEY'S ANIMAL KINGDOM

¢–$ ✕**Flame Tree Barbecue.** This counter-service eatery is one of the relatively
FAST FOOD   undiscovered gems of Disney's culinary offerings. There's nothing fancy
here but you can dig into St. Louis ribs, barbecued chicken, and pulled
pork and barbecued beef sandwiches with several sauce choices. For
something with a lower calorie count, try the smoked turkey served in a
multigrain bun. There is also a great barbecued chicken and crisp green
salad with vinaigrette dressing. The outdoor tables, set beneath intricately carved wood pavilions, make great spots for a picnic and they're
not usually crowded. ✉*Discovery Island* ▭*AE, MC, V* ✛*1:A4.*

$$–$$$ ✕**Rainforest Café.** You don't have to pay park admission to dine at the
AMERICAN   Rainforest Café, the only full-service eatery in the Animal Kingdom
area, with entrances both inside the park and at the gate. Since it resembles the one in Downtown Disney Marketplace, complete with the long
lines for lunch and dinner, go early or late. If you can, make reservations
by phone ahead of time. The most popular entrée is "mojo bones,"
slow-roasted pork ribs in a tangy barbecue sauce. Other good choices
include chicken-fried steak with country gravy, and shrimp *en brochette*
(broiled jumbo shrimp stuffed with crabmeat, jalapeños, four cheeses,
and wrapped in bacon). The coconut bread pudding with apricot filling and whipped cream is great. The best dessert choice is a toss-up
between Gorillas in the Mist (chocolate-topped banana cheesecake) and
the peanut butter pie, topped with whipped cream, chocolate sauce, and
peanuts. Breakfast, ranging from steak and eggs to excellent French
toast, is served beginning at 7:30 in the morning. ✉*Disney's Animal
Kingdom* ☎*407/938–9100 or 407/939–3463* ⊕*www.rainforestcafe.
com* ▭*AE, D, DC, MC, V* ✛*1:A5.*

$$–$$$
AMERICAN

✕ **Tusker House.** This restaurant offers all-buffet dining three meals a day, starting with a character breakfast (Donald's Safari Breakfast; $19 for adults, $11 for kids 3–9) and buffets with no character appearances for lunch ($20 for adults, $11 for kids) and dinner ($27 for adults, $13 for kids). Tusker's offers healthier fare like rotisserie chicken, curry chicken, prime rib, rotisserie pork loin, and a big garden salad served with focaccia bread on the side, along with the standard kids' fare like mac and cheese and chicken drumsticks served with mashed potatoes. Breakfast includes eggs, ham, biscuits and gravy, and lighter options like fruit cups and cereal. ⊠ *Harambe* ⊟ *AE, MC, V* ✛ *1:A4.*

$$–$$$
ASIAN

✕ **Yak & Yeti.** The location of this pan-Asian cuisine, sit-down eatery—the only full-service restaurant inside Disney's Animal Kingdom—certainly makes sense. It's just at the entrance to the Asia section, in a two-story, 250-seat building that won't necessarily make you think you're somewhere on the outskirts of Bangkok, but is pleasantly faux-Asian, with cracked plaster walls, wood carvings, and tile mosaic tabletops. Standout entrées include the maple tamarind chicken, with coconut-ginger rice and stir-fried shiitake mushrooms, and the tempura pork or chicken from the wok, both cooked with broccoli, carrots, and a honey sauce. Also tasty, if not authentically Asian, are the baby back ribs with a hoisin barbecue sauce and sweet chili slaw. The grown-ups will like the Yak Attack, a mango daiquiri made with rum, and the Bonsai Blast, made with vodka, banana liqueur, schnapps, and curacao. ⊠ *Disney's Animal Kingdon* ☎ *407/938–9100 or 407/939–3463* ⊟ *AE, D, DC, MC, V* ✛ *1:A4.*

DOWNTOWN DISNEY

Downtown Disney has three sections: the Marketplace, a small shopping-and-dining area; Pleasure Island, a complex that as of this writing was closing its nightclubs, though maintaining its dining venues; and, close by, Disney's West Side, a group of hipper-than-hip entertainment, dining, and shopping spots. The edge of Disney property is about a block away.

$$$–$$$$
CARIBBEAN

✕ **Bongos Cuban Café.** Singer Gloria Estefan's Cuban eatery is inside a two-story building shaped like a pineapple. Hot-pressed Cuban sandwiches, black-bean soup, deep-fried plantain chips, and beans and rice are mainstays on the menu for the lunch crowd. For lunch or dinner you can chow down on *ropa vieja* (which literally means "old clothes," but is in fact a hugely popular dish of shredded beef in a tomato sauce with mild peppers, served on a bed of rice with fried plantains). Another popular Cuban mainstay is *chuletas de puerco*, marinated pork chops, grilled and served with grilled onions, rice, and plantains. Other worthwhile offerings include *masitas de puerco* (pork chunks served with grilled onions) and *vaca frita*, marinated flank steak served with rice and yucca. There's live Latin music on Friday and Saturday, and a great walk-up bar from which you can get Cuban coffee, Miami-style. ⊠ *West Side* ☎ *407/828–0999* ⊕ *www.bongoscubancafe.com* ⌂ *Reservations not accepted* ⊟ *AE, D, DC, MC, V* ✛ *1:F4.*

$$$–$$$$ ✕**Fulton's Crab House.** Set in a faux riverboat docked in a lagoon between
SEAFOOD Pleasure Island and the Marketplace, this fish house offers fine, if expen-
sive, dining. The signature seafood is flown in daily. Dungeness crab
from the Pacific coast, Alaskan king crab, Florida stone crab: it's all
fresh. Start with the crab and lobster bisque, then try one of the many
combination entrées like the gulf shrimp and crab cake platter. If you
have no budget constraints, go for Louis Fulton's Ultimate Crab and
Lobster Experience for two, which includes generous servings of Alas-
kan king crab, snow crab, and golden crab, plus a 1¼-pound Maine
lobster, for $42 a person. Also excellent and in that upper echelon price
range is the lobster Narragansett, which includes a whole 1¼-pound
Maine lobster, stuffed with shrimp and scallops and served with red
skin potatoes. Or if you really want to shell out the bucks, try the king
crab claws and lobster dinner. Lunch is considerably less expensive than
dinner. ⊠ *Marketplace* ☎ *407/934–2628* ☱ *AE, MC, V* ✛*1:F4.*

$$–$$$ ✕**House of Blues.** You are unlikely to like this place unless you enjoy listen-
AMERICAN ing to high-decibel music during your meal. But if you do, this is a great
place to chow down from an eclectic menu that offers everything from
baby back ribs, to shrimp and scallop diablo, to a tasty and healthy Thai
salad with chicken skewers and Thai noodles. The smoked pulled pork
sandwich with Jim Beam barbecue sauce is a great menu mainstay item,
as is the brick oven pizza. A worthy dessert is the white chocolate banana
bread pudding. The Gospel Sunday Brunch ($32 for adults, $18 for chil-
dren) offers a Southern cooking buffet and live gospel music. ⊠ *West
Side* ☎ *407/934–2583* ⊕ *www.houseofblues.com* ⚲ *Reservations avail-
able only for Sunday brunch* ☱ *AE, D, DC, MC, V* ✛*1:F4.*

$$–$$$ ✕**Olivia's Café.** This is like a meal at Grandma's—provided she lives
AMERICAN south of the Mason-Dixon line. The menu ranges from barbecued grou-
per to grilled pork chops with sweet mashed potatoes. The best dessert
choice is also a bargain: apple pie with vanilla bean ice cream. The
indoor palms and rough wood walls resemble those of a venerable Key
West abode, but other than that the atmosphere is not that special. The
outdoor seating, which overlooks a waterway, is a nice place to dine
any time the midsummer's heat is not bearing down. ⊠ *Old Key West
Resort* ☎ *407/939–3463* ☱ *AE, D, DC, MC, V* ✛*1:E3.*

$$–$$$ ✕**Planet Hollywood.** This place used to have one of the longest lines
AMERICAN in Pleasure Island, as patrons flocked to see the movie memorabilia
assembled by celebrity owners like Schwarzenegger, Stallone, and Willis.
The wait has been abated by a system that allows you to sign in, take a
number, and get an assigned time window to return. The restaurant–bar
covers 20,000 square feet if you count the indoor waterfall. The most
popular menu item here is still the burger (the barbecue-bacon-cheddar
version is the best). Also notable are the grilled specialties, including
the New York strip steak, salmon, ribs, fajitas and Philly steak sand-
wiches. You can also indulge in unusual pastas and salads. Also wor-
thy are the smoothies as well as and a wide variety of frozen alcoholic
drinks. ⊠ *West Side, at entrance to Pleasure Island* ☎ *407/827–7827*
⊕ *www.planethollywood.com* ⚲ *Reservations not accepted* ☱ *AE, D,
DC, MC, V* ✛*1:F4.*

$$$–$$$$ ✕**Portobello.** The northern Italian cuisine here is uniformly good. The
ITALIAN chicken meatballs with orrechiette pasta, oven dried tomatoes, spinach,

and chicken broth is an excellent choice, and at least gives you the feeling that you are cutting calories. Other fine options include linguine *alla vongole*, which includes manila clams, lemon, white wine, and garlic, and the farfalle pasta, with wood-roasted chicken, snow peas, asparagus, and Parmesan cream sauce. There's always a fresh-catch special, as well as tasty wood-oven pizza. If you are ready to unload your wallet, go for the excellent filet mignon with roasted mushrooms. A true bargain at this place is the minestrone (served with lots of fresh bread), which is still $5 a bowl even after years of popularity. Reservations are accepted 30 days in advance, and are difficult to get with shorter notice. ✉ *Pleasure Island* ☎ *407/934–8888* ▤ *AE, MC, V* ✛ *1:F4.*

$$–$$$
AMERICAN

✕ **Rainforest Café.** People start queuing up a half hour before the 10:30 AM opening of this 30,000-square-foot jungle fantasy in Downtown Disney's Marketplace, drawn as much by the gimmicks (manmade rainstorms, volcano eruptions) as the menu. But the food, a mix of American fare with imaginative names, is nevertheless worthwhile. Top choices include the Paradise Pot Roast, served with roasted veggies and mashed potatoes; and "mojo bones," tender ribs with barbecue sauce. For dessert, try "gorillas in the mist," a banana cheesecake topped with chocolate and whipped cream. ✉ *Marketplace* ☎ *407/827–8500 or 407/939–3463* ⊕ *www.rainforestcafe.com* ▤ *AE, D, DC, MC, V.*

$$$–$$$$
IRISH

✕ **Raglan Road Irish Pub.** Some would argue that the phrase "authentic Irish pub at Disney's Pleasure Island" is oxymoronic, particularly when that pub seats 600 people. But if Irish grub's your thing, Raglan's is on target: the shepherd's pie is prepared with the traditional beef, lamb, and mashed potatoes and jazzed up with house spices. And you don't have to settle for plain fish-and-chips here (though you can for $17); there's also panfried lemon sole and chips. You can also get lots of hearty soups and plenty of Irish beer and whiskey. Three massive and ornate bars, all imported from Ireland and all more than a century old, help anchor the pub. The entertainment (which runs from 9 AM until 2 AM Monday–Saturday) alone makes this place worth the visit. A good, four-person Irish house band, Tuskar Rock, performs nightly as does Danielle Fitzpatrick, herself an Irish import, who performs lively folk dances on stage each evening. ✉ *Pleasure Island, Downtown Disney* ☎ *407/938–0300* ▤ *AE, D, MC, V* ✛ *1:F4.*

$$$–$$$$
AMERICAN

✕ **Wolfgang Puck.** There are lots of choices here, from wood-oven pizza at the informal Puck Express to five-course meals in the upstairs formal dining room, where there's also a sushi bar and an informal café; the café is quite literally a happy medium and may be the best bet for families hoping for a bit of elegance without the pressure of a formal dinner. At Express try the barbecue chicken, or spinach and mushroom pizza, or the real standout, Wolfgang's smoked salmon pizza. The dining room always offers inspired pastas with sublime sauces like the shrimp scampi risotto with garlic, white wine, and lemon. Always worth coming back for is the veal Wiener schnitzel with warm potato salad, which has been on the menu for years because of its popularity. Special five-course prix-fixe dinners ($110 with wine, $75 without) require 24-hour notice. ✉ *West Side* ☎ *407/938–9653* ⊕ *www.wolfgangpuck.com* ▤ *AE, MC, V* ✛ *1:F4.*

DISNEY'S BOARDWALK

$$–$$$ ✕ **Big River Grille & Brewing Works.** Strange but good brews, like Pale
AMERICAN   Rocket Red Ale, Southern Flyer Light Lager, and Gadzooks Pilsner,
abound here. You can dine inside among the giant copper brewing
tanks, or sip your suds outside on the lake-view patio. The menu
emphasizes meat, with pork ribs slow-cooked in red barbecue sauce,
barbecue pork, and a house-special flame-grilled meat loaf made with
ground beef and Italian sausage. The cheddar cheese–mashed potatoes
are a perfect accompaniment. There's also a worthwhile grilled Atlantic
salmon fillet with dill butter and a very credible meat loaf made with
ground beef and pork sausage and finished off on a grill. ⊠ *Disney's
BoardWalk* ☎ *407/560–0253* ▤ *AE, MC, V* ✥ *1:C4.*

$–$$ ✕ **ESPN Club.** Not only can you watch sports on a big-screen TV here,
AMERICAN   but you can also periodically see ESPN programs being taped in the
club itself and be part of the audience of sports radio talk shows. Food
ranges from an outstanding half-pound burger, made with Angus chuck,
to an excellent Reuben with plenty of corned beef, sauerkraut, and
cheese. If you want an appetizer, try the Macho Nachos, crispy corn
tortilla chips piled high with ground beef, shredded cheddar cheese, sour
cream, spicy salsa, and sliced jalapeños. The hot apple pie is a satisfying
dessert. This place is open quite late by Disney standards—until 2 AM
on Friday and Saturday, but beware, the place can be pretty loud during any broadcast sports event, especially football games. ⊠ *Disney's
BoardWalk* ☎ *407/939–5100* ▤ *AE, MC, V* ✥ *1:C4.*

$$–$$$ ✕ **Flying Fish.** One of Disney's better restaurants, Flying Fish, is elegantly
SEAFOOD   decorated with murals along the upper portion of the walls, and a chic-
looking bar adjoining the dining area. This is a place where you put on
your "resort casual" duds and go to "dine," as opposed to putting on
your flip-flops and shorts to go "chow down." Flying Fish's best dishes
include potato-wrapped red snapper, which is so popular it has been
on the menu for several years, and oak-grilled Bay of Fundy salmon. A
tasty and creative light offering is the Maine lobster and a sandwich.
Save room for the spiced pumpkin cheesecake or the warm chocolate
peanut butter bread pudding. ⊠ *Disney's BoardWalk* ☎ *407/939–2359*
▤ *AE, MC, V* ✥ *1:C4.*

$$–$$$ ✕ **Spoodles.** The international tapas-style menu draws on the best foods
MEDITERRANEAN   of the Mediterranean—from Italy to Greece to Lebanon with dishes
ranging from grilled steak kebabs with multigrain pilaf and *harissa*
(a piquant red pepper paste that is a staple in North African cooking) to Italian lemon-garlic shrimp linguine. Another good main dish
is Israeli-inspired: the pan-roasted red snapper fillet with couscous,
chorizo, wilted greens, and spicy tomato broth. Oak-fired flatbreads
with toppings such as roasted peppers make stellar appetizers. For dessert, try the mascarpone cheesecake or the house-made Italian gelato.
There are also great breakfast offerings, like an Italian frittata (omelet)
for $10, and flatbreads with scrambled eggs, roasted red peppers, spin-
ach and other Mediterranean-style ingredients. ⊠ *Disney's BoardWalk*
☎ *407/939–3463* ▤ *AE, MC, V* ✥ *1:C4.*

WDW RESORTS

$$$–$$$$
Fodor'sChoice
★
AMERICAN

✕ **Artist Point.** If you're not a guest at the Wilderness Lodge, a meal here is worth it just to see the giant totem poles and huge rock fireplace in the lobby. The specialty is cedar-plank salmon and roasted potatoes with smoked pork belly and truffle butter (worth its $34 price tag). Another good option: braised buffalo short ribs with parsnip potato gratin, caramelized leeks, and red wine jus. For dessert, do not fail to order the seasonal berry cobbler with house-made blackberry ice cream. There's a good northwestern U.S. wine list, and wine pairings for the meal cost $28 per person. ⊠ *Wilderness Lodge* ☎ *407/939–3463* ⌕ *Reservations essential* ⊟ *AE, MC, V* ✛ *1:C1.*

$$$
Fodor'sChoice
★
AFRICAN

✕ **Boma.** Boma takes Western-style ingredients and prepares them with an African twist. The dozen or so walk-up serving stations have entrées such as spit-roasted pork, spiced roast chicken, pepper steak, and banana leaf–wrapped sea bass or salmon. Don't pass up the soups, as the hearty chicken corn porridge is excellent. The zebra bones dessert is chocolate mousse covered with white chocolate and striped with dark chocolate. Breakfast includes conventional choices like omelets and pap, a porridge made with white corn meal. All meals are prix fixe (breakfasts are $17 for adults and $10 for kids 3–9; dinner is $27 for adults, $13 for children ages 3–9). The South African wine list is outstanding. Priority seating reservations are essential if you're not a guest at the hotel. ⊠ *Disney's Animal Kingdom Lodge* ☎ *407/939–3463* ⌕ *Reservations essential* ⊟ *AE, D, DC, MC, V* ◔ *No lunch* ✛ *1:A5.*

$$–$$$
AMERICAN

✕ **California Grill.** The view of the surrounding Disney parks from this rooftop restaurant is as stunning as the food, especially at night, when you can watch the nightly Magic Kingdom fireworks from the patio. The menu changes periodically, but choices might include pan-roasted grouper with olive-crushed potatoes and a red wine sauce, oak-fired beef fillet with three-cheese potato gratin and tamarind barbecue sauce, or Japanese pumpkin ravioli with spinach and Parmesan. Good dessert choices might include a warm chocolate cake with raspberry ice cream and raspberry sauce or a dessert that is always on the menu, butterscotch crème brûlée with banana cakes and caramelized bananas. ⊠ *Contemporary Resort* ☎ *407/939–3463* ⌕ *Reservations essential* ⊟ *AE, MC, V* ✛ *1:B1.*

$$$
AMERICAN

✕ **Chef Mickey's.** This is the holy shrine for character meals, with Mickey, Minnie, and Goofy always around for breakfast and dinner, so it's not a quiet spot to read the *New York Times*. Folks come here for entertainment and comfort food. The dinner buffet ($30 adults, $15 for kids 3–9) includes prime rib, baked ham, and changing specials like beef tips with mushrooms or baked cod with tarragon butter. The Parmesan mashed potatoes have been a popular menu item for years, but you can also get more unusual offerings like broccoli with black olives and feta. The all-you-can-eat dessert bar has sundaes and chocolate cake. The breakfast buffet ($23 for adults and $13 for kids) also includes character appearances and includes omelets cooked to order, mountains of pancakes, and even a breakfast pizza. ⊠ *Contemporary Resort* ☎ *407/939–3463* ⊟ *AE, MC, V* ✛ *1:B1.*

$$$–$$$$ ✕ **Citricos.** Although the name implies that you might be eating lots of
ECLECTIC local citrus-flavor specialties, you won't find them here, aside from
drinks like a "Citropolitan" martini, infused with lemon-and-lime
liqueur, and a tropical fruit crème brûlée for dessert. Standout entrées
include grilled swordfish Provençal with orzo pasta, grape tomatoes,
and clams, and roasted breast of chicken with prosciutto and pasta.
The wine list, one of Disney's most extensive, includes vintages from
around the world. ⊠ *Grand Floridian* ☎ *407/939–3463 Reservations
essential* ⊟ *AE, MC, V* ✛ *1:A1.*

$$$–$$$$ ✕ **Garden Grove.** Formerly Gulliver's at Garden Grove, this place has
AMERICAN dropped the Gulliver fantasy and turned into what one might call
"The Rotating Buffet Kingdom." Sunday, Tuesday, and Thursday, it's
Mediterranean Night ($29 for adults, $13 for kids), with all the great
Italian pasta, Greek moussaka, and Israeli couscous you care to eat.
On Monday and Friday it's Fisherman's Wharf Night ($32 for adults,
$13 for kids), with all the claim chowder, peel-and-eat shrimp, orzo,
and crab, seafood risotto, and other treats from the sea you can con-
sume. And on Wednesday and Saturday, it's Southern Barbecue Night
($29 for adults, $13 for kids), with everything caloric from barbecued
beef brisket to fried chicken to Texas-style chili. ⊠ *Walt Disney World
Swan* ☎ *407/934–3000* ⊜ *Reservations essential* ⊟ *AE, D, DC, MC, V*
☾ *No lunch* ✛ *1:C4.*

$$$–$$$$ ✕ **Jiko.** The name of this restaurant means "the cooking place" in Swa-
Fodor's Choice hili, and it is certainly that. The dining area surrounds two big, wood-
★ burning ovens and grill area where you can watch cooks in North
AFRICAN African–style caps cooking up your meal. Simply smelling the aroma
generated by the oven tells you this is going to be a great dining experi-
ence. The menu here is more African-inspired than purely African, but
does include authentic entrées like Swahili curry shrimp from an East
African recipe and short ribs with a Kenyan coffee barbecue sauce. The
menu changes periodically but typically includes entrées, such as roasted
chicken with mashed potatoes, and braised lamb shank with toasted
couscous. After dinner, try the Tanzanian cheesecake with lavender ice
cream. The restaurant offers more than 65 wines by the glass, including
a large selection of African vintages. And if you want to have a private
party (for up to 40 people), there's a wine room decorated with Afri-
can sculptures. ⊠ *Disney's Animal Kingdom Lodge* ☎ *407/939–3463*
⊜ *Reservations essential* ⊟ *AE, D, MC, V* ☾ *No lunch* ✛ *1:A5.*

$$–$$$ ✕ **Kimonos Sushi Bar.** Knife-wielding sushi chefs prepare world-class sushi
JAPANESE and sashimi but also excellent beef teriyaki and other Japanese treats
good for a full dinner or just a snack. One of the best bets here is the
sushi-sashimi combination, which gives you a generous amount of both
for the price. Popular rolls include the California roll (crab, avocado,
and cucumber), Mexican roll (shrimp tempura), and the bagel roll
(smoked salmon, cream cheese, and scallion). At $5 to $10 per sushi
roll, your tab can add up fast, but a bargain strategy involves the chef's
choice combinations, in which you get 8 to 10 pieces for $20 to $24.
⊠ *Walt Disney World Swan* ☎ *407/934–3000* ⊟ *AE, D, DC, MC, V*
☾ *No lunch* ✛ *1:C4.*

$$–$$$
ECLECTIC

✕ **Kona Cafe.** Desserts get a lot of emphasis at this eclectic restaurant, with choices like caramel-banana crème brûlée and white chocolate cheesecake. Some notable entrées include breaded shrimp and pan-seared scallops with sticky rice and the pomegranate barbecued pork chop. The best lunch option is the Polynesian plate, with sticky rice and your choice of chicken in peanut sauce or Teriyaki steak with grilled pineapple salsa. If you want a cocktail, the Lapu Lapu, made with rum, orange juice, and chunks of pineapple, makes for soothing liquid solace at the end of a long day on your feet. As the name of the place hints, coffee is a specialty, too. ⊠ *Polynesian Resort* ☎ *407/939–3463* ⊟ *AE, MC, V* ⊹ *1:B2.*

$$$–$$$$
SEAFOOD

✕ **Narcoossee's.** The dining room, with Victorian-style columns, high ceilings and hard-wood floors, makes a great place not only to enjoy great steaks and seafood, but to gaze out the windows at the nightly fireworks shows over the Seven Seas Lagoon. (And while the restaurant has its own elegant style, they expect your wardrobe to have that quality as well—no shorts or flip-flops.) Among the best menu choices, grilled salmon and grilled filet mignon are popular entrées, as is the traditional surf-and-turf centerpiece: Maine lobster and a tender filet mignon. Other good choices include crab-crusted flounder with lemon butter and roasted free-range chicken breast with mashed potatoes. For dessert, don't miss the strawberry cheesecake with a cherry sauce and the key lime crème brûlée. The name of the place, incidentally, was not a word coined by Disney Imagineers, it's the name of a river and a small Central Florida town, both which predate Disney. ⊠ *Grand Floridian Resort* ☎ *407/939–3463* ⊟ *AE, MC, V* ⊹ *1:A1.*

$$$
HAWAIIAN

✕ **'Ohana.** The only option here is an all-you-can-eat prix-fixe meal ($26 for adults, $12 for kids) of shrimp, or grilled pork, beef, or turkey sliced directly onto your plate from mammoth skewers. The chef performs in front of an 18-foot fire pit, grilling the meats as flames shoot up to sear in the flavors and entertain the diners. ⊠ *Polynesian Resort* ☎ *407/939–3463* ⊟ *AE, MC, V* ⊹ *1:A1.*

¢–$
AMERICAN

✕ **Picabu Buffeteria.** This buffet in the Walt Disney World Dolphin would be forgettable were it not for its hours and reasonable prices—Picabu serves up relatively inexpensive hot food around the clock. You can find lots of kids' favorites here, like pizza, hot dogs, hamburgers, and grilled-chicken sandwiches, plus a supply of nonfood necessities like laundry detergent and disposable diapers. A buffet breakfast ($10 for adults, $5 for kids) is served from 6 to 11:30 AM. ⊠ *Walt Disney World Dolphin* ☎ *407/934–4000* ⊟ *AE, MC, V* ⊹ *1:C4.*

$$$–$$$$
STEAK

✕ **Shula's Steak House.** The hardwood floors, dark-wood paneling, and pictures of former Miami Dolphins coach Don Shula make this restaurant resemble an annex of the NFL Hall of Fame. Among the best selections are the porterhouse and prime rib. Finish the 48-ounce porterhouse and you get a football with your picture on it, but it's not easy to eat three pounds of red meat at one sitting unless you're a polar bear. The least expensive steak is still hefty at 16 ounces and $38. If you're not a carnivore, go for the Norwegian salmon, the Florida snapper, or the huge (up to 4 pounds) Maine lobster (market price). For dessert, the molten lava chocolate cake is a worthy choice. ⊠ *Walt Disney World Dolphin* ☎ *407/934–1362* ⊟ *AE, D, DC, MC, V* ⊗ *No lunch* ⊹ *1:C4.*

$$–$$$ ✕**Shutters at Old Port Royale.** This bright and breezy restaurant is a good
AMERICAN   place to put your feet up after a long day and sample cuisine inspired
by the flavors of the Caribbean, and it is relatively inexpensive for Disney hotel restaurants. Dishes with a Caribbean flair include plantain-
crusted Red snapper with tropical black bean salsa and grilled skirt
steak with mashed sweet potatoes. There's also a host of classic American offerings, such as the New York strip steak, and tasty chocolate
cake. Wash it all down with a tangerine margarita or a Red Stripe beer
from Jamaica. ⊠ *Caribbean Beach Resort* ☎ 407/939–3463 ⊟ *AE, D,
DC, MC, V* ✛ *1:D4.*

$$$–$$$$ ✕**Todd English's bluezoo.** Celebrity chef Todd English opened this cutting-
AMERICAN   edge seafood eatery in late 2003. The sleek, modern interior resembles
an underwater dining hall, with blue walls and carpeting, aluminum
fish suspended from the ceiling, and bubblelike lighting fixtures. The
menu is creative and pricey, with entrées like roasted sea bass with white
bean puree and lemon caper emulsion, or spiced swordfish with faro
risotto. If you don't care for fish, alternatives include salted, braised
pork loin with charred sweet corn, flame-grilled beef fillet with horse-
radish fingerling potatoes, and a half chicken cooked in a cast iron
skillet. The chocolate caramel cake, with mango sauce and caramel
sorbet, is worthy of its $13 price tag. ⊠ *Walt Disney World Dolphin*
☎ 407/934–1111 ⊟ *AE, D, DC, MC, V* ⊘ *No lunch* ✛ *1:C4.*

$$$$ ✕**Victoria & Albert's.** At this Disney fantasy, you are served by "Vic-
Fodor'sChoice   toria" and "Albert," who recite the menu in tandem. There's also a
★   sommelier to explain the wine pairings. Everyone, of course, is dressed
CONTINENTAL   in period Victorian costumes. This is one of the plushest fine-dining
experiences in Florida: a regal meal in a lavish, Victorian-style room.
Perhaps because of this regal atmosphere, WDW made a policy change
and in January 2008 announced it no longer allows children under 10
in the restaurant. The six-course, prix-fixe menu ($125; wine is an addi-
tional $60) changes daily, but it's not as if they are suddenly going to
switch from $380-an-ounce caviar (which they do) to hot dogs and mac
and cheese (which they most certainly don't). Appetizer choices might
include chorizo crusted duck, or walnut oil-seared duck with hearts
of palm and a cheese fondue; entrées may be Florida Black Grouper
with artichokes, fennel, leeks, and *Jamón Ibérico* (Spanish ham), or
Kurobuta pork tenderloin and belly with beets and sherry bacon vin-
aigrette. The restaurant also features a vegetarian menu with exotics
such as rutabaga napoleon with melted leeks and ramps. Every female
diner gets a long-stem rose. For most of the year, there are two seatings,
at 5:45 and 9 PM. In July and August, however, there's generally just
one seating—at 6:30 PM. Make your reservations at least 90 and up to
180 days in advance. Disney considers this the biggest of the "big deal"
restaurants on the property, and most long-time Disney World fans do,
too. ⊠ *Grand Floridian* ☎ 407/939–3463 ⌖ *Reservations essential,
jacket required* ⊟ *AE, MC, V* ⊘ *No lunch* ✛ *1:A1.*

$$–$$$ ✕**Whispering Canyon Cafe.** No whispering goes on here. The servers,
AMERICAN   dressed as cowboys and cowgirls, deliver corny jokes and other talk
designed to keep things jovial at this family-style restaurant, where huge
stacks of pancakes and big servings of spare ribs are the orders of the

day. The all-you-can-eat breakfast platter puts eggs, sausage, biscuits, and tasty waffles in front of you for $12. For dinner, the $25 all-you-can-eat skillet with pork ribs and roasted chicken is the best deal for big eaters. It includes pork ribs, pulled pork, roast chicken, beef stew, and sides like roasted red potatoes and corn on the cob. Kids love the warm chocolate s'more cake with graham cracker meringue cookie for dessert. ⊠ *Wilderness Lodge* ☎407/939–3463 ☐*AE, MC, V* ✛*1:C1.*

$$$–$$$$ ✗**Yachtsman Steak House.** Aged beef, the attraction at this steak house
STEAK in the ultrapolished Yacht and Beach Club, can be seen mellowing in the glassed-in butcher shop near the entryway. They are proud of their beef here, and the prices seem to prove it. The slow-roasted prime rib is great, especially if you're good with $39 for a 14-ounce serving. The pan-seared sea bass with spinach ravoli makes a great option for those who want to eschew red meat. The 12-ounce New York Strip with potato gratin is quite tasty but at $42 it's not soft on your wallet. For dessert, try the white chocolate macadamia nut pie or the dessert sampler for two, a bargain at $11. ⊠ *Yacht and Beach Club* ☎407/939–3463 ☐*AE, MC, V* ☽*No lunch* ✛*1:C4.*

LAKE BUENA VISTA

The community of Lake Buena Vista stretches north of Downtown Disney and southeast to the other side of I–4, off Exit 68. This is where most off-site visitors to Disney World stay, and there are some good mealtime options.

$–$$ ✗**Chevy's.** True, the ersatz cantina motif here looks like that of every
MEXICAN other Mexican place in every suburb you've ever seen. But the food is a shocker: it's quite good. Try the hot tamales, or the shrimp-and-crab enchiladas topped with pesto-cream sauce. The menu, geared to appeal to a gringo audience, includes some very non-Mexican offerings like barbecued chicken wings and a big chicken Caesar salad, but the mainstays on the menu include very credible burritos, soft tacos, chicken flautas (with roasted red peppers), and a massive chimachanga grande. A specialty here is the selection of quesadillas—a traditional dish with melted cheese between two tortillas—but in this case the stuffing is pretty nontraditional, including chicken in barbecue sauce. For dessert, look for "deep-fried" ice cream topped with cinnamon-dusted tortilla strips. ⊠*12547 Rte. 535, Lake Buena Vista* ☎407/827–1052 ⊕*www.chevys.com* ☐*AE, MC, V* ✛*1:G3.*

$$$$ ✗**La Coquina.** This restaurant, just outside Disney property, bills itself as
FRENCH French with an Asian influence, and if you sample the buffalo tenderloin or the red pepper–marinated duck, you'll approve of its methods. Come for Sunday brunch, when the generous selection of goodies makes the price ($64 adults, $32 kids) almost seem like a bargain. In an unusual touch, during brunch your waiter takes you into the kitchen, where you pick out what you want and watch the chef cook it to order. For a closer look at the chef in action, ask the manager about sitting at the special chef's table in the kitchen. ⊠*Hyatt Regency Grand Cypress, 1 Grand Cypress Blvd.* ☎407/239–1234 ⊕*www.hyattgrandcypress.com* ☐*AE, D, DC, MC, V* ✛*1:F3.*

$$$–$$$$ ✕**LakeView Restaurant.** When the former Grosvenor Resort spent $25
ECLECTIC million to reinvent itself as the Regal Sun Resort, one of its smart moves
was *not* to eliminate or radically change its popular main dining room,
now called LakeView because of its great view of the lake for which the
town is named. This is not so much an epicurean haven as an eclectic
eatery, offering everything from a big breakfast buffet to the ultimate
carnivore's dream: a nightly prime rib buffet ($22 per person). If you
elect to order from the menu, standouts include the Cajun shrimp wrap
at lunch and the pork chops with a piquant pineapple ginger jerk mari-
nade at dinner. A Disney character breakfast with Pluto and Goofy is
offered from 8:30 to 10:30 AM on Tuesday, Thursday, and Saturday, at
$22 for adults and $11 for kids 4–9. ⊠ *1850 Hotel Plaza Blvd., Lake
Buena Vista* ⊕*www.regalsunresort.com* ☎*407/828–4444* ⌖*Reserva-
tions recommended* ▤*AE, D, DC, MC* ⊹*1:F4.*

$$$–$$$$ ✕**Landry's Seafood House.** Set in a fake warehouse building—popular
SEAFOOD architecture in Central Florida—this branch of a nationwide chain deliv-
ers seafood at reasonable prices. The food is first-rate, especially Cajun
dishes like the fresh-caught fish Pontchartrain, a broiled fish with slightly
spicy seasoning and a creamy white-wine sauce that's topped with a
lump of crabmeat. Because this chain traces its roots to New Orleans, it
offers some great Louisiana-style cooking, such as a hearty gumbo with
plenty of shrimp, crab, and oysters, along with good po'boy sandwiches
packed with your choice of shrimp, oysters, or white fish. Combination
platters abound, including a $22 one that includes white fish, stuffed
crab, fried oysters, and stuffed shrimp. ⊠*8800 Vineland Ave., Rte.
535, Lake Buena Vista* ☎*407/827–6466* ⊕*www.landrysseafood.com*
▤*AE, D, DC, MC, V* ⊹*1:G3.*

UNIVERSAL ORLANDO AREA

With more than a dozen restaurants and the world's largest Hard Rock
Cafe, Universal Orlando's CityWalk is a culinary force. At Islands of
Adventure, each of the six lands has between two and six eateries—not
all of them strictly burgers-and-fries affairs. But the food is generally
of a higher quality and greater variety at the CityWalk eateries than
those inside the two parks. Universal has done a good job of provid-
ing information and access to these eateries, with a special **reservation
and information line** (☎*407/224–9255* ⊕*www.universalorlando.com*)
and a Web site that includes menus for many of the restaurants. To get
to Universal, take I–4 Exit 75A from eastbound lanes, Exit 74B when
you're westbound.

UNIVERSAL MEAL DEAL TICKETS

Universal Studios now offers an all-you-can-eat, all-day-long deal for
the walk-up eateries inside the two theme parks (but not the restaurants
in CityWalk). All-you-can-eat fees are $25 a day for adults (those 10
and older), $13 daily for kids 9 and under; likewise, all-you-can-drink
soft drinks are $9 daily for all. The meal deal costs $21 for adults and
$11 for kids if you only want to visit one theme park. And, if you

buy the unlimited meal deal tickets, you can also purchase a $6 ticket (same fee for adults and children) good for one entrée at four CityWalk restaurants on the same deal that your meal deal ticket is valid; participating restaurants are Bob Marley's, Pat O'Brien's, Latin Quarter, and Pastamore. Tickets can be purchased at the theme-park ticket office, or at ⊕ *www.universalorlando.com.*

CHARACTER MEALS

Universal Studios offers meals with its characters, specifically Scooby-Doo, Spider-Man, Thing One and Thing Two, Woody Woodpecker, and Curious George, although the line-up is not nearly as extensive as what is offered at Disney World. It's important to check by phone at the numbers listed below before making your plans, because the number of days per week that the character meals are offered expands and contracts with the seasons.

BREAKFAST
On Thursday through Sunday, you can catch the Dr. Seuss characters, including the Cat in the Hat, for breakfast at the **Confisco Grille** (☎407/363–8000), at the entrance to Islands of Adventure, with seatings from 9 to 10:15 AM. The meal costs $17 for adults (those 10 and older), $14 for children 3–9, and free for kids under 3.

DINNER
Character dinners at Universal take place at the three on-property hotels, and are by reservation only. Characters appearing at these restaurants vary, so call the restaurant in advance to see which of the following will be appearing: Shrek, Shaggy, Scooby-Doo, Woody Woodpecker, or Curious George. Reservations can be made at the **character meal reservation line** (☎407/224–4012).

Character dinners at **Islands Dining Room** (☎407/503–3430), in the Royal Pacific Resort, take place Monday, Tuesday, and Saturday from 6:30 to 9:30 PM. Children age 12 and under eat from the buffet ($9.25), while adults order from a menu ($15–$25), except on Saturday, when the buffet is open to everyone and costs $24.50 for adults. Dinners at **Trattoria del Porto** (☎407/503–1430), in the Portofino Bay Hotel, take place on Friday and Saturday from 6:30 PM and cost $18.50 for adults, $10 for children 12 and under. **The Kitchen** (☎407/503–2430) at the Hard Rock Hotel hosts character dinners Saturday from 6 to 9 PM. Menu entrées range from $8 to $34. Character breakfasts at Universal hotels are handled by the **Loews Orlando reservations line** (☎407/503–3463).

UNIVERSAL STUDIOS

$–$$ ✕**Finnegan's Bar & Grill.** In an Irish pub that would look just right in
IRISH   downtown New York during the Ellis Island era, Finnegan's offers classic Irish comfort food like shepherd's pie, Scotch eggs (eggs wrapped in sausage and bread crumbs and fried), corn beef and cabbage, bangers and mash (sausage and mashed potatoes), and fish-and-chips, plus Guinness, Harp, and Bass on tap. If shepherd's pie isn't your thing, there are also steaks, burgers, and a darn good chicken salad. Irish

folk music, sometimes live, completes the theme. ⊠*Production Central* ☎*407/363–8757* ▭*AE, D, MC, V* ✢*2:E2.*

$$–$$$ ✕**Lombard's Landing.** Fresh grilled or fried fish, fried shrimp, and steamed
SEAFOOD clams and mussels are the specialty at this restaurant designed to resemble a Fisherman's Wharf warehouse from 19th-century San Francisco. You can also get a Boursin steak sandwich with fried onion strips, lemon pepper chicken with pasta, hamburgers, chicken sandwiches, and big salads. The New England clam chowder is a standout, especially for the price. ⊠*San Francisco/Amity* ☎*407/224–6400* ▭*AE, D, MC, V* ✢*2:D1.*

$–$$ ✕**Mel's Drive-In.** At the corner of Hollywood Boulevard and 8th Ave-
AMERICAN nue—which turns into Sunset Boulevard along the bottom shore of the lagoon—is a flashy '50s eatery with a pink-and-white 1956 Ford Crown Victoria parked out in front. For burgers and fries ($8 for a cheeseburger basket), this is one of the best choices in the park, and it comes complete with a roving doo-wop group. You're on vacation—go ahead and have that extra-thick shake or the decadent chili cheese fries. Mel's is also a great place to meet-up, in case you decide to go your separate ways in the park. ⊠*Hollywood Boulevard* ☎*407/363–8766* ⌘*Reservations not accepted* ▭*AE, D, MC, V* ✢*2:D1.*

ISLANDS OF ADVENTURE

$–$$ ✕**Confisco Grille.** You could walk right past this eatery, but if you want
AMERICAN a good meal and sit-down service, don't pass by too quickly. This is one of the better eateries inside the theme parks (as opposed to outside in CityWalk). The menu changes often, but typical entrées include a good beef fillet with mashed potatoes and sautéed spinach, baked cod with spinach and mashed potatoes, and Thai noodles with chicken, shrimp, tofu, and bean sprouts. Save room for desserts like chocolate-banana bread cake with peanut butter ice cream or crème brûlée. You can catch the Dr. Seuss characters here at breakfast, Thursday through Sunday. Wine is available by the glass. ⊠*6000 Universal Blvd., Port of Entry* ☎*407/224–4404* ▭*AE, D, MC, V* ☾*No lunch* ✢*2:D2.*

$–$$ ✕**Mythos.** The name is Greek, but the dishes are eclectic. The eatery
ECLECTIC rivals the Confisco Grille for the best restaurant inside the Islands of Adventure. The menu, which changes frequently, usually includes mainstays like pistachio-crusted roast pork tenderloin, cedar-plank salmon with citrus butter and assorted wood-fired, personal pan pizzas. Among the creative desserts is banana cake with peanut butter ice cream. The building itself is enough to grab your attention. It looks like a giant rock formation from the outside and a huge cave (albeit one with plush upholstered seating) from the inside. Mythos also has a waterfront view of the big lagoon in the center of the theme park. (When it's slow in the park, Mythos is only open for lunch.) ⊠*6000 Universal Blvd., Lost Continent* ☎*407/224–4534* ▭*AE, D, MC, V* ✢*2:D1.*

CITYWALK

$$–$$$
SEAFOOD

✕**Bubba Gump Shrimp Co.** The fare at this "Forrest Gump"–inspired chain doesn't constitute fine cuisine, but it's tasty and creative. For a good cross section, go for the Shrimper's Heaven, which, as Bubba might explain, comes with fried shrimp, chilled shrimp, and coconut shrimp (as well as hush puppies and fries). Another worthwhile option is the "I'm Stuffed" shrimp, with shrimp stuffed with crabmeat and covered with Monterey Jack cheese. The shrimp po'boy sandwich is a good bet with plenty of shrimp and a tangy sauce. Hamburgers and steak are also available, but the best red-meat option is the huge slab of baby back ribs with a side of fries. For dessert, try the chocolate cookie sundae with vanilla ice cream and whipped cream. The faux-warehouse interior adds to the fun, especially if you're a fan of the film. ⊠ *6000 Universal Blvd. #73, Universal CityWalk* ☎*407/903–0044* ⚐*Reservations not accepted* ☰*AE, D, DC, MC, V* ✛*2:E1.*

$$$–$$$$
Fodor'sChoice
★
CREOLE

✕**Emeril's.** The popular eatery is a culinary shrine to Emeril Lagasse, the famous Food Network chef who occasionally makes an appearance. And while the interior of the restaurant with its modernistic interior of blond woods and lots of wrought iron looks nothing like the Old French Quarter, the hardwood floors and linen tablecloths create an environment befitting the stellar nature of the cuisine. Entrées may include andouille-crusted Texas redfish with toasted pecans and crispy shoestring potatoes; grilled filet mignon au poivre with garlic stuffed potatoes; lemongrass roasted duck with ginger rice pilaf; and double-cut pork chops with caramelized sweet potatoes. And Emeril knows your 9-year-old is not a New York food critic, so there are kids' offerings like chicken tenders and fries for $8.50. Save room for Emeril's ice-cream parfait or the German chocolate cake with vanilla bean ice cream and coconut shavings. Reservations are usually essential, but there's a chance of getting a walk-in seating if you show up early for lunch (11:30 AM) or dinner (5:30 PM). ⊠*6000 Universal Blvd.* ☎*407/224–2424* ⊕*www.emerils.com* ⚐*Reservations essential* ☰*AE, D, MC, V* ✛*2:D2.*

$$–$$$
AMERICAN

✕**Hard Rock Cafe Orlando.** Built to resemble Rome's Coliseum, this 800-seat restaurant is the largest of the 100-odd Hard Rocks in the world, but getting a seat at lunch can still require a long wait. The music is always loud and the walls are filled with rock memorabilia. Appetizers range from spring rolls to chicken tenders. The most popular menu item is still the $15 cheeseburger, but the baby back ribs and the beef fajitas are strong contenders. If you don't eat meat, try the Mediterranean veggie sandwich or the grilled salmon fillet with penne pasta. The best dessert is the hot fudge brownie sundae. Parking is $8 until 6:30 PM, and free afterward. ⊠*6000 Universal Blvd.* ☎*407/351–7625* ⊕*www.hardrockcafe.com* ⚐*Reservations not accepted* ☰*AE, D, DC, MC, V* ✛*2:D2.*

$$–$$$
AMERICAN

✕**Jimmy Buffett's Margaritaville.** Parrotheads can probably name the top two menu items before they even walk in the door. You've got your cheeseburger, featured in the song "Cheeseburger in Paradise," and, of course, your Ultimate Margarita. The rest of the menu is an eclectic mix of quesadillas, crab cakes, fish tacos, jerk salmon (marinated in spicy sauce), and a salute to Cajun cooking, a worthwhile jambalaya.

This place wouldn't be true to Buffet's heritage without Key West–style conch chowder; this version is quite piquant. Worthy dessert choices include chocolate banana bread pudding, the obligatory key lime pie, and a New York–style cheesecake topped with seasonal fruit. ☒*6000 Universal Blvd.* ☎*407/224–2155* ⊕*www.margaritaville.com* ▭*AE, D, MC, V* ⊹*2:E1.*

$$–$$$

LATIN AMERICAN

✕ **The Latin Quarter.** This grottolike restaurant and club, with domed ceilings and stone walls, is one of those jumping-by-night, dormant-by-day spots, but the food is good all the time. Cuisines from 21 Latin nations are on the menu, as is a wide selection of South American beers. Good entrée choices include the Chilean salmon served over mixed greens with avocado and orange-mango dressing; marinated *churrasco* (grilled skirt steak); *paella* with chorizo and three seafood ingredients; red snapper with chorizo; guava-spiced spare ribs; and fajitas with chicken, steak, snapper or a combo of meats. Most main dishes come with black beans and rice. This place can be a little loud in the evenings, but the live Latin music has a grand energy. ☒*6000 Universal Blvd.* ☎*407/224–2800* ⊕*www.universalorlando.com* ▭*AE, D, MC, V* ⊹*2:D1.*

$$–$$$

AMERICAN

✕ **NASCAR Sports Grille.** Filled with race-car simulator games and racing memorabilia, this eatery might not look like the place to grab a sublime meal, but that's not the case since the café stepped up its menu. The beef is cooked with care here, with the $25, 12-ounce rib eye being the best of the offerings. Other selections worth trying include the ultra-thick pork chop with apple chutney, and the slow-roasted baby back rib platter with sweet potatoes; the Talladega cheeseburger with a side of fries is a cut above the standard theme park burger. The best of the desserts is key lime pie topped with whipped cream and strawberries. ☒*6000 Universal Blvd.* ☎*407/224–7223* ⊕*www.nascarsportsgrille. com* ▭*AE, D, MC, V* ⊹*2:E2.*

$$–$$$

AMERICAN

✕ **NBA City.** The NBA memorabilia and video games are great, but the food is actually the real draw here. The best appetizers include spring rolls filled with snow crab, and pecan-crusted chicken tenders with orange marmalade sauce, although the flat breads, with toppings like baked cheese and tomatoes, are also worthy. For an entrée, try the grilled salmon with bowtie pasta. The brick-oven pizzas include a tasty Buffalo chicken version with blue cheese crumbles. Finish off with the cinnamon apple tart baked in the restaurant's brick oven. The big-screen TVs, which naturally broadcast nonstop basketball action, probably won't surprise you, but the relatively quiet bar upstairs with elegant blond-wood furniture, probably will. If you haven't already worked up an appetite walking through the parks, there is a half basketball court outside, suitable for free-throws or a pick-up game. ☒*6000 Universal Blvd.* ☎*407/363–5919* ⊕*www.nbacity.com* ▭*AE, D, MC, V* ⊹*2:E2.*

$$–$$$

ITALIAN

✕ **Pastamoré.** Since it doesn't have marquee appeal like its neighbor Emeril's, Pastamoré is something of a CityWalk sleeper. But this could be the best uncrowded restaurant at Universal, with wood-fired pizza, fresh pastas, and good versions of classics like fettucine Alfredo, chicken parmigiana and veal marsala—plus Italian beer and wines. Especially notable are the huge Italian sandwiches, with ingredients like marinated chicken, peppers, and sun-dried tomatoes, as well as a good tiramisu. If you want a treat you probably won't find at your neighborhood Italian eatery, go for the Italian wedding soup, with chicken broth, veal meatballs, veggies, and pasta. In another unusual touch, you can also come here for Italian breakfast breads—the place opens at 8 AM. The breakfast pizza, topped with sausage and eggs, will make you glad you didn't opt for a McMuffin. ⊠*6000 Universal Blvd.* ☎*407/224–3663* ▤*AE, D, MC, V* ✚*2:E1.*

HARD ROCK HOTEL

$$$–$$$$ ✕**The Palm.** With its dark-wood interior and hundreds of framed celebrity caricatures, this restaurant resembles its famed New York City namesake. As you might guess, a hearts of palm salad is a specialty here, but for most diners, the steaks are the star of the show. Aged beef is the predominant house specialty, and the 16-ounce strip steak cooked on a hot stone with onions and peppers is another standout. There are several veal dishes on the menu, including veal piccata, veal parmigiana, and veal Milanese along with a 3-pound Maine lobster (market price, but somewhere north of $70), and linguine with clam sauce, either red or white. For fish lovers, the peppercorn-encrusted Atlantic salmon is a tasty option. ⊠*1000 Universal Studios Plaza* ☎*407/503–7256* ⊕*www.thepalm.com* ▤*AE, D, DC, MC, V* ◷*No lunch weekends* ✚*2:E1.*

STEAK

PORTOFINO BAY HOTEL

$$$$ ✕**Bice.** In 2004 trendy, pricey Bice replaced the hotel's former top-billed restaurant, Delfino Riviera. Bice (pronounced "*beach*-ay") is an Italian nickname for Beatrice, as in Beatrice Ruggeri, who founded the original Milan location of this family restaurant in 1926. But the word "family" does not carry the connotation "mom and pop" here, where white starched tablecloths set the stage for sophisticated cuisine. The restaurant retains its frescoed ceilings, marble floors, and, of course, picture windows overlooking great views of the artificial (but appealing) bay just outside. This restaurant is expensive (a simple spaghetti bolognese is $25), but some of the entrées that seem worth it include the osso buco with saffron risotto. While you're running up your tab, you may as well try a tasty appetizer; the chilled lobster served with arugula salad, ripe tomatoes, and hearts of palm. Desserts, ranging from tiramisu to baked apple tart with vanilla ice cream, are delicious. Outdoor seating overlooks a lake. ⊠*5601 Universal Blvd.* ☎*407/503–1415* ⊕*www. biceorlando.com* ▤*AE, D, DC, MC, V* ◷*No lunch* ✚*2:E1.*

Fodor'sChoice
★
ITALIAN

$$$ ✕**Mama Della's.** The premise here is that Mama Della is a middle-age Italian housewife who has opened up her home as a restaurant. "Mama" is always on hand (this is a coveted job for middle-aged actresses who do a good Italian accent), strolling among the tables, wearing an apron and making small talk. The food, which is served family style (or diners can order individually), is no theme park fantasy—it's excellent. The menu has Italian classics like chicken marsala, veal parmigiana, and spaghetti with veal or sirloin meatballs and bolognese sauce, and all

ITALIAN

of the pastas are made in-house. If you like seafood, go for the frutti di mare, with shrimp, scallops and grouper with roasted tomatoes in a garlic olive oil sauce. Tiramisu and white chocolate praline crunch cake with raspberry sorbet are sure bets for dessert. Outdoor seating, on a second-story patio that overlooks the adjacent lake, is pleasant. ⊠*5601 Universal Blvd.* ☎*407/503–3463* ⊕*www.portofinobay.com* ⊟*AE, D, DC, MC, V* ⊗*Closed Mon. No lunch* ✛*2:E1.*

ROYAL PACIFIC RESORT

$$$–$$$$ ✕**Tchoup Chop.** With its cathedral ceiling, the inside of this restaurant
ASIAN   looks almost churchlike, and the food at Emeril Lagasse's Pacific-influenced restaurant is certainly righteous. Following the theme of the Royal Pacific Resort, the decorators included a tiki bar with lots of bamboo, a couple of indoor waterfalls, and a long pool with porcelain lily pads running the length of the dining room. The menu combines Lagasse's own New Orleans–style cuisine with an Asian theme. Entrées change periodically, but representative dishes include lemon grass–crusted shrimp with noodles and curry sauce, and pepper-grilled Hereford fillet with potato sticks, hot and sour peppers, and bacon ginger steak sauce. One of the mainstay dishes is basil-seared mahi-mahi with wild mushroom lobster sauce—something to give you that Asian fusion feeling. For dessert try the banana cream pie with Graham cracker crust, caramel sauce, and chocolate shavings. If you want an experience to remember, try the Teppenyaki Tasting, a limited seating event, held every second Saturday of the month, with a five-course, prix-fixe menu and a serving at which a staff chef presides. ⊠*6300 Hollywood Way* ☎*407/503–2467* ⊕*www.emerils.com* ✍*Reservations essential* ⊟*AE, D, DC, MC, V* ✛*2:E2.*

KISSIMMEE

Although Orlando is the focus of most theme-park visitors, Kissimmee is actually closer to Walt Disney World; it offers a huge number of dining choices, although many are of the "burger barn" variety. But there are notable exceptions. To visit the area, follow I–4 to Exit 64A. Allow about 15 to 25 minutes to travel from WDW, or about 35 minutes from I-Drive.

$$$–$$$$ ✕**Old Hickory Steak House.** If paying $44 for a 10-ounce Angus steak
STEAK   (and an extra $7 for a side of mashed potatoes) and eating it inside a barn seems a bit surreal, remember that this is not your average restaurant. The barn, like many of the unusual eateries in the Orlando area, is a fake, movie-set kind of edifice designed for effect. Dine on the deck adjacent to the main building and you'll overlook the hotel's faux Everglades, where electronic alligators cavort with fiberglass frogs. The experience is designed to entertain, and it does; the food is worth the roughly $50 a person you'll spend for dinner. Or if you really want to go all-out, you can indulge in the surf and turf, with Angus fillet and lobster tail, which costs approximately $66. For dessert, go for the chocolate soufflé, or the white chocolate raspberry bread pudding. ⊠*Gaylord*

Palms Resort, 6000 W. Osceola Pkwy., I–4 Exit 65 ☎*407/586–1600* ⊕*www.gaylordhotels.com* ▤*AE, DC, MC, V* ⊘*No lunch* ✛*1:E6.*

$$–$$$ ✕**Romano's Macaroni Grill.** You may have a branch of this prolific chain
ITALIAN in your hometown, and the popular Orlando locations deliver a known quantity—good but not great Italian cuisine. It's friendly, it's casual, and it's comfortable. For starters, try the Romano's Sampler, which includes tomato bruschetta, fried mozzarella, and calamari. For an entrée, try the chicken and shrimp scallopini, with generous portions of sautéed chicken and shrimp, mushrooms, capers, and smoked prosciutto in a lemon butter sauce, served over capellini pasta. If you're counting dollars (but not calories), go for the fettuccine Alfredo, with an excellent cream sauce, and lots of butter and Parmesan cheese. The brick-oven pizzas are quite good, especially the pesto chicken pizza. House wines are brought to the table in gallon bottles—you serve yourself and then report how many glasses you've had. Your kids can pass the time doodling with crayons on the white-paper table covering. ✉*5320 W. Irlo Bronson Memorial Hwy.* ☎*407/396–6155* ✉*12148 S. Apopka–Vineland Rd., Lake Buena Vista* ☎*407/239–6676* ⊕*www.macaroni-grill.com* ▤*AE, D, DC, MC, V* ✛*1:G6.*

$$$–$$$$ ✕**Sunset Sam's Fish Camp.** Often restaurants with a great decor or an
SEAFOOD architectural gimmick don't bother to back it up with good food. But that's not the case with Sunset Sam's. The cuisine here, focused on great fish offerings, is on par with the grand look of the place, with its 60-foot sailboat floating in a giant indoor lake. Starters are big enough to be a meal, and include blue point oysters with mashed potato, and tamarind-braised short ribs with fried polenta. Entrées are pricey but not exorbitant, and include blackened swordfish, seared ahi tuna, and lemongrass-glazed salmon. Other worthy dishes include the papardelle pasta with shrimp, scallops, and lobster in a garlic cream sauce and crab cakes with purple potato salad with smoked bacon. For dessert, go for the "Banana Mama" split, with three kinds of ice cream, bananas, caramelized pineapple slices, and, of course, lots of whipped cream. ✉*Gaylord Palms Resort, 6000 W. Osceola Pkwy., I–4 Exit 65, Gaylord Palms Resort* ☎*407/566–1101* ▤*AE, D, DC, MC, V* ✛*1:E6.*

$$$$ ✕**The Venetian Room.** Inside the Caribe Royale Resort, one of Orlando's
CONTINENTAL bigger convention hotels, this place was definitely designed for execs on expense accounts. But the serene, luxurious, and romantic atmosphere makes it a great place for dinner with your significant other. The architecture alone is enough to lure you in. It's designed to look like Renaissance Venice: the entryway has a giant copper dome over the door and the dining room has dark-wood furniture, crystal chandeliers, and carpets that could grace a European palace. A good starter is the roasted red beets and tenderloin beef carpaccio with white truffle oil, capers, and micro green salad. You can follow that with a good filet mignon, or braised bison short ribs, or if you don't like red meat, go for the Dover sole with roasted caper and butter sauce. Finish off your meal with the Grand Marnier soufflé or the fresh fruit and berries in a white chocolate shell. ✉*Caribe Royale Resort, 8101 World Center Dr., International Drive Area* ☎*407/238–8060* ⊕*www.thevenetianroom.com* ▤*AE, D, DC, MC, V* ⊘*No lunch* ✛*1:F5.*

$$$ ╳ **Villa de Flora Marketplace and Restaurant.** At lunch and dinner, you can
ECLECTIC see people going back to the dessert buffet again and again, loading
up on the house specialty strawberry short cake. And why not? With
relatively inexpensive all-you-can-eat buffets, this is a great place to
load up on the food without unloading your wallet. Lunch and dinner
buffets ($20 and $27.50, respectively), rotate cuisine themes from day
to day—Italian, French, and Greek. Breakfast buffets feature American-
style meals seven days a week, but the Sunday breakfast buffet steps
everything up a notch with the addition of dishes like prime rib and
roast pork. All the breakfasts offer made-to-order omelets, eggs Bene-
dict, Belgian waffles, and biscuits and gravy. Lunch and dinner, depend-
ing on the day you eat there, offer tasty dishes ranging from chicken
cacciatore and osso buco (Italian), to banana leaf salmon crusted with
banana chips (Spanish), to coq au vin and roasted pork loin au poivre
(French). With the prices and quality of the food, it make dollars-and-
cents sense to drive here from other Disney-area hotels. ⊠ *6000 W.
Osceola Pkwy., I–4 Exit 65, Gaylord Palms Resort* ☎ *407/586–1114*
⊟ *AE, D, DC, MC, V* ✛ *1:E6.*

CELEBRATION

If this small town with Victorian-style homes and perfectly manicured
lawns reminds you a bit of Main Street, U.S.A., in the Magic Kingdom,
it should. The utopian residential community was created by Disney,
with all the Disney attention to detail. Every view of every street is warm
and pleasant, though the best are out the windows of the town's four
restaurants, all of which face a pastoral (though artificial) lake. There's
even an interactive fountain in the small park near the lake, giving kids
a great place to splash. Homes here are quite expensive, and restaurants
reflect the upscale nature of the local customers. To get here take I–4 to
Exit 64A and follow the "Celebration" signs.

$$–$$$ ╳ **Café d' Antonio.** The wood-burning oven and grill are worked pretty
ITALIAN hard here, and the mountains of hardwood used in the open kitchen
flavor the best of the menu—the pizza, the grilled fish and chicken, the
steaks and chops, and even the lasagna. Standouts include *pappardella
al salmon* (wide, ribbon pasta with salmon, sweet peas, and a brandy
and cheese sauce) and ravioli stuffed with lobster and ricotta cheese,
tossed in tarragon cream with brandy and capers. At lunch, you can
pick your own ingredients for a personal, wood-oven pizza. For dessert,
try the chocolate walnut cake. Italian vintages dominate the wine list.
As at the rest of Celebration's restaurants, there's an awning-covered
terrace overlooking the lagoon. ⊠ *691 Front St.* ☎ *407/566–2233*
⊕ *www.antoniosonline.com* ⊟ *AE, D, MC, V* ✛ *1:H6.*

$$–$$$ ╳ **Celebration Town Tavern.** This New England–cuisine eatery, operated by
AMERICAN a family with Yankee roots, has a double personality. The interior is a
brass, glass, and dark-wood paneling kind of place, with lots of urbane
eatery treats, like baby back ribs, prime rib, and gargantuan burgers.
The quiet courtyard outside is the Boston Garden area, with exquisite
seafood ranging from Ipswich clams to 2-pound lobsters (market price),
plus a salute to the Sunshine State with its Florida stone crabs in season

(also market price). Theoretically, the two dining areas are two restaurants, but you can order anything on the menu from either seating area. While the place has a clearly ultra-affluent demeanor, there are plenty of menu choices right out of a working-class Boston bar—meatball hoagies, Philly cheese steak sandwiches, and Buffalo-style chicken wings. For dessert there's great—what else?—Boston cream pie. ⊠ *721 Front St.* ☎ *407/566-2526* ⊕ *www.celebrationtowntavern.com* ⊟ *AE, D, MC, V* ✣ *1:H6.*

$$–$$$ ✕ **Columbia Restaurant.** Celebration's branch of this family-owned chain
LATIN AMERICAN is generally as good as the original in Tampa, which has been operating for a century now. Start with the black bean cakes with guacamole and sour cream, empanadas stuffed with beef, roasted corn and black beans, or the house specialty appetizer, *croquetas y croquetas* (two chicken croquettes and two crab croquettes). For your main course you should zero in on the paella—either *à la Valenciana,* with clams, shrimp, scallops, squid, chicken, and pork mixed into tasty yellow rice; or the *paella campesina,* a "farmer's" paella from Spain, with no seafood, but beef, pork, and chicken. The best dessert, *brazo gitano cien anos,* was created for the restaurant chains' 100th anniversary in 2005 (a sponge cake with strawberries that is soaked in syrup and Spanish sherry and flambéed table-side), and is well worth its price just for the show. ⊠ *649 Front St.* ☎ *407/566-1505* ⊕ *www.columbiarestaurant. com* ⊟ *AE, D, DC, MC, V* ✣ *1:H6.*

$–$$ ✕ **Market Street Café.** The menu at this informal diner ranges from the
AMERICAN house-special baked-potato omelet, which is served until 5 PM, as are other breakfast classics like waffles and French toast, to chicken Alfredo and prime rib. One appetizer, the chili cheese nachos plate is large enough to make a meal, although perhaps not if you are trying to eat healthy. Standout entrées include the pot roast and meat loaf. In addition to a hearty version of the quintessential American hamburger, there's also a salmon and veggie burger for the cholesterol wary. The excellent house-made potato chips come with a blue cheese sauce. If you're looking for that quintessentially Southern dish, chicken-fried steak, they have an excellent version here. For dessert, go for the hot brownie topped off with vanilla ice cream or the coconut pie. There's a pleasant outdoor seating section in front of the restaurant. ⊠ *701 Front St.* ☎ *407/566-1144* ⌕ *Reservations not accepted* ⊟ *AE, D, MC, V* ✣ *1:H6.*

$$–$$$ ✕ **Seito Celebration.** Operated by the Seils, the Japanese family that owns
JAPANESE Seito Sushi in downtown Orlando, this quiet and casual eatery offers the same excellent sushi as its sister location. You can dine on your favorite rolls while overlooking the lake in the center of Celebration. Selections range from the quintessentially Eastern Seito Roll (tuna, salmon, and crab) to a highly Occidental TGIF Roll (tuna, shrimp, avocado, and white fish). There are also combination sushi and sashimi platters that range from $14 to $18. Non-sushi entrées like salmon teriyaki and a tender filet mignon are also available. The house specialties, which include marinated sea bass, are worthwhile and inexpensive. Although cold tofu may sound like a health-food freak's revenge, it's actually a great appetizer here, livened up with ginger, scallions, and soy sauce.

The bananas fried in tempura batter make an excellent dessert. The restaurant also offers several prix-fixe meals, with a representative sampling of the chef's best work. ✉ *671 Front St., Suite 100* ☎ *407/566–1889* ⊕ *www.seitosushi.com* ▤ *AE, D, DC, MC, V* ✛*1:H6.*

ORLANDO METRO AREA

INTERNATIONAL DRIVE

A number of restaurants are scattered among the hotels that line manicured International Drive. Many are branches of chains, from fast-food spots to theme coffee shops and up. The food is sometimes quite good. To get to the area, take I–4 Exit 72 or 74A. Count on it taking about a half hour from the Kissimmee area or from a WDW property.

$$$$
AMERICAN
×**A Land Remembered.** The name of this place is somewhat enigmatic (it's named for a locally famous novel about Florida by Patrick Smith) but then, so is the location—it's in the golf clubhouse of the Rosen's Shingle Creek Resort complex. But if you're a steak lover, it's worth your while to find this place. Chef James Slattery, who spent several years working for Emeril Lagasse in Lagasse's two Orlando restaurants, has obvious skill. Worthwhile choices include the 1½-pound slab of prime rib, and if the sticker shock of its price doesn't get you, the 24-ounce porterhouse with a Vidalia onion sauce, shouldn't disappoint the most ardent beef connoisseur. If you don't like beef, you're still in a good place here, with choices that include spit-roasted free-range chicken with tangerine and thyme butter, and lamb Tequesta, rubbed with roasted garlic and dry mustard. The strawberry cheesecake and the key lime pie are wise dessert choices. ✉ *9939 Universal Blvd., International Drive, Rosen Shingle Creek Resort* ☎ *407/996–3663* ⌖ *Reservations recommended* ▤ *AE, DC, MC, V* ⊘ *No lunch* ✛*2:D5.*

$$–$$$
AMERICAN
×**B-Line Diner.** As you might expect from its location in the Peabody Hotel, this slick, 1950s-style diner with red-vinyl counter seats is not exactly cheap, but the salads, sandwiches, and griddle foods are tops. The classic combo—a thick, juicy burger with fries and a milk shake—is done beautifully. You can also get southern favorites like crispy fried red snapper or hickory-smoked chicken, both with sides like white beans or collard greens. And there are lots of selections you'd never expect to find at the traditional 1950s-style dinner, like sautéed seafood piccata, soy-glazed salmon, and roasted pork in Dijon mustard sauce. Desserts range from hazelnut-orange cake to coconut cream pie to banana splits. It's open 24 hours, so if you crave eggs Benedict at 3 AM, B-Line is the place to go. ✉*Peabody Orlando, 9801 International Dr.* ☎*407/352–4000* ⊕*www.peabodyorlando.com* ▤*AE, D, DC, MC, V* ✛*2:D6.*

$$–$$$
CARIBBEAN
×**Bahama Breeze.** Even though the lineage is corporate, the menu here is creative and tasty. The big outdoor dining area, casual style, and the Caribbean cooking draw a crowd: so be prepared for a wait. Meanwhile, you can sip piña coladas and other West Indian delights on a big wooden porch. The food is worth the wait. Start with fire-roasted jerk shrimp or barbecued chicken flatbread, and move on to the shrimp

linguine with garlic, scallions, and a creole sauce, or the West Indian–style baby back ribs with a sweet and smoky guava barbecue glaze. Warm chocolate pineapple upside-down cake is the perfect finish. ✉*8849 International Dr.* ☎*407/248–2499* ✉*8735 Vineland Ave., I–4 Exit 68, I-Drive Area* ☎*407/938–9010* ⊕*www.bahamabreeze.com* ⌲*Reservations not accepted* ▤*AE, D, DC, MC* ✛*2:D5.*

$$$–$$$$ ✕**Bergamo's.** If you like Broadway show tunes with your spaghetti, and ITALIAN opera with your osso buco, then head here for the booming voices as well as the good food, both of which are provided by servers in satin vests. Management does not rely on the entertainment alone to fill seats: the food is very worthwhile. Start with the assorted antipasti, which gets you a sampling of roasted peppers, roasted marinated mushrooms, frittata, and bruschetta with white anchovies. Then try the linguine *pescatore* (fisherman's linguine), with lobster, shrimp, crabmeat, and mussels; or the classic osso buco with risotto Milanese. And while the idea of a mango–basil cheesecake sounds a tad strange, you'll probably love it, too. Bergamo's is open for dinner only. ✉*8445 International Dr., I–4 Exit 74A* ☎*407/352–3805* ⊕*www.bergamos.com* ▤*AE, D, DC, MC, V* ☽*No lunch* ✛*2:D4.*

$$$–$$$$ ✕**Café Tu Tu Tango.** The food here is served tapas-style—everything is ECLECTIC appetizer-size but plentiful, and inexpensive. The eclectic menu is fitting for a restaurant on International Drive. If you want a compendium of cuisines at one go, try the black-bean soup with cilantro sour cream, mango duck quesadillas, the pan-seared pork pot stickers, or the baby chipotle lobster tails. The wine list includes more than 30 wines from half a dozen countries, both by the bottle and the glass. The restaurant is supposed to resemble a crazy artist's loft; artists paint at easels while diners sip drinks like Matisse Margaritas. ✉*8625 International Dr.* ☎*407/248–2222* ⊕*www.cafetututango.com* ⌲*Reservations not accepted* ▤*AE, D, DC, MC, V* ✛*2:D5.*

$$–$$$ ✕**Capriccio's.** From the marble-top tables in this Italian restaurant you ITALIAN can view the open kitchen and the wood-burning pizza ovens, which turn out whole-wheat flour pies ranging from pizza *salsiccia,* with pepperoni and Italian sausage, to pizza *formaggio* with Gorgonzola, pecorino, Parmesan, mozzarella, and garlic cream. However, this Italian eatery is more noted for steaks that are "flash-seared" to seal in the juices, like the house signature cut, the 24-ounce rib eye, which will easily feed two people. Other standouts include seafood dishes like New Zealand lobster (flown in daily) and an excellent *zuppa di pesce,* an Italian seafood stew that is worth its $27.50 price tag. Because the hotel in which the restaurant is located does a huge convention attendee business, reservations are essential. ✉*Peabody Orlando, 9801 International Dr.* ☎*407/352–4000* ▤*AE, DC, MC, V* ☽*Closed Mon.* ✛*2:D6.*

$$$ ✕**Cuba Libre.** This restaurant, a branch of a popular chain that began in CUBAN Philadelphia, is not exactly like the down-home *Cubano* kinds of eateries you'll find in the *Calle Ocho* district of Miami, but it presents great Caribbean cooking in an Orlando sort of way—with movie-set style flair. The restaurant concept is from chef Guillermo Pernot, a James Beard Award winner and one of the creators of what is called "New Latin Cuisine." The *Plato Cuba Libre* dish is very representative of the

menu in this huge (20,000-square-foot) International Drive eatery. Contents of the plate, which costs $29.50, rotate daily and include typical Cuba Libre entrées like spice-rubbed New York strip steak, or lime-garlic marinated chicken breast, served with a bevy of sides like black beans and rice, fried plantains, and watercress salad. Other main dishes of note include the slow-cooked, guava glazed barbecued ribs, and the *churrasco a la Cubana* (grilled skirt steak), the daily staple in Cuban restaurants in Miami or Havana. There's also a worthwhile pressed Cuban sandwich and a good version of a traditional Latin dish *ropa vieja*, shredded beef brisket with tomatoes, bell peppers, and onions in a red wine sauce. ⊠ *9101 International Dr. 32819* ☎ *407/226–1600* ⊟ *AE, DC, MC, V* ✛ *2:D5.*

$$$ ✕ **Fiorella's Cucina Toscana.** Newly incarnated in January 2009 when chef
ITALIAN Robert Mason, formerly the executive chef at the Grand Bohemian Hotel in downtown Orlando came aboard at the new Westin Imagine Orlando, this restaurant was something of an undiscovered gem in its early months of operation. The hotel is easy for the average tourist to miss, tucked behind the Orange County Convention Center on Universal Boulevard. But this quiet little eatery is just off International Drive, and the Tuscan cooking makes it worth the short trip. The decor is vibrant but not gaudy, with dark woods accented by bright, 21st-century-style artwork on the walls. Open for three meals a day, the restaurant offers an Italian but eclectic breakfast, with selections like three-egg omelets with lobster and mascarpone, a breakfast panini with two eggs, tomatoes, mozzarella, and basil, and traditional American pancakes with Vermont maple syrup. Lunchtime brings offerings like Italian panini sandwiches with salami, prosciutto, tomatoes, and fontina cheese, a variety of personal-size pizzas and entrées like sautéed grouper with Swiss chard and chianti butter. Dinner selections include Maine lobster ravioli, and Black Angus tenderloin of beef with Gorgonzola cheese and fingerling potatoes. Worthy desserts on the menu at both lunch and dinner include amaretto cheesecake with white peach puree and raspberry chocolate flourless cake. ⊠ *9501 Universal Dr., Westin Imagine Hotel, Universal Drive area* ☎ *407/233–2200* ⊟ *AE, DC, MC, V* ✛ *2:D56.*

$$$–$$$$ ✕ **Maggiano's Little Italy.** With red-checkered tablecloths, lots of hearty
ITALIAN pasta dishes, and Frank Sinatra music playing nonstop in the cavernous (320-seat) dining room, this place seems like the ideal locale for a family evening, and in fact, that's the specialty of this chain restaurant. For about $25 a person, your family can dive into a huge meal, with traditional Italian mainstays like fettucine Alfredo, rib-sticking spaghetti with meat sauce, linguine with clams (with either red or white sauce), or baked lasagna with both crumbled meat balls and Italian sausage. A standout is the Italian pot roast, and a particularly good, not-so-Italian choice at lunch is the salmon, bacon, and avocado sandwich. The tiramisu is a solid dessert choice. ⊠ *9101 International Dr., Pointe Orlando, International Drive* ☎ *407/241–8650* ⊟ *AE, D, DC, MC, V* ✛ *2:D5.*

$$–$$$ ✕ **Ming Court.** A walled courtyard and serene pond make you forget
CHINESE you're on International Drive. The extensive menu includes simple

chicken Szechuan, jumbo shrimp with honey-glaze walnuts, and aged filet mignon grilled in a spicy sauce. Ming Court features an extensive selection of dim sum, including pepper stuffed shrimp, and grilled petite lamb chops. And there's an extensive sushi menu, including two sampler plates. There's also an extensive array of dishes from the wok, including a house specialty, chicken and basil in a flaming wok, with thin chicken slices sautéed in barbecue sauce with basil, ginger, and roasted garlic. The flourless chocolate cake, certainly not Asian, has been a popular standard for years. Ming Court is within walking distance of the Orange County Convention Center and can be quite busy at lunchtime. ✉ *9188 International Dr.* ☎ *407/351–9988* ⊕ *www.ming-court.com* ▭ *AE, D, DC, MC, V* ✛ *2:D6.*

$$$$
AMERICAN
✕ **Norman's.** Chef-entrepreneur Norman Van Aken brings impressive credentials to the restaurant that bears his name, as you might expect from the headline eatery in the first and only Ritz-Carlton in Orlando. Van Aken's culinary roots go back to the Florida Keys, where he's credited with creating "Floribbean" cuisine, a blend that is part Key West, part Havana, and part Kingston, Jamaica. In the '90s, Van Aken became a star in Miami with his Coral Gables restaurant. The Orlando operation is a formal restaurant with marble floors, starched tablecloths, waiters in black-tie, and a creative, if expensive, prix-fixe menu. The offerings change frequently, but representative selections include Florida Gulf Pompano with ham hash, mahimahi with whipped potatoes and mussel chorizo salad, and grilled rib-eye steak with fingerling potatoes. For dessert, try the Pink Lady apple beignet with caramelized molasses ice cream. This place is not for those on a budget. ✉ *Ritz-Carlton Grande Lakes, 4000 Central Florida Pkwy.* ☎ *407/393–4333* ▭ *AE, D, DC, MC, V* ☾ *No lunch* ✛ *2:H6.*

$$$–$$$$
SEAFOOD
✕ **Oceanaire Seafood Room.** Don't let the 1930s-era ocean liner interior fool you: as theme restaurants go, this place is a good one, packing everything from Coromandel oysters from New Zealand to Alaskan halibut to bluefin tuna from Baja California's Sea of Cortez. The straightforward preparation here—grilled or broiled, brushed with sea salt, olive oil, and fresh lemon juice—is also a welcome break from some of this eatery's more flamboyant counterparts. Standouts include the grand shellfish platter and the grilled black Florida grouper. A worthy side dish for those who aren't carbohydrate conscious is the sour cream and onion mashed potatoes. Make sure to save room for the caramel deluxe brownie. ✉ *9101 International Dr., Suite 1002, International Drive* ☎ *407/363–48011* ⊕ *www.theoceanaire.com* ⌔ *Reservations essential* ▭ *AE, DC, MC, V* ☾ *Closed Sun. No lunch* ✛ *2:D5.*

$$–$$$
JAPANESE
✕ **Ran-Getsu.** The surroundings are a Disney-style version of Asia, but the food is fresh and carefully prepared, much of it table-side. Unless you're alone, you can have your meal Japanese family-style at the low tables overlooking a carp-filled pond and decorative gardens. You might start with fried grouper "*Tasuta Age,*" grouper bites with ginger soy sauce, and continue with the *Sukiyaki,* made tableside with USDA choice beef for $26 per person or Kobe beef for $50 per person. Another standout is the seafood *Yosenabe,* a hearty Japanese soup made with seafood, chicken, and duck meat. If you feel adventurous, try the

deep-fried alligator bits glazed in a ginger–soy sauce. ✉ *8400 International Dr.* ☎ *407/345–0044* ⊕ *www.rangetsu.com* ▭ *AE, DC, MC, V* ⊙ *No lunch* ✛ *2:D4.*

$$$–$$$$
GREEK

✕ **Taverna Opa.** This high-energy Greek restaurant bills itself as offering "fun with a capital F," possibly because the ouzo flows like a mountain stream, the Greek music almost reaches the level of a Red Hot Chili Peppers concert, and the roaming belly dancers actively encourage diners to take part in the mass Zorba dancing (which often happens on the tops of dining tables). The only thing missing is the Greek restaurant tradition of throwing dinner plates, made up in part by the throwing of torn-up paper napkins, which sometimes reaches near-blizzard level. The food, by the way, is also excellent. Standouts include traditional staples like *spanakopita* (phyllo pastry with spinach and feta cheese), *saganaki* (the traditional flaming cheese appetizer), *avegolemono* (lemon chicken rice soup), and perhaps the most famous Greek entrée, *mousaka* (layers of roasted eggplant, potatoes, and ground meat, topped with béchamel sauce). Other standouts include the slow-roasted lamb and the "meat platter," with chicken kebab, beef tenderloin kebob, pork loin, gyro, and a lamb chop thrown in to make sure your carnivorous urges are totally satisfied. The best dessert is the *baklava* (phyllo filled with walnuts, cinnamon, cloves, and honey). ✉ *9101 International Dr., Pointe Orlando* ☎ *407/879–2481* ▭ *AE, D, DC, MC, V* ✛ *2:D5.*

$$$$
STEAK

✕ **Texas de Brazil.** The chain that brought this restaurant to Orlando is from Texas, but the concept is straight out of Rio, where the *churrascarias* (barbecue restaurants) offer you the option of eating yourself into oblivion. Just as it is in Rio, here you'll find a card on your table, red on one side and green on the other. As long as you leave the green side up, an endless cavalcade of waiters will bring expertly grilled and roasted beefsteak, pork, chicken, and sausage. Buffet stations offer sides like garlic-mashed potatoes, baked potatoes, black beans and rice, a wide assortment of salads, and decadent desserts such as Brazilian papaya cream. Brazil's national drink, the high-octane *caipirnha* (made with cachaca, in turn derived from Brazilian sugarcane) is well worth trying. The fixed-price meal costs $45, but you can often catch specials at $39 for the meal (call first). For an additional cost you can choose from more than 700 wines. Children 12 and under eat for half price, and kids under 6 eat free. You can dine outdoors or in, where the restaurant has bright red walls, dark furniture, and white tablecloths. ✉ *5259 International Dr.* ☎ *407/355–0355* ⊕ *www.texasdebrazil.com* ▭ *AE, D, DC, MC, V* ⊙ *No lunch Mon.–Sat.* ✛ *2:F2.*

$$$–$$$$
CARIBBEAN

✕ **Tommy Bahama's Tropical Café.** Adjoining a Tommy Bahama's clothing store at the Pointe Orlando complex, this big dining room with cozy booths is not a bad respite after a day trudging up and down I-Drive. Eclectic Caribbean-inspired entrées include the Trinidad tuna, the Tortolla tortilla soup, the Sanibel stuffed chicken, and the Santiago sea bass—but don't be put off by the forced alliteration—the food is actually quite good. A good appetizer choice is the crab Calloway (actually two coconut-encrusted crab cakes). Also worthy is the house signature dessert, the Piña Colada cake, in which the white cake is sandwiched between layers of white chocolate mouse and pineapple chunks. ⊠ *9101 International Dr., Pointe Orlando* ☎*321/281–5888* ▤*AE, D, MC, V* ✛*2:D5.*

$$–$$$$ ✕**Vito's Chop House.** There's a reason why they keep the blinds closed
STEAK most of the time: it's for the wines' sake. The dining room doubles as
the cellar, with hundreds of bottles stacked in every nook and cranny.
The lobsters weigh in at 2 to 3 pounds, so you may need a doggie bag
if you go for one of the larger ones. The steaks are sliced by hand and
flame broiled over mesquite wood from Texas, and the Porterhouse
veal chop is 2-inches thick. A popular entrée is the cedar plank roasted
king salmon, and a second house favorite is the lobster Diablo. Worthwhile desserts include grilled peach di Vito, an excellent key lime pie,
and Italian wedding cake. Finish your meal by enjoying a glass of aged
cognac, Armagnac, or grappa in the lounge. ⊠*8633 International Dr.*
☎*407/354–2467* ⊕*www.vitoschophouse.com* ⚑*Reservations essential* ▤*AE, D, DC, MC, V* ⊗*No lunch* ✛*2:D5.*

SAND LAKE ROAD

This is the part of the city nearest the main Disney tourism area, a
mere five minutes or so northeast of International Drive or Universal
Orlando. Because the neighborhood has many expensive homes, with
high incomes to match, it's where you'll find some of the city's more
upscale stores and restaurants. Over the past few years one of the most
significant dining sectors in Orlando has sprung up along Sand Lake
Road, Exit 74A, just about a mile west of crowded International Drive,
where the quality of the average restaurant is not up to par with the
eateries on Sand Lake.

$$–$$$ ✕**Antonio's.** This pleasant trattoria has great service, welcoming sur-
ITALIAN roundings, and a good chef with plenty of world-class talent. Tasty
creations include *lombata al forno,* a veal chop stuffed with prosciutto,
fontina cheese, and spinach, sautéed and finished in the wood-fire oven;
ravioli de argosta (ravioli with lobster, brandy, and a cream sauce); and
the lasagna with ground beef, also baked in a wood-fired oven. Daily
specials include a consistently great *zuppa del giorno* (soup of the day),
at a market price; plenty of fish (like Florida grouper); and red meat.
There is also excellent wood-oven pizza. ⊠*Fountains Plaza, 7559 W.
Sand Lake Rd., I–4 Exit 74A* ☎*407/363–9191* ⊕*www.antoniosonline.
com* ▤*AE, D, DC, MC, V* ⊗*Closed Sun. No lunch* ✛*2:C4.*

$$$ ✕**Ayothaya.** Although it is not as fancy or as highly themed as its Sand
THAI Lake neighbors, the menu here is solid. Start with the mandatory (if you
are a true Thai fan) chicken satay or the Thai dumplings with shrimp
and chicken stuffing, or go for the Ayothaya sampler with chicken satay,
spring rolls, tulip dumplings (dumplings stuffed with chicken and crab-
meat with sweet and sour sauce), crab cakes, fried wonton, and Thai
shrimp rolls. There's no sensible need to eat more after that, but forge
ahead and put aside thoughts of your own gluttony. The main dishes
are worth loosening your belt a bit. Standouts include four great curry
dishes and pad Thai noodles dishes ranging from simple pad Thai with
no meat, to pad Thai with salmon. A house creation called Gulf of
Thai is the pinnacle of the menu (at $36) and includes prawns, squid,

Not-Bad Chains

When all you want is a quick bite, consider these chain restaurants. They seem to crop up everywhere, and most have tables where you can sit for a few moments before heading back out to the shops and attractions

California Pizza Kitchen: There's usually a line at the Mall at Millenia location, but the wait is worth it. The specialty is individual-size pizza, served on a plate with toppings ranging from Jamaican jerk chicken to spicy Italian peppers. You can also get fettuccine with garlic–cream sauce, and Santa Fe chicken topped with sour cream, salsa, and guacamole.

Don Pablo's: Chicken enchiladas and beef fajitas are on the bill of fare at this Tex-Mex outpost. The I-Drive location is in a big, barnlike building.

Johnny Rockets: Burgers and chili dogs are served in a vibrant, '50s-diner-style environment here. There are branches at the Mall at

Millenia, on International Drive, and in Winter Park.

Moe's: Burritos with names like Joey Bag of Donuts seem geared to make you laugh, but once you taste them, your mouth will be happy to just chew. This is good, fast, fresh Mex for the road.

Panera Bread: Fresh-baked pastries, bagels, and espresso drinks are the mainstays here, although you can grab a hearty and inexpensive meal like smoked-chicken panini on onion focaccia and still have change left from a $10 bill. Lake Eola and Mall at Millenia are standouts in this chain.

Wolfgang Puck Express: At Puck's café, a meal is an event. But at the two Downtown Disney express walk-up windows, a meal is poetry in motion. Grab a wood-oven pizza or soup and salad, and you're out of there in 10 minutes.

---

scallops, steamed mussels, and deep-fried soft shell crab with jasmine rice. For dessert, go for the sticky sweet rice with coconut milk and fresh mangoes. Ayothaya has an extensive take-out menu. ✉ *7555 Sand Lake Rd., Sand Lake Road* ⊕ *www.ayothaythai.com* ☎ *407/345–0040* ☰ *AE, MC, V* ✛*2:C4.*

$$–$$$
Fodor'sChoice
★
SEAFOOD

✕ **Bonefish Grill.** After perfecting its culinary act in the Tampa Bay area, this Florida-based seafood chain has moved into the Orlando market with a casually elegant eatery that offers seafood from around the world. Anglers (waiters) serve standout dishes like wood-grilled salmon in mango sauce, mahimahi in a pan-Asian sauce, and pistachio-crusted rainbow trout. Meat-lovers may prefer the center-cut, wood-grilled filet mignon or the boneless pork chop with Fontina cheese. For the record, there's no bonefish on the menu. It's an inedible game fish, caught for sport (and usually released) in the Florida Keys. ✉*7830 Sand Lake Rd., I–4 Exit 74A* ☎*407/355–7707* ⊕*www.bonefishgrill.com* ☰*AE, D, DC, MC, V* ✆*No lunch* ✛*2:B4.*

$$–$$$
Fodor'sChoice
★
ITALIAN

✕ **Bravo! Cucina Italiana.** Just when you thought the Sand Lake dining district had all the appealing, positive-energy eateries it needed, another one opens. Such is the case with Bravo! Cucina Italiana, an Italian bistro and trattoria in the Via Dellagio shopping court, two blocks east of the "main drag" along Sand Lake's restaurant row. This place caters to an upscale crowd, but there's no mandatory coat and tie, or any other culinary anachronisms to deal with. Starched tablecloths give the place a formal feel, and there's a great bar area, including a patio bar with sun umbrellas over the tables just out the back door. All the traditional Italian dishes you'd expect at a good eatery are on the menu; veal Marsala, chicken scaloppini, and a humble but tasty spaghetti bolognese. There's a wood-fired grill here, which means everything from hickory-grilled salmon to grilled, marinated pork chops grace the menu. The house specialty, Pasta Bravo! (rigatoni with wood-grilled chicken, roasted peppers, and a pepper-cream sauce) is quite good, as are the wide variety of pizzas, many of which have wood-grilled meats as toppings. ⊠ *7924 Via Dellagio Way, Sand Lake Road* ☎*888/452–7286 or 888/452–7286* ⚏*Reservations recommended* ⊕*www.bravoitalian. com* 🍽*AE, D, DC, MC, V* ✛*2:B4.*

$$–$$$ ✕**Cantina Laredo.** You can tell that this is an upscale Mexican eatery
MEXICAN   first by the Porsches in the parking lot, and then by the aged Mexican tequila that fetches up to $46 a bottle on the menu. The food is of course pricey, but satisfying. Among the great *platos especiales* (special plates) is *camaron Poblano asada*—a Mexican steak wrapped around a mild Pablano pepper stuffed with shrimp and Jack cheese. But if you want representative Mexican dining, go for the Laredo Platter, with a cheese chile *relleno* (breaded, mild pepper stuffed with cheese and fried), handmade tamale (not even in the same universe with something you'd get out of a can), a chicken enchilada, and a taco al carbon made with shredded steak. Brunch (11 AM–3 PM on Sunday) brings out a great menu that includes crab cakes Benedict (with poached egg and Hollandaise) and a dish called *"Migas con huevos"* (scrambled eggs with pieces of fried corn tortillas with peppers and bacon)—a great, authentically Mexican taste. If you enter from the front, you may never notice there is a small covered dining area out back that faces a courtyard with what is clearly the most spectacular fountain in central Florida (and that is saying a lot), with 20-foot-high statues that look like they came from Renaissance Europe, if it were not for the fact that the concrete just dried last month. ⊠*8000 Via Dellagio Way, Sand Lake Road* ☎*407/345–0186* ⚏*Reservations recommended* ⊕*www. cantinalaredo.com* 🍽*AE, D, DC, MC, V* ✛*2:B4.*

$$–$$$ ✕**Cedar's Restaurant.** Set in a small strip shopping center that's become
MIDDLE EASTERN   part of a restaurant row, this family-owned Lebanese eatery includes Middle Eastern standards like shish kebab, falafel, and hummus, as well as tasty daily specials. One of the best of the regular entrées is the *samak hara* (sautéed red snapper topped with onions, tomatoes, and cilantro). You may also want to try the mixed grille with three different meats or the tasty rack of lamb. They do wonderful things with poultry here, including chicken Cedar's, sautéed chicken breast stuffed with tomatoes, onions, garlic, and cilantro; marinated Cornish game hen; and marinated quail. There's a lunch combo for $9.50 and sandwiches to go for $6.50. A tad more formal than the average Orlando-area Middle Eastern restaurant, Cedar's has tables with white linen tablecloths and diners who tend to sport resort-casual attire. ⊠*7732 W. Sand Lake Rd.,*

I–4 Exit 74A ☎*407/351–6000* ⊕*www.cedarsoforlando.com* ▭*AE, D, DC, MC, V* ✛*2:C4.*

$$$–$$$$ ✗ **Chatham's Place.** In Florida, grouper is about as ubiquitous as Coca-
SEAFOOD Cola, but to discover its full potential, try the rendition here: it's sau-
téed and topped with pecan butter and scallions. Other good entrées
include the chicken piccata, and the filet mignon served with a Madiera
sauce. A worthy appetizer is the crabmeat *en croute,* lump crabmeat
and shiitake mushrooms in a garlic butter sauce, served over puff pas-
try. The chef does wonders with desserts like pecan–macadamia nut
pie and the classic bananas Foster for those who like to see their des-
sert in flames before consuming it. Take I–4 Exit 74A. ✉*7575 Dr.
Phillips Blvd.* ☎*407/345–2992* ⊕*www.chathamsplace.com* ▭*AE, D,
DC, MC, V* ✛*2:C4.*

$$$–$$$$ ✗ **Christini's.** Locals, visitors, and Disney execs alike love to spend money
ITALIAN at Christini's, one of the city's best places for northern Italian cuisine.
Try the chicken Marsala or the fettuccine *alla Christini,* the house ver-
sion of fettuccine Alfredo, or the veal scaloppine, topped with roasted
peppers, prosciutto, and provolone, and then flambéed in sherry and
brandy. The multicourse dinner often takes a couple of hours or more,
but if you like Italian minstrels at your table, this place should please
you. Take I–4 Exit 74A. ✉*Dr. Phillips Marketplace, 7600 Dr. Phillips
Blvd.* ☎*407/345–8770* ⊕*www.christinis.com* ▭*AE, D, DC, MC, V*
✛*2:B4.*

$$$$ ✗ **The Melting Pot.** This fondue restaurant keeps you busy while you
SWISS eat—as you'll be doing part of the cooking. Diners dip morsels ranging
from lobster tails (market price) to sirloin slices into flavorful broths
and oils in stainless steel pots built into the center of the table. The
lineup also includes the traditional cheese fondues, as well as chocolate
fondues for dessert. ✉*Fountains Plaza, 7549 W. Sand Lake Rd., I–4
Exit 74A* ☎*407/903–1100* ⊕*www.meltingpot.com* ▭*AE, D, DC,
MC, V* ✛*2:C4.*

¢–$ ✗ **Moe's.** The Moe in this equation could almost be the guy who cavorted
MEXICAN with Larry and Curly. There are several oddly named dishes, including
an "Ugly Naked Guy" taco, "The Homewrecker" (formerly called "The
Other Lewinsky," but updated when the world forgot Monica), and
"Joey Bag of Donuts." But the food is more sublime than the nomencla-
ture. The Art Vandalay, for instance, is a vegetarian burrito with beans,
rice, pico de gallo, guacamole, and sour cream. And the Joey Bag of
Donuts burrito offers a choice of meats including fajita steak, chicken,
ground beef, or pork. Everything on the menu comes with chips and
four different salsas (the most clever name among the salsas: "Who is
Kaiser Salsa?"). The burritos here are gargantuan. In fact the Joey Jr.
special, a smaller burrito and a soft drink, is enough to feed the aver-
age adult. The dessert list is short but good—oatmeal raisin cookies
and chocolate chip cookies. Moe's is a great fast-food alternative with
most meals costing well south of $10. This is an immensely casual fast
food joint with music blaring over the sound system, but by no means
a dive. It has a young vibrancy, and makes a great place for a quick
meal. ✉*7541D W. Sand Lake Rd., I–4 Exit 74A* ☎*407/264–9903*

✉ *847 S. Orlando Ave., Winter Park* ☎ *407/629–4500* ⊕ *www.moes. com* ⌦ *Reservations not accepted* ▭ *AE, D, MC, V* ✛ *2:C4.*

$$$–$$$$
SEAFOOD

✕ **MoonFish.** The big waterfall on the sign out front will grab your attention, but once you get inside you'll find the gimmicks give way to solid cuisine served in a serene space. Dark-wood paneling and white tablecloths abound. The menu is a blend of Pan-Asian, Pacific Rim, Cajun, and Floribbean fare. Specialties range from grilled lobster tail (market price) to seared bluefin tuna mignon, to Florida stone crab (market price). The restaurant also specializes in aged beef, which you can view in a big refrigerated cabinet as you walk in the door, then served up in every variety, including a house specialty Oscar Mignon, which is a sirloin with Hollandaise and a crabmeat topping. There's also a raw bar with oysters (baked, wood-roasted, or raw) and a sushi bar with the usual selections, including yellowtail tuna, octopus, squid, and eel. More than 300 wines are sold by the glass. ✉ *7525 W. Sand Lake Rd., I–4 Exit 74A* ☎ *407/363–7262* ⊕ *www.fishfusion.com* ▭ *AE, D, DC, MC, V* ✛ *2:C4.*

$$$–$$$$
STEAK

✕ **Morton's of Chicago.** Center stage in the kitchen is a huge broiler, kept at 900°F to sear in the flavor of the porterhouses, sirloins, T-bones, and other cuts of aged beef. Morton's looks like a sophisticated private club, and youngsters with mouse caps are not common among the clientele of this nationwide chain's Orlando restaurant. It's not unusual for checks to hit $80 a head, but if beef is your passion, this is the place you'll want to go. Soufflés are a specialty here and there are four: chocolate, raspberry, lemon, and Grand Mariner. (Order at the beginning of your meal.) The wine list has about 500 vintages from around the world. Take I–4 Exit 74A. ✉ *Dr. Phillips Marketplace, 7600 Dr. Phillips Blvd., Suite 132* ☎ *407/248–3485* ⊕ *www.mortons.com* ▭ *AE, DC, MC, V* ✛ *2:B4.*

$$$–$$$$
HAWAIIAN

✕ **Roy's.** Chef Roy Yamaguchi has more or less perfected his own cuisine type—Hawaiian fusion, replete with lots of tropical fruit–based sauces and lots of imagination. The menu changes daily, but typical dishes include treats like Hawaiian-style butterfish with a sizzling Chinese vinaigrette or Hibachi-style grilled Atlantic salmon with Japanese citrus sauce. If your tastes remain on the mainland, go for classics like garlic-honey-mustard beef short ribs or the "Cowboy" center-cut 16-ounce, bone-in rib eye. The crunchy golden lobster pot stickers are one of the best appetizers in Orlando. The prix-fixe menu, at $35 per person, is a relative bargain, as you get your choice between two entrées, an appetizer, and a dessert. ✉ *7760 W. Sand Lake Rd., I–4 Exit 74A* ☎ *407/352–4844* ⊕ *www.roysrestaurant.com* ▭ *AE, D, DC, MC, V* ⊘ *No lunch* ✛ *2:C4.*

$$–$$$
LATIN AMERICAN

✕ **Samba Room.** Although owned by the same company that operates the TGI Friday's chain, this big, vibrant restaurant is a good version of an "authentic" Latin experience. You may agree once you've heard the bongos and tasted the *barbacoa* (barbecue with a Latin flare), the best of which is the pork barbacoa cooked in banana leaves. To sample the extensive menu, go for the *bocaditas*, or tapas-style appetizers, including the Peruvian calamari and the empanada sampler. A standout on the main course menu is the seared jumbo scallops with mashed potatoes, *ropa vieja* (shredded flank steak with yellow rice, yucca, and beans), and citrus emulsion. For dessert, try the banana crème brûlée or the *pudin de zanahoria* (sweet carrot cake). There is a limited menu at lunch, but you can grab the Latin lunch boxes for $11–$13 with great ingredients like empanadas, soup, and skirt steak. There is live Latin music nightly and free wireless access. ✉ *7468 W. Sand Lake Rd., I–4 Exit 75A* ☎ *407/226–0550* ⊕ *www.e-brands.net* ▤ *AE, D, MC, V* ✛ *2:C4.*

$$$–$$$$
Fodor's Choice
★

AMERICAN

✕ **Seasons 52.** Parts of the menu change every week at this innovative restaurant, which began with the concept of serving different foods at different times, depending on what's in season. Meals here tend to be light, healthy, and very flavorful. You might have the grilled rack of lamb with Dijon sauce, pork tenderloin skillet with polenta, or salmon cooked on a cedar plank and accompanied by grilled vegetable, or if you prefer a light meal, go for what the menu calls "entrée salads," like the tamarind glazed salmon salad with a cumin-lime vinaigrette. An impressive wine list complements the long and colorful menu. Another health-conscious concept adopted at Seasons 52 is the "mini indulgence" dessert: classics like chocolate cake, butterscotch pudding, and rocky road ice cream served in portions designed not to bust your daily calorie budget. Although the cuisine is haute, the prices are modest—not bad for a snazzy, urbane, dark-wood-walled bistro and wine bar. It has live music nightly. ✉ *7700 Sand Lake Rd.* ☎ *407/354–5212* ✉ *463 E. Altamonte Dr., Altamonte Springs* ☎ *407/767–1252* ⊕ *www.e-brands. net* ▤ *AE, D, DC, MC, V* ✛ *2:C4.*

$$–$$$
ITALIAN

✕ **Timpano Italian Chophouse.** You may feel like you're on the set of the movie *Oceans 11*—the original version—as you slide into the black-leather booth at a table with a starched tablecloth and a cabaret lamp, while Frank Sinatra croons in the background and the waiters sing along—but the place is not boisterous or silly; it's laid back. American beef definitely gets plenty of attention here, but that doesn't cancel out any of the Italian flair. A very worthy appetizer is the tuna carpaccio with kalamata olives, red onions, and lemon aïoli served with Timpano's signature flatbread, but perhaps the best starter is the Italian wedding soup, with spinach, meatballs, Parmesan, and orzo pasta. Along with the 12-ounce New York strip and 16-ounce double-bone pork chops, there's a credible version of veal Marsala with herbs and tomatoes and a fine rock shrimp and lobster ravioli. Your cardiologist will be proud of you if you go for the roasted salmon with artichokes and spinach, but if cholesterol fighting is not your idea of a great vacation activity, go for the spaghettini bolognese, made with tomato sauce and Angus beef. There's also a good variety of to-go boxes at lunch. ✉ *7488 W. Sand Lake Rd., I–4 Exit 75A* ☎ *407/248–0429* ⊕ *www. timpanochophouse.net* ▤ *AE, D, DC, MC, V* ✛ *2:C4.*

$$$–$$$$
AMERICAN

✕ **Vines Grill & Wine Bar.** Live jazz and blues music fills the night at this strip-mall bar, but don't worry—the food and drink here aren't second-rate warm-up acts. They're headliners in their own right. The kitchen specializes in double cut Kurobuta pork chops, essentially as thick as *Webster's New Collegiate Dictionary,* plus charcoal cooked steaks, like the 22-ounce rib eye and sublime fish dishes like crab-crusted black grouper. And, if you just won the Florida lottery, there is a burger that is perhaps the most expensive in Orlando, the Kobe cheeseburger with bacon, which goes to $39 if you want to add foie gras. The wine list here is extensive, with offerings from Napa Valley, New Zealand, Australia, Chile, Italy, and France. The crowd tends to dress up, but suit jackets and ties are not required. Wood tables and ceramic tile floors give the place a rustic, elegant look. ⊠*7563 W. Sand Lake Rd.* ☎*407/351– 1227* ⊕*www.vinesgrille.com* ▤*AE, D, DC, MC, V* ✛*2:C4.*

ORLANDO INTERNATIONAL AIRPORT

$$–$$$
ECLECTIC

✕**Hemisphere.** The view competes with the food on the ninth floor of the Hyatt Regency Orlando International hotel. Although Hemisphere overlooks a major runway, you don't get any jet noise, just a nice air show. Start with the escargot in phyllo pastry. Entrées change frequently, but often include selections like lamb chops with apple mint chutney, or cedar plank roasted wild Pacific salmon with mustard ginger glaze, and you can always find classics on the menu like filet mignon. Desserts change daily, but there's always a good chocolate cake or Key lime pie. Even though it's been open for years, a lot of experienced travelers consider this place somewhat of an undiscovered gem because it's relatively hard to find. Ask for directions at the hotel front desk. ⊠*Hyatt Regency* ☎*407/825–1234 Ext. 1900* ▤*AE, DC, MC, V* ☺*No lunch* ✛*2:H6.*

$$$–$$$$
STEAK

✕**Porterhouse.** Orlando International Airport is like Orlando itself in microcosm—filled with virtually every fast-food chain one can imagine, yet offering opportunities for a quiet, quality dining experience. An example is Porterhouse, opened in 2007 in the Orlando Airport Marriott, which is connected to the main terminal of the airport itself. The dining room is elegant but casual, with dark-wood walls and butcher-block tabletops. The aged Angus beef is a treat for your palate if not your wallet—a 10-ounce filet is $39, and the house specialty, the 36-ounce Porterhouse for two, will cost you $70. If beef is not your ideal meal, alternatives include grouper with sun-dried tomato, and pan-seared breast of duck with an orange-lavender syrup. And if you can't decide twixt surf and turf, eat both—an 8-ounce center-cut fillet and a 6-ounce lobster tail ($65). A worthwhile appetizer is fried lobster fritters with Key lime mustard sauce, and a house specialty side dish is the bacon-wrapped free-range chicken with blue cheese and mustard sauce. ⊠ *7499 Augusta National Dr., Orlando Airport Marriott, Orlando International Airport* ☎*407/851–9000* ▤*AE, D, DC, MC, V* ✛*2:H6.*

CENTRAL ORLANDO

The center of Orlando shows what the town as a whole was like before it became a big theme park. Quiet streets are lined with huge oaks covered with Spanish moss. Museums and galleries are along main thoroughfares, as are dozens of tiny lakes, where herons, egrets, and, yes, alligators, peacefully coexist with human city dwellers. This is quintessential urban Florida.

The restaurants in this area, a good half hour from the Disney tourism area via I–4, tend to have more of their own sense of character and style than the eateries going full tilt for your dollars in Kissimmee or on International Drive.

\$–\$\$ ✗**Alfonso's Pizza & More.** This is a strong contender for the best pizza
ITALIAN   in Orlando (in the non-wood-fired oven division). Since it's across the street from a high school, things get frenzied at lunch. The hand-tossed pizzas' toppings range from pepperoni to pineapple—but the calzones and some of the pasta dishes, such as fettuccine Alfredo, are quite worthy as well. There are also subs and salads for lighter fare. The secret to the superior pizza is simple: the dough and all the sauces are made from scratch each and every day. For dessert, opt for the apple pie. Take I–4 Exit 84 to the College Park neighborhood area. ⊠*3231 Edgewater Dr., College Park* ☎*407/872–7324* ▭*Reservations not accepted* ▭*MC, V* ✛*3:C3.*

\$\$–\$\$\$ ✗**Amura.** A quiet respite from the vibrant—and loud—bars around it,
JAPANESE   Amura, Japanese for "Asian village," is comfortable and sophisticated. The sushi menu has about 40 choices, from *aoyagi* (round clams) to yellowtail tuna. For a taste of everything, try the Tokyo Plate, piled high with chicken teriyaki, salmon teriyaki, ginger pork, California roll, and tempura veggies. The Mexican roll—with avocado, shrimp, and jalapeño peppers—makes for an unusual appetizer. The Sand Lake Road location has a big, performance-style dining room, where the tables all surround grills and the chef cooks while you watch. The original downtown location has a quieter, more familylike atmosphere. The Sand Lake location has a great feature if you're headed to nearby Universal Studios—boxed lunch specials with everything from chicken terriyiki to Chilean seas bass with black bean sauce. ⊠*7786 W. Sand Lake Rd., I–4 Exit 74A, Sand Lake Road Area* ☎*407/370–0007* ⊠*55 W. Church St. 170, Downtown Orlando* ☎*407/316–8500* ⊠*950 Market Promenade Ave., Suite 1210* ☎*407/936–6001* ⊕*www.amura.com* ▭*AE, D, DC, MC, V* ☉*No lunch Sun.* ✛*3:D6.*

\$–\$\$ ✗**Anthony's Pizzeria and Restaurant.** This neighborhood spot in Thorn-
ITALIAN   ton Park is well known to locals for its deep-dish pizza, but the pasta is worthy in its own right—and correctly priced for those on a budget. All the traditional Italian fare is available, and the chicken piccata and eggplant parmigiana are house favorites. If you're in a hurry, go for pizza by the slice, ranging from \$2 for plain cheese to \$4.50 for a slice of the stuffed pizza with ham, salami, pepperoni, peppers, onions, provolone, and mozzarella. The outdoor seating area is a great option, except in summer when the heat is unbearable. ⊠*100 N. Summerlin Ave., Thornton Park* ☎*407/648–0009* ⊕*www.anthonyspizza.com* ▭*MC, V* ✛*3:E6.*

¢–\$ ✗**Baja Burrito Kitchen.** Because of the excellent fish tacos, as well as a spe-
MEXICAN   cialty called the L.A. Burrito (grilled chicken or steak, plus guacamole and jack cheese), Baja Burrito calls itself a "Cal-Mex" palace. However, the mainstays of the menu—like the "Burrito Maximo," a gargantuan flour tortilla–wrapped monster filled with chicken or steak, pinto beans, guacamole, and sour cream—will be familiar to denizens of the American heartland. The place offers great variety in its *comida* (food)

that makes it palatable to even the most trendy Gringo tastes, like the fajita with grilled chicken, basil pesto, romano and mozzarella cheeses, and plum tomatoes, and, of course, a vegetarian burrito, with grilled peppers and onions, black beans, jack cheese, sour cream, and salsa Mexicana. It's not fancy, but it also won't drain your wallet. ⊠ *2716 E. Colonial Dr., near Fashion Sq. Mall, Central Orlando* ☎*407/895–6112* ⊠*931 N. State Rd. 434, Altamonte Springs* ☎*407/788–2252* ⚒ *Reservations not accepted* ▤*AE, D, MC, V* ✛*3:F5.*

$$$–$$$$ ✕ **The Boheme Restaurant.** The Grand Bohemian, a downtown boutique
ECLECTIC luxury hotel, is the setting for one of the central city's better restaurants. As a prelude to your main, try the Bohemian tapas, with braised short rib, blue cheese–crusted scallop, and seared duck breast in plum sauce. For a main course, try roasted Chilean sea bass with fingerling potatoes and rock crab minestrone, or the double-cut pork chop stuffed with pecorino arugula. At breakfast, the French toast with a triple sec–strawberry glaze is an excellent way to awaken your palate. The Sunday brunch here ($49 per person) is a worthwhile experience: you can get prime rib and sushi as well as omelets. ⊠ *Westin Grand Bohemian, 325 S. Orange Ave., Downtown Orlando* ☎*407/313–9000* ⊕*www.grandbohemianhotel.com* ⚒ *Reservations essential* ▤*AE, D, DC, MC, V* ✛*3:B6.*

$$$–$$$$ ✕ **Cityfish.** In downtown Orlando's trendy Thornton Park district, this
SEAFOOD casual dining spot aims to be urbane and caters to locals, but if your kids are wearing mouse ears when you go here you won't be frowned upon. With the general ambience of a city sports bar—including flat screen TVs on all the walls—Cityfish dispenses basic, well-prepared, fresh fish, served up in creative ways, as with the seafood nachos, layered with shrimp and scallops, corn, black beans, salsa, and shredded cheese. A good choice on the brunch menu is the seafood skillet, with sautéed tilapia, shrimp, scallops, red potatoes, tomatoes, and onion, nestled in the skillet under a layer of fried scrambled eggs with white cheese on top. A brunch menu bargain is the $2 mimosas, some 50¢ cheaper than the ice tea or sodas, although those two beverages come with unlimited refills. The big patio filled with tables shaded by big umbrellas, is a great place to spend a few unhurried hours in spring or fall. ⊠ *617 E. Central Blvd., Thornton Park* ☎*407/849–9779* ⚒ *Reservations not accepted* ▤*AE, D, MC, V* ✛*3:E6.*

$$$–$$$$ ✕ **Del Frisco.** Locals like this quiet, uncomplicated steak house, which
STEAK delivers carefully prepared, corn-fed beef and attentive service. When your steak arrives, the waiter asks you to cut into it and check that it was cooked as you ordered. The menu is simple: T-bones, porterhouses, filet mignon. Seafood such as Alaskan crab, and lobster bisque fill out the "surf" side of the menu. Bread is baked daily at the restaurant, and the bread pudding, with a Jack Daniels sauce, is worth a try, as is the carrot cake. There's a piano bar next to the dining room. ⊠ *729 Lee Rd., North-Central Orlando* ☎*407/645–4443* ⊕*www.delfriscosorlando. com* ▤*AE, D, DC, MC, V* ◷*Closed Sun. No lunch* ✛*3:C2.*

$$$–$$$$ ✕ **HUE.** On the ground floor of a condo high-rise on the edge of Lake
ECLECTIC Eola, this place takes its name from a self-created acronym: Hip Urban Environment. While it may not be quite as cool as its press clippings, the

food is both good and eclectic, with offerings ranging from blackened fish tacos with cheddar cheese, black beans, and white rice in a flour tortilla to double-cut pork chops in Asian barbecue sauce. The wood grilled rack of lamb with chive mashed potatoes and sautéed vegetables, the crispy oysters with garlic mayo, or the wood-grilled New York strip steak with a red wine demi-glace are also notable dishes. Unfortunately, the large outdoor dining area overlooks the street and not the lake. Brunch is served Sunday 11 AM– 4 PM. ⊠ *629 E. Central Blvd., Thornton Park* ☎ *407/849–1800* ⊕ *www.huerestaurant.com* ⚐ *Reservations not accepted* ⊟ *AE, D, DC, MC, V* ✛ *3:E6.*

¢–$　　✕ **Johnny's Fillin' Station.** In a building that once housed a gas station, this
AMERICAN　burger joint and sports bar is a monument to the fact that good eating can sometimes be had in extremely humble surroundings. Orlando residents rave about the burgers, which are straightforward half-pounders infused with what the management calls a "family recipe." Generous portions of onions, tomatoes, and other less common ingredients— like grilled mushrooms and peppers—make these burgers wonderfully sloppy. Make sure to grab extra napkins. The bacon-and-blue cheeseburger is the most popular item on the menu. Other options include chicken wings, cheesesteaks, and a worthwhile corned beef sandwich. This place is also a sports bar and can get pretty loud and crowded. ⊠ *2631 Ferncreek Ave., Central Orlando* ☎ *407/894–6900* ⊕ *www. johnnysfillinstation.com* ⊟ *MC, V, D* ✛ *3:D6.*

$$$–$$$$　✕ **K Restaurant & Wine Bar.** This dark-wood-paneled spot for locals of
AMERICAN　College Park—a quiet and quintessentially residential neighborhood about 2 mi northeast of downtown—features upscale eclectic American cuisine in an urbane, intimate setting. For those who love fine dining, this trip is well worth making. Most visitors from out of town don't make it here. The "K" stands for Kevin, as in Kevin Fonzo, the Culinary Institute of America graduate who created the place. Menus change daily, but there are several regular dishes that stand out. Start with the fried-green-tomato and blue-cheese appetizer. For entrées, check out the porcini-dusted filet mignon with red wine sauce or the grilled ahi tuna with rice noodles. K also has some much-lauded desserts like the pecan pie with house-made ice cream, and the chocolate lava cake with vanilla ice cream. There is an extensive wine list, and many selections are available by the glass. ⊠ *2401 Edgewater Dr., College Park* ☎ *407/872– 2332* ⊕ *www.kwinebar.com* ⊟ *MC, V* ☾ *Closed Sun.* ✛ *3:C4.*

$$$–$$$$　✕ **Le Coq au Vin.** Chef-owner Louis Perrotte is something of a culinary
Fodor's Choice　god in Orlando, but he doesn't let it go to his head. He operates a
★　modest little kitchen in a small house in south Orlando, seating 100
FRENCH　people in three dining rooms. Perrotte's homey eatery is usually filled with locals who appreciate the lovely traditional French fare: roasted halibut with manchego cheese on a bed of potatoes; rack of lamb with potatoes au gratin; and of course, the house namesake dish, *Poulet Coq au Vin,* braised chicken with red wine, mushrooms, bacon, and onion with creamed potatoes. The menu changes seasonally, but the house namesake dish is always available and always excellent. For dessert, try the Grand Marnier soufflé. One caveat: the menu somewhat patronizingly proclaims "We accept well-behaved children." ⊠ *4800*

S. Orange Ave., South-Central Orlando ☎*407/851–6980* ⊟*AE, DC, MC, V* ⊗*Closed Mon.* ✛*3:D6.*

$$$–$$$$
STEAK

✕ **Linda's La Cantina.** A favorite among locals since the Eisenhower administration, this down-home steak house serves good cuts of meat, cooked expertly and served at a reasonable price. The menu is short and to the point, including about a dozen steaks and just enough ancillary items to fill a single page. The beef is relatively inexpensive here, with an 18-ounce sirloin going for $23 and a 2-pound T-bone—more beef than most can handle—for $40. Among the fish selections, the 12-ounce blackened red snapper is perhaps the best. With every entrée you get a heaping order of spaghetti (which isn't particularly noteworthy) or a baked potato. The chicken, veal, or eggplant Parmesan topped with marinara sauce is good for nonsteak lovers. ⊠*4721 E. Colonial Dr., near Orlando Executive Airport, Central Orlando* ☎*407/894–4491* ⊕*www.lindaslacantina.com* ⊟*AE, D, MC, V* ✛*3:G5.*

$–$$
VIETNAMESE

✕ **Little Saigon.** This local favorite is one of the best of Orlando's ethnic restaurants. Even though there are more than 100 menu items, you can still create your own dish, and everything is inexpensive. Sample the summer rolls (spring-roll filling in a soft wrapper) with peanut sauce, or excellent Vietnamese crepes (stuffed with shredded pork and noodles). Move on to the *Com Heo Xao Bong Cai* (sautéed pork, onion, and broccoli over rice) or the traditional soup filled with noodles, rice, vegetables, and your choice of either chicken or seafood; ask to have extra meat in the soup if you're hungry, and be sure they bring you the mint and bean sprouts to sprinkle in. And if you have never experienced the strong, sweet Vietnamese iced coffee, it's almost like a dessert in itself. But if you prefer a dessert you can eat, go for the *Wuong Xo Hat Luu* (Vietnamese jello with coconut juice). ⊠*1106 E. Colonial Dr., South-Central Orlando* ☎*407/423–8539* ⊕*www.littlesaigonrestaurant.com* ⊟*MC, V* ✛*3:E5.*

$$–$$$
LATIN AMERICAN

✕ **Numero Uno.** To the followers of this long-popular Latin restaurant, the name is no mere hyperbole. Downtowners have been filling the place at lunch for years. It bills itself as "the home of paella," so just take their word for it and order some. If you have a good appetite and you either called ahead to order or can spare the 75-minute wait, try the *boliche* (a tender pork roast stuffed with chorizo sausage) and a side order of plantains. Otherwise, go for traditional Cuban fare like *ropa vieja* (shredded flank steak), *arroz con pollo* (rice with chicken), or paella. Finish with the *tres leches* (three-milk) cake, made with regular, evaporated, and sweetened-condensed milk. Take I–4 Exit 81A or 81B. ⊠*2499 S. Orange Ave., South-Central Orlando* ☎*407/841–3840* ⊟*AE, D, DC, MC, V* ✛*3:D6.*

$
ITALIAN

✕ **NYPD Pizza.** In business since 1996, this pizza place offers as wide a variety of brick-oven, hand-tossed pizza as you'll find in Orlando, ranging from the Hawaiian-style ham and pineapple pizza, to the Brooklyn blue cheese and buffalo chicken pizza, with grilled chicken, a layer of mild wing sauce, mozzarella, and chunks of rich blue cheese. Lasagna and chicken parmigiana are also available. Coney Island–style potato knishes make good snacks. Dessert standouts include a credible cannoli and, of course, New York cheesecake. Hardwood floors and brick walls make this place feel old-fashioned, and live music at night keeps things interesting. ⊠*2589 S. Hiawassee Rd., MetroWest* ☎*407/293–8880* ⊠*2947 Vineland Rd., Kissimmee* ☎*407/390–0170* ⊕*www.nypdpizza. net* 🖃*AE, D, MC, V* ✛*3:D6.*

$$–$$$
JAPANESE

✕**Shari Sushi Lounge.** Resplendent with chrome and glass, this trendy eatery has more of the atmosphere of a fast-lane singles bar than of an Asian oasis, but the dishes from the kitchen—fresh sushi and daily fresh fish entrées—acquit the place well as a legit dining establishment. If you're just there for the sushi, the place will not disappoint—there are 25 different varieties, including sea urchin and baby octopus. Start with the *tako* (not taco) salad, a delicious arrangement of octopus, cucumber, enoki mushrooms, mandarin oranges, and spicy kimchi sauce, then move on to one of the entrées like shrimp tempura or cedar-baked salmon in soy lime glaze. ⊠*621 E. Central, Thornton Park* ☎*407/420–9420* ⊕*www.sharisushilounge.com* 🖃*AE, D, DC, MC, V* ☽*No lunch* ✛*3:E6.*

$$$–$$$$
SEAFOOD

✕**Straub's Fine Seafood.** With offerings like escargots for $8.50—less than the price of a burger in the theme parks' sit-down restaurants—Straub's proves that the farther you drive from Disney, the less you pay. Owner Robert Straub, a fishmonger for many years, prepares a fine mesquite-grilled Atlantic salmon with béarnaise sauce on the side. He fillets all his own fish and says he won't serve anything he can't get fresh. The Captain's Platter, with lobster tail, mesquite-grilled shrimp, and broiled sea scallops is a great choice. The menu states the calorie count and fat content of every fish item, but for the tasty coconut-banana cream pie you just don't want to know. If you care to join a loyal crowd of locals, Straub's offers an "early bird" seating that begins daily at 4:30 PM, and features dishes like a seafood platter with haddock, scallops with crabmeat stuffing, and mesquite grilled shrimp. ⊠*5101 E. Colonial Dr., near Orlando Executive Airport, Central Orlando* ☎*407/273–9330* ⊠*512 E. Altamonte Dr., Altamonte Springs* ☎*407/831–2250* ⊕*www. straubsseafood.com* 🖃*AE, D, DC, MC, V* ✛*3:H5.*

OUTLYING TOWNS

WINTER PARK

Winter Park is a charming suburb on the northern end of Orlando, 25 minutes from Disney. It's affluent, understated, and sophisticated—and can be pleasurable when you need a break from the theme parks. To get into the area, follow I–4 to Exit 87.

$–$$
AMERICAN

✕**Briarpatch Restaurant & Ice Cream Parlor.** With a faux country store facade, this small eatery makes quite a contrast to its upscale neighbors, stores like Gucci and its ilk. But Briarpatch makes a great place to catch a hearty and inexpensive meal. The locals favor the thick burgers, which are topped with your choice of cheese, bacon, or mushrooms. Good breakfast choices include Belgian waffles, raisin-bread French toast, freshly made scones, and there is a wide variety of omelets, served with toast, and home fries or grits. About 30 flavors of ice cream are available to help cool off on those long strolls down Park Avenue. ⊠*252 Park Ave. N* ☎*407/628–8651 or 407/645–4566* ⌀*Reservations not accepted* ▤*AE, D, DC, MC, V* ✛*3:F1.*

$$–$$$ ✕**Brio Tuscan Grille.** Head to this trendy restaurant for wood-grilled

ITALIAN pizzas and oak-grilled steaks, lamb chops, veal scaloppine, and even lobster. Try the strip steak topped with Gorgonzola, or the pasta alla pesto, with wood-grilled chicken with mozzarella sun-dried tomatoes and pine nuts. A good appetizer choice is the *brio bruschetta,* a wood-baked flatbread covered with roasted chicken, pine nuts, mozzarella, and roasted peppers. The dining room's Italian archways are elegant, but the sidewalk tables are also a good option. ⊠*480 N. Orlando Ave.* ☎*407/622–5611* ⊠*4200 Conroy Rd., Mall at Millenia Orlando* ☎*407/351–8909* ⊕*www.brioitalian.com* ▤*AE, MC, V* ✛*3:E2.*

$$–$$$ ✕**Cheesecake Factory.** You can select from more than three dozen vari-

AMERICAN eties of the namesake treat, from chocolate Oreo mudslide cheesecake to southern pecan cheesecake. If you just don't like cheesecake, try the excellent apple dumplings. But this big restaurant also offers many full-meal options inluding Angus beef ribs, fish tacos with a spicy citrus salsa, chicken picatta, wood-oven pizza, and miso-marinated fillet of salmon. Great appetizers include avocado and sun-dried-tomato egg rolls, and bruschetta topped with chopped tomato, garlic, basil, and olive oil. ⊠*520 N. Orlando Ave.* ☎*407/644–4220* ⊠*4200 Conroy Rd., Mall at Millenia* ☎*407/226–0333* ⊕*www.thecheesecakefactory.com* ⌀*Reservations not accepted* ▤*AE, D, DC, MC, V* ✛*3:E2.*

$$–$$$ ✕**Chef Justin's Park Plaza Gardens.** Sitting at the sidewalk café and bar

CONTINENTAL is like sitting on the main street of the quintessential American small town. But the locals know the real gem is hidden inside—an atrium with live ficus trees, a brick floor, and brick walls that give the place a Vieux Carré feel. Chef Justin Plank's menu combines the best of French and Italian cuisine with an American twist. Much of the dinner menu is composed of traditional Continental fare, like rack of lamb or ten-derloin topped with Boursin cheese. One Florida touch is baked grou-per with lemon jasmine rice and tomato ginger coulis. Lunch offerings are lighter, with selections like glazed salmon and a good blue-cheese burger. ⊠*319 Park Ave. S* ☎*407/645–2475* ⊕*www.parkplazagardens. com* ▤*AE, D, DC, MC, V* ✛*3:F1.*

$$–$$$ ✕**Dexter's.** The good wine list and imaginative menu tend to attract

ECLECTIC quite a crowd of locals. Dexter's has its own wine label and publishes a monthly newsletter about wine. Two of the best entrées here are the chicken tortilla pie—a stack of puffy, fried tortillas layered with chicken and cheese—and the Bourbon Street Jambalaya, with andouille sau-sage and salmon. The rotating fish of the day often features various slants on Florida black grouper. There's often live music on Thursday night. The Thornton Park location is just east of downtown Orlando; you may be the only out-of-towner here. If you're north of town, stop at the Lake Mary location in Colonial Town Park. ⊠*558 W. New England Ave.* ☎*407/629–1150* ⊠*808 E. Washington St., Thornton Park* ☎*407/648–2777* ⊠*950 Market Promenade Ave., Lake Mary* ☎*407/805–3090* ⊕*www.dexwine.com* ⌀*Reservations not accepted* ▤*AE, D, DC, MC, V* ✛*3:E2.*

$$–$$$ ✕**Houston's.** This Atlanta-based chain restaurant sits on a prime spot
AMERICAN on Lake Killarney, which gives it a prime spot view. As you watch the
egrets and herons you can savor some meaty fare. The fancy wood-
grilled burger acquits itself well, but there's nothing like the steaks,
which are wood-grilled or pan-seared to your specifications, a good
example being the center-cut tenderloin. The grilled fish entrées, such
as tuna and salmon (sold at a market price that changes day to day),
offer tasty alternatives. On the lighter side, the club salad with chicken,
bacon, avocados, and croutons (definitely pick the blue-cheese dressing)
could easily satisfy two. Of the excellent soups, the New Orleans–style
red beans and rice is the best. The patio makes a great place for a drink
at sunset. Houston's has an extensive wine lists and offers some Latin-
style drinks like the Cuba Libre and Mojito. ⊠*215 S. Orlando Ave.,
U.S. 17–92* ☎*407/740–4005* ⊕*www.houstons.com* ⚓*Reservations
not accepted* ▤*AE, MC, V* ✛*3:E2.*

$$$–$$$$ ✕**Luma on Park.** Park Avenue, once an ultra-upscale enclave, was itself
AMERICAN a tourist attraction decades before the advent of Walt Disney World.
Although Luma on Park is a 21st-century place, serving what some call
"new American cuisine," it's also very much in line with Winter Park's
19th-century past. The chic contemporary setting includes terrazzo
floors accented by plush carpets and seating areas in alcoves that cre-
ate a cozy feel. A high point is the wine cellar, which holds 95 varieties
of fine wine. The menu changes periodically, but on recent visits stand-
outs included two appetizers; the blue crab cannollini with peppercorn
and sherry sauce, and the wood-fired pizza with pear, smoked bacon,
arugula, and blue cheese. Notable entrées include flounder with truffled
potato gnocchi, artichokes, and lobster cream, and the pork tenderloin
and Italian sausage with fingerling potatoes, brussel sprouts, and apple
coulis. Save room for the warm chocolate truffle cake with banana ice
cream and chocolate sauce. The restaurant offers an extensive wine
list with vintages from all over the world, by the bottle or glass, and
also offers a dinner with wine pairings for $45 per person. ⊠*250 S.
Park Ave.* ☎*407/599–4111* ⊕*www.lumaonpark.com* ⚓*Reservations
essential* ▤*AE, MC, V* ✛*3:F2.*

$–$$ ✕**Pannullo's.** The view of the tidy little downtown park across the street
ITALIAN rivals the quality of the Italian cuisine when you dine in the sidewalk
seating area. But when the rain or the heat drives you indoors, you've
still got the consistently great cooking at this place, which includes an
excellent veal piccata. Pizza by the slice starts at $3—a good choice
if you are in a hurry or on a budget. Perhaps the best entrée is the
lobster-stuffed ravioli, but the fettucine Alfredo with chicken is excellent as well. ⊠*216 Park Ave. S* ☎*407/629–7270* ⊕*www.pannullos.
com* ▤*AE, D, DC, MC, V* ✛*3:F2.*

$–$$ ✕**P. F. Chang's.** Two huge, faux-stone, Ming dynasty–style statues of
CHINESE horses stand guard outside this Chinese restaurant. There's a lengthy
wine list and very un-Asian desserts such as chocolate macadamia-
nut pie and fruit tarts. You might start with shrimp dumplings, fried
or steamed, and continue with Kung Pao chicken with peanuts, chili
peppers, and scallions, or perhaps crispy catfish in Szechuan sauce.
You can even get the calorie count of any dish, but you probably don't

want to know that the succulent spare ribs are 1,280 calories. The Mall at Millenia location has an outdoor dining area. ✉ *423 N. Orlando Ave., U.S. 17–92* ☎*407/622–0188* ✉*4200 Conroy Rd., Mall at Millenia, Orlando* ☎*407/345–2888* ⊕*www.pfchangs.com* ☰*AE, MC, V* ✛*3:E2.*

$$$–$$$$ ✕**The Ravenous Pig.** A trendy, vibrant bar in one of Orlando's most
AMERICAN affluent enclaves, the Pig dispenses delicacies, such as roast suckling pig with rye gnocci dumplings and lobster tacos. A good if strange dessert is the "Pig Tail," a pig tail–shaped piece of sweet, tender dough with a chocolate espresso dipping sauce. There's an amply sized bar area separate from the dining room. ✉ *1234 N. Orange Ave., Winter Park* ☎*407/628–2333* ⊕*www.theravenouspig.com* ⌖*Reservations essential* ☰*AE, D, MC, V* ⊘*Closed Sun.* ✛*3:D5.*

$$–$$$ ✕**Seito Sushi.** Tucked into a corner of Winter Park Village, this pleasant
JAPANESE eatery combines two great elements: sushi and sidewalk dining. Order a Japanese beer (or some hot sake) and sample the raw fish offerings, including the signature Seito roll, composed of tuna, whitefish, salmon, and crabmeat in a cucumber skin. Another favorite roll is the lobster Katsu, with deep-fried lobster topped with snow crab and avocado. There's also plenty of inspired cooked cuisine, including tasty sea bass with Asian rice, excellent salmon teriyaki, and even a good New York strip steak. Top off your meal with some red-bean ice cream or fried bananas. ✉*510 N. Orlando Ave.* ☎*407/644–5050* ⊕*www.seitosushi. com* ☰*AE, MC, V* ✛*3:E2.*

LONGWOOD

A northern suburb 45 minutes from Disney, Longwood is a long way from the tourism treadmill. The community has some worthy restaurants as well. To get into the area, follow I–4 to Exit 94.

$$$–$$$$ ✕**Enzo's on the Lake.** This is one of Orlando's favorite restaurants, even
ITALIAN though it's on a tacky stretch of highway filled with used-car lots. Enzo Perlini, the Roman charmer who owns the place, has turned a rather ordinary lakefront house into an Italian villa. And the view of the serene little lake it overlooks makes lunch a good idea. It's worth the trip, about 45 minutes from WDW, to sample the antipasti. Mussels in the shell, with a broth of tomatoes, olive oil, and garlic, make a great appetizer. Try the aged tenderloin grilled with Gorgonzola cheese, the *bucatini alla Enzo* (a thick, hollow pasta tossed with prosciutto, peas, bacon, mushrooms, and Parmesan), or the simple sphagetti carbonara, served in a skillet. ✉*1130 S. U.S. 17–92* ☎*407/834–9872* ⊕*www. enzos.com* ☰*AE, DC, MC, V* ⊘*Closed Sun* ✛*3:E1.*

ALTAMONTE SPRINGS

A northern suburb 40 minutes from Disney, Altamonte Springs is immediately south of Longwood. The community is popular for its upscale shopping. To get into the area, follow I–4 to Exit 92.

$$–$$$ ✕**Terramia Winebar Trattoria.** Don't let the nondescript exterior fool
ITALIAN you; the Northern Italian pasta dishes here have a special twist: lobster

ravioli, rigatoni with eggplant, mozzarella and basil, or fettucine with braised rabbit. A huge local following for this trattoria may come in part from the ample antipasto plate, which includes roasted peppers, Italian sausage, polenta, and bruschetta. The desserts are dreamy as well, including an excellent tiramisu and a rich and creamy cannoli. Part of the charm of the place is a big, dark-wood bar, behind which you'll find dozens of bottles of fine Italian wines. ✉ *1185 S. Spring Center Blvd.* ☎ *407/774–8466* ▭ *MC, V* ⊗ *Closed Sun* ✛ *3:D1.*

DAVENPORT

This small town is the closest community to the Disney World exits if you go southwest on I–4 instead of northeast toward Orlando. It's largely a collection of budget motels along U.S. 27 South, but it also includes the big Omni Orlando Resort at Champions Gate.

$$$$ ╳ **Zen.** The signature restaurant at the Omni Orlando Resort at Cham-
ASIAN   pionsGate, this pan-Asian delight includes Chinese soups, Thai noo-
dles, and sushi. Your best bet is the Zen Experience—an Asian sampler plate that includes Thai-style chicken wings, Chinese barbecued spareribs, and a trio of salmon, pork, and chicken dishes. The sashimi and sushi combo platter is also a good bet. Zen serves dinner only. ✉ *1500 Masters Blvd., I–4 Exit 58* ☎ *407/390–6664* ⊕ *www.omnihotels.com* ▭ *AE, DC, MC, V* ⊗ *No lunch* ✛ *1:A1.*

Where to Stay

WORD OF MOUTH

"I've stayed off site and on. Even for a frugal person like me, there is still no comparison. Stay on site."

—horsemom

"When you arrive at your hotel, ask the front desk for a list of the special events at the parks. This will tell you the 'magic hours' (the days and times you can get in early and/or stay late as a guest of a Disney resort)."

—Attnymom

Updated
by Rowland
Stiteler

With literally tens of thousands of hotel rooms in Orlando at every price point, it's easy, especially for a first-time visitor, to get overwhelmed upon first glance at the choices. If you find the choices daunting, don't despair. Everything becomes more logical and easy to understand if you first ask yourself what your basic goal for the trip is going to be, and then look what the various neighborhoods in the metro Orlando area have to offer.

Orlando entertains almost 50 million visitors a year, making it the most popular tourism destination on the planet, and consequently it has a huge and complex inventory of hotel rooms at all price points, themes, color schemes, brands, meal plans, guest room amenities—including kitchens that allow you to cook for yourself—you name it. This is Hotel World. With nearly 130,000 hotel rooms and counting in the metro area, Orlando is second only to Las Vegas in the total number of guest rooms in the city, and certainly in a dead heat with Las Vegas for another distinction—number of hotels built with the idea of not just housing their guests but entertaining them as well.

There are no slot machines or big show rooms in Orlando, of course, but there are plenty of hotels that offer everything from clowns and characters in costume performing for the kids to massive indoor amusements—like the Gaylord Palms, which offers re-creations of the Everglades, old St. Augustine, and Key West under a gargantuan glass roof that creates the biggest hotel atrium in town—so far.

I-Drive, at least in the area around the Orange County Convention Center, is going more upscale as the center draws more convention attendees ready to spring for more expensive rooms. But you can still find relative bargains throughout the Orlando area by researching your trip well and shopping wisely.

In recent years, for instance, Disney World itself has entered the bargain hotel room market, with roughly 9,000 sub-$100-per-night hotel rooms in its All-Star Sports, Music, and Movies and Pop Century Resorts alone. And a family can still find a few clean, efficient, and safe hotel rooms in the $50-a-night range in the off-season (late summer) in parts of Kissimmee and the International Drive and Universal Orlando areas.

Even though 2009 was clearly a tough year for Orlando, economically—three big new resort hotels were scheduled to open their doors in October, including the 1,400-room Hilton Orlando, the first Waldorf Astoria outside of New York City, and the Hilton Orlando Bonnet Creek adjacent to the Waldorf.

BEST BETS FOR ORLANDO LODGING

With thousands of hotels to choose from, ask yourself first what your family truly wants to do in Orlando during your visit. This will invariably lead to the "on-property/off property" debate, and more questions. To assist you, here are our top recommendations by price (any property listed here has at least some rooms in the noted range) and experience. The very best properties—those that provide a particularly remarkable experience in their price range—are designated in the listings with the Fodor's Choice logo.

Fodor'sChoice ★

All-Star Sports, Music & Movies Resorts, p. 350
The Courtyard at Lake Lucerne, p. 387
Grand Floridian Resort & Spa, p. 346
Hyatt Regency Grand Cypress Resort, p. 362
Nickelodeon Family Suites by Holiday Inn, p. 363
Ritz-Carlton Orlando Grande Lakes, p. 383
Royal Pacific Resort, p. 373
Wilderness Lodge, p. 347

By Price

¢

Celebrity Resorts Kissimmee, p. 367

Holiday Inn Express & Suites Orlando South, p. 372
South Gate Inn, p. 390

$

All-Star Sports, Music & Movies Resorts, p. 350
Extended Stay Deluxe Orlando-Universal Studios, p. 371
Hyatt Place Orlando/Convention Center, p. 379
Hyatt Place Orlando/Universal, p. 372
Parc Corniche Condominium Suite Hotel, p. 381
Pop Century Resort, p. 350

$$

The Courtyard at Lake Lucerne, p. 387
Caribbean Beach Resort, p. 348

Coronado Springs Resort, p. 349
Gaylord Palms Resort, p. 368
Lake Buena Vista Resort, p. 355
Nickelodeon Family Suites by Holiday Inn, p. 363

$$$

Contemporary Resort, p. 344
Fort Wilderness Resort Cabins, p. 345
Grand Bohemian, p. 388
Hyatt Regency Grand Cypress Resort, p. 362
Royal Pacific Resort, p. 373
Walt Disney World Dolphin, p. 353
Walt Disney World Swan, p. 354

Wilderness Lodge, p. 347

$$$$

Grand Floridian Resort & Spa, p. 346
Ritz-Carlton Orlando Grande Lakes, p. 383
Polynesian Resort, p. 347

By Experience

MOST KID-FRIENDLY

All-Star Sports, Music & Movies Resorts, p. 350
Contemporary Resort, p. 344
Doubletree Castle, p. 375
Grand Floridian Resort & Spa, p. 346
Nickelodean Family Suites by Holiday Inn, p. 363
Pop Century Resort, p. 350

BEST POOLS

Boardwalk Inn & Villas, p. 348
Hyatt Regency Grand Cypress Resort, p. 362
JW Marriott Orlando Grande Lakes, p. 379
Omni Orlando Resort at ChampionsGate, p. 369
Portofino Bay Resort, p. 373
Ritz-Carlton Orlando Grande Lakes, p. 383

TOP 5 DISNEY HOTELS

All-Star Movies Resort. Kids love the giant *Toy Story* figures and Disney-movie themes everywhere, and parents love the price.

BoardWalk Inn & Villas. The price is right and the location can't be beat for adults more interested in Epcot and nightlife than being close to the Magic Kingdom.

Grand Floridian Resort & Spa. If you want to be on the monorail line just minutes from the Magic Kingdom's gate and you can splurge to

stay in a gorgeous luxury hotel, the Grand Floridian is for you.

Wilderness Lodge. Close to the Magic Kingdom yet surprisingly secluded, this stunning retreat is perfect for families who prefer a lodge theme in a good location.

Yacht & Beach Club Resorts. With a man-made beach, spacious family suites, and a relaxed, luxurious, Ralph Lauren–esque feel, the Yacht and Beach clubs appeals to families looking for tranquillity and beauty closer to Epcot.

DO WE STAY ON-PROPERTY?

If you stay on-property, which means anywhere within the Walt Disney World Resort, you can, for the most part, put aside your car keys, because Disney buses and monorails are efficient enough to make it possible to visit one park in the morning and another after lunch with a Park Hopper pass. You have the freedom to return to your hotel for R&R when the crowds are thickest, and if it turns out that half the family wants to spend the afternoon in Epcot and the other half wants to float around Typhoon Lagoon, it's not a problem.

Rooms in the more expensive Disney-owned properties are large enough to accommodate up to five, and villas sleep six or seven. All rooms have cable TV with the Disney Channel and a daily events channel.

If you're an on-site guest at a Disney lodging, you're guaranteed entry to parks even when they have reached capacity, as the Magic Kingdom, Disney–MGM Studios, Blizzard Beach, and Typhoon Lagoon sometimes do. You also get other perks like meal plans ($39 a day); the chance to enter Disney parks earlier and stay later than nonguests; and the ability to use the Magical Express service to check your bags through to the hotel from your home airport when departing for Orlando and back again on return.

Though rates are often better at non-Disney owned hotels on Disney property (e.g., the Swan, the Dolphin, and the hotels on the so-called Hotel Row just outside Downtown Disney), the perks are fewer. Be sure to clarify what you'll get for the money at each type of property.

The hotels closest to WDW are clustered in a few principal areas: along I-Drive; in the U.S. 192 area and Kissimmee; and in the Downtown Disney–Lake Buena Vista Area, just off I–4 Exit 68. Nearly every hotel in these areas provides frequent transportation to and from WDW. In addition, there are some noteworthy, if far-flung, options in the suburbs and in the greater Orlando area. If you're willing to make the commute,

BEST BETS FOR ORLANDO LODGING

With thousands of hotels to choose from, ask yourself first what your family truly wants to do in Orlando during your visit. This will invariably lead to the "on-property/off property" debate, and more questions. To assist you, here are our top recommendations by price (any property listed here has at least some rooms in the noted range) and experience. The very best properties—those that provide a particularly remarkable experience in their price range—are designated in the listings with the Fodor's Choice logo.

TOP 5 DISNEY HOTELS

All-Star Movies Resort. Kids love the giant *Toy Story* figures and Disney-movie themes everywhere, and parents love the price.

BoardWalk Inn & Villas. The price is right and the location can't be beat for adults more interested in Epcot and nightlife than being close to the Magic Kingdom.

Grand Floridian Resort & Spa. If you want to be on the monorail line just minutes from the Magic Kingdom's gate and you can splurge to stay in a gorgeous luxury hotel, the Grand Floridian is for you.

Wilderness Lodge. Close to the Magic Kingdom yet surprisingly secluded, this stunning retreat is perfect for families who prefer a lodge theme in a good location.

Yacht & Beach Club Resorts. With a man-made beach, spacious family suites, and a relaxed, luxurious, Ralph Lauren–esque feel, the Yacht and Beach clubs appeals to families looking for tranquillity and beauty closer to Epcot.

DO WE STAY ON-PROPERTY?

If you stay on-property, which means anywhere within the Walt Disney World Resort, you can, for the most part, put aside your car keys, because Disney buses and monorails are efficient enough to make it possible to visit one park in the morning and another after lunch with a Park Hopper pass. You have the freedom to return to your hotel for R&R when the crowds are thickest, and if it turns out that half the family wants to spend the afternoon in Epcot and the other half wants to float around Typhoon Lagoon, it's not a problem.

Rooms in the more expensive Disney-owned properties are large enough to accommodate up to five, and villas sleep six or seven. All rooms have cable TV with the Disney Channel and a daily events channel.

If you're an on-site guest at a Disney lodging, you're guaranteed entry to parks even when they have reached capacity, as the Magic Kingdom, Disney–MGM Studios, Blizzard Beach, and Typhoon Lagoon sometimes do. You also get other perks like meal plans ($39 a day); the chance to enter Disney parks earlier and stay later than nonguests; and the ability to use the Magical Express service to check your bags through to the hotel from your home airport when departing for Orlando and back again on return.

Though rates are often better at non-Disney owned hotels on Disney property (e.g., the Swan, the Dolphin, and the hotels on the so-called Hotel Row just outside Downtown Disney), the perks are fewer. Be sure to clarify what you'll get for the money at each type of property.

The hotels closest to WDW are clustered in a few principal areas: along I-Drive; in the U.S. 192 area and Kissimmee; and in the Downtown Disney–Lake Buena Vista Area, just off I–4 Exit 68. Nearly every hotel in these areas provides frequent transportation to and from WDW. In addition, there are some noteworthy, if far-flung, options in the suburbs and in the greater Orlando area. If you're willing to make the commute,

TOP 5 OFF-SITE HOTELS

Gaylord Palms Resort. The interior of this place is like a Cecil B. DeMille movie—about Florida. Just walking around in the 4-acre atrium is an adventure in itself: the Everglades, old St. Augustine. The wow-factor isn't exclusive to the theme parks.

Hyatt Regency Grand Cypress Resort. A top-class resort with sprawling grounds almost on top of Walt Disney World property, the Hyatt is perfect for families who want to be near the Mouse but need to take a break from Disney each night.

Nickelodeon Family Suites by Holiday Inn. For the same amount you'd spend on a basic room at a Disney value resort, you get a suite with a separate area for the kids, a Nickelodeon-theme pool, and tons of kids' activities at this family-oriented hotel.

Ritz-Carlton Orlando Grande Lakes. Ultraluxurious rooms, restaurants, and spa programs, plus a championship golf course, make this resort one of the best in the Orlando area.

Royal Pacific Resort. Like roller coasters? Got teens? You might want to stay at Universal Orlando instead of Disney. A stay at this South Pacific–theme hotel gets you into the Express lines on an unlimited basis for free.

12

you'll probably save a bundle. Whereas the Hilton near Downtown Disney charges about $200 a night in season, another Hilton about 45 minutes away in Altamonte Springs has rates that start at $140. Other costs, such as gas and restaurants, are also lower in the northeast suburbs. One suburban caveat: traffic on I-4 in Orlando experiences typical freeway gridlock during morning (7–9 AM) and evening (4–6 PM) rush hours.

RESERVATIONS

Reserve your hotel several months in advance if you want to snag the best rooms during high season. You can book all on-site accommodations—including Disney-owned hotels, non-Disney-owned hotels, and the Hotel Row properties—through the **WDW Central Reservations Office** (✉ Box 10100, Suite 300, Lake Buena Vista 32830 ☎ 407/934–7639 ⊕ www.disneyworld.com). People with disabilities can call **WDW Special Request Reservations** (☎ 407/939–7807) to get information or book rooms at any of the on-site Disney properties.

When you book a room, be sure to mention whether you have a disability or are traveling with children and whether you prefer a certain type of bed or have any other concerns. You may need to pay a deposit for your first night's stay within three weeks of making your reservation. At many hotels you can get a refund if you cancel at least five days before your scheduled arrival. However, individual hotel policies vary, and some properties may require up to 15 days' notice for a full refund. Check before booking.

If neither the WDW Central Reservations Office nor the off-site hotels have space on your preferred dates, look into packages from American Express, Delta, or other operators, which have been allotted whole blocks of rooms. In addition, because there are always cancellations, it's worth trying at the last minute; for same-day bookings, call the property directly. Packages, including airfare, cruises, car rentals, and hotels both on and off Disney property, can be arranged through your travel agent or **Walt Disney Travel Co.** (⊠ *7100 Municipal Dr., Orlando* ☎ *407/828–3232* ⊕ *www.disneyworld.com*).

RATES

There's an inverse corollary between the reading on the thermometer and the room rate. Hot and humid weather in September and October ("fall" is not certain to arrive until after Thanksgiving) bring low prices. Conversely, the entire population of North America seems to want to be in Orlando in February, March, and April, and hotel owners know that and charge accordingly. One note about hurricane season—it officially begins in June, but in reality—there have been virtually no hurricanes in Florida before August during the past century. One other thing to remember, Orlando is 50 mi from the nearest ocean—hurricane activity of any consequence in Orlando is quite rare.

Like everywhere else, Orlando experienced an upward drift in hotel prices during 2005 and 2006. Although it used to be quite easy to find worthwhile lodging for less than $80 per room night, now that threshold has drifted closer to $100. The lodgings we list are the top selections of their type in each category. Rates are lowest from early January to mid-February, from late April to mid-June, and from mid-August to the third week in December.

Always call several places—availability and special deals can often drive room rates at a $$$$ hotel down into the $$ range—and don't forget to ask whether you're eligible for a discount. Many hotels offer special rates for members of, for example, the American Automobile Association (AAA) or the American Association of Retired Persons (AARP). Don't overlook the savings to be gained from preparing your own breakfast and maybe a few other meals as well, which you can do if you choose a room or suite with a kitchenette or kitchen. In listings, we always name the facilities that are available, but we don't specify whether they cost extra.

DISCOUNT RESERVATIONS To save money, look into discount reservations services with Web sites and toll-free numbers, which use their buying power to get a better price on hotels, airline tickets, even car rentals. When booking a room, always call the hotel's local toll-free number (if one is available) rather than the central reservations number—you'll often get a better price. Always ask about special packages or corporate rates.

Hotel Rooms Accommodations Express (☎ *800/444–7666 or 800/277–1064* ⊕ *www.accommodationsexpress.com*). **Central Reservation Service** (*CRS* ☎ *800/555–7555 or 800/548–3311* ⊕ *www.crshotels.com*). **Hotels.com** (☎ *800/246–8357* ⊕ *www.hotels.com*). **Quikbook** (☎ *800/789–9887* ⊕ *www. quikbook.com*). **Turbotrip.com** (☎ *800/473–7829* ⊕ *www.turbotrip.com*).

WHERE TO STAY

	VIBE	PROS	CONS
Disney Parks and Properties	Literally thousands of rooms at every price point; extremely convenient to Disney's four theme parks, with free transportation to get you all over the huge WDW complex.	Perks like early park entry, free transportation system, and Disney's Magical Express, which permits you to circumvent airport bag checks.	Without a rental car, you likely won't be seeing, eating, or drinking anything during your entire stay that Disney has not produced.
Lake Buena Vista	Many hotel and restaurant chains have a presence in this area immediately adjacent to WDW. Almost every guest in your hotel is headed for a WDW park.	Really close to WDW; plenty of dining and shopping options; easy access to I-4 for vacationers who want to see other parts of Orlando as well.	Heavy traffic during peak hours. As it is with all neighborhoods near Disney, a gallon of gas will be a good 10%-15% more than you will pay in Central Orlando.
Kissimmee	Another tourism district that goes back almost 40 years, Kissimmee is replete with more mom 'n pop motels and restaurants than any other part of the metro area.	Located just outside Disney, it's very close to the Magic Kingdom. If you like quintessential Old Florida venues like places to buy salt-water taffy, you'll love Kissimmee.	Some of the motels here can be a little seedy. Petty crime in which tourists are victims is rare—but not unheard of.
Universal Orlando Area/I-Drive	The oldest and most diverse tourism district in Orlando, I-Drive has a free shuttle to the myriad attractions, shops, and restaurants along the lengthy boulevard.	Plenty of dining and shopping options; convenient to Universal Orlando, SeaWorld, and big Pointe Orlando dining and shopping plaza.	If you're driving, traffic can be heavy at peak hours; some parts of I-Drive are considered garish (but not unsafe) by some visitors—this place is proletariat world.
Downtown Orlando	Parts of town have the high-rises you'd expect of a modern city. Other areas have old-South charm: imagine brick streets winding among small, cypress ringed lakes.	Lots of locally owned restaurants and some quaint B&Bs are here. If you plan to head to nearby Florida cities, this is a great place to access I-4.	You will need to rent a car. And that traffic headed toward WDW from central Orlando? You'll be part of it. Expect the 25-mi drive to take at least 45 minutes.
Davenport	It is what it is: Off a busy interstate, a small collection of inexpensive chain hotels and motels.	Quite close to WDW; location on the southwest side of the Orlando metro area means little traffic.	Not really a garden spot, just a small motel and hotel stop.
Winter Park	This old-money enclave has plenty of tony dining and shopping options; quaint downtown.	Lots of lakes, museums, and shopping. Tree-lined brick streets and pleasant, small parks.	Renting a car will be a must, and this is another 10 minutes farther from WDW than downtown Orlando.

12

WHAT IT COSTS					
	¢	$	$$	$$$	$$$$
FOR TWO PEOPLE	under $80	$80–$140	$140–$220	$220–$280	over $280

Price categories reflect the range between the least and most expensive standard double rooms in nonholiday high season, based on the European Plan (with no meals) unless otherwise noted. City and state taxes (10%–12%) are extra.

WHAT TO CONSIDER FOR YOUR FAMILY

If you're coming to Orlando with kids, you're the quintessential target customer that hotels in Orlando have literally spent billions of dollars trying to attract. Only a few hotels in Orlando are not kid-friendly. A good hint how kid-friendly a big hotel might be, for example, is whether the hotel has a "lazy river" style pool, like the Ritz-Carlton Orlando Grande Lakes or the Omni Orlando Resort at Champions-Gate, for instance—which one might normally think of as "adult oriented" hotels. That swimming pool feature means the hotel has spent $1 million or so on something their research tells them will attract customers with children. You can bet they're kid-friendly. A step in your research is to ask, before booking, if your hotel has a children's program, babysitting available, or a policy by which kids eat free with a paying adult in their restaurant. This is a market in which travelers with youngsters can expect a lot.

Walt Disney World has strong children's facilities and programs at the BoardWalk, Contemporary, Dolphin, Grand Floridian, Polynesian, Swan, Wilderness Lodge, and Yacht and Beach Club resorts. The Polynesian Resort's Neverland Club has an enchanting Peter Pan–theme clubhouse and youngsters-only dinner show. Parents also rave about the Sand Castle Club at the Yacht and Beach Club resorts. The BoardWalk's child-care facility, Harbor Club, provides late-afternoon and evening child care for children ages 4–12.

Many hotels have supervised children's programs with trained counselors and planned activities as well as attractive facilities; some even have mascots. Standouts are the Hyatt Regency Grand Cypress, near Downtown Disney, and the Camp Holiday programs at the Holiday Inn SunSpree Resort Lake Buena Vista.

East of International Drive, the connected JW Marriott and Ritz-Carlton Grand Lakes resorts have rooms with adjoining kids' suites, complete with miniature furniture and toys. Additionally, the JW Marriott has a 24,000-square-foot "lazy river" pool, and the Ritz-Carlton has a Kids Club with a play area and daily scheduled activities.

Nickelodeon Family Suites by Holiday Inn, in Lake Buena Vista, offers suites with separate kid-friendly bedrooms decorated with images of cartoon characters. Plus, there are scheduled breakfasts and shows featuring Nick characters.

BABYSITTING

The **Kid's Nite Out** (☎407/828–0920 or 800/696–8105 🌐*www.kidsniteout.com*) program works in participating hotels throughout the Orlando area, including the Disney resorts. It provides infant care and in-room babysitting for children ages 6 weeks to 12 years (a waiver must be signed for older children who are under the care of the sitter). Fees start at $14 an hour for one child, and increase by $2.50 for each additional child. There's a four-hour minimum, plus a transportation fee of $10 for the sitter to travel to your hotel room. When you make a reservation, you must provide a credit-card number. There's a 24-hour cancellation policy; if you cancel with less than 24 hours' notice, your credit card is charged the four-hour minimum fee ($56 for one child, higher rates for multiple children booked). The service recommends booking from two weeks to 90 days in advance.

DELIVERY ROOM

If you're staying in a room, suite, or condo and need to rent baby equipment, such as a stroller, bassinet, high chair, or even pool toys, call **A Baby's Best Friend** (☎407/891–2241 or 888/461–2229 toll-free in U.S. 🌐*www.abbf.com*), for swift delivery and fair rates. You can order online, and the company also carries refrigerators and microwaves if your hotel or resort doesn't provide them.

PEOPLE WITH DISABILITIES

Hotels and motels at Walt Disney World are continually being renovated to comply with the Americans with Disabilities Act. Most resorts here in every price range have rooms with roll-in showers or transfer benches in the bathrooms. Especially worthwhile and convenient are the luxurious Grand Floridian and the Port Orleans–French Quarter.

Outside Disney World, the definition of accessibility seems to differ from hotel to hotel. Some properties may be accessible by ADA standards for people with mobility problems but not for people with hearing or vision impairments, for example. One of the most accommodating off-Disney resorts is the Orlando World Center Marriott; its level of commitment is especially notable each morning, when the Solaris Restaurant hosts a bountiful, wheelchair-accessible buffet breakfast.

Newer hotels, such as the JW Marriott Orlando Grand Lakes, are fully accessible. In most properties, only elevators are Braille-equipped, but some have programs to help employees understand how best to assist guests with visual impairments. Particularly outstanding is the Buena Vista Palace Hotel & Spa. The Embassy Suites hotels offer services such as talking alarm clocks and Braille or recorded menus.

Most area properties have purchased the equipment necessary to accommodate guests with hearing impairments. Telecommunications devices for the deaf, flashing or vibrating phones and alarms, and closed captioning are common; an industry-wide effort to teach some employees sign language is under way. The Regal Sun Resort, on Hotel Plaza Boulevard, has excellent facilities but no Teletype reservations line.

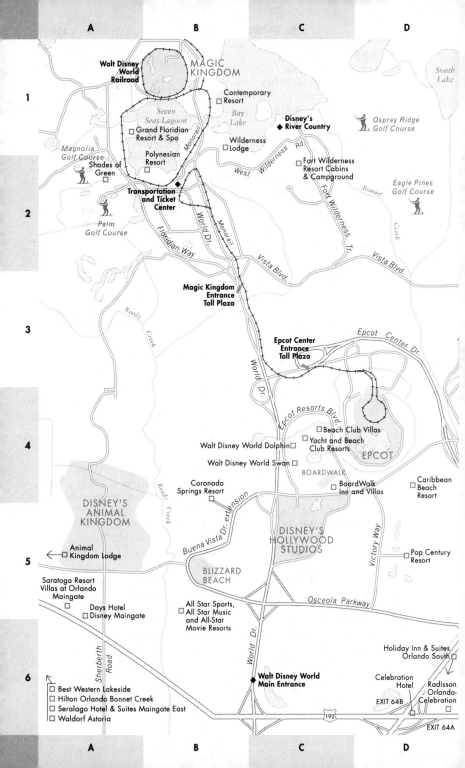

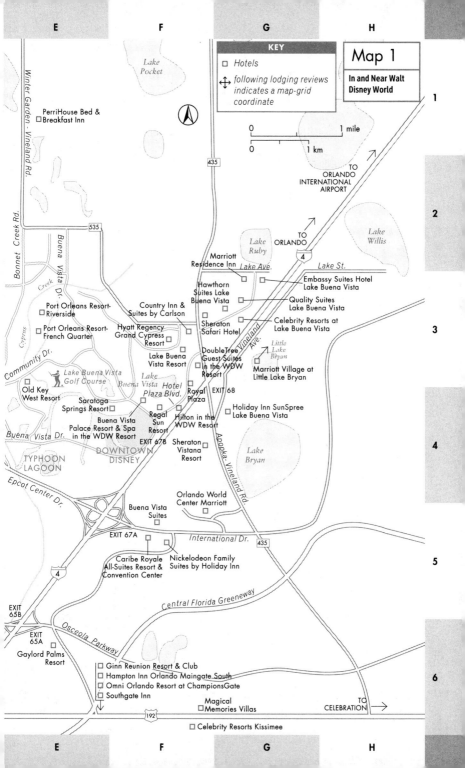

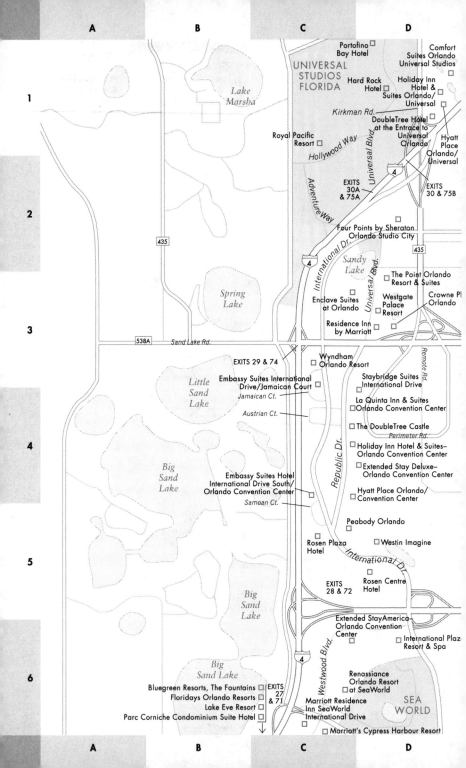

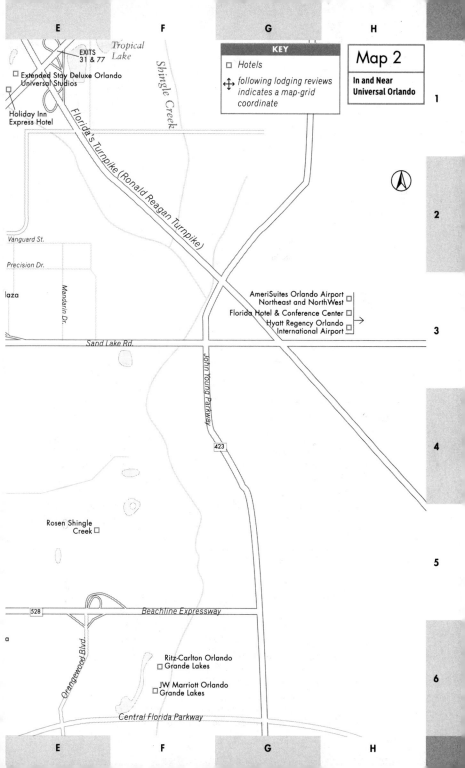

KEY

□ Hotels

⬍ following lodging reviews indicates a map-grid coordinate

Map 2

In and Near Universal Orlando

E F G H

1

2

3

4

5

6

Tropical Lake

EXITS 31 & 77

□ Extended Stay Deluxe Orlando Universal Studios

□

Holiday Inn Express Hotel

Shingle Creek

Florida's Turnpike (Ronald Reagan Turnpike)

Vanguard St.

Precision Dr.

laza

Mandarin Dr.

Sand Lake Rd.

AmeriSuites Orlando Airport Northeast and NorthWest □
Florida Hotel & Conference Center □
Hyatt Regency Orlando International Airport □ →

John Young Parkway

423

Rosen Shingle Creek □

528

Beachline Expressway

a

Orangewood Blvd.

Ritz-Carlton Orlando
□ Grande Lakes

JW Marriott Orlando
□ Grande Lakes

Central Florida Parkway

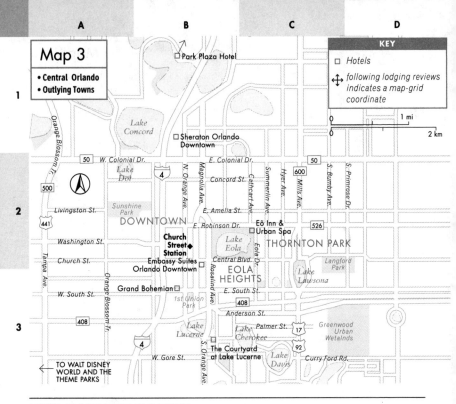

Map 3
- Central Orlando
- Outlying Towns

KEY

□ Hotels

following lodging reviews indicates a map-grid coordinate

Park Plaza Hotel

Sheraton Orlando Downtown

Eō Inn & Urban Spa

THORNTON PARK

Church Street Station

Embassy Suites Orlando Downtown

Grand Bohemian

The Courtyard at Lake Lucerne

TO WALT DISNEY WORLD AND THE THEME PARKS

THE DISNEY PARKS

Disney-operated hotels are fantasies unto themselves. Each is immaculately designed according to a theme (quaint New England, the relaxed culture of the Polynesian Islands, an African safari village, etc.) and each offers the same perks: free transportation from the airport and to the parks, the option to charge all your purchases to your room, special guest-only park-visiting times, and much more. If you stay on-site, you'll have better access to the parks and you'll be more immersed in the Disney experience.

MAGIC KINGDOM RESORT AREA

Take I–4 Exit 62, 64B, or 65.

The ritzy hotels near the Magic Kingdom all lie on the monorail route and are only minutes away from the park. Fort Wilderness Resort and Campground, with RV and tent sites, is a bit farther southeast of the Magic Kingdom, and access to the parks is by bus.

$$$–$$$$ **Contemporary Resort.** You're paying for location, and perhaps tradition, when you stay here. This 15-story, flat-topped pyramid, the first hotel to open here more than 37 years ago, has been completely renovated several times. The 2006–07 upgrade brought workstation desks, flat-panel TVs, blond-wood furniture that is truly "contemporary" and marble bathroom vanities. The monorail runs through the lobby, so it

12

takes just minutes to get to the Magic Kingdom and Epcot. Upper floors of the main tower (where rooms are more expensive) offer great views of all the activities in and around the Magic Kingdom, including the nightly fireworks. For the fireworks alone, at least one dinner at the California Grill (atop the building) is worth the pricey dinner tab. **Pros:** easy access to Magic Kingdom; Chef Mickey's is here, the epicenter of the character-meal world; launching point for romantic sunset Bay Lake cruises. **Cons:** a mix of conventioneers and vacationers (there's an on-site convention center) means that it is sometimes too frenzied for the former and too staid for the latter; among the most kid-intensive of the pricier Disney hotels, so if you don't like children around, look elsewhere; pricey for what you get, unless location is a huge priority for your family. ☎407/824–1000 ➹1,013 rooms, 25 suites ♿In-room: safe, refrigerator, Internet. In-hotel: 3 restaurants, room service, tennis courts, pools, gym, beachfront, concierge, concierge floor, children's programs (ages 4–12), laundry facilities, laundry service, executive floor, public Wi-Fi, no-smoking rooms ▤AE, D, DC, MC, V ✛1:B1.

¢ – $ 🏕 **Fort Wilderness Resort Campground.** Bringing a tent or RV is one of the cheapest ways to stay on WDW property, especially considering that sites accommodate up to 10. Tent sites with water and electricity are real bargains. RV sites cost more but are equipped with electric, water, and sewage hookups as well as outdoor charcoal grills and picnic tables. Even with just a good tent and cozy sleeping bag you'll be relatively comfortable, since the campground has 15 strategically located comfort stations where you can take a hot shower, as well as laundry facilities, restaurants, a general store—everything you need. There are many activities to keep you occupied, such as tennis and horseback riding. Tents can be rented for $30 a night, so it's easy to camp here with virtually no gear of your own. **Pros:** Disney's most economical lodging; pets allowed ($5 nightly fee per campsite, not per pet). **Cons:** amount of walking within the camp (to reach the store, restaurants, etc.) can be a bit much for some; shuttle rides to Disney parks take too long; the bugs can be irritating especially around twilight, except in winter. ☎407/824–2742 or 407/ 934–7639 ➹788 campsites, 695 with full hookups, 90 partial hookups ♿pools, flush toilets, full hookups, dump station, drinking water, guest laundry, showers, picnic tables, food service, electricity, public telephone ▤AE, D, DC, MC, V ✛1:C2.

$$$–$$$$ 🏕 **Fort Wilderness Resort Cabins.** This 700-acre campground is a resort in itself. With its dozens of entertainment options—including biking, outdoor movies, and singing around the campfire—and the very popular Hoop-Dee-Doo Musical Review character event, a family can have a truly memorable vacation. The campground is so big that you may want to rent a golf cart (about $45 a day) or a bike ($22 a day). There's a shuttle bus system, but it's about 20 minutes between departures. The larger cabins can accommodate four grown-ups and two youngsters; the bedroom has a double bed and a bunk bed, and the living room has a double sleeper sofa or Murphy bed. Each cabin has a fully equipped kitchen, and daily housekeeping is provided. **Pros:** cabins don't constitute roughing it (they have air-conditioning); you can save a fortune by cooking, but you don't have to, thanks to the three-meals-a-day

Perks for Disney Resort Guests

■ **Location! Location! Location!**
You'll probably get to the parks faster than guests staying off-site, and if you plan to stay at Disney for your whole trip, you won't need to rent a car.

■ **Extra Magic Hour.** You get special early- and late-night admission to certain parks on specified days—call ahead for information about each park's "magic hours" days to plan your early- and late-visit strategies.

■ **Magical Express.** This perk answers that bothersome question, "How do I get there from the airport?" If you're staying at a Disney hotel, you don't need to rent a car, and you don't even have to think about finding a shuttle or taxi. With Disney Magical Express, once you get off your plane at Orlando International, you're met by a Disney rep who leads you to a coach that takes you directly to your hotel. You don't even have to worry about picking up your luggage; it is delivered separately and usually arrives at your hotel room an hour or two after you do. Participating airlines include American, Continental, Delta, JetBlue, Northwest, Southwest, and United. When you're ready to leave, the process works in reverse (though only on some participating airlines,

so check in advance). You get your boarding pass and check your bags at the hotel. Then you go to the airport and go directly to your gate, skipping check-in. You won't see your bags until you're in your hometown airport. Best of all, the service is free.

■ **Package Delivery.** Anything you purchase, whether at one of the parks, one of the hotels, or even in Downtown Disney, can be delivered to the gift shop of your Disney hotel free of charge. It's a big plus not to have to carry your packages around all day.

■ **Priority Reservations.** Hotel guests get priority reservations at Disney restaurants by calling 407/939–3463. Hotel guests also get the choicest tee times at Disney golf courses. Reserve them up to 30 days in advance by calling 407/939–4654.

■ **Charging Privileges.** You can charge most meals and purchases throughout Disney to your hotel room.

■ **Free Parking.** Parking is free for hotel guests, and that extends beyond hotel parking lots. Show your parking pass when you go to any of the Disney parks and you won't be charged for parking.

---

restaurant and nightly barbecue. **Cons:** shuttle to Disney theme parks is free, but slow; coin-op laundry is pricey ($2 to wash, $2 to dry). ☎407/824–2900 ⇗408 cabins ♿In-room: kitchen, Internet. In-hotel: restaurant, tennis courts, pools, beachfront, bicycles, laundry facilities, no-smoking rooms ▤AE, D, DC, MC, V ✛1:C2.

$$$$ ☷ **Grand Floridian Resort & Spa.** On the shores of the Seven Seas Lagoon,
Fodor'sChoice   this red, gable-roof Victorian is all delicate gingerbread, rambling veran-
★   das, and brick chimneys. It's Disney's flagship resort, with everything from its best-appointed guest rooms to the high-quality hotel amenities, like a dock from which you can rent a boat or take the ferry across the adjoining lake. The place isn't bad to just look at, either, with faux Victorian architecture that makes it look like some of the grand old wooden hotels built in Florida in the 19th century. Add a dinner at one

12

of the two on-site restaurants, Victoria & Albert's or Cítricos and you may spend more in a weekend here than on your mortgage payment—but you'll have great memories. Although you won't look out of place walking through the lobby in flip-flops, afternoon high tea and a pianist playing nightly in the lobby are among the high-scale touches. The Mouseketeer Clubhouse on the ground floor offers children's programs until midnight daily. **Pros:** on the monorail; Victoria & Albert's, one of the state's best restaurants is located here; if you're a couple with no kids, this can be among the least noisy of the on-property Disney hotels. **Cons:** some say it's not ritzy enough to match the room rates; conference center and convention clientele lend to the stuffiness; Victoria & Albert's no longer seats kids 10 and under. ☎407/824–3000 *900 rooms, 90 suites* ⌂ *In-room: safe, Internet, Wi-Fi. In-hotel: 5 restaurants, room service, tennis courts, pools, gym, spa, beachfront, concierge, children's programs (ages 4–12), laundry facilities, laundry service, executive floor, no-smoking rooms* ▭*AE, D, DC, MC, V* ✢*1:A1.*

$$$$ ▦**Polynesian Resort.** You may not think you're in Fiji, but it's not hard to pretend here, especially after downing a few of the tropical drinks available in the Great Ceremonial House—aka the lobby. In the three-story atrium lobby orchids bloom alongside coconut palms and banana trees, and water cascades from volcanic-rock fountains. At the evening luau, Polynesian dancers perform before a feast with Hawaiian-style roast pork. Rooms sleep five, since they all have two queen-size beds and a daybed. Most rooms also have a balcony or patio. Lagoon-view rooms—which overlook Magic Kingdom fireworks—are peaceful but costly. **Pros:** on the monorail; great aloha-spirit atmosphere. **Cons:** pricey; not good for those bothered by lots of loud children. ☎407/824–2000 *853 rooms, 5 suites* ⌂ *In-room: safe, Internet. In-hotel: 4 restaurants, room service, bar, pools, gym, beachfront, children's programs (ages 4–12), laundry facilities, laundry service, concierge, executive floor, public Wi-Fi, no-smoking rooms* ▭*AE, D, DC, MC, V* ✢*1:B2.*

$$$–$$$$ ▦**Wilderness Lodge.** The architects outdid themselves with this seven-
Fodor's Choice   story hotel modeled after the majestic turn-of-the-20th-century lodges
★   of the American Northwest. The five-story lobby, supported by towering tree trunks, has an 82-foot-high, three-sided fireplace made of rocks from the Grand Canyon and lighted by enormous tepee-shaped chandeliers. Two 55-foot-tall hand-carved totem poles complete the illusion. Rooms have leather chairs, patchwork quilts, cowboy art, and a balcony or a patio. The hotel's showstopper is its Fire Rock Geyser, a faux Old Faithful, near the large pool, which begins as an artificially heated hot spring in the lobby. This hotel is a good option if you're a couple without kids looking for more serenity than is found at Disney's other hotels. **Pros:** high-wow-factor architecture; one of the restaurants, Artist Point, is among the best at Disney; boarding point for romantic Bay Lake sunset cruises. **Cons:** ferry toots its horn at every docking; no direct shuttle to Magic Kingdom. ☎407/824–3200 *728 rooms, 31 suites* ⌂ *In-room: safe, Internet. In-hotel: 3 restaurants, room service, pool, beachfront, bicycles, children's programs (ages 4–12), laundry facilities, laundry service, concierge, executive floor, public Wi-Fi, no-smoking rooms* ▭*AE, D, DC, MC, V* ✢*1:B1.*

EPCOT RESORT AREA

Take I–4 Exit 64B or 65.

From the Epcot resorts you can walk or take a boat to the International Gateway entrance to Epcot, or you can take the shuttle from your hotel or drive to the Future World (front) entrance.

$$$$ **Beach Club Villas.** Each villa has a separate living room, kitchen, and one or two bedrooms; studios are more like hotel rooms. Interiors are soft yellow and green with white iron bedsteads. Private balconies on the upper levels or porches at street level ensure that you can enjoy your morning coffee in the sun with a view of the lake. The villas are marketed as time-share properties for Disney Vacation Club members, but available rooms are also rented on a per-night basis. You'll have access to all the facilities of the adjacent Yacht and Beach Club resorts, including Stormalong Bay. The Studio Villas do not have full kitchens; the more expensive, one and two-bedroom villas, which cost up to $665 a night during high-season (for the one bedroom unit), have all the furnishings of a nice home. **Pros:** short walk to Epcot's BoardWalk area; in-suite kitchens let you save money on meals. **Cons:** can be noisy; not close to Magic or Animal Kingdoms. ☎407/934–8000 ⤶205 villas ⚫ In-room: safe, Internet. In-hotel: restaurant, room service, tennis courts, pools, gym, beachfront, laundry service, concierge, public Wi-Fi, no-smoking rooms ▤AE, D, DC, MC, V ✛1:C4.

$$$$ **BoardWalk Inn and Villas.** Disney's smallest deluxe hotel is a beautiful re-creation of Victorian-era Atlantic City inn. Architectural master Robert A.M. Stern designed it to mimic 19th-century New England building styles. Rooms have floral-print bedspreads and blue-and-white painted furniture. Those overlooking Crescent Lake cost the most and are the noisiest. A 200-foot waterslide in the form of a classic wooden roller coaster cascades into the pool area. The property opens directly onto Disney's BoardWalk entertainment complex, where you can ride surrey bikes, watch a game at the ESPN Sports Club, or dine in some of Disney's better restaurants. The hotel is also a 15-minute walk from Disney–MGM Studios. **Pros:** quick access to nighttime fun; rooms are larger than average (390 square feet). **Cons:** shuttle to Magic Kingdom and other parks is slow. ☎407/939–5100 inn, 407/939–6200 villas ⤶370 rooms, 19 suites, 526 villas ⚫ In-room: safe, Internet. In-hotel: 4 restaurants, room service, tennis court, pool, gym, concierge, children's programs (ages 4–12), laundry facilities, laundry service, public Wi-Fi, no-smoking rooms ▤AE, D, DC, MC, V ✛1:C4.

$$–$$$ **Caribbean Beach Resort.** Six palm-studded "villages," all awash in dizzying pastels and labeled with Caribbean names like Barbados and Trinidad, share 45-acre Barefoot Bay and its white-sand beach. Bridges connect to a 1-acre path-crossed play and picnic area called Parrot Cay. You can rent boats to explore the lake, or rent bikes to ride along the 1½-mi lakefront promenade. The Old Port Royale complex, decorated with cannons, statues, and tropical birds, has a food court, lounge, and pool area with falls and a big slide. Rooms, which have painted-wood furniture, are fresh and done in soft pastels like turquoise and peach. **Pros:** restaurants sell Jamaica's Red Stripe beer; plenty of on-site

outdoor activities, giving the place a lush "summer camp" feel; convenient to Epcot, Disney-MGM, and Downtown Disney. **Cons:** you don't truly feel swept away to a tropical island; the only crystalline and swimmable waters are in the pools; walks from your room to the beach or a restaurant can be up to 15 minutes. ☎407/934–3400 ➷2,112 rooms ⬧In-room: safe, Internet. In-hotel: restaurant, room service, pools, beachfront, bicycles, no elevator, laundry facilities, laundry service, public Wi-Fi, no-smoking rooms ☰AE, D, DC, MC, V ✛1:D4.

$$–$$$ 🏨 **Coronado Springs Resort.** Because of its 95,000-square-foot convention center and the adjacent 84,000-square-foot exhibit hall, this is Disney's most popular convention hotel. But since the meeting space is in its own wing, the moderately priced resort is also popular with families who appreciate its casual Southwestern architecture, its lively, Mexican-style food court, and its elaborate swimming pool, which has a Mayan pyramid with a big slide. There's a full-service health club and spa, and if you like jogging, walking, or biking you're in the right place—a pleasant path circles the lake. You can rent bikes, kayaks, canoes, and paddleboats. **Pros:** great pool with a play area/arcade for kids and a bar for adults; lots of outdoor activities. **Cons:** some accommodations are a half-mile from the restaurants; standard rooms are on the small side (314 square feet); kids may find the subdued atmosphere boring. ☎407/939–1000 ➷1,967 rooms ⬧In-room: safe, Internet. In-hotel: 2 restaurants, room service, bar, pools, gym, spa, bicycles, laundry service, public Wi-Fi, no-smoking rooms ☰AE, D, DC, MC, V ✛1:B4.

$$$$ 🏨 **Yacht and Beach Club Resorts.** These big Seven Seas Lagoon inns seem straight out of a Cape Cod summer, if perhaps a tad institutional because of their sheer size. The five-story Yacht Club has hardwood floors, a lobby full of gleaming brass and polished leather, an oyster-gray clapboard facade, and evergreen landscaping; there's even a lighthouse on its pier. Rooms have floral-print bedspreads and a small ship's wheel on the headboard. At the Beach Club, a croquet lawn and cabana-dotted white-sand beach set the scene. Stormalong Bay, a 3-acre water park with slides and whirlpools, is part of this club. Both lodgings have "quiet pools," which are secluded and largely kid-free, albeit nondescript. **Pros:** location, location, location—it's easy to walk to Epcot and the BoardWalk, and Disney–MGM is a fun, 20-minute ferry ride away. **Cons:** distances within the hotel—like, from your room to the front desk—can seem vast; high-noise factor. ☎407/934–8000 Beach Club, 407/934–7000 Yacht Club ➷1,213 rooms, 112 suites ⬧In-room: safe, Internet, Wi-Fi. In-hotel: 4 restaurants, room service, tennis courts, pools, gym, beachfront, bicycles, children's programs (ages 4–12), laundry service, concierge, public Wi-Fi, no-smoking rooms ☰AE, D, DC, MC, V ✛1:C4.

ANIMAL KINGDOM RESORT AREA

Take I–4 Exit 64B.

In the park's southwest corner, Disney's third resort area comprises the fabulous Africa-theme Animal Kingdom Lodge, plus two budget-price hotel complexes: All-Star Village, not far from U.S. 192, and the Pop Century Resort, on Osceola Parkway.

$–$$
Fodor's Choice
★
☺
All-Star Sports, All-Star Music, and All-Star Movies Resorts. Stay here if you want the quintessential Disney-with-your-kids experience, or if you're a couple that feels all that pitter-pattering of little feet is a reasonable tradeoff for a good deal on a room. (Hint: for a little peace, request a room away from pools and other common areas.) In the Sports resort, Goofy is the pitcher in the baseball-diamond pool; in the Music resort you'll walk by giant bongos; and in the Movies resort,

WORD OF MOUTH

"I'd also recommend staying at the All-Star resorts or Pop Century, if they're available, primarily based on the size of your group. At an outside resort, you'd probably need a rental car, which would have to be a minivan to accommodate everyone, which eats into your savings and costs more for gas."   –karameli

huge characters like *Toy Story*'s Buzz Lightyear frame each building. Each room has two double beds, a closet rod, an armoire, and a desk. At 260 square feet, these are the smallest rooms in any Disney hotel, which helps keep the room rate down. The food courts sell standard fare, and you can have pizza delivered to your room. **Pros:** unbeatable price for a Disney property. **Cons:** no kids' clubs or programs, possibly because this is on the bottom tier of Disney hotels in terms of room rates; distances between rooms and on-site amenities can seem vast. ☎407/939–5000 *Sports, 407/939–6000 Music, 407/939–7000 Movies* ⌁*1,920 rooms at each* ⌂*In-room: safe, Internet. In-hotel: room service, bars, pools, laundry facilities, laundry service, public Internet, public Wi-Fi, no-smoking rooms* ⊟*AE, D, DC, MC, V* ⊹*1:B5.*

$$$–$$$$
Animal Kingdom Lodge. Giraffes, zebras, and other wildlife roam three 11-acre savannas separated by wings of this grand hotel. In the atrium lobby, a massive faux-thatched roof hovers almost 100 feet above hardwood floors with inlaid carvings. Cultural ambassadors give talks about their African homelands, the animals, and the artwork on display; evenings include storytelling sessions around the fire circle on the Arusha Rock terrace. All the romantic rooms (with drapes descending from the ceiling to lend a tentlike feel) have a bit of African art, including carved headboards, pen-and-ink drawings, or original prints. Most rooms also have balconies overlooking the wildlife reserve. **Pros:** extraordinary wildlife and cultural experiences; Jiko and Boma restaurants serve authentic African cuisine, although the menus have become a little less pure African and a little more American in recent years. **Cons:** shuttle to parks other than Animal Kingdom can take more than an hour; guided savannah tours available only to guests on the concierge level, where the least expensive room is $100 a night higher than the least expensive rooms in other parts of the hotel. ☎407/934–7639 ⌁*1,293 rooms* ⌂*In-room: safe, Internet. In-hotel: 3 restaurants, bar, pools, gym, spa, children's programs (ages 4–12), laundry facilities, laundry service, public Wi-Fi, no-smoking rooms* ⊟*AE, D, DC, MC, V* ⊹*1:A5.*

$–$$
Pop Century Resort. Giant jukeboxes, 65-foot-tall bowling pins, an oversized Big Wheel and Rubik's Cube, and other pop-culture memorabilia are scattered throughout the grounds. Items from mood rings to eight-track tapes are incorporated into the architecture; wall-mounted

shadow boxes display toys, fashions, and fads from each decade since the 1950s. Brightly colored rooms are functional for families, with two double beds or one king. A big food court and a cafeteria serve reasonably priced fare. This megahotel was opened in 2003 after the All-Star Resorts at Disney proved that a low price point was a big draw for many families. **Pros:** great room rates; hotel provides a trip down memory lane; proximity to ESPN Wide World of Sports and Disney-MGM. **Cons:** big crowds at the front desk; big crowds (and noise) in the food court; small rooms; lots of small kids around. ☎407/934–7639 ⚓2,880 rooms ⚲In-room: safe, Internet. In-hotel: room service, bar, pools, gym, laundry service, public Wi-Fi, no-smoking rooms ▤AE, D, DC, MC, V ⚑1:D5.

DOWNTOWN DISNEY RESORT AREA

Take I–4 Exit 64B or 68.

The Downtown Disney–Lake Buena Vista resort area, east of Epcot, has two mid-price resorts with an Old South theme, plus the upscale Old Key West Resort. From here shuttles are available to all of the parks.

$$$$ 🏨 **Old Key West Resort.** A red-and-white lighthouse helps you find your way through this marina-style resort. Freestanding villas resemble turn-of-the-20th-century Key West houses, with white clapboard siding and private balconies that overlook the waterways winding through the grounds. The one-, two-, or three-bedroom houses have whirlpools in the master bedrooms, full-size kitchens (which could save you a fortune on food if you shop at an off-site grocery store), washers and dryers, and patios. The 2,265-square-foot three-bedroom grand villas accommodate up to 12 adults—so bring some friends. The resort is part of the Disney Vacation Club network, but rooms are rented to anyone when they're available. A ferry service will transport you across the lake to Downtown Disney, which can be a fun experience in itself. **Pros:** quiet and romantic; abundance of accommodations with whirlpool baths. **Cons:** distances between rooms and restaurants, recreation facilities, bus stops. ☎407/827–7700 ⚓761 units ⚲In-room: safe, Internet, Wi-Fi. In-hotel: restaurant, tennis courts, 4 pools, gym, spa, bicycles, laundry facilities, laundry service, no-smoking rooms ▤AE, D, DC, MC, V ⚑1:E3.

$$–$$$ 🏨 **Port Orleans Resort–French Quarter.** Ornate Big Easy–style row houses with vine-covered balconies cluster around squares planted with magnolias. Lamp-lighted sidewalks are named for French Quarter thoroughfares. Because this place is relatively quiet, it appeals more to couples than families with kids, although, like any WDW hotel, it is not devoid of youngsters. The food court serves Crescent City specialties such as jambalaya and beignets. Scat Cat's Lounge is a serene little bar.

Doubloon Lagoon, one of Disney's most exotic pools, includes a clever "sea serpent" slide that swallows and then spits you into the water. **Pros:** authentic, fun New Orleans–style atmosphere; lots of water recreation options, including boat rentals; "Standard View" rooms have a view of the parking lot, but in peak season they are $25 a night cheaper than the rooms with better views. **Cons:** even though there are fewer kids here, public areas can still be quite noisy; shuttle service is slow; food court is the only on-site dining option. ☎407/934–5000 ⌂1,008 rooms ♿ In-room: safe, Internet. In-hotel: pool, bicycles, laundry facilities, laundry service, public Wi-Fi, no-smoking rooms ▤AE, D, DC, MC, V ✚1:E3.

$$–$$$ 🏨**Port Orleans Resort–Riverside.** Buildings look like plantation-style mansions (in the Magnolia Bend section) and rustic bayou dwellings (in the Alligator Bayou section) and you can typically pick which section you want. Rooms accommodate up to four in two double beds and have wooden armoires, quilted bedspreads, and gleaming brass faucets; a few rooms have king-size beds. The registration area looks like a steamboat interior, and the 3½-acre, old-fashioned swimming-hole complex called Ol' Man Island has a pool with slides, rope swings, and a nearby play area. Recreation options here include fishing trips on the Sassagoula River, paddleboat and canoe rentals, and evening carriage rides. **Pros:** carriage rides; river cruises; lots of recreation options for kids. **Cons:** shuttle can be slow; no shortage of extremely noisy youngsters, if that's a concern. ☎407/934–6000 ⌂2,048 rooms ♿ In-room: safe, Internet. In-hotel: restaurant, pools, gym, bicycles, laundry facilities, laundry service, no-smoking rooms ▤AE, D, DC, MC, V ✚1:E3.

$$$$ 🏨**Saratoga Springs Resort.** This large Disney Vacation Club has hundreds of units on 16 acres. Three- and four-story buildings, decorated inside and out to look like the 19th-century resorts of upstate New York, overlook a giant pool with artificial hot springs and faux boulders. Standard rooms, with 355 square feet, have microwaves and refrigerators; suites have full kitchens. Three-bedroom family suites—as big as most homes, with 2,265 square feet—occupy two levels and have dining rooms, living rooms, and four bathrooms. Rich woods, Early American–style furniture, and overstuffed couches lend a homey, country-chic look. You can walk to Downtown Disney in 10 minutes or take the ferry, which docks near Fulton's Crab House. **Pros:** in-room massage available; abundance of rooms with whirlpool baths. **Cons:** it's a fair hike from some accommodations to the restaurant and other facilities. ☎407/934–7639 ⌂828 units ♿ In-room: safe, Internet. In-hotel: restaurant, tennis courts, pools, gym, spa, bicycles, public Wi-Fi, no-smoking rooms ▤AE, D, DC, MC, V ✚1:F4.

OTHER ON-SITE HOTELS

Although not operated by the Disney organization, the Swan and the Dolphin just outside Epcot, Shades of Green near the Magic Kingdom, and the hotels along Hotel Plaza Boulevard near Downtown Disney call themselves "official" Walt Disney World hotels. While the Swan, Dolphin, and Shades of Green have the special privileges of on-site

Disney hotels, such as free transportation to and from the parks and early park entry, the Downtown Disney resorts have their own systems to shuttle hotel guests to the parks.

MAGIC KINGDOM RESORT AREA

$-$$$ 🏨**Shades of Green.** Operated by the U.S. Armed Forces Recreation Center, the resort is open only to active-duty and retired personnel from the armed forces, as well as reserves, National Guard, active civilian employees of the Department of Defense, widows or widowers of service members, disabled veterans, and Medal of Honor recipients. Rates vary with your rank, but are significantly lower than at Disney hotels open to the public. You'll find a Tuscan-style restaurant, a ballroom for weddings and other events, 11 family suites that sleep up to eight adults each, and two swimming pools surrounded by expansive decks and lush, tropical foliage. A little-known fact is that the resort is a short walk from the Polynesian, so it's easy to use the Monorail stop at the Polynesian to expedite your travels around Disney World. **Pros:** large standard rooms (480 square feet); on Disney's shuttle line; Army–Air Force Exchange store discounts deeply for people with military IDs. **Cons:** three-night minimum stay; fee ($7 a day) for Internet usage. ☎407/824–3600 or 888/593–2242 ⊕*www.shadesofgreen.org* ⇨*586 rooms, 11 suites* ♿*In-room: safe, refrigerator, Internet. In-hotel: 4 restaurants, room service, bars, outdoor tennis courts, pools, gym, children's programs (ages 4–12), laundry facilities, laundry service, public Wi-Fi, no-smoking rooms* ▭*AE, D, MC, V* ✚*1:A2.*

EPCOT RESORT AREA

Take I–4 Exit 64B or 65.

$$$-$$$$ 🏨 **Walt Disney World Dolphin.** World-renowned architect Michael Graves designed the neighboring Dolphin and Swan hotels. Outside, a pair of 56-foot-tall sea creatures bookend this 25-story glass pyramid. The fabric-draped lobby resembles a giant sultan's tent. All rooms have either two queen beds or one king, and bright, beach-inspired spreads and drapes. The pillow-top mattresses, down comforters, and multitude of overstuffed pillows make the beds here some of the kingdom's most comfortable. Extensive children's programs include Camp Dolphin summer camp and the five-hour Dolphin Dinner Club. **Pros:** access to all facilities at the Walt Disney World Swan; easy walk to BoardWalk; good on-site restaurants. **Cons:** rooms only dip below $250 in off-season; self-parking is $9 a day; the hotel rolled out a $10 a day "resort fee" in 2008 that covers Internet access and local phone calls; room charge privileges stop at the front door, and don't extend to the Disney parks. ⊠*1500 Epcot Resorts Blvd., Lake Buena Vista* ☎407/934–4000 or 800/227–1500 ⊕*www.swandolphin.com* ⇨*1,509 rooms, 136 suites* ♿*In-room: safe, Internet. In-hotel: 9 restaurants, room service, tennis courts, pools, gym, spa, beachfront, children's programs (ages 4–12), executive floor, concierge, public Wi-Fi, no-smoking rooms* ▭*AE, D, DC, MC, V* ✚*1:C4.*

$$$–$$$$ 🏨 **Walt Disney World Swan.** Facing the Dolphin across Crescent Lake, the Swan is another example of the postmodern "Learning from Las Vegas" school of entertainment architecture characteristic of Michael Graves. Two 46-foot swans grace the rooftop of this coral-and-aquamarine hotel, and the massive main lobby is decorated with a playful mix of tropical imagery. Guest rooms are quirkily decorated with floral and geometric patterns, pineapples painted on furniture, and exotic bird-shaped lamps. Every room has two queen beds or one king, two phone lines (one data port), and a coffeemaker; some have balconies. The Grotto, a 3-acre water playground complete with waterslides, waterfalls, and all the trimming, is nearby, as is Disney's BoardWalk and the Fantasia Gardens miniature golf complex. You can walk for miles around here and always be in a super-pleasant Disney environment. **Pros:** charge privileges and access to all facilities at the Dolphin (but not inside Disney World); easy walk to BoardWalk; good on-site restaurants. **Cons:** rooms only dip below $250 in off-season; like the Dolphin, the Swan now levees a $10 per night resort fee, which at least eliminates charges for in-room Internet access, and gives you 60 minutes a day of free local phone calls. ⌂ *1200 Epcot Resorts Blvd., Lake Buena Vista* ☎ *407/934–3000 or 800/248–7926* ⊕ *www.swandolphin.com* ⌲ *756 rooms, 55 suites* ⌂ *In-room: safe, Internet. In-hotel: 6 restaurants, room service, tennis courts, pools, gym, spa, beachfront, children's programs (ages 4–12), executive floor, concierge, public Wi-Fi, no-smoking rooms* ⊟ *AE, D, DC, MC, V* ⊕ *1:C4.*

DOWNTOWN DISNEY RESORT AREA

Take I–4 Exit 68.

A number of non-Disney-owned resorts are clustered on Disney property not far from Downtown Disney, and several more sprawling, high-quality resorts are just outside the park's northernmost entrance. Several of these hotels market themselves as "official" Disney hotels, meaning that they have special agreements with Disney that allow them to offer their guests perks such as early park admission. The hotels on Hotel Plaza Boulevard are within walking distance of Downtown Disney Marketplace, though most offer shuttle service anyway.

$–$$$ 🏨 **Buena Vista Palace Resort & Spa in the WDW Resort.** This hotel gets kudos as much for its on-site charms as for its location—100 yards from the Wolfgang Puck's restaurant in Downtown Disney. All rooms have patios or balconies, most with great views of Downtown Disney. As a guest, you receive free transportation to all Disney parks, the chance to sign up for Disney character meals at your hotel, access to Disney golf courses, and early entrance to the Disney theme parks, just like in the Disney on-property hotels. **Pros:** easy walk to Downtown Disney; spa is huge and luxurious. **Cons:** inconvenient to Universal and downtown Orlando. ⊠*1900 Buena Vista Dr., Lake Buena Vista* ☎*407/827–2727* ⊕*www.luxuryresorts.com* ☞*1,014 rooms, 209 suites* ♿*In-room: safe, Internet. In-hotel: 4 restaurants, room service, tennis courts, pools, gym, spa, children's programs (ages 4–12), laundry facilities, laundry service, concierge, public Wi-Fi, no-smoking rooms* ▤*AE, D, DC, MC, V* ✠*1:F4.*

12

$$–$$$$ 🏨 **Doubletree Guest Suites in the WDW Resort.** The lavender-and-pink exterior that used to leap out at you, and not in a good way, has given way to a more sedate beige, and the interior has gotten a makeover as well. Comfortable one- and two-bedroom suites are decorated in tasteful hues, with blue carpeting and bedspreads and raspberry colored furniture. Each bedroom has either a king bed or two doubles. Units come with three TVs, including one in the bathroom, and a wet bar, microwave, refrigerator, and coffeemaker. The small lobby has a charming feature—a small aviary with birds from South America and Africa. There's a special "registration desk" for kids, where they can get coloring books, balloons, and chocolate chip cookies. **Pros:** within walking distance of Downtown Disney; free shuttle to all Disney attractions. **Cons:** inconvenient to Universal and downtown Orlando. ⊠*2305 Hotel Plaza Blvd., Lake Buena Vista* ☎*407/934–1000 or 800/222–8733* ⊕*www.doubletreeguestsuites.com* ☞*229 units* ♿*In-room: safe, refrigerator, Internet. In-hotel: restaurant, room service, bars, tennis courts, pool, gym, laundry facilities, laundry service, public Wi-Fi, no-smoking rooms* ▤*AE, DC, MC, V* ✠*1:F3.*

$–$$$ 🏨 **Hilton in the WDW Resort.** An ingenious waterfall tumbles off the covered entrance and into a stone fountain surrounded by palm trees. Although not huge, rooms are upbeat, cozy, and contemporary, with flat-screen TVs and work tables, and many on the upper floors have great views of Downtown Disney, which is just a short walk away. The hotel offers two good eateries: Andiamo Italian Bistro, specializing in pasta and grilled seafood, and a Benihana Steakhouse and Sushi Bar. Guests can enter Disney parks an hour before they officially open. The Hilton is one of the Orlando hotels certified by the Florida Green Lodging program, meaning it follows prescribed environmental standards for recycling, and water and electric consumption. **Pros:** close to Downtown Disney; because this is an "official" Disney hotel (although not a Disney-operated one) you get the same early-entrance privileges to Disney Parks; free shuttle bus; kids program. **Cons:** pricier than similar lodgings farther from Disney; inconvenient to Universal and downtown Orlando. ⊠*1751 Hotel Plaza Blvd., Lake Buena Vista* ☎*407/827–4000, 800/782–4414 reservations* ⊕*www.hilton.com* ☞*814 rooms, 27 suites* ♿*In-room: safe, Internet. In-hotel: 7 restaurants, room service, pools, gym, children's programs (ages 3–12), laundry facilities, laundry service, public Wi-Fi, no-smoking rooms* ▤*AE, DC, MC* ✠*1:F4.*

$–$$$ 🏨 **Lake Buena Vista Resort.** A 2008 renovation of the lobby, and the adjoining restaurant and bar, has given this place a much cleaner, less-smaltzy look, without doing away with one of the hotel's best assets—the great green view of the wetlands that back up to the building.

They also added an in-house Pizza Hut that offers to-go goodies, and the renovation in its entirety has brought a more current feel to the place. Most rooms have private, furnished balconies with spectacular views of the nightly Disney fireworks. Disney shuttles are available, but you can walk to Downtown Disney in 10 minutes or less. The resort also offers free shuttle service to Orlando outlet malls. Pros: one of the best bargains on Hotel Row; close to Downtown Disney. Cons: not as plush as other Hotel Row properties; inconvenient to Universal and downtown Orlando. ⊠ *2000 Hotel Plaza Blvd., Lake Buena Vista* ☎ *407/828–2424 or 800/937–8376* ⊕ *www.lakebuenavistaresorthotel. com* ↪ *325 rooms* ♿ *In-room: Internet. In-hotel: restaurant, room service, pool, laundry facilities, laundry service, no-smoking rooms* ☰ *AE, D, DC, MC, V* ⊕ *1:F3.*

$–$$$ ▦ **Regal Sun Resort.** Any hotel that's an easy walk from Downtown Disney is by its very nature a great draw for tourists, so that's why the investors in this hotel poured $25 million into upgrading it when they re-invented the former Grosvenor Resort and turned it into the Regal Sun Resort in 2007. The multimillion-dollar makeover included redoing the lobby area with bamboo decor and new hardwood floors. The 619 guest rooms and seven suites were completely refurbished and now have red bed coverings and bright blue carpeting. The pool area was also totally redone with the addition of a clover-leaf "beach entry"–style swimming pool. Pros: within walking distance of Downtown Disney; free shuttle to all Disney attractions. Cons: inconvenient to Universal and downtown Orlando. ⊠ *1850 Hotel Plaza Blvd., Downtown Disney, Lake Buena Vista* ☎ *407/828–4444 or 800/624–4109* ⊕ *www. regalsunresort.com* ↪ *619 rooms, 7 suites* ♿ *In-room: safe, refrigerator, Internet. In-hotel: 3 restaurants, lobby bar, pool bar, room service, tennis courts, pools, laundry service, no-smoking rooms* ☰ *AE, DC, MC, V* ⊕ *1:F4.*

$$–$$$$ ▦ **Royal Plaza.** Spruced-up guest rooms have plasma-screen TVs, pillow-top mattresses, and granite bathroom counters. Some ground-level rooms have semiprivate, gated patios that overlook the swimming pool. The restaurant, the Giraffe Café, is informal but pleasant and specializes in gourmet pizzas with toppings like Boursin cheese and lump crabmeat. Kids under 10, accompanied by parents, eat free at the restaurant, and on check-in, adults can book a length-of-stay all you can eat breakfast buffet for $37.50 per person. You can rent microwaves and refrigerators for your room, for $75 (each) per stay. Pros: within walking distance of Downtown Disney; free shuttle to all Disney attractions. Cons: inconvenient to Universal and downtown Orlando; airport shuttle costs $48. ⊠ *1905 Hotel Plaza Blvd., Lake Buena Vista* ☎ *407/828–2828* ⊕ *www.royalplaza.com* ↪ *394 rooms, 5 suites* ♿ *In-room: safe, Internet. In-hotel: 2 restaurants, room service, tennis courts, pools, laundry service, public Wi-Fi, no-smoking rooms* ☰ *AE, DC, MC, V* ⊕ *1:F3.*

OFF-SITE HOTELS NEAR WALT DISNEY WORLD

LAKE BUENA VISTA AREA

12

Many people stay in resorts a bit farther northeast of Downtown Disney because, though equally grand, they tend to be less expensive than those right on Hotel Plaza Boulevard. If you're willing to take a five-minute drive or shuttle ride, you might save as much as 35% off your room tab.

Perennially popular with families are the all-suites properties, many with in-room kitchens, just east of Lake Buena Vista Drive. And this is an area in which it is safe to walk, even in the evening, although you should be careful crossing streets—traffic is heavy. Furthermore, the 1,100-room Marriott Village at Lake Buena Vista, across I–4 from Downtown Disney, has made a splash in hotel-laden Orlando with its utter comprehensiveness. The gated, secure village has three hotels, a multi-restaurant complex, a video-rental store, a 24-hour convenience store, and a Hertz rental-car station. There's also an on-property Disney booking station, staffed by a Disney employee who can answer questions and make suggestions.

$–$$ Buena Vista Suites. In this all-suites property you get a bedroom, a living room with a foldout sofa bed, two TVs, two phones, and a small kitchen with a coffeemaker, sink, microwave, and refrigerator. King suites have a single king bed and a whirlpool bath. This is the sister property of the Caribe Royale, next door, so you effectively have five restaurants (including the three at the Caribe) and you can charge meals to your room at all of them. **Pros:** free hot breakfast buffet; free Disney shuttle. **Cons:** not much of interest within walking distance, besides the hotel next door (but there is a convenience store across the street). ✉*8203 World Center Dr., Lake Buena Vista Area* ☎*407/239–8588 or 800/537–7737* ⏏*www.buenavistasuites.com* ↪*280 suites* ⟺*In-room: safe, refrigerator, Internet. In-hotel: 2 restaurants, room service, tennis courts, pool, gym, laundry facilities, public Wi-Fi, no-smoking rooms* ▭*AE, D, DC, MC, V* ⏍*BP* ✛*1:F5.*

$$–$$$ Caribe Royale All-Suites Resort & Convention Center. This big pink palace of a hotel, with flowing palm trees and massive artificial waterfalls, wouldn't look out of place in Vegas. Huge ballrooms attract corporate conferences, but there are key family-friendly ingredients, too: free transportation to Disney (10 minutes away) and a huge children's recreation area, including a big pool with a 65-foot slide. Suites are 450 to 500 square feet and have spacious living rooms with pull-out sofa beds, kitchenettes, and one or more bedrooms; most suites have Jacuzzis. **Pros:** family-friendly; great pool area; good on-site restaurants; free shuttle to Disney; reciprocal room-charge privileges at the restaurants in the Buena Vista suites hotel next door. **Cons:** too far to walk to shops and restaurants. ✉*8101 World Center Dr., Orlando* ☎*407/238–8000 or 800/823–8300* ⏏*www.cariberoyale.com* ↪*1,218 suites, 120 villas* ⟺*In-room: kitchen (some), refrigerator, Internet. In-hotel: 4 restaurants, room service, tennis courts, pool, fitness center, concierge,*

laundry facilities, laundry service, no-smoking rooms ⊟*AE, D, DC, MC, V* ⍚│*BP* ✛*1:F5.*

$–$$$ ⊞ **Celebrity Resorts at Lake Buena Vista.** The large, comfortable, one- to three-bedroom suites here can sleep 4 to 10 people. Add full kitchens, dining and living areas, and washer-dryer sets, and you have excellent accommodations for families who want more space and amenities for their money. The Spanish-style architecture gives way to tastefully furnished interiors, although doors between rooms in the same suite are a little thin. Master bedrooms have floor-to-ceiling mirrors on two walls, and whirlpool tubs in the bathrooms. A small playground and a large, attractive outdoor pool are surrounded by pretty landscaping, and Downtown Disney is just a mile away. **Pros:** upscale atmosphere; convenient to Disney; in-suite hot tubs. **Cons:** no theme-park shuttles; need a car to reach most things of interest. ✉*8451 Palm Pkwy., Lake Buena Vista* ☎*407/238–1700 or 800/423–8604* ⊕*www.celebrityresorts.com* ⇱*66 suites* ♿*In-room: safe, kitchen (some), Internet. In-hotel: restaurant, basketball court, racquetball court, tennis court, 3 pools, gym, children's programs (ages 4–12), laundry facilities, laundry service, no-smoking rooms* ⊟*AE, D, MC, V* ✛*1:G3.*

$–$$ ⊞ **Country Inn & Suites by Carlson.** The signature lobby fireplace looks a little ridiculous in Orlando, but the in-room amenities and proximity to Downtown Disney (½ mi away) make this hotel a good bet for either families or couples. For $120–$144 (depending on the date) you can book what the hotel calls a one-bedroom Country Kids Suite, with two beds, two TVs (one of which is hooked up for video games), a refrigerator, and a microwave. And the place is within easy walking distance of a lot of restaurants, a shopping mall, and Disney Hotel Row, where you can catch the Disney Shuttle busses to the parks—for free. **Pros:** within walking distance of Downtown Disney; refrigerators in every room; free shuttle to Disney World; free Continental breakfast. **Cons:** no on-site restaurant; no room service (but there are plenty of restaurants within walking distance and it's quite safe to walk in this neighborhood). ✉*12191 S. Apopka Vineland Rd., Orlando* ☎*407/239–1115 or 800/456–4000* ⊕*www.countryinns.com* ⇱*170 rooms, 50 suites* ♿*In-room: safe, refrigerator, Internet (fee). In-hotel: pool, gym, laundry facilities, public Wi-Fi, no-smoking rooms* ⊟*AE, D, DC, MC, V* ⍚│*CP* ✛*1:F3.*

$$–$$$ ⊞ **Embassy Suites Hotel Lake Buena Vista.** The peach facade of this hotel, clearly visible from I–4, makes it something of a local landmark. But even if you find the color scheme too much, it's attractive for other reasons. It's 1 mi from Downtown Disney, 3 mi from SeaWorld, and 7 mi from Universal Orlando. Each suite has a separate living room and two TVs, along with a microwave and mini-refrigerator. The atrium lobby, loaded with vegetation and soothed by the sounds of a rushing fountain, is a great place to enjoy the free cooked-to-order breakfast and evening cocktails. **Pros:** convenient to Downtown Disney; free shuttle to all Disney parks; within walking distance of restaurants and shops, including downtown Disney. **Cons:** public areas are noisy. ✉*8100 Lake Ave., Orlando* ☎*407/239–1144, 800/257–8483, or 800/362–2779* ⊕*www. embassysuites.com* ⇱*333 suites* ♿*In-room: safe, refrigerator, Internet.*

In-hotel: 2 restaurants, room service, basketball court, tennis court, pool, gym, children's programs (ages 4–12), no-smoking rooms ▭*AE, D, DC, MC, V* ⦿*BP* ✛*1:G3.*

$–$$ ▦**Hawthorn Suites Resort Lake Buena Vista.** Every suite has a bedroom and a full kitchen, including a dishwasher, a two-burner stovetop, a microwave, and a refrigerator, but if you don't want to cook breakfast, there's a free hot breakfast buffet, even though there is no on-site restaurant other times of the day. Twenty-four-hour room service is available from an outside provider with which the hotel has a contract. Downtown Disney is 1 mi away, and it's a pleasant walk if you're inclined for a stroll. **Pros:** affordable; full kitchens; easy walk to shops. **Cons:** pool area gets noisy; two-night minimum during peak season in March and April. ✉*8303 Palm Pkwy., Orlando* ☎*407/597–5000 or 866/756–3778* ⊕*www.hawthornlakebuenavista.com* ⤴*120 suites* ♿*In-room: safe, kitchen, refrigerator, Internet. In-hotel: bar, pool, outdoor Jacuzzi, basketball court, room service, laundry facilities, public Wi-Fi, no-smoking rooms* ▭*AE, D, DC, MC, V* ⦿*CP* ✛*1:G3.*

$$$–$$$$ ▦**Hilton Orlando Bonnet Creek.** Next door to the Waldorf-Astoria hotel, and connected via a convention hall between the two buildings, the Hilton Orlando Bonnet Creek is part of Hilton's new, 428-acre resort immediately adjacent to Disney World's own vast forest lands, making it a pristine, über-resort that is the most ambitious luxury resort to come to Orlando since the Ritz-Carlton Grande Lakes half a dozen years ago. The Hilton, open in October 2009, is not quite as plush as the Waldorf, but it is an amenity-laden property just the same. The Hilton shares a 122,000 square-foot convention hall and a championship golf course with the Waldorf. It targets corporate meetings, but also offers great appeal for families, with its 2-acre lagoon pool, resort pool, children's program, and, of course, transportation to Disney World. Guests at the Hilton can use the facilities at the Waldorf, including the Waldorf Astoria Spa by Guerlain and the Waldorf restaurants. The Hilton offers four restaurants of its own, La Luce, featuring signature Chef Donna Scala, Harvest, Sucre, and Beech. Rooms include amenities like 42-inch, flat-screen television sets. **Pros:** wonderful setting for a hotel—remote feeling while being close to Disney World; next door to the Waldorf, with its amenities easily at hand. **Cons:** nothing within walking distance; you will need to rent a car. ✉*14100 Bonnet Creek Resort Land, Bonnet Creek* ☎*407/597–5500* ⊕*www.hiltonbonnetcreek.com* ⤴*964 rooms, 36 suites* ♿*In-room: Internet, safe. In-hotel: 4 restaurants, room service, 2 bars, 18-hole golf course, pool, gym, spa, concierge, children's programs (ages 4–12), laundry service, executive floor, public Wi-Fi, no-smoking rooms* ▭*AE, D, DC, MC, V* ✛*1:A6.*

$–$$ ▦**Holiday Inn SunSpree Lake Buena Vista.** This family-oriented hotel has a children's registration desk. Off the lobby you'll find the CyberArcade; a small theater where clowns perform weekends at 7 PM; and a buffet restaurant where kids accompanied by adults eat free at their own little picnic tables. Families love the Kidsuites: playhouse-style rooms within a larger room, which only costs about $25 a night more than a room for two adults. **Pros:** extremely kid-friendly; great deal for families; you can walk to some off-property restaurants, and a very handy,

CLOSE UP

Spas That Pamper With Panache

Once upon a time something crucial was missing in Central Florida's vacation kingdom. There were castles and thrill rides, performing whales and golf meccas, but there were no standout spas, no havens of respite for the millions who trekked their feet flat and rubbed their shoulders raw lugging backpacks from one attraction to the next.

Now weary travelers can rejoice. It's a spa-world after all in Central Florida. Several pampering palaces at first-rate resorts can add blessed balance to your visit. Some of the finest spas have seized on Florida's reputation as a citrus production center and will baste and massage you with essences of lemon, lime, orange, and grapefruit. Others import exotic treatments from Bali, Japan, and Thailand. Each spa offers signature treatments in addition to the usual massages, facials, and pedicures. You can even find leg-relief treatments for exhausted park hoppers. All resort spas offer bottled water, teas, and fresh-fruit snacks, and with any treatment you'll have access to saunas, steam rooms, whirlpools, and fitness facilities.

The **Buena Vista Palace Hotel & Spa** has one of the area's most popular full-service rejuvenation centers, with intimate, beautiful surroundings, reasonable prices, and light lunches in the courtyard. If you're like many spa guests here, you'll indulge in a tropical body polish and moisturizing massage—the Royal Velvet Sugar Scrub, featuring mango-ginger sugar crystals and moisturizing mango body butter (80 minutes, $175). Or you might try the ultra-relaxing, skin-smoothing European Rose Body Treatment (80 minutes, $160), a cream-based body polish with sun-dried rose clay wrap and essential oil treatment. Say "ahh" as African Shea Butter is gently massaged into your skin. To extend the feeling, add on the Delicate Skin Soother Facial (50 minutes, $135). Take your beautified body to Downtown Disney afterward for shopping, lunch or dinner—it's just across the street.

Fruit-enhanced fantasies can be realized at the lavish spa in the **Ritz-Carlton Orlando Grande Lakes,** where the two-hour Relax Body Ritual ($330) is one of several signature treatments featuring organic products that range from cranberry pomegranate to pear and green apple. You retire to a special suite where you choose your favorite flavor for a body-smoothing exfoliation. Your therapist next applies aromatic moisturizers for a hydrating body wrap that precedes an invigorating massage. Finally, you ease into the suite's tub for a hydrotherapy soak—you can control the jets to suit your mood. The Ritz has an excellent spa with 42 treatment rooms in a 40,000-square-foot facility. It also has the highest prices. But if you want to indulge in the royal lifestyle, this is the place to do it.

A stone's throw from the theme parks is the **Canyon Ranch SpaClub at Gaylord Palms.** Here the Canyon Stone Massage (80 minutes, $190) paves the path to nirvana. Smooth volcanic stones of several sizes are heated to a temperature between 115°F and 124°F. After applying oil to the stones, your therapist works them along your body using either Swedish, deep tissue, shiatsu, or Reiki techniques. If you've already experienced a traditional massage, this is a wonderfully soothing alternative.

A Balinese paradise in landlocked Central Florida? It's right there at Universal Orlando's Portofino Bay Hotel, where the **Mandara Spa** delivers the signature Mandara Four Hand Massage (50 minutes, $230), in which two therapists massage you simultaneously, and the Balinese Massage (50 minutes, $125), involving acupressure and Swedish techniques. There's also a **Mandara Spa** on Disney property at the Walt Disney World Dolphin.

Almost as soon as you enter Disney's **Grand Floridian Resort & Spa** you can feel the stress melt away. Established in 1997, the Grand's spa has kept up its flawless reputation with its signature treatments, such as the Citrus Zest Therapies (80 minutes, $190), in which a soothing dose of grapefruit body oil is used in an aromatherapy massage, followed by reflexology. Families can enjoy the experience together—there's a couples treatment room, and there's a menu of facials, manicures, and pedicures for kids. Arrive an hour or so ahead of your appointment for complimentary use of the fitness center and a soak in the hot tub.

Healing spring waters of turn-of-the-20th-century Saratoga, New York, inspired the theme for the **Spa at Disney's Saratoga Springs**—it's the perfect place to sink into the luxury of a hydro-massage or emerge with the glow from a maple-enhanced body treatment. The Mineral Spring Hydro-Massage (45 minutes, $115) uses herbs to detoxify and awaken your skin. The Maple Sugar Body Polish (50 minutes, $125) deep cleans and exfoliates to boost circulation and hydrate your skin. Heated stones do the work during the Adirondack Stone Therapy Massage (80 minutes,

$185)—you'll be utterly relaxed. Kids' treatments include first facials, manicures, and pedicures. You can order a flavorful, nourishing lunch from nearby Artist's Palette.

Florida's settlers would have marveled at the luxury of the **Spa at Shingle Creek** at one of Orlando's newest resorts evoking an Old Florida mood. Tired pioneers might have traded valuable livestock for the stress-relieving Calusa Cocoon (50 minutes, $120) or the binge-worthy Chocolate and Raspberry Facial (50 minutes, $120, or 80 minutes, $170). The Cocoon begins with an apricot scrub for skin silkening. Next, your therapist massages a blend of essential oils like lavender and ylang ylang into your skin before wrapping you like a burrito in a foil-like blanket. A scalp massage completes the blissful experience. The facial starts with gentle steam and exfoliation and a soothing shoulder and neck massage featuring chocolate-raspberry oil. A detoxifying berry mask freshens tired skin; a firming anti-aging mask revitalizes more mature skin. A cup of ginger-peach tea paired with oatmeal cranberry cookies in the spa lounge helps prolong the tranquil escape.

Most spas can book treatments on short notice, but your best bet is to call ahead and reserve the indulgence you don't want to miss. Be sure to inquire about any gratuity—often 18% to 20%—that will be added to your spa package or treatments.

—Jennie Hess

24-hour convenience store, without crossing the street. **Cons:** too noisy at times for adults; street is a tad busy for pedestrians to try to cross, especially at night. ✉ *13351 Rte. 535, Orlando* ☎ *407/239–4500 or 800/366–6299* ⊕ *www.kidsuites. com* ⇲ *507 rooms* ⚫ *In-room: safe, refrigerator, Internet. In-hotel: restaurant, bar, pool, gym, children's programs (ages 4–12), laundry facilities, laundry service, public Wi-Fi, no-smoking rooms* ▭*AE, D, DC, MC, V* ✛*1:G4.*

$$$–$$$$
Fodor'sChoice
★

🏨**Hyatt Regency Grand Cypress Resort.** On 1,500 acres just outside Disney's north entrance, this spectacular resort has a private lake, three golf courses, and miles of trails for bicycling, jogging, and horseback riding. The 800,000-gallon pool has a 45-foot slide and is fed by 12 waterfalls. Tropical birds and plants and Chinese sculptures fill the 18-story atrium. All rooms were refurbished in 2008 and early 2009 in the first phase of a $65 million total renovation of the entire resort. Rooms offer iPod stations, 42-inch HDTVs, and green and blue carpeting and wall covers in a style that gives them a tastefully contemporary look. All rooms have a private balcony overlooking either the Lake Buena Vista Area or the pool. Villas have fireplaces and whirlpool baths. Accommodations are divided between the hotel and the **Villas of Grand Cypress** (✉*1 N. Jacaranda Dr., Lake Buena Vista* ☎*407/239–1234 or 800/835–7377*), with 200 villas. **Pros:** great Sunday brunch at La Coquina; huge pool; lots of recreation options, including nearby equestrian center. **Cons:** pricey; inconvenient to Universal Orlando, SeaWorld, and downtown Orlando. ✉*1 Grand Cypress Blvd., Lake Buena Vista Area, Orlando* ☎*407/239–1234 or 800/233–1234* ⊕*www.hyattgrandcypress.com* ⇲*750 rooms* ⚫*In-room: safe, Internet. In-hotel: 5 restaurants, room service, 18-hole golf courses, 9-hole golf course, tennis courts, pools, gym, spa, bicycles, children's programs (ages 4–12), laundry service, public Wi-Fi, no-smoking rooms* ▭*AE, D, DC, MC, V* ✛*1:F3.*

$$–$$$
🏨**Marriott Residence Inn.** Billing itself as a Caribbean-style oasis, with lush palms and a waterfall near the swimming pool, this all-suites hotel's most compelling features are more pragmatic: every room has a full kitchen with a stove and dishwasher, and there's an on-site convenience store. (A supermarket is a few blocks down Palm Parkway.) Suites include a separate living room–kitchen and bedrooms. Two-bedroom suites have two baths. The recreation area has both a kids' pool and a putting green. **Pros:** sequestered, resortlike atmosphere; convenient to Disney and I-Drive; free Disney shuttle; free hot breakfast buffet. **Cons:** public areas can be a bit noisy; not within walking distance of much. ✉*11450 Marbella Palm Ct., Orlando* ☎*407/465–0075 or 800/331–3131* ⊕*www.marriott.com* ⇲*210 suites* ⚫*In-room: safe,*

kitchen, refrigerator, Internet. *In-hotel: pool, gym, laundry facilities, laundry service, no-smoking rooms* ⊟AE, D, DC, MC, V ⊹1:G3.

$–$$ 🏨**Marriott Village at Little Lake Bryan.** The private, gated Marriott Village has three hotels. The **Courtyard** welcomes both families and business travelers with 3,000 square feet of meeting space and large standard rooms decorated with yellow and green floral patterns and blond-wood furniture. Each room has a coffeemaker and Web TV, and the indoor-outdoor pool has a swim-up bar. At **SpringHill Suites,** accommodations have kitchenettes, separate sleeping and dining areas, and Sony Playstations, and the hotel serves a free, hot breakfast. The **Fairfield Inn** is the least expensive of the three, but rooms are as bright and pleasant, if not quite as amenity laden. It also has family suites with bunk beds and a Hawaiian theme that kids will love. Continental breakfast is included in the rates, and there are several chain restaurants in the complex. Best of all, there's an on-site Disney planning center where you can buy park tickets. **Pros:** lots of informal dining options; lower room rates than hotels on the other side of I–4; you can walk to a few chain restaurants just off of the hotel property. **Cons:** Disney shuttle costs $7 per person round-trip (hotels across I–4 have free shuttles). ⊠*8623 Vineland Ave., Orlando* ☎*407/938–9001 or 877/682–8552* ⊕*www.marriottvillage. com* ⇆*650 rooms, 450 suites* ♿*In-room: safe, refrigerator, Internet. In-hotel: 8 restaurants, room service, bars, pools, gym, children's programs (ages 4–12), laundry facilities, laundry service, public Wi-Fi, no-smoking rooms* ⊟AE, D, DC, MC, V ⍻CP ⊹1:G3.

$$–$$$$ 🏨**Nickelodeon Family Suites by Holiday Inn.** The Nickelodeon theme
Fodor's Choice extends everywhere, from the suites, where separate kids' rooms have
★ bunk beds and SpongeBob wall murals, to the two giant pools built up
☻ like water parks. Kids will look forward to wake-up calls from Nickelodeon stars, character breakfasts, and live entertainment. The accommodations are so thoroughly designed for kids, it is not the best place for those without youngsters. You can choose between one-, two- and three-bedroom suites, with or without full kitchens. **Pros:** extremely kid-friendly; free Disney, Universal Orlando, and SeaWorld shuttles; massive discounts (up to 50% off standard rates) for active duty military, and you can save about $20 on a room a night with memberships like AAA and AARP; 9-hole golf course. **Cons:** not within walking distance of Disney or Downtown Disney; may be too frenetic for folks without kids. ⊠*14500 Continental Gateway, I–4 Exit 67, Orlando* ☎*407/387–5437 or 866/462–6425* ⊕*www.nickhotels.com* ⇆*777 suites* ♿*In-room: safe, kitchen (some), refrigerator, Internet. In-hotel: 3 restaurants, room service, pools, 9-hole golf course, gym, children's programs (ages 4–12), laundry facilities, laundry service, public Wi-Fi, no-smoking rooms* ⊟AE, D, DC, MC, V ⊹1:F5.

$$–$$$$ 🏨**Orlando World Center Marriott.** With 2,000 rooms, this is one of Orlando's largest hotels, and it's very popular with conventions. (In fact, it has more convention space within the hotel that any other hotel in Orlando, which means more that any hotel in Florida. The place is a convention factory.) All rooms have patios or balconies, and the lineup of amenities and facilities seems endless—there's even on-site photo processing. You can rent the upscale Royal Palms, Imperial Palms,

12

and Sabal Palms villas by the day or by the week. Golf at the 6,800-yard championship Hawk's Landing golf course becomes a bargain for guests—a golf package including one round costs about $20 more than the standard rate for a deluxe room, depending on the season. Other package deals include admission to SeaWorld, Discovery Cove. **Pros:** good steak house; golf course, lobby Starbucks. **Cons:** on-site restaurants have expense account-size tabs; nothing worth seeing within walking distance, in fact the hotel fronts a highway that would be unwise to walk on. ⊠ *8701 World Center Dr., I–4 Exit 65, Orlando* ☎ *407/239–4200 or 800/228–9290* ⊕ *www.marriottworldcenter.com* ⇄ *2,000 rooms, 98 suites, 259 villas* ♿ *In-room: Internet. In-hotel: 7 restaurants, room service, 18-hole golf course, pool, gym, children's programs (ages 4–12), laundry facilities, laundry service, public Wi-Fi, no-smoking rooms* ⊟ *AE, D, DC, MC, V* ✛ *1:F5.*

$–$$ ⛫ **PerriHouse Bed & Breakfast Inn.** This place offers great respite from the typical Orlando fast-lane tourism experience. An eight-room bed-and-breakfast inside a serene bird sanctuary, the PerriHouse offers you a chance to split your time between sightseeing and spending quiet moments bird-watching: the 16-acre sanctuary has observation paths, a pond, a feeding station, and a small birdhouse museum. It's attractive to bobwhites, downy woodpeckers, red-tail hawks, and the occasional bald eagle. The inn is a romantic getaway, with four-poster and canopy beds and some fireplaces. And the resort recently added a freestanding villa that can sleep six. The staff can book some interesting adventures—anything from bass fishing trips to sessions at an Orlando skydiving simulator. You're free to use the kitchen, and there is a free hot breakfast for all guests. **Pros:** intimate and private; great bird-watching. **Cons:** not an easy walk to much of interest; need a rental car. ⊠ *10417 Vista Oak Court, Lake Buena Vista* ☎ *407/876–4830 or 800/780–4830* ⊕ *www.perrihouse.com* ⇄ *8 rooms* ♿ *In-room: safe, Internet. In-hotel: pool* ⊟ *AE, D, DC, MC, V* ⦿*CP* ✛ *1:E1.*

$–$$$ ⛫ **Quality Suites Lake Buena Vista.** Both the prices and location make this a great home base for a family vacation. You won't think you are in the Ritz-Carlton, but the suites are pleasant, if not enormous. Each suite sleeps up to six if you fold out the living room's sofa bed, and kitchens are well equipped. A nice perk is the free hot breakfast buffet and free high-speed Internet. **Pros:** you can save big bucks on food; Downtown Disney Market Place, with a reasonably priced Publix supermarket, is ½ mi from hotel (although you should watch the traffic if you walk there). **Cons:** with the maximum capacity of six people, suites would be cramped. ⊠ *8200 Palm Pkwy., Orlando* ☎ *407/465–8200 or 800/370–9894* ⊕ *www.qualityinn.com* ⇄ *123 suites* ♿ *In-room: safe, kitchen, refrigerator, Internet. In-hotel: pool, gym, public Wi-Fi, no-smoking rooms* ⊟ *AE, D, DC, MC, V* ⦿*CP* ✛ *1:G3.*

$$–$$$ ⛫ **Sheraton Safari Hotel.** From the pool's jungle motif to the bamboo enclosures around the lobby pay phones, this little piece of Nairobi in the hotel district adjacent to Downtown Disney is a trip. Although there are some leopard skin–print furniture coverings and wild-animal portraits on the walls, the guest rooms are relatively sedate. Suites have kitchenettes with microwaves; six deluxe suites have full kitchens. Watch your kids play on 79-foot-long python waterslide in the pool area while you sip drinks at the poolside Zanzibar. **Pros:** kid-attractive pool area; short walk to shops and restaurants; free Disney shuttle; small pets allowed with deposit. **Cons:** pool area can get loud; close to Downtown Disney, but a tad too far to walk there (about 1 mi). ⊠ *12205 Apopka Vineland Rd., Orlando* ☎ *407/239–0444 or 800/423–3297* ⊕ *www.sheratonsafari.com* ⇄ *489 rooms, 96 suites* ♿ *In-room: safe, kitchen (some), refrigerator (some), Internet. In-hotel: 2 restaurants, room service, pool, gym, public Wi-Fi, no-smoking rooms* ▤ *AE, D, DC, MC, V* ✛ *1:F3.*

$$–$$$ 🖼**Sheraton Vistana Resort.** Consider this peaceful resort, just across I–4 from Downtown Disney, if you're traveling with a large family or group of friends. The spacious, tasteful, one- and two-bedroom villas and town houses have living rooms, full kitchens, and washers and dryers. Tennis players take note: the 13 clay and all-weather courts are free to guests; private or semiprivate lessons are available for a fee. With seven outdoor heated pools, five kiddie pools, and eight outdoor hot tubs, you can spend the whole day just soaking up the sun. Or, you can have a family barbecue with one of the outdoor grills that are ubiquitous around the grounds. **Pros:** kitchens let you save money on food (plenty of nearby grocery shopping options); lots of on-site recreation choices. **Cons:** not within walking distance of Downtown Disney (across I–4); shuttles to Disney ($10 round-trip) and Universal and I-Drive ($12 round-trip) are slow. ⊠ *8800 Vistana Center Dr., Orlando* ☎ *407/239–3100 or 800/325–3535* ⊕ *www.starwoodvo.com* ⇄ *1,700 units* ♿ *In-room: safe, kitchen, refrigerator, Internet. In-hotel: 2 restaurants, tennis courts, volleyball court, bicycle rentals, pools, gym, concierge, children's programs (ages 4–12), public Wi-Fi, no-smoking rooms* ▤ *AE, D, DC, MC, V* ✛ *1:F4.*

$$$$ 🖼**Waldorf Astoria Orlando.** Anyone familiar with the titans of the five-star hotel world knows that the one and only Waldorf-Astoria is in New York City. That was true until Oct. 1, 2009 (the 78th anniversary of the opening of the original hotel) when Hilton, now parent company of the Waldorf, branched out to a 428-acre tract of pristine forest, immediately next to Walt Disney World property, called Bonnet Creek. As the name connotes, the new hotel is at the top of the luxury class. The centerpiece of the lobby is a clock that is essentially a copy of the big clock that started ticking in the lobby of the New York Waldorf in 1931. Rooms and suites are, of course, quite plush, and butler service is available to all guests. The Waldorf is connected to, and shares a convention hall with, the new Hilton Orlando Bonnet Creek. Amenities at the resort include a luxurious spa, a new, par-72 Reese Jones–designed golf course, and a signature Waldorf swimming pool surrounded by private, air-conditioned, and amenity-laden cabanas for rent to hotel guests, and five restaurants. The hotel is a 10-minute drive from the gates of Disney World, 15 mi from Orlando International Airport, and for those of you with private jets, 5 mi from a corporate jetport in Kissimmee. **Pros:** this is a lavish hotel with lots of amenities; in a lush, green-forested area that seems a million miles away from any tourist strip. **Cons:** you will definitely need to rent a car here as nothing is within walking distance. ⊠ *14200 Bonnet Creek Resort La., Orlando* ☎ *407/597–5500* ⊕ *www.waldorfastoriaorlando.com* ⇄ *328 rooms,*

169 suites ⚹*In-room: Internet, safe. In-hotel: 5 restaurants, room service, bars, 18-hole golf course, pool, gym, spa, concierge, children's programs (ages 4–12), laundry service, executive floor, public Wi-Fi, no-smoking rooms* ▭ *AE, D, DC, MC, V* ⊹*1:A6.*

KISSIMMEE

Take I–4 Exit 64A, unless otherwise noted.

If you're looking for anything remotely quaint, charming, or sophisticated, move on. With a few exceptions (namely, the flashy Gaylord Palms Resort), the U.S. 192 strip—aka the Irlo Bronson Memorial Highway—is a neon-and-plastic strip crammed with bargain-basement motels, fast-food spots, nickel-and-dime attractions, overpriced gas stations, and minimarts where a small bottle of aspirin costs $8. In past years, when Disney was in its infancy, this was the best place to find affordable rooms. But now that budget hotels have cropped up all along I-Drive, you can often find better rooms closer to the theme parks by passing the Kissimmee motel strip and heading a few exits north.

There are exceptions, however—a few big-name companies like Marriott have excellent lodging on or near U.S. 192, and some of the older hotels have maintained decent standards and kept their prices very interesting. You can find clean, simple rooms in Kissimmee for $40 to $80 a night, depending on facilities and proximity to Walt Disney World.

One Kissimmee caveat: beware of the word "maingate" in many hotel names. It's a good 6 mi from Kissimmee's "maingate" hotel area to the Walt Disney World entrance. The "maingate west" area, however, is about 2 mi from the park. Of course, the greater the distance from Walt Disney World, the lower the room rates. A few additional minutes' drive may save you a significant amount of money, so shop around. And if you wait until arrival to find a place, don't be bashful about asking to see the rooms. It's a buyer's market.

$ 🏨**Best Western Lakeside.** Fifteen two-story, balconied buildings make up this 27-acre hotel complex. A small man-made lake offers pedal boating, and four outdoor tennis courts are available on a first-come, first-served basis. Rooms come with two double beds or one king. Children's activities involve arts and crafts, movies, or miniature golf in a comfortable play area. The on-property "general store" serves Pizza Hut pizza all day long. **Pros:** this is one of the few Orlando hotels with a sub-$60 rate (in the off season) that is not a dump; feels almost like a family summer camp; on an idyllic lake; free breakfast for kids 10 and under; free Disney shuttle. **Cons:** on a stretch of highway that you wouldn't want to walk along; rates have crept up for a basic room in high season (March–April), but the place is still a bargain. ✉*7769 W. Irlo Bronson Memorial Hwy., 2 mi west of I–4, Kissimmee* ☎*407/396–2222 or 800/848–0801* ⊕*www.bestwesternlakeside.com* ⤏*651 rooms* ⚹*In-room: safe, refrigerator. In-hotel: 2 restaurants, room service, tennis courts, pools, gym, children's programs (ages 4–12), laundry facilities, laundry service, no-smoking rooms* ▭*AE, D, DC, MC, V* ⊹*1:A6.*

$$–$$$$ 🏨**Celebration Hotel.** Like everything in the Disney-created town of Celebration, this 115-room hotel borrows from the best of the 19th and

21st centuries. The lobby resembles those of Victorian grand dames, with hardwood floors and decorative millwork throughout. Rooms may look as if they date from the early 1900s, but each has a plasma-screen TV, two phone lines, high-speed Internet access, and a six-channel stereo system. Even though it's less than 1 mi south of the U.S. 192 tourist strip in Kissimmee, the hotel's surroundings are serene. The hotel is part of the locally owned Kessler Hotel "collection," which also owns the Grand Bohemian in downtown Orlando, and has some of the Kessler trademark amenities, like a display of some of the Kessler art collection, and a lobby piano bar with high-brow music. The restaurant, and many of the hotel rooms, look out onto a serene little lake. The entire hotel is no-smoking. **Pros:** a mere block from good restaurants; rental bikes and golf carts make touring a breeze; free shuttle to Disney World, Celebration Golf and Fitness Center. **Cons:** need a rental car (or lots of cab money) to get around off-site. ⊠*700 Bloom St., Celebration* ☎*407/566–6000 or 888/499–3800* ⊕*www.celebrationhotel.com* ⤴*115 rooms* ⌂*In-room: Internet. In-hotel: 2 restaurants, pool, gym, laundry service, public Wi-Fi, no-smoking rooms* ▤*AE, D, DC, MC, V* ✛*1:D6.*

¢–$ 🏨**Celebrity Resorts Kissimmee.** A collection of villas a few blocks south of U.S. 192, this resort puts you far enough from the highway to avoid the clutter of the tourist strip, but close enough to conveniently reach its shops and restaurants. And it's about 4 mi from the Walt Disney World entrance. As at the Celebrity Resort in Lake Buena Vista, accommodations here range from standard hotel rooms to two-bedroom deluxe suites that can sleep up to 10 people. Suites have living rooms with sofa beds and separate dining areas. A general renovation of the properties in 2008 gave everything a fresh, spruced-up look. **Pros:** feels miles off the tourist strip; short drive to shops. **Cons:** not within an easy walk of much; Disney shuttle costs $10 per person round-trip; a $4 daily "resort fee" for standards such as phone usage and self-parking; two-night minimum during high season. ⊠*2800 N. Poinciana Blvd., Kissimmee* ☎*407/997–5000 or 800/423–8604* ⊕*www.celebrityresorts. com* ⤴*311 suites* ⌂*In-room: safe, kitchen (some), refrigerator, Internet, Wi-Fi. In-hotel: restaurant, room service, tennis court, pools, gym, children's programs (ages 4–12), laundry facilities, laundry service, no-smoking rooms* ▤*AE, D, MC, V.*

¢–$ 🏨**Days Hotel Disney Maingate.** This six-story, former Holiday Inn has large standard rooms with two double beds. Kids' suites have queen beds for the adults and an extra room for the kids with bunk beds, a TV, CD player, Nintendo 64, and board games. And there are options to get your kids out in the sunshine without leaving the hotel, like a sand volleyball court and pool complex with an adjacent wading pool. The hotel also allows small pets with a $50 deposit. **Pros:** kids' play area in main restaurant; free Disney shuttle; golf and tennis centers nearby; bargain room rates. **Cons:** feels very much on the tourist strip. ⊠*7601 Black Lake Rd., 2 mi west of I–4, Kissimmee* ☎*407/396–1100 or 800/365–6935* ⊕*www.legacygrand.com* ⤴*295 rooms, 30 suites* ⌂*In-room: safe, refrigerator, Internet, Wi-Fi. In-hotel: restaurant, room service, pool, gym, laundry facilities, laundry service, public Wi-Fi, no-smoking rooms* ▤*AE, D, DC, MC, V* ✛*1:A5.*

$$–$$$$ **Gaylord Palms Resort.** Built in the style of a grand turn-of-the-20th-century Florida mansion, this resort is meant to awe. Inside its enormous atrium, covered by a 4-acre glass roof, are re-creations of Florida icons such as the Everglades, Key West, and old St. Augustine. Restaurants include Sunset Sam's Fish Camp, on a 60-foot fishing boat docked on the hotel's indoor ocean, and the Old Hickory Steak House in an old warehouse overlooking the faux alligator-ridden Everglades. Rooms carry on the Florida themes with colorful, tropical decorations. With extensive children's programs, two pool areas, and a huge Canyon Ranch spa, the hotel connives to make you never want to leave. The newest room amenity is Gaylord iConnect, complete with a 15-inch flat-screen monitor, that connects you to the Internet plus a hotel network for booking dinner and activity reservations. **Pros:** you could have a great vacation without ever leaving the grounds; free shuttle to Disney; Villa de Flora, the resort's all-buffet restaurant, offers international cuisine that's a cut above what the word "buffet" typically connotes. **Cons:** rooms are pricey; not much within walking distance (although the hotel is so big, you can take quite a hike inside the building). ⊠ *6000 Osceola Pkwy., I–4 Exit 65, Kissimmee* ☎ *407/586–0000* ⊕ *www.gaylordpalms.com* ⇗ *1,406 rooms, 86 suites* ⊘ *In-room: safe, Internet. In-hotel: 5 restaurants, bars, pools, gym, spa, children's programs (ages 4–12), laundry service, public Wi-Fi, no-smoking rooms* ⊟ *AE, D, DC, MC, V* ⊹ *1:E6.*

$$$–$$$$ **Ginn Reunion Resort & Club of Orlando.** It's on 28,000 tranquil acres of a former orange grove, far from the bustle of I–4, and yet it's only 12 minutes from Disney. A stay here includes access to three private world-caliber golf courses designed by Tom Watson, Arnold Palmer, and Jack Nicklaus. (And the property adjoins the ANNIKA Academy, operated by LPGA great Annika Sorenstam, if you want to polish your game.) The resort was developed as a residential and vacation-home complex, but its condo-style villas are available on a per-night basis. Activities include walking and horseback riding on meandering trails. Kids love the swim pavilion with a winding lagoon, wave pool, slide, and beach volleyball area. **Pros:** secluded atmosphere; proximity to Disney and ChampionsGate area. **Cons:** no Disney shuttle; you need a rental car, but if you are staying here, you can likely afford one. ⊠ *7593 Gathering Dr., Reunion* ☎ *407/396–3200 or 888/418–9611* ⊕ *www. reunionresort.com* ⇗ *60 units* ⊘ *In-room: safe, Internet. In-hotel: restaurant, room service, bar, 18-hole golf courses, pools, gym, spa, bicycles, children's programs (ages 4–12), laundry facilities, laundry service, no-smoking rooms* ⊟ *AE, D, DC, MC, V* ⊹ *1:E6.*

$–$$ **Magical Memories Villas.** Despite the name, this resort is not affiliated with Disney, but you'll probably feel the magic anyway when you get your bill. Two-bedroom villas with full kitchens start at $89 a night. (Although in the high season, you're likely to pay approximately $110 for the least expensive units.) Three- and four-bedroom villas are also available. (But, the resort requires a three-night minimum stay in peak demand periods; March–May.) Although the furnishings are standard, the villas are spacious and bright, with large windows and pastel pink walls. All of the suites include a washer and dryer, and a set of linens.

Pros: sequestered and homey; free long-distance calls with mid-price and premium rooms. **Cons:** not an easy walk to area shops or restaurants; extra charge for daily housekeeping (which is required). ✉*5075 U.S. 192 W, Kissimmee* ☎*407/390–8200 or 800/736–0402* ⊕*www. magicalmemories.com* ⇥*140 villas* ♿*In-room: kitchen, refrigerator, Internet. In-hotel: tennis court, pool, gym, laundry facilities, no-smoking rooms, some pets allowed (fee)* ▭*D, MC, V.*

12

$$–$$$$ ⊡**Omni Orlando Resort at ChampionsGate.** Omni took over a 1,200-acre golf club with two Greg Norman–designed courses and a David Ledbetter academy to create this huge Mediterranean-style hotel complex in 2007. With a 70,000-square-foot conference center, the resort definitely attracts the corporate crowd. But there's family appeal, too, thanks to an 850-foot-long, lazy-river-style pool (one of the most popular in the Orlando area) and excellent children's programs. And the hotel is a 10-minute drive from Disney. Rooms are attractive if not distinctive, with earth-color walls, gold carpets and drapes, and marble bathroom vanities. There are also one-, two-, and three-bedroom villas. **Pros:** big European-style spa; huge, water-park-style pool; good restaurant; golf school and two golf courses. **Cons:** rooms and food are pricey; need a rental car, as the only place you could walk to from here is the golf course. ✉*1500 Masters Blvd., I–4 Exit 58, Championsgate South of Kissimmee* ☎*407/390–6664 or 800/843–6664* ⊕*www.omnihotels. com* ⇥*730 rooms, 32 suites, 57 villas* ♿*In-room: Internet. In-hotel: 5 restaurants, room service, bars, 18-hole golf courses, tennis courts, pools, gym, spa, children's programs (ages 1–12), laundry facilities, laundry service, public Wi-Fi, no-smoking rooms* ▭*AE, D, DC, MC, V* ✛*1:E6.*

$–$$ ⊡**Radisson Resort Orlando-Celebration.** This bright, spacious Radisson has an attractive location amid 1½ acres of foliage, good facilities, and competitive prices. The focal point is the giant pool, with wide, gentle waterfalls, a 40-foot slide; and whirlpools. The lively sports bar off the lobby has a massive TV. On-site refueling options include Starbucks, Krispy Kreme, and Pizza Hut. Generously proportioned rooms are decorated with blond-wood furniture and white down comforters. A free shuttle makes 20-minute trips to Disney. **Pros:** kids 10 and under eat free at hotel restaurants; kids' suites have bunk beds; free Disney, Universal Orlando, and SeaWorld shuttles. **Cons:** not an easy walk to area shops or restaurants; entrance to the place is on a rather garish tourist strip. ✉*2900 Parkway Blvd., Kissimmee* ☎*407/396–7000 or 800/634–4774* ⊕ *www.radisson.com/kissimmeefl* ⇥*712 rooms, 8 suites* ♿*In-room: Internet. In-hotel: 2 restaurants, bar, tennis courts, pools, gym, laundry facilities, laundry service, public Wi-Fi, no-smoking rooms* ▭*AE, D, DC, MC, V* ✛*1:D6.*

$–$$ ⊡**Saratoga Resort Villas at Orlando Maingate.** The red-tile-and-stucco villas have between one and three bedrooms, living and dining areas, and well-equipped kitchens. With 1,200 square feet, three-bedroom units sleep up to eight comfortably. Because there is a full kitchen, you can cook your own meals, but room service dining is also available. And most everyone can have his or her own flat-screen HDTV to watch, since there is one in each bedroom and one in the living room. The hotel added a health and beauty spa in 2008. **Pros:** rates are hard to beat: a family of four can get a two-bedroom villa for $129 a night in high season; free shuttle to Disney. **Cons:** on unattractive tourist strip; can't really walk around off the grounds. ⊠*4787 W. Irlo Bronson Hwy., Kissimmee* ☎*407/397–0555 or 800/222–8733* ⊕*www.saratogaresortvillas. com* ⤴*150 villas* ⅋*In-room: safe, Internet. In-hotel: restaurant, room service, tennis court, pool, gym, spa, laundry facilities, no-smoking rooms* ▱*AE, D, DC, MC, V* ✛*1:A5.*

¢–$ ▯**Seralago Hotel & Suites Maingate East.** It's within walking distance of the Old Town shopping and entertainment complex and 3 mi from Disney. Special kids' suites have a room designed to look like a Wild West fort, with bunk beds, TVs, and video games. All rooms have kitchenettes with refrigerators and microwaves. Kids under 12 eat free (with a paying adult) at the restaurant. **Pros:** easy walk to shops and restaurants; pets are welcome ($50 nonrefundable deposit; dogs must be 40 pounds or less); free shuttle to all Disney parks. **Cons:** on a touristy strip of highway about as far from Walden Pond as you could imagine. ⊠*5678 W. Irlo Bronson Memorial Hwy., Kissimmee* ☎*407/396–4488, 800/366–5437, or 800/465–4329* ⊕*www.orlandofamilyfunhotel.com* ⤴*614 rooms, 110 suites* ⅋*In-room: kitchen. In-hotel: restaurant, room service, bar, tennis courts, 2 pools, children's programs (ages 3–12), laundry facilities, laundry service, no-smoking rooms* ▱*AE, D, DC, MC, V* ✛*1:A6.*

UNIVERSAL ORLANDO AREA

Take I–4 Exit 74B or 75A, unless otherwise noted.

Universal Orlando's on-site hotels, all managed by Loews, were built in a little luxury enclave that has everything you need, so you never have to leave Universal property. In minutes you can walk from any hotel to CityWalk, Universal's dining and entertainment district, or take a ferry that cruises the adjacent artificial river. If you need something as mundane as a new toothbrush, there's plenty of shopping just across the street from Universal on Kirkman Road.

A significant perk is that your hotel key lets you go directly to the head of the line for most Universal Orlando attractions. Other special services at some hotels include a "Did You Forget?" closet that offers everything from kid's strollers to dog leashes to computer accessories.

If the on-property Universal hotels are a bit pricey for your budget, don't worry, a burgeoning hotel district has sprung up across Kirkman Road, offering convenient accommodations and some room rates less than $50 a night. Although these off-property hotels don't have the perks of the on-site places, you'll probably be smiling when you see your hotel bill.

¢–$ ▯**Comfort Suites Orlando/Universal Studios.** The brick exterior with Victorian-style architectural touches makes the place look like a dorm in a small-town college, but the amenities inside are far more extensive than what you probably had at your alma mater. Each studio has a full kitchen, complete with microwave, stovetop, refrigerator, dishes, and dishwasher. There's no on-site gym, but a Bally's fitness center is a short walk away, and the neighborhood has lots of entertainment and dining options. Take Exit 75B off I–4. **Pros:** half-mile walk to Universal and area shops and restaurants; low room rates. **Cons:** free Continental breakfast, but no on-site restaurant or room service. ⊠*5617 Major Blvd., Orlando* ☎*407/363–1967 or 800/951–7829* ⊕*www.suburbanhotels.com* ⇆*150 suites* ⚐*In-room: safe, kitchen, refrigerator, Internet, Wi-Fi. In-hotel: laundry facilities, no-smoking rooms* ▤*AE, D, DC, MC, V* ✛*2:D1.*

12

$$ ⌂**Doubletree Hotel at the Entrance to Universal Orlando.** The name sounds awkward, but it's very descriptive, and the conveniently located hotel is typically sold out during the high season of April and May. It's a hotbed of business-trippers that also attracts pleasure-seekers thanks to a location right at the Universal Orlando entrance. Don't worry about noisy conventioneers—the meeting and convention facilities are completely isolated from the guest towers. If you happen to stay here on business, though, note that the teleconferencing center lets you connect with points all over the world. **Pros:** within walking distance of Universal and area shops and restaurants. **Cons:** on a fast-lane tourist strip; need a rental car to reach Disney, I-Drive, or downtown Orlando. ⊠*5780 Major Blvd., I–4 Exit 75B* ☎*407/351–1000* ⊕*www.doubltreeorlando. com* ⇆*742 rooms, 15 suites* ⚐*In-room: safe, Internet. In-hotel: restaurant, room service, pool, gym, laundry facilities, laundry service, public Wi-Fi, no-smoking rooms* ▤*AE, D, DC, MC* ✛*2:D1.*

$ ⌂**Extended Stay Deluxe Orlando–Universal Studios.** This is no luxury resort, but the rooms are spacious, tidy, and pleasant. What's more, every suite has a full kitchen, so you can save money on meals if you enjoy cooking. Each suite also has a work table with broadband access, a queen-size bed, and a sofa bed that folds out to sleep two adults. The hotel is within walking distance of a good variety of dining and shopping options— including a grocery store from which to stock your kitchen—and the neighborhood is safe to walk in at night. **Pros:** in-suite kitchens; short walk to Universal and area shops and restaurants. **Cons:** on a touristy strip; need a rental car to reach Disney. ⊠*5610 Vineland Rd., Orlando* ☎*407/370–4428 or 800/398–7829* ⊕*www.extendedstayhotels.com* ⇆*84 suites* ⚐*In-room: kitchen, refrigerator, Internet. In-hotel: pool, gym, laundry facilities, public Wi-Fi, no-smoking rooms* ▤*AE, D, DC, MC, V* ✛*2:E1.*

$$$$ ⌂**Hard Rock Hotel.** Inside the California mission–style building you'll find rock memorabilia such as the slip Madonna wore in her "Like a Prayer" video. Rooms have black-and-white photos of pop icons and serious sound systems with CD players. Stay in a suite, and you'll get a big-screen TV and a wet bar. Kid-friendly suites have a small extra room for children. Your hotel key card lets you bypass lines at Universal. The Kitchen, one of the hotel's restaurants, occasionally hosts visiting musicians cooking their favorite meals at the Chef's Table. **Pros:** short walk to Universal and CityWalk; preferential treatment at Universal rides; charge privileges on your room extend to the two other on-property Universal hotels. **Cons:** rooms and meals are pricey; loud rock music in public areas may annoy some people. ⊠*5800 Universal Blvd., Universal*

Studios ☎*407/503–7625 or 800/232–7827* ⊕*www.universalorlando. com* ⌧*621 rooms, 29 suites* ⚷*In-room: safe, refrigerator, Internet. In-hotel: 3 restaurants, room service, bars, pools, gym, children's programs (ages 4–14), laundry service, public Wi-Fi, no-smoking rooms, some pets allowed (fee)* ▭*AE, D, DC, MC, V* ✛*2:D1.*

¢–$ 🖼️**Holiday Inn Express Hotel & Suites Universal Orlando.** Rooms in this 11-story hotel have two double beds or one king; suites add full kitchens and a sofa bed. As the result of a 2007 renovation, all rooms have 32-inch, flat screen HDTV and free wired, high-speed Internet access, along with a small work table and two chairs, which could double for a table for two. Note that there are no kitchen-oriented amenities in the rooms besides a mini-refrigerator. Roll-away beds that sleep two are available for $10 a night. **Pros:** within walking distance of Universal and area shops and restaurants; free shuttle to Universal, SeaWorld, and Wet 'n Wild; free hot buffet breakfast (although there is no restaurant open at the hotel other times of day). **Cons:** need a rental car to reach Disney or downtown Orlando; no on-site restaurant or room service. ⌧*5605 Major Blvd., Orlando* ☎*407/363–1333* ☎*888/465-4329* ⊕*www.hixuniversal.com* ⌧*196 rooms, 40 suites* ⚷*In-room: safe, kitchen (some), refrigerator, Internet. In-hotel: pool, gym, laundry facilities, laundry service, no-smoking rooms* ▭*AE, D, DC, MC, V* ⏐○⏐*CP* ✛*2:E1.*

$ 🖼️**Holiday Inn Hotel & Suites Orlando/Universal.** Staying at this hotel directly across the street from Universal could eliminate your need for a rental car if Universal, SeaWorld, Wet 'n Wild, and I-Drive are your only planned stops. There's a free shuttle to all four, though you can easily walk to Universal. Rooms have coffeemakers, hair dryers, irons, and ironing boards; one- and two-bedroom suites also have refrigerators, microwaves, dishwashers, and tableware. Suites cost about $20 more per night than the standard guest rooms. **Pros:** you can walk to Universal and area shops (although there's a free shuttle); small pets allowed ($50 nonrefundable deposit) **Cons:** need a rental car to reach Disney and downtown Orlando. (Cab fare would cost more than a rental car.) ⌧*5905 S. Kirkman Rd., I–4 Exit 75B, Orlando* ☎*407/351–3333 or 800/327–1364* ⊕*www.hiuniversal.com* ⌧*390 rooms, 120 suites* ⚷*In-room: safe, refrigerator (some), Internet. In-hotel: restaurant, room service, bar, pool, gym, laundry service, public Wi-Fi, no-smoking rooms, some pets allowed* ▭*AE, D, DC, MC, V* ✛*2:D1.*

$–$$ 🖼️**Hyatt Place Orlando/Universal.** This new Hyatt Place is geared to support what Hyatt calls the "24/7" lifestyle, which means essentially that any of the hotel amenities that are available at 3 in the afternoon are also on tap for hotel guests at 3 in the morning. For instance, in the Gallery (aka the lobby) you can check in at a touch-screen kiosk, order hot food 24/7 in the casual Gallery Kitchen, or watch a big-screen flat-panel TV in the Gallery Den while sipping espresso or wine. Rooms, done in gold and earth tones, have a pleasant, contemporary feel and have flat-panel TVs equipped with docking ports, to which you can hook up your own DVD, laptop, video game system, or MP3 player to the screen. There are also a couple of PCs (with a printer) available in a small room off the lobby, in case you did not bring your own. **Pros:** walking distance to Universal Orlando, and there's also a free shuttle; free high-speed wireless Internet access throughout the hotel. **Cons:** no kids' programs or babysitting service; no room service. ✉ *5859 Caravan Court, Universal Orlando area* ☎ *407/351-0627* ⊕ *www.orlandouniversal. place.hyatt.com* ⟳ *151 rooms* ⚘ *In-room: safe, refrigerator, Internet. In-hotel: restaurant, room service, bar, pool, gym, laundry facilities, laundry service, public Wi-Fi, no-smoking rooms* ▤ *AE, DC, MC, V* ⊕ *2:D1.*

$$$–$$$$ ⊞ **Portofino Bay Hotel.** The charm and romance of Portofino, Italy, are conjured up at this lovely luxury resort. The illusion is so faultless, right down to the cobblestone streets, that you might find it hard to believe that the different-color row houses lining the "bay" are a facade. Large, plush rooms here are done in cream and white, with down comforters and high-quality wood furnishings. There are two Italian restaurants, Mama Della's and Bice, and gelato machines surround the massive pool. The Feast of St. Gennaro (the patron saint of Naples) is held here in September as are monthly Italian wine tastings. **Pros:** incredible, Italian villa atmosphere; large spa; short walk or ferry ride to Universal Studios and Islands of Adventure; preferential treatment at Universal rides; you can charge meals and services (and use the pools and spa) at the Hard Rock and the Royal Pacific Resort; two great Italian eateries, Momma Della's and Bice, on property. **Cons:** rooms and meals are noticeably expensive; in-room high-speed Internet access costs $10 a day. ✉ *5601 Universal Blvd., Universal Studios* ☎ *407/503-1000 or 800/232-7827* ⊕ *www.universalorlando.com* ⟳ *699 rooms, 51 suites* ⚘ *In-room: safe, Internet. In-hotel: 3 restaurants, room service, bar, pools, gym, spa, children's programs (ages 4–14), laundry service, public Wi-Fi, some pets allowed (fee)* ▤ *AE, D, DC, MC, V* ⊕ *2:D1.*

$$–$$$$
Fodor's Choice
★   ⊞ **Royal Pacific Resort.** The entrance—a footbridge across a tropical stream—sets the tone for the South Pacific theme of this hotel, which is on 53 acres planted with tropical shrubs and trees, most of them palms. The focal point is a 12,000-square-foot, lagoon-style pool, which has a small beach and an interactive water play area. Indonesian carvings decorate the walls everywhere. An $8.5 million makeover transformed all guest rooms in late 2007, with bright, tropical bed coverings, bamboo ceiling accents, and electronics that include iPod station clock radios and 32" flat panel televisions, plus in-room Wi-Fi. Emeril Lagasse's restaurant, Tchoup Chop, draws crowds. The hotel hosts Polynesian-style luaus every Saturday. **Pros:** Emeril's restaurant (don't fail to eat there at least once); preferential treatment at Universal rides. **Cons:** rooms can feel cramped; $10-a-day fee for Internet access unwarranted given rates. ✉ *6300 Hollywood Way, Universal Orlando* ☎ *407/503-3000 or 800/232-7827* ⊕ *www.universalorlando.com* ⟳ *1,000 rooms, 113 suites* ⚘ *In-room: safe, Wi-Fi. In-hotel: 3 restaurants, room service, bars, pool, gym, children's programs (ages 4–14), laundry facilities, laundry service, executive floor, public Wi-Fi, no-smoking rooms, some pets allowed (fee)* ▤ *AE, DC, MC, V* ⊕ *2:C1.*

12

ORLANDO METRO AREA

INTERNATIONAL DRIVE

Take I–4 Exit 72, 74A, or 75A, unless otherwise noted.

The sprawl of newish hotels, restaurants, malls, and dozens of small attractions known as International Drive "I-Drive" to locals—makes a convenient base for visits to Walt Disney World, Universal, and other Orlando attractions. Parallel to I–4, this four-lane boulevard stretches from Universal in the north to Kissimmee in the south. Each part of I-Drive has its own personality. The southern end is classier, and south of SeaWorld there's still, amazingly, quite a lot of wide-open space just waiting for new hotels and restaurants to open up. The concentration of cheaper restaurants, fast-food joints, and T-shirt shops increases as you go north, and the stretch north of Sand Lake Road has a clearly markedly tacky ambience these days.

I-Drive's popularity makes it a crowded place to drive in any season. Try to avoid the morning (7–9 AM) and evening (4–6 PM) rush hours. If you're planning a day visiting I-Drive attractions, consider riding the I-Ride Trolley, which travels the length of I-Drive from Florida's Turnpike to the outlet center on Vineland Avenue, stopping at Wet 'n Wild and SeaWorld. Cost: $1.25 per trip for adults; free for kids under 12, and 25¢ for anyone 65 and older. (This trolley does not go to Universal Orlando, even though it's nearby.) And I-Ride can be more of a worthy transportation tool than you might think. Lots of hotels don't offer shuttle service to Disney, even for a fee; but you can ride I-Ride to hotels that do offer the fee-based Disney shuttle, which is far cheaper than a cab.

$$–$$$ **⚇Bluegreen Resorts, The Fountains.** As you drive along the newer section of International Drive, this resort, which opened in early 2009, would appear to take its name from the blue-green roofs on the multi-story buildings in the complex, with walls all painted different colors to make it look like an upscale, high-rise, town home neighborhood. But the hue of the roofs becomes the least important thing about this big condo community, which rents out lodging to nonowners of the condos, just like a regular hotel. This place is like summer camp for the entire family, and a good one, in terms of its amenities. On the edge of Lake Eve, with a dock with boat rentals, there are two large pools (the biggest is 6,000 square feet), and a 20,000-square-foot recreational center, with a store, a kids' club, and all sorts of organized activities going on inside, like bingo, kids' karaoke, face painting, and a regular session of "Margarita Madness" for adults. The pool is the site of a regular "Dive-in Movie," by which you jump in the water to watch outdoor movies at night. One- and two-bedroom units have all the comforts of a typical suburban home. **Pros:** self-contained resort that you'd never have to leave to have a great vacation. **Cons:** roughly equidistant between Disney and Universal, this resort is close to neither; nothing outside the resort is within easy walking distance. ✉*12400 International Dr. S, International Drive* ☎*407/905–4100* ⊕*www.bluegreenonline.com*

539 rooms △ *In-room: safe, Internet, kitchens, washer/dryer. In-hotel: 2 restaurants, bar, 2 pools, Jacuzzis, gym, bicycles, bike trail, boat rentals, lake, laundry service, public Wi-Fi, no-smoking room* ▤ *AE, D, DC, MC, V* ✛ *2:C6.*

$-$$$ 🏨 **Crowne Plaza Orlando Universal.** This hotel has convenience going for it—it's a couple of minutes off I–4, within walking distance of the better part of International Drive, and has free shuttles to Universal Orlando, SeaWorld, and Disney World. (Free shuttles to all three locations is a rarity among I-Drive hotels.) Suites, which run $40 to $50 a night more than regular guest rooms, offer mini-refrigerators and microwaves, and some suites offer an in-room Jacuzzi. A downside for families is that this is largely a convention hotel, with not much in kid-friendly features besides a small playground. **Pros:** convenient location; good hotel for adults who want a break from the child-dominated atmosphere that is the bulk of the Orlando experience; free shuttles to the big three of Orlando attractions (SeaWorld, Universal, and Disney); I-Ride takes you to anywhere on I-Drive for $1.25 fare. **Cons:** not a particularly kid-friendly property; no kids' club. ✉ *7800 Universal Blvd., International Drive* ☎ *407/355–0550* ⊕ *www.cporlando.com* *400 rooms, 72 suites* △ *In-room: safe, Internet. In-hotel: 3 restaurants, 2 bars, pool, gym, laundry service, business center, public Wi-Fi, no-smoking rooms* ▤ *AE, D, DC, MC, V* ✛ *2:D3.*

$$-$$$ 🏨 **The Doubletree Castle.** You won't really think you're in a castle at this mid-price hotel, although the tall gold-and-silver spires, medieval-style mosaics, arched doorways, hotel "creature" in the entry hall and a bevy of British tourists may make you feel like reading Harry Potter. Take your book to either the rooftop terrace or the inviting courtyard, which has a big, round swimming pool. Rooms have gold-framed mirrors and black-velvet headboards. Don't worry about the benign looking creature, it won't scare your kids. Two good restaurants, Café Tu Tu Tango and Vito's Chophouse, are each less than a block from the hotel, and Pointe Orlando, a popular dining, entertainment, and shopping complex with lots of new restaurants, is an easy walk. **Pros:** kid-friendly; easy walk to I-Drive eateries and attractions; free theme-park shuttle, including Disney (a rarity in this neighborhood). **Cons:** on a congested stretch of I-Drive. ✉ *8629 International Dr., I-Drive Area, Orlando* ☎ *407/345–1511 or 800/952–2785* ⊕ *www.doubletreecastle. com* *216 rooms* △ *In-room: safe, refrigerator, Internet, Wi-Fi. In-hotel: 2 restaurants, bar, room service, pool, gym, laundry service, public Wi-Fi, no-smoking rooms* ▤ *AE, D, DC, MC, V* ✛ *2:D4.*

$-$$ 🏨 **Embassy Suites Hotel International Drive South/Convention Center.** This all-suites hotel has an expansive Mediterranean-style lobby with marble floors, pillars, hanging lamps, and old-fashioned ceiling fans. The atrium is all about fountains and palm trees. Elsewhere, tile walks and brick arches lend more flavor. The hotel has a number of good amenities, such as a health club with a fine steam room. **Pros:** free breakfast and nightly beverages; easy walk to convention center and Pointe Orlando; free shuttle to Disney and Universal; walking distance to Convention Center and lots of shopping and dining. **Cons:** on congested stretch of I-Drive. ✉ *8978 International Dr., I-Drive Area, Orlando* ☎ *407/352–1400 or*

800/433–7275 ⊕*www.embassysuitesorlando.com* ⇲*244 suites* ☟*In-room: safe, Internet. In-hotel: restaurant, pool, gym, public Wi-Fi, no-smoking rooms* ▤*AE, D, DC, MC, V* ⦾*BP* ⊹*2:C4.*

$–$$ 🖭**Embassy Suites International Drive/Jamaican Court.** The atrium of this all-suites hotel has a lounge where a piano player sets the mood. Each suite has a living room with a wet bar, pullout sofa, and two TVs—all at a better price than for many area single rooms. Two-room suites can sleep six. The shuttle to Disney World has been eliminated, but you can catch the free shuttle at the Embassy Suites four blocks down International Drive. **Pros:** within walking distance of I-Drive eateries and attractions; free breakfast; free cocktails and sandwiches; free shuttle to Universal, SeaWorld, and Wet 'n Wild. **Cons:** convention center traffic can be bad; shuttle to Disney isn't free. ⊠*8250 Jamaican Court, I-Drive Area, Orlando* ☏*407/345–8250 or 800/327–9797* ⊕*www. orlandoembassysuites.com* ⇲*246 suites* ☟*In-room: safe, refrigerator, Internet, Wi-Fi. In-hotel: room service, pool, gym, public Wi-Fi, no-smoking rooms* ▤*AE, D, DC, MC, V* ⦾*BP* ⊹*2:C3.*

$–$$ 🖭**Enclave Suites at Orlando.** With three 10-story buildings surrounding a private lake, an office, restaurant, and recreation area, this all-suites lodging is less a hotel than a condominium complex. Here, what you would spend for a normal room in a fancy hotel gets you an apartment with a living room, a full kitchen, two bedrooms, and small terraces with lake views. Kids Quarter suites, which can sleep six, have small children's rooms with bunk beds and whimsical murals of Shamu. There's free transportation to Universal, SeaWorld, and Wet 'n Wild. The food court is replete with popular-brand snacks like Mrs. Fields, Pizza Hut, Block and Barrel Deli, and Seattle's Best. **Pros:** good deals on spacious suites; within walking distance of I-Drive eateries and attractions; free breakfast; free shuttle to Universal, SeaWorld, and Wet 'n Wild. **Cons:** area traffic can be a hassle; public facilities, like the pools are not exceedingly large, considering the size of the resort. ⊠*6165 Carrier Dr., I-Drive Area, Orlando* ☏*407/351–1155 or 800/457–0077* ⊕*www.enclavesuites.com* ⇲*321 suites* ☟*In-room: safe, kitchen, refrigerator, Internet. In-hotel: restaurant, food court, tennis court, pools, gym, laundry facilities, laundry service, public Wi-Fi, no-smoking rooms* ▤*AE, D, DC, MC, V* ⦾*BP* ⊹*2:D3.*

¢–$ 🖭**Extended StayAmerica Orlando Convention Center–Westwood Boulevard.** Don't confuse this hotel with the Extended Stay Deluxe Orlando Convention Center—the Universal Boulevard branch of which is just up the street. The StayAmerica (on Westwood Boulevard) has slightly lower room rates, slightly smaller rooms, and fewer amenities. It's tucked behind a pine forest and feels remote, but SeaWorld, the convention center, and Pointe Orlando are all within a 1-mi drive. **Pros:** very economical; within walking distance of I-Drive restaurants and shops; free shuttle to Disney and Universal. **Cons:** a tad farther from the Convention Center than its sister property; small pool; limited amenities; I-Drive traffic can be heavy; Disney is 30 minutes away. ⊠*6451 Westwood Blvd., I–4 Exit 72, I-Drive Area, Orlando* ☏*407/352–3454 or 800/398–7829* ⊕*www. extstay.com* ⇲*113 suites* ☟*In-room: safe, kitchen, Internet. In-hotel:*

pool, laundry facilities, public Wi-Fi, no-smoking rooms ⊟*AE, D, DC, MC, V* ✛*2:C6.*

$ ⊞**Extended Stay Deluxe Orlando Convention Center.** Both the Pointe Orlando and the Westwood Boulevard branches are designed for business travelers: each room has voice mail, two phone lines, free local phone calls and incoming faxes, speakerphone, and good-size work tables. But families also get a lot for their money. There's a full kitchen with everything you need to avoid restaurant tabs, including a dishwasher. The earth-tone color scheme is warm if not memorable, and the suites have two queen- or one king-size bed, plus a sofa bed. Although neither hotel has a restaurant, lots of eateries are within walking distance of both. **Pros:** very economical; within walking distance of I-Drive restaurants and shops; free shuttle to Disney and Universal. **Cons:** I-Drive traffic can be heavy; no on-site restaurant; no room service; Disney is 30 minutes away. ⊠*8750 Universal Blvd., I–4 Exit 74A, I-Drive Area, Orlando* ☎*407/903–1500* ⤳*137 suites* ⊠*6443 Westwood Blvd., I–4 Exit 72, I-Drive Area, Orlando* ☎*407/351–1982* ⤳*125 suites* ⊕*www.extendedstayhotels.com* ⌖*In-room: safe, kitchen. In-hotel: pool, gym, laundry facilities, laundry service, public Wi-Fi, no-smoking rooms* ⊟*AE, D, DC, MC, V* ✛*2:D4.*

$$–$$$ ⊞**Floridays Resort.** The ad slogan of the place is "in the middle of the Magic," but if you interpret that to mean you are going to look out the window and see Disney World, you'll be disappointed. You won't see any theme parks out your window—and that's a good thing. This 35-acre resort is roughly equidistant between Disney and Universal Orlando, which means it is not close to either, and it's within walking distance of virtually nothing. All of those geographical facts are more than offset by the great things Floridays does have going for itself. They are not exaggerating in their self-description as an "oasis." This 430-unit, all-suites resort has all the amenities on the grounds you'll need for perfect Florida days (if not "Floridays"), including a couple of swimming pools, a health club, a game room and kids' activity center, an on-site restaurant, business center and more. The two-bedroom suites are 1,005 square-feet (the size roomy one-family apartment or condo) and the three-bedroom units are 1,295 square feet. All have kitchens, washer and dryer, flat-screen TVs, free high-speed Internet, and a 70-square-foot balcony with a table where you can eat meals and enjoy those Florida days they are selling here. There is a free shuttle to Disney, Universal, and SeaWorld, all of which are about a 15-minute ride to the front gate. **Pros:** great, self-contained environment for a family vacation; free shuttle to theme parks; it's also on the I-Ride route. **Cons:** too far to walk to almost anything meaningful; grocery shopping via shuttle or I-Ride can be problematic. ⊠*12550 Floridays Resort Dr., immediately off International Dr., International Drive area* ☎*407/238–7700* ⊕*www.floridaysresort.com* ⤳*430 suites* ⌖*In-room: safe, Internet, kitchens, washer/dryer. In-hotel: restaurant, bar, pools, outdoor Jacuzzis, gym, laundry service, public Wi-Fi, no-smoking rooms* ⊟*AE D, DC, MC, V* ✛*2:C6.*

$$–$$$ ▦ **Four Points by Sheraton Orlando Studio City.** Atop this Sheraton is a giant silver globe suitable for Times Square on New Year's Eve. But the interior has a Hollywood theme, with movie posters and black-and-white art deco touches throughout the public spaces and rooms, most of which have two queen beds. The 21st floor has 15 extra-large rooms with floor-to-ceiling windows. **Pros:** convenient to Universal; free shuttle to theme parks and outlet malls; great night views from upper floors. **Cons:** located on an unattractive stretch of I-Drive. ✉ *5905 International Dr., I-Drive Area, Orlando* ☎ *407/351–2100 or 800/327–1366* ⊕ *www.starwoodhotels.com/fourpoints* ⤳ *302 rooms* ♨ *In-room: safe, Internet. In-hotel: restaurant, room service, bar, pool, concierge, laundry service, public Wi-Fi, no-smoking rooms* ▤ *AE, D, DC, MC, V* ✛ *2:D2.*

$$$ ▦ **Hilton Orlando.** Newly opened in September 2009, this 1,400-room property adjacent to the Orange County Convention Center is the largest hotel to open in the midst of a recession year, but there is nothing about this big hotel that will make you think of hard times. The hotel's target clientele is corporate meeting groups, with 175,000 square feet of meeting space inside the hotel. But Hilton is eager to entice conventioneers who want to bring their families (and spend more money as a result), so the place is laden with amenities like a big, "lazy-river style" pool, basketball court, kids' club, and other family-attractive amenities. A big draw for those with money to spend are the 12 poolside cabanas, complete with air-conditioning, 42-inch, flat-screen TVs, and wireless and wired Internet, which also happens to be how the guest rooms are outfitted. **Pros:** the same walkway that conventioneers can use to reach the convention center also allows anyone to walk to the center and out the other side and end up on International Drive, near Pointe Orlando, Ripley's Believe It Or Not, and other attractions; free shuttle to Universal Studios, SeaWorld; 13 mi from Orlando International Airport. **Cons:** About 80% of the guests here will be conventioneers; no free shuttle to Disney World. ✉ *6001 Canadian Court, Universal Blvd.* ☎ *407/313–4300* ⊕ *www.hilton.com* ⤳ *1,400 rooms* ♨ *In-room: Internet. In-hotel: 5 restaurants, room service, bars, 9-hole golf course, basketball court, bocce ball court, tennis court, 3 pools, gym, spa, kids club, concierge, laundry service, executive floor, public Wi-Fi, no-smoking rooms, small pets allowed* ▤ *AE, D, DC, MC, V.*

$–$$ ▦ **Holiday Inn Hotel & Suites–Orlando Convention Center.** A bright yellow facade fronted by palm trees welcomes you to this six-story family-friendly hotel. Furnishings are simple, but rooms are large, with either two queen beds or one king. Suites, which have full kitchens, are a bargain at about $160 a night—even in high season. A stay here puts you a block from the Mercado shopping and dining complex, with plenty of inexpensive meal options. Universal, SeaWorld, and Wet 'n Wild are all within 2 mi. **Pros:** very economical; less than a block from I-Drive; free theme-parks shuttle; kids 10 and under eat free with parents. **Cons:** I-Drive traffic can be heavy; Disney is 30 minutes away, and there's no shuttle from this hotel. ✉ *8214 Universal Blvd., I–4 Exit 74A, I-Drive Area, Orlando* ☎ *407/581–9001 or 800/881–3152* ⊕ *www. holidayinnconvention.com* ⤳ *150 rooms, 35 suites* ♨ *In-room: safe,* *kitchen (some), refrigerator, microwave, Internet. In-hotel: restaurant, bar, pools, outdoor Jacuzzis, gym, laundry facilities, laundry service, no-smoking rooms* ▭*AE, D, DC, MC, V* ⊕*2:D4.*

12

$–$$ ▦ **Hyatt Place Orlando/Convention Center.** Youngish, high-tech-consuming business travelers and vacationing Orlando families will find value here because of the location. While it's three blocks from the Orange County Convention Center, which attracts tens of thousands of attendees every day, it's also just a block from a highly tourist-friendly part of I-Drive, making it an easy walk to dozens of restaurants, shops, and attractions like the Pointe Orlando, which geared up with a handful of new, family-friendly restaurants in late 2007. Like other Hyatt Places, this one is hooked into the 24/7 lifestyle, with a computer touch screen in the lobby restaurant from which you can order food at all hours (a kitchen staff is always on duty). At the 24-hour "E-Center," you'll have use of a desktop computer and free printouts. Guest rooms, decorated in pleasant earth tones, offer plenty of tech touches, like a docking station permitting you to use virtually any of your own electronics with the flat-panel HDTV. There's also a wet bar with a mini-refrigerator. **Pros:** free I-Drive, SeaWorld, and Universal Orlando shuttle; convenient to Convention Center and Pointe Orlando. **Cons:** no kids program or babysitting services; no Disney shuttle. ⊠*8741 International Dr., I-Drive* ☎*407/370–4720 or 888/492–8847* ⊕*www.orlandoconventioncenter. place.hyatt.com* ⟿*149 rooms* ⌂*In-room: safe, refrigerator, Internet. In-hotel: restaurant, room service, bar, pool, gym, laundry service, public Wi-Fi, no-smoking rooms* ▭*AE, DC, MC, V* ⊕*2:D4.*

$$–$$$ ▦ **International Plaza Resort & Spa.** On 28 acres just south of the convention center, this 17-story hotel welcomes families as well as conventioneers. It's roughly midway between the airport and Disney, less than a mile from SeaWorld, and a five-minute drive from Universal. There are free shuttles to all major theme parks, including Disney. The hotel went through a multimillion-dollar upgrade in 2008 that gave the place a fresh look for 2009, and it restored the miniature golf course, which had been a putting green for a while. **Pros:** close to SeaWorld, I-Drive, and convention center; on-site miniature golf course; free theme-parks shuttle. **Cons:** few shops and restaurants within walking distance. ⊠*10100 International Dr., I-Drive Area, Orlando* ☎*407/352–1100 or 800/327–0363* ⊕*www.intlplazaresort.com* ⟿*1,102 rooms, 68 suites* ⌂*In-room: safe, Internet. In-hotel: 3 restaurants, room service, pools, gym, spa, putting green, laundry service, public Wi-Fi, no-smoking rooms* ▭*AE, D, DC, MC, V* ⊕*2:D6.*

$$–$$$$ ▦ **JW Marriott Orlando Grande Lakes.** With more than 70,000 square feet of meeting space, this hotel caters to a convention clientele. But because it's part of a lush resort that includes a European-style spa and a Greg Norman–designed golf course, it also appeals to those looking to relax. Rooms are large (420 square feet), and most have balconies that overlook the huge pool complex. The good news about this place is that you get Ritz-Carlton amenities at JW Marriott prices. Wander down a long connector hallway to the adjoining Ritz-Carlton, where you can use your room charge card in the restaurants and shops. **Pros:** pool is great for kids and adults; shares amenities with the Ritz, including

a world-class, albeit expensive, health and beauty spa. **Cons:** things are spread out on the grounds; you need a rental car to reach Disney and other area offerings. ✉ *4040 Central Florida Pkwy., I-Drive Area, Orlando* ☎ *407/206–2300 or 800/576–5750* ⊕ *www.grandelakes.com* ⬗ *1,000 rooms, 57 suites* ♿ *In-room: Internet. In-hotel: 4 restaurants, room service, bars, 18-hole golf course, pool, gym, spa, concierge, laundry service, executive floor, public Wi-Fi, no-smoking rooms* ▭ *AE, D, DC, MC, V* ✛ *2:F6.*

$–$$ 🖬 **La Quinta Inn & Suites Orlando Convention Center.** It's a family-oriented hotel on the more upscale part of I-Drive, near the convention center. The entrance is on Universal Boulevard, the relatively undiscovered thoroughfare a block east of I-Drive, so, despite the proximity to the tourist strip, things are still serene here, but it's easy to walk to I-Drive and shop and dine around the Pointe Orlando complex. The king rooms and suites have refrigerators and microwaves, and although there's no restaurant, the hotel provides free Continental breakfast daily (which includes a make-your-own waffle option), and there are a half-dozen eateries nearby. Round-trip shuttle service to Universal is free. **Pros:** within walking distance of I-Drive restaurants and attractions; free breakfast; free shuttle to Universal. **Cons:** no restaurant; no room service, no Disney shuttle; shuttle to SeaWorld has been discontinued, but you can walk one block and catch I-Ride for $1.25 to SeaWorld. ✉ *8504 Universal Blvd., I–4 Exit 74A, I-Drive Area, Orlando* ☎ *407/345–1365* ⊕ *www.orlandolaquinta.com* ⬗ *170 rooms, 15 suites* ♿ *In-room: safe, refrigerator (some), Internet. In-hotel: bar, pool, gym, laundry facilities, laundry service, no-smoking rooms, some pets allowed* ▭ *AE, D, DC, MC, V* ✛ *2:D4.*

$$–$$$ 🖬 **Lake Eve Resort.** Even though the address is on International Drive (in the newer section of the big tourism thoroughfare, south of Central Florida Parkway), this all-suites resort actually offers serenity as its salient attribute. The hotel building is set well off the street, and the primary visual element you will experience outside the windows is Lake Eve, a place of refuge for migratory birds that don't seem to care that an Interstate Highway and a major tourism strip are each about a half-mile away. Accommodations are all one-, two-, and three-bedroom suites with full kitchens, in-room Jacuzzis, and clothes washer/dryer combos. You probably would not want to stay here without a rental car, but the resort offers some great perks, like free shuttles to Disney, Universal, and SeaWorld, plus free grocery shopping service, with delivery to your room. **Pros:** relatively secluded, especially for I-Drive; free shuttle to both Disney and Universal, a rarity for I-Drive hotels. **Cons:** too far to walk anywhere. ✉ *12388 International Dr. S., International Drive* ☎ *866/934–7985 or 407/597–0370* ⊕ *www.lakeeveresort.com* ⬗ *167 suites* ♿ *In-room: safe, Internet, kitchens, Jacuzzis, washer/dryer. In-hotel: restaurant, bar, 2 pools, gym, bicycles, children's programs (ages 4–12), babysitting, laundry service, public Wi-Fi, no-smoking rooms* ▭ *AE, D, DC, MC, V* ✛ *2:C6.*

$$ 🖬 **Marriott Residence Inn SeaWorld International Center.** The longish name hints at all the markets the hotel is attempting to tap: SeaWorld, I-Drive, and the convention center. All are within a 2-mi radius; all are served

by hotel shuttles. Even the least expensive suites can sleep five people. A free breakfast is served daily, and several nearby restaurants will deliver to your room. The recreation area around the pool is like a summer camp, with a basketball court, playground equipment, picnic tables, and gas grills. Get a firm grip on directions if you're driving. The hotel is adjacent to I–4, but it's 2 mi from the interstate via two expressways, including Beachline Expressway. There's free shuttle service to Universal and SeaWorld. **Pros:** well-equipped kitchens; free breakfast; pets allowed ($75 deposit); free shuttles to lots of places, including Disney World (which is uncommon among I-Drive hotels) **Cons:** not much within walking distance; hard to find from I–4, even though you can see the hotel from the freeway. ⊠ *11000 Westwood Blvd., I–4 Exit 72, I-Drive Area, Orlando* ☎ *407/313–3600 or 800/331–3131* ⊕ *www.residenceinnseaworld.com* ⇨ *350 suites* ⚲ *In-room: safe, kitchen, Internet, Wi-Fi. In-hotel: restaurant, bar, pool, gym, laundry facilities, laundry service, no-smoking rooms* ▤ *AE, D, DC, MC, V* ❙⚬❙ *BP* ✛ *2:C6.*

$$$–$$$$ ☷**Marriott's Cypress Harbour Resort.** This big, elaborate resort is a destination unto itself, with boating on a private lake, golf, tennis, and many other on-site amenities. The two-bedroom, two-bathroom villas sleep up to eight people and include washers and dryers. An on-property market has groceries, liquor, cigars, and video rentals. There's also a Pizza Hut Express and Edy's ice-cream shop. Because the resort is a half-mile from the Nick Faldo Golf Institute by Marriott, the place is popular with those who want a golf getaway. (And you can book golf packages here that get you two rounds of golf at the nearby Grande Pines Golf Club for $339 a night.) **Pros:** lots of outdoor activities (biking, beach volleyball, boating). **Cons:** not much within walking distance. ⊠ *11251 Harbour Villa Rd., I-Drive Area, Orlando* ☎ *407/238–1300 or 800/845–5279* ⊕ *www.vacationclub.com* ⇨ *510 villas* ⚲ *In-room: safe, DVD, Internet. In-hotel: 2 restaurants, bar, tennis courts, pools, gym, beachfront, children's programs (ages 4–12), laundry facilities, laundry service, concierge, public Wi-Fi, no-smoking rooms* ▤ *AE, D, DC, MC, V* ✛ *2:C6.*

$ ☷**Parc Corniche Condominium Suite Hotel.** A Joe Lee–designed golf course frames this property, and it's a quiet location, set back from International Drive a bit. Each of the one- and two-bedroom suites, which are full of pastels and tropical patterns, has a kitchen (with a dishwasher) plus a patio or balcony with golf-course views. The largest accommodations, with two bedrooms and two baths, can sleep up to six. A free Continental breakfast is served daily. SeaWorld is only a few blocks away. And if you're interested in taking your golf game to a higher level, Orlando's famous Faldo Golf Institute is just across International Drive from Parc Coniche. Becomes a good buy for families—you can rent a two-bedroom suite that sleeps up to eight people for around $160. **Pros:** great for golf lovers; well-equipped kitchens; free themeparks shuttle; free breakfast. **Cons:** not much within walking distance. ⊠ *6300 Parc Corniche Dr., I-Drive Area, Orlando* ☎ *407/239–7100 or 800/446–2721* ⊕ *www.parccorniche.com* ⇨ *210 suites* ⚲ *In-room: Internet. In-hotel: restaurant, room service, 18-hole golf course, pool,* *laundry facilities, laundry service, no-smoking rooms* ▤*AE, D, DC, MC, V* ⏅*CP* ⊹*2:C6.*

$$–$$$ 🏨**Peabody Orlando.** Every day at 11 AM the celebrated Peabody ducks exit a private elevator and waddle across the lobby to the marble fountain where they pass the day, basking in their fame. At 5 PM they repeat the ritual in reverse. Built by the owners of the landmark Peabody Hotel in Memphis, this 27-story structure resembles a trio of high-rise office towers, but don't be put off by the austerity. The interior impresses with gilt and marble halls. Some of the oversize upper-floor rooms have views of Disney. A lobby concierge can answer your questions about attractions and cultural events. You can leave your cares behind at the spa or health club. A round-trip shuttle to Disney or Universal is $10 per person. This hotel is about to double in size at the end of 2009, when a brand new high-rise tower will be built and connected to the Orange County Convention Center. This will bring a new luxury spa, and plenty of conventioneers. **Pros:** adjacent to convention center (business travelers take note); good spa; short walk to shops and restaurants. **Cons:** pricey; adjacent to convention center (leisure travelers take note); on a congested section of I-Drive. ✉*9801 International Dr., I-Drive Area, Orlando* ☎*407/352–4000 or 800/732–2639* ⊕*www.peabodyorlando. com* ⬅*891 rooms* ⅃*In-room: safe, Internet. In-hotel: 3 restaurants, room service, tennis courts, pool, gym, spa, concierge, public Wi-Fi, no-smoking rooms* ▤*AE, D, DC, MC, V* ⊹*2:C5.*

$$–$$$ 🏨**The Point Orlando Resort & Suites.** Not to be confused with the Pointe Orlando, the chic shopping and dining complex on International Drive, this high-rise complex on Carrier Drive (just over a mile from the Pointe) has the same things going for it as most any hotel in the area—close proximity to Universal Orlando, the Sand Lake Restaurant Row, and the area along I-Drive that's one of Orlando's more popular tourism strips. The Point, an all-suites property, offers one- and two-bedroom accommodations that are a good fit for families, with mini-kitchens with sinks, microwaves, and mini-refrigerators. (Executive Suites, which run about $20 a night more than the standard "junior" suites, have full kitchens and washer/dryers.) The Point has the advantage of being less frenzied than hotels on I-Drive, which is a couple of blocks away. A shuttle to Disney or Universal (or the airport) is available for a fee. **Pros:** suites are family-friendly; hotel is slightly off the beaten I-Drive path, while still being on the route for I-Ride, the trolley that will take you all the way to SeaWorld. **Cons:** no free shuttles to attractions, so you'll likely need a rental car if you want to go to Disney or downtown Orlando, each a good 10 mi away; no on-site restaurant. ✉*6039 Carrier Dr., International Drive* ☎*407/956–2000 or 866/956–2015* ⊕*www.thepoint-orlando.com* ⬅*197 suites* ⅃*In-room: safe, Internet. In-hotel: pool, gym, laundry facilities, laundry service, public Wi-Fi, no-smoking rooms* ▤*AE, D, DC, MC, V* ⊹*2:D3.*

$$–$$$$ 🏨**Renaissance Orlando Resort at SeaWorld.** The 10-story atrium brims with ponds and palm trees, much of which you can ogle from above as you shoot skyward in sleek glass elevators. Rooms and bathrooms have more floor space than the average Central Florida hotel, plus nice touches like high-speed Internet connections. Try the Neu Lotus Spa, with Oriental-style massage and beauty treatments. **Pros:** FedEx/Kinkos and Starbucks storefronts on-site; good restaurants; across from Sea-World; shuttles to Disney ($10 round-trip) and Universal (free); new Neu Lotus Spa, with Oriental-style massage and beauty treatments, opened in 2008. **Cons:** unless you're near an elevator it's a long walk around each floor to reach rooms; shuttles aren't free; many conventioneers afoot; the once-legendary Sunday brunch has been dropped. ✉ *6677 Sea Harbor Dr., I-Drive Area, Orlando* ☎ *407/351–5555 or 800/468–3571* ⊕ *www.renaissancehotels.com* ⤴ *781 rooms* ♿ *In-room: Internet. In-hotel: 4 restaurants, room service, tennis courts, pool, gym, spa, laundry service, concierge, public Wi-Fi, no-smoking rooms* ▤ *AE, D, DC, MC, V* ✛ *2:C6.*

$–$$ ⌂ **Residence Inn by Marriott.** In a hotel enclave just off International Drive that has been around for at least 25 years, this recently renovated, all-suites property offers a great place for families, with home-like accommodations complete with everything from full kitchens to separate living rooms with fireplaces. It is an easy walk to Fishbones restaurant and the world's largest McDonald's, although hot breakfast at the hotel is free. (But there is no restaurant open beyond breakfast.) Wet 'n Wild and Pointe Orlando are about a mile south on I-Drive on the trolley bus system, I-Ride, and a plethora of outlet stores are within a mile north. **Pros:** convenient to Universal Orlando, Universal Drive attractions; pleasant atmosphere inside the hotel complex. **Cons:** this is a traffic-heavy and somewhat tacky area of the International Drive area, somewhat unpleasant outside the hotel grounds; no shuttle to anywhere, and it's too far to walk to any theme park. ✉ *8800 Universal Blvd., International Drive* ☎ *407/226–0288* ⊕ *www.marriott.com* ⤴ *210 suites* ♿ *In-room: safe, kitchen, refrigerator, Internet. In-hotel: pool, gym, basketball court, sand volleyball court, laundry facilities, laundry service, no-smoking room* ▤ *AE, D, DC, MC, V* ✛ *2:D3.*

$$$$ ⌂ **Ritz-Carlton Orlando Grande Lakes.** Orlando's first and only Ritz is

Fodor's Choice a particularly extravagant link in the luxury chain. Service is exem-

★ plary, from the fully attended porte-cochere entrance to the 18-hole golf course and 40-room spa. Rooms and suites have large balconies, elegant wood furnishings, down comforters, and decadent marble baths (with separate showers and tubs). A lovely, Roman-style pool area has fountains and a hot tub. Make reservations for dinner at Norman's when you reserve your room (Norman's is hugely expensive, but if you can afford the Ritz, you can probably afford Norman's). An enclosed hallway connects the Ritz to the nearby JW Marriott Hotel, where you'll find more restaurants and a kid-friendly water park. And the Ritz offers 480-square-foot Kids Suites, complete with child-size furniture, toys and games, which attach to the Executive Suites (the catch is you need to stay in an Executive Suite, which costs about $500 a night). **Pros:** truly luxurious; impeccable service; great spa; golf course; shares amenities with Marriott. **Cons:** pricey; need a rental car to reach Disney and area shops and restaurants. ✉ *4012 Central Florida Pkwy., I-Drive Area, Orlando* ☎ *407/206–2400 or 800/576–5760* ⊕ *www.grandelakes.com* ⤴ *520 rooms, 64 suites* ♿ *In-room: Internet. In-hotel: 4 restaurants, room service, bars, 18-hole golf course, pool, gym, spa, concierge,* *children's programs (ages 4–12), laundry service, executive floor, public Wi-Fi, no-smoking rooms ☰AE, D, DC, MC, V ✥2:F6.*

$$–$$$ 🏨 **Rosen Centre Hotel.** This 24-story palace is adjacent to the convention center and within walking distance of I-Drive attractions such as the Pointe Orlando shopping and entertainment center and Ripley's Believe It or Not! There's a massive pool surrounded by vegetation and a couple of good restaurants, including the Everglades Room and Cafe Gauguin. Universal ticket services are available, and so is the BAGS service offered by all Rosen conference and Disney properties. With it, you can get a boarding pass and check your luggage in at the hotel, eliminating check-in at Orlando International. A round-trip shuttle to Disney, Universal, or SeaWorld costs $9 to $16. Banshoo (which means "Sunset" in Japanese), a sushi bar adjoining the lobby, opened in the spring of 2009, offering a full range of sushi and sashimi, as well as sake, the Japanese rice wine. **Pros:** easy walk to convention center, Pointe Orlando, and other I-Drive attractions; BAGS check-in service; priority golf reservations at Rosen's Shingle Creek Golf course, 2 mi from Rosen Centre. **Cons:** theme-park shuttles aren't free; feels very much like a business hotel; convention center traffic can be a problem. ✉*9840 International Dr., I-Drive Area* ☎*407/996–9840 or 800/204–7234* ⊕*www.rosencentre.com* ⬳*1,334 rooms, 80 suites* ♿*In-room: safe, Internet. In-hotel: 3 restaurants, room service, bars, pool, gym, laundry service, public Wi-Fi, no-smoking rooms* ☰*AE, D, DC, MC, V* ✥*2:D5.*

$–$$ 🏨 **Rosen Plaza Hotel.** Harris Rosen, Orlando's largest independent hotel owner, loves to offer bargains, and you can definitely find one here. Although it's essentially a convention hotel, leisure travelers like the prime location and long list of amenities. Rooms have two queen-size beds and are larger than those at many hotels. Two upscale restaurants, Jack's Place and Café Matisse, offer great steaks and a great buffet, respectively. Rossini's serves good pizza, and you can also grab quick eats at the reasonably priced 24-hour deli. With the BAGS service, you can get your airline boarding pass and check your suitcases in the hotel lobby, so you can go straight to the gate at Orlando International. There's a free shuttle to Universal Orlando and SeaWorld; a round-trip shuttle to Disney costs $16 per person. **Pros:** within walking distance of I-Drive eateries and attractions; free shuttle to Universal and SeaWorld; BAGS check-in service; guests in all seven Rosen-owned hotels in Orlando get priority reservations at the 18-hole golf course at Rosen's Shingle Creek, a couple of blocks away from the Rosen Plaza. **Cons:** convention center traffic can be bad; shuttle to Disney isn't free. ✉*9700 International Dr., I-Drive Area, Orlando* ☎*407/996–9700 or 800/627–8258* ⊕*www.rosenplaza.com* ⬳*810 rooms* ♿*In-room: safe, Internet. In-hotel: 2 restaurants, room service, bar, pool, laundry facilities, laundry service, public Wi-Fi, no-smoking rooms* ☰*AE, D, DC, MC, V* ✥*2:C5.*

$$–$$$$ 🏨 **Rosen Shingle Creek.** It may be close to the convention center, but make no mistake: this place has plenty for those seeking fun and relaxation. There's the 13,000-square-foot spa, for instance, and the championship golf course and golf academy. (Both the course and the academy have appeared on top 25 and top 100 lists in *Golfweek* and *Golf* magazines.)

There are also four swimming pools and recreation options that include kayaking on a creek. The architecture recalls the Spanish-revival palaces you find in Palm Beach County. (In fact, the place also looks a lot like the Ritz-Carlton Grande Lakes in Orlando, from a distance.) Standard guest rooms are large (436 square feet) and have plasma-screen TVs and NXTV, a system that turns the TV into an Internet-linked computer. Thanks to the BAGS service, you can get a boarding pass for your flight and check in your luggage at the hotel, thus eliminating check-in at Orlando International. **Pros:** golf course; spa; free shuttle to Universal; BAGS check-in service; the only four-star level resort in town with a self-service coin laundry. **Cons:** large grounds mean long walks to on-site amenities; no shuttle to I-Drive, and the walk is about 3 mi. ⊠*9939 Universal Blvd., I-Drive Area, Orlando* ☎*407/996–9939, 866/996–6338 reservations* ⊕*www.rosenshinglecreek.com* ⇆*1,500 rooms, 109 suites* ♿*In-room: safe, Internet. In-hotel: 3 restaurants, room service, 4 pools, gym, golf course, tennis courts, spa, children's programs (ages 4–14), laundry facilities, laundry service, public Wi-Fi, no-smoking rooms* ⊟*AE, D, DC, MC, V* ✛*2:E5.*

$–$$ ⬚ **Staybridge Suites International Drive.** The one- and two-bedroom units at this all-suites hotel sleep four to eight people. Each has a living room and kitchen with simple but up-to-date furnishings. The signature unit in this hotel is the 750-square-foot, two-bedroom, two-bath suite with a full kitchen, plus a big, foldout sofa in the living room, which makes it practical to house up to eight people comfortably. Suites have televisions with a DVD player in each sleeping area, including the living room. The hotel is within walking distance of plenty of I-Drive shopping and restaurants. Lush landscaping makes the place seem secluded even though it's on I-Drive. **Pros:** within walking distance of I-Drive eateries and attractions; close to Universal. **Cons:** no restaurant; no room service; on a congested stretch of I-Drive. ⊠*8480 International Dr., I–4 Exit 74A, I-Drive Area, Orlando* ☎*407/352–2400 or 800/238–8000* ⊕*www.sborlando.com* ⇆*146 suites* ♿*In-room: safe, kitchen, refrigerator, Internet. In-hotel: pool, gym, laundry facilities, laundry service, no-smoking rooms* ⊟*AE, D, DC, MC, V* ❤️*CP* ✛*2:D4.*

$–$$ ⬚ **Westgate Palace Resort.** This place has quite an architectural history, having stood for years as twin, 18-story, bright pink condo towers that were visible from I-4, but were never actually finished by their former developers. But that's ancient history by I-Drive neighbor standards, where the average person needs to look at his or her wrist watch to determine how long they've been in Orlando. Now, with a tasteful white paint job, these two towers collectively offer 408 two-bedroom suites that offer a great deal for travelers because of price and location (about $130 a night for a 610-square-foot suite with two bedrooms, three TV sets, and a full kitchen, and within easy walking distance of most of the northern I-Drive attractions.) This is still a condo development, but functions as a hotel because you can walk in and rent suites by the night or by the week. Although the resort has no kids' programs on property, an unusual perk is free usage of the facilities at the **Westgate Lakes Resort & Spa** (⊠*1000 Turkey Lake Rd., Orlando*), 4 mi away. Westgate Lakes not only has a kids' program, but a massive and extensive activities program for visitors of all ages, ranging from bingo and crafts for seniors to teen dances to kayaking expeditions on the lake that adjoins the resort. The bad news is that you need to get there on your own—no Westgate-provided shuttle between the resorts. **Pros:** good location and rates; I-Ride can take you anywhere along I-Drive, including SeaWorld, but there is a fee; within walking distance of outlet malls. **Cons:** no free shuttles to anywhere, including Universal Studios, about 3 mi away; no restaurant, but plenty within walking distance, and this neighborhood is take-out or order-in Nirvana. ⊠ *6145 Carrrier Dr., International Drive* ☎ *888/808–7410* ⊕ *www.westgatgedestinations. com* ⇔ *408 suites* ⊘ *In-room: safe, Internet (fee), kitchen, washer/ dryer. In-hotel: pool, gym, arcade, public Wi-Fi, no-smoking rooms* ▭ *AE, D, DC, MC, V* ✛ *2:D3.*

$$–$$$$ ▣ **Westin Imagine.** Directly across Universal Boulevard from the mammoth Orange County Convention Center, this 12-story hotel attracts scores of conventioneers, but it's also strategically situated near Sea-World, Universal Orlando, and I-Drive one block away. The design of the place is legitimately art deco, but won't make you think you're among the 1930s architectural treasures of Miami's South Beach. Guest rooms are decorated in subdued gold-and-green tones, with creature comforts like the chain's trademark Heavenly Beds. The hotel also has one- and two-bedroom suites; all rooms and one-bedroom suites have kitchenettes, and two-bedroom suites have full kitchens. The hotel has some inviting amenities like a big lagoon pool and huge pool deck area with outdoor hot tubs. The Westin Kids Club program is available for kids 3–12. The hotel got its name from the Village of Imagine, a giant, ultra-upscale condo community to be built around the hotel over the next few years. **Pros:** free shuttle to SeaWorld and Universal; easy walk to Convention Center, Pointe Orlando, I-Drive; kids' programs. **Cons:** no Disney shuttle, 20–25 minutes away from Disney World. ⊠ *9501 Universal Blvd., I-Drive area* ☎ *888/946–9501* ⊕ *www.starwoodhotels. com* ⇔ *312 rooms* ⊘ *In-room: safe, Internet. In-hotel: restaurants, bar, room service, tennis courts, pool, gym, spa, concierge, public Wi-Fi, no-smoking rooms* ▭ *AE, D, DC, MC, V* ✛ *2:D5.*

$–$$ ▣ **Wyndham Orlando Resort.** Two-story villas, palm trees, and romantic lagoons evoke a Caribbean getaway. There's a children's entertainment center and an upscale shopping court. The villas are comfortable, if not necessarily candidates for *Architectural Digest.* And you can't beat the location five minutes from Universal. If you choose the Family Fun Suites option, your youngsters get a separate room with bunk beds. There's a free shuttle to Universal and SeaWorld. **Pros:** convenient to Universal, SeaWorld, I-Drive, and outlet malls; pets allowed ($50 non-refundable fee, pets can't weigh more than 50 pounds and no more than two are allowed). **Cons:** no shuttle to Disney, which is about 30 minutes away. ⊠ *8001 International Dr., I-Drive Area, Orlando* ☎ *407/351–2420 or 800/996–3426* ⊕ *www.wyndham.com* ⇔ *1,064 rooms* ⊘ *In-room: safe, refrigerator, Internet. In-hotel: 3 restaurants, room service, tennis courts, jogging track, pools, gym, spa, massage, laundry service, public Wi-Fi, no-smoking rooms, some pets allowed (fee)* ▭ *AE, D, DC, MC, V* ✛ *2:C3.*

DOWNTOWN ORLANDO

Downtown Orlando, north of Walt Disney World and the I-Drive area, is a thriving business district during weekdays, and, as a result of the economic climate, had become relatively dead at nights and on weekends by 2009. Overbuilding of downtown residence condos has not helped. There are still some good restaurants and bars, especially in the nearby Thornton Park area. And there are still good museums and galleries just north of downtown. Lake Eola is still beautiful, but much of the vibrancy that used to attract tourism has moved south and west of Sand Lake Road—12 mi from downtown Orlando. To get there take Exit 83B off I-4 westbound, Exit 84 off I-4 eastbound.

$-$$$
Fodor'sChoice
★

The Courtyard at Lake Lucerne. These four beautifully restored Victorian houses that surround a palm-lined courtyard were architectural treasures more than 50 years before Disney came to Orlando, and have kept their own brand of magic even now, as they collectively make up one of the better historic inns you'll find in the southeast United States. Although it's almost under an expressway bridge, there's no traffic noise. You can sit on one of the porches and imagine yourself back in the time when citrus ruled and the few visitors arrived at the old railroad station on Church Street, six blocks away. Rooms have hardwood floors, Persian rugs, and antique furniture. A real treat is the Turret Room, which overlooks the lake across the street. **Pros:** serenity; great Victorian architecture; the azaleas in this neighborhood are alive with color in spring and summer; short walk to Lake Eola and Church Street. **Cons:** far from theme parks and I-Drive; walking in some parts of downtown can be a bit dicey. ⊠ *211 N. Lucerne Circle E, Downtown, Orlando* ☎ *407/648–5188* ⊕ *www.orlandohistoricinn. com* ↪ *15 rooms, 15 suites* ♿ *In-room: Internet. In-hotel: no elevator, no-smoking rooms* ☐ *MC, V* ⦿ *CP* ✚ *3:B3.*

$-$$
Embassy Suites Orlando Downtown. Although designed for business travelers, this property has nice touches for vacationers, too. All suites have two TVs—one in each room. Many suites overlook nearby Lake Eola, and a balcony suite overlooking the lake is one of the great undiscovered bargains in Orlando at $200 a night. The hotel is a short walk from a half-dozen sidewalk cafés. The seven-story indoor atrium gives the hotel a classy touch. **Pros:** short walk to Lake Eola and Church Street; some suites have stunning lake views; free Continental breakfast. **Cons:** traffic can be heavy; finding on-street parking is hard and on-site valet parking costs $12 a day; Disney is at least 45 minutes away (or an hour or more during rush hours); no room service, but you can order delivery from half a dozen restaurants nearby (ask the front desk for menus). ⊠ *191 E. Pine St., Downtown, Orlando* ☎ *407/841–1000 or 800/609–3339* ⊕ *www.embassysuites.com* ↪ *167 suites* ♿ *In-room: safe, refrigerator, Internet. In-hotel: pool, gym, laundry service, public Wi-Fi, no-smoking rooms* ☐ *AE, D, DC, MC, V* ⦿ *BP* ✚ *3:B2.*

$$-$$$
Eō Inn & Urban Spa. The entrance is at the rear of the building, behind Panera Bread, the bakery–restaurant that occupies the ground floor. Consequently, this three-story boutique hotel in a 1923 building is an undiscovered charmer. The spa does a brisk business on its own, but as

a hotel guest you can always get in for a Swedish massage or a beauty treatment. Rooms have black-and-white photographs, thick down comforters, and high-speed Internet connections. Best of all, Lake Eola, with its 1-mi walking path, is across the street—treat yourself to a king suite, with a balcony overlooking the lake. **Pros:** good spa; very short walk to Lake Eola; short walk to Thornton Park and Church Street; these areas have plenty of restaurants and are safe to walk to at night. **Cons:** you have to battle I–4 traffic; Disney is 30–45 minutes away. (Don't believe the hotel Web site statement that Disney is 20 minutes away. Without lights and a siren on your car, or a helicopter, that won't happen.) ✉ *227 N. Eola Dr., off E. Robinson St., Thornton Park, Orlando* ☎ *407/481–8485 or 888/481–8488* ⊕ *www.eoinn.com* ➘ *17 rooms* ⌂ *In-room: safe, Internet. In-hotel: spa, laundry service, public Wi-Fi, no-smoking rooms* ⊟ *AE, D, DC, MC, V* ✛ *3:C2.*

$$$–$$$$ 🏨**Grand Bohemian.** This European-style property is downtown Orlando's only luxury hotel. Opposite city hall, the Grand Bohemian showcases more than 100 pieces of art—including an Imperial Grand Bösendorfer piano, one of only two in the world, which sits in a posh ground-floor lounge. Rooms have dark-wood furnishings with brushed-silver accents. Tall headboards are upholstered in iridescent fabrics. The owner of the property has an extensive art collection, and displays it in a gallery in the hotel. **Pros:** art gallery; quiet, adult-friendly atmosphere; great restaurant; short walk to Lake Eola and Church Street. **Cons:** kids may find it boring; meals are relatively expensive. ✉ *325 S. Orange Ave., Downtown, Orlando* ☎ *407/313–9000 or 866/663–0024* ⊕ *www.grandbohemianhotel.com* ➘ *250 rooms, 36 suites* ⌂ *In-room: Internet. In-hotel: restaurant, room service, bar, pool, gym, concierge, executive floor, public Wi-Fi, parking (fee), no-smoking rooms* ⊟ *AE, D, DC, MC, V* ✛ *3:B3.*

$–$$ 🏨**Sheraton Orlando Downtown.** A business hotel with a 20,000-square-foot conference center, this relatively undiscovered gem's location also holds value for families. Within walking distance is pleasant little Lake Ivanhoe and a neighborhood with a handful of mom-and-pop restaurants and antiques shops. Within easy driving distance is the Orlando museum district, including great kid-friendly programs at the Orlando Science Museum. There are also a concierge level and a nice little on-property Italian restaurant, 60 South Bar and Trattoria. This is a good base from which to see the "real" Orlando, miles away from the nearest tourist strip. Rooms have 42" plasma screen TVs and work desks. **Pros:** easy walk to pleasant downtown lakes; close to museum district, arts and antiques district; you can jump on 1–4 and be in Daytona Beach (60 mi away) about as quickly as you can be in Downtown Disney; the bulk of the nasty I–4 traffic is between your hotel and Disney, not between the hotel and points east and north. **Cons:** no children's program or babysitting services. ✉ *60 S. Ivanhoe Blvd., Orlando* ☎ *407/425–4455* ⊕ *www.starwoodhotels.com* ➘ *341 rooms* ⌂ *In-room: safe, refrigerator, Internet. In-hotel: restaurant, room service, bar, pool, gym, laundry facilities, laundry service, public Wi-Fi, no-smoking rooms* ⊟ *AE, DC, MC, V* ✛ *3:B1.*

ORLANDO INTERNATIONAL AIRPORT

The area around the airport, especially the neighborhood just north of the Beachline Expressway, has become hotel city over the past few years, with virtually every big-name hotel you can think of, including plenty of family-style choices, such as suites with kitchens. All the hotels listed include free airport shuttle service.

$–$$ ⊞ **AmeriSuites Orlando Airport Northeast and Northwest.** These two hotels (one on each side of State Road 436, north of the airport) offer suites with bedrooms and living room–kitchen areas. With red carpeting, gold drapes, an overstuffed couch and lounge chair, and of course, a coffeemaker, the living area has the warm feeling of the quintessential American home. This is largely a business-traveler-oriented chain, but the rates make it attractive to families. **Pros:** good rates; efficient rooms with all the essentials; free airport shuttle. **Cons:** no shuttle to theme parks; not much within walking distance. ⊠ *7500 Augusta National Dr., Orlando International Airport, Orlando* ☎ *407/240–3939* ⟋ *128 suites* ⊠ *5435 Forbes Pl., Orlando International Airport* ☎ *407/816–7800 or 800/833–1516* ⟋ *135 suites* ⊕ *www.amerisuites.com* ⟍ *In-room: safe, refrigerator, Internet. In-hotel: pool, gym, laundry facilities, laundry service, public Wi-Fi, no-smoking rooms* ⊟ *AE, D, DC, MC, V* ⫿○⫿ *BP* ⊹ *2:H3.*

$–$$$ ⊞ **The Florida Hotel & Conference Center.** Five miles from the airport gates, the Florida Hotel is right between Orlando International and I-Drive. You're in for a treat if you like to shop: the hotel is connected to the upscale Florida Mall, with seven major department stores and 250 specialty shops. The hotel feels upscale, too, with polished marble floors, fountains in the lobby, and a good in-house restaurant, Le Jardin, as well as a Starbucks. Rooms have either two queen beds or a king and a foldout sofa; microwaves and refrigerators are available for a small fee. There's free shuttle service to Disney, Universal, and SeaWorld. **Pros:** access to the mall's shopping and dining options; in-room spa services; short drive to airport. **Cons:** neighborhood is less than scenic; besides the interior of the adjoining mall, there's nothing to walk around the hotel; Disney is 18 mi away. ⊠ *1500 Sand Lake Rd., at S. Orange Blossom Trail, Orlando International Airport, Orlando* ☎ *407/859–1500 or 800/588–4656* ⊕ *www.thefloridahotelorlando. com* ⟋ *510 rooms* ⟍ *In-room: Internet. In-hotel: restaurant, room service, pool, gym, laundry service, public Wi-Fi, no-smoking rooms* ⊟ *AE, D, DC, MC, V* ⊹ *2:H3.*

$$$ ⊞ **Hyatt Regency Orlando International Airport.** If you have to catch an early-morning flight, this hotel inside the main terminal complex is a good option. Counting the time you spend waiting for the elevator, your room is a five-minute walk from the nearest ticket counter. Rooms have views of either the runways or a 10-story-tall terminal atrium; terminal-side rooms have balconies. Hemisphere, the hotel's upscale restaurant, offers an eclectic menu that changes seasonally and spectacular runway views. An in-house health club, open 24 hours, and pool provide places to unwind. Shuttles to Disney and Universal are $29 per person round-trip. **Pros:** quiet and sublime; the terminal's

24-hour shopping and dining options are available; all rooms have mini-refrigerators, not mini-bars. **Cons:** nothing around but the airport; downtown Orlando and the theme parks are at least 30 minutes away. ⊠ *9300 Airport Blvd., Orlando International Airport, Orlando* ☎ *407/825–1234 or 800/233–1234* ⊕ *www.orlandoairport.hyatt.com* ➘ *446 rooms* ⬥ *In-room: Internet. In-hotel: 3 restaurants, room service, pool, gym, massage, laundry service, no-smoking rooms* ▤ *AE, D, DC, MC, V* ✛ *2:H3.*

OUTLYING TOWNS

Travel farther afield and you can get more comforts and facilities for the money, and maybe even some genuine Orlando charm—of the cozy country-inn variety.

DAVENPORT

Take I–4 Exit 55.

The beauty of Davenport is that virtually no one in Orlando has ever heard of it, even though it's only 13 mi southwest of Disney's south entrance. The relative obscurity of this town makes it a bargain oasis. If you don't mind the absence of nightlife and entertainment, you'll save 30% or more at Davenport hotels, which surround I–4 at Exit 55, compared with the same chains on I-Drive. Both areas are about the same distance from Disney but in opposite directions.

$ 🏨 **Holiday Inn Express & Suites, Orlando South.** This hotel makes a great place for families who want to see Disney on a budget for many reasons. Every room has a mini-refrigerator and microwave, so you can buy your food at the grocery store; the room rates are relatively cheap and the hotel is the best (and newest, opened in February 2009) in this little town; and to top it all off, you'll spend a lot less time in Orlando traffic, because the hotel is 10 mi from Disney's front gate and on the other side of Disney World from all the traffic to and from Orlando. **Pros:** good location; free Internet; microwave, and mini-refrigerator in every room; good shopping within a mile. **Cons:** no theme park shuttle; nothing to walk to; you will definitely need a rental car; located near the Interstate but tricky to get to, so call the hotel for instructions. ⊠ *4050 Hotel Dr., Davenport* ☎ *863/420–6611* ⊕ *www.hiexpress.com* ➘ *132 rooms* ⬥ *In-room: safe, Internet. In-hotel: restaurant, pool, gym, coin laundry, business center, public Wi-Fi, no-smoking rooms* ▤ *AE, D, DC, MC, V* ✛ *1:D6.*

¢–$ 🏨 **South Gate Inn.** The hotel, which changed its brand name in 2008, is nothing extraordinary, but offers a nice palm-lined courtyard with a swimming pool and outdoor hot tub. Rates are low here, even in high season. (You can, for instance, get a room for two, on a weeknight during April, which is ultrahigh season in the Disney environs, for $59 and for $69 on weekends.) Rooms, with pink-and-blue floral-pattern spreads and blue carpets, are pleasant but not palatial. There's no restaurant, but a Bob Evans Family Restaurant is just across the parking

12

lot, and there's a free Continental breakfast in a small dining area adjacent to the lobby. **Pros:** free breakfast; free Disney shuttle; small pets allowed ($10 per night fee); easy drive to WDW and Orlando metro area; virtually every franchises burger or pizza joint in the western hemisphere has a branch just across the bridge on the other side of I-4. **Cons:** shuttles to SeaWorld and Universal cost $15 round-trip; located in less-than-picturesque Davenport. ✉ *2425 Frontage Rd., Davenport* ☎ *863/424–2596 or 800/424–1880* ⊕ *www.southgateinnorlandosouth. com* ⤶ *113 rooms* ♿ *In-room: Internet. In-hotel: pool, laundry facilities, no-smoking rooms, some pets allowed (fee)* ▭ *AE, D, DC, MC, V* �'O'*CP* ✛ *1:E6.*

$–$$ ⊡ **Hampton Inn Orlando Maingate South.** They've taken some poetic (or marketing) license with the name here. For the record, the hotel is 27 mi from Disney's main entrance. The park's south entrance is 13 mi away, however, the hotel offers good bargains and access to attractions west of Orlando, like Cypress Gardens and Fantasy of Flight. Rooms are bright and pleasant—some come with DVD players—and you get a free hot breakfast and local phone calls. **Pros:** lots of freebies (Disney shuttle, breakfast, local calls); small pets allowed (nonrefundable $25 deposit); good location—easy drive to Disney, the Orlando metro area, and even Tampa (an hour west). **Cons:** Davenport is more of a nondescript interstate stop than a picturesque hamlet; nothing worthwhile within walking distance. ✉ *44117 U.S. 27 N, Davenport* ☎ *863/420–9898* ⊕ *www.hamptoninn.com* ⤶ *83 rooms* ♿ *In-room: Internet. In-hotel: pool, laundry facilities, no-smoking rooms* ▭ *AE, D, DC, MC, V* �'O'*CP* ✛ *1:E6.*

WINTER PARK

Take I–4 Exit 87 or 88.

A small college town and greater Orlando's poshest and best-established area, Winter Park is full of chichi shops and restaurants. It feels a million miles from the tourist track, but it's just a short drive from the major attractions.

$–$$$$ ⊡ **Park Plaza Hotel.** Small and intimate, this 1922 establishment feels almost like a private home. The best accommodations are front garden suites with a living room that opens onto a long balcony usually abloom with impatiens and bougainvillea. Balconies are so covered with shrubs and ferns that they are somewhat private, inspiring more than a few romantic interludes. A half-dozen sidewalk cafés and many more upscale boutiques and shops surround the hotel. Also, the Charles Hosmer Morse Museum of Art, which features the world's largest collection of Tiffany glassworks, is within two blocks. Park Plaza Gardens, the restaurant downstairs, offers quiet atrium dining and excellent food. **Pros:** romantic; great balconies overlooking Park Avenue; short walk to shops and restaurants; in-house restaurant is in a charming, brick-walled courtyard; you can walk to the nearest Amtrak station, about a block away. **Cons:** the railroad tracks are a lot closer than the station is, and you can sometimes hear train noise at night; no small children allowed; small rooms; Disney is 60 minutes away. ⊠*307 Park Ave. S, Winter Park* ☎*407/647–1072 or 800/228–7220* ⊕*www. parkplazahotel.com* ⇦*27 rooms* ☼*In-room: Internet. In-hotel: restaurant, room service, laundry service, public Wi-Fi, no kids under 5, no-smoking rooms* ⊟*AE, DC, MC, V* ✛*3:B1.*

Nightlife

WORD OF MOUTH

"If you have a car and it's Friday or Saturday, go downtown. There are a lot of clubs and restaurants in Thornton Park (Hues) and lots of places on South Orange Avenue. The Grand Bohemian hotel at Orange Avenue and Jackson has great jazz combos (check the Website for times). Although the restaurant is pricey, the bar—where the music is—has delicious food and drinks that cost no more than that at Disney. It's a hip and arty hotel; not the usual Disney experience. And there won't be screaming kids everywhere. I'm not dissing kids, it's just that we're talking about nightlife here!"

—Thorspecken

Updated
by Gary
McKechnie

Not only must Orlando provide nightlife for more than 50 million visitors each year, it must also make it memorable enough to bring people back again and again. The city's main domestic rival, Las Vegas, accomplishes this with stage spectaculars, free drinks at the slots, and promises of money for nothing. But for Orlando it's more difficult. Why? Because its visitors are more diverse. They can be a family from Canada, newlyweds from the Midwest, or retirees from Japan, and Orlando is required by law to provide appropriate entertainment for them all.

When you enter the fiefdom known as Walt Disney World, you're likely to see as many watering holes as cartoon characters—and this is true even after the closing of Disney's Pleasure Island nightlife complex. You have a choice of nightlife at various Disney shopping and entertainment complexes—from the casual down-by-the-shore BoardWalk to the much larger multi-area Downtown Disney, which comprises the Marketplace and West Side. Two long-running dinner shows provide an evening of song, dance, and dining, all for a single price. You can also frequent a wide range of themed bars, lounges, and clubs at Disney resorts before hitting a theme park after dark to see a stage show or catch fireworks or a parade.

At Universal, the after-hours action has seeped out of the parks and into CityWalk, an eclectic and eccentric 30-acre pastiche of shops, restaurants, clubs, and concert venues. CityWalk's attitude is as hip and sassy as anywhere in the Universal domain.

Although CityWalk—with all its clubs, concert venues, and nightly shows like those by Blue Man Group—is your best one-stop place for nightlife, it's not your only option. The downtown clubs may have lost their monopoly on nighttime entertainment when Disney and Universal muscled their way onto the scene. As the pendulum swings, though, more locals are making their way back downtown.

There are many independent clubs and venues scattered throughout Orlando and into Kissimmee. Among the noteworthy spots are BB King's Blues Club and ICEBAR, both on International Drive. Although completion is several years away, the city has approved a multibillion package to bring in a new performing arts center and other venues. Developers, too, are hoping to jump-start a downtown revival by salvaging old buildings and adding new nightclubs.

TOP 5 AFTER DARK EXPERIENCES

Cirque du Soleil—*La Nouba.* If you haven't yet seen one of the surreal Cirque du Soleil shows, or if you have and you were wowed, you'll love this high-energy acrobatics performance.

Blue Man Group. How many marshmallows can one Blue Man catch in his mouth? It's worth your while to head over to Universal's Sharp-Aquos Theatre to find out.

House of Blues. This concert hall in Downtown Disney is the best live-music venue in Orlando and always hosts major headliners.

IllumiNations. Epcot's nighttime spectacular, featuring lasers, fireworks, and floating movie screens, is a not-to-be-missed crowd-pleaser.

SpectroMagic. Millions of tiny white lights decorating the floats, carriages, and even costumes in this parade will absolutely mesmerize you. Kids can't tear their eyes away from the spectacle and usually end up watching the whole thing with their mouths silently agape.

13

WALT DISNEY WORLD

Don't assume that all after-dark activities revolve solely around adult bars and expensive shows. A wealth of free shows is performed at Epcot's pavilions and stages at the Magic Kingdom and Disney's Hollywood Studios. Even if you head back to your hotel for an afternoon nap or swim, you can always return to a theme park to catch the fireworks show. Get information on WDW nightlife from the **Walt Disney World information hotline** (☎ *407/824–2222 or 407/824–4500*) or check online at www.waltdisneyworld.com. Disney nightspots accept American Express, MasterCard, and Visa. And cash. Lots of it.

DISNEY'S BOARDWALK

At the turn of the 20th century, Americans escaping the cities for the Atlantic seaside spent their days on breeze-swept boardwalks above the strand, where early thrill rides kept company with band concerts and other activities. Here, across Crescent Lake from Disney's Yacht and Beach Club Resorts, WDW has created its own version of these amusement areas, a shoreside complex that's complete with restaurants, bars and clubs, souvenir sellers, surreys, saltwater taffy vendors, and shops. When the lights go on after sunset, the mood is festive in a family way. For information on events call the **BoardWalk entertainment hotline** (☎ *407/939–3492 or 407/939–2444*).

Atlantic Dance Hall. This club started out as a hypercool room recalling the Swing Era, with martinis, cigars, and Sinatra soundalikes, but that didn't last, so it reopened as a Latin club. That didn't last either, so now it's a typical high energy Top 40 dance club. These days it has a huge screen showing videos requested by the crowd. You must be 21 to enter. ☎ *407/939–2444 or 407/939–2430* 🎟 *No cover* ⊙ *Tues.–Sat.* 9 PM–2 AM.

Big River Grille & Brewing Works. Disney World's first (and only) brewpub, Big River has warm wood surfaces and intimate tables where brewmasters tend to their potions, adding to the charm of this retreat. Inside stainless-steel vats are a variety of beers, including the popular Rocket Red Ale. If you're not ready to settle on one, order up a $5 sampler that includes up to six 4-ounce shots of whatever's on tap that day, from the Red Rocket, Southern Flyer Light Lager, Gadzooks Pilsener, and Steamboat Pale Ale to Sweet Magnolia Brown and Winter's Nip Porter. Upscale pub grub and sandwiches round out the offerings. The brewery's sidewalk café is a great place for people-watching and good conversation. ☎*407/560–0253* 📧*No cover* ⊘*Daily 11:30* AM*–12:30* AM.

> ## WORD OF MOUTH
>
> "Jellyrolls at the Boardwalk is a must! Dueling pianos have never been better.... Write your requests on a napkin, take it up to the [pianists] with a couple of bucks, and you're sure to get your songs played."
>
> –shellybyjosh

ESPN Club. As with all themed things at Disney, the sports motif here is carried into every nook and cranny. The arcade is jammed with sports-themed video games, and the main dining area looks like a sports arena, with a basketball-court hardwood floor and a giant scoreboard that projects the big game of the day. Sportscasters originate programs from a TV and radio broadcast booth, and there are more than 100 TV monitors throughout the facility, even in the restrooms. If you want to watch NFL on Sunday, get here about two hours before kickoff, because the place is packed for back-to-back games. On special game days, like those of the World Series or Super Bowl, count on huge crowds and call in advance to see if special seating rules are in effect. ☎*407/939–1177* 📧*No cover* ⊘*Daily 11:30* AM*–1* AM

Jellyrolls. In this rugged, rockin', and boisterous piano bar, comedians act as emcees and play dueling grand pianos nonstop. In a Disney version of "Stump the Band," they promise "You Name It. We Play It." You may have gone to piano bars before, but the steady stream of conventions at Disney makes this the place to catch CEOs doing the conga to Barry Manilow's "Copacabana"—if that's your idea of a good time. You must be 21 to enter. ☎*407/560–8770* 📧*$10 cover after* 7 PM ⊘*Daily 7* PM*–2* AM.

DOWNTOWN DISNEY

WEST SIDE

Disney's West Side is a hip outdoor complex of shopping, dining, and entertainment with the main venues being the House of Blues, Disney-Quest, and Cirque du Soleil. Aside from this trio, there are no cover charges. Whether you're club hopping or not, the West Side is worth a visit for its waterside location, wide promenade, and diverse shopping and dining. Opening time is 11 AM, closing time around 2 AM; crowds vary with the season, but weeknights tend to be less busy. For

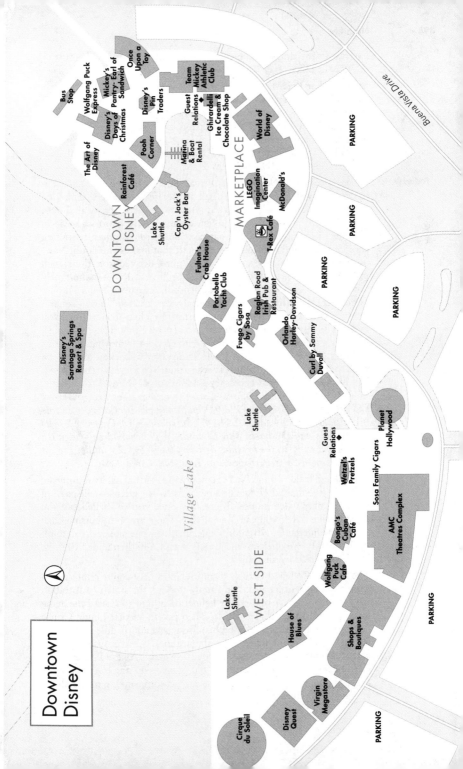

entertainment times and more information, call 407/824–4500 or 407/824–2222.

Bongos Cuban Café. Latin rhythms provide the beat at this enterprise owned by pop singer Gloria Estefan. Although this is primarily a restaurant, you may get a kick out of the pre-Castro Havana interior, the three bars, and the Latin band that plays *muy caliente* music every Friday and Saturday evening. Samba, tango, salsa, and merengue rhythms are rolling throughout the week. Drop by for a beer and a "babalu." ☎407/828–0999 ⊘ *Daily 11* AM–2 AM.

FodorsChoice
★

Cirque du Soleil—*La Nouba*. This surreal show by the world-famous circus company starts at 100 MPH and accelerates from there. Although the ticket price is high compared with those for other local shows, you'd be hard-pressed to hear anyone complain. The performance is 90 minutes of extraordinary acrobatics, avant-garde stagings, costumes, choreography, and a thrilling grand finale that makes you doubt Newton's law of gravity. The story of La Nouba—derived from the French phrase *faire la nouba* (which translates to "live it up")—is alternately mysterious, dreamlike, comical, and sensual. A cast of 72 international performers takes the stage in this specially constructed, 70,000-square-foot venue. The original music is performed by a live orchestra that you might miss if you don't scrutinize the towers on either side of the stage, which is a technical marvel in itself, with constantly moving platforms and lifts. A couple of hints: call well in advance for tickets to improve your chances of getting front-row seats (there are four levels of seating) and hire a babysitter if necessary—admission is charged for infants. ☎407/939–7600 *reservations* ⊕*www.cirquedusoleil.com* ✉*Front and center $121.41 adults, $96.92 children under 10; Category 1 seats (front sides) $105.44 adults, $84.14 children under 10; Category 2 seats (to the side and the back) $86.27 adults, $69.23 children under 10; Category 3 seats (to the far sides and very back) $69.23 adults, $55.38 children under 10* ⊘ *Performances Tues.–Sat. 6 and 9* PM.

DisneyQuest. Inside an enclosed five-floor video/virtual reality minitheme park, they've figured out that some suckers—er, guests—will pay big bucks to play video games. To be fair, once you've shelled out the considerable cover, you can play all day. There are some cutting-edge games and interactive adventures here, but save your money if you think you'll quickly tire of electronic arcade noises. Children under 10 must be accompanied by an adult.

The Explore Zone is a virtual adventureland where you're immersed in exotic and ancient locales. You can fly through the streets of Agrabah with the help of a virtual-reality helmet on a hunt to release the genie on Aladdin's Magic Carpet Ride. Then take a Virtual Jungle Cruise down the roiling rapids of a prehistoric world and paddle (yes, *really* paddle) to adventure in the midst of volcanoes, carnivorous dinosaurs, and other cretaceous threats. End your stay in this zone at Pirates of the Caribbean: Battle for Buccaneer Gold, where you and the gang must brave the high seas from the helm of your ship, sinking pirate ships, and acquiring treasure.

The Score Zone is where you can match wits and game-playing skills against the best. Battling supervillains takes more physical energy than you'd think as you fly, headset firmly intact, through a 3-D comic world in Ride the Comix. Escape evil aliens and rescue stranded colonists with your crew during Invasion! An ExtraTERRORestrial Alien Encounter. Or hip-check your friends in a life-size Mighty Ducks Pinball Slam game.

In the **Create Zone** you can let your creative juices flow in this studio of expression and invention. You can learn the secrets of Disney animation at the Animation Academy, where magic overload led one man who attended to propose to his girlfriend—she said yes! Create your own twisted masterpiece at Sid's Create-A-Toy, based on the popular animated film *Toy Story*. Or, at Living Easels, create a *living* painting on a giant electronic screen. All of the above creative ventures are quite popular with the elementary-school crowd. The real thrills await at Cyberspace Mountain, where you can design your own roller coaster on a computer screen, then climb aboard a 360-degree pitch-and-roll simulator for the ride of your dreams. At Radio Disney SongMaker, produce your own hit in a sound booth equipped with a computer and audio system that helps incorporate all kinds of sounds into your recording (DisneyQuest claims there are 2 billion possible combinations of songs, lyrics, and musical styles). You can buy what you've created at the Create Zone counter.

Classic free-play machines, like SkeeBall and Whack A Alien, reside in **the Replay Zone**. You can also sit with a partner in an asteroid cannon–equipped bumper car and blast others to make their cars do a 360-degree spin in Buzz Lightyear's AstroBlaster.

DisneyQuest attractions all are wheelchair accessible, but most require transfer from wheelchair to the attraction itself, including the virtual thrill ride Cyberspace Mountain. You can, however, wheel right on to Pirates of the Caribbean: Battle for Buccaneer Gold, Aladdin's Magic Carpet Ride, and Mighty Ducks Pinball Slam. Wheelchairs can be rented ($10 with a major credit card or Disney resort ID card) at the DisneyQuest Emporium or in the Marketplace at the Wonderful World of Memories shop. Electronic wheelchairs available at the Marketplace location cost $45 per day with a major credit card only. If you have your own wheelchair, it pays to bring it along. Guide dogs are permitted in all areas but are unable to ride several attractions.

Strollers are *not* permitted at DisneyQuest, which really doesn't provide much for very small children, though baby-changing stations are in both men's and women's restrooms.

As you enter the building, children will pass a height check and if they're at least 51" tall receive a wristband that allows access to all rides. The four attractions that have height requirements are Cyberspace Mountain (51"), Buzz Lightyear's Astro Blaster (51"), Mighty Ducks Pinball Slam (48"), and Pirates of the Caribbean: Battle for Buccaneer Gold (35"). Little ones 2–7 can enjoy a new Kids' Area on the fourth floor, where they can play smaller versions of popular video and other games like mini air hockey, basketball, and bowling.

13

Lost and Found is at the **admissions** window, film can be purchased at the Emporium, and cash is available at ATMs inside the House of Blues merchandise shop not far from the DisneyQuest entrance and inside Wetzel's Pretzels near the bridge to Pleasure Island.

Lost children are first walked through the building accompanied by a security guard. If that method is not successful, then the children are taken to the manager's office to wait for their mom or dad. ☎*407/828–4600* ✏ *$40 adults, $34 children 3–9; fees do not include sales tax* ⊗*Sun.–Thurs. 11:30 AM–11 PM, Fri. and Sat. 11:30 AM–midnight.*

FodorsChoice
★
House of Blues. The restaurant hosts cool blues nightly (alongside its rib-sticking Mississippi Delta cooking), but it's the HOB's concert hall next door that garners the real attention. The hall has showcased local and nationally known artists including Aretha Franklin, David Byrne, Steve Miller, Los Lobos, Willie Nelson, and even Journey. From rock to reggae to R&B, this is arguably the best live-music venue in Orlando, and standing a few feet from your guitar heroes is the way music should be seen and heard. ☎*407/934–2583* ✏*Covers vary* ⊗*Daily, performance times vary.*

DOWNTOWN DISNEY MARKETPLACE

Although the Marketplace offers little in the line of typical nightlife, there's hardly a more enjoyable place for families to spend a quiet evening window-shopping, enjoying ice cream at a courtyard café, or strolling among eclectic Disney stores. Aside from this, there's not much "nightlife," per se, but **Cap'n Jack's Restaurant** (☎*407/828–3971*) is a nice, quiet waterfront restaurant where you can gulp down some oysters or sip on a huge strawberry margarita made with strawberry tequila. For a sweeter tooth, the **Ghirardelli Soda Fountain & Chocolate Shop** makes a nice after-dinner stop for sundaes, malts, and shakes. Both **Rainforest Café** and **T-Rex: A Prehistoric Family Adventure** combine theme dining and shopping which includes favorites such as The Art of Disney, Team Mickey Sports, and the **Bibbidi Bobbidi Boutique,** where children can get princess makeovers complete with pixie-dust "reveals." ⊗*Daily 11:30–10:30.*

HOTEL BARS

DISNEY RESORT HOTELS

With more than a dozen resort hotels on Walt Disney World property, the hotel-bar scene is understandably active. Depending on whether the resort is geared to business or romance, the lounges can be soothing or boisterous—or both. You do not have to be a resort guest to visit the bars and lounges, and a casual tour of them may well provide an evening's entertainment. To reach any of these hotel bars directly, you can call the Disney operator at 407/824–4500 or 407/824–2222.

Belle Vue Room. Settle back in this lovely 1930s-style sitting room to escape the crowds, play board games, savor a quiet drink, and listen to long-ago shows played through old radios. Step out onto the balcony for a soothing view of the village green and lake. ✉*Boardwalk Inn* ⊗*Daily 5 PM–midnight.*

California Grill. High atop the Contemporary Resort, this utterly chic restaurant–lounge offers a fantastic view of the Magic Kingdom, especially when the sun goes down and the tiny white lights on Main Street start to twinkle. Add nightly fireworks (usually at 10 PM), and there's no better place to order a glass of wine and enjoy the show. An observation deck, which extends to the end of the hotel, adds a breezy vantage point from which to see all this, plus surrounding Bay Lake. In high season, you may need dinner reservations to gain access to the observation deck. ⌂ *Contemporary Resort* ☾ *Daily 5 PM–11:30 PM, dinner 6 PM–10 PM.*

> ## WORD OF MOUTH
>
> "Go to Epcot's World Showcase day or night. Eat in Paris. Drink margaritas in Mexico. Definitely (depending on your budget) dine at the California Grill in Contemporary Resort overlooking Magic Kingdom. Hang out at Downtown Disney and go to Wolfgang Pucks."
> –lindapie

13

Martha's Vineyard Lounge. This is a cozy, refined hideaway where you can sit back and sip domestic and European wines. Each evening 18 wines are poured for tasting. After facing the maddening crowd, it's worth a detour if you're looking for a quiet retreat and a soothing glass of zinfandel. ⌂ *Beach Club Resort* ☾ *Daily 5:30 PM–midnight.*

Mizner's. At the stylish Grand Floridian, a refined alcove is tucked away at the far end of the second-floor lobby. Even on steroids, this place wouldn't approach rowdy—it's a tasteful getaway where you can unwind with ports, brandies, and mixed drinks while overlooking the beach and the elegance that surrounds you. ⌂ *Grand Floridian* ☾ *Daily 5 PM–11 PM.*

Narcoossee's. Inside the restaurant is a bar that serves ordinary beer in expensive yard glasses, but the porch-side views of the Seven Seas Lagoon (and the nightly Electrical Water Pageant) are worth the premium you pay. Find a nice spot and you can also watch the Magic Kingdom fireworks. ⌂ *Grand Floridian* ☾ *Daily 5:30 PM–10 PM.*

Tambu Lounge. Beside 'Ohana's restaurant at the Polynesian Resort, Disney bartenders ring up all the variations on rum punch and piña coladas. Festooned with South Seas–style masks, totems, and Easter Island head replicas, this place is exotic—with the exception of the large-screen TV. ⌂ *Polynesian Resort* ☾ *Daily 1 PM–midnight.*

Territory Lounge. Nestled within a carbon copy of the magnificent Yellowstone Lodge, this lounge is a frontier-theme hideout that pays tribute to the Corps of Discovery (look overhead for a Lewis and Clark expedition trail map). In between drinks, check out the props on display: surveying equipment, daguerreotypes, large log beams, parka mittens, maps, and what the lounge claims is a pair of Teddy Roosevelt's boots. ⌂ *Wilderness Lodge* ☾ *Daily 4:30 PM–midnight.*

Victoria Falls. The central lounge at the extraordinary Animal Kingdom Lodge is a second-floor retreat that overlooks the Boma restaurant. The exotic feel of an obligatory safari theme extends to leather directors' chairs, native masks, and the sounds of a stream flowing past. Across the hall near the front desk, a small alcove beckons. Although no drinks are served in the sunken den called the Sunset Overlook—with arti-facts and photos from 1920s safaris of Martin and Osa Johnson—it's a popular spot for late-night conversation. ⊠*Animal Kingdom Lodge* ☉*Daily 4* PM–*midnight, dinner 5:30* PM–*10* PM.

DISNEY'S DINNER SHOWS

★ **Hoop-Dee-Doo Revue.** Staged at Fort Wilderness's rustic Pioneer Hall, this show may be corny, but it's also the liveliest dinner show in Walt Disney World (and reportedly the world's longest-running dinner show). A troupe of jokers called the Pioneer Hall Players perform an old-fashioned saloon-style show that includes romantic ballads, corny tunes, festive sing-alongs, and add a lot of lowbrow slapstick humor while the audience chows down on barbecued ribs, fried chicken, corn on the cob, strawberry shortcake, and all the fixin's. There are three shows nightly, and the prime times sell out months in advance in busy seasons. But you're better off eating dinner too early or too late rather than miss-ing the fun altogether—so take what you can get since this is a real honest-to-goodness family favorite. If you arrive in Orlando with no reservations, try for a cancellation. Prices vary by seat selection. ⊠*Fort Wilderness Resort* ☎*407/939–3463 advance tickets, 407/824–2803 day of show* ▣*$50.99–$59.99 adults, $25.99–$30.99 children 3–9, including tax and gratuity* ☉*Daily 5, 7:15, and 9:30.*

Spirit of Aloha. Formerly the Polynesian Luau, this show is still an out-door barbecue with entertainment in line with its colorful South Pacific style. Its fire jugglers and hula-drum dancers are entertaining for the whole family, if never quite as endearing as the napkin twirlers at the Hoop-Dee-Doo Revue. The hula dancers' navel maneuvers, however, are something to see. You should try to make reservations at least a month in advance. ⊠*Polynesian Resort* ☎*407/939–3463 advance tickets, 407/824–1593 day of show* ▣*$50.99–$59.99 adults, $25.99–$30.99 children 3–9, including tax and gratuity. Prices vary by seat selection* ☉*Tues.–Sat. 5:15 and 8.*

FIREWORKS, LIGHT SHOWS, AND PARADES

Both in the theme parks and around the hotel-side waterways, Walt Disney World offers up a wealth of fabulous sound-and-light shows after the sun goes down. In fact WDW is one of the earth's largest single consumers of fireworks—perhaps even rivaling mainland China. Tradi-tionally, sensational short shows have been held at the Magic Kingdom at 10. Starting times vary throughout the year, but you can check them at Guest Services.

Fireworks are only part of the evening entertainment. Each park hosts shows staged with varying degrees of spectacle and style. For the best of the best, head to Epcot, which hosts visiting shows that are free with admission. Regular performers include a Beatles soundalike group in the United Kingdom, acrobats in China, mimes in France, musicians in a smaller African kiosk, and rock-and-roll bagpipers in Canada. Catching any of these parades and/or performances easily soothes the sting of what you may feel is an overpriced admission.

Electrical Water Pageant. One of Disney's few remaining small wonders (it premiered three weeks after the WDW opened in 1971) is this 10-minute floating parade of sea creatures outlined in tiny lights, with an electronic score highlighted by Handel's *Water Music.* Don't go out of your way, but if you're by Bay Lake and the Seven Seas Lagoon, look for it from the beaches at the Polynesian (at 9), the Grand Floridian (9:15), Wilderness Lodge (9:35), Fort Wilderness (9:45), the Contemporary (10:05), and, in busy seasons, the Magic Kingdom (10:20). Times occasionally vary, so check with Guest Services.

★ **Fantasmic!** Disney–MGM's blockbuster after-dark show is held once nightly (twice on weekends and in peak seasons) in a 6,500-seat amphitheater. The throngs of people filing into the Hollywood Bowl–style amphitheater give you the distinct sense that you're in for something amazing. The special effects are superlative indeed, as Mickey Mouse in the guise of the Sorcerer's Apprentice emcees a revue full of song and dance, pyrotechnics, and special effects. Several scenes from Disney films and historic events are staged amid music, special lighting, and fireworks. Arrive an hour in advance for the best seats, 20 minutes if you don't mind sitting to the side of the stage. Or sign up for the Fantasmic! **Dinner Package,** which includes reservations at either the Studio's Brown Derby, Hollywood & Vine, or Mama Melrose restaurants, plus seating in a special VIP area of the Fantasmic! amphitheater. You should still show up at least 20 minutes early so you don't have to sit at the very back of the VIP section, which comprises all the risers at one end of the theater.

Fodor'sChoice **IllumiNations: Reflections of the Earth.** It's worth sticking around until
★ dark to see Epcot's light and fireworks show, which takes place over the reflective World Showcase lagoon. As orchestral music fills the air, accompanied by the whoosh and boom of lasers and pyrotechnic bursts, a 30-foot globe on a barge floats across the lagoon, revealing the wonders of the seven continents on its curved LED screens. Meanwhile, each of the World Showcase pavilions is illuminated with more than 26,000 feet of lights. Check the wind direction before staking a claim, since smoke can cloak some views. Some of the better vantage points are the Matsu No Ma Lounge in the Japan pavilion, the patios of the Rose & Crown in the United Kingdom pavilion, and Cantina de San Angel in Mexico. Another good spot is the World Showcase Plaza between the boat docks at the Showcase entrance, but this is often crowded with those who want to make a quick exit after the show. If you decide to join them here, claim your seat at least 45 minutes in advance. It's worth waiting to see this spectacle.

Fodor'sChoice **SpectroMagic.** This splendidly choreographed parade of lights is one of
★ the Magic Kingdom's don't-miss attractions. It's a colorful, flickering, luminescent parade with cartoonish floats and a complete lineup of favorite Disney characters. This is a seasonal parade; times vary, so check the schedule before you set out, or ask any Disney staffer while you're in the park. The early showing is for parents with children,

while the later ones attract night owls and others with the stamina and the know-how to enjoy the Magic Kingdom's most pleasant, least-crowded time of day.

★ **Wishes.** This show defines the magic of Disney better than any you'll see during your trip. To the accompaniment of Disney melodies, the fireworks of Wishes are launched from 11 locations around the park, as Jiminy Cricket reminds you that "anything your heart desires" can come true. The fireworks and music recall scenes from Disney films in which a fairy-tale character did indeed get his or her wish. The best place to watch the show is on Main Street—try to snag the few seats on the second floor of the Walt Disney World train station. It's a wonderful way to wrap up the day at the Magic Kingdom.

UNIVERSAL ORLANDO

CityWalk. Armed with a catchy headline ("Get a Nightlife"), CityWalk met the challenge of diverting the lucrative youth market from Disney and downtown Orlando. In fact, it did it so well that, in 2008, Disney blinked, got out of the after-dark entertainment business, and began turning their Pleasure Island nightclubs into stores. This left Universal with a virtual monopoly in the world of Orlando entertainment complexes.

When you arrive, you'll enter an open and airy gathering place with quiet jazz retreats, over-the-top discotheques, and the theater that's home to the fabulous and extremely popular Blue Man Group. On weeknights the crowd is a mix of families and conventioneers; weekends draw a decidedly younger demographic whose members trickle in through to the wee hours.

Although clubs have individual cover charges, it's far more economical to pay for the whole kit and much of the caboodle. You can buy a variety of admissions and accessories including a Party Pass (a one price–all clubs admission) for $11.99; or a Party Pass-and-a-Movie for $15.98 (plus tax); or a Movie-and-a-Meal for $21.95; or a Party Pass-and-a-Meal for $21. The movies are those at the Universal cineplex, and the meals (tax and gratuity included) are served at City Walk restaurants including Jimmy Buffett's Margaritaville, the Hard Rock Cafe, NASCAR Sports Grille, and others. What makes these deals even better is the fact that after 6 PM the $11 parking fee drops to $3. It is, however, a long walk from the parking garage to CityWalk (even longer when you stumble out at 2 AM and realize it's a ¼-mi walk to your car). Then again, you shouldn't be driving in this condition, so have a good time and call a cab. Taxis run at all hours. ☎407/224–2692, 407/363–8000 Universal main line ⊕www.citywalkorlando.com.

AMC–Loew's Universal Cineplex. Why spend your time watching a movie when you're on vacation? Who cares? It's your vacation. The 20-screen,

5,000-seat, bi-level theater offers an escape from the crowds. You can purchase tickets in advance by telephone. ☎*407/354–5998 recorded information and tickets, 407/354–3374 box office.*

Blue Man Group. What began in a small New York theater has evolved into a worldwide phenomenon. So, with Universal creating a permanent theater specifically for the Blue Man Group, it means the resort has raised the "nightlife" bar considerably in an effort to compete with Disney's long-running Cirque show, La Nouba. At the Sharp-Aquos Theatre, the preshow is entertaining in itself, with LED signs instructing the waiting crowd to participate in simple tasks such as speaking—not singing—"Happy Birthday" to an audience member. Sounds simple, but mighty weird. When the Blue Men appear, it kicks off 90 minutes of surreal and silly routines that are greatly appreciated by anyone who enjoys juvenile humor—which happens to be everyone. How many marshmallows can one Blue Man catch in his mouth? Many. Is it really art when a Blue Man spits paint onto a spinning canvas? Yes. Can they really create music out of a spaghetti twist of PVC tubing? Absolutely. How much paper can be unraveled at one show? Miles of it. Kidlike fun that's creative and colorful (just watch the fluorescent paints splatter as they play their drums). One of the new highlights of an Orlando vacation. ☎*407/BLUE–MAN (258–3626)* ✉*Adults advance purchase $64–$74, children 9 and under $54–-$64 (add $10 when buying at the box office)* ☉*Daily showtimes vary, call for schedule.*

★ **Bob Marley—A Tribute to Freedom.** The beauty of this place is that even if you can't dance, you can easily pretend just by swaying to the syncopated reggae rhythms. This museum-club is modeled after the "King of Reggae's" home in Kingston, Jamaica, complete with intimate low ceilings and more than 100 photographs and paintings reflecting pivotal moments in Marley's life. Off the cozy bar is a patio area where you can be jammin' to a (loud) live band that plays from 8 PM to 1:30 AM nightly. Red Stripe Rastafarian Thursday—soon to be a national holiday—lasts from 4 PM until closing, and offers $3.25 Red Stripes and Captain Morgan specials. You must be 21 or over to be admitted on Friday and Saturday after 9 PM. ☎*407/224–2692* ✉*$7 after 8* PM ☉*Weekdays 4* PM*–2* AM, *weekends 2* PM*–2* AM.

CityWalk's Rising Star. It's a wonder someone didn't think of this earlier. Rising Star gives hopeful (and hopeless) singers a chance to reveal their talent in one of the nicest karaoke clubs around. Instead of singing to recorded music, you're accompanied by a band complete with back-up singers—and all before an audience. Although the band's not here on Sunday and Monday, the back–up singers are on hand every single night so you can get yourself one step closer to opening for U2. ☎*407/224– 2692* ✉*$7* ☉*Nightly 8* PM*–2* AM, *21 and up; 18 and up on Thurs.*

the groove. The very sound of this place can be terrifying to the uninitiated: images flicker rapidly on several screens and the combination of music, light, and mayhem appeals to a mostly under-30 crowd. Within the cavernous hall, every nook and cranny is filled with techno pop. If you need to escape, the dance floor leads to three rooms: the '70s-style Green Room, filled with beanbag chairs and everything you threw out

The Birth of Walt Disney World

It'd be a great question for a game show: Florida was founded by (a) Juan Ponce de León, (b) Millard Fillmore, (c) Sonny Bono, or (d) Walt Disney. For travelers who can't fathom Florida without Walt Disney World, the final answer is "d"—at least Central Florida. The theme park's arrival spawned a multibillion-dollar tourism industry that begat a population boom that begat new roads, malls, and schools that begat a whole new culture.

So how did it happen? Why did Walt pin his hopes on forlorn Florida ranchlands 3,000–mi from Disneyland? In the 1950s, Walt barely had enough money to open his theme park in California, and lacking the funds to buy a buffer zone, he couldn't prevent cheap hotels and tourist traps from setting up shop next door. This time he wanted land. And lots of it. Beginning in the early 1960s, Walt embarked on a super-secret four-year project: he traveled the nation in search of a location with access to a major population center, good highways, a steady climate, and, most important, cheap and abundant land. Locations were narrowed down and, in the end, Orlando was it.

In May 1965, major land transactions were being recorded a few miles southwest of Orlando. By late June, the *Orlando Sentinel* reported that more than 27,000 acres had been sold so far. In October, the paper revealed that Walt was the mastermind behind the purchases. Walt and his brother Roy hastily arranged a press conference. Once Walt described the $400 million project and the few thousand jobs it would create, Florida's government quickly gave him permission to establish the autonomous Reedy

Creek Improvement District. With this, he could write his own zoning restrictions and plan his own roads, bridges, hotels—even a residential community for his employees.

Walt played a hands-on role in the planning of Disney World, but just over a year later, in December 1966, he died. As expected, his faithful brother Roy took control and spent the following five years supervising the construction of the Magic Kingdom. Fittingly, before the park opened on October 1, 1971, Roy changed the name of his brother's park to "Walt" Disney World. Roy passed away three months after the park's opening, but by then WDW was hitting its stride. For the next decade, it became part of Florida's landscape. Families that once saw Orlando merely as a whistle-stop on the way to Miami now made their vacation base at WDW.

Behind the scenes, however, a few cracks began to appear in the facade. In its first decade, growth was stagnant. By 1982, when Epcot opened, construction-cost overruns and low attendance created a 19% drop in profits. Meanwhile, the Disney Channel and Disney's film division were also sluggish. Eventually, in 1984, Michael Eisner came aboard as CEO and company chairman, along with Frank Wells as president and CFO. Their arrival got Disney out of the doldrums. Disney's unparalleled film catalog was brought out of storage with rereleases in theaters and on video. Jeffrey Katzenberg was put in charge of the Disney Studios, and with him came the release of "new classics" such as *Aladdin, Beauty and the Beast, The Little Mermaid,* and *The Lion King.*

In 1988 the Grand Floridian and Caribbean Beach resorts opened. The following year Disney–MGM Studios (now Disney's Hollywood Studios) opened along with Typhoon Lagoon and the ever-evolving Pleasure Island. Five resort hotels opened in the early 1990s. By 1997 Blizzard Beach, ESPN Wide World of Sports, and Downtown Disney West Side had opened; and by 1998 Disney's Animal Kingdom had come to life. Also arriving in this decade of growth were the planned community of Celebration, Disney Cruise Line, the book-publishing arm of Hyperion, and the purchase of Miramax Films and ABC television.

Since the profitable mid-1990s, however, Disney has suffered its share of economic trouble and political unrest. Following a dip in earnings in 2002, and several box-office bombs (think: *The Alamo*), Roy E. Disney, Walt's nephew, resigned from his position as vice chairman of the board of directors to lead a movement to oust Michael Eisner from the company. When Eisner came up for re-election to the Disney board in early 2004, 43% of shareholders withheld their votes. By September 2005, Robert Iger had replaced Eisner as CEO. Despite the big changes at its parent company, Walt Disney World continues to grow and improve. A score of new shows and attractions opened in 2006, 2007, and 2008, including the exciting "runaway train" ride Expedition Everest, the brilliant "Finding Nemo—The Musical," Monsters, Inc. Laugh Floor, and Toy Story Mania! Disney has also tapped into the concept of special yearlong celebrations that give you a reason to return.

Also, the next time you put Disney on your vacation schedule, consider setting your sights on the coast. In 2011 and 2012, the impressively successful Disney Cruise Line will christen two new super ships.

And it all started with a man who didn't have the cash to buy a little more land in Anaheim.

–Gary McKechnie

13

when Duran Duran hit the charts; the sci-fi Jetson-y Blue Room; and the Red Room, which is hot and romantic in a bordello sort of way. Prepare yourself for lots of fog, swirling lights, and sweaty bodies. This is another 21-and-up club. ☎*407/224–2692* ✉*$7* ⊙*Daily 9* PM–2 AM.

Hard Rock Cafe. This Hard Rock Cafe is the largest on earth, and the one that seems to play the loudest music. The best objects adorn a room on the second floor: Beatles rarities such as cutouts from the *Sgt. Pepper* cover, John Lennon's famous "New York City" T-shirt, Paul's original lyrics for "Let It Be," and the doors from London's Abbey Road studios. Buddy Holly's Boy Scout booklet and favorite stage suit are also here. Wow. Start with dinner and stay for the show, since much of the attraction here is at the adjoining Hard Rock Live. The concert hall's exterior resembles Rome's Coliseum, and almost every evening an entertainer performs here; occasionally it's one you recognize (Ringo Starr, Elvis Costello, Jerry Lee Lewis, etc.). Although the seats are hard and two-thirds don't face the stage, it's one of Orlando's top venues. Cover prices vary. Warning: you can't bring large purses or bags inside and there are no lockers at CityWalk, so leave big baggage in your car. ☎*407/224–2692* ⊕*www.hardrocklive.com* ⊙*Daily from 11* AM, *with varying closing times, generally around midnight.*

★ **Jimmy Buffett's Margaritaville.** Jimmy Buffett may be the most savvy businessman in America. He took a single concept, wrapped it up in a catchy tune, and parlayed it into books, clothing, musicals, and a hot club at Universal. It seems that Florida law requires residents to play Buffett music 24 hours a day, but if you're from out of state you might still not be over "Cheeseburger in Paradise." Attached to the restaurant are three bars (Volcano, Land Shark, and 12 Volt). There's a Pan Am Clipper suspended from the ceiling, music videos projected onto sails, limbo and Hula-Hoop contests, a huge margarita blender that erupts "when the volcano blows," live music nightly, and all the other subtleties that give Parrotheads a place to roost. ☎*407/224–2692* ⊕*www. margaritaville.com* ✉*$7 after 10* PM ⊙*Daily 11:30* AM–2 AM.

Latin Quarter. This tribute to Latin music and dance is especially popular with local Hispanics. It's easy to overlook the restaurant here, as most attention is paid to the nightclub, which is crowded with partygoers in eye-catching clothing. The club feels like a 21st-century version of Ricky Ricardo's Tropicana, although the design is based on a mix of Aztec, Inca, and Maya architecture. There's even an Andes mountain range, complete with waterfalls, around the dance floor. If you can get your hips working overtime, pick a rhumba from 1 to 10 and swivel . . . And tango and merengue and salsa . . . ☎*407/224–2692* ✉*$7; price may vary for certain performances* ⊙*Mon.–Thurs. 5* PM–2 AM, *Fri. and Sat. noon–2* AM.

Pat O'Brien's. A legend in pre-Katrina New Orleans, this exact reproduction of the original is doing all right in Orlando, with its flaming fountain, dueling pianists, and balcony that re-creates the Crescent City. The draw here is the Patio Bar, where abundant tables and chairs allow you to do nothing but enjoy a respite from the madding crowd—and drink a potent, rum-based hurricane. You must be 21 to enter.

☎407/224–2692 ⊕*www.patobriens.com* ✉*$7 after 9* PM ⊗*Patio Bar daily 4* PM*–2* AM; *Piano Bar daily 6* PM*–2* AM.

Red Coconut Club. Swank and hip, the interior of CityWalk's newest nightclub is an ultralounge that features a full bar, signature martinis, an extensive wine list, and VIP bottle service. Loaf around the Rat Pack–era lounge, hang out on the balcony, or mingle with the happening crowd at the bars. If you're on a budget, take advantage of the daily happy hours and a gourmet appetizer menu. A DJ and live music pushes the energy with tunes from rock to Sinatra. You must be 21 to enter. ☎407/224–2692 ✉*$7 after 9* PM ⊗*Sun.–Wed. 8* PM*–2* AM, *Thurs.–Sat. 6* PM*–2* AM.

ORLANDO

CLUBS AND BARS

INTERNATIONAL DRIVE

BB King's Blues Club. The blues great was already doing quite well as a musician, and then went and added to his legend as an entrepreneur. Following the success of his eponymous blues clubs in Memphis and Nashville, it's Orlando's turn. Like the others, the root of the club is music, with dance floors and two stages for live performances by the BB King All-Star Band as well as by visiting musicians. You can't really experience Delta blues without Delta dining, so the club serves double duty as a restaurant with fried dill pickles, catfish bites, po' boys, ribs, and other comfort foods, plus a full bar. ⊠*Pointe Orlando, 9101 International Dr.,Orlando* ☎407/370–4550 ⊗*Daily 11* AM*–2* AM.

ICEBAR. Thanks to the miracle of refrigeration, this is Orlando's coolest bar—literally and figuratively. Fifty tons of pure ice is kept at a constant 27°F and has been cut and sculpted by world-class carvers into a cozy (or as cozy as ice can be) sanctuary of tables, sofas, chairs, and a bar. The staff loans you a thermal cape and gloves, and when you enter the frozen hall you receive a complimentary drink served in a glass made of crystal-clear ice. There's no cover charge if you just want to hang out in the Chill Lounge or outdoor Polar Patio, but you will pay $30 to spend 45 minutes in the sub-freezing ICEBAR. There's no beer or wine inside; it's simply too cold. ⊠*Pointe Orlando, 8967 International Dr., Orlando* ☎407/426–7555 ⊕*www.icebarorlando.com* ⊗*Daily 11* AM*–2* AM.

DOWNTOWN ORLANDO

Bösendorfer Lounge. One of only two Imperial Grand Bösendorfer pianos takes center stage at this, perhaps the classiest gathering spot in Orlando. The highly civilized (but not stuffy) lounge attracts a cross-section of trendy Orlandoans, especially the after-work crowd, among which the conversation and camaraderie flow as smoothly as the champagne, beer, wine, and cocktails. Art on the walls, comfortable couches, rich fabrics, sleek black marble, and seductive lighting invite you to stay awhile. If music is what attracts you, call in advance for the schedule of jazz combos and solo pianists who perform in the lounge. Many of the players are among the area's finest and most talented musicians. ⊠ *Westin Grand Bohemian Hotel, 325 S. Orange Ave.,Orlando* ☎*407/313–9000* ⊕*www.grandbohemianhotel.com* ⊗*Thurs.–Sat. 11* AM*–2* AM, *Sun.–Wed. 11* AM*–midnight.*

Bull and Bush Pub. It's a mile or so east of downtown, but you might not mind the trek for a good pint, a bite of shepherd's pie, some fish-and-chips, and a game of darts. Besides the bar, there are small booths for privacy. The tap lineup covers 11 imported beers and ales. ⊠*2408 E. Robinson St., Orlando* ☎*407/896–7546* ⊗*Mon.–Sat. 4* PM*–2* AM.

Cheyenne Saloon. After an absence of many years, Cheyenne is back. The tri-level structure has a quarter-million board feet of golden oak rails, spindles, banisters, and balustrades, spiffed up Remington art and sculptures, fantastically elaborate cut glass doors, and beautiful chandeliers. While it may sound like a museum, the purpose is to party with Grand Ol' Opry–style country music performed by the Cheyenne Stampede band. There's red-hot music, dancing, food, nickel beer Wednesday 5–7, and a poker parlor. There's a $5 cover charge. ⊠*128 W. Church St., Orlando* ☎*407/839–3000* ⊗*Daily 4* PM*–2* AM*; closed Mon.*

Social. Perhaps the favorite live-music venue of locals, Social is a great place to see touring and local musicians. It serves full dinners Wednesday through Saturday and offers up live music seven nights a week. You can sip trademark martinis while listening to anything from alternative rock to rockabilly to undiluted jazz. Several now-national acts got their start here, including Matchbox Twenty, Seven Mary Three, and other groups that don't have numbers in their names. ⊠*54 N. Orange Ave., Orlando* ☎*407/246–1419* ⊕*www.thesocial.org* ⊠*$7–$30, depending on entertainment* ⊗*Check Web site; hrs. determined by concert schedule.*

Wally's. One of Orlando's oldest bars (circa 1953), this longtime local favorite is a hangout for a cross section of cultures and ages. Some would say it's a dive, but that doesn't matter to the students, bikers, lawyers, and barflies who land here to drink surrounded by the go-go-dancer wallpaper and '60s-era interior. Just grab a stool at the bar to take in the scene and down a cold one. ⊠*1001 N. Mills Ave., Orlando* ☎*407/896–6975* ⊗*Mon.–Sat. 7:30* AM*–1* AM, *Sun. noon–10* PM.

DINNER SHOWS

Dinner shows are an immensely popular form of nighttime entertainment around Orlando. For a single price (which seems like an ever-increasing price), you get a theatrical production and a multicourse dinner. Performances run the gamut from jousting to jamboree tunes, and meals tend to be better than average; unlimited beer, wine, and soda are usually included, but mixed drinks (and often *any* drinks before dinner) cost extra. What the shows lack in substance and depth they make up for in grandeur and enthusiasm. The result is an evening of light entertainment, which youngsters in particular enjoy. Seatings are usually between 7 and 9:30, and there are usually one or two performances a night, with an extra show during peak periods. You might sit with strangers at tables for 10 or more, but that's part of the fun.

Always reserve in advance, especially for weekend shows, and always ask about discounts although you can often find online coupons (sometimes for half off) that you can print out yourself. Since performance schedules can vary depending on the tourist season, it's always smart to call in advance to verify show times. When buying tickets, ask if the cost includes a gratuity—servers anxious to pocket more cash may hit you up for an extra handout.

Arabian Nights. An elaborate palace on the outside, this arena has seating for more than 1,200 on the inside. Its 25-act dinner show centers around the quest for an Arabian princess to find her true love, and includes a buffoonish genie who may or may not be amusing, a chariot race, an intricate Western square dance on horseback, and 60 fabulous horses that perform in such acts as bareback acrobatics by gypsies. Dinner is served during the show, so you might end up not paying much attention to the food—which is not a bad idea since the meal of prime rib or vegetable lasagna is functional, not flavorful. Extra shows are added in summer. Make reservations in advance and ask about discounts, which are also available when booking online. ✉6225 W. Irlo Bronson Memorial Hwy., Kissimmee ☎407/239–9223 or 800/553–6116, 800/533–3615 in Canada ⊕www.arabian-nights.com ☜$56.60 adults, $72.60 adult VIP, includes seating in first 3 rows, poster, and drink, $29 children 3–11, $43 children VIP 3–11 ☉Shows nightly, times vary ▤AE, D, MC, V.

Capone's Dinner and Show. This show brings you back to the era of 1931 gangland Chicago, when mobsters and their dames were the height of underworld society. The evening begins in an old-fashioned ice-cream parlor, but say the secret password and you're ushered inside Al Capone's private Underworld Cabaret and Speakeasy. After 15 years, a new show presented as the "sequel" to the long-running original premiered in 2007. Dinner is an unlimited Italian buffet that's heavy on pasta. ✉4740 W. Irlo Bronson Memorial Hwy., Kissimmee ☎407/397–2378 ⊕www.alcapones.com ☜$49.99 adults , $29.99 children 4–12 ☉Daily 7:30 ▤AE, D, MC, V.

Medieval Times. In a huge, ersatz-medieval manor house, this evening out presents a tournament of sword fights, jousting matches, and other games on a good-versus-evil theme. No fewer than 30 charging horses and a cast of 75 knights, nobles, and maidens participate. Sound silly? It is. But it's also a true extravaganza. That the show takes precedence over the meat-and-potatoes fare is obvious: everyone sits facing forward at long, narrow banquet tables stepped auditorium-style above the tournament area. Additional diversions include tours through a dungeon and torture chamber and demonstrations of antique blacksmithing, woodworking, and pottery making. ✉4510 W. Irlo Bronson Memorial Hwy., Kissimmee ☎407/396–1518 or 800/229–8300 ⊕www.medievaltimes.com ☜$63.08 adults, $40.61 children ☉Castle daily 9–4, village daily 4:30–8, performances usually daily at 8 but call ahead ▤AE, D, MC, V.

Sleuths Mystery Dinner Show. If Sherlock Holmes has always intrigued you, head on over for a four-course meal served up with a healthy dose of conspiracy. There are 14 rotating whodunnit performances staged throughout the year in three different theaters. The show begins during your appetizer, and murder is the case by the time they clear your plates for this course. You'll get to discuss clues and question still-living characters over dinner and solve the crime during dessert. ⊠*8267 International Dr., Orlando* ☎*407/363–1985 or 800/393–1985* ⊕*www. sleuths.com* ✑*$52.95–$55.95 adults, $23.95–$26.95 children (3–11)* ☺*Performances usually daily at 7:30 but call ahead for all times and shows* ⊟*AE, D, MC, V.*

Sports and the Outdoors

WORD OF MOUTH

"When my family of now-adult children has gone [to Disney] in recent years, we've really enjoyed renting a boat in Downtown Disney for an hour or so on a down-day. There are these nice boats with canopies that comfortably seat at least the 6 of us adults, and you can tool around past Port Orleans and the treehouses. It's pretty reasonably priced too."

—alyssabc

Updated
by Rowland
Stiteler

Northern travelers were flocking to central Florida's myriad lakes, streams, and golf resorts decades before there was a Disney World. There's nothing that can quite compare to an afternoon paddling down a Florida river, watching the alligators splash into the water and snowy egrets glide among the palm trees. It's an experience that will make you feel that you're miles, and perhaps decades, away from the theme park incarnation of Florida.

You can find just about every outdoor sport in the Orlando area—unless it involves a ski lift. There are plenty of tennis courts and more than 155 golf courses, plus 18 golf or tennis academies, staffed by nearly three dozen PGA pros within a 40-mi radius. Some of the world's best-known golfing champions—huge names such as Arnold Palmer and Tiger Woods—have homes in the Orlando area. Anglers soak up the Orlando sun on the dozens of small lakes, and the metropolitan area has as many big-league professional bass fishermen as big-league baseball stars and PGA golf luminaries. And when you're ready to soothe those aching muscles from a day hiking the parks or the links, you can book yourself a treatment at one of the dozens of world-class spas in the Orlando area.

As a professional sports town, Orlando holds a hot ticket. The Orlando Magic basketball team is big-time, and baseball fans have plenty of minor-league action to enjoy. The Southern Professional Hockey League franchise, the Florida Seals, has a rabid fan base, and the Walt Disney World Speedway is the home of the Indy 200 and the Richard Petty Driving Experience. At ESPN Wide World of Sports you can watch or you can play. The complex hosts participatory and tournament-type events in more than 25 individual and team sports, including basketball, softball, and track-and-field; and it serves as the spring-training home of the Atlanta Braves.

But not everything in Orlando is wholesome, Disney-style family fun. Wagering a wad of cash at the jai-alai fronton or the dog track is guaranteed to wipe the refrain from "It's a Small World" right out of your head. Most of the tracks and frontons now have closed-circuit TV links with major horse-racing tracks, so you can bet on the ponies and then watch the race on a big-screen TV. And even if you bet and lose steadily, you won't necessarily spend more than you would at most Disney attractions—that is, depending on how much you wager.

AUTO RACING

★ **The Richard Petty Driving Experience** allows you to ride in or even drive a NASCAR-style stock car on a real racetrack. Depending on what you're willing to spend—prices range from $116 to $1,383—you can

TOP 5 OUTDOOR EXPERIENCES

Fishing excursions. You can almost walk across Bay Lake on the backs of the bass, and that's not a fishing story.

Grand Cypress Equestrian Center. Take a trail ride, learn dressage, or just stop by to see the stabled horses (some are for sale) at this world-class equestrian center just north of Walt Disney World.

Osprey Ridge Golf Course. This gorgeous, secluded, Tom Fazio–designed course is on Disney property but it's a world away from the cheerful insanity of the theme parks.

Players on one hole can't see players on another.

Sky Venture. Totally safe skydiving? That's right, you can fly like a bird without jumping out of an airplane or even getting that far off the ground.

Winter Summerland Minigolf. This is kind of what you might expect Christmas in the Bahamas to look like, minus the snowman, of course. The giant sand castle is a small replica of Cinderella's not-so-humble abode.

14

do everything from riding shotgun for three laps on the 1-mi track to taking driving lessons, culminating in your very own solo behind the wheel. The riding cost for 3 laps is $116; 8 laps, $478; 18 laps, $904; 30 laps, $1,383; the experience, priceless. The Richard Petty organization has a second Central Florida location at the Daytona International Speedway, but it involves riding in the car with an experienced race-car driver rather than driving a car yourself. ⊠ *Walt Disney World Speedway* ☎ *800/237–3889* ⊕ *www.1800bepetty.com.*

BALLOONING

Fodor's Choice **Bob's Balloons** offers one-hour rides over protected marshland and will
★ even fly over Disney World if wind and weather conditions are right. You meet in Lake Buena Vista at dawn, where Bob and his assistant take you by van to the launch site. It takes about 15 minutes to get the balloon in the air and then you're off on an adventure that definitely surpasses Peter Pan's Flight in the Magic Kingdom.

From the treetop view you'll see farm and forest land for miles, along with horses, deer, wild boar, cattle, and birds flying *below* you. Bob may take you as high as 1,000 feet, from which point you'll be able to see Disney's landmarks: the Expedition Everest mountain, the Epcot ball, and more. Several other balloons are likely to go up near you—there's a tight-knit community of balloonists in the Orlando area—so you'll view these colorful sky ornaments from a parallel level. There are seats in the basket, but you'll probably be too thrilled to sit down. ☎ *407/466–6380 or 877/824–4606* ⊕ *www.bobsballoons.com* ⊠ *$175, $90 per child under 90 lbs or 12 yrs* ⊟ *D, MC, V.*

BIKING

WALT DISNEY WORLD

The most scenic biking in Orlando is on Disney property, along roads that take you past forests, lakes, golf courses, wooded campgrounds, and resort villas. Most locations have children's bikes with training wheels and bikes with baby seats, in addition to adult bikes. You must be 18 to rent, you can only use bikes only in the area where you rent them. Management also asks that you wear helmets, which are free with all rentals.

You can rent bikes for $9 per hour and surrey bikes for $20 per half hour (two seats) and $22 per half hour (four seats) at the **Barefoot Bay Marina** (☎407/934–2850), open daily from 10 to 5. At the **BoardWalk Resort** (☎407/939–6486 *surrey bikes*), near Disney–MGM Studios, two types of bikes are available at two separate kiosks. Surrey bikes cost $20, $22, and $25 per half hour, depending on the size of the bike. Regular bicycles are $7 per hour.

Regular bikes at **Coronado Springs Resort** (☎407/939–1000), near Disney–MGM Studios, rent for $9 per hour or $22 per day, and surrey bikes rent for $20 (two seats) and $22 (four seats) per half hour. The surrey bikes look like old-fashioned carriages and are a great way to take your family on a sightseeing tour. The covered tops provide a rare commodity at Disney—shade. At **Fort Wilderness Bike Barn** (☎407/824–2742), bikes rent for $9 per hour and $22 per day.

ORLANDO AREA

Thanks to the Orlando community's commitment to the nationwide Rails to Trails program, the city now has several bike trails, converted from former railroad lines, in both rural and urban surroundings. You can venture into the city of Winter Park and pick up a trail that starts at the mall, or travel into the backwoods through heavily vegetated landscape and by scenic lakes. The Clermont–Lake County region is out in the boonies, where orange groves provide great scenery, and some hills afford challenges. Information about Orlando bike trails can be obtained from the **Orlando City Transportation Planning Bureau** (☎407/246–3347 ⊕*www.cityoforlando.net*).

★ **The West Orange Trail,** the longest bike trail in the Orlando area, runs some 20 mi through western Orlando and the neighboring towns of Winter Garden and Apopka. Highlights of the trail are the xeriscape–butterfly garden a mile east of the Oakland Outpost and views of Lake Apopka. You can access the trail at **Chapin's Station** (⊠*501 Crown Point Cross Rd., Winter Garden* ☎407/654–1108). **West Orange Trail Bikes & Blades** (⊠*17914 State Rd. 438, Winter Garden* ☎407/877–0600) rents bicycles and in-line skates, $6 per hour for either.

A favorite of local bikers, joggers, and skaters, **the Cady Way Trail** connects eastern Orlando with the well-manicured enclave suburb of Winter Park. The pleasant trail is 3½ mi long, with water fountains and shaded seating along the route. The best access point is the parking lot on the east side of the **Orlando Fashion Square Mall** (⊠*3201 E. Colonial Dr., about 3 mi east of I–4 Exit 83B*). You can also enter the trail at its east end, in **Cady Way Park** (⊠*1300 S. Denning Ave.*).

FISHING

Central Florida freshwater lakes and rivers swarm with all kinds of fish, especially largemouth black bass but also perch, catfish, sunfish, and pike.

LICENSES

To fish in most Florida waters (but not at Disney) anglers over 16 need a fishing license, available at bait-and-tackle shops, fishing camps, most sporting-goods stores, and Wal-Marts and Kmarts. Some locations may not sell saltwater licenses, or they may serve non-Florida residents only; call ahead. For nonresidents of Florida, freshwater or saltwater licenses cost $17 for three consecutive days, $30 for seven consecutive days and $47 for one year. For Florida residents under age 65, a freshwater or saltwater license is $17 per year for each, or $32.50 for both. A five-year fishing license costs Florida residents $79 for both. Information on obtaining fishing licenses is available from the **Florida Game & Fish Commission** (☎850/488–3641). Fishing on a private lake with the owner's permission—which is what anglers do at Disney—doesn't require a state fishing license.

WALT DISNEY WORLD

★ You can sign up for two-hour **fishing excursions** (☎407/939–7529) on regularly stocked Bay Lake and Seven Seas Lagoon. In fact, Bay Lake is so well stocked, locals joke that you can almost walk across the lake on the backs of the bass. The trips work on a catch-and-release program, though, so you can't take fish home.

Departing from the Fort Wilderness, Wilderness Lodge, Contemporary, Polynesian, Port Orleans Riverside, and Grand Floridian resort marinas, trips include boat, equipment, and a guide for up to five anglers. Your guide is happy to bait your hook, unhook your catches, and even snap pictures of you with your fish.

These organized outings are the only way you're allowed to fish on the lakes. Reservations are required. Yacht and Beach Club guests and Boardwalk Hotel guests can book a similar fishing excursion on Crescent Lake for the same fee as the Bay Lake trip. Two-hour trips for up to five people, which depart daily at 7, 10, and 1:30, cost $260 for the morning departures and $239 for the afternoon departure, plus $100 for each additional hour. Live bait and fishing equipment are free.

On **Captain Jack's Guided Bass Tours** (☎407/939–7529), bass specialists go along for the two-hour fishing expeditions on Lake Buena Vista. Anglers depart from the Downtown Disney Marketplace marina at 7, 10, and 1:30. Trips for groups of two to five people cost $260 for the morning departures and $230 for the afternoon departure. Per-person admission, available only for the 1:30 trip, is $110.

The Fort Wilderness Bike Barn (☎407/824–2742), open daily 8–6, rents poles and tackle for fishing in the canals around the Port Orleans–Riverside (formerly Dixie Landings) and Port Orleans resorts and at Fort Wilderness Resort and Campground. Fishing without a guide is permitted in these areas. Rod and reel with tackle is $6 per hour and $12.50 per day. You must be at least 18 to rent a rod and reel. Policy stipulates that rod users must be at least 12 years old, though this is not strictly enforced.

🌣 **Ol' Man Island Fishing Hole** (✉ *Port Orleans–Riverside* ☎ *407/939–2277*) has fishing off a dock. Catch-and-release is encouraged, but you can have fish packed in ice to take home—you have to clean them yourself. Cane poles and bait are $4 per half hour or $9 per day. You must rent equipment here to use the dock. Two-hour excursions in a boat with a driver are $110 per person, and include rod, reel, and bait. The Fishing Hole is open daily 7 to 2:30; reservations are required.

ORLANDO AREA

Top Central Florida fishing waters include Lake Kissimmee, the Butler and Conway chains of lakes, and Lake Tohopekaliga—a Native American name that means "Sleeping Tiger." (Locals call it Lake Toho.) The lake got its centuries-old name because it becomes incredibly rough during thunderstorms and has sent more than a few fishermen to a watery grave. Be careful in summer when you see storm clouds. Your best chance for trophy fish is between November and April on Toho or Kissimmee. For good creels, the best bet is usually the Butler area, which has the additional advantage of its scenery—lots of live oaks and cypresses, plus the occasional osprey or bald eagle. Toho and Kissimmee are also good for largemouth bass and crappie. The Butler chain yields largemouth, some pickerel, and the occasional huge catfish. Services range from equipment and boat rental to full-day trips with guides and guarantees. Like virtually all lakes in Florida, the big Orlando-area lakes are teeming with alligators, which you'll find totally harmless unless you engage in the unwise practice of swimming at night. Small pets are more vulnerable than humans, and should never be allowed to swim in Florida lakes or rivers.

FISHING   **East Lake Fish Camp** (✉ *3705 Big Bass Rd., Kissimmee* ☎ *407/348–*
CAMPS   *2040*), on East Lake Tohopekaliga, has a restaurant and country store, sells live bait and propane, and rents boats. You can also take a ride on an airboat. The camp has 286 RV sites that rent at $30–$45 per night for two people. The RV sites rent for $148 a week or $450 per month. Simple, rustic cabins are $65 per night for two people and $5 per night for each additional person with a limit of five per cabin. Try to reserve one of the 24 cabins at least two weeks in advance in winter and spring.

Lake Toho Resort (✉ *4715 Kissimmee Park Rd., St. Cloud* ☎ *407/892–8795* ⊕ *www.laketohoresort.com*), on West Lake Tohopekaliga, has 200 RV sites. Most of the full hookups are booked year-round, but electrical and water hookups are usually available, as are live bait, food, and drinks. The RV sites are $28 per night and $350 per month, plus electricity. An initial $50 refundable deposit is charged. Boat slips start at $50 a month, depending on the length of your boat.

Richardson's Fish Camp (✉ *1550 Scotty's Rd., Kissimmee* ☎ *407/846–6540*), on West Lake Tohopekaliga, has 7 cabins with kitchenettes, 16 RV sites, 6 tent sites, boat slips, and a bait shop. The RV sites are $30 per night, tent sites are $24.50, and cabins are $44 for one bedroom, about $68 for two bedrooms, and $79 for three bedrooms.

GUIDES Guides fish out of the area's fishing camps, and you can usually make arrangements to hire them through the camp office. Rates vary, but for two people a good price is $250 for a half day and $350 for a full day. Many area guides are part-timers who fish on weekends or take a day off from their full-time job.

> ### NON-DISNEY LAKES
>
> The key difference between the public lakes and the Disney lakes is that you have the option of keeping the fish you catch on the public lakes. Disney has a catch-and-release policy.

Bass Challenger Guide (BCG) (✉ *195 Heather Lane Dr., Deltona* ☎ *407/273–8045 or 800/241–5314* ⊕ *www.basschallenger.com*) takes you out in Ranger boats and equips you with tackle, license, bait, and ice. Transportation can be arranged between fishing spots and hotels. Bass is the only quarry. Half-day trips for one or two people begin at $275; six-hour trips are $300; full-day trips begin at $350. Each additional person pays $75 more. You can buy your license and bait here. If you want a multiday trip or need accommodations, Captain Eddie Bussard may book you a hotel room for $59 a night.

Overstreet Fish Camp (✉ *4500 Joe Overstreet Rd., Kenansville* ☎ *407/436–1966 or 800/347–4007* ⊕ *www.all-florida-fishing.com*) takes you on half- and full-day trips to go after the big bass that make the Kissimmee chain of lakes southeast of Disney ideal for sportfishing. Captain Rob Murchie also leads full-day saltwater expeditions in the Indian River Lagoon and Atlantic, an hour's drive east, in pursuit of tarpon and other game fish. Half-day freshwater trips are $225; a six-hour trip is $275 and full-day trips are $325. Saltwater trips (full day only) are $375. Prices are for one to two people. A third participant costs $76 more. You can buy your license and bait here.

GOLF

Sunny weather practically year-round makes Central Florida a golfer's haven, and there are about 150 golf courses and 17 golf academies within a 45-minute drive of Orlando International Airport. Most of Florida is extremely flat, but many of the courses listed here have man-made hills that make them more challenging. Many resort hotels let nonguests use their golf facilities. Some country clubs are affiliated with particular hotels, and their guests can play at preferred rates. If you're staying near a course you'd like to use, call and inquire. Because hotels have become so attuned to the popularity of golf, many that don't have golf courses nearby might still have golf privileges or discounts at courses around town. Check with your hotel about what it offers before you set out on your own.

In general, even public courses have dress codes—most courses would just as soon see you stark naked as wearing a tank top, for instance—so call to find out the specifics at each, and be sure to reserve tee times in advance. The yardages quoted are those from the blue tees. Greens fees usually vary by season, but the highest and lowest figures are provided, and virtually all include mandatory cart rental, except for the few 9-hole walking courses.

Golfpac (✉ *483 Montgomery Pl., Altamonte Springs* ☎ *407/260–2288 or 800/327–0878* ⊕ *www.golfpactravel.com*) packages golf vacations and prearranges tee times at more than 78 courses around Orlando. Rates vary based on hotel and course, and at least 60 to 90 days' advance notice is recommended to set up a vacation.

Numbers in the margin correspond to properties on the Golf Courses in and near WDW map.

WALT DISNEY WORLD

Where else would you find a sand trap shaped like the head of a well-known mouse? Disney has 99 holes of golf on five championship courses—all on the PGA Tour route—plus a 9-hole walking course. Eagle Pines and Osprey Ridge are the newcomers, flanking the Bonnet Creek Golf Club just east of Fort Wilderness. WDW's original courses, the Palm and the Magnolia, flank the Shades of Green Resort to the west and the Lake Buena Vista course near Downtown Disney's Marketplace. All courses have a driving range, pro shop, locker room, snack bar–restaurant, and PGA-staffed teaching and training program. Disney provides a perk to any guest at a WDW hotel who checks in specifically to play golf: free cab fare for you and your clubs between the hotel and the course you play. Ask at the front desk when you check into the hotel or call ☎ 407/939–7529.

GREENS FEES There are lots of variables here, with prices ranging from $20 for a youngster 17 or under to play 9 holes at Oak Trail walking course, to an adult nonhotel guest paying $174 to play 18 holes at one of Disney's newer courses in peak season. Disney guests get a price break, with rates ranging from $94 for a Disney hotel guest playing Monday through Thursday at the Lake Buena Vista course to $174 for a day visitor playing the Osprey Ridge course. All have a twilight discount rate, $38–$80 for the 18-hole courses, which goes into effect at 2 PM from January 16 to February 28 and at 3 PM from March 11 to October 26. The 9-hole, par-36 Oak Trail course is best for those on a budget, with a year-round rate of $20 for golfers 17 and under and $39 golfers 18 and older, and can be played for a twilight rate of $15 for adults and $10 for youngsters under 17 after 3 PM between May 14 and September 27. Rates at all courses except Oak Trail include an electric golf cart. No electric carts are allowed at Oak Trail, and a pull cart for your bag is $6. If you've got the stamina and desire to play the same course twice in the same day, you can do so for half price the second time around, but you can't reserve that option in advance, and this "Re-Play Option," as Disney calls it, is subject to availability. Golf shoes rent for $10 a pair, and range balls cost $7 a bucket. Rental clubs cost $55 for adults and nothing for juniors (17 and under). Tee times must be cancelled at least 48 hours in advance to avoid being charged. Note that golf rates change frequently, so double-check them.

TEE TIMES AND RESERVATIONS Tee times are available daily from 6:45 AM until dark. You can book them up to 90 days in advance if you're staying at a WDW-owned hotel, 30 days ahead if you're staying elsewhere from May through December, and four days in advance from January through April. For tee times and private lessons at any course, call **Walt Disney World Golf & Recreation Reservations** (☎️ *407/939–7529*).

GOLF
INSTRUCTION

One-on-one instruction from PGA-accredited professionals is available at any Disney course. Prices for private lessons vary: 45-minute lessons cost $75 for adults and $50 for youngsters 17 and under. Call the **Walt Disney World Golf & Recreation Reservations** to book a lesson.

COURSES

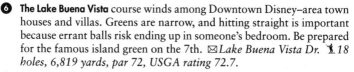

Eagle Pines, one of the newer Walt Disney World courses, was designed by golf-course architect Pete Dye. The dish-shaped fairways and vast sand beds are lined with pines and punctuated by challenging bunkers. *Golf Digest* gave this course 4½ stars. ⊠*Bonnet Creek Golf Club* ⛳️*18 holes, 6,772 yards, par 72, USGA rating 72.3.*

The Lake Buena Vista course winds among Downtown Disney–area town houses and villas. Greens are narrow, and hitting straight is important because errant balls risk ending up in someone's bedroom. Be prepared for the famous island green on the 7th. ⊠*Lake Buena Vista Dr.* ⛳️*18 holes, 6,819 yards, par 72, USGA rating 72.7.*

The Magnolia, played by the pros in the Disney–Oldsmobile Golf Classic, is long but forgiving, with extra-wide fairways. More than 1,500 magnolia trees line the course. ⊠*Shades of Green, 1950 W. Magnolia-Palm Dr.* ⛳️*18 holes, 7,190 yards, par 72, USGA rating 73.9.*

Oak Trail is a 9-hole, par-36 walking course, designed to be fun for the entire family. It was designed by Ron Garl and is noted for its small, undulating greens. ⊠*Shades of Green, 1950 W. Magnolia-Palm Dr.* ⛳️*9 holes, 2,913 yards, par 36.*

FodorśChoice
★

Osprey Ridge, sculpted from some of the still-forested portions of the huge WDW acreage, was transformed into a relaxing tour in the hands of designer Tom Fazio. However, tees and greens as much as 20 feet above the fairways keep competitive players from getting too comfortable. The course was rated 4½ stars by *Golf Digest*. Rental clubs require photo ID and a major credit card for refundable deposit of $500 per set. ⊠*Bonnet Creek Golf Club, 3451 Golf View Dr.* ⛳️*18 holes, 7,101 yards, par 72, USGA rating 73.9.*

The Palm, one of WDW's original courses, has been confounding the pros as part of the annual Disney–Oldsmobile Golf Classic for years. It's not as long as the Magnolia, or as wide, but it has 9 water holes and 94 bunkers. ⊠*Shades of Green, 1950 W. Magnolia-Palm Dr.* ⛳️*18 holes, 6,957 yards, par 72, USGA rating 73.*

ORLANDO AREA

Greens fees at most non-Disney courses fluctuate with the season. A twilight discount applies after 2 PM in busy seasons and after 3 PM during the rest of the year; the discount is usually half off the normal rate. Because golf is so incredibly popular around Orlando, courses raise their rates regularly.

Annika Academy. Named for its owner and chief golf guru, world-renowned pro golfer Annika Sorenstam, the academy offers golf instruction, fitness training, and nutritional counseling. A special Healthy Back program, with guidance on how to avoid back injuries, is offered

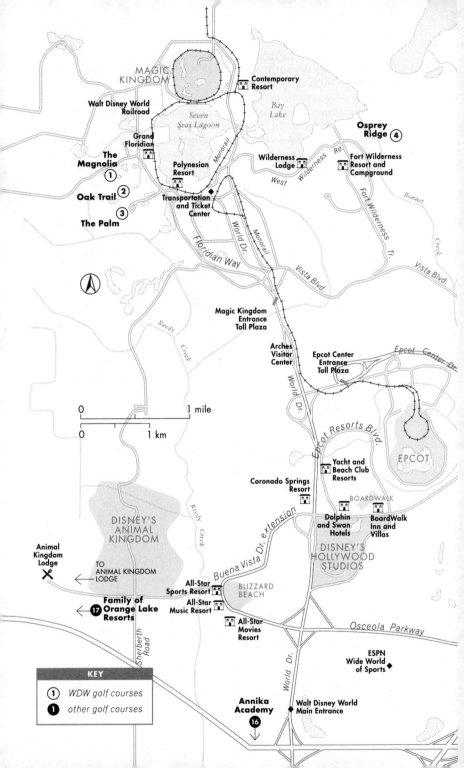

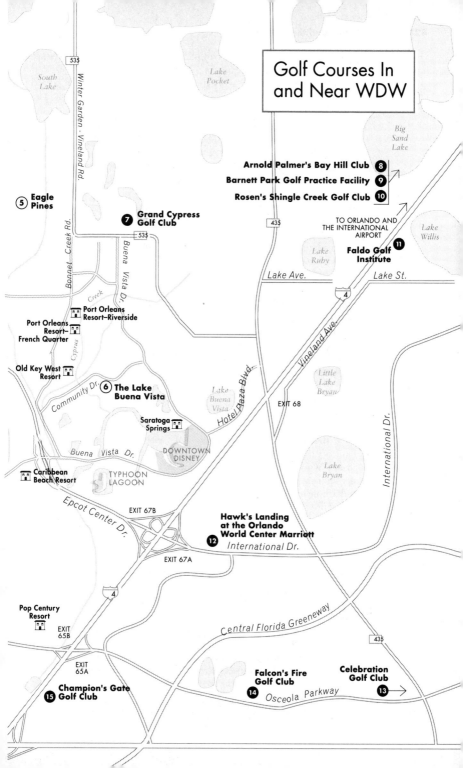

Golf Courses In and Near WDW

periodically. Prices are steep: from $2,500 for a two-day package that includes lodging, golf instruction, computer/video swing analysis, and 18 holes to $12,000 for a three-day package that includes a round with Annika herself as well as fitness and nutritional instruction. The academy has its own driving range and putting green and is at the Ginn Reunion Resort, which has three championship golf courses on which academy attendees can play. ✉ *7450 Sparkling Court, Reunion* ☎ *407/662–4653 or 888/266–4522* ⊕ *www.theannikaacademy.com.*

❽ Arnold Palmer's Bay Hill Club & Lodge golf courses are open only to those who have been invited by a member or who book lodging at the club's 65-room hotel. But with double-occupancy rates for rooms overlooking the course running as low as $571 in summer, including a round of golf, many consider staying at the club an interesting prospect. The course is the site of the annual Bay Hill Invitational, and its par-72, 18th hole is considered one of the toughest on the PGA tour. ✉ *9000 Bay Hill Rd., Orlando* ☎ *407/876–2429 or 888/422–9445* ⊕ *www.bayhill.com* ♣ *18 holes, 7,207 yards, par 72, USGA rating 75.1; 9 holes, 3,409 yards, par 36* ☜ *Greens fees included in room rates* ☞ *Restaurant, private lessons, club rental.*

❾ Barnett Park Golf Practice Facility, besides having an attractive course, has a great asset: it's free. All a golfer has to do is show up to use the net-enclosed driving range (with 10 pads), the three chipping holes with grass and sand surroundings, and the 9-hole putting green. As a special bonus, children ages 7–13 can spend time with a pro at no charge from 3 to 4:30 PM on Wednesday. ✉ *4801 W. Colonial Dr., Orlando* ☎ *407/836–6248* ☜ *Free.*

❸ Celebration Golf Club course—in addition to its great pedigree (it was designed by Robert Trent Jones Jr. and Sr.)—has the same thing going for it that the Disney-created town of Celebration, Florida, has: it's 1 mi off the U.S. 192 tourist strip and a 10-minute drive from Walt Disney World, yet it's lovely and wooded, and as serene and bucolic as any spot in Florida. In addition to the 18-hole course, driving range, and 3-hole junior course, the club includes a quaint, tin-roof clubhouse with a pro shop and restaurant, flanked by a tall, wooden windmill that is a local landmark. The club has golf packages, which include lodging at the nearby Celebration Hotel. ✉ *701 Golf Park Dr., Celebration* ☎ *407/566–4653* ⊕ *www.celebrationgolf.com* ♣ *18 holes, 6,783 yards, par 72, USGA rating 73* ☜ *Greens fees $69–$145, depending on time of year, time of day you play, whether you're a Florida resident, and whether you're a Celebration resident; daily discount rates begin at 2 PM* ☞ *Restaurant, pro shop, private lessons, club rental.*

★ ❿ Champions Gate Golf Club, which has the David Leadbetter Golf Academy on its property, has courses designed by Greg Norman. The club is less than 10 mi from Walt Disney World at Exit 72 on I–4. The two courses have distinct styles; the 7,406-yard International has the feel of the best British Isles courses, whereas the 7,048-yard National course is designed in the style of the better domestic courses, with a number of par-3 holes with unusual bunkers. ✉ *1400 Masters Blvd., Champions Gate* ☎ *407/787–3330 Champions Gate, 888/633–5323 Ext.*

23 Leadbetter Academy ⊕*www.championsgategolf.com* ⚑*International: 18 holes, 7,406 yards, par 72, USGA rating 73.7; National: 18 holes, 7,048 yards, par 72, USGA rating 72.0* ✉*Greens fees $65–$187, depending on time of year and time of day you play. Golf lessons at Leadbetter Academy are $225 per hr and $1,888 per day for private lessons; group lessons are $325 for 3 hrs; a 3-day minischool is $975; a 3-day complete school is $3,000* ☞*Pro shop, golf school, private lessons, club rental.*

⑭ **Falcon's Fire Golf Club,** designed by Rees Jones, has strategically placed fairway bunkers that demand accuracy off the tee. This club is just off the Irlo Bronson Highway and is convenient to the hotels in the so-called Maingate area. ✉*3200 Seralago Blvd., Kissimmee* ☎*407/239–5445* ⊕*www.falconsfire.com* ⚑*18 holes, 6,901 yards, par 72, USGA rating 73.8* ✉*Greens fees $79–$145, $80 after 2* PM ☞*Tee times 8–60 days in advance. Restaurants, private and group lessons, club rental, lockers, driving range, putting green.*

⑪ **Faldo Golf Institute by Marriott** is the team effort of world-famous golf pro Nick Faldo and Marriott Corp. An extensive-curriculum golf school and 9-hole golf course occupy the grounds of the corporation's biggest time-share complex, Marriott's Grande Vista. Here you can do anything from taking a one-hour, $160 lesson with a Faldo-trained pro (although not with the great Faldo himself, of course) to immersing yourself in a three-day extravaganza ($895–$1,400) in which you learn more about golf technique than most nonfanatics would care to know. Among the high-tech teaching methods at the school is the Faldo Swing Studio, in which instructors tape you doing your initial, unrefined swing; analyze the tape; and then teach you how to reform your physical skills the Faldo Way. The Club Fitter's Workshop offers a one-hour fitting session where your unique measurements will be determined to create your personal equipment recommendation. The course, designed by Ron Garl, is geared to make you use every club in your bag—and perhaps a few you may elect to buy in the pro shop. As with virtually everything else in Florida, prices go up in peak seasonal months, but there's always a group discount at the Faldo Institute, even for groups as small as two people. ✉*Marriott Grande Vista, 12001 Avenida Verde, Orlando* ☎*407/903–6295 or 888/800–4352 Ext. 6295* ⊕*www.gofaldo.com* ⚑*9 holes, 2,400 yards, par 32.*

⑰ **Family of Orange Lake Resorts,** about five minutes from Walt Disney World's main entrance, has two 18-hole courses (the Legends and the Reserve) and two 9-hole courses (Crane's Bend, Legends Walk). The Legends is an Arnold Palmer–designed championship course; the Reserve was designed by Mike Dasher and has unique land and water challenges. Crane's Bend is family-friendly and great for corporate outings as well. Legend's Walk is an executive course open until 9 PM nightly and is designed as a walker's course. Distances aren't long, but fairways are very narrow, and there's a great deal of water, making the courses difficult. The signature hole for the entire group of courses is the Island Oak, #13, a 432-yard, par 4 hole in the Pines section (the back 9) of the Legends Course. ✉*8505 W. Irlo Bronson Memorial Hwy., Kissimmee* ☎*407/239–0000 or 800/877–6522* ⊕*www.orangelakegolf.com*

14

🏌 *The Legends: 18 holes, 7,072 yards, par 72, USGA rating 72.2; The Reserve: 18 holes, 6,670 yards, par 71, USGA rating 72.6; Crane's Bend: 9 holes, 1,901 yards, par 30; Legend's Walk: 9 holes, 1,581 yards, par 30* ✉ *Greens fees $35–$145 for resort guests; $45–$155 nonguests* ☞ *Tee times 2 days in advance. Restaurant, private and group lessons, club rental, driving range, putting green.*

❼ Grand Cypress Golf Resort, fashioned after a Scottish glen, is comprised of four 9s: the North, South, East, and New courses. In addition, the Grand Cypress Academy of Golf, a 21-acre facility, has golf lessons and clinics. The North and South courses have fairways constructed on different levels, giving them added definition. The New Course was inspired by the Old Course at St. Andrews, and has deep bunkers, double greens, a snaking burn, and even an old stone bridge. ✉ *1 N. Jacaranda, Orlando* ☎ *407/239–1909 or 800/835–7377* ⊕ *www.grandcypress.com* 🏌 *North: 9 holes, 3,521 yards, par 36; South: 9 holes, 3,472 yards, par 36; East: 9 holes, 3,434 yards, par 36; New: 9 holes, 6,773 yards, par 72. USGA rating 72* ✉ *Greens fees $120–$250* ☞ *Tee times 7:30 AM– 5 PM. Restaurant, club rental, shoe rental, locker room, driving range, putting green, free valet parking.*

❿ Hawk's Landing at the Orlando World Center Marriott, originally designed by Joe Lee, was extensively upgraded with a Robert E. Cupp III design in 2000. The 220-acre course includes 16 water holes, lots of sand, and exotic landscaping. ✉ *Orlando World Center Marriott, 8701 World Center Dr., Orlando* ☎ *407/238–8660 or 800/567–2623* ⊕ *www. golfhawkslanding.com* 🏌 *18 holes, 6,810 yards, par 72, USGA rating 73.2* ✉ *Greens fees $89–$169* ☞ *Tee times 7 days in advance for public, 90 days in advance for World Center guests. Restaurants, private and group lessons, club and shoe rental.*

❿ Rosen's Shingle Creek Golf Club, designed by David Harman, lies alongside a lovely creek, the headwaters of the Everglades. The course is challenging yet playable, with dense stands of oak and pine trees and interconnected waterways. The golf carts even have GPS yardage systems. Universal Studios and the Orange County Convention Center are within a few minutes' drive. ✉ *9939 Universal Blvd., Orlando* ☎ *407/996–9933 or 866/996–9933* ⊕ *www.shinglecreekgolf.com* 🏌 *18 holes, 7,205 yards, par 72, USGA rating 69.8* ✉ *Greens fees $65–$119* ☞ *Tee times 7–dusk. Restaurant, club rental, shoe rental, driving range, putting green.*

HORSEBACK RIDING

WALT DISNEY WORLD

☾ **Fort Wilderness Resort and Campground** (✉ *Fort Wilderness Resort* ☎ *407/824–2832*) offers tame trail rides through backwoods. Children must be at least 9 to ride, and adults must weigh less than 250 pounds. Trail rides are $42 for 45 minutes; hours of operation vary by season. You must check in 30 minutes prior to your ride, and reservations are essential. Both horseback riding and the campground are open to nonguests.

ORLANDO AREA

Fodor'sChoice
★

Grand Cypress Equestrian Center gives private lessons in hunt seat, jumping, combined training, dressage, and Western riding. Supervised novice and advanced group trail rides are available daily 8:30 to 5. Trail rides, which depart from a rustic Barn and wind through Florida scrub pines and shaded trails, are $45 per hour. Private lessons are $55 per half hour and $100 per hour. Call at least a week ahead for reservations in winter and spring. ⊠ *Hyatt Regency Grand Cypress Resort, 1 Equestrian Dr., Lake Buena Vista Area* ☎ *407/239–1938* ⊕ *www. grandcypress.com.*

☾ **Horse World Riding Stables,** open daily 9 to 5, has basic and longer, more advanced nature-trail tours along beautifully wooded trails near Kissimmee. The stables area has picnic tables, farm animals you can pet, and a pond where you can fish. Trail rides are $43 for basic, $52 for intermediate, and $74 for advanced. Trail rides for children 5 and under are $17, and the stables offer birthday party packages for kids, as well as hayrides for groups. Reservations a day in advance are recommended for the advanced trails. ⊠ *3705 S. Poinciana Blvd., Kissimmee* ☎ *407/847–4343* ⊕ *www.horseworldstables.com.*

14

MINIATURE GOLF

☾ **Fantasia Gardens Mini-Golf** (☎ *407/560–4870*), near Disney-MGM Studios and the Swan and Dolphin resorts, recalls Disney's *Fantasia* with a huge statue of Mickey in his sorcerer's outfit directing dancing broomsticks. Music from the film plays over loud speakers. Games cost $11.75 for adults, $9.75 for children ages 3 to 9, and there's a 50% discount for the second consecutive round played.

☾
Fodor'sChoice
★

Winter Summerland Mini-Golf (☎ *407/560–7161*) has everything from sand castles to snowbanks, and is allegedly where Santa and his elves spend their summer vacation. The course is close to Disney's Animal Kingdom and the Coronado Springs and All-Star resorts. Adults play for $11.75 and children ages 3 to 9 play for $9.75, including tax. A 50% discount applies to your second consecutive round.

RUNNING

WALT DISNEY WORLD

Walt Disney World has several scenic running trails. Pick up maps at any Disney resort. Early in the morning all the roads are fairly uncrowded and make for good running. The roads that snake through Downtown Disney resorts are pleasant, as are the cart paths on the golf courses. At the **Caribbean Beach Resort** (☎ *407/934–3400*) there's a 1½-mi running promenade around Barefoot Bay. **Fort Wilderness Campground** (☎ *407/824–2900*) has a 2-mi running course with woods, as well as numerous exercise stations along the way.

ORLANDO AREA

Orlando has two excellent bike trails, the West Orange Trail and the Cady Way Trail, which are also good for running. Rural Orlando has some unbelievable hiking trails with long, densely wooded, nonrocky stretches that are tremendous for running, and often you can run for a half hour and not see any other living being—except wild game.

Turkey Lake Park, about 4 mi from Disney, has a 3-mi biking trail that's popular with runners. Several wooded hiking trails also make for a good run. The park closes at 5 PM, and fees are $4 per car. ⊠*3401 S. Hiawassee Rd., Orlando* ☎*407/299–5581.*

SKYDIVING AND PARASAILING

Sammy Duvall's Water Sports Centre (⊠*Disney's Contemporary Resort* ☎*407/939–0754*) a great way to get a birds'-eye view of WDW Resort and Orlando is by parasailing on Bay Lake. Flights, $95 per outing, reach a height of 450 feet and last 7 to 10 minutes. Individual participants must weigh at least 100 pounds, but youngsters may go aloft accompanied by an adult. Tandem flights are $160.

Fodor's Choice **Sky Venture,** is a 12-foot-high, 1,000 horsepower wind tunnel that lets
★ you experience everything skydivers do but close to the ground. The experience starts with instruction, after which you suit up and hit the wind tunnel, where you soar like a bird under your instructor's watchful eye. While you're "falling" on the wind stream, you even experience what divers called "ground rush," because you're surrounded by a video depiction of a dive. The experience is so realistic that skydiving clubs come to Sky Venture to hone their skills. You must be less than 250 pounds and at least 4 feet tall to participate. You can purchase a video of your jump for $16. ⊠*6805 Visitors Circle, I-Drive Area, Orlando* ☎*407/903–1150* ⊕*www.skyventure.com* ⌨*$45 per jump* ⊙*Weekdays 2–midnight, weekends noon–midnight.*

TENNIS

WALT DISNEY WORLD

You can play tennis at any number of Disney hotels, and you may find the courts a pleasant respite from the milling throngs in the parks. All have lights and are open 7 AM to 8 PM, unless otherwise noted, and most have lockers and rental rackets for $3 to $5 a day. There seems to be a long-term plan to move from hard courts to clay. Most courts are open to all players—court staff can opt to turn away nonguests when things get busy, but that doesn't often happen. Disney offers group and individual tennis lessons at all of its tennis complexes.

The Contemporary Resort, with its sprawl of six HydroGrid courts, is the center of Disney's tennis program. It has two backboards and an automatic ball machine. Reservations are available up to 24 hours in advance, and there's an arrange-a-game service. ☎*407/939–7529 reservations* ⌨*Free; lessons $80 per hr or $40 per half hr per individual and $15 per person for group lessons* ⊙*Daily 7–7.*

Fort Wilderness Resort and Campground has two tennis courts in the middle of a field. They're popular with youngsters, and if you hate players who are too free about letting their balls stray to their neighbors' court, this is not the place for you. There's no instruction or court reservations. ⊠*3520 N. Fort Wilderness Trail* ☎*407/824–2742* ⌨*Free* ⊙*Daily 8–6.*

The Grand Floridian has two Har-Tru clay courts that attract a somewhat serious-minded tennis crowd. Court reservations are available up to 24 hours in advance. Courts cost $80 hour, $40 per half hour, and $15 person for groups. ☎407/939–7529 ✉Free ◷Daily 8–8.

The Yacht and Beach Club Resorts have two blacktop tennis courts. Court reservations are not required. Equipment is available at the towel window at no charge. ☎407/939–7529 ✉Free ◷Daily 7 AM–10 PM.

ORLANDO AREA

Family of Orange Lake Resorts has, in addition to its golf courses, seven lighted, all-weather hard tennis courts. It's five minutes from Walt Disney World's main entrance. Court reservations are necessary. ✉8505 *W. Irlo Bronson Memorial Hwy., Kissimmee* ☎407/239–0000 or 800/877–6522 ✉*Free for guests, $5 per hr nonguests, $60 per hr for private lessons with pro Ernie Sink, $10 per ½ hr for group clinics, $2 per hr and $5 per day racket rental* ◷*Daily dawn–11* PM.

14

WALT DISNEY WORLD SPORTS

★ **ESPN Wide World of Sports Complex** is proof that Disney doesn't do anything unless it does it in a big way. The 220-acre facility, formerly Disney's Wide World of Sports Complex, plays host to more than 170 amateur and professional events each year. The huge complex contains a 7,500-seat baseball stadium—housed in a giant stucco structure that from the outside looks like a Moroccan palace—a 5,000-seat field house, and a number of fan-oriented commercial ventures such as the Official All-Star Cafe and shops that sell clothing and other items sanctioned by Major League Baseball, the NBA, and the NFL. During spring training, the perennially great Atlanta Braves play here, and the minor-league Orlando Rays have games during the regular season. But that's just the tip of the iceberg. The complex hosts all manner of individual and team competitions, including big-ticket tennis tournaments. In all, some 30 spectator sports are represented among the annual events presented, including Harlem Globetrotters basketball games, baseball fantasy camps held in conjunction with the Braves at the beginning of spring training each year, and track events ranging from the Walt Disney World Marathon to dozens of annual Amateur Athletic Union (AAU) championships. The complex has softball, basketball, and other games for group events ranging from family reunions to corporate picnics. ✉*Osceola Pkwy.* ☎407/828–3267 *events information* ⊕*www. disneyworldsports.com.*

A key source for sports information on all things Disney is the **Sports Information and Reservations Hotline** (☎407/939–7529).

WATER SPORTS

WALT DISNEY WORLD

Boating is big at Disney, and it has the largest fleet of for-rent pleasure craft in the nation. There are marinas at the Caribbean Beach Resort, Contemporary Resort, Downtown Disney Marketplace, Fort Wilderness Resort and Campground, Grand Floridian, Old Key West Resort,

Polynesian Resort, Port Orleans Resort, Port Orleans–Riverside Resort, and the Wilderness Lodge. The Yacht and Beach Club Resorts rent Sunfish sailboats, catamarans, motor-powered pontoon boats, pedal boats, and tiny two-passenger Water Sprites—a hit with children—for use on Bay Lake and the adjoining Seven Seas Lagoon, Club Lake, Lake Buena Vista, or Buena Vista Lagoon. Most hotels also rent Water Sprites. The Polynesian Resort marina rents outrigger canoes. Fort Wilderness rents canoes for paddling along the placid canals in the area. And you can sail and water-ski on Bay Lake and the Seven Seas Lagoon; stop at the Fort Wilderness, Contemporary, Polynesian, or Grand Floridian marina to rent sailboats or sign up for waterskiing. Call 407/939–7529 for parasailing, waterskiing, and Jet Skis reservations.

Sammy Duvall's Water Sports Centre (✉ *Disney's Contemporary Resort* ☎*407/939–0754*) offers waterskiing, wakeboarding (like waterskiing on a small surfboard; usually done on your knees), and parasailing on Bay Lake. Boat and equipment rental is included with waterskiing (maximum of five people) and wakeboarding (maximum of four people), as are the services of an expert instructor. Parasailing is $95 single for an 8- to 10-minute ride, and $170 for tandem. Wakeboard is $85 per half hour and $165 per hour for up to five people.

ORLANDO AREA

★ **Wekiwa River,** a great waterway for nature lovers, runs through 6,397-acre **Wekiwa Springs State Park** (✉*1800 Wekiva Circle, I–4 Exit 94, Apopka* ☎*407/884–4311, 407/884–2009 for camp site bookings* ⊕*www.dep.state.fl.us/parks*) into the St. Johns River. Bordered by cypress marshlands, its clear, spring-fed waters showcase Florida wildlife, including otters, raccoons, alligators, bobcats, deer, turtles, and numerous birds. Canoes and campsites can be rented near the southern entrance of the park in Apopka. Canoes are available for $16 for two hours and $3.20 per hour after that. The park has 60 campsites, some of which are "canoe sites," in that they can only be reached via the river itself, while others are "trail sites," meaning you must hike a good bit of the park's 13.5-mi hiking trail to reach them. Most sites, however, are for the less hardy among us—you can drive right up to them. Sites go for $20 a night with electric hookups. Tents are available for $4 per night, and it costs $5 per vehicle to enter the park.

Shopping

WORD OF MOUTH

"There are so many malls and outlets in Orlando that you really will be able to shop till you drop. Most outlets also have discount coupon books; ask about them at your hotel or at the mall. They'll make big difference in total costs."

—travelbuff

Updated
by Alicia
Callanan
Mandigo

From fairy-tale kingdoms to Old West–style trading posts to sophisticated malls, Walt Disney World and Orlando have lots of shopping opportunities that won't leave you disappointed. The colors are bright and energetic, the textures soft and cuddly, and the designs fresh and thoughtful. Before you board a roller coaster or giggle at a show, you'll catch yourself window-shopping and delighting in the thought of making a purchase. When it comes time to actually shop, you may have a hard time deciding what to buy.

Even if you're not inclined to make a purchase, the shops on Disney property are worth a look. Across the board, they're open, inviting, cleverly themed, and have beautiful displays. And don't let the price tags scare you. Small souvenirs like key chains, pens, and toys for less than $10 are available in almost every establishing.

Downtown Disney—a shopping and entertainment complex made up of the Marketplace, West Side, and what was formerly known as Pleasure Island—has the largest concentration of on-property stores. (At this writing the Pleasure Island area is being revamped, with only a few restaurants remaining open during the renovations.)

At Universal, every ride and attraction has its affiliated theme shop; in addition, Rodeo Drive and Hollywood Boulevard are pockmarked with money pits. To spice up the mix of CityWalk's entertainment and nightlife, Universal added stores geared to trendy teens and middle-age conventioneers who can't go back home without a little something.

Orlando's International Drive area is filled with factory outlet stores, most on the northeast end. These outlets are clumped together in expansive malls or scattered along the drive, and much of the merchandise is ostensibly discounted 20%–75%. You can find just about anything, some of it top quality, but be advised: retailers have learned that they can fool shoppers into believing they must be getting a deal because they're at a stripped-down outlet store. Actually, prices may be the same as or higher than those at other locations.

Park Avenue, a central street in the Winter Park suburb north of Orlando and 25 minutes from Disney, is definitely a shopper's heaven. It's easy to spend a pleasant day here wandering this inviting brick street with its boutiques, sidewalk cafés, restaurants, and hidden alleyways that lead to peaceful nooks and crannies with even more restaurants and shops.

WALT DISNEY WORLD

You can easily pick up $100 worth of goods before you've ventured even 10 feet into a Disney store, but you're better off practicing some restraint. Enjoy the experience of just looking first. If you see something you like, think about it while you enjoy the rest of your day. You might see something even better in the next store. If you're still thinking of that beautiful stuffed Cheshire Cat or Cinderella snow globe at the end of the day, you can always go back to get it. That way you don't weigh yourself down with purchases until you're ready to leave. If you're a Disney hotel guest, you never have to carry off your purchases—Disney stores will deliver your merchandise to your room for free.

Of course, your best bet is to wait a couple of days before you buy anything; survey the scene a little before spending all the money in your budget. Better yet, save shopping for the last day of your trip. Just be careful with souvenir-hungry kids. Many attractions exit directly into gift shops. Even if you put your kid on a strict budget, he may be overwhelmed by the mind-boggling choices at hand and be completely unable to make a selection. If you return home and realize that you've forgotten a critical souvenir, call WDW's Merchandise Mail Order service at 407/363–6200.

MAGIC KINGDOM

Everywhere you turn in the Magic Kingdom there are shops and stalls urging you to take home a little piece of the magic.

MAIN STREET, U.S.A.

Fodor's Choice ★ Main Street, U.S.A., which serves as your gateway to the Magic Kingdom, is end to end with little shops selling clothing and memorabilia.

The Chapeau sells those classic monogrammed mouse ears. The hats won't stay on all day, though, and they'll get squished in a backpack, so this is another good souvenir to get at the end of the day. You could also consider buying a Disney baseball cap to protect you from the sun.

Crystal Arts is one of many shops you'll find on-property that will dazzle you with engraved crystal. If a sparkling Cinderella coach has always been your dream, this is the place to find one, along with the iconic glass slipper. Offered in a variety of sizes, none of which will actually fit your foot, a glass slipper will set you back about $95. Dreamy newlyweds can buy a bride and groom to "crystallize" their moment of union for about $125. Crystal Arts is next to Arribas Brothers, so be sure to pass through from one shop to another and check out the in-house glass-blowers working their craft in a custom studio created just for them. And yes, the glass blowers will custom-make something just for you that you are, of course, expected to buy.

Uptown Jewelers is a great spot for window-shopping. Along with a dazzling display of jewelry, figurines, and collectible Disney lithographs, you can see Disney artists at work in the Watchmaker's corner. The artists sketch Disney characters and themes for the watch faces that are then built into watches. Ranging in price $200–$350, these

Best Disney Souvenirs

According to Fodors.com forums users . . .

"My friend who is almost 25 still wears her Indiana Jones hat she bought on a senior-year spring break trip to Disney." –jayne1973

"My girls bought inexpensive fans (about $5) in the Epcot China pavilion gift shop. Then the fans were personalized right there (free) with the girls' names written in Chinese." –ajcolorado

"I bought a silver Tinker Bell necklace that I love. They also have these memo holders that are miniatures of the princess dresses. I have Snow White, Cinderella, and Sleeping Beauty, and of course, each is holding the picture of my kids with that princess. So cute!" –missypie

"My best Disney souvenir? Pictures of my kids doing stuff like freaking out on Splash Mountain, etc. These will be around a lot longer than any souvenir. But to officially answer your question it would be the Minnie dress I bought my two-year-old. She did not take it off forever!!" –momof5

"When we went for our honeymoon, we bought the Mickey and Minnie bride-and-groom stuffed toys. Every time I look at them, I think of our honeymoon. And they look so cute in the tux and dress, too!" –travel_addict

"We just returned and we got a Tinkerbell cookie jar and the Cinderella waffle iron." –jetprincess

---

one-of-a-kind watches are exclusive to this store and cannot be purchased anywhere else.

Serious collectors of Disney memorabilia stop at **Main Street Gallery,** next to City Hall. Limited-edition sculptures, dolls, posters, and sometimes even park signs are available. You can buy a Pal Mickey plush toy stuffed with a receiver and audio device that plays sound tracks at various attractions—it's as if Mickey is giving you a personal guided tour of his kingdom.

The big daddy of all Magic Kingdom shops is the **Emporium.** This 17,000-square-foot store stocks thousands of Disney character products, from sunglasses to stuffed animals. Girls will be thrilled to see lots of princess items, including pillows and pajamas. One of the best souvenirs ever is a princess cameo ring encircled with feathers. At $2 each, the rings are a very inexpensive way to give your little princess a gem of her own. Although perpetually crowded and absolutely mobbed at closing time, the Emporium is, hands down, one of the best sources for souvenirs. Hang on to your kids in here; they're likely to wander away as they spot yet another trinket they have to have.

ADVENTURELAND

Just outside the Pirates of the Caribbean ride, the **Pirate's Bazaar** is a good place to shop for your next Halloween costume. The pirate hats, swords, and hooks-for-hands are hits with everyone who has a bit of the scoundrel in them. And if you think you're too cool for a souvenir T-shirt, the Bazaar's hip and slightly Gothic shirts will make you reconsider. There are gritty, almost sinister skull-and-bones appliqués on biker vests, skullcaps, and even beer koozies. Movie novelty collectors can buy any number of items with the logo of the *Pirates of the Caribbean* films.

Nearby, the **Agrabah Bazaar** has Aladdin-wear and the all-important Jasmine costume, as well as Moroccan-made carpets, carvings, and masks.

FRONTIERLAND

Emporia in Frontierland are generally referred to as "posts," as in the **Frontier Trading Post,** which is largely devoted to Disney collector pin trading. Large signs with advice for pin traders indicate that this place is a real trading post as well as a store.

> **DRUMROLL, PLEASE . . .**
>
> The number-one best store on Disney property is World of Disney in the Marketplace section of Downtown Disney. You could actually skip all of the stores in the theme parks and find everything you want here in an hour. And it may be a cliché, but there really is something for everyone, whether you're looking for something small and inexpensive, like the $3 princess pen, or a Disney collectible, like a Mickey watch or figurine.

15

The **Prairie Outpost & Supply** has been repurposed into an old-fashioned candy store, complete with giant suckers, taffy, and old-fashioned fudge.

Popular among boys are the Davy Crockett coonskin hats and personalized sheriff badges at **Big Al's,** across from the Country Bear Jamboree.

The **Briar Patch,** next door to Splash Mountain, looks like the inside of a tree hollow, with big, snarled roots across the ceiling and a pair of old wooden rockers in front of the hearth. If you're lucky enough to grab one of the rockers, you can rest your feet a spell while your kids snuggle and cuddle the many plush toys in the shop.

History buffs can find presidential and Civil War memorabilia at Liberty Square's **Heritage House.**

FANTASYLAND

For the famous black Mouseketeer hats, head to **Sir Mickey's.**

After you ride the Many Adventures of Winnie the Pooh, you end up at **Pooh's Thotful Spot** a small store devoted entirely to Pooh merchandise, although these items are also available in other Disney stores.

Tinker Bell's Treasures is pretty much princessland, with sparkly, shimmering dresses, hats, dolls, and jewelry. You can even take home your very own Cinderella Castle, but it will cost you better than $70. Toontown's **County Bounty** is a voluminous carnival-tent-like store centered around a giant, cylindrical Mr. Potato Head dispenser. For $20, you get a potato head, a box, and all the accessories you can stuff inside the box. Some of the pieces are classic Mr. Potato Head parts, others are all Disney. There are mouse ears, Goofy hats, Minnie Bows, and so on. With an estimated 40 different parts to choose from, this may be the most interactive purchase you ever make.

Inside Cinderella Castle, the **King's Gallery** sells items to help you furnish your own castle, like imported European clocks, chess sets, and tapestries.

EPCOT

There are a few stores in Future World, but it's the World Showcase that has the really unique gifts.

WORLD SHOWCASE

Fodor's Choice
★

Each of the countries represented has at least one gift shop loaded with things reflective of the history and culture of that nation's homeland, and many of the items are authentic imported handicrafts.

If your shopping time is limited, check out the two shops at the entrance to World Showcase. **Disney Traders** sells Disney dolls dressed in various national costumes as well as the requisite T-shirts and sweatshirts. Also sold here—and at some scattered kiosks throughout the park—is a great keepsake for youngsters: a World Showcase Passport ($9.95). At each pavilion, children can present their passports to be stamped—it's a great way to keep their interest up in this more adult area of Epcot. At **Port of Entry** you'll find lots of merchandise for kids, including clothing and art kits.

CANADA

With its recently revamped movie, Canada is worth a new look, as is its Northwest Mercantile. Along with an abundance of hockey-related merchandise and maple syrup, the shop offers a number of things not otherwise available in the United States, such as the lighthearted Hatley clothing line and the Roots fragrance and clothing line.

UNITED
KINGDOM

Anglophiles will find their hearts gladdened upon entering the cobble-stoned village at the United Kingdom, where an English Pub sits on one side, and a collection of British, Irish, and Scottish shops beckon you on the other. The **Queen's Table** is devoted to smelling good, or smelling like David Beckham, as his signature scent is available here. You can also pick up a dainty sterling ring stamped with authentic Celtic designs. At $10, it's a unique little trinket with some definite heritage.

World Cup fans will want to take their time exploring the **Crown & Crest**, which has a full selection of team jerseys, soccer balls, and more. If you wish you still had that Beatles lunch box from childhood, you might be able to buy a replacement here.

FRANCE

Your nose will alert you to your approach to France, and it won't be the foie gras. France has become perfume land beyond the original Guerlain perfume and cosmetics at **La Signature. Plume et Palette** no longer sells Limoges, but it has plenty of high-end French perfumes like Dior and lots of chances to enjoy a spritz. At **Les Vins de France** you can do some wine tasting and then pick up a bottle of your favorite.

MOROCCO

Morocco has an **open-air market** like something out of an Indiana Jones movie. It's also a great place to pick up something really different, like a Moroccan tarboosh or fez for $17. If you're feeling really exotic, you can buy a belly-dancing kit, complete with a scarf, hat, finger cymbals, and a CD for $120.

JAPAN

Instead of another princess doll, go to **Mitsukoshi** for one of Japan's most popular toys, Hello Kitty. Or instead of another T-shirt, consider a silk kimono, some authentic Japanese sandals, or some anime-inspired merchandise.

ITALY For chic Italian handbags, accessories, and collectibles, stop in at **Il Bel Cristallo.** Other gifts to look for include Venetian beads and glasswork, olive oils, pastas, and Perugina cookies and chocolate kisses (*baci*).

GERMANY In Germany pay a visit to the **Weinkeller,** where you can sample German wines by the glass. There are plenty to choose from, including rare German ice wines. For a good conversation piece, check out the hefty German steins at **Die Weinachts Ecke.**

SALUTING AFRICA OUTPOST At the **Village Traders,** wood carvers from Kenya whittle beautiful giraffes, elephants, and other animals while you watch. If you ask, the carvers may tell you stories about their homeland as they work. Each piece is unique, and some are a bit pricey, but you can buy an intricately carved wooden flute for $15. You'll find items from India and Australia for sale, too.

CHINA **Yong Feng Shangdian** is considered by some well-traveled guests to be the largest Chinese department store in the United States. It has exquisite desks, cabinets, and chairs featuring heavy lacquer and beautiful inlays. There's also a huge selection of tea sets ranging in style from traditional to contemporary, and fabulously fragranced candles that are sure to align your chi.

NORWAY You can find Norwegian pewter, leather goods, and colorful sweaters at the **Puffin's Roost.** Viking wannabes can check out the spears, shields, and helmets.

MEXICO For a fun and colorful gift for kids, consider the piñatas at **Plaza de los Amigos,** in Mexico. Other fun souvenirs include brightly colored paper blossoms, sombreros, baskets, pottery, and leather goods, but the Folk Art Gallery at the entry is where the most interesting things are found. You can watch artisans from Oaxaca hand-paint wood figurines with brilliant colors and intricate designs. Prices start at $20 and go up from there: some of these pieces can take as much as a day to complete.

FUTURE WORLD

Future World shopping won't tempt you to spend much money unless you're heavily into the art of Disney animation. For the serious collector, the **Art of Disney** sells limited-edition figurines and cels (the sheets of celluloid on which cartoons are drawn). **Green Thumb Emporium,** in the Land pavilion, sells kitchen- and garden-related knickknacks—from hydroponic plants to vegetable refrigerator magnets. **Mouse Gear,** the biggest Disney apparel store at Epcot, has an impressive selection of Disney and Epcot logo items. Racing and automobile enthusiasts will likely be a bit disappointed by **Inside Track** near the Test Track exit. It sells some racing merchandise and other car-related items, but with less of a selection than a racing hobbyist store.

DISNEY'S HOLLYWOOD STUDIOS

HOLLYWOOD BOULEVARD

Hollywood Boulevard is set up like Main Street, U.S.A., in the Magic Kingdom—you can bypass the shops on your way in because you'll pass them again on the way out.

Of the shops here, **Sid Cahuenga's One-of-a-Kind,** an antiques and curios store, is the most interesting. With its bungalow-style architecture and 1930s phonograph music playing in the background, this very cool little shop might trick you into thinking it's actually a vintage store. You can pick up autographed items ranging in age from the 1950s to now. There's a wide price range, too. An autographed picture of race-car driver Danica Patrick is available for a few hundred bucks, while an Elizabeth Taylor's signature commands $1,400. Sid's even sells clothes worn by your favorite soap star. A dress worn by Susan Lucci might set you back a couple of hundred bucks.

If you're in the market for something you can actually wear, pop in to **Keystone Clothiers.** This store is full of Mickey clothing that is clearly geared to adults. The styles are hip and trendy, with some items capitalizing on popular vintage styles. Backpacks, for instance, sport vintage Mickey or vintage 1930s Sleeping Beauty artwork. For kid's clothing, go to **L.A. Prop Cinema Storage,** at the corner of Sunset and Hollywood.

ECHO LAKE

Almost as popular as the pirate swords and hats in the Magic Kingdom are the Indiana Jones bullwhips and fedoras sold at the **Indiana Jones Adventure Outpost,** next to the stunt amphitheater, and the Darth Vader and Wookie masks at **Tatooine Traders,** outside of Star Tours. Serious Star Wars collectors might also find the action figure that's been eluding them, as well as books and comics. It's a busy store that inspires browsing.

NEW YORK STREET

The Writer's Stop offers one of the few decent cups of coffee to be had in Disney parks, as well as Earl Grey tea. If you happen to hit it right, you might get a book signed by a celebrity author, but the shop is small, the book selection is limited, and it's not conducive to hanging around. It is, however, a good place to pick up an autograph book.

ANIMATION COURTYARD

Budding animators can hone their talents with Paint-a-Cel, a kit with two picture cels ready to be illustrated, sold at the **Animation Gallery.**

SUNSET BOULEVARD

These days, **Legends of Hollywood** on Sunset Boulevard is more like Legends of Disney Channel, with all the gear, games, clothing, and accessories a preteen aficionado of the channel could want. There's "High School Musical" merchandise galore and an entire section devoted to Hannah Montana.

Making the most of villains in vogue, the **Beverly Sunset** has Disney's best bad guys: Cruella DeVil, Mufasa, and the Siamese cats from *Lady and the Tramp*. You can also pick up weird Tim Burton wear featuring characters from *The Nightmare Before Christmas*.

DISNEY'S ANIMAL KINGDOM

Before you pass through the turnstiles on your way into the Animal Kingdom, stop at the **Outpost Shop** for a must-have safari hat with Mouse ears.

If you're traveling with small children, you won't escape Animal Kingdom without a visit to DinoLand U.S.A., where you'll find **Chester & Hester's Dinosaur Treasures.** This purposely tacky tourist outlet is the Animal Kingdom's premier toy store, with the toys mostly being of the prehistoric sort.

For African imports and animal items, as well as T-shirts, toys, and trinkets, check out the Harambe village shops. **Mombasa Marketplace and Ziwani Traders,** which you'll spot as you leave Kilimanjaro Safaris, has a few areas clearly geared toward grown-up tastes, such as South African wines and an interesting selection of books on Africa. Less serious-minded souvenirs include plush safari animals, and T-shirts with sparkly, leopard-print, Mickey silhouettes. Kids will be drawn to the unique African percussion and wind instruments—flutes cost just $4.50.

At **Creature Comforts** (before you cross from Discovery Island to Harambe), you can get a Minnie Mouse headband with a safari-style bow, sunglasses, prince and princess costumes, and great kiddie togs. **Island Mercantile,** to the left as you enter Discovery Island, has loads of little trinkets, like Mickey pens and key chains, plus cute safari, Tigger, and Pooh backpacks for $30, and Disney headgear for your dog.

15

Disney Outfitters, directly across from Island Mercantile and by the Tip Board, is another spot for finding some unique items. Along with a broad selection of clothing and hats, there are some handcrafted items to be had. Handmade beaded jewelry and hammered metal jewelry ranges in price from $40 to $80. There are also some cleverly painted pottery animals with soft multicolor geometric shapes. Crafted by African artisans, each piece of pottery carries a label of authenticity guaranteeing that your purchase is contributing to sustainability.

DOWNTOWN DISNEY

⓫ The shopping and entertainment complex known as **Downtown Disney** has two areas: the Marketplace and Westside. New shops are slated to be introduced in the area that was once known as Pleasure Island.

Fodor'sChoice
★

MARKETPLACE

A lakefront outdoor mall with meandering sidewalks, hidden alcoves, jumping fountains that kids can splash around in, and absolutely fabulous toy stores, the Marketplace is a great place to spend a relaxing afternoon or evening, especially if you're looking for a way to give the kids a break from standing in line. There are plenty of spots to grab a bite, rest your feet, or enjoy a cup of coffee while taking in the pleasant water views and the hustle and bustle of excited tourists. The Marketplace is generally open from 9:30 AM to 11 PM. If you happen to run out of cash while you're shopping, you can apply for instant Disney credit at any register. How convenient.

Mickey's Mart. The sign proclaims "Everything Ten Dollars and Under," undoubtedly a welcome sight for those who've been reaching for their wallets a little too frequently. Look for the Surprise Grab Bags and the Item of the Week specials. ☎ *407/828–3864.*

LEGO Imagination Center. An impressive backdrop of large and elaborate LEGO sculptures and piles of colorful LEGO pieces wait for children and their parents to build toy kitties, cars, or cold fusion chambers. ☏407/828–0065.

Once Upon A Toy. A joint venture by Disney and Hasbro, this huge toy store is the kind of place childhood dreams are made of. There are tons of classic games redesigned with Disney themes. You'll find Princess Monopoly and the Pirates of the Caribbean Game of Life, just to name a couple. Overhead are a massive Tinker Toy creation and an oversize toy train making the rounds on a suspended track. Toys in the main room seem to be mostly for boys, but another room has a huge faux-candy castle and a My Little Pony Creation Station. You can test-drive many of the toys and play with touch-screen computers. With so many things to do, this is one store that might let you escape without making a purchase. ☏407/934–7775.

World of Disney. You might make it through Once Upon a Toy without pulling out your wallet, but you probably won't be so lucky at World of Disney. For Disney fans, this is *the* Disney superstore. It pushes you into sensory overload with nearly a half-million Disney items from Tinker Bell wings to Tigger hats. But if you have girls in your party, it's the Princess Room that will get you into the most trouble. Five-foot-tall likenesses of Cinderella and Sleeping Beauty stand watch over hoards of little misses scrambling to pick out just the right accessories. Besides princess dolls, clothes, shoes, and jewelry, you can buy a Belle (or Cinderella or Sleeping Beauty) wig to complete the look. Be warned, if you have a princess-obsessed child, one of the dazzling $65 princess dresses is going to be a must-have in her eyes, and people will be plucking them off the racks left and right of her. Add to that the new Bibbidi Bobbidi Boutique, where girls just like yours will be receiving princess makeovers ranging in price from $45 to $180, and you could land your budget in a royal mess. Of course there are things in the $10 to $30 range, including some cute pajamas, but it's hard to compare with those dresses. For grown-ups there are elegant watches, limited-edition artwork, and stylish furniture pieces with a Disney twist. ☏407/828–1451.

Pin Traders. It's nice to know that you can visit the biggest and best location for pin collectors without paying park admission. The Marketplace location has not only the largest selection, it also sells many limited-edition pins that are hard to find elsewhere. There are enough pins lining the walls to make you go cross-eyed, but the employees in this shop know their inventory very well, so if you're looking for something in particular, be sure to ask. And if you're having trouble managing your collection, you can buy additional lanyards, pin bags, and corkboards, too. ☏407/828–1451.

Mickey's Pantry is the only store on the property dedicated to cooking related items. This is where you'll find Mickey Mouse waffle irons, fun Mickey coffee mugs, cookie cutters, and the like. ☏407/828–1451.

WEST SIDE

The West Side is mainly a wide promenade bordered by an intriguing mix of shops and restaurants. There are also gift shops attached to **Cirque du Soleil, DisneyQuest**, the **House of Blues**, and **Planet Hollywood.**

Magic Masters. This small shop is arguably the most popular one here. As the magician on duty performs close-up card tricks and sleight of hand, an enraptured audience packs the shop for the free show. After the trick is finished, the sales pitch begins with a promise that (if you buy) they'll teach you how to do that particular feat of prestidigitation before you leave. ☎407/827–5900.

Magnetron. As the name implies, this place sells magnets—some 20,000 of them. So what's the big attraction? Well, they light up, change color, glow in the dark, and come in every shape, size, color, and pop culture character (check out magneto-Elvis). ☎407/827–0108.

Sosa Family Cigar Company. Cigars are kicking ash at this family-owned business. A fella's usually rolling stogies by hand in the front window and there's even a humidor room filled with see-gars. Smoking! ☎407/827–0114.

Starabilia's. If you're comfortable paying a few hundred simoleons for a framed, autographed picture of the cast of your favorite '70s sitcom, stop by Starabilia's. Although prices for the memorabilia run high—shoppers have paid from $195 for a Pee-Wee Herman autograph to $250,000 for a Hofner bass signed by the Beatles—you can't lose any money window-shopping, and the turnover of goods means the inventory's always entertaining. ☎407/827–0104.

There are several smaller, yet still enjoyable, shops along the **West Side pedestrian mall.** If you need a boost of sugar, the **Candy Cauldron** is filled with chocolate, fudge, hard candy, and other similarly wholesome foods. **Sunglass Icon** carries designer sunglasses with inspired designs from around the globe. **Mickey's Groove** has hip lamps, posters, greeting cards, and souvenirs inspired by the rodent. **Hoypoloi** adds art to the mix, with beautifully creative sculptures in various mediums—glass, wood, clay, and metals.

UNIVERSAL ORLANDO

UNIVERSAL STUDIOS FLORIDA

It's important to remember that few attraction-specific souvenirs are sold outside of their own shop. So if you're struck by a movie- and ride-related pair of boxer shorts, seize the moment—and the shorts.

The Simpsons-inspired **Kwik-E-Mart is** touted as the world's first permanent Kwik-E-Mart. In addition to picking up some authentic Simpsons memorabilia, you can also grab an authentic squishee. Yum. Other choice souvenirs include Universal Studios' trademark movie clipboard, available at the **Universal Studio Store**; sepia prints of Richard Gere, Mel Gibson, and Marilyn Monroe from **Silver Screen Collectibles**; supercool

TOP 5 SHOPPING DESTINATIONS

Downtown Disney. Why spend valuable touring time shopping in the theme parks when you come here (for no entry fee) on your first or last day? The perfect place for one-stop souvenir shopping, Downtown Disney has dozens of stores, including World of Disney, easily the largest and best store on Disney property.

Epcot World Showcase. Trinkets from all over the world, some handcrafted and incredibly unique, are sold at the pavilions representing individual countries here. Check out the Japanese bonsai trees and Moroccan fez hats.

Main Street, U.S.A., Magic Kingdom. The Main Street buildings are so adorable with their forced perspective architecture, pastel colors, and elaborately decorated facades that you want to go inside them and start examining the wares immediately. Don't waste precious touring time shopping in the morning, but definitely come back to check them out in the afternoon or evening.

Mall at Millenia. Visiting this mall is like going to New York for the afternoon. One look at the store names—Gucci, Dior, Chanel, Jimmy Choo, Cartier, Tiffany—and you'll think you've died and gone to the intersection of 5th and Madison.

Park Avenue, Winter Park. If you have the chance to visit the quaint village of Winter Park north of Orlando, carve out an hour or two to stroll up and down this thoroughfare.

Blues Brothers sunglasses from **Shaiken's Souvenirs**; plush animals, available at **Safari Outfitters, Ltd.** Stop by Hollywood's **Brown Derby** for the perfect topper, from fedoras to bush hats from Jurassic Park.

ISLANDS OF ADVENTURE

From your own stuffed Cat in the Hat to a Jurassic Park dinosaur and a Blondie mug, you can find just about every pop-culture icon in take-home form here. The **Dinostore** in Jurassic Park has a *Tyrannosaurus rex* that looks as if he's hatching from an egg, and (yes, mom) educational dino toys, too. Watch for—or watch out for—the **Comics Shop.** Kids may not be able to leave without a Spider-Man toy.

Merlin wannabes should head for **Shop of Wonders** in the Lost Continent to stock on magic supplies. And poncho collectors can get one at **Gasoline Alley** in Toon Lagoon, along with clever blank books and cartoon-character hats and wigs that recall Daisy Mae and others. For a last-minute spree, the **Universal Studios Islands of Adventure Trading Company,** in the Port of Entry, stocks the park's most popular souvenirs.

CITYWALK

❻ Most of CityWalk's stores are tucked between buildings on your left and right when you exit the moving walkway that rolls in from the parking garages, and a few are hidden upstairs—watch for the large overhead signs. Hours vary but are generally 11 AM–11 PM, closing at midnight on weekends. CityWalk parking is free after 6 PM. You can call the shops directly or get complete theme-park, nightlife, and shopping information from **Universal Orlando CityWalk** (☎*407/363–8000* ⊕*www.citywalkorlando.com*).

Cigarz. You have to duck down an alley to find this store, but the heavy aroma wafting from within might help to guide you. Just be careful not to walk into the giant Indian as you step through the doorway. Cigarz has a walk-in humidor, a full-length bar, and plenty of tables and ashtrays for enjoying your newly acquired stogie. Employees here take great pride in having hard-to-find smokes always in stock. Labels like OpusX, Ashton VSG, and Diamond Crown Maximus can be had for $9–$20 each, but you have to ask. Cigarz is open daily from 11 AM to 2 AM. ☎*407/370–2999*.

Endangered Species. Designed to resemble a jungle, this store aims to raise awareness of endangered species, ecosystems, and cultures worldwide. Some items, such as plush toys made by Aurora World Inc., clearly state on the tags that a portion of the proceeds are donated to conservation efforts. Periodically, artists, authors, and educators come in to discuss issues regarding the preservation of the planet. ☎*407/224–2310*.

Fresh Produce Sportswear. Bright, colorful beach clothes for women are sold here. Everything is made from 100% cotton, and the styles are loose and relaxed. You won't find much for dad, but moms and daughters can pick up matching outfits. ☎*407/363–9363*.

Hart and Huntington Tattoo Company. Universal Studios never wants you to forget that it's edgy and wild, so go ahead, pick out your design and then go home and show off your Orlando ink. ☎*407/373–0718*.

Jimmy Buffett's Margaritaville. If you absolutely *must* buy a Jimmy Buffett souvenir and can't make it to Key West, this is the next best thing. You can stock up on JB T-shirts, books, toy guitars, margarita glasses, sunglasses, picture frames, license plates, key chains, and theme hats (cheeseburger, parrot, and toucan). ☎*407/224–2144*.

Katie's Candy Company. This shop is full of all the old time favorites, like fresh fudge and candied apples. But the biggest surprise here may be discovering 21 different colors of M&M's. Yum. ☎*407/363–8000*.

Quiet Flight. Florida has managed to turn a natural detriment (small waves) into an asset—Florida's Cocoa Beach is the "Small Wave Capital of the World." This explains Quiet Flight, which sells surf brands like Billabong, Quicksilver, and Oakley. You'll find plenty of clothes but no surfboards. You can, however, shop for a skateboard. Quiet Flight opens a little earlier than other CityWalk stores, so you can start shopping at 9 AM. ☎*407/224–2126*.

Universal Studios Store. Although impressive in size, this store does not have all of the merchandise that's available in the individual park gift shops. Only the best-sellers are for sale here—T-shirts, stuffed animals, and limited-edition comic-book artwork. What's exclusive to this store are the mini movie posters, featuring some of Universal Studios greatest monster movies, priced at $11.99. It's also one of the few places on the property selling Universal trading pins. While you're here, be sure to check the back of the store for clearance racks. ☎*407/224–2207*.

15

SEAWORLD

Just as Disney offers all things Mickey, SeaWorld offers all things Shamu. If the classic plush Shamu toy isn't your thing, then perhaps you'd like a hand-painted Shamu martini glass from **Fins** at the Waterfront. The **Waterfront,** a promenade lined with open-air restaurants and shops, resembles an international bazaar. You'll find wood carvings, hand-crafted jewelry, and dinnerware painted with brilliant tropical flowers.

Since the Budweiser Clydesdale is the only animal at SeaWorld that could possibly overshadow Shamu, the **Anheuser-Busch Trading Company** certainly seems fitting. This is where you'll find beer mugs and Anheuser-Busch signs to add to your collection, along with souvenir Clydesdales.

Allura's Treasure Trove is very appealing to young girls with its enchanting assortment of mermaid toys and mermaid apparel.

If you've promised your little one a stuffed toy, you might want to hold out until you've been through the **Wild Arctic gift shop,** which has an irresistible collection of soft, white, baby seals and fluffy polar bears. It's hard to walk past them without hugging at least one. You might also consider a soft manatee toy, available from **Manatee Gifts,** west of Dolphin Stadium. Proceeds from the toys go to benefit a manatee preservation organization.

During your visit, a park photographer may shoot a picture of you interacting with the animals. You can buy the souvenir photograph at **Keyhole Photo,** near Shamu's Emporium. You can also have your picture taken with one of the famous Budweiser Clydesdales at Clydesdale Hamlet. And if you're a real Anheuser-Busch enthusiast, then you might want to hit **Bud's Shop** near Turtle Point.

If you've left the park before realizing that you simply must have a Shamu slicker, visit **Shamu's Emporium,** just outside the entrance. Also, any purchase you make inside the park can be sent to Shamu's Emporium for pickup as you exit.

THE ORLANDO AREA

CENTERS AND MALLS

❸ Festival Bay. Taking a new approach to retailing, Festival Bay has an indoor miniature golf course called Putting Edge and a 55,000-square-foot Vans Skatepark, with ramps for skateboarders and in-line skaters. Shops include Ron Jon Surf Shop, Steve & Barry's University Sportswear, Hot Topic, Shepler's Western Wear, and Journeys. There's also a 20-screen Cinemark Theater. Festival Bay is adjacent to the Factory Outlet Mall. ✉ *5250 International Dr.* ☎ *407/351–7718* ⊕ *www.belz.com* ☾ *Mon.–Sat. 10–10, Sun. 11–7.*

❹ Florida Mall. With 260-plus stores, this is easily the largest mall in Central Florida. Anchor stores and specialty shops include Nordstrom, ★ Sears Roebuck, JCPenney, Dillard's, Saks Fifth Avenue, Restoration

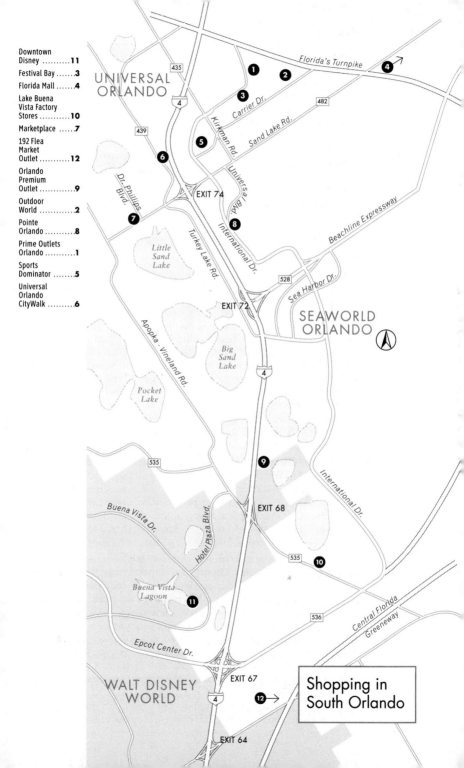

Shopping in
South Orlando

Hardware, J. Crew, Pottery Barn, Brooks Brothers, Cutter & Buck, Harry & David Gourmet Foods, and Swarovski. A 17-restaurant food court and four sit-down restaurants assure you won't go hungry. Stroller and wheelchair rentals are available, along with concierge services and, because the mall attracts crowds of Brazilian and Puerto Rican tourists, foreign-language assistance. The mall is minutes from the Orlando International Airport and 4½ mi east of I–4 and International Drive at the corner of Sand Lake Road and South Orange Blossom Trail. ⊠ *8001 S. Orange Blossom Trail* ☎ *407/851–6255* ⊕ *www.simon.com* ☼ *Mon.– Sat. 10–9:30, Sun. 11–7.*

★ **Mall at Millenia.** The best way to describe this mall is "high-end." Designers such as Gucci, Dior, Burberry, Chanel, Jimmy Choo, Hugo Boss, Cartier, and Tiffany have stores here. You'll also find Anthropologie, Neiman Marcus, Bloomingdale's, Bang & Olufsen, and an Apple store. But in case you're thinking the shopping here is too high end, there is also now a new freestanding IKEA store immediately adjacent to Bloomingdale's. The **Millenia Gallery** (☎ *407/226–8701* ⊕ *www. milleniagallery.com*) treats window-shoppers and serious art buyers to paintings by Picasso, pop art by Warhol, and hand-blown glass art by Chihuly. Beyond the gallery's three exhibit halls is a second-floor balcony displaying outdoor sculptures. A few minutes northwest of Universal, the mall is easy to reach via Exit 78 off I–4. ⊠ *4200 S. Conroy Rd.* ☎ *407/363–3555* ⊕ *www.mallatmillenia.com* ☼ *Mon.– Sat. 10–9:30, Sun. 11–7.*

❼ Marketplace. Convenient for visitors staying on or near International Drive, the Marketplace (not to be confused with Disney's Marketplace) provides all the basic necessities in one spot. Stores include a pharmacy, post office, one-hour film processor, stationery store, bakery, dry cleaner, hair salon, optical shop, natural-food grocery, and 24-hour supermarket. Take the I–4 Sand Lake Road exit (Exit 74AB) and head west. ⊠ *7600 Dr. Phillips Blvd.* ☎ *No phone* ☼ *Hrs vary.*

❽ Pointe Orlando. Strategically located within walking distance of the Peabody Orlando and Orange County Convention Center, this impressive retail center along the I-Drive corridor has also undergone a massive renovation and upgrade designed to make it even more appealing to expense-account-rich conventioneers. In addition to WonderWorks and the enormous Muvico Pointe 21 theater, the complex houses more than 60 specialty shops, including A/X Armani Exchange, Foot Locker Superstore, Chico's, the Grape, and Victoria's Secret. It also has a wide range of dining options, including the very high-end Capital Grille, and the Oceanaire Seafood Room, entertainment-centered restaurants such as B.B. King's Blues Club and Taverna Opa, and more casual choices such as Hooters and Johnny Rockets. There are also a few dozen pushcart vendors selling hair ribbons, sunglasses, and other small items. Considering you have to pay to park ($2 for 15 minutes–2 hours, $5 daily), the nearby ATM is more than convenient. ✉ *9101 International Dr.* ☎ *407/248–2838* ⊕ *www.pointeorlando.com* ☯ *Sun.–Thurs. 10–10, Fri. and Sat. 10* AM–*11* PM.

FACTORY OUTLETS

❶ ★ **Prime Outlets Orlando.** Two malls and four annexes make Prime Outlets Orlando the area's largest collection of outlet stores. One of the best places to find deals is Off 5th, the Saks Fifth Avenue Outlet. There are almost always sales under way, allowing you to pick up high-end labels at sometimes ridiculously low prices. The same is true for the Nieman Marcus Last Call Clearance Center, which joined the Prime Outlet shopping area as part of a massive remodel.

There are tons of apparel stores to choose from, along with few stores specializing in housewares, jewelry, perfume and even luggage if you didn't bring enough. Among the trendy shops to search out while here are 7 For All Mankind, Juicy Couture, Aeropostale, and Polo Ralph Lauren Factory Store.

15

Don't worry about carting home breakable or cumbersome articles: these stores will ship your purchases anywhere in the United States by UPS. And just to be sure you don't run out of steam before you run out of money, Prime Outlets runs a free trolley between its Design Center, Mall 1, and Annex. ✉ *5401 W. Oak Ridge Rd., at northern tip of International Dr.* ☎ *407/352–9600* ⊕ *www.primeoutlets.com* ☯ *Mon.–Sat. 10–9, Sun. 10–6.*

❿ **Lake Buena Vista Factory Stores.** Although there's scant curb appeal, this is a nice gathering of standard outlet stores. The center is roughly 2 mi south of I-4 and includes Reebok, Nine West, Big Dog, Sony, Liz Claiborne, Wrangler, Disney's Character Corner, American Tourister, Murano, Sony/JVC, Tommy Hilfiger, Ralph Lauren, Jockey, Casio, Osh-Kosh, Fossil, and the area's only Old Navy Outlet. If you can, check the Web site before traveling as some stores post online coupons. Take Exit 68 at I-4. ✉ *15591 State Rd. 535, 1 mi north of Hwy. 192* ☎ *407/238–9301* ⊕ *www.lbvfs.com* ☯ *Mon.–Sat. 10–9, Sun. 10–6.*

❾ **Orlando Premium Outlet.** This outlet capitalizes on its proximity to Disney (it's at the confluence of I-4, Highway 535, and International Drive). It can be tricky to reach—you have to take I-4 Exit 68 at Highway 535, head a few blocks east, and find the very subtle entrance to Little Lake Bryan Road (it parallels I-4). Parking is painful, and on peak days it can take as much as 30 minutes just to get from the highway to the parking lot, where you'll then spend another frustrating 20 minutes or so vying for a spot. But the center's design makes this almost an open-air market, so walking can be pleasant on a nice day. You'll find the Gap, Nike, Adidas, Timberland, Polo, Giorgio Armani, Burberry, Tommy Hilfiger, Dockers, Reebok, Versace, Guess?, Bebe, Mikasa, Max Mara, Nautica, Calvin Klein, and about 100 other stores. This mall has many of the same stores as Prime Outlets Orlando, so if you've hit one, you may find you can skip the other. ✉ *8200 Vineland Rd.* ☎ *407/238–7787* ⊕ *www. premiumoutlets.com/orlando* ☯ *Mon.–Sat. 10–10, Sun. 10–9.*

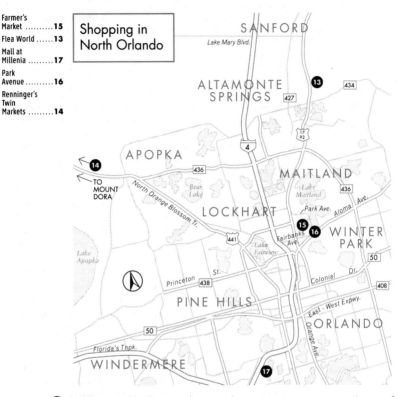

Shopping in
North Orlando

② Outdoor World. The very large and very nice megastore carries goods and provisions for every aspect of outdoor life. In a sparkling 150,000-square-foot Western-style lodge accented by antler door handles, fishing ponds, deer tracks in the concrete, and a massive stone fireplace, the store packs in countless fishing boats, RVs, tents, rifles, deep-sea fishing gear, freshwater fishing tackle, scuba equipment, fly-tying materials (classes are offered, too), a pro shop, outdoor clothing, Uncle Buck's Cabin (a restaurant and snack bar), and a shooting gallery. If you're an outdoors enthusiast, this is a must-visit. ⊠*5156 International Dr.* ☎*407/563–5200* ⊕*www.basspro.com* ☾*Mon.–Sat. 9 AM–10 PM, Sun. 10–7.*

⑤ Sports Dominator. The huge, multilevel Sports Dominator could probably equip all the players of Major League Baseball and the NFL, NBA, and NHL combined. Each sport receives its own section, crowding the floor with soccer balls, golf clubs, catcher's mitts, jerseys, bows, and a few thousand more pieces of sports gear. The prices may not be lower than anywhere else, but the selection is a winner. ⊠*6464 International Dr.* ☎*407/354–2100* ⊕*www.sportsdominator.com* ☾*Daily 9 AM–10 PM.*

FLEA MARKETS

⑬ Flea World. It's a long traffic-choked haul from the attractions area (about 30 mi northeast), but Flea World claims to be America's largest flea market under one roof. Merchants at more than 1,700 booths sell predominately new merchandise—everything from car tires, Ginsu knives, and pet tarantulas to gourmet coffee, biker clothes, darts, NASCAR souvenirs, rugs, books, incense, leather lingerie, and beaded evening gowns. It's also a great place to buy cheap Florida and Mickey Mouse T-shirts. In one building, 50 antiques and collectibles dealers cater to people who can pass up the combination digital ruler and egg timer for some authentic good old junk and collectibles. A free newspaper, distributed at the parking lot entrance, provides a map and directory. Children are entertained at Fun World next door, which offers two unusual miniature golf courses, arcade games, go-karts, bumper cars, bumper boats, children's rides, and batting cages. Flea World is 3 mi east of I–4 Exit 98 on Lake Mary Boulevard, then 1 mi south on U.S. 17–92. ⊠ *U.S. 17–92, Sanford* ☎ *407/321–1792* ⊕ *www.fleaworld. com* ⊠ *Free* ⊗ *Fri.–Sun. 9–6.*

⑫ 192 Flea Market Outlet. With 400 booths, this market is about a fourth the size of Sanford's Flea World, but it's much more convenient to the major Orlando attractions (about 10 mi away in Kissimmee) and is open daily. The all-new merchandise includes "tons of items": toys, luggage, sunglasses, jewelry, clothes, beach towels, sneakers, electronics, and the obligatory T-shirts. ⊠ *4301 W. Vine St., Hwy. 192, Kissimmee* ☎ *407/396–4555* ⊗ *Daily 9–6.*

⑭ Renninger's Twin Markets. In the charming town of Mount Dora (30 mi
★ northwest of downtown Orlando), Renninger's may be Florida's largest gathering of antiques and collectibles dealers. At the top of the hill, 400 flea-market dealers sell household goods, garage-sale surplus, produce, baked goods, pets, and anything else you can think of. At the bottom of the hill, 200 antiques dealers set up shop to sell ephemera, old phonographs, deco fixtures, antique furniture, and other stuff Granny had in her attic. If you have the time, hit the flea market first, since that's where antiques dealers find many of their treasures. Both markets are open every weekend, but on the third weekend of the month the antiques market has a fair attracting about 500 dealers. The really big shows, however, are the three-day extravaganzas held on the third weekends of November, January, and February—these draw approximately 1,500 dealers. These events can be all-day affairs; otherwise, spend the morning at Renninger's and then move on to downtown Mount Dora in time for lunch. From I–4, take the Florida Turnpike north to Exit 267A to reach Highway 429 east and, 8 mi later, Highway 441 north to Mount Dora. Summers are very slow, the pace picks up from October through May. ⊠ *U.S. 441, Mount Dora* ☎ *352/383–8393* ⊕ *www.renningers. com* ⊠ *Markets and Antiques Fairs free; Extravaganzas $10 Fri., $6 Sat., $4 Sun.* ⊗ *Markets, weekends 9–5; Antiques Fairs, Mar.–Oct., 3rd weekend of month, 9–5; Extravaganzas Nov., Jan., and Feb., 3rd weekend of month, Fri. 10–5, weekends 9–5.*

15

WINTER PARK

⓰
Fodor'sChoice
★

Unquestionably one of the most inviting spots in Central Florida, **Park Avenue** in downtown Winter Park offers a full day of shopping and entertainment. The last couple of years have seen a mass exodus of the chain stores that came to dominate shopping on Park Avenue, leaving the street open to the return of boutique shopping. Most of these stores are privately owned and offer merchandise that cannot be easily found elsewhere.

On the north end of Park Avenue is the **Charles Hosmer Morse Museum of American Art,** of which the centerpiece is the work of Louis Comfort Tiffany. It's a great little museum with a fantastic shop selling lots of Tiffany-theme gifts and books. On the other side of the street is **10,000 Villages,** a fascinating little store dealing exclusively in fair-trade items. Across the street is **Shoooz,** which sells funky but functional Euro shoes. Just a short walk from there, **Jacobson's** is a chic clothing boutique.

Toward the south end of Park Avenue, you'll find **Peterbrooke Chocolatier,** which makes all of its chocolates on premises and almost always has something on hand to sample, such as its to-die-for chocolate-covered popcorn. Next door is **Red Marq,** a truly hip card shop that goes way beyond anything Hallmark has to offer. Across the street, **NFX Apothecary** sells indulgent soaps, lotions, and cosmetics. **Shoúture,** a high-end shoe boutique, stocks such designers as Hollywould, Constanca Basto, and Lily Holt. And if your feet are weary from shopping, don't worry, most Shoúture purchases will qualify you for a complimentary pedicure. If you're looking for the popular upscale pet boutique that used to be called the Doggie Door, go north a block. This shop has been combined with another venture owned by the same people, a former gourmet food and wine shop known as Olive This Relish That, to create **Bullfish.** A pet store–wine shop might sound like an odd combination, but the new combined business is as popular as the old separate businesses were.

For shoppers and nonshoppers alike part of the fun of Park Avenue is exploring the little nooks and crannies that divert you from the main drag. Tucked in an alley between Lyman and New England Avenues is **Palmano's,** a great little coffee bar that will sell you a hot cup of brew or a pound of its fresh roasted beans. It's also a great place to grab a glass of wine in the evening. Between Welbourne and Morse avenues, around the corner from Barnie's Coffee, you find **Greeneda Court.** A walk to the back reveals a delightful fountain and wrought-iron tables and chairs where you can sit and relax with a cappuccino from Barnie's. Of course the antiques store hidden there could keep you on your feet.

In the middle of the next block are the **Hidden Garden Shops.** Also on Park Avenue are numerous art galleries, antique jewelry stores, a cigar shop, and a gentlemen's barbershop where you can treat yourself to a haircut and a shave.

The third weekend in March brings the **Winter Park Sidewalk Art Festival** (☎407/672–6390); more than 40 years after its debut it still attracts thousands of art aficionados and a few hundred of America's better artists. ✉*Park Ave. between Fairbanks and Canton Aves.* ◷*Most shops Mon.–Sat. 10–5, some also Sun. noon–5.*

🕔 **Farmer's Market.** If you know you want to hit Park Avenue while you're in Central Florida, you might try to schedule your visit on a Saturday. Then you can begin your day at the Winter Park Farmer's Market, which takes place every week at the city's old train depot, two blocks west of Park Avenue. It's a bustling, vibrant market with vendors selling a wide selection of farm-fresh produce, dazzling flowers, and prepared foods. On any given morning you may find a chef stirring a steaming pot of Irish oatmeal, or a woman selling made-to-order crepes. There are plenty of baked goods and hot coffee available, along with places to sit and enjoy your treats.

Those willing to cross the railroad tracks that run through Winter Park will find the recently gentrified **Hanibel Square.** Centered on the intersection of New England and Pennsylvania avenues, the upscale dining and shopping found here is slowly working its way eastward toward Park Avenue with every additional boutique and art gallery.

15

INDEX

NOTES

NOTES

ABOUT OUR WRITERS

Jennie Hess is a travel and feature writer based in Orlando. When she's not trekking through theme parks, she's looking for hidden treasures across the Orlando landscape. Formerly a publicist for Walt Disney World Resort, Jennie enjoys sharing noteworthy gems ranging from the hottest live entertainment to the latest high-tech innovations at new and updated attractions. She gives us the inside scoop on the evolving Disney kingdom and "don't miss"–sights beyond the theme parks, with added perspective gleaned from her husband and two teenage sons.

Alicia Callanan Mandigo, our Shopping updater, is a freelance broadcast journalist and writer. Though technically a transplant, she considers herself a Central Florida native. Alicia worked at Epcot while she was in college, and she still considers it the best job she's ever had.

Gary McKechnie knows a lot about Florida—his native state—and its many attractions. During his student days, he worked as a Walt Disney World ferryboat pilot, Jungle Cruise skipper, steam-train conductor, double-decker bus driver, and was also an improv comedian at Epcot. His award-winning book *Great American Motorcycle Tours* is the nation's best-selling motorcycle guidebook and, following years of travel and research, in May 2009 released *National Geographic's USA 101,* a book that highlights 101 American icons, events, and festivals.

Good meals stick to your ribs; great meals stick in your mind. That's the belief of Rowland Stiteler, who has served as editor and dining critic of *Orlando* and *Central Florida* magazines. During the past 10 years he's researched more than 500 Florida hotels and restaurants for travel publications and the convention and resort industry.

31901046481000